Written and Edited by

Richard C. Edwards
University of Massachusetts, Amherst

Michael Reich
University of California, Berkeley

Thomas E. Weisskopf
University of Michigan, Ann Arbor

The Capitalist System

A RADICAL ANALYSIS OF AMERICAN SOCIETY

SECOND EDITION

PRENTICE-HALL, INC., Englewood Cliffs, New Jersey 07632

Library of Congress Cataloging in Publication Data

Edwards, Richard C   comp.
    The capitalist system.

    Includes bibliographical references.
    1. United States—Economic conditions—1945–
—Addresses, essays, lectures.   2. United States—
Social conditions—1945–   —Addresses, essays,
lectures.   I. Reich, Michael, joint comp.
II. Weisskopf, Thomas E., joint comp.   III. Title.
HC106.5.E393 1977   330.9′73′092   77–1495
ISBN 0–13–113597–X

Printed in the United States of America

10   9   8   7   6

PRENTICE-HALL INTERNATIONAL, INC., *London*
PRENTICE-HALL OF AUSTRALIA PTY. LIMITED, *Sydney*
PRENTICE-HALL OF CANADA, LTD., *Toronto*
PRENTICE-HALL OF INDIA PRIVATE LIMITED, *New Delhi*
PRENTICE-HALL OF JAPAN, INC., *Tokyo*
PRENTICE-HALL OF SOUTHEAST ASIA PTE. LTD., *Singapore*
WHITEHALL BOOKS LIMITED, *Wellington, New Zealand*

Contents

PART **II**

A THEORETICAL APPROACH TO CAPITALISM   *37*

PART **III**

MONOPOLY CAPITALISM IN THE UNITED STATES   *115*

Preface

This book analyzes modern capitalism from the perspective of radical political economy, with a primary focus on the experience of the United States. We have organized the book around a variety of different readings selected and edited from the work of many different authors. Our own contributions as author-editors include the choice and arrangement of readings, the authoring of several original articles, and the writing of extensive introductions to all the chapters and readings in order to bind the diverse materials into a coherent whole. Though we have conceived the book as the basis for an independent radical course in political economy, it can also serve as a useful collection of readings for other courses in the social sciences.

The first edition of this book was published in 1972. During the six years since then, the issues and problems that we analyzed have continued to confront our society, and the world capitalist system as a whole has been subjected to new sources of stress and strain. At the same time, radical political economists in the United States and abroad have continued to develop and enrich their analyses of the operation and the contradictions of modern capitalism. It seemed to us important, then, that we revise our book so as to make it more relevant to present-day concerns and more representative of the current state of radical political economy.

In preparing this second edition, we have benefited from additional years of teaching and research and from the opportunity to draw on a great deal of new work by our colleagues in the Union for Radical Political Economics.[1] As a result, we have made many changes in the organization and content of the book; more than 75 percent of this second edition is entirely new, and much of the rest has been modified or updated. We have thoroughly reorganized every chapter and rewritten all introductions, and we have added several new chapters. The major innovations include a greatly expanded treatment of the development and functioning of monopoly capitalism in the United States (Chapters 4, 5 and 6) and a radical analysis of capitalist economic crises (Chapter 12).

We have edited judiciously most of the readings being reprinted. The editing, we trust, improves the clarity of exposition, avoids unnecessary repetition, and focuses on points that are most germane to our analysis. Deletions from the original text are indicated by ellipses. Each source is cited in full so that readers can consult the original text as desired. In excerpting readings, we removed footnotes that were not essential to the understanding or documentation of the piece and renumbered the footnotes and tables for con-

[1]Founded in 1968 at the height of the radical political movement in the United States, URPE has continued to thrive through the 1970s, providing an organizational network for radical political economists engaged in teaching, research, communication, and political action. URPE publishes a quarterly *Review of Radical Political Economics*, sponsors a monthly bulletin of economic affairs, *Dollars and Sense*, and promotes sundry other activities; the URPE national office is located at 41 Union Square West, Room 901, New York, New York 10003.

tinuity. Finally, we have included at the end of the book a bibliography of additional readings that we have found particularly useful.

Our work on the first edition of the book was greatly facilitated by the fact that we were together at Harvard University. Although we have since gone to different universities, we have communicated regularly and met as often as possible over the past two years to prepare the second edition. The resulting book thus represents a truly collective effort at every stage, from the selection of materials to the drafting of chapter introductions to the final editing process. Although we have not burdened our individually authored articles with acknowledgments to one another, we have benefited enormously from each other's advice in every case.

We have also benefited greatly from the help of other friends and colleagues during the course of our work on both the first and second editions of the book. We wish especially to thank Nancy Chodorow for her major contribution to the writing of the introduction to the new Chapter 9. We also would like to thank Coburn Everdell, whose drawings for the chapter openings have added greatly to the attractiveness of the book. Rather than try to identify here everyone else to whom we are indebted, we will limit ourselves to an expression of profound gratitude to all who have contributed in different ways to the making of this book.

RICHARD C. EDWARDS,
University of Massachusetts, Amherst

MICHAEL REICH,
University of California, Berkeley

THOMAS E. WEISSKOPF,
University of Michigan, Ann Arbor

Introduction

Despite its wealth and democratic promise, our society suffers grievous problems. American troops and bombers are no longer decimating the people of Indochina, but we keep learning about new parts of the world where well-funded American agents are fighting against movements of popular liberation. The United States government ignores pressing needs for health care and environmental protection while facilitating the growth of the military-industrial complex and serving the interests of giant multinational corporations. Most people's jobs are alienating; wealth and power are concentrated in the hands of a privileged elite; poverty, racism, and sexism persist despite highly publicized efforts to diminish them. Perhaps the most important new development in recent years has been the failure of our economic system to do one thing it had done tolerably well since World War II: maintain a fairly low level of unemployment with a reasonable degree of price stability. In the 1970s we have experienced rates of unemployment and inflation unprecedented in the last three decades, and we have learned that in spite of the best efforts of sophisticated economists our capitalist society is not immune to economic crises.

Why do all these problems continue to afflict us? Are they simply the modern equivalents of age-old forms of oppression, to be expected in any society because people are inherently greedy, selfish, and power-seeking? Or, formidable as they may seem, are they merely aberrations of a basically just and humane society, problems that can be solved with enough intelligence and determination on the part of our leaders?

We reject both of these explanations. We believe instead that human behavior is significantly shaped by the socioeconomic environment within which people work and live. Oppression has its roots in the basic economic institutions of a society, and the various forms of oppression we observe in our own society today derive in large part from its capitalist institutions.

The perspective we bring to this book is that of radical political economy, which draws its inspiration and its basic analytical framework from the Marxist tradition of critical theory, interdisciplinary analysis, and struggle for change. We do not find everything that Marx or his followers have written to be useful, or even relevant or correct. On the contrary, readers familiar with the Marxist literature will notice (and may complain) that many strands of Marxist thought are not represented in this book. Nonetheless, our approach is fundamentally Marxist and our primary intellectual debt is to Karl Marx.

The following quotation from Ernesto (Che) Guevara describes well our position.[1]

> *The merit of Marx is that he suddenly produces a qualitative change in the history of social thought. He interprets history, understands its dynamic, predicts the future, but in addition to predicting it (which would satisfy his scientific obligation), he expresses a*

[1] "Notes for the Study of the Ideology of the Cuban Revolution," *Studies on the Left*, Vol. 1, No. 3, 1960.

revolutionary concept: the world must not only be interpreted, it must be transformed.

Explanation alone is not enough. The purpose of social and economic analysis should be to help to eradicate the current sources of oppression rather than merely to describe them, or—still worse—to obscure them. We want to place our analysis squarely on the side of the growing movement for radical social change. For, as a result of our studies and our association with the radical movement in the United States, it has become clear to us that to achieve a better society the capitalist system must be challenged.

We do not imply that *all* forms of oppression can be attributed *solely* to capitalism, nor that they will automatically disappear when capitalism is replaced by a new social order. We have respect for the tenacity of such phenomena as sexism and military expansion, which predate the rise of capitalism and are not unique to capitalist societies today. Yet we do believe that most often capitalism makes use of and reinforces these forms of oppression. To eradicate them it is therefore necessary, but not sufficient, to transform the basic institutions of the capitalist system itself. To achieve a truly humane society, the struggle against capitalism must be intimately linked with struggles against all forms of oppression.

The purpose of this book is to contribute to these struggles by analyzing the structure and the dynamics of the capitalist system in the United States. In so doing, we seek to illuminate the relationships between capitalist institutions and the various forms of oppression discussed above, and we seek to identify those forces in the development of American capitalism that create the potential for a radical transformation of the social order.

CAPITALISM AND SOCIALISM

Throughout this book we will be criticizing the capitalist system that dominates the Western world today. In Part II we define quite explicitly what we mean by the capitalist mode of production and how it is to be distinguished from alternative modes. But it will be useful at the outset to clarify our understanding of the differences between capitalism and socialism, since the meaning of both terms has been subject to much confusion.

A common view, which we find inappropriate, is that the difference between capitalism and socialism depends solely upon the legal relations of ownership of the means of production. Capitalism is often equated with private ownership of capital, while socialism is equated with public or state ownership of capital.

In many advanced capitalist countries—such as England, France, or Sweden—the state-owned branches of production have grown in importance in recent decades, and the state has taken on the responsibility of regulating and managing the entire economy. These countries are often said to be examples of mixed systems, in that they embody elements of both capitalism and socialism. However, the state-owned production sectors in these countries tend to differ only marginally, if at all, from the private sectors of the economy, inasmuch as the state employs capitalist-oriented criteria in organizing its activities. These countries are examples of what we would call *state capitalism*.

At the same time, in the Soviet Union and the Eastern European countries, virtually the entire economy is run by a centralized state apparatus. This system has resulted in a stratified, bureaucratic, and hierarchical society in which the maximization of material goods production—subject to the constraint of preserving hierarchical control—is a primary objective. Such a society might best be called *state socialism*. In Serge Mallet's apt analogy, the state socialist societies of the Soviet Union and Eastern Europe are to true socialism what "the monsters of the paleolithic era are to present animal species: clumsy, abortive, prototypes."[2] It would be

[2]Serge Mallet, "Bureaucracy and Technology in the Socialist Countries," *Socialist Revolution*, 1, No. 3 (May/June 1970), p. 45.

incorrect to equate mechanically state socialism and state capitalism, for the two systems
do differ in significant respects. For example,
the state socialist societies have gone much
further toward equalizing the distribution of
essential goods and services such as food,
housing, medical care, and transportation.
Yet state socialism and state capitalism are
akin in many respects: neither are model
societies of socialism to be emulated.

For us, socialism is more than a juridical
change in the legal relations of ownership.
Socialism means democratic, decentralized,
and *participatory* control for the individual: it
means having a say in the decisions that affect
one's life. Such a participatory form of socialism certainly requires equal access for all to
material and cultural resources, which in turn
requires the abolition of private ownership of
capital and the redistribution of wealth. But
it also calls for socialist men and women to
eliminate alienating, destructive forms of
production, consumption, education, and
community and family life. Participatory
socialism requires the elimination of corporate
bureaucracies and all such hierarchical forms,
and their replacement, not by new state or
party bureaucracies, but by a self-governing
and self-managing people with directly-
chosen representatives subject to recall and
replacement. Participatory socialism entails a
sense of egalitarian cooperation, of solidarity
of people with one another; but at the same
time it respects individual and group differences and guarantees individual rights. It
affords to all individuals the freedom to exercise human rights and civil liberties that are
not mere abstractions but have concrete day-
to-day meaning.[3]

Our vision of a radical social transformation of the United States clearly involves far

[3]We pursue further our conception of socialism in
Chapter 14, where it is described in greatest detail by
Lerner, Section 14.3, p. 532. By our criteria, no existing
country has as yet achieved full participatory socialism,
although some countries that call themselves "socialist"
(e.g., China and Cuba) appear to have progressed
further in that direction than others (e.g., the Soviet
Union).

more than formal changes in political and
economic institutions. Such changes must be
part of an ongoing process of change in social
and cultural consciousness that will constitute
a revolution of social relations among people.

ORGANIZATION OF THE BOOK

We have organized this book so as to facilitate
its use as an independent and coherent text in
political economy. The content of the book
has been divided into six parts and fourteen
chapters which follow one another in a logically continuous sequence.

Part I, "Inside the Capitalist System," consists of one introductory chapter, "The Seamy
Side of American Capitalism." The selected
readings are intended to illustrate briefly but
vividly some of the forms of oppression that
are so prevalent and so intractable in the
United States today. Each of the readings has
its counterpart in a full chapter in Part IV
or Part V of the book, where the issues are
related to the structure and dynamics of
capitalist institutions.

Part II, "A Theoretical Approach to Capitalism," is designed to lay the basic theoretical
groundwork for a Marxist analysis of capitalist
society. Chapter 2, "Historical Materialism
and the Rise of Capitalism," introduces the
reader to the Marxist materialist conception
of history and discusses from this perspective
the rise of capitalism in the Western world.
Chapter 3, "The Capitalist Mode of Production," presents the essential elements of a
Marxist theory of how capitalism works.
Because of their theoretical nature these
chapters do not make easy reading, but they
are important for the development of a radical
analytical approach to the study of our
society.

Part III, "Monopoly Capitalism in the
United States," focuses attention on some of
the salient characteristics of the contemporary
stage of capitalism in the United States—
monopoly capitalism. Chapter 4, "Capital
Accumulation and the Capitalist Class," and
Chapter 5, "Wage-Labor and the Working

Class," discuss the evolution and current situation of capital and labor in the United States. Chapter 6, "Class Conflict and the State," discusses the role of the American state in the context of the continuing struggle between capital and labor.

Parts IV and V contain the chapters devoted to analyzing specific forms of oppression in the United States today. In addition to examining the current situation, these chapters seek to throw light on potential future developments that could prove contradictory for the capitalist system. Part IV, "Class Structure and Exploitation," groups together chapters dealing with "micro" processes of production, reproduction, and distribution within our society: Chapters 7 to 10 examine "Alienation," "Inequality," "Sexism," and "Racism." Part V, "Contradictions of the Macroeconomy," includes the chapters dealing with the "macro" behavior of the society as a whole: Chapters 11 to 13 discuss "Irrationality," "Economic Crises," and "Imperialism."

Part VI of the book, "Toward an Alternative to the Capitalist System," consists of a single chapter, "From Capitalism to Socialism." This chapter explores our vision of a socialist alternative to capitalism and considers some possible strategies for achieving such a society in the context of the contradictions of advanced capitalism. These issues are extremely important and deserve a far more extensive treatment than we can provide in this book. We hope, nonetheless, that by presenting an analysis of the existing capitalist system we will have contributed to the process of forming a strategy to bring about the truly free and humane alternative society that we call participatory socialism.

PART I

INSIDE
THE CAPITALIST
SYSTEM

The Seamy Side
of American Capitalism

AMERICAN CAPITALISM HAS PRODUCED the most stupendous wealth any society has ever known. In the process, it has advertised its bright side and drummed into our heads its benefits. Its triumphs are shown to us in the happy faces of the Coca-Cola commercial, in the impressive technology of the moon landing, in the endless procession of rising economic indexes. We know only too well how a poor farm boy named Henry Ford (or John D. Rockefeller or J. Paul Getty or H. Ross Perot or Edwin Land) was able to parlay "freedom of opportunity" into a billion-dollar fortune. We see pictures of vast piles of wheat and soybeans being loaded for export to countries that cannot feed themselves. We are dazzled, especially at Christmas-time, by the new toys, the newly essential "feminine hygiene" products, new recreation vehicles, pocket calculators, cameras, clothes fashions, "natural" foods. We observe the tide of state lotteries and TV game shows in which the process of becoming rich is telescoped from a "lifetime of sacrifice" to a convenient half-hour. Life is increasingly pictured for us through the carefully nurtured images of "celebrities"—those affluent, happy, witty, and active personalities who people the movies, professional sports, TV's situation comedies, rock music, and politics. American capitalism's wealth has produced much that glitters.

Yet as we proceed through the last quarter of the twentieth century, we hardly need to be told that American capitalism has another side as well, a less affluent, less eternally happy, less secure, less sensible, and less decent side: there is a seamy side to its advertised froth. After all, situation comedies alternate with shows of crime and violence. Henry Ford's fortune (now Henry Ford II's) stands in stark contrast to the underpaid auto workers' plight. The lunar module has proved unsuited for mass transit. Rising economic indexes can measure rising prices, unemployment, and misery as well as increasing output. And what are we to make of the booming sales of valium and other drugs that seem to be necessary to keep masses of Americans from being chronically overanxious or depressed? Or of the continued massive scarring of Appalachia and, increasingly, Montana, Wyoming, Arizona, and elsewhere as strip-mining literally eats up the land? Or of the startling but repeated reports of children's malnutrition at home as the food stamp program is unable to service all those who need aid? Or of the visible deterioration in urban housing? Or of the race riots that erupt from the attempts to desegregate Boston and Louisville? Or of the disclosures of a far-reaching domestic spying apparatus run by the federal government to disrupt political opposition and prepare for "emergency detention" of opponents? Or of the CIA's assistance to the fascist generals or corrupt politicians in Italy, Greece, and Chile? These are also very much a part of modern American capitalism.

A major theme of this book is the relationship in a capitalist society between the accumulation of wealth and the degradation of human life. We will attempt to illuminate this relationship by studying the basic social and economic processes of capitalism.

Before beginning such an analysis, however, we shall focus directly on some of the social problems that confront our society. For people who are not the most immediate victims, there is a persistent air of unreality about the disastrous news reports or chilling exposés that regularly remind us of our society's deep troubles. Just as we casually switch channels from the most vicious rape scene to the most inane comedy, so we are able to pass crumbling neighborhoods and clusters of unemployed on our way to the new-car showroom or the sports arena. We should not let ourselves lose sight of these desperate and massive social problems.

In the readings in this chapter we draw attention to several such aspects of contemporary capitalism, each of which we examine in greater detail in Parts IV and V. Alienation, inequality, sexism, racism, irrationality, economic crises, and imperialism are illustrated by brief accounts that are both per-

sonal and well-informed. Our choices here are intended to be more illustrative than comprehensive, but our selection of topics is not random. The readings reflect issues of such social significance and urgency that they have become focal points for resistance, opposition, and struggle. This connection between the conditions created by the capitalist system and the efforts of people to change those conditions is a second major theme in our analysis.

It is an understandable fact of life that the most directly oppressed people are rarely in a position to articulate their oppression in written form. Instead, oppression is more often described by sympathetic observers whose background and education have spared them from the most obvious forms of oppression and enabled them to communicate effectively in writing. Most of the readings in this chapter conform to this rule. By reprinting reports by persons directly or closely involved, we hope to convey some insight into the seamy side of American capitalism.

1.1   *Inside the New York Telephone Company*

Much of every person's adult life is spent working. Yet the effect of work on working people is rarely considered from the perspective of what might help workers achieve their aspirations or what might make their work lives meaningful. Life on the job is seldom fulfilling, as Elinor Langer found out at the New York Telephone Company, a privately owned utility whose mode of operations is typical of large corporations.

From October to December 1969 I worked for the New York Telephone Company as a Customer's Service Representative in the Commercial Department. My office was one of several in the Broadway–City Hall area

of lower Manhattan, a flattened, blue windowed commercial building in which the telephone company occupies three floors. The room was big and brightly lit—like the city room of a large newspaper—with perhaps one hundred desks arranged in groups of five or six around the desk of a Supervisor. The job consists of taking orders for new equipment and services and pacifying customers who complain, on the eleven exchanges (although not the more complex business accounts) in the area between the Lower East Side and 23rd Street on the North and bounded by Sixth Avenue on the West.

My Supervisor is the supervisor of five women. She reports to a Manager who manages four supervisors (about twenty women) and he reports to the District Supervisor along with two other managers. The offices of the managers are on the outer edge of the main room separated from the floor by glass partitions. The District Supervisor is down the hall in an executive suite. A job identical in rank to that of the district supervisor is held by four other men in Southern Manhattan alone. They report to the Chief of the Southern Division, himself a soldier in an army of division chiefs whose territories are five boroughs, Long Island, Westchester, and the vast hinterlands vaguely referred to as "Upstate." The executives at ———— Street were only dozens among the thousands in New York Tel alone.

Authority in their hierarchy is parceled out in bits. A representative, for example, may issue credit to customers up to, say, $10.00; her supervisor, $25.00; her manager, $100.00; his supervisor, $300.00; and so forth. . . .

I brought to the job certain radical interests. I knew I would see "bureaucratization," "alienation," and "exploitation." I knew that it was "false consciousness" of their true role in the imperialist economy that led the "workers" to embrace their oppressors. I believed those things and I believe them still. I know why, by my logic, the workers should rise up. But my understanding was making reality an increasing puzzle: Why didn't people move? What things, invisible to me, were holding them back? What I hoped to learn, in short, was something about the texture of the industrial system: what life within it meant to its participants.

I deliberately decided to take a job which was women's work, white collar, highly industrialized and bureaucratic. I knew that New York Tel was in a management crisis notorious both among businessmen and among the public and I wondered what effect the well-publicized breakdown of service was having on employees. Securing the position was not without hurdles. I was "overqualified," having confessed to college; I performed better on personnel tests than I intended to do; and I was inspected for symptoms of militance by a shrewd but friendly interviewer who noticed the several years' gap in my record of employment. "What have you been doing lately?" she asked me. "Protesting?" I said: "Oh, no, I've been married," as if that condition itself explained one's neglect of social problems. She seemed to agree that it did.

My problem was to talk myself out of a management traineeship at a higher salary while maintaining access to the job I wanted. This, by fabrications, I was able to do. I said: "Well, you see, I'm going through a divorce right now and I'm a little upset emotionally, and I don't know if I want a career with managerial responsibility." She said: "If anyone else said that to me, I'm afraid I wouldn't be able to hire them," but in the end she accepted me. I had the feeling it would have been harder for her to explain to her bosses why she had let me slip away, given my qualifications, than to justify to them her suspicions.

I nonetheless found as I began the job that I was viewed as "management material" and given special treatment. I was welcomed at length by both the District Supervisor and the man who was to be my Manager, and given a set of fluffy feminist speeches about "opportunities for women" at New York Tel. I was told in a variety of ways that I would be smarter than the other people in my class; "management" would be keeping an eye on me. Then the Manager led me personally to the back classroom where my training program was scheduled to begin.

·   ·   ·

LEARNING

The Representative's course is "programmed." It is apparent that the phone company has spent millions of dollars for high-class management consultation on the best way to train new employees. The two principal criteria are easily deduced. First, the course should be made so routine that any employee can teach it. The teacher's material—the remarks she makes, the examples she uses—are all printed in a loose-leaf notebook that she follows. Anyone can start where anyone else leaves off. I felt that I could teach the course myself, simply by following the program. The second criterion is to assure the reproducibility of results, to guarantee that every part turned out by the system will be interchangeable with every other part. The system is to bureaucracy what Taylor was to the factory: it consists of breaking down every operation into discrete parts, then making verbal the discretions that are made.

At first we worked chiefly from programmed booklets organized around the principle of supplying the answer, then rephrasing the question. For instance:

> *It is annoying to have the other party to a conversation leave the line without an explanation.*
> *Before leaving, you should excuse yourself and*
> ———*what you are going to do.*

Performing skillfully was a matter of reading, and not actual comprehension. . . .

Soon acting out the right way to deal with customers became more important than self-instruction. The days were organized into Lesson Plans, a typical early one being: How to Respond to a Customer if You Haven't Already Been Trained to Answer his Question, or a slightly more bureaucratic rendering of that notion. Sally [the instructor] explained the idea, which is that you are supposed to refer the call to a more experienced Representative or to the Supervisor. But somehow they manage to complicate this situation to the point where it becomes confusing even for an intelligent person to handle it. You mustn't say: "Gosh, that's tough, I don't know anything about that, let me give the phone to someone who does," though that in effect is what you do. Instead when the phone rings, you say: "Hello. This is Miss Langer. May I help you?" (The Rule is, get immediate "control of the contact" and hold it lest anything unexpected happen, like, for instance, a human transaction between you and the customer.)

He says: "This is Mr. Smith and I'd like to have an additional wall telephone installed in my kitchen."

You say: "I'll be very glad to help you, Mr. Smith (Rule the Second: Always express interest in the Case and indicate willingness to help), but I'll need more information. What is your telephone number?"

He tells you, then you confess: "Well, Mr. Smith, I'm afraid I haven't been trained in new installations yet because I'm a new representative, but let me give you someone else who can help you." (Rule the Third: You must get his consent to this arrangement. That is, you must say: *May* I get someone else who can help you? *May* I put you on hold for a moment?)

The details are absurd but they are all prescribed. What you would do naturally becomes unnatural when it is codified, and the rigidity of the rules makes the Representatives in training feel they are stupid when they make mistakes. . . . The logic of training is to transform the trainees from humans into machines. The basic method is to handle any customer request by extracting "bits" of information: by translating the human problem he might have into bureaucratic language so that it can be processed by the right department. For instance, if a customer calls and says: "My wife is dying and she's coming home from the hopsital today and I'd like to have a phone installed in her bedroom right away," you *say*, "Oh I'm very sorry to hear that sir, I'm sure I can help you, would you be interested in our Princess model? It has a dial that lights up at night," meanwhile *writing* on your ever-present CF-1: "Csr wnts Prn inst bdrm immed," issuing the order, and placing it in the right-hand side of your work-file where it gets picked up every fifteen minutes by a little clerk.

. . .

SELLING

It is largely since World War II that the Bell System abandoned being a comparatively simple service organization and began producing such an array of consumer products as to rival Procter and Gamble. It is important to realize what contribution this proliferation makes both to creating the work and to making it unbearable. If the company restricted itself to essential functions and services—standard telephones and standard types of service—whole layers of its bureaucracy would not need to exist at all, and what did need to exist could be both more simple and more humane. The pattern of proliferation is also crucial, for among other things, it is largely responsible for the creation of the "new"—white collar—"working class" whose job is to process the bureaucratic desiderata of consumption.

In our classroom, the profit motivation behind the telephone cornucopia is not concealed and we are programmed to repeat its justifications: that the goods were developed to account for different "tastes" and the "need of variation." Why Touchtone Dialing? We learn to say that "it's the latest thing," "it dials faster," "it is easier to read the letters and numbers," and "its musical notes as you depress the buttons are pleasant to hear." We learn that a Trimline is a "spacesaver," that it has an "entirely new feature, a recall button that allows you to hang up without replacing the receiver," and that it is "featured in the Museum of Modern Art's collection on industrial design." Why a night-light? we were asked. I considered saying, "It would be nice to make

love by a small sexy light," but instead helped to contribute the expected answers: "It gives you security in the bedroom," "it doesn't interfere with the TV."

. . .

Selling is an important part of the Representative's job. Sally introduced the subject with a little speech (from her program book) about the concept of the "well-telephoned home," how that was an advance from the old days when people thought of telephone equipment in a merely functional way. Now, she said, we stress "a variety of items of beauty and convenience." Millions of dollars have been spent by the Bell System, she told us, to find out what a customer wants and to sell it to him. She honestly believed that good selling is as important to the customer as it is to the company: to the company because "it makes additional and worthwhile revenue," to the customer because it provides services that are truly useful. We are warned not to attempt to sell when it is clearly inappropriate to do so, but basically to use every opportunity to unload profitable items. This means that if a girl calls up and asks for a new listing for a roommate, your job is to say: "Oh. Wouldn't your roommate prefer to have her own extension?"

The official method is to avoid giving the customer a choice but to offer him a total package which he can either accept or reject. For instance, a customer calls for new service. You find out that he has a wife, a teen-age daughter, and a six-room apartment. The prescription calls for you to get off the line, make all the calculations, then come back on and say all at once: "Mr. Smith, suppose we installed for you a wall telephone in your kitchen, a Princess extension in your daughter's room and one in your bedroom, and our new Trimline model in your living room. This will cost you only X dollars for the installation and only Y dollars a month."

Mr. Smith will say, naturally, "That's too many telephones for a six-room apartment," and you are supposed to "overcome his objections" by pointing out the "security" and "convenience" that comes from having telephones all over the place.

Every Representative is assigned a selling quota—so many extensions, so many Princesses—deducted and derived in some way from the quota of the next largest unit. In other words, quotas are assigned to the individual because they are first assigned to the five-girl unit; they are assigned to the unit because they are assigned to the twenty-girl section; and they are assigned to the section because they are assigned to the district: to the Manager and the District Supervisor. The fact that everyone is in the same situation— expected to contribute to the same total—is one of the factors that increase management-worker solidarity.

The women enact the sales ritual as if it were in fact in their own interest and originated with them. Every month there is a sales contest. Management provides the money—$25.00 a month to one or another five-girl unit—but the women do the work: organizing skits, buying presents, or providing coffee and donuts to reward the high sellers. At Thanksgiving the company raffled away turkeys: the number of chances one had depending on the number of sales one had completed.

SURVIVING

Daily life on the job at the New York Telephone Company . . . consists largely of pressure. To a casual observer it might appear that much of the activity on the floor is random, but in fact it is not. The women moving from desk to desk are on missions of retrieving and refiling customers' records; the tête-à-têtes that look so sociable are anxious conferences with a Supervisor in which a Representative is Thinking and Planning What to Do Next. Of course the more experienced women know how to use the empty moments that do occur for social purposes. But the basic working unit is one girl: one telephone, and the basic require-

ment of the job is to answer it, perhaps more than fifty times a day.

For every contact with a customer, the amount of paperwork is huge: a single contact can require the completion of three, four, or even five separate forms. No problems can be dispensed with handily. Even if, for example, you merely transfer a customer to Traffic or Repair you must still fill out and file a CF-1. At the end of the day you must tally up and categorize all the services you have performed on a little slip of paper and hand it in to the Supervisor, who completes a tally for the unit: it is part of the process of "taking credit" for services rendered by one unit vis-à-vis the others.

A Representative's time is divided into "open" and "closed" portions, according to a recent scientific innovation called FADS (for Force Administration Data System), of which the company is particularly proud; the innovation consists in establishing how many Representatives have to be available at any one moment to handle the volume of business anticipated for that month, that day, and that hour. Under this arrangement the contact with the customer and the processing of his request are carried out simultaneously: that is, the Representative does the paperwork needed to take care of a request while she is still on the line. For more complex cases, however, this is not possible and the processing is left for "closed" time: a time when no further calls are coming in.

This arrangement tends to create a constant low-level panic. There is a kind of act which it is natural to carry to its logical conclusion: brushing one's teeth, washing a dish, or filling out a form are things one does not leave half done. But the company's system stifles this natural urge to completion. Instead, during "open" time, the phone keeps ringing and the work piles up. You look at the schedule and know that you have only one hour of "closed" time to complete the work, and twenty minutes of that hour is a break.

The situation produces desperation: How am I to get it done? How can I call back all those customers, finish all that mail, write all those complicated orders, within forty minutes? Occasionally, during my brief time at the job, I would accidentally press the wrong button on my phone and it would become "open" again. Once, when I was feeling particularly desperate about time, I did that twice in a row and both times the callers were ordering new telephone service —a process which takes between eight and ten minutes to complete.

My feeling that time was slipping away, that I would never be able to "complete my commitments" on time was intense and hateful. Of course it was worse for me than for the experienced women—but not much worse. Another situation in which the pressure of time is universally felt is in the minutes before lunch and before five o'clock. At those times, if your phone is open, you sit hoping that a complex call will not arrive. A "new line" order at five mintues to five is a source of both resentment and frustration.

· · ·

CONSUMING

The women of the phone company are middle class or lower middle class, come from a variety of ethnic backgrounds (Polish, Jewish, Italian, Irish, Black, Puerto Rican), mainly high-school graduates or with a limited college education. They live just about everywhere except in Manhattan: the Bronx, Brooklyn, Staten Island, or Queens. Their leisure time is filled, first of all, with the discussion of objects. Talk of shopping is endless, as is the pursuit of it in lunch hours, after work, and on days off. The women have a fixation on brand names, and describe every object that way: it is always a London Fog, a Buxton, a White Stag. This fixation does not preclude bargain-hunting: but the purpose of hunting a bargain is to get the brand name at a lower price. Packaging is also important: the women will describe not only the thing but also the box or wrapper it comes in. They are especially fascinated

by wigs. Most women have several wigs and are in some cases unrecognizable from day to day, creating the effect of a continually changing work force. The essence of wiggery is escapism: the kaleidoscopic transformation of oneself while everything else remains the same. Anyone who has ever worn a wig knows the embarrassing truth: it *is* transforming.

Consumerism is one of the major reasons why these women work. Their salaries are low in relation to the costs of necessities in American life; ... barely enough, if one is self-supporting, to pay for essentials. In fact, however, many of the women are not self-supporting, but live with their families or with husbands who also work, sometimes at more than one job. Many of the women work overtime more than five hours a week (only for more than five extra hours do they get paid time and a half) and it seems from their visible spending that it is simply to pay for their clothes, which are expensive, their wigs, their color TV's, their dishes, silver, and so forth.

What the pressures of food, shelter, education, or medical costs contribute to their need to work I cannot tell, but it seems to me the women are largely trapped by their love of objects. What they think they need in order to survive and what they endure in order to attain it is astonishing. Why this is so is another matter. I think that the household appliances play a real role in the women's family lives: helping them to run their homes smoothly and in keeping with a (to them) necessary image of efficiency and elegance. As for the clothes and the wigs, I think they are a kind of tax, a tribute exacted by the social pressures of the work-place. For the preservation of their own egos against each other and against the system, they had to feel confident of their appearance on each and every day. Outside work they needed it too: to keep up, to keep their men, not to fall behind.

The atmosphere of passionate consuming was immeasurably heightened by Christmas, which also had the dismal effect of increasing the amount of stealing from the locker room. For a period of about three weeks nothing was safe: hats, boots, gloves. The women told me that the same happens every year: an overwhelming craving, a need for material goods that has to find an outlet even in thievery from one another.

The women define themselves by their consumerism far more than by their work, as if they were compensating for their exploitation as workers by a desperate attempt to express their individuality as consumers. Much of the consuming pressure is generated by the women themselves: not only in shopping but in constant raffles, contests, and so forth in which the prize is always a commodity—usually liquor. The women are asked to participate in these raffles at least two or three times a week.

But the atmosphere is also deliberately fostered by the company itself. The company gave every woman a Christmas present: a little wooden doll, about four inches tall, with the sick-humor look that was popular a few years ago and still appears on greeting cards. On the outside the doll says "Joy is . . ." and when you press down the springs a little stick pops up that says "Extensions in Color" (referring to the telephone extensions we were trying to sell). Under that label is another sticker, the original one, which says "Knowing I wuv you." The doll is typical of the presents the company distributes periodically: a plastic shopping bag inscribed with the motto "Colorful Extensions Lighten the Load"; a keychain with a plastic Princess telephone saying "It's Little, It's Lovely, It Lights"; plastic rain bonnets with the telephone company emblem, and so forth.

There were also free chocolates at Thanksgiving and, when the vending machine companies were on strike, free coffee for a while in the cafeteria. The women are disgusted by the company's gift-giving policies. Last year, I was told, the Christmas present was a little gold-plated basket filled with velour fruit and adorned with a flag containing a company motto of the "Extensions in Color" type. They think it is a cheap

trick—better not done at all—and cite instances of other companies which give money bonuses at Christmas.

It is obvious that the gifts are all programmed, down to the last cherry-filled chocolate, in some manual of Personnel Administration that is the source of all wisdom and policy; it is clear from their frequency that a whole agency of the company is devoted to devising these gimmicks and passing them out. In fact, apart from a standard assortment of insurance and pension plans, the only company policy I could discover which offers genuine advantage to the employees and which is not an attempt at manipulation is a tuition support program in which the company pays $1000 out of $1400 of the costs of continuing education.

Going still further, the company, for example, sponsors a recruiting game among employees, a campaign entitled "People Make the Difference." Employees who recruit other employees are rewarded with points: 200 for a recommendation, an additional thousand if the candidate is hired. Employees are stimulated to participate by the circulation of an S&H-type catalogue, a kind of encyclopedia of the post-scarcity society. There you can see pictured a GE Portable Color Television with a walnut-grained polystyrene cabinet (46,000 points), a Silver-Plated Hors d'Oeuvres Dish By Wallace (3,900 points), and a staggering assortment of mass-produced candelabra, linens, china, fountain pens, watches, clothing, luggage, and—for the hardy—pup tents, power tools, air mattresses.

Similarly, though perhaps less crudely, the company has institutionalized its practice of rewarding employees for longevity. After every two years with the company, the women receive a small gold charm, the men a "tie-tac." These grow larger with the years and after a certain period jewels begin to be added; rubies, emeralds, sapphires, and eventually diamonds and bigger diamonds. The tie-tac evolves over the years into a tie-clasp. After twenty-five years you may have either a ceremonial luncheon or an inscribed watch: the watches are pre-fixed, pre-selected, and pictured in a catalogue.

The company has "scientifically structured" its rewards just as it has "scientifically structured" its work. But the real point is that the system gets the women as consumers in two ways. If consumption were less central to them, they would be less likely to be there in the first place. Then, the company attempts to ensnare them still further in the mesh by offering as incentives goods and images of goods which are only further way stations of the same endless quest.

·   ·   ·

1.2   *The Elderly Poor*

In the United States the vast fortunes of the wealthy few exist alongside the pressing poverty of millions. Unemployed workers, racial minorities, migrant laborers, women who are heads of households, employees in low-wage industries, the unskilled, and many others make up this country's poor. In the following reading, Harold Freeman describes the plight of one of the most neglected groups in our society—the elderly poor.

Consider a single group of [capitalism's victims,] the elderly poor; of the 25 million Americans now below the federal poverty line, approximately 5 million are over 65. Being old they find it hard to get around; in many smaller communities bus service during the middle hours of the day is poor. So they shop in nearer, smaller, and more expensive stores. If hot food is served at a center few can get to it. They are particularly vulnerable to assault and theft; to the dissident young, as Marvin Wolfgang has explained, the elderly poor are attractive targets. Occupational opportunities are few, though a surprising part of their small current income does come from whatever work they can get—often as part-time janitors, watchmen, house and baby sitters. The work-at-home offers to which some are drawn are often fraudulent. They cannot read the fine print, they have slender legal recourse against misrepresentation. They are many among the fifteen million who come annually to the bar of justice with anxious complaints but without

funds, and now even the limited capacity of the Office of Economic Opportunity to provide help for them has been reduced by the elimination of its vital back-up research funds.

Medical burdens are particularly heavy on the elderly poor. They cannot readily reach a clinic or private doctor or dentist and when they do the hours they face in out-patient corridors and waiting rooms are tiring. In some areas the long clinic lines now have an added feature—for the elderly poor among the twenty-five million who have no Medicare, Medicaid, or private health insurance, up to $21 a visit is payable in advance. In New York City, only 23% of doctors accept Medicaid patients and 4% of the city's doctors collect 85% of all Medicaid fees. In Chicago, 73 of the county's 6000 private doctors see over half of the county's 285,000 Medicaid recipients—1 doctor per 2000 persons on Medicaid—and the ratio gets worse as these doctors, with their increased income from Medicaid fees, leave the poorer sections of the city; in

New York City there are 280 doctors per 100,000 population, but in the impoverished South Bronx area this figure has fallen to 10. In the nation's capital, about 20 persons, a high percentage of them elderly poor, die each year in the process of transfer from private hospital *emergency rooms*, where they are not wanted, to the District of Columbia General Hospital. In 1970 in Chicago, 18,000 persons, again with a disproportion of the elderly poor, were turned away from private hospital emergency rooms, and more than 100 of them died in the process of turnaway or transfer to Cook County Hospital which cares for half of Chicago's Medicaid patients. The turnaway, known in medical circles as patient dumping, generally consists of suggested use of a car or taxi, or simply pointing out the nearest bus stop.

Some are still involved in the consequences of unwise installment buying; harassment and repossession are occasional. Some have discovered that not only can an item on which one default has occurred be repossessed, but other items sold on prior contracts by the same merchant can also be repossessed. They have learned that dealers sometimes sell the notes of cheated buyers to finance houses, thereby nullifying complaints of fraud against the dealers. The few loans available to them are seldom from banks and always at high interest rates, up to 1000% per year in the experience of Justice William Douglas. With their too-small last-ditch savings (40% have assets under $1,000) they are the favorite prey of flim-flam specialists. They are exploited in stores skilled at offering special merchandise to the elderly and to welfare recipients, and careful not to show prices. Side street merchants have discovered the optimal way to deal with the elderly poor— get all you can now. Generally living alone they are found in declining residential hotels and tenements. In Lawrence, Massachusetts, after brief experience, one can confidently describe the room before seeing it—the rust-locked window, the artificial flowers, slow plumbing, framed family pictures and the inevitable two-burner hot plate. Thirty per-

cent of the residences of the elderly poor have no inside flush toilets, 40% no hot water bath, 54% minimal winter heat. Except in seven states, the tenant's obligation to pay rent is absolute while the landlord's obligation to maintain the premises is unmentioned, and the consequence for some of the elderly poor is eviction. Contrary to a few dramatic situations noted by the press, most rental evictions are quiet; for different reasons neither the landlord nor the tenant is eager for publicity.

Arrests of the elderly poor for shoplifting food are up sharply in the United States. A fair number of the elderly poor have discovered the greater protein value of dog food, that it is fairly edible though bland, that the health hazard is probably small, that it is somewhat cheaper than the food previously bought, and they have quietly made the change; the Washington *Post* estimates that the elderly poor purchase more dog food than do dog owners.

Except for burial policies, insurance either is not available or is outside their means; a furniture fire insurance policy is uncommon. Against even more primitive menaces like hunger, prolonged illness and eviction, protection is slight. Protection could come from savings or income, but their savings are small and their principal source of life-time income —their own modest earnings—have often come to an end. For the elderly poor with their small inflation-damaged income and their improved life span, insecurity is even more threatening than poverty; it saps much of their remaining vitality. As they age, we watch them drain their children's resources, then move or be moved to the lower strata of rest and nursing homes, the latter, 23,000 in all and three-quarters of them profit-making (documented in the report by Van Halamandaris to the Senate Special Committee on Aging), forming on average one of America's most destructive industries. Edith Stern describes these homes under the title *Buried Alive*. Even final dignity is denied them: they are cheated on funeral and cemetery arrangements.

Among these people you find no general

absence of character, not even irremediable loss of initiative. Their strength is diminished but it is not negligible; it has been paralyzed by forces against which they cannot, acting separately as the elderly poor do, prevail. Researches by David Blau and others have shown the alacrity with which, given some support, the elderly poor can recover mental and physical strength. But in the common absence of such support, degradation sets in. Seeing those who are better off express by indifference their doubt of the elderly poor's value to the community, so finally the elderly poor themselves doubt their value. For many the consequence is to turn inward, to protect what little they still have, not reaching out at all. Watching such a person, who wanted no help, get a solid block of ice out of a toilet in an apartment on Western Avenue —a street in Cambridge halfway between Harvard University and the Massachusetts Institute of Technology—one learns to respect the characteristic reaction of the elderly poor to all indignities, silence.

The tragedy of the elderly poor is unmistakable. Yet it would be difficult to find Americans in ordinary walks of life who would decline to support measures insuring a better deal for these people; in a Harris poll in 1975, 76% of Americans questioned stated that a person should be able to live comfortably during retirement no matter how much was earned during his or her worklife. But nothing like this prevails and the situation improves minimally. Why?

In the logic of capitalism the elderly poor are a problem, simply because they are unproductive. In a society which rewards according to contribution, they have no proper place. As a consequence, their dilemmas must multiply and reinforce each other, and in the process, much of the joy of life must be ground away. Like the sick and disabled, like all who can produce but little, the elderly poor are an externality to the theory of capitalism; they are found, if at all, in a chapter toward the end of the textbook. They have no solution within the system. Duncan Foley writes,

> Capitalism offers no systematic support to these people so that more or less effective devices outside the capitalist distribution system become necessary. Charity, welfare, public housing, socialized medicine . . . exist to support or help support persons of low productivity but they are all unnatural in a capitalist society, conflict with its basic principles, and as a result tend automatically to be controversial, badly run, inadequate and ineffective.

1.3 *We Usually Don't Hire Married Girls*

In recent years women have struggled to redefine the "female role"; this reading suggests some of the reasons why.

The following was written anonymously and first published in *Quicksilver Times* (Washington, D.C.)

I am 23 years old, I have a B.A. in Spanish literature, I am well traveled, I can speak Spanish and French, and I am a prostitute . . . I am a secretary, a wastebasket, a file-cabinet, a hostess, a messenger boy, and a slave. I am everything but a woman and a human being.

THE INTERVIEW

During my interview for this job my entire body was numbed. My interviewer kept looking at my legs and talking about how interesting he thought the job would be for me because I would be around men doing interesting work (not mentioning that my work would be boring).

He then looked at my legs again and looked up and gave me a very big paternalistic smile. "We usually don't hire married girls," he said. "We like to have young, pretty and available girls around the office. You know," he added, "it cheers things up a lot."

No wonder so many women fall apart in job interviews—our minds and our abilities are not questioned. It is our bodies and our smiles that are checked out to see if they will fit properly behind a mahogany desk.

I was hired and took the job because I was desperate. I was told I was awfully pretty and would most certainly be an asset to the office. For the first two weeks all the older women did was smile at me with their huge wide plastic smiles. They are not young, pretty or available anymore, so all they can offer is their smiles.

THE JOB

When I was hired I was told that two people constitute a team that would work on a specific project. "Teamwork" and "togetherness" were the key words used. It didn't take long to realize the real situation—racism, male supremacy, prejudice (you name it), all in one carpeted, IBM-filled office.

The "team" turned out to be a male, making around $15,000, and a female, making $6,000. Most girls have the same degrees as the men, or higher ones, but are still in the lower positions. The reason for this, I was told, was that most foreigners (whom the office deals with) don't "respect" women and would feel slighted if they had to deal with "one." (Wasn't that the reason given for not hiring blacks in offices and shops?—blacks would turn away customers!)

My job consists of serving coffee, answering the telephone, typing boring letters, and taking constant orders from my male "partner." I love "taking" letters for him. This gives him a chance to show me how really important he thinks he is. He leans back in his chair, takes a deep breath, and tries real hard to use the biggest words he knows. Dictating letters is a real ego-trip for these guys. It is incredible that the brainwashed females in this office will not admit that they have terrible jobs.

I have now been at this job for two months. My partner has never asked me anything about myself nor asked me to lunch. All he knows about me is that I type and take shorthand. Once in a while he will joke with me, but I am unable to respond. I would only be more of a whore if I did.

LUNCHTIME

We secretaries, nurses and administrative assistants have one hour to enjoy the day—lunchtime—and we usually are not even paid for that period. During the summer I attended a "Summer in the Parks" concert every Wednesday from 12 to 1 P.M. Sometimes the concert would run a little after the scheduled time. One could notice that exactly at 1 all the females would get up to go back to work. The males, who had no time clocks to punch, would stay to hear the rest of the concert.

There are few things we can do during that short time. It is too expensive and not easy to take a bus home to have lunch. A nice relaxing lunch would be nice—but at People's Drug or Linda's Cafeteria that is hardly possible. Have you ever gone to an expensive place at lunchtime? All men. How many working women can afford to spend more than $1 for lunch? How many restaurants are there that are cheap, relaxing, have good food and are not anxious to get rid of you after you have swallowed the last bite?

I tried taking my lunch and a book and going to the park for lunch. A chance to be outside and read and enjoy the sunshine was very appealing. One day a man masturbated behind me in the bushes as I tried to read. The next day a guy asked me to come to his hotel. On different days I was told various parts of my body were "really fine." For four days I was followed, touched, and generally harassed. On the fifth day I ate lunch at my desk.

The only thing that is open for us to do during that time is shop—whether it's food, clothes or shoes, the stores are all waiting (and panting) with cash registers ready. These stores are the only places where we can be comfortably accommodated during that hour. The drawback is that we must buy.

In my office all the men go out to eat together and all the women go out to eat together. No one has ever broken that unwritten law. The three blacks in the mailroom eat inside. They are not permitted to go out to eat.

When I mention women's liberation to the men in my office they always reply that we women at least have to admit that things have gotten better—equal opportunity act, equal pay and all that. But when you are being oppressed so severely, $1,000 or even $2,000 extra a year doesn't mean very much. Because men are so hung up on money and titles on the door, they feel that we too should be appeased with a larger paycheck and a fancy title like "administrative assistant" instead of plain "secretary."

At the end of my working day I am tired and depressed. The entire day I have been used as an instrument. So I get on a pollution-emitting bus and go home. There I find the baby, the dishes in the sink, dinner to be made, and a husband who wants me to look like Twiggy. And people ask why women want to be liberated.

1.4 *Going to School in Boston*

At various times in our country's past, Irish, Chinese, Jews, Italians, Greeks, and others have been discriminated against. In the 1840s it was common for employers, when advertising a job, to add "Irish need not apply." The slaughter of American Indians was so great as to justify the term "genocide." One of the most persistent and vicious forms of discrimination has been that directed against blacks. The following reading shows that white racism remains an important feature of the American landscape.

This essay was excerpted from "Going to School in Boston" by STEPHEN R. BING from *The Docket* (Civil Liberties Union of Massachusetts), December 1975. Copyright © 1975 by the Civil Liberties Union of Massachusetts. Reprinted by permission of the publisher.

Black elementary school children assigned to the Fairmount School in the Hyde Park section of Boston have learned a lot during this New England autumn. The quality, type and substance of their education, however, may not be what was envisioned by the architects of school desegregation in the city nor what was projected by authorities charged with the protection of the physical and psychological well-being of these children.

Ride the bus route to that school. Shortly before you arrive you see a black mannequin hung in effigy from the porch of a typical Boston three decker home, the kind of building lyrically invoked in any description of one of Boston's white neighborhoods. If you were one of the black children who travel that route daily, you would step off your bus onto a sign painted on the sidewalk. "WHITE POWER" is its message. To avoid this greeting, you might then look up to your school, across the playground and past the basketball court. Four foot high letters painted on the school say "HITLER WAS RIGHT." Quickly going to the school door reserved for those who ride the bus, lunch box banging against your knee and these images banging in your head, you would go to your classroom to begin to learn the three R's. Maybe, just maybe, the fourth one, racism, is left on the school wall, on the sidewalk, and in those streets the bus has just travelled.

Black students geocoded to other schools learn too. An adult white male wanders the halls of Charlestown High School, with the full knowledge of the federal court, the U.S. Marshalls and the Civil Rights Division of the Department of Justice, clothed in his own personal pledge of allegiance. His jacket says, "ROAR" [Restore Our Alienated Rights—a militant anti-busing group]. His presence is authorized by the federal court order.

The students are told by law enforcement personnel that nothing can be done; the jacket raises "grave First Amendment problems." In the phrase of one frequent apologist for this kind of conduct, "never mind" that last year a young black male student was assaulted and then suspended from South Boston High School for appearing in class in a Progressive Labor Party shirt. In that case, of course, his expression was "shouting fire in a crowded theatre."

But what of the presence of avowed and visible supporters of ROAR in the school? Could there be any significance greater than the fact that the position of that organization, already painfully clear to black children in Boston, is simply restated to them inside the school building? Perhaps.

·   ·   ·

It should be made quite explicit that the fear and terror are beginning to work. . . . Students who observe ROAR's impunity in Charlestown High School have grave doubts about whether the process is worth it. We

cannot even speculate on the damage done to the smaller, younger children.

·   ·   ·

Today, November 14, 1975, during third period (9:35–10:15) an assault occurred in my algebra class. The four black students in the class sit up front. Suddenly, without any warning (the class had been peaceful all year) I looked up and saw a white boy holding a chair up over one of the black boys' head. The next thing I knew, the white boy had hit the black boy two times over the head. The black boy was stunned but seemed to recover and started to get out of his chair.

Right after this happened, the rest of us blacks in the class got up to go after the white boy who had hit the black boy. All the whites were sitting behind us and got up and started to go to the back of the room. Before we got to the back of the room, a state trooper came in and grabbed the white boy who assaulted the black boy and took him out of the room.

Right after the white boy was taken out of the room, another white boy in our class jumped up and said. "Are you going to arrest him? You didn't arrest that nigger when he hit me with a chair." He was then taken from the room.

Everyone in the room was upset and we couldn't work for the rest of the period. Our teacher was shaking and crying, and said to the police that the white boy had no reason to assault the black boy. She suggested to us blacks that we sit in the back of the room from now on.

On Saturday, October 18, the Boston Globe [Boston's largest daily newspaper] reported that on the previous day a black student at South Boston High School had been suspended for striking a white student over the head with a chair. The white student had been taken to the hospital where several stitches were required to close the wound.

The few facts in the Globe story were accurate but by no means told the full story. The truth was quite the opposite of the impression created by the newspaper account. The incident is described in one of the affidavits filed with the court:

I was sitting in my homeroom class early in the morning before first period. My teacher, Mr. Moore, was there and a Spanish student whose name I don't know and two other black students. We were just sitting in our homeroom minding out own business, waiting for classes to start. All of a sudden, a lot of white boys, perhaps ten or twenty, came into the room and started to jump all of us. There was fighting all over the room, and we looked to our teacher Mr. Moore for help, but there was nothing that he could do about it. One of the white boys whose name I know is Sean.

During the melee, one of the outnumbered black students hit one of the white students over the head with a chair. The police arrived, broke up the fight and took all three blacks and three of the whites to the detention rooms. The students were suspended, but after adults in the school had corroborated the black students' version of events, the blacks' suspensions were, with some difficulty, lifted or expunged.

Mr. Moore corroborated the black students' story, and Headmaster Reid has admitted that the black students were attacked, completely without provocation, by a large number of whites, but the general public has never been given the true story of this and other incidents within the school. The original Globe story was never followed up or corrected, and the South Boston Information Center [run by ROAR] cites the incident to prove that blacks instigate violent attacks on whites.

The student we identify here as "Sean" has been involved in many incidents of violence within the school. Indeed, his continued presence inside the school is an intense irritant to the black students. The day before the attack described above, Sean had been found guilty in South Boston District Court of a similar assault, and had been ordered to be committed to the Department of Youth Services. But he and his gang seem to be able to roam the halls at will. How they get in is no mystery. One student describes it:

I have seen white aides letting white kids come into the school by the side doors two different times. Nobody is supposed to come in the side doors, because everybody is supposed to come in the front door where the metal detectors are.

Other student affidavits describe Sean's activities:

Some days I see gangs of white boys, headed by a student they call Sean, just roaming around the halls of the school. Some days they all wear green army jackets, and it seems like there is trouble on days when that happens.

. . .

One day early in October, I saw a white student named Sean come into the school on crutches with his foot wrapped in a bandage. During homeroom, before first period started, I saw Sean unwrapping the bandage from his foot. I heard him say, "This is my new nigger beater. I am going to use this crutch on the first nigger that says anything to me."

Although Sean and his gang are responsible for a lot of the violence, numerous other reports suggest that the aggression is not limited to any one white attacker or small group. The black students' affidavits tell a grim story.

The fighting started when a white boy threw a book at a black girl and hit her in the head with it. I saw this happen very clearly because I was standing only about four feet away from the white boy. She turned to come at the white boy and fell down, and a lot of other whites started hitting her, too. Then some other black kids tried to help defend her by pulling off the whites. She got arrested for this fight. . . . The white boy who had thrown the book to start it was not even detained.

. . .

On Tuesday, October 7, I was walking in the school hall. The only other people there were Mr. Gizzi, the Assistant Headmaster, and one white student. When the white student passed me, he swung his elbow at me and hit me and knocked me aside. I said to Mr. Gizzi, "You saw that. What are you going to do about that?" Mr. Gizzi replied, "That's just the way he walks."

. . .

Three black students were walking with me, all in single file. When we got to the lobby, I saw a long row of white students the whole length of the corridor. One of the white students pushed Jack and said something about "nigger mothers" and "all niggers suck." Jack said, "Whose mother are you talking about?" The white said, "Yours, nigger." The whites all started dropping their books and started to make a big circle around us. The one started swinging at Jack, and I tried to pull him away. Other whites started fighting us all. The police ran in and started pulling people apart and it was over in about twenty seconds. I was suspended for three days for this incident.

POLICE NOT NEUTRAL EITHER, STUDENTS SAY

Many of the black students' complaints involve the conduct of the police officers stationed inside South Boston High School. Now in general kids don't like cops—there's a natural antagonism that exists. But even allowing for that antagonism, there is enough corroborated evidence to indicate that, at the minimum, police inside the school are not neutral. One indication of their attitude is indicated by the mathematical precision with which they collar exactly equal numbers of blacks and whites following any incident, even when the incident involved a small number of blacks and a very large number of white students. The following incidents illustrate why black students do not feel safe and protected inside South High:

During that meeting, a black aide came in. She had been handcuffed by a state trooper. I asked her what happened, and she told me that she had been walking with six black students to the office. They had been jumped by white students, and one of them had grabbed for the guard's gun. The police jumped the black students and also slammed the black aide into a locker before he handcuffed her. . . . The police took all six black students, but no white students, to the school office. When a white teacher told the police that the black aide had not tried to get his gun, he apologized to her and asked her not to press charges against him. She also told me that he had hit her in the head with his stick. I know she was hit because I could see the knot on her head.

. . .

I was out in the hall near a state trooper. A white student passed me and said: "If there's one thing I hate, it's the smell of niggers," and spit on the floor. I said to the trooper: "You heard that." The trooper turned away from me and didn't do anything about it.

. . .

I am 17 years old and a sophomore at South Boston High School. I went there last year, too. I have five brothers and sisters in school in South Boston, three in the Gavin, one at L Street, and a sister with me at G Street. I am black.

All year long I have not been in any fights, and I have not been suspended.

One morning, Friday, October 31, 1975, I was walking to my first period Health class, going right in front of the office. Three white boys were walking behind me, and one of them named John started to push me. A teacher named Mr. Marc Scarsella was standing right there by the office and saw this happen, Mr. Scarsella grabbed that white boy John real quick. But John grabbed me anyway and ripped my coat and the other two white boys grabbed me, too, and I was knocked to the ground. I did not try to fight back. I did not raise my hands. I kept holding on to my books until I dropped them when I was knocked to the ground. A lot of state troopers came running over and grabbed me, and the white boys continued to hit me and kick me as the troopers held me.

Three or four of those troopers picked me up and carried me downstairs to the holding room. I didn't try to fight back or anything and I would have walked down, but they carried me anyway. When we got downstairs, one of the troopers, Badge No. 665, who I have seen lots of times in front of the office, said "Drop the nigger." They just dropped me on the floor like I was a dog or something. Then the troopers wanted to take my picture but they didn't tell me what for, and I didn't want them to. I turned my head away and put my new leather coat over my head. One of the troopers who wears shades, whom I have seen lots of times, said something like "Break his arms" and "You grab one arm. I'll hold his other, and we'll break his arms, if he won't stand for this picture." They tore my new leather coat even more.

Later a little short man who works in the school office came in and asked me to write a report about this incident. I told him what had happened and he wrote it down. I told him that Mr. Scarsella had seen the whole thing, and that I did not start anything, and that I did not fight back.

Mr. Gorovitch, the Assistant Head Master, came in and told me I was suspended for fighting. He told me that I would have to go home, and they took me home in a van.

I have been trying to get along out there at South Boston this year, and have not been involved in any trouble until this. Now this white boy John, who also pushed me and wanted to fight me last year, is starting that stuff this year.

THE "MONKEY TEACHER"

One of the charges made by the black students at the recent hearing in federal court involved the conduct of a South Boston High School teacher, Mr. Scalese. The students claimed that he ridiculed them by making monkey sounds and gestures. On the stand, one student was unable to identify Mr. Scalese or his homeroom. But others, describing a different incident on another day, could and did. Their testimony is as follows:

I was walking with a group of black students to a meeting we had arranged with the head of the state troopers stationed inside South Boston High. We walked by Tyson's homeroom, and his room teacher, Mr. Scalese, was not going to let him go to the meeting. Clyde told Mr. Scalese about the meeting, and we were starting to walk on down the hall to go to the meeting when I saw Scalese making monkey sounds in front of me. Mr. Scalese was standing in the doorway, making gestures and sounds like a monkey at us. I heard students inside the class behind him laughing and clapping and pounding their desks.

.   .   .

At the hearing, Mr. Scalese denied the students' allegations. Another teacher testified that Mr. Scalese was only fiddling with the flaps on his jacket pockets. The students insist the incident occurred as they described it.

.   .   .

[A black student summed up the atmosphere as follows.]

There is something about being in South Boston that does something to the white students. There is one white boy who was with us in the Burke [School] last year, who was really friendly and nice to black kids. This year at Southie [South High], he runs with that Sean gang and is always getting into fights.

1.5 *Caution: The Food May Be Hazardous to Your Health*

An economic system ought to provide the material things that can best meet the needs of people in society. From this perspective, our society is fundamentally irrational: it spends a hundred billion dollars on armaments while basic human needs go unmet; it fosters technologies and products that destroy the natural environment; and it produces consumer goods and a style of consumption that, as the following reading indicates, are detrimental to even the consumers' interests.

This essay was excerpted from "Food Pollution" by DANIEL ZWERDLING in *Ramparts*, June 1971. Copyright © 1971 by *Ramparts*; reprinted by permission of the author.

Canterbury, England (AP)—A 23-year-old woman starved to death because she believed nearly all human food was produced by the suffering of animals, the Canterbury coroner's court was told. Miss Brenda Holton, an office secretary, had a horror of all meat and other foods that she thought had been tainted by chemical sprays. She tried to live on a diet of honey, cereals and dandelion coffee, but her appetite faded and she wasted away.

Brenda Holton, poor masochist, at least had a glimpse of the problem: namely, that the Western World, and especially the United

States, is slowly eating itself to death as it stokes down nutty doddle snacks, hot dogs, balloon bread, chickens and steaks, canned orange juice, dehydrated soups, soft drinks, cakes made from mixes and imitation whipped cream sodden with 3000 different synthetic flavors, colors, thickeners, acidifiers, bleachers, preservatives, package contaminants, antibiotics and poison pesticides. Virtually no food on the grocery shelves is free from chemical additives which have no nutritive value, are probably harmful, and whose main purpose is to make eaters think they're eating something they aren't. Even Brenda's honey was contaminated with benzaldehyde, a toxic bee-repellent, her cereals tainted with preservatives and traces of grain pesticides, and her pathetic dandelions choked by herbicides and automobile exhaust fumes.

No one knows for sure whether synthetic additives in our food poison us in normal, everyday eating as many scientists suspect— traceable instances of human poisoning are rare—but there are well-founded suspicions, and no one knows that they *don't*. "We never know for sure whether additives are safe or not," warns Marvin Legator, chief biochemist at the Food and Drug Administration. "Long-term usage of additives can in no way be rated with safety. We have so many cases of common diseases like mental retardation and cancer, which we can't account for through epidemiological studies, for which we can't find a cause and effect." In other words, it might be chronic poisoning from food additives—but it will take years to find out. "The only reason we ever pinpointed thalidomide poisoning," Legator admits, "was because its effects were such gross abnormalities which are so damn rare. And even then it took us five years to find out."

Even if the 93 possible different additives in your daily bread aren't bad for you (and there's good evidence that they are), it is clear that they do nothing positive. At best you pay for synthetic color and taste, signifying nothing—except booming profits for the multi-billion dollar drug and food industry. Food companies are beginning to devote themselves exclusively to processed, synthetic foods—and it's no surprise. "The profit margin on food additives is fantastically good," a top food marketer says, "much better than the profit margin on basic, traditional foods."

The word to the industry is out: the more additives, "the higher the potential profit-margin," writes *Food Engineering*, the leading trade journal, which advises food corporations. Shy away from price-oriented "commodity" items and look to "highly manufactured" products in the decades ahead.

So much the worse for us and our polluted inner environment.

· · ·

The food industry has flooded the market's shelves with synthetic products, saturated the airwaves with their ads and created a demand for additives which never before existed. They have succeeded in making it appear retrograde to eat plain old food. "You can say that a demand was created for convenience foods," *Food Engineering*'s Trauberman confides. "The function of advertising is to create a demand for a product and to point out its virtues. Of course, all the advertising in the world isn't going to make me buy a product I don't like. Ads tell the housewife over and over again that if she likes the product, it's still around to be bought."

With over $100 million per year spent on its advertising, a corporation like General Foods can keep its synthetic products going pretty well. Consider Tang, the imitation orange drink: When a severe freeze in Florida several years ago decimated the orange crop, GF saw an instant opportunity for a new product: a simulated orange drink containing nothing but some citric acid, calcium phosphate, sodium citrate, hydrogenated vegetable oils, BHA, and some artificial color and flavoring. GF promotion did the rest. Do consumers want and need this kind of orange juice? Some never had a chance to decide. "My daughters won't touch natural orange juice," says Trauberman. "They drink only the packaged or canned concentrates. But it's only because that's what they're used to. Natural orange juice is unfamiliar."

. . .

[Or] take a long cooling swig of Mountain Dew, the tart beverage from Pepsi-Cola. Mountain Dew, like most tart soft drinks from the nation's $4 billion soft drink industry, gets its zip from brominated vegetable oils—artificial flavorings which have been stabilized in vegetable oil by a reaction process with poisonous bromine. Scientists at the Canadian Food and Drug Directorate discovered in 1969 that BVO causes liver, heart, kidney and spleen damage in rats. Here's what different diet levels did to the rats:

> *Growth retardation and impaired food utilization were observed in the 2.5 percent group, in which there was evidence of slight anemia. Enlargement of the heart occurred at the 0.5 percent level, and of the liver, heart, kidneys and spleen at the 2.6 percent level. All rats fed the brominated oil displayed thyroid hyperplasia, myocarditis, fatty changes in the liver, arrested testicular development, vacuolation of the renal tubular epithelium and reduced liver glucose . . . activities . . .*

. . .

Geneticists like Nobel prize winner Joshua Lederberg and Bruce Ames at the University of California, Berkeley, fret about the human gene pool. They think synthetic food additives may be fouling it up only we won't discover what we've done to the human race for generations, when it's too late. "It's not that the food additive is a large individual risk, but it may be an epidemiological problem." says Ames. "If out of one million people one person's genes are mutant, that's a serious problem. Cigarettes were around a long time before we knew that they caused lung cancer. If we're filling ourselves now with mutant genes, they're going to be around for generations and generations."

. . .

In any case, . . . you'd better look out for the following . . . .

SODIUM NITRITE AND SODIUM NITRATE

The all-purpose meat color fixatives. Americans just can't abide brown hot dogs and bologna and breakfast sausage, food industry motivational research has decided, so it keeps the meat blood-red with nitrite and nitrate (which keep the hemoglobin in the blood from turning brown when exposed to air). Sodium nitrite and nitrate hold a firm place in toxicological literature as potent human poisons and as laboratory carcinogens and mutagens. Consider this unfortunate case reported in the *New England Journal of Medicine:* "A 48-year-old factory worker was admitted to the hospital with intense cyanosis. . . . Twenty minutes earlier he complained of increasing nausea, became vertiginous, vomited three times, collapsed to the pavement and turned a bluish color." Only one hour before he had eaten a pound of New York Polish sausage—a typical market sausage made of pork, coarse cereal filler, beef blood, artificial flavor and color, and sodium nitrite and nitrate. His doctors figure the sausage had poorly distributed nitrite clusters.

Scientists worry particularly about sodium nitrate fertilizer residues in spinach and other leafy vegetables. Intestinal bacteria change the nitrates into nitrites, which then react with hemoglobin and turn children and babies blue in fits of methemoglobinemia, an acute blood poisoning. Medical journals are full of these cases. (California faces possible mass poisonings because it has an extraordinary nitrate level in drinking water due to fertilizer runoffs.) Nitrites, which are used to preserve smoked fish, like herring, salmon and tuna, also react with certain substances (secondary amines) in the fish, and at stomach acidic levels form nitrosamines, which are powerful cancer agents. Or, warns Dr. Lederberg, if nitrite gets to the DNA in human cells as it does in laboratory tests with microorganisms, it will mutate the genes.

"Sodium nitrite is going to have to come

out of our food sooner or later," says geneticist Ames. "If nitrite were coming up now as a new additive, FDA probably wouldn't let it on the market. But it's been around so long it will be hard to get it off.

"If the public can get used to brown hot dogs (even Germany, home of the wurst, eats its sausages without nitrite and nitrate), it would be a lot better off."

PRESERVATIVES

No one in the United States government can get aroused by BHT and BHA, the most widely used antioxidants in the country—which Britain has heavily restricted, and completely banned from all foods intended for babies or children. American kids eat them every day in their Wheaties and Cheerios—every breakfast cereal and every packaged slice of bread on the market and countless other packaged fatty foods they eat daily. Rats fed BHT often show increased liver enlargement, and British scientists have found that BHA induces tumors. BHT poses a peculiar problem because although 70 percent of it is excreted from the body within 24 hours, the rest lingers and accumulates in body fats. None of the damaging evidence is conclusive—numerous tests have not found harmful effects—so the FDA takes the easy way out and leaves the additives on the market.

Sodium benzoate and benzoic acid, the most popular preservatives in margarine, fish, fruit juices, confections, jams, jellies and soft drinks, have worried biochemists for years. The FAO/WHO committee on food additives reports that benzoates killed all the rats in one experiment—they died with convulsions, hyper-excitability, urinary incontinence and loss of body weight. Benzoic acid, reports *Food and Cosmetic Toxicology*, the respected science journal published by the University of Albany, is "markedly toxic" in mice, reducing their survival rates and body weights and possibly contributing to cancer.

That was enough evidence for the State of Wisconsin, which has banned sodium benzoate and benzoic acid from all its foods. From the FDA and food industry—not a murmur.

SYNTHETIC COLORS

They account for the color in 95 percent of the food on the market. Since Congress passed the Color Additive Amendment in 1960, a large number of colors have dropped from use because they are strongly suspected carcinogens. The last color to go, sort of, was FD&C Red No. 2, which causes cancer in laboratory mice. You'll still eat it in every maraschino cherry, though, because the maraschino lobbyists convinced the FDA that no one could possibly want to eat more than one or two at a time.

But the handful of synthetic colors left are making plenty of scientists uneasy—especially the coal-tar dyes. "Artificial colors are very suspicious," warns Dr. Lederberg, who says their molecular structures look like potent carcinogens. Laboratory tests by the FDA's own researchers show colors form skin tumors and ulcers on rats, and the Kaiser hospitals in California have documented numerous artificial color-caused asthmatic and other allergic attacks in children and adults. An FDA spokesman insists that "all artificial colors are continually under review"; meanwhile, almost every orange in the nation is dyed with sunshiny Citrus Red No. 2, which the FAO/WHO additive experts have flatly denounced as a potent danger—although FDA doubts that anyone would want to eat the peel.

CONDITIONERS AND BLEACHES

Virtually every loaf of bread or cookie or cake or doughnut you buy has been made with flour bleached and conditioned by poisons like hydrogen acetone and benzyl peroxides, chlorine dioxide, nitrogen oxides, nitrosyl chloride—and they all end up in your stomach. If you swallow any one of them straight you will probably die. In trace amounts in the markets, "they might have a chronic mutagenic effect," warns Lederberg: "If bleach is going to change the color of flour, it's certainly going to produce other chemical alterations."

Chlorine, another potent poison, is also used in flour manufacturing—"it gets into the food abundantly," says Lederberg. "It's clear that chlorine reacts badly with DNA in microorganisms—the question is how it reacts in the body. These may be long shots," says Lederberg, "but there may be some bad surprises; I just don't want any surprises discovered late in the game."

But some surprises have already popped up. Like in South Africa, where flour with potassium bromate—a common ingredient in many American flours—caused poisoning outbreaks. The FAO additive committe has reported that potassium and ammonium persulfates, common flour strengtheners, give bakers dermatitis, and it warns that nitrogen oxides can form—nitrites again!—in the products. As far as anyone knows, Americans have been lucky with their bakery goods—up to 14 pounds worth every week in every American home. But it's conceivable that our Wonder Bread, baked in the kitchens of Continental Bakery (of IT&T), is poisoning us—if not in 12 ways, at least in more than one.

· · ·

FOOD AND COSMETIC TOXICOLOGY

Or consider modified food starch, which thickens pie-fillings and gravies: the FAO warns it "may harm the very young, the old, and patients with gastrointestinal troubles."

Most foods, including salad oils, which contain shortening, a supersaturated vegetable oil, contribute as much as or more than animal fat toward heart disease. Even disodium salts of EDTA—which is used in canned vegetables and fruits to keep the juice clear and the color bright—FAO would discourage because they raise the calcium level of the blood in rats and erode their teeth.

The moral is not that all of these additives will poison you (though they *do* poison rats). But we can assume they won't do much good for humans who eat them every day in every food. One big area of concern to biochemists is how all of these different chemicals react in combinations in the normal diet. For they're always tested separately. But emulsifiers, the most widely used additives on the entire market, probably increase the chances that many additives which would normally be quickly excreted are instead absorbed in the bloodstream. Hydroxylated lecithin and the glycerides—the most widely used emulsifiers —all are enormous unknowns. The experiments aren't going on yet in the laboratories —but they're going on continually in your stomachs.

· · ·

Pesticides pose a nasty health problem because they destroy body enzymes and derange metabolism in the organs, and affect the body in other ways that even biochemists don't yet understand. Scientific literature does have disturbing cases of pesticides destroying the body's chlorinesterase enzyme, which normally detoxifies certain toxins at nerve endings and synapses. The result: headaches, cramps, nausea, diarrhea, twitching, vomiting—maybe death. Scientists speculate that common chronic disorders, usually untraceable, are really due to chronic pesticide poisoning.

The problems aren't restricted to produce. The grocery store's plump chickens and steaks didn't get fat from corn meal—they've been primed with antibiotics and synthetic growth hormones which are passed on to you. DES (diethylstilbestrol), the super growth hormone, fattens 75 percent of the beef cattle in the United States. (Poultry used to get it, but that was outlawed—although hens still eat arsenic to make them lay more eggs.) FDA requires that all cattle be taken off these hormones, which are implanted below their ears, 48 hours before slaughter; therefore, meat should end up on your table without any residues. But in 1969, a random study found .6 percent of all beef livers still contained some DES residue—a small percentage, but in human terms, it means 12,000 people at any given time are munching beef hormones.

The antibiotics usually end up in the food (they're even used as uncooked poultry dips, or on ice packed around fresh fish) and in our bodies. Chronic exposure to antibiotics immunizes the body against their useful therapeutic effects, so when bacterial infections strike, there aren't any drugs which can do the job. Antibiotics also disrupt the intestinal flora, fouling up the digestive system and body metabolism. Tetracyclines, as FAO additive experts warn, bind to teeth and calcium and inhibit skeletal growth in children. Or, as numerous medical journals point out, antibiotics will cause allergies. Some researchers speculate that the nagging allergies which so many kids suffer come from the same milk, meat and fish which their school health textbooks promise will make them strong.

In a fitting ironic twist, a perverse salute to the last bit of technology to touch our food, contamination is also caused by polyethylene bags, cans, paper bags and cardboard boxes —the sterile 20th century wrappings which smother our food in order to keep out dirt. Meats, crackers, soups, cereals, vegetables, fruits, crisp snacks: they all suck up several thousand additives used in the packaging, more bits of BHT and BHA, more sodium nitrite, methylcellulose and potassium hydroxide all in the wrappings this time—lime, zinc, chloride, soap, animal glue, shellac, peroxides—every additive that is also put directly into the food and more. Rest assured (by the FDA) that the package-to-food migration is very small. Also remember that you get the additives from every package, from every wrapper, from every food. The levels add up.

You can forego all packaged food and spend the rest of your life munching fruits and vegetables which haven't touched a paper or polyethylene bag. A warning, though: they've all been rinsed with soaps and detergents to clean off the field dirt (which you could rinse in your kitchen sink); and in a last compulsive act to seal them for market, 75 percent have been soaked with mixtures of carcinogenic coal-tar waxes, paraffin and petroleum naptha—the prime ingredient of napalm.

Caveat emptor. Let the buyer beware.

1.6   *Working People Who Can't Find Work*

The unemployment rate is one of those abstract, impersonal indexes that measure how well or how poorly the economy is performing. But behind the numbers are real people for whom the experience of being unemployed is a wrenching personal disaster. Rosie Washington, Frank Martinez, and Charles Phillips were interviewed in the Buffalo area in 1975, and their own accounts are reproduced here. Also in 1975 Alfred Prato was laid off from his job in New York City, and his story is told by *The New York Times.*

This essay was excerpted from *The New York Times Magazine,* February 12, 1975, pp. 9–11, 34–35, and *The New York Times,* November 3, 1975, p. 35. Copyright © 1975 by The New York Times Company; reprinted by permission.

ROSIE WASHINGTON

Unemployed and on welfare, 27; in the small apartment she shares with her daugher, 6, and another woman, from which they are about to be evicted.

You look in the paper, see all these jobs in Cheektowaga, Williamsville; no way to get to them, bus don't even go that way. You go up and go looking for a job; the jobs they send you to, 50 per cent of the time there's not a job anyway. "Well, we're not hiring now, but we'll take your application." Then they send you out to jobs that they know you're either overqualified for or underqualified for. I was an administrative assistant at a community center; I've been an employment coach on a Federal program, then a counselor. I've done all this, and I really like it. But my biggest problem is that I don't have that piece of paper that says I'm qualified, so now, well, I went to the restaurants, hotels, plants. I've said I never wanted to work in any plant. I wish I could get a plant job now—I have applications in at Bethlehem, Chevy, Ford. You can't get any answers, you can't get any services, just sit around and wait, just to be told to come back and go through it again. Honest to God.

And the welfare system. Isn't that a design, a design to fail? They just give you enough money so you don't starve to death, so you're always hungry. They don't give you enough to live, just to exist. You know, I think these clerks, they look at me as an imposition on their paychecks. They're paying for me: "If it wasn't for her, I might have a nickel or a dime more." But you know, they want us here. They always got to have somebody on the bottom, so they know they're closer to the top. A crummy welfare recipient chewing up their tax dollar, you dig it? With me here, I can make you feel better. . . .

I'm tired. I really am. I have a child, and she's part of me. She sees me doing nothing, never going out to work, depressed, worried, sometimes crying. I mean, I try. I try to play with her. When I have some money, we even go out together. We can't afford the movies, but I take her to Henry's and buy her a hamburger. I do love her. I do care, but with all the pressure, sometimes I can't even talk to her—you know. She comes home: "Hi, Mommy." "Hi, how was school today?" "Fine." She wants to play, but I can't. I think it's going to affect her emotionally. I went to school with her and the teacher said, "She's a good, bright child, but she's so sad. Why?" I said, "Because that's all we got in our home. Sadness. No hope. No future."

And this country thinks it's so damn great. It's *not*. It's hard to believe, but I really feel we're going to have a revolution, because this Government ain't doing it, not to say any other kind is better. What I'd like to know, really, is what am I supposed to do with my life? I had my goals, but no means to make them. I'm just at the breaking point. And when I break, what am I going to do? You're just never right for anything. At first you're too young; then you don't have experience; by the time you're 35 or 40 years, you're too old. So all through your life you were never right for anything. You know, it's everything—job and experience, no experience, no job. To get a job you gotta have money; you gotta have a job to get money. So it's just a vicious circle of nothing. And you're all locked up in this thing, crossed in it all your life. One circle that leads nowhere. That makes you pretty angry. Angry isn't even the word for it. I don't even *know* how to describe that feeling.

· · ·

FRANK MARTINEZ

Works at Chevrolet's Tonawanda complex, in the metal-casting plant; four children, ages 7 to 14.

Myself, I'm practically in a state of financial bankruptcy. As of two years ago, when wage and price controls went into effect, since that time, Sally and I have withdrawn a sizable amount from our savings, and see no conceivable way we're going to put it back. . . .

Last week we had a layoff, they laid off a number of men; there were 22 in our department, the maintenance department, and three men from our shop, two sheet-metal workers and one apprentice-trainee. What the foreman said is, he had no idea there was a layoff at all, and he controls a lot of men. He thought if anyone should know about a layoff it would be him, but he wasn't expecting it. In fact, in our department, which is short-handed, he thought they'd be hiring, and instead they laid off. They just sent the word out, with a list of names to lay off these people. Corporations have their way of operating. I have heard this is a big corporation and conglomerate scheme; in other words, they have made their profit, they can afford to give the workingman the business: Let him take a vacation, they could care less.

It looks hopeless, unless somebody really takes hold of the whole situation, reverses the trend, or at least stabilizes it. This is something I've recently read into, and it seemed to be the general thinking when Nixon got into office that we were going to have a lot of unemployment, because the philosophy is to take the money out of the working people and put it back in the hands of the rich and the corporations.

· · ·

The experts say that unemployment is necessary. . . . Some of the people I work with, we discuss these things, we really don't know what it's all about because we're not intellectuals. Most fellas just throw up their arms in the air, curse, and walk away, saying, "I've heard enough; I don't want to talk about it anymore." It seems as though they feel hopeless; there's nothing they can do. They're just a cog in the wheel; the wheel's going to turn; the cog's going to go to the other side, and that's the way working fellas that I work with feel.

CHARLES (BILL) PHILLIPS

Bethlehem Steel worker; 58.

Well, I marvel, I have to marvel at the Establishment, because they can make a person believe they are at fault for not working. Now I don't know whether it is the mentality of the general population, or what it is. Me, I'm nothing, a mere cipher, that's what I call myself. But I don't buy the Establishment package. This is it—you have your one pull at the brass ring, and you can't do it without money in this society, you can't do it without a job. The young person who goes out, they're the hardest hit. For one thing, they've swallowed everything they've been taught. Then they go out and can't get the jobs. And yet they blame themselves. Just as everybody in my day blamed themselves, except me. I say, "You don't blame me, buddy, it's the system —the jobs aren't there." That's the part that makes me angry, because anyone with a little bit of common sense can see that there aren't the jobs, and there never were enough jobs.

ALFRED PRATO

Unemployed laborer, laid off from the New York City Parks Department. [Story told by The New York Times.]

Sometimes at night, after another lonely disappointment-filled day, Alfred Prato will try to still the apprehensions in his household by letting the children climb into bed with him and Marie for a few minutes.

They hug and say how much they love one another.

But sometimes that is not enough to overcome the anxieties of the Pratos' eldest son, 7-year-old Anthony, who hears the talk about the mortgage, the cost of food and the lack of a job.

"He's worried," said Mr. Prato the other day. "He expects to wake up and find us out in the street."

When Anthony starts asking, "What's going to happen to us?" Mr. Prato wraps his arms about his son and roughhouses a bit with him. "I tell him, 'You concentrate on being a little boy, you don't have to worry about grown-up stuff yet.' "

Mr. Prato is 30 years old and lives on Staten Island. He is one of an estimated 20,000 New York City employes who have lost their jobs this year as the result of budget cuts.

For 10 years, Mr. Prato was a proud laborer for the city Parks Department. He made $12,000 a year, owned a 1972 Chevrolet Nova automobile for which he paid $2,600 cash and he and his wife bought a small ranch-style house.

Last June, along with 500 other park laborers, Mr. Prato was laid off.

He is no longer proud.

"She Is My Strength"

Alfred Prato is unsure of himself. After more than 20 job interviews, he has not had an offer.

He worries constantly.

"It's with you 24 hours a day," he said. "When I got laid off, I weighed 172 pounds. Now I weigh 157."

Mr. Prato was born in Manhattan. His mother died when he was born. The aunt who raised him now lives in Italy. His father has remarried and lives at Port Richey, Fla.

When he was a student at Chelsea Vocational High School, Mr. Prato went to Coney Island one day with a "couple of my friends" and there he met Marie, a red-haired girl who was born in Italy.

They were married in September 1965. In November of that year he was hired by the Parks Department and he has worked there ever since.

Five months of job hunting has left Mr.

Prato with nervous trembling in his fingers and the beginnings of a facial tic. He feels that he might disintegrate, were it not for his wife.

"She is a good woman." he said. "She is my strength. She keeps me going. She tells me that someday I'll walk into a place and get a job. She's sure of it."

When Mr. Prato was a little boy, growing up under the guidance of his thrift-conscious aunt from Italy, he was constantly urged, "Make something of yourself."

He and Marie refused to live on credit after they married. She worked for Metropolitan Life until she was eight months pregnant with Anthony, and they saved their money to buy a house.

"Everything Was Fine"

"Everything was just fine." said Mr. Prato, sitting with his wife in soft lamplight at evening, playing with the new baby, Dominick, while Anthony struggled with his first-grade readers.

"Then came June; everything just ended," Mr. Prato said. "We had a little money saved. We cashed in my insurance policy."

He applied for unemployment benefits and gets $95 a week. "I'm eligible until next July," he said.

For a time after he was laid off, Mr. Prato tried to do some unpaid union work, going to Albany to help lobby through the General Assembly a special appropriation of $330-million. When that became law, 235 of the park laborers were rehired. Mr. Prato was 255th on the seniority list.

When it became evident that there was little likelihood that he would get his city job back soon, Mr. Prato began a serious search for work.

"I went to the unemployment center," he said. "I wasn't even interviewed. The woman there wrote on my application, 'Come back Jan. 26.'

"I remember one day the United States Public Health Service hospital on Staten

Island was hiring. Marie and I both went down. I said I would take any job. The hospital said they had 50 teachers that came in to look for menial work. That got to me—all those well-educated people who couldn't find jobs.

"I heard about an opening at another place. We got up early. My wife said. 'Don't be nervous, you'll do fine.' When I got there, there were 50 guys waiting for the job. What bothered me was that I'm 30 years old and I was the oldest guy there.

"My wife saw an ad in the paper for a girl. They were giving interviews on Monday and Tuesday. My wife got dressed up to go apply for it. I told her to telephone first because it was a holiday. She did. The girl who answered the phone said, 'I already got the job.'

"At the unemployment center, the lines are running out the doors. It's really pathetic. Firemen, policemen, laborers, teachers—decent people who put a lot of time and energy on their jobs.

"I had 10 years with the city. Those are 10 years blown away. I'm put on the preferred list for four years. If I don't get called back, forget it.

"Nobody really cares. Politicians don't care. The people who are supposed to represent you don't care. You don't hear nothing from them The President, the Governor, the Mayor, the Senators. They're playing games. We are pawns. They are playing with our lives."

A Feeling of Helplessness

The Pratos, with the help of their savings, are almost able to handle the mechanics of living. They eat a lot of macaroni. Mrs. Prato saves an estimated $4 a week on foods by using coupons clipped from newspapers. The Pratos do not drink, smoke or entertain. On Fridays Mr. Prato's older brother comes over and brings a cake for the children.

Mr. Prato is sometimes tempted to stop trying, to sit back and let the future wash over him.

"The worst thing, I guess, that could happen to someone is when someone you love dies," he said. "The next-worst thing is for a man to lose his job."

He said that some nights after everybody else in the family has gone to bed, he takes a final check of his sleeping sons.

"I stand there looking at them and thinking. 'I brought them into the world, and I can't even provide for them.' You feel like a failure. Less than a man."

1.7 *Guatemala—Occupied Country*

For Americans, the seamy side of American capitalism is lived here at home: crises, inequality, racism, and the other social evils described in this chapter are visible aspects of American cities and towns. But the oppression that results from American capitalism does not end at the water's edge. Vietnam, as the most direct and brutal instance of American oppression, naturally comes to mind. The millions of Vietnamese who were killed, maimed, or made homeless are also victims of our system. The disclosures of the CIA's role in setting up a fascist military government in Chile has focused attention on another aspect of American oppression abroad. The following account by Eduardo Galeano describes the consequences of American involvement in yet another country.

"My pilots are blond with blue eyes," Guatemalan ex-President Miguel Ydígoras Fuentes once said, "but that doesn't mean they're North American." In this country of Indians the physical coincidence was hardly accidental. The United States has been intervening in Guatemala's internal affairs for a long time, on every level. The imperial presence in the country is the very essence of crudity—an unadorned model of the exploitation endured by the tormented lands south of the Rio Grande. Guatemala is the clumsily masked face of all Latin America, the face of the suffering and of the hope of our countries, plundered of their wealth and of the right to choose their destiny.

It is from the United States that presidents and dictators are installed and removed in Guatemala. The economy is controlled from Wall Street through investments, trade, and credits. The army receives weapons, training, and orientation from North American officials who often participate personally in military operations within the country. Press and television depend in large degree on the advertising of foreign firms. Officials and technicians of the United States Embassy or "international" organizations operate a parallel government which becomes the only government at decisive moments. Coca-Cola has replaced natural fruit juices and the God of the Protestants and the Mormons competes with the Mayan divinities, who have survived hidden behind Catholic altars.

Of course the domination and exploitation of Guatemala, as if it were a piece of private property, is nothing new. It has assumed peculiar characteristics since 1954, because the criminal invasion which imperialism organized in that year has marked the country's present history with fire. The fall of Arbenz [in 1954] was a decisive link in a long chain of aggressions which neither began nor ended at that point. The present situation cannot be explained without keeping very much in mind the revolutionary process of the decade beginning in 1944, and its tragic end. From those winds come today's storms. The same forces which bombed Guatemala City, Puerto Barrios, and Puerto San José at 4 P.M. on June 18, 1954, are now in power. They exercise *real* power behind the screen of a civilian regime which hypocritically proclaims itself heir to the defeated revolution. Ever since that disaster the defeated people have been learning to rise up in other ways. The lost revolution is also the key to the consolidation and development of today's guerrillas.

The colony wanted to make itself a nation: until 1944, the country had been witness and victim of its history but not a protagonist. For a long time Guatemala's fate had been at the mercy of foreign money staked by gamblers in Wall Street or Washington or the Pentagon. Led by university men and young nationalist army officers, the revolution exploded and [in 1944] put an end to the long dictatorship of Ubico—an old general whose pro-German sympathies did not prevent him from serving the interests of North American enterprises, and whose proclaimed cult of honesty raised no obstacles to his excellent relations with the local oligarchy.

This small country of illiterate Indians dying of hunger raised itself up on two legs. Arévalo and Arbenz, successively elected by popular vote, had the job of leading the

difficult venture of national affirmation—
"national" in a sense that transcended the
frontiers of Guatemala. Under these administrations the best and sturdiest efforts were
made to rebuild Central America's lost unity
on new foundations.

.   .   .

Offshoots of the Guatemalan revolution
throughout Central America could have
materialized only through other revolutions
which never occurred. Guatemala felt nothing but hostility or indifference from its
small neighbor countries, ruled by straw men
for United Fruit or by life dictators. Yet within the country's borders, the revolution followed its course until its final destruction by
troops prepared by the CIA in Honduras and
Nicaragua. Its successes are still very much
alive in the people's memory. A vigorous
educational program was launched; workers
of country and city organized into unions protected by the Labor Code. The United Fruit
Company, a state within a state, master of the
land and railroad and port, exempt from
taxes and free from controls, ceased to be
omnipotent on its vast properties. The new
labor and social security laws enabled the
internal market to develop by raising purchasing power and the workers' living standards. Construction of highways and creation
of the port at Matías de Gálvez on the Atlantic broke the United Fruit monopoly of
transport and trade. Ambitious economic
development projects such as electrification
of the country were undertaken *with national
capital*. As Arévalo said, "In Guatemala we
have received no loans, because we know very
well that when one gets dollars with the right
hand one yields sovereignty with the left."
(But this was a very different Arévalo from
the man who ended up advising armed intervention against the Cuban revolution.)
Guatemala was beginning to show all of
Latin America that a country can break
underdevelopment, emerge from misery,
without humiliating itself as a beggar at the
door of the imperium. There was a new Constitution which for the first time was not a

rhetorical trap framed by intellectuals behind
the people's backs. Above all there was a new
conscience: the obstacles convinced Guatemala of its newborn strength. The Mayas'
descendants recaptured a sense of dignity
badly wounded by the Spanish conquest and
never healed.

On June 17, 1952, the Arbenz government approved the agrarian reform law. In
his farewell speech on leaving the government, Arévalo had revealed that his administration had had to deal with 32 coups d'état
promoted by the United Fruit Company.
The agrarian reform was "too much": an
impermissibly dangerous example for Latin
America. The North American Embassy
decided that the Arbenz government smelled
strongly of "Communism" and was a peril to
hemispheric security. It was not the first time
that a bourgeois nationalist regime aiming at
independence had been thus described. Certainly neither Arévalo nor Arbenz proposed
to socialize the means of production and
exchange. The agrarian reform law laid
down as its basic objective *the development of
the peasant capitalist economy and the capitalist
agricultural economy in general*. The other measures taken by both governments were
oriented toward the same end. This "confusion" would not be the last, as witness the
blood spilled in other countries in years to
come. The good health of North American
investments south of the Rio Grande and the
United States' power politics in its "natural
sphere of influence" rest on sacred socioeconomic structures which determine that
every minute of every day more than one
Latin American child shall die of disease or
hunger. Whoever touches these structures
commits sacrilege: a scandal erupts.

An overpowering international propaganda campaign was launched against
Guatemala. *That is the plague-spot*, it was proclaimed. "The Iron Curtain is falling over
Guatemala." In the first months of 1954 over
100,000 families had benefited from agrarian
reform, which *affected only idle lands* for which
indemnities in bonds were paid to expro-

priated owners, United Fruit cultivated only eight percent of its properties extending from ocean to ocean; now its vast unused lands began to be distributed among poor peasants who were ready to work them. The president of United Fruit said in a confidential interview: "From here on out it's not a matter of the people of Guatemala against the United Fruit Company: the question is going to be Communism against the right of property, the life and security of the western hemisphere." The Organization of American States met to give its blessing to the invasion that the CIA was preparing against Guatemala. Among the indignant democrats who then raised their hands to condemn the Arbenz regime at the Caracas Conference were representatives of the bloodiest dictators in the continent's history, living guarantees of Latin American "stability": Batista, Somoza, Trujillo, Pérez Jiménez, Rojas Pinilla, Odría; even now such a conglomeration of corruption would break any computer into which it was fed. "We had neither doubts nor hopes," Guatemalan foreign minister Toriello wrote later about the Conference. That was Guatemala's last chance, on the eve of the agony, to raise its voice for the independent foreign policy which was born of the revolution and died with it. In Chapultepec, San Francisco, Rio de Janeiro, Bogotá, and many other European and American cities, that small voice had spoken loudly and bravely enough to demonstrate, for the United States, inadmissible insolence.

The OAS gave its approval and Castillo Armas—the man-of-the-hour on a white horse, trained at Fort Leavenworth, Kansas —led his U.S.-trained and paid troops into Guatemala. Supported by North American "volunteers" piloting B-47 bombers, the invasion succeeded. Cornered by the enemy, betrayed by his military commanders whom he trusted to the end, Arbenz did not want— perhaps was unable—to fight. On that tragic night in 1954 the people listened on the radio to his recorded speech of resignation, not to the hoped-for proclamation of resistance.

The same thing was to happen later with leaders of similar movements elsewhere in Latin America. Popular leaders or Presidents with bourgeois-nationalist-type reformist intentions would wind up their days in power by abandoning it without firing a shot. Perhaps scared by the contradictions they had stirred up, and fearing that they would be swamped by the popular forces they had set in motion, neither Perón nor Bosch nor Goulart gave arms to the workers to defend their regimes against the challenge of successive military coups.

Soon after the invasion of Guatemala, Washington officially conceded that the machinery for the crime had been assembled, oiled, and set rolling by North American hands. It was a nice job by the CIA. A year later one of its heads, Gen. Walter Bedell Smith, joined the board of United Fruit, one of whose chairs had already been occupied by the then No. 1 man of the CIA, Allen Dulles. Allen's brother, John Foster Dulles, had been the most impatient of the foreign ministers at the OAS meeting. This is no enigma: it was in his law office that the contracts between United Fruit and the Guatemalan Government had been drafted in 1930 and 1936.

Castillo Armas fulfilled his mission. He returned the expropriated idle lands to United Fruit and other landlords, and delivered to the international oil cartel the subsoil of 4,600,000 hectares—almost half of the country. The Oil Agreement was drawn up in English and arrived in English at the Congress. It was translated into Spanish at the request of a deputy who still retained a shred of shame. The revolution had declined to surrender the oil despite the pressures brought to bear during its decade of government. "For whom are you keeping this oil?" "For Guatemala," Arévalo had replied to a Standard Oil agent. Today the cartel keeps in reserve, without exploiting them, the deposits where oil has been located—a policy it also follows in other Latin American countries.

Castillo Armas governed by terror. He closed down the opposition press, which had functioned freely in Arbenz's time, and sent militant democratic politicians and labor and student leaders to jail, to the grave, or to exile. Finally he himself was assassinated. Eisenhower bewailed his death: "It is a great loss for his own nation and for the whole free world," he said. After new elections, which were annulled, and a brief military junta government, Gen. Ydígoras Fuentes became President. Before the Castillo Armas invasion the CIA had invited Ydígoras to head the expedition. He himself now tells how he turned down the offer. Interviewed by the newspaperwoman Georgie Anne Geyer in San Salvador, Ydígoras said that he had hardly won the elections before four CIA men approached him to threaten reprisals if he didn't pay the balance on the $3 million debt incurred by Castillo Armas to finance his glorious invasion.

Ydígoras put his signature to an unconstitutional and infamous agreement guaranteeing present or future foreign investments, which later served as a model for other Latin American governments with equally dubious ideas about national dignity. He also made his own effort at agrarian reform—a reform with such peculiar characteristics that only big landlords benefited, as a recent official report shows. It was Ydígoras who offered Guatemalan land to train the forces that stormed Cuban beaches in April 1961, in exchange for some commitments to help his government. But in spite of this, his business relations with the CIA continued to be disastrous. He still bitterly complains that the United States did not keep its part of the bargain, and says he obtained the promised sugar quota only after threatening to boycott Alliance for Progress conferences.

According to the *Miami Herald*, which is no more Communist than Lyndon Johnson [was,] the decision to unseat Ydígoras was adopted at a meeting between Kennedy and his "top advisers" early in 1963. The [then] head of CIA, Richard Helms, was there and so was the then ambassador to Guatemala, John O. Bell. Both showed great concern about a possible new electoral victory for Juan José Arévalo, who had announced his candidacy from exile. They attached no value to Arévalo's repeated blasts against the regime in Cuba, his public denunciations of Castro as "a danger to the continent, a menace." Bell was convinced that Arévalo was "a Communist." His view prevailed despite President Kennedy's doubts. Colonel Peralta Azurdia brought off the coup d'état at the end of March, 1963. Three days earlier Arévalo had secretly entered Guatemala; a journalist interviewed him. This "provocation" was enough to make the military unsheathe their swords.

So began another brutal dictatorship. One of its first acts was the murder of eight political and trade union leaders in Puerto Barrios, the United Fruit port. Trucks laden with rocks drove over them, crushing them alive.

Three years later Julio César Méndez Montenegro, a liberal Catholic lawyer who had been involved in the revolution of 1944, defeated his two opponents—both colonels—in the elections. The results were only made public a week after polling day. By then the winning candidate had been forced to sign a pact with the purportedly defeated dictatorship. Among other things the pact provided that the military commands must remain unchanged; that no officer involved on the side of the 1944 revolution could fill a post of command in the armed forces; and that Col. Rafael Arriage Bosque must remain as Minister of Defense. Arriaga Bosque had actively plotted against Arévalo and Arbenz, and later also against Ydígoras; he had been the "strong man" of the Peralta Azurdia administration. He was the "strong man" of the Méndez Montenegro administration (of which Méndez Montenegro was the "weak man") until his attempted coup met with failure and the U.S. gave the go-ahead for his replacement. The names changed but the power structure remained the same. The President plays a pathetic role. He provides the cover of an apparently civil administration for the military dictatorship which actually rules. Had it not been for the above-mentioned pact, the military men would not have surrendered the government to Mén-dez Montenegro. Government, not power: Méndez Montenegro's hands are tied. He survives, openly backed by the United States Embassy, but only on the basis that he can do nothing. Nothing except talk with intimate friends in strictly private gatherings about his good reformist intentions, receive imposing loans from foreign banks that are mortgaging the country, and watch with impotent complicity the savage violence from the Right. Many activists of the President's own party have been murdered by armed bands which the army organizes and protects: the hunt for "Communists" has been launched with blind fury in Guatemala.

Appendix to 1.7

The following is part of a list of American invasions of other countries and the purposes for such actions published by the Committee on Foreign Affairs of the U.S. House of Representatives. Only actions of uniformed services were reported; in all, the Committee identified 165 interventions between 1798 and 1970. We have added the items in brackets to the Committee list in order to include cases where the Central Intelligence Agency (CIA) rather than the U.S. military was involved.

U.S. Congress, Committee on Foreign Affairs, *Background Information on the Use of United States Armed Forces in Foreign Countries*, 91st Congress, 2nd Session (1970).

1899–1901 *Philippine Islands:* To protect American interests following the war with Spain, and to conquer the islands by defeating the Filipinos in their war for independence.

1900 *China:* A permanent legation guard was maintained in Peking, and was strengthened at times as troubles threatened. It was still there in 1934.

1901 *Colombia (State of Panama):* To protect American property on the Isthmus and to keep transit lines open during serious revolutionary disturbances.

1902 *Colombia; State of Panama.*

1903. *Honduras:* To protect the American consulate and the steamship wharf at Puerto Cortez during a period of revolutionary activity.

1903 *Dominican Republic:* To protect American interests in the city of Santo Domingo during a revolutionary outbreak.

1903 *Syria.*

1903–14 *Panama:* To protect American interests and lives during and following the revolution for independence from Colombia over construction of the [Panama] Canal. With brief intermissions, United States Marines were stationed on the Isthmus from 1903 to 1914, to guard American interests.

1904 *Dominican Republic:* To protect American interests in Puerto Plata and Sosua and Santo Domingo City during revolutionary fighting.

1904–5 *Korea; Morocco; Panama; Korea.*

1906–9 *Cuba:* Intervention to restore order, protect foreigners, and establish a stable government after serious revolutionary activity.

1907–11 *Honduras: Nicaragua; Honduras.*

1911 *China:* Approaching stages of the nationalist revolution.

1912 *Honduras:* Small force landed to prevent seizure by the government of an American-owned railroad at Puerto Cortez. Forces withdrawn after the United States disapproved the action.

1912 *Panama: Cuba; Turkey.*

1912 *China:* To protect Americans and American interests during revolutionary activity.

1912–41 *China:* In 1927, the United States had 5,670 troops ashore in China and 44 naval vessels in its waters. In 1933 we had 3,027 armed men ashore. All this protective action was in general terms based on treaties with China ranging from 1858 to 1901.

1912–25 *Nicaragua:* To protect American interests during an attempted revolution. A small force serving as a legation guard and as a promoter of peace and governmental stability remained until 1925.

1913–14 *Mexico; Haiti.*

1914 *Dominican Republic:* During a revolutionary movement, United States naval forces by gunfire stopped the bombardment of Puerto Plata, and by threat of force maintained Santo Domingo City as a neutral zone.

1914–17 *Mexico.*

1915–34 *Haiti:* To maintain order during a period of chronic and threatened insurrection.

1916–24 *Dominican Republic:* To maintain order during a period of chronic and threatened insurrection.

1917–18 *Europe:* World War I. Fully declared.

1917–22 *Cuba:* To protect American interests during an insurrection and subsequent unsettled conditions.

1918–20 *Panama; Mexico.*

1918–20 *Soviet Russia:* Marines were landed at and near Vladivostok in June and July. In August the project expanded. Then 7,000 men were landed in Vladivostok and remained until January 1920, as part of an allied occupation force. In September 1918, 5,000 American troops joined the allied intervention force at Archangel, suffered 500 casualties and remained until June 1919. All these operations were to offset effects of the Bolsheviki revolution in Russia and were partly supported by Czarist or Kerensky elements.

1919 *Honduras:* A landing force was sent ashore to maintain order in a neutral zone during an attempted revolution.

1920–22 *Russia (Siberia); China; Guatemala; Panama–Costa Rica; Turkey.*

1924 *Honduras:* To protect American lives and interests during election hostilities.

1924–25 *China.*

1925 *Honduras:* To protect foreigners at LaCeiba during a political upheaval.

1925 *Panama:* Strikes and rent riots led to the landing of about 600 American troops to keep order and protect American interests.

1926–33 *Nicaragua:* The coup d'état of General Chamorro aroused revolutionary activities leading to the landing of American marines to protect the interests of the United States. United States forces came and went, but seem not to have left the country entirely until 1933. Their work included activity against the outlaw leader Sandino in 1928.

1926–27 *China.*

1933 *Cuba:* During a revolution against President Gerardo Machada naval forces demonstrated but no landing was made.

1940 *Newfoundland, Bermuda, St. Lucia, Bahamas, Jamaica, Antigua, Trinidad,* and *British Guiana:* Troops were sent to guard air and naval bases obtained by negotiation with Great Britain.

1941 *Greenland:* Taken under protection of the United States in April.

1941 *Netherlands (Dutch Guiana):* In November the president ordered American troops to occupy Dutch Guiana.

1941 *Iceland; Germany.*

1941–45 *Germany, Italy, Japan,* etc. World War II. Fully declared.

1950–53 *Korea.*

[1953 *Iran:* CIA-sponsored coup overthrew popular government, installed Shah as ruler.]

[1954 *Guatemala:* CIA-sponsored coup overthrew popular Arbenz government and installed pro-U.S. ruler.]

1958 *Lebanon.*

[1961 *Cuba:* Bay of Pigs invasion organized by CIA to overthrow revolutionary government.]

1962 *Cuba:* [Missile crisis, naval blockade].

1962–7[5] *Laos:* From October 1962 until [1975] the United States played a role of military support in Laos.

1964–197[5] War in *Vietnam.*

[1964 *Brazil:* CIA-supported coup overthrew elected Goulart government, installed dictatorship.]

1965 *Dominican Republic:* Intervention to protect lives and property during a Dominican revolt. More troops were sent as the U.S. feared the revolutionary forces were coming increasingly under Communist control.

[1965 *Indonesia:* CIA-sponsored coup overthrew government, installed military regime.]

[1967 *Greece:* CIA-sponsored coup overthrew democratic government, installed "colonels" regime.]

1970 *Cambodia:* U.S. troops were ordered into Cambodia. The object of this attack, which lasted from April 30 to June 30, was to ensure the continuing safe withdrawal of American forces from South Vietnam and to assist the program of Vietnamization.

[1972–1975 *Cambodia:* Support of military government.]

[1973 *Chile:* CIA-supported coup overthrew elected government, installed military regime.]

[1975–76 *Portugal, Angola:* Support of right-wing factions.]

PART II

A THEORETICAL
APPROACH
TO CAPITALISM

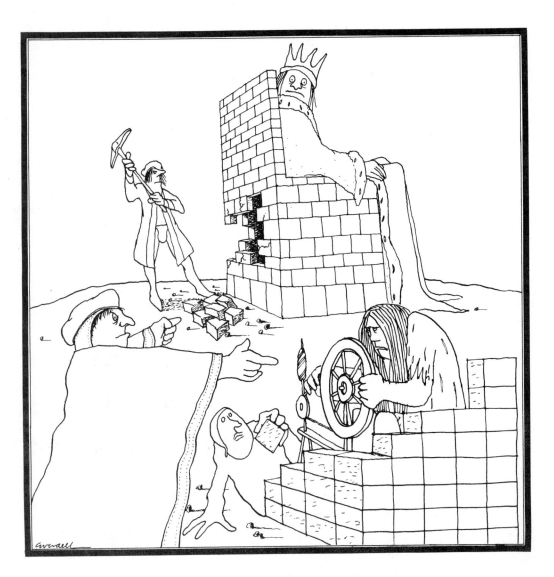

Historical Materialism
and the Rise
of Capitalism

"EVERY CHILD KNOWS," Karl Marx once wrote, "that a country that ceased to work would die."[1] Every society must organize the production, distribution, and consumption of the necessities of life if it is simply to survive. Every society must, moreover, organize its own reproduction if it is not to disappear. There must be some particular social arrangement for these tasks to be achieved; in fact, there are a dazzling variety of ways in which different human societies have organized and divided these tasks in the course of human history. *Why* is any particular society organized the way it is, how did it come to be that way, and what makes it change? Is there any logic to the complex patterns of development of different societies? What is the relationship between the "economic" and the "noneconomic" spheres of a society?

This chapter presents one approach to these questions: the conceptual approach to history developed by Marx and known as historical materialism. We shall use this approach to analyze the emergence of capitalism itself, to ask such questions as: How did the social system that we call capitalism, with its particular way of organizing production, distribution, consumption, and reproduction, come into being? In the following chapter we will examine in greater detail the essential features of the capitalist system.

The materialist approach to history begins its analysis of any society by examining the particular social arrangement of production.

The act of production always has two main aspects. First, people produce by transforming an object, a raw material of the physical world, into another object, using some sorts of tools or means of production. Second, while engaging in this production process, people simultaneously enter into particular social relationships with one another. These relationships can take a variety of forms. In a rural patriarchal farm family, for example, the hierarchical kinship relations of age and sex in the family determine the way the labor of the family is carried out, the way tasks are divided, and the specific tasks assigned to each family member. In an egalitarian cooperative farm, by contrast, the organization and allocation of tasks will be determined quite differently. Marx argues that people's social relations, their ideas about themselves and their social world (their consciousness), as well as their laws, morality, ethics and religion can only be understood in relation to the way they organize their productive and reproductive activity.

We begin the presentation of historical materialism by introducing the important concepts that we need to analyze the dominant mode of production in any society: forces of production, social surplus, social class, relations of production, mode of production, base and superstructure. The *forces of production* consist of the raw materials, tools, instruments, machines, buildings, and equipment used in the process of production as well as the state of science and technology, the organizational techniques of production and,

[1]Marx, Letter to Dr. Kugelmann, July 1868.

ortantly, the abilities, skills, and
ge of people themselves. The degree
opment of the productive forces mea-
society's capacity to produce.

social surplus is that part of a society's
potential product remaining once it
met the basic requirements needed to
intain the society at a subsistence level.
his subsistence level is not simply a biolog-
cal minimum; it is conditioned by historical
and social factors. The surplus can be determined with adequate precision for any given
society.

In all but the most primitive societies, the
productive forces have developed beyond a
rudimentary level, and a social surplus is or
potentially could be produced. It is then generally possible to identify two different
groups: those who *produce* the surplus, or the
producing class, and those who, through
some form of direct or indirect coercion,
appropriate the surplus, or the appropriating
class. A *social class* is thus defined as a group
of people who have a common relation to the
production and appropriation of the surplus.
The appropriating class benefits whenever it
increases the surplus it appropriates from the
producing class. Because the two classes have
antagonistic interests, *class struggle* is an inherent element of any class society.

The *social relations of production* are defined
by the specific manner in which the surplus is
produced and then appropriated from the
direct producers. These relations of production can be described by answering four questions: (1) Who possesses the instruments or
means of production? (2) What are the direct
social relations in the production process between the producers and appropriators of
surplus? (3) By what manner does the appropriating class arrange to appropriate the
surplus? and (4) Are things produced for
direct use or for exchange on a market?

We define the *mode of production* as the combination of the existing forces of production
and the existing relations of production. This
mode of production provides us with a way to
periodize history, for every society can be
characterized by its particular dominant
mode of production. At any given time an

actual society will contain a variety of modes
of production within it, but one of them can
usually be identified as dominant.

An elaboration of slave, feudal, petty commodity, and capitalist social relations of production will help to clarify the concept of a
mode of production. In each example, we will
address the four questions that were just
listed. In slave societies, the producers (the
slaves) do not own or control the instruments
or means of production. The slaves are owned
by the master as pieces of property that he or
she is legally free to sell. The slave is supervised in the process of production by the
master or his or her assistant, who organizes
in detail the tasks and process of production.
The master through direct coercive force
appropriates the total product of the slaves'
labor, using some of the products to provide
the slaves' subsistence. Slave production can
be either for use or for exchange; on the slave
plantations of the pre-Civil War South cotton
was grown not for internal consumption but
for external sale on a world market.

In feudal societies, the most importnat
means of production, the land, cannot be sold
by either lords or serfs, and so is not subject to
private ownership. The producers (the serfs)
possess the instruments of production, and
work on allocated plots of land. They organize the production process themselves and
are responsible for providing for their own
subsistence. The serfs are tied to the land and
cannot be removed by the lord. The lord
extracts surplus from the serf through traditional obligations on the serf to perform certain annual economic services; the lord
provides in return basic military protection.
Most production is for internal consumption
by the serfs and the lord of the manor, with
little being exchanged on a market.

A petty commodity mode of production is
characterized by a class of free, independent
small producers, usually artisans (crafts people) and small farmers. These producers own
the means of production, the craft tools, and
the land. They organize and control their
own production process and sell their products on a market, thereby obtaining funds to
purchase other commodities for their needs.

Petty commodity production is thus for exchange rather than for use. There is no apparent appropriating class here. The petty commodity mode is an example of an incomplete or transitional mode. It often exists in a relation to another predominant mode or tends to become fairly quickly transformed into another mode as some of the producers begin to accumulate their surplus and develop into an appropriating class.

Capitalist relations of production are characterized by the complete separation of the producers (wage-workers) from the means of production. Capitalists as a class have a monopoly on the means of production while workers have only their labor-power, which they must sell to the capitalists for a wage if they are to subsist. The capitalist directly organizes the labor process, so that workers labor under the supervision of capitalists or their managers. In respect to control of the work process and ownership of the means of production, capitalism resembles slavery and differs from feudalism and petty commodity production. The objective of the capitalists is to expand their initial capital by combining labor and means of production and selling the resultant commodities, which are their property, for a profit. Hence, capitalist production is for exchange, not for use. Workers are free to change employers, while capitalists are free to hire and fire workers as needed. Capitalist relations of production thus differ from slavery and feudalism in that the relationship between the worker and the owner of the means of production is purely contractual, with no direct coercion involved. The appropriation of the surplus occurs by means of a market exchange.

As we have just seen, each of these four types of class societies are characterized by profoundly different relations of production; they provide our starting point for analyzing these societies. For example, by examining capitalist relations of production we shall see not only the role of class struggle between workers and capitalists but also the constant need of capitalism to expand.

Each of the four different relations of production is associated with a particular set of property laws, or concepts of property and possession. These in turn necessita legal and juridical institutions and some ort of political structure or state to articula and enforce those laws. In addition, each node of production will also have a corresponding ideology and institutions to promote that ideology. An ideology is a set of commonly held values that contributes to the stability and cohesion of a given society by legitimizing the position of the dominant class that appropriates the surplus. The legal, political, and ideological institutions form part of the *superstructure* of a society; this superstructure rests upon and is also essential for the maintenance of the social relations of production that constitute the economic *base*. The legal, political, and ideological functions of the superstructure may be carried out directly by the appropriating class, or by social groups dependent upon it—for example, a state bureaucracy.

The social relations of production are in these ways crucial to understanding the general character of a society. But the connection between the base and the superstructure of the society is not simple. A purely unidirectional analysis of base and superstructure would be grossly inadequate, for social custom, tradition, culture, ideology, philosophical views, kinship and family relations, religion, politics, judicial forms, etc. all certainly have a historical dynamic of their own and to some extent condition the base. While economic factors are determining, they are so only in the last instance.

The relationship between the base and the superstructure may be different in societies based on different modes of production. When the appropriation of the surplus involves transparent coercion, as in a feudal society, the superstructure takes on a more important role, as religion did in feudal times. Serfs accepted the appropriation of the surplus they produced as a part of their station in a religious order created by God. In a capitalist society, the appropriation of surplus is indirect, obscured by market relations, and the base plays a particularly dominant role. Instead of society controlling material life, the economic base dominates all of social life, and the entire social product takes the form of commodities.

Social surplus, social class, mode of production, base and superstructure: these concepts describe a society from an objective structural viewpoint. But societies consist of people. An adequate understanding of a society requires a theory of how people act as well, how human activity is situated in, and in turn shapes, these objective structures. Class struggle, for example, emerges from the recognition by members of a class of their common interests and opposition to another class.

A consideration of human activity in a structural context enables us to understand historical change, how societies are transformed from one dominant mode of production to another, from one class structure to another. The key to historical change is the unfolding contradiction within a mode of production between the forces of production and the relations of production. The forces of production develop and grow over the long run, although in a manner and rate that depends on the given social relations of production. But the social relations of production tend to be much less dynamic than the forces of production because of the vested interests of the dominant class in preserving the social *status quo*. The contradiction between the forces and the relations of production provides the evolving context in which struggle between opposing classes occurs and develops.

The contradiction is likely to intensify as the social relations of production become a fetter on the further development of the forces of production. For example, in England traditional feudal ties and monopolistic charters granted by the Crown inhibited the development of productive possibilities that could only be realized with free markets in land, labor, and other commodities—i.e., with capitalist social relations. An emergent capitalist class thus found itself in direct conflict with the feudal landed aristocracy and the crown. But a dominant class is unlikely to give up its privileged status peacefully. The contradiction between the forces of production (represented in England by the rising capitalists) and the social relations of production (represented by the ruling feudalists) grows in intensity and is expressed in cultural, ideological, and political as well as economic forms, producing a generalized social and political crisis. The crisis is resolvable only by a decisive and often violent rupture with the *status quo* that transforms the existing class structure. Historical examples of such ruptures include the English Revolution with its beheading of King Charles in 1649 (in large part, a capitalist rebellion against the absolutist monarchy and feudalism); the French Revolution in 1789 (a revolt against the feudal nobility and clergy); the American Civil War in 1861–65 (the destruction of slavery allowed the full development of capitalist relations of production); the Russian Revolution in 1917; and the Chinese Revolution in 1949.

The first reading in this chapter further elaborates the method of historical materialism, while the next three apply the method to the emergence of the capitalist mode of production itself. The final reading applies historical materialism to explore the ways that the rise of capitalism affected the family, profoundly changing its form and ideology.

2.1 The Materialist Conception of History

Because the exposition of historical materialism requires more than a short chapter introduction, it is worth going over the same ground again in a somewhat more detailed fashion. This is what John Gurley does in the following reading.

THE MATERIALIST CONCEPTION OF HISTORY

Marx and Engels developed a theory about the movement of history that purports to explain why feudalism gave way to capitalism and why the latter will be succeeded by socialism. It is essential to understand this view of social development, which they called "the materialist conception of history," if one is to have any grasp of Marxism, for it lies at the heart of almost all Marxian reasoning today.

According to this theory, which is principally Marx's, people in a society, at any given time, have a certain level of productive ability. This depends on their own knowledge and skills, on the technology (machines, tools, draft animals, and so on) available to them, and on the bountifulness of the natural environment in which they live. These together are called "the material forces of production" or, in short, the productive forces. Marx alleged that the productive forces determine the way people make their living (for example, in hunting and gathering, agriculture, or industry) and, at the same time, the way they relate to one another in producing and exchanging the means of life (for example, as lord and serf, master and slave, or capitalist and worker). These production and exchange relationships are what Marx ca[lls] [social] relations of production." Th[e produc]tive forces plus the relations of pro[duction] which Marx referred to as "the e[conomic] structure of society," shape the "supe[rstruc]ture" of people's religious, political, an[d legal] systems and their modes of thought and [ways] of life. That is, people's material lives d[eter]mine their ideas and their supporting ins[titu]tions.

In a famous passage, which deserves ca[re]ful attention, Marx summarized the theo[ry] that "became the guiding principle of m[y] studies":

> In the social production of their existence, people inevitably enter into definite relations, which are independent of their will, namely relations of production appropriate to a given stage in the development of their material forces of production. The totality of these relations of production constitutes the economic structure of society, the real foundation, on which arises a legal and political superstructure and to which correspond definite forms of social consciousness. The mode of production of material life conditions the general process of social, political and intellectual life. It is not the consciousness of people that determines their existence, but their social existence that determines their consciousness.

The key relationships are depicted below, with the main causal connections shown run-

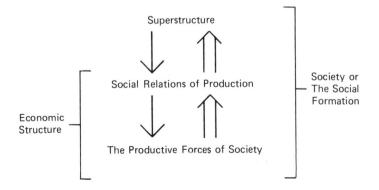

ith downward reciprocal
ning upw nt. These components are
relations or expository purposes; in
separate means independent of the
fact, e
others ally the materialist conception ach of its major components
wil iscussed more fully to give
re ortunity to get their bearings.
A e theory will be illustrated in

ctive Forces

ductive forces are the material
roduction that people fashion and
a livelihood from nature. Produc-
include machines, instruments and
materials, and natural resources;
include human beings themselves—
nowledge, talents, aspirations, and
Productive forces develop through the
and activity that people expend in
acting a living from their natural environ-
nt. Part of their development includes the
rowth of human abilities and needs. As people change their world, they develop their
own capabilities as well as their desires to
change the world still further. People thus
make their living and themselves simultaneously. Human activity is, therefore, an integral part of the productive forces; an interpretation of the Marxian theory as being a form
of "technological determinism" emasculates it
by excising the human factor.

Human beings differ from animals in that
they engage in purposeful productive activity
—they *produce* their means of subsistence, consciously and not instinctively. At any one
time, this purposive labor is performed with
a certain technology, in a given environment,
and within a particular class society—that is,
it is performed within a certain mode of production. Human nature, according to Marx
and Engels, is determined by the mode of
production that people work in to maintain
human life, and since the mode of production
changes, so does human nature.

Feudal man, for example, within his own
mode of production, had different values,
aspirations, abilities, and needs than has capitalist man within his higher mode of production. The change from the feudal to the
capitalist mode of production, however, was
made by human beings themselves, as they
fashioned better tools, altered and controlled
their environment, and, in this very process,
changed themselves. Thus, capitalism could
succeed feudalism not only because people designed superior technology, but also because,
in the process of doing this, they changed
their values and skills, their outlook on what
is important, and so on.

This Marxian view of social development is
important because it stresses that such development is not imposed on us from the "outside," nor do we simply adapt, in passive
ways, to social changes. We, in fact, initiate
those changes and, by so doing, make ourselves worthy of the new conditions. Thus,
human nature, as seen by Marx and Engels,
is essentially subject to change: man makes
himself through productive activity.

The scheme below traces out these relationships which underlie the productive forces of
the previous diagram.

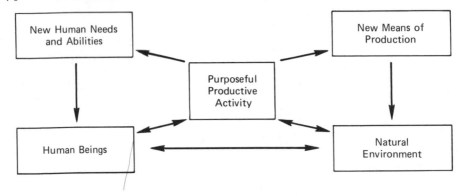

Social Relations of Production

According to Marx's formulation, the stage of development of society's material means of production—its productive forces—determines the social relations of production and exchange. The latter are the institutions and practices most closely associated with the way goods are produced, exchanged, and distributed. This includes property relations; the way labor is recruited, organized, and compensated; the markets or other means for exchanging the products of labor; and the methods used by the ruling classes to capture and dispose of the surplus product. The social relations of production are, in effect, the class structure of a society that is revealed in the work process. The mode of production of a society is seen principally through its class structure. A mode of production could be of the slave type, feudalist, capitalist, or anything else which describes the dominant manner in which people organize to make their living. Although societies may contain more than one mode of production, one mode is usually dominant.

As people change the world, they develop their own abilities and needs to change it further. Thus, productive forces grow over time. Sooner or later, the developing productive forces come into conflict with the prevailing class structure—the social relations of production. The newly developed ways that people extract a living from their natural environment become incompatible with the older ways they relate to one another in the work process. For instance, the rise of trade and commercial activity in the 16th century became incompatible with feudal relations in the countryside and with guilds in the towns.

This growing contradiction takes the form of a class struggle between the rising class associated with the new means of production and the old ruling class whose dominance was based on its control of the older, waning forces. This class struggle, under appropriate conditions, intensifies the contradiction between the means of production and the class structure until, as a result of revolution, new relations of production which are compat-

ible with the superior produc[...] established. Thus, the bourgeo[...] gradually gained strength on [...] new productive forces, such as [...] improved weaponry, new ener[...] machinery, factory processes, acc[...] of technical knowledge, and so on. [...] ductive forces under their control[...] them to challenge successfully the old[...] ruling classes, whose privileged positi[...] depended on land rights and control [...] work processes as well as the judicia[...] military systems. The mode of produ[...] was changed, in a series of revolutions, s[...] times spreading over a century or more, f[...] feudalism to capitalism, from a class struct[...] of lords and vassals, guildmasters and appre[...] tices, to one of capitalists and wage-laborer[...] As Marx once put it, "The handmill gives you[...] a society with the feudal lord; the steam-mill,[...] society with the industrial capitalist." Even[...] though coming from Marx, this is a grossly simplified aphorism that overemphasizes the technological to the neglect of the dialectical.

Marx has expressed these transformations in the following passage known by heart to many people around the world:

> At a certain stage of development, the material productive forces of society come into conflict with the existing relations of production or—this merely expresses the same thing in legal terms—with the property relations within the framework of which they have operated hitherto. From forms of development of the productive forces these relations turn into their fetters. Then begins an era of social revolution. The changes in the economic foundation lead sooner or later to the transformation of the whole immense superstructure.

The Superstructure

Marx postulated that the economic structure of society molds its superstructure of social, political, and intellectual life, including sentiments, morality, illusions, modes of thought, principles, and views of life. The superstructure contains the ideas and systems of authority (political, legal, military, etc.) which support the class structure of that society—that is, the dominant position of the ruling class. In brief, how people make their

mental conceptions and
living sh...ions. It follows that the
supporti... the economic structure of
transfor... causes the character of the
society... change—after ideological
super... erthrow of older systems of
strug... ttrition have taken their toll.
aut... he feudal ruling classes by the
Th... example, not only opened the
b... irther development of society's
... rces but in addition spelled the
... al values, ideas, and institutions
... ich supported the feudal ruling
... fettered the rising capitalists. The
... ociated with vows of homage and
... instance, were vital to manorial life
... ly got in the way of—and were
... ent with—commerce and market
... ions.

... nuch as human beings change them-
... by labor, it is clear that they alter, at
... me time, at least some of their mental
... ceptions. They produce both material
... ods and their ideas. Thus, productive activ-
... ity and the attending class struggles change
not only the economic structure of society but
the superstructure as well. Since this is so,
interactions between the two are inevitable
and are, in fact, both numerous and intricate.
That is, the way people make a living determines their ideas, but these ideas in turn affect
the way they make their living. However,
modes of thought are shaped and limited, in
the first place, by the mode of production.
Accordingly, the ideas that become influential in a society cover only the narrow range
reflecting the material activities and interests
of the dominant class. Many ideas do not gain
prestige because they conflict with real positions of class domination which themselves
rest on a certain attained level of the productive forces. For example, the current idea of
"no growth" is incompatible with the fortunes
of a capitalist class that are generated by
industrial growth.

History is not the development of ideas,
Marx and Engels tell us, but rather the development of productive forces, and the formation of ideas is explained by these underlying

material changes. "Life is not determined by
consciousness, but consciousness by life."
Their theory of history "does not explain
practice from the idea but explains the formation of ideas from material practice." This
leads Marx and Engels to the conclusion that
in every society the ideas of the ruling class
are the ruling ideas. This does not mean that,
at any given time, there is only a single set of
ideas which serves the ruling class. The class
structure of a society is often complex and the
ideas of each class are likely to be expressed
in complex ways in the superstructure. Therefore, revolutionary ideas may exist side by
side with conventional ones because of the
existence of a revolutionary class. (Marxism
thus explains itself by the rise of an industrial
proletariat in the first half of the 19th century.) But these revolutionary ideas can at
best displace some other ideas; they cannot by
themselves overthrow the prevailing class
structure, which gave rise to the ruling ideas.
So Marx and Engels write that "not criticism
but revolution is the driving force of history."
From the Marxist view this means, to use our
previous example, that the idea of "no
growth" can become dominant, not through
criticism of the idea of "growth," but only by
the revolutionary overthrow of the capitalist
class.

The superstructure contains not only ideas
but also institutions and activities that support the class structure of society—the state,
legal institutions, family structures, art forms,
and spiritual processes. The Marxian presup-
position is that the superstructure of ideas and
supporting institutions, although in some
respects and to some degree capable of developing a life of its own, strongly reflects the
economic structure of society. Thus, according to some Marxists, the prehistoric cave-
wall paintings of animals in southern France
and northern Spain reflected the magical
need of hunters to depict their prey accurately
and naturally. The later geometric pottery
designs of settled agriculturalists, it is claimed,
were reflections of the more abstract, mysteri-
ous forces that determined whether crops
would prosper or die. This revolutionary

change from hunting and gathering to settled agriculture, which occurred because of radically new productive forces (which in turn transformed the relations of production), also altered other elements of the superstructure, such as family structures, religions, rules and laws, governing bodies, the games played, and military organizations.

Marx regarded the religious world as "the reflex of the real world." Religion is a consolation for man's degraded condition; it is the imaginary realization of human perfection. It will finally vanish "when the practical relations of everyday life offer to man none but perfectly intelligible and reasonable relations with regard to his fellowmen and to Nature." For capitalism, Marx reasoned, "Christianity with its *cultus* of abstract man, more especially in its bourgeois developments, Protestantism, Deism, etc., is the most fitting form of religion." Engels carried the analysis further by linking some changes in religious views to changes in material life over a period of 2,000 years. But Engels was careful to note that once an ideology (such as a set of religious views) arises, it develops in part independently of the economic structure, subject to its own laws.

In Marxian thought, the state, a product of society at a certain stage of development, as a rule is the institution that protects the property and privileges of the ruling classes and preserves order among the oppressed and exploited classes. It is an instrument of class rule, the manifestation of the irreconcilability of class antagonisms. Nevertheless, Engels added: "By way of exception, however, periods occur in which the warring classes balance each other so nearly that the state power, as ostensible mediator, acquires, for the moment, a certain degree of independence of both." Marxists assert that over long periods the form of the state has changed—for example, from decentralized to centralized monarchies, to constitutional governments, bourgeois democracies, fascist dictatorships, and so on—in response to changes in economic structures. The state is the guarantor of a given set of property relations, and in capitalist society its highest function is the protection of private property. Marx believed that the bourgeois state would have to be smashed by the proletariat and a dictatorship of that class established in the new socialist society. As socialism gives way to communism . . . , the state will wither away because, in a classless society, no organ of class rule is required. The state, however, as an administrator of things, such as a five-year plan, rather than an oppressor of subordinate classes, remains.

Dialectical Materialism

Marx's view of social development has been called by others "dialectical materialism." The phrase refers to Marx's method of analyzing social change, a method that is strongly present in all of his major works. Marxian materialism reverses the idealist approach of viewing abstract ideas, concepts, and consciousness as divorced from real people and their activities. According to Marx, materialism begins with "real, active men, and on the basis of their real life-process demonstrates the development of the ideological reflexes and echoes of this life-process." The ideas in the human brain (morality, religion, and all the rest of ideology) do not live completely independent lives. A person, in trying to understand social history, should not start with these phantoms—with, say, the concept of "freedom"—for they are all sublimates of the real material life-process. For example, the 16th century is not explainable by "the idea of expansion," as though some people got this idea around 1500 and then proceeded to carry it out. Instead, the idea of expansion came from revolutionary changes in the economic structures of Western European societies, attended by transformations of the relations of production.

To understand the world, a person must begin with what is basic—with real human beings and their activities in the world. Marx and Engels felt that work was the most basic and most important of all human activities. Most of people's lives are spent working and much of the rest is spent in an environment which is shaped by the kind of productive technology available to them. For example, Indians lived in huts or tents near the rivers they fished, while early industrial workers lived in the company towns built around the factories. In both cases, the work process exerted an all-pervading influence on their lives, shaping the conditions of their existence and therefore of their thoughts. Marxian materialism maintains that ideas, philosophies, religions, and so forth all take form within the influence of real material conditions and are therefore determined by them.

Materialism is also at the base of the Marxian concept of social class, for classes are the result of people's lives being formed by the work process within a strict hierarchical work structure. Marx and Engels believed that two major classes, the bourgeoisie and the proletariat (along with several minor ones), emerged with capitalism. The bourgeoisie and the proletariat are distinct classes because the former owns and controls the physical means of production—raw materials, energy, and capital goods—while the latter owns only its labor-power and must sell it to the bourgeoisie to survive.

Although Marx believed, along with other materialists, that objects exist independently of human beings and their consciousness, still his materialism was quite different from that of the 18th century, as anticipated in the writings of John Locke. Bertrand Russell, in his *A History of Western Philosophy*, has best delineated this difference by pointing out that the older materialism regarded sensation of the subject as passive, with activity attributed to the object. Russell explains that in Marx's view, on the other hand, "all sensation or perception is an interaction between subject and object; the bare object, apart from the activity of the percipient, is a mere raw material, which is transformed in the process of becoming known." Consequently, knowledge is not passive contemplation, as Locke and others would have it. Rather, Russell continues, "both subject and object, both the knower and the thing known, are in a continual process of mutual adaptation." Russell then connects Marx's materialism to his economics:

> For Marx, matter, not spirit, is the driving force [of human history]. But it is matter in the peculiar sense that we have been considering, not the wholly dehumanized matter of the atomists. This means that, for Marx, the driving force is really man's relation to matter, of which the most important part is his mode of production. In this way Marx's materialism, in practice, becomes economics.

Marx stated that we can really know an object only by acting on it successfully. "And since we change the object when we act upon it," Russell appends, "truth ceases to be static, and becomes something which is continually changing and developing. That is why Marx calls his materialism 'dialectical.'" When a person gains knowledge through investigation of the material world he not only changes that world—and hence "the truth"—but changes himself at the same time, for in the process of knowing an object he acquires new information, abilities, and needs. This has been phrased very well by Ernst Fischer, the Austrian poet and critic, who wrote in *The Essential Marx*:

> From the very start the species man has not appropriated the world passively but actively, through practice, labor, the setting of goals, the giving of form. As men changed *the world they expanded and refined their ability to* know *it, and the growing capacity for cognition again enhanced their ability to change it.*

What Fischer is describing is the dialectical relation between human beings and their natural environment, an important instance of the dialectical process that Marx and Engels believed pervaded human societies. In its broadest sweep, the dialectic method stresses the following elements:

1. All things are in constant change;
2. the ultimate source of the change is within the thing or process itself;
3. this source is the struggle of opposites, the contradiction, within each thing;
4. this struggle, at nodal points, brings about qualitative changes, or leaps, so that the thing is transformed into something else; and
5. practical-critical activity resolves the contradictions.

Formal logic, which has dominated Western thought for some 2,000 years, is based on the simplest and seemingly most common sense axioms, such as *A* is equal to *A* and *A* is not equal to *non-A*. But by being based on axioms like these, which freeze reality into fixed categories, formal logic loses its ability to explain structural change. Thus, one difference between the bourgeois (traditional) and Marxian approach to economics is that the former postulates only *quantitative* change, with each element maintaining its basic identity as it grows or contracts, whereas Marxian change allows for *qualitative transformation*, with each thing capable of turning into something new by becoming a synthesis of itself and its opposite.

Marxian dialectics is the logic of constant change: *A*, which includes not only itself but its opposite, *non-A*, is in continuous evolution. The fundamental cause of change in all things lies in their internal contradictions, in the struggle of opposites, in their self-movement. Whatever *is* has emerged from something else. Capitalism has evolved out of feudalism; socialism will emerge out of the contradictions of capitalism, not because it is "a better idea." Within capitalism, wealth exists in unity with its opposite, poverty; the very same economic processes have created both wealth and poverty, and one cannot exist or even be defined independently of the other. Similarly, workers in capitalism can only be discussed in relation to their opposite, capitalists. The one is inconceivable without the other, and

social change occurs as a result of the struggle between these opposites.

Dialectical thought, which Marx learned from the work of the German philosopher Hegel (1770–1831), has been called the power of negative thinking. This is because, according to the dialectical view, everything includes its opposite (its negative); a thesis has an antithesis. The struggle of these opposites leads to the transformation of the thesis into some other and higher form of being—a synthesis. The development of the thesis which results from the contradiction does not stop at the opposite of what it was, but rather moves to a synthesis of itself and its opposite. Thus, a thing or process is never simply this or that; it is always both. "The simple-minded use of the notion 'right or wrong,'" English philosopher Alfred Whitehead wrote, "is one of the chief obstacles to the progress of understanding." This is because right includes wrong and wrong contains right. Likewise, Engels wrote that one knows "that which is recognized now as true has also its latent false side which will later manifest itself, just as that which is now regarded as false has also its true side by virtue of which it could previously have been regarded as true. One knows that what is maintained to be necessary is composed of sheer accidents and that the so-called accidental is the form behind which necessity hides itself."

Marx can hardly be understood unless his dialectical approach is kept constantly in mind.

2.2   *The Essence of Capitalism*

How should we define capitalism? What are its distinguishing features? In the following reading Maurice Dobb argues from a historical materialist perspective that capitalism can be characterized as a system of production for the market in which labor-power itself has become a commodity like any other article of exchange. With this definition, capitalism can be identified as a distinct historical epoch. The prerequisite for the capitalist mode of production was the creation of a class of producers separated from the means of production and the concentration of those means of production in the hands of another class, the capitalists. Thus for capitalism to exist, there must be two types of people, capitalists and workers, who come together and meet in a market.

Dobb divides history into periods, each characterized by a different mode of production; the antagonistic social classes of each period are defined by the manner in which surplus product is produced and appropriated. The analysis of the capitalist mode of production that Dobb begins in this selection is continued in greater detail in Chapter 3.

The following is excerpted from Chapter 1 of *Studies in the Development of Capitalism* by MAURICE DOBB. Revised edition copyright © 1963 by Maurice Dobb. Reprinted by permission of International Publishers, Inc.

I

It is perhaps not altogether surprising that the term Capitalism, which in recent years has enjoyed so wide a currency alike in popular talk and in historical writing, should have been used so variously, and that there should have been no common measure of agreement in its use. What is more remarkable is that in economic theory, as this has been expounded by the traditional schools, the term should have appeared so rarely, if at all. There is even a school of thought, numbering its adherents both among economists and historians, which has refused to recognize that Capitalism as a title for a determinate economic system can be given an exact meaning. . . .

To-day, after half a century of intensive research in economic history, this attitude is rarely regarded by economic historians as tenable, even if they may still hold the origin of the term to be suspect. . . . But if to-day Capitalism has received authoritative recognition as an historical category, this affords no assurance that those who claim to study this system are talking about the same thing. . . . If it is the pattern which historical events force upon us, and not our own predilections, that is decisive in our use of the term Capitalism, there must then be one definition that accords with the actual shape which historical development possesses, and others which, by contrast with it, are wrong. Even a believer in historical relativism must, surely, believe that there is one picture that is right from the

standpoint of any given homogeneous set of historical observations.

. . .

We [accept] the meaning originally given by Marx, who sought the essence of Capitalism neither in a spirit of enterprise nor in the use of money to finance a series of exchange transactions with the object of gain, but in a particular mode of production. By mode of production he did not refer merely to the state of technique—to what he termed the state of the productive forces—but to the way in which the means of production were owned and to the social relations between men which resulted from their connections with the process of production. Thus Capitalism was not simply a system of production for the market —a system of commodity-production as Marx termed it—but a system under which labour-power had "itself become a commodity" and was bought and sold on the market like any other object of exchange. Its historical prerequisite was the concentration of ownership of the means of production in the hands of a class, consisting of only a minor section of society, and the consequential emergence of a propertyless class for whom the sale of their labour-power was their only source of livelihood. Productive activity was furnished, accordingly, by the latter, not by virtue of legal compulsion, but on the basis of a wage-contract. It is clear that such a definition excludes the system of independent handicraft production where the craftsman owned his own petty implements of production and undertook the sale of his own wares. Here there was no divorce between ownership and work; and except where he relied to any extent on the employment of journeymen, it was the purchase and sale of inanimate wares and not of human labour-power that was his primary concern. What differentiates the use of this definition from others is that the existence of trade and of money-lending and the presence of a specialized class of merchants or financiers, even though they be men of substance, does not suffice to constitute a capitalist society. Men of capital, however acquisitive, are not enough: their capital must be used to yoke labour to the creation of surplus-value in production.

. . .

II

If it be right to maintain that the conception of socio-economic systems, marking distinct stages in historical development, is not merely a matter of convenience but an obligation—not a matter of suitable chapter-headings but something that concerns the essential construction of the story if the story is to be true—then this must be because there is a quality in historical situations which both makes for homogeneity of pattern at any given time and renders periods of transition, when there is an even balance of discrete elements, inherently unstable. It must be because society is so constituted that conflict and interaction of its leading elements, rather than the simple growth of some single element, form the principal agency of movement and change, at least so far as major transformations are concerned. If such be the case, once development has reached a certain level and the various elements which constitute that society are poised in a certain way, events are likely to move with unusual rapidity, not merely in the sense of quantitative growth, but in the sense of a change of balance of the constituent elements, resulting in the appearance of novel compositions and more or less abrupt changes in the texture of society. To use a topical analogy: it is as though at certain levels of

development something like a chain-reaction is set in motion.

Clearly the feature of economic society which produces this result, and is accordingly fundamental to our conception of Capitalism as a distinctive economic order, characteristic of a distinctive period of history, is that history has been to-date the history of *class societies*: namely, of societies divided into classes, in which either one class, or else a coalition of classes with some common interest, constitutes the dominant class, and stands in partial or complete antagonism to another class or classes. The fact that this is so tends to impose on any given historical period a certain qualitative uniformity; since the class that is socially and politically dominant at the time will naturally use its power to preserve and to extend that particular mode of production—that particular form of relationship between classes—on which its income depends. If change within that society should reach a point where the continued hegemony of this dominant class is seriously called in question, and the old stable balance of forces shows signs of being disturbed, development will have reached a critical stage, where either the change that has been proceeding hitherto must somehow be halted, or if it should continue the dominant class can be dominant no longer and the new and growing one must take its place. Once this shift in the balance of power has occurred, the interest of the class which now occupies the strategic positions will clearly lie in accelerating the transition, in breaking up the strongholds of its rival and predecessor and in extending its own. The old mode of production will not necessarily be eliminated entirely; but it will quickly be reduced in scale until it is no longer a serious competitor to the new.[1] For a period the new mode of production, associated with new pro-

[1] It is not necessary to assume that this is done as part of a conscious long-term plan; although, in so far as the dominant class pursues a definite political policy, this will be so. But it assumes at least that members of a class take common action over particular questions (e.g., access to land or markets or labour), and that greater strength enables them to oust their rivals.

ductive forces and novel economic potentialities, is likely to expand far beyond the limits within which the old system was destined to move; until in turn the particular class relations and the political forms in which the new ruling class asserts its power come into conflict with some further development of the productive forces, and the struggle between the two is fought to a climax once again.

The common interest which constitutes a certain social grouping, a class in the sense of which we have been speaking, does not derive from a quantitative similarity of income, as is sometimes supposed: a class does not necessarily consist of people on the same income level, nor are people at, or near, a given income level necessarily united by identity of aims. Nor is it sufficient to say simply that a class consists of those who derive their income from a common source; although it is source rather than size of income that is here important. In this context one must be referring to something quite fundamental concerning the roots which a social group has in a particular society: namely to the relationship in which the group as a whole stands to the process of production and hence to other sections of society, In other words, the relationship from which in one case a common interest in preserving and extending a particular economic system, and in the other case, an antagonism of interest on this issue can alone derive, must be a relationship with a particular mode of extracting and distributing the fruits of surplus labour, over and above the labour which goes to supply the consumption of the actual producer. Since this surplus labour constitutes its life-blood, any ruling class will of necessity treat its particular relationship to the labour process as crucial to its own survival; and any rising class that aspires to live without labour is bound to regard its own future career, prosperity and influence as dependent on the acquisition of some claim upon the surplus labour of others. "A surplus of the product of labour over and above the costs of maintenance of the labour," said Friedrich Engels, "and the formation and enlargement, by means of this surplus, of a social production and reserve fund, was and

is the basis of all social, political and intellectual progress. In history up to the present, this fund has been the possession of a privileged class, on which also devolved, along with this possession, political supremacy and intellectual leadership."[2]

The form in which surplus labour has been appropriated has differed at different stages of society; and these varieties of form have been associated with the use of various methods and instruments of production and with different levels of productivity. Marx spoke of Capitalism itself as being, "like any other definite mode of production, conditioned upon a certain stage of social productivity and upon the historically developed form of the productive forces. This historical prerequisite is itself the historical result and product of a preceding process, from which the new mode of production takes its departure as from its given foundation. The conditions of production corresponding to this specific, historically determined, mode of production have a specific, historical passing character."[3] At a stage of social development when the productivity of labour is very low, any substantial and regular income for a leisured class, living on production but not contributing thereto, will be inconceivable unless it is grounded in the rigorous compulsion of producers; and in this sense, as Engels remarked, the division into classes at a primitive stage of economic development "has a certain historical justification."[4] In a predominantly agricultural society the crucial relationships will be connected with the holding of land; and since the division of labour and exchange are likely to be little developed, surplus labour will tend to be performed directly as a personal obligation or to take the form of the delivery of a certain quota of his produce by the cultivator as tribute in natural form to an overlord. The growth of industry, which implies the invention of new and varied instruments of production, will beget new classes and by creating new economic prob-

[2]*Anti-Dühring*, 221.
[3]*Capital*, Vol. III, 1023–24.
[4]*Anti-Dühring*, 316.

lems will require new forms of appropriating surplus labour for the benefit of the owners of the new instruments of production. Mediæval society was characterized by the compulsory performance of surplus labour by producers: producers who were in possession of their own primitive instruments of cultivation and were attached to the land. Modern society, by contrast, is characterized, as we have seen, by a relationship between worker and capitalist which takes a purely contractual form, and which is indistinguishable in appearance from any of the other manifold free-market transactions of an exchange society. The transformation from the mediæval form of exploitation of surplus labour to the modern was no simple process that can be depicted as some genealogical table of direct descent. Yet among the eddies of this movement it is possible for the eye to discern certain lines of direction of the flow. These include, not only changes in technique and the appearance of new instruments of production, which greatly enhanced the productivity of labour, but a growing division of labour and consequently the development of exchange, and also a growing separation of the producer from the land and from the means of production and his appearance as a proletarian. Of these guiding tendencies in the history of the past five centuries a special significance attaches to the latter; not only because it has been traditionally glossed over and decently veiled behind formulas about the passage from status to contract, but because into the centre of the historical stage it has brought a form of compulsion to labour for another that is purely economic and "objective"; thus laying a basis for that peculiar and mystifying form whereby a leisured class can exploit the surplus labour of others which is the essence of the modern system that we call Capitalism.

III

The development of Capitalism falls into a number of stages, characterized by different levels of maturity and each of them recognizable by fairly distinctive traits. But when we seek to trace these stages and to select one of them as marking the opening stage of Capitalism, there is an immediate consideration about which it is of some importance that there should be no confusion. If we are speaking of Capitalism as a specific mode of production, then it follows that we cannot date the dawn of this system from the first signs of the appearance of large-scale trading and of a merchant class, and we cannot speak of a special period of "Merchant Capitalism," as many have done. We must look for the opening of the capitalist period only when changes in the mode of production occur, in the sense of a direct subordination of the producer to a capitalist. This is not just a point of terminology, but of substance; since it means that, if we are right, the appearance of a purely trading class will have of itself no revolutionary significance; that its rise will exert a much less fundamental influence on the economic pattern of society than will the appearance of a class of capitalists whose fortunes are intimately linked with industry; and that, while a ruling class, whether of slave-owners or feudal lords, may take to trading or enter into a close alliance with traders, a merchant class, whose activities are essentially those of an intermediary between producer and consumer, is unlikely to strive to become a dominant class in quite that radical and exclusive sense of which we were speaking a moment ago. Since its fortunes will tend to be bound up with the existing mode of production, it is more likely to be under an inducement to preserve that mode of production than to transform it. It is likely to struggle to "muscle in" upon an existing form of appropriating surplus labour; but it is unlikely to try to change this form.

When we look at the history of Capitalism, conceived in this way, it becomes clear that we must date its opening phase in England, not in the twelfth century as does Pirenne (who is thinking primarily of the Netherlands) nor even in the fourteenth century with its urban trade and guild handicrafts as others have done, but in the latter half of the sixteenth and the early seventeenth century when capital began to penetrate production on a considerable scale, either in the form of a fairly matured relationship between capitalist and hired wage-earners or in the less developed form of the subordination of domestic handicraftsmen, working in their own homes, to a capitalist on the so-called "putting-out system." It is true that already prior to this, fairly numerous examples are to be found of a transitional situation where the craftsman had lost much of his independence, through debt or in face of the monopoly of wholesale traders, and already stood in relations of some dependence on a merchant, who was a man of capital. It is also true that in the fourteenth century or even earlier there was a good deal of what one may call (to use modern terminology) *kulak* types of enterprise—the well-to-do peasant in the village or the local trader or worker-owner in town handicrafts, employing hired labour. But these seem to have been too small in scale and insufficiently matured to be regarded as much more than adolescent Capitalism, and scarcely justify one in dating Capitalism as a new mode of production, sufficiently clear-cut and extensive to constitute any serious challenge to an older one, as early as this. At any rate, one can say with considerable assurance that a capitalist mode of production, and a special class of capitalists specifically associated with it, did not attain to any decisive significance as an influence on social and economic development until the closing decades of the Tudor era.

In the career of Capitalism since this date it is evident that there are two decisive moments. One of them resides in the seventeenth century: in the political and social transformations of that decisive period, including the struggle within the chartered corporations, which the researches of Unwin have brought to light, and the Parliamentary struggle against monopoly, reaching its apex in the Cromwellian revolution, the results of which were very far from being submerged, despite a certain measure of compromise and reaction at the Restoration. The second consists of the industrial revolution of the late eighteenth and earlier half of the nineteenth century, which was primarily of economic significance; it had a less dramatic, but far from unimportant, reflection in the political sphere. So decisive was it for the whole future of capitalist economy, so radical a transformation of the structure and organization of industry did it represent, as to have caused some to regard it as the birth pangs of modern Capitalism, and hence as the most decisive moment in economic and social development since the Middle Ages. Maturer knowledge and judgment today clearly indicate, however, that what the industrial revolution represented was a transition from an early and still immature stage of Capitalism, where the pre-capitalist petty mode of production had been penetrated by the influence of capital, subordinated to capital, robbed of its independence as an economic form but not yet completely transformed, to a stage where Capitalism, on the basis of technical change, had achieved its own specific production process resting on the collective large-scale production unit of the factory, thereby effecting a final divorce of the producer from his remaining hold on the means of production and establishing a simple and direct relationship between capitalist and wage-earners.

2.3   *The Transition from Feudalism to Capitalism*

Having defined the capitalist mode of production as a distinctive economic system, we can now apply the materialist conception of history to the emergence of capitalism out of feudal society. In the following reading E. K. Hunt describes the nature of the feudal system, discussing its organization of production as well as its values and ideology. He shows how both the basic economic institutions and the superstructural ideas and values were transformed by the dissolution of feudalism and the rise of the capitalist mode of production. The breakup of feudalism occurred because of contradictions between the developing forces of production and the feudal relations of production. The creation of the new capitalist mode of production involved considerable violence and force; its history, Marx said, could be written "in letters of blood and fire."

Hunt also describes how capitalism from its very beginning in the sixteenth century was a worldwide system. The European powers in the center of the system developed a colonial system to exploit systematically their treasures and cheap labor. We shall investigate capitalism as a world system in Chapter 13.

The following is an abridgement of pp. 12–24 from *Property and Prophets*, 2nd Edition by E. K. HUNT. Copyright © 1972, 1975 by E. K. Hunt. Reprinted by permission of Harper and Row, Publishers, Inc.

FEUDALISM

The decline of the western part of the old Roman Empire left Europe without the laws and protection the empire had provided. The vacuum was filled by the creation of a feudal hierarchy. In this hierarchy, the serf, or peasant, was protected by the lord of the manor, who, in turn, owed allegiance to and was protected by a higher overlord. And so the system went, ending eventually with the king. The strong protected the weak, but they did so at a high price. In return for payments of money, food, labor, or military allegiance, overlords granted the fief, or feudum—a hereditary right to use land—to their vassals. At the bottom was the serf, a peasant who tilled the land. The vast majority of the population raised crops for food or clothing or tended sheep for wool and clothing.[1]

Custom and tradition are the key to understanding medieval relationships. In place of laws as we know them today, the *custom of the manor* governed. There was no strong central authority in the Middle Ages that could have enforced a system of laws. The entire

[1]For a more complete discussion of the medieval economic and social system, see J. H. Claphan and Eileen E. Power, eds., *The Agrarian Life of the Middle Ages*, 2d ed. The Cambridge Economic History of Europe, vol. I (London: Cambridge University Press, 1966).

medieval organization was based on a system of mutual obligations and services up and down the hierarchy. Possession or use of the land obligated one to certain customary services or payments in return for protection. The lord was as obligated to protect the serf as the serf was to turn over a portion of his crop to or perform extensive labor for the lord.

Customs were broken, of course; no system always operates in fact as it is designed to operate in theory. One should not, however, underestimate the strength of custom and tradition in determining the lives and ideas of medieval people. Disputes between serfs were decided in the lord's court according to both the special circumstances of each case and the general customs of the manor for such cases. Of course, a dispute between a serf and a lord would usually be decided in his own favor by the lord. Even in this circumstance, however, especially in England, an overlord would impose sanctions or punishments on a lord who, as his vassal, had persistently violated the customs in his treatment of serfs. This rule by the custom of the manor stands in sharp contrast to the legal and judicial system of capitalism. The capitalist system is based on the enforcement of contracts and universally binding laws, which are softened only rarely by the possible mitigating circumstances and customs that often swayed the lord's judgment in medieval times.

The extent to which the lords could enforce their "rights" varied greatly from time to time and from place to place. It was the strengthening of these obligations and the nobleman's ability to enforce them through a long hierarchy of vassals and over a wide area that eventually led to the emergence of the modern nation-states. This process occurred during the period of transition from feudalism to capitalism. Throughout most of the Middle Ages, however, many of these claims were very weak because political control was fragmented.

The basic economic institution of medieval rural life was the manor, which contained within it two separate and distinct classes: noblemen, or lords of the manors, and serfs (from the Latin word *servus*, "slave"). Serfs were not really slaves. Unlike a slave, who was simply property to be bought and sold at will, the serf could not be parted from either his family or his land. If his lord transferred possession of the manor to another nobleman, the serf simply had another lord. In varying degrees, however, obligations were placed upon the serfs that were sometimes very onerous and from which there was often no escape. Usually, they were far from being "free."

The lord lived off the labor of the serfs who farmed his fields and paid taxes in kind and money according to the custom of the manor. Similarly, the lord gave protection, supervision, and administration of justice according to the custom of the manor. It must be added that although the system did rest on reciprocal obligations, the concentration of economic and political power in the hands of the lord led to a system in which, by any standard, the serf was exploited in the extreme.

The Catholic church was by far the largest owner of land during the Middle Ages. While bishops and abbots occupied much the same place as counts and dukes in the feudal hierarchy, there was one important difference between the religious and secular lords. Dukes and counts might shift their loyalty from one overlord to another, depending on the circumstances and the balance of power

involved, but the bishops and abbots always had (in principle at least) a primary loyalty to the church in Rome. This was also an age during which the religious teaching of the church had a very strong and pervasive influence throughout western Europe. These factors combined to make the church the closest thing to a strong central government throughout this period.

Thus the manor might be secular or religious (many times secular lords had religious overlords and vice versa), but the essential relationships between lord and serfs were not significantly affected by this distinction. There is little evidence that serfs were treated any less harshly by religious lords than by secular ones. The religious lords and the secular nobility were the joint ruling classes; they controlled the land and the power that went with it. In return for very onerous appropriations of the serf's labor, produce, and money, the nobility provided military protection and the church provided spiritual aid.

In addition to manors, medieval Europe had many towns, which were important centers of manufacturing. Manufactured goods were sold to manors and, sometimes, traded in long-distance commerce. The dominant economic institutions in the towns were the guilds—craft, professional, and trade associations that had existed as far back as the Roman Empire. If anyone wanted to produce or sell any good or service, he had to join a guild.

The guilds were as involved with social and religious questions as with economic ones. They regulated their members' conduct in all their activities: personal, social, religious, and economic. Although the guilds did regulate very carefully the production and sale of commodities, they were less concerned with making profits than with saving their members' souls. Salvation demanded that the individual lead an orderly life based on church teachings and custom. Thus the guilds exerted a powerful influence as conservators of the status quo in the medieval towns.

· · ·

Any account of medieval social and economic thought must also stress the great disdain with which people viewed trade and commerce and the commercial spirit. The medieval way of life was based on custom and tradition; its viability depended on the acceptance by the members of society of that tradition and their place within it. Where the capitalist commerical ethic prevails, greed, selfishness, covetousness, and the desire to better oneself materially or socially are accepted by most people as innate qualities. Yet they were uniformly denounced and reviled in the Middle Ages. The serfs (and sometimes the lower nobility) tended to be dissatisfied with the traditions and customs of medieval society and thus threatened the stability of the feudal system. It is not surprising, therefore, to find pervasive moral sanctions designed to repress or to mitigate the effects of these motives.

One of the most important of such sanctions, repeated over and over throughout this period, was the insistence that it was the moral duty of merchants and traders to transact all trade or exchanges at the just price. This notion illustrates the role played by paternalistic social control in the feudal era. A *just price* was one that would compensate the seller for his efforts in transporting the good and in finding the buyer at a rate that was just sufficient to maintain the seller at his *customary* or *traditional* station in life. Prices above the just price would, of course, lead to profits, which would be accumulated as material wealth.

It was the lust for wealth that the Christian paternalist ethic consistently condemned. Thus the doctrine of the just price was intended as a curb on such acquisitive and socially disruptive behavior. Then as now, accumulation of material wealth was a passport to greater power and upward social mobility. This social mobility was eventually to prove totally destructive of the medieval system because it put an end to the status relationships that were the backbone of medieval society.

Another example of this condemnation of acquisitive behavior was the prohibition of usury, or the lending of money at interest. A "bill against usury" passed in England reflected the attitudes of most of the people of those times. It read in part:

> But forasmuch as usury is by the word of God utterly prohibited, as a vice most odious and detestable . . . which thing, by no godly teachings and persuasions can sink in to the hearts of divers greedy, uncharitable and covetous persons of this Realm . . . be it enacted . . . that . . . no person or persons of what Estate, degree, quality or condition so ever he or they be, by any corrupt, colorable or deceitful conveyance, sleight or engine, or by any way or mean, shall lend, give, set out, deliver or forbear any sum or sums of money . . . to or for any manner of usury, increase, lucre, gain or interest to be had, received or hoped for, over and above the sum or sums so lent . . . as also of the usury . . . upon pain of imprisonment.

The church believed usury was the worst sort of acquisitive behavior because most loans on which interest was charged were granted to poor farmers or peasants after a bad crop or some other tragedy had befallen them. Thus, interest was a gain made at the expense of one's brother at a time when he was most in need of help and charity. Of course, the Christian ethic strongly condemned such rapacious exploitation of a needy brother.

Many historians have pointed out that bishops and abbots as well as dukes, counts, and kings often flagrantly violated these sanctions. They themselves granted loans at interest, even while they were punishing others for doing so. We are more interested, however, in the values and motives of the period than in the sins and infractions of the rules. The values of the feudal system stand in stark, antithetical contrast to those that were shortly to prevail under a capitalist system. The desire to maximize monetary gain, accumulate material wealth, and advance oneself socially and economically through acquisitive behavior was to become the dominant motive force in the capitalist system.

The sins that were most strongly denounced within the context of the Christian paternalist ethic were to become the behavioral assumptions on which the entire capitalist market economy was to be based. It is obvious that such a radical change would render the Christian ethic, at least in its medieval version, inadequate as the basis of a moral justification of the new capitalist system. The ethic would have to be modified drastically or rejected completely in order to elaborate a defense for the new system.

. . .

THE TRANSITION TO EARLY CAPITALISM

The medieval society was an agrarian society. The social hierarchy was based on individuals' ties to the land, and the entire social system rested on an agricultural base. Yet, ironically, increases in agricultural productivity were the original impetus to a series of profound changes. These changes, occurring over several centuries, resulted in the dissolution of medieval feudalism and the beginnings of capitalism.

CHANGES IN TECHNOLOGY

The most important technological advance in the Middle Ages was the replacement of the two-field system of crop rotation with the three-field system. Although there is evidence that the three-field system was introduced into Europe as early as the eighth century, its use was probably not widespread until around the eleventh century.

Yearly sowing of the same land would deplete the land and eventually make it unusable. Consequently, in the two-field system half of the land was always allowed to lie fallow in order to recover from the previous year's planting.

With the three-field system, arable land was divided into three equal fields. Rye or winter wheat would be planted in the fall in the first field. Oats, beans, or peas would be planted in the spring in the second, and the third would lie fallow. In each subsequent

year there was a rotation of these positions. Any given piece of land would have a fall planting one year, a spring planting the next year, and none the third year.

A dramatic increase in agricultural output resulted from this seemingly simple change in agricultural technology. With the same amount of arable land, the three-field system could increase the amount under cultivation at any particular time by as much as 50 percent.

. . .

Improvements in agriculture and transportation contributed to two important and far-reaching changes. First, they made possible a rapid increase in population growth. The best historical estimates show that the population of Europe doubled between 1000 and 1300.[2] Second, closely related to the expansion of population was a rapid increase in urban concentration. Before the year 1000, most of Europe, except for a few Mediterranean trade centers, consisted of only manors, villages, and a few small towns. By 1300, there were many thriving cities and larger towns.

The growth of towns and cities led to a growth of rural-urban specialization. With urban workers severing all ties to the soil, the output of manufactured goods increased impressively. Along with increased manufacturing and increased economic specialization came many additional gains in human productivity. Interregional, long-distance trade and commerce was another very important result of this increased specialization.

THE INCREASE IN LONG-DISTANCE TRADE

Many historians have argued that the spread of trade and commerce was the single most important force leading to the disintegration of medieval trade and customs. The impor-

[2]Harry A. Miskimin, *The Economy of Early Renaissance Europe, 1300–1460* (Englewood Cliffs, N.J.: Prentice-Hall, 1969), p. 20.

tance of trade cannot be doubted, but it must be emphasized that this trade did not arise by accident or by factors completely external to the European economy, such as increased contact with the Arabs. On the contrary, it was shown in the previous section that this upsurge in trade was prepared for by the internal economic evolution of Europe itself. The growth of agricultural productivity meant that a surplus of food and handicrafts was available for local and international markets. The improvements in power and transportation meant that it was possible and profitable to concentrate industry in towns, to produce on a mass scale, and to sell the goods in a widespread, long-distance market. Thus the basic agricultural and industrial developments were necessary prerequisites for the spread of trade and commerce—which then further encouraged industry and town expansion.

The expansion of trade, particularly long-distance trade in the early period, led to the establishment of commercial and industrial towns that serviced this trade. And the growth of these cities and towns, as well as their increased domination by merchant capitalists, led to important changes in both industry and agriculture. Each of these areas of change, particularly the latter, brought about a weakening and ultimately a complete dissolving of the traditional ties that held together the feudal economic and social structure.

From the earliest part of the medieval period, some long-distance trade had been carried on throughout many parts of Europe. This trade was very important in southern Europe, on the Mediterranean and Adriatic seas, and in northern Europe, on the North and Baltic seas. Between these two centers of commercialism, however, the feudal manorial system in most of the rest of Europe was relatively unaffected by commerce and trade until the later Middle Ages.

From about the eleventh century onward, the Christian Crusades gave the impetus to a marked expansion of commerce. . . . The development of trade with the Arabs—and with the Vikings in the North—led to increased production for export and to the great trade fairs that flourished from the twelfth through the late fourteenth centuries. Held annually in the principal European trading cities, these fairs usually lasted for one to several weeks. Northern European merchants exchanged their grain, fish, wool, cloth, timber, pitch, tar, salt, and iron for the spices, silks, brocades, wines, fruits, and gold and silver that were the dominant items in southern European commerce.[3]

By the fifteenth century the fairs were being replaced by commercial cities where year-round markets thrived. The trade and commerce of these cities was incompatible with restrictive feudal customs and traditions. Generally the cities were successful in gaining independence from church and feudal lords. Within these commercial centers there arose complex systems of currency exchange, debt-clearing, and credit facilities, and modern business instruments like bills of exchange came into widespread use. New systems of commercial law developed. Unlike the system of paternalistic adjudication based on custom and tradition that prevailed in the manor, the commercial law was fixed by precise code. Hence it became the basis of the modern capitalistic law of contracts, negotiable instruments, agency sales, and auctions.

In the manorial handicraft industry, the producer (the master craftsman) was also the seller. The industries that burgeoned in the new cities, however, were primarily export industries in which the producer was distant from the final buyer. Craftsmen sold their goods wholesale to merchants, who, in turn, transported and resold them. Another important difference was that the manorial craftsman was also generally a farmer. The new city craftsman gave up farming to devote himself to his craft, with which he obtained a

[3]For a more complete discussion of the rise of trade and commerce, see Dudley Dillard, *Economic Development of the North Atlantic Community* (Englewood Cliffs, N.J.: Prentice-Hall, 1967), pp. 3–178.

money income that could be used to satisfy his other needs.

THE PUTTING-OUT SYSTEM AND THE BIRTH OF CAPITALIST INDUSTRY

As trade commerce thrived and expanded, the need for more manufactured goods and greater reliability of supply led to increasing control of the productive process by the merchant-capitalist. By the sixteenth century the handicraft type of industry, in which the craftsman owned his workshop, tools, and raw materials and functioned as an independent, small-scale entrepreneur, had been largely replaced in the exporting industries by the *putting-out system*. In the earliest period of the putting-out system, the merchant-capitalist would furnish an independent craftsman with raw materials and pay him a fee to work the materials into finished products. In this way the capitalist owned the product throughout all stages of production, although the work was done in independent workshops. In the later period of the putting-out system, the merchant-capitalist owned the tools and machinery and often the building in which the production took place. He hired workers to use these tools, furnished them with the raw materials, and took the finished products.

The worker no longer sold a finished product to the merchant. Rather, he sold only his labor power. The textile industries were among the first in which the putting-out system developed. Weavers, spinners, fullers, and dyers found themselves in a situation where their employment, and hence their ability to support themselves and their families, depended on the merchant-capitalists, who had to sell what the workers produced at a price that was high enough to pay wages and other costs and still make a profit.

Capitalist control was, then, extended into the process of production. At the same time, a labor force was created that owned little or no capital and had nothing to sell but its labor power. These two features mark the appearance of the economic system of capitalism. Some writers and historians have defined capitalism as existing when trade, commerce, and the commercial spirit expanded and became more important in Europe. Trade and commerce, however, had existed throughout the feudal era. Yet as long as feudal tradition remained the organizing principle in production, trade and commerce were really outside the social and economic system. The market and the search for money profits replaced custom and tradition in determining who would perform what task, how the task would be performed, and whether a given worker could find work to support himself. When this occurred, the capitalist system was created.

Capitalism became dominant with the extension to most lines of production of the relationship that existed between capitalists and workers in the sixteenth-century export industries. For such a system to evolve, the economic self-sufficiency of the feudal manor had to be broken down and manorial customs and traditions undermined or destroyed. Agriculture had to become a capitalistic venture in which workers would sell their labor power to capitalists, and capitalists would buy labor only if they expected to make a profit in the process.

A capitalist textile industry existed in Flanders in the thirteenth century. When for various reasons its prosperity began to decline, the wealth and poverty it had created led to a long series of violent class wars, starting around 1280, that almost completely destroyed the industry. In the fourteenth century a capitalist textile industry flourished in Florence. There, as in Flanders, adverse business conditions led to tensions between a poverty-stricken working class and their affluent capitalist employers. The results of these tensions were violent rebellions in 1379 and 1382. Failure to resolve these class antagonisms significantly worsened the precipitous decline in the Florentine textile industry, as it had earlier in Flanders.

In the fifteenth century England dominated the world textile market. Its capitalist textile industry solved the problem of class conflict by ruralizing the industry. Whereas the earlier capitalist textile industries of Flanders and Florence had been centered in the densely populated cities, where the workers were thrown together and organized resistance was easy to initiate, the English fulling mills were scattered about the countryside. This meant that the workers were isolated from all but a small handful of other workers, and effective organized resistance did not develop.

The later system, however, in which wealthy owners of capital employed propertyless craftsmen, was usually a phenomenon of the city rather than of the countryside. From the beginning, these capitalistic enterprises sought monopolistic positions from which to exploit the demand for their products. The rise of livery guilds, or associations of merchant-capitalist employers, created a host of barriers to protect their position. Different types of apprenticeships, with special privileges and exemptions for the sons of the wealthy, excessively high membership fees, and other barriers, prevented ambitious poorer craftsmen from competing with or entering the new capitalist class. Indeed, these barriers generally resulted in the transformation of poorer craftsmen and their sons into a new urban working class that lived exclusively by selling its labor power.

THE DECLINE OF THE MANORIAL SYSTEM

Before a complete system of capitalism could emerge, however, the force of capitalist market relations had to invade the rural manor, the bastion of feudalism. This was accomplished as a result of the vast increase of population in the new trading cities. Large urban populations depended on the rural countryside for food and much of the raw materials for export industries. These needs fostered a rural-urban specialization and a large flow of trade between the rural manor and the city. The lords of the manors began to depend on the cities for manufactured goods and increasingly came to desire luxury goods that merchants could sell to them.

The peasants on the manor also found that they could exchange surpluses for money at the local grain markets; the money could be used by the peasants to purchase commutation of their labor services.[4] Commutation often resulted in a situation in which the peasant became very nearly a independent small businessman. He might rent the land from the lord, sell the produce to cover the rents, and retain the remaining revenues himself. This system gave peasants a higher incentive to produce and thereby increased their surplus marketings, which led to more commutations, more subsequent marketings, and so forth. The cumulative effect was a very gradual breaking down of the traditional ties of the manor and a substitution of the market and the search for profits as the organizing principle of production. By the middle of the fourteenth century, money rents exceeded the value of labor services in many parts of Europe.

Another force that brought the market into the countryside and was closely related to commutation was the alienation of the lords' demesnes. The lords who needed cash to exchange for manufactured goods and luxuries began to rent their own lands to peasant farmers rather than having them farmed directly with labor service obligations. This process led increasingly to a situation in which the lord of the manor was simply a landlord in the modern sense of that term. In fact, he very often became an absentee landlord, as many lords chose to move to the cities or were away fighting battles.

The breakup of the manorial system, however, stemmed more directly from a series of catastrophies in the late fourteenth and fifteenth centuries. The Hundred Years' War

[4]Commutation involved the substitution of money rents for the labor services required of the serf.

between France and England (1337–1453) created general disorder and unrest in those countries. The Black Death was even more devastating. On the eve of the plague of 1348–1349, England's population stood at 4 million. By the early fifteenth century, after the effects of the wars and the plague, England had a scant 2.5-million population. This was fairly typical of trends in other European countries. The depopulation led to a desperate labor shortage, and wages for all types of labor rose abruptly. Land, now relatively more plentiful, began to rent for less.

These facts led the feudal nobility to attempt to revoke the commutations they had granted and to reestablish the labor service obligations of the serfs and peasants (peasants were former serfs who had attained some degree of independence and freedom from feudal restrictions). They found, however, that the clock could not be turned back. The market had been extended into the country-side, and with it had come greater freedom, independence, and prosperity for the peasants. They bitterly resisted efforts to reinstate the old obligations, and their resistance did not go unchallenged.

The result was the famous peasant revolts that broke out all over Europe from the late fourteenth through the early sixteenth centuries. These rebellions were extreme in their cruelty and ferocity. . . .

England experienced a series of such revolts in the late fourteenth and fifteenth centuries. But the revolts that occurred in Germany in the early sixteenth century were probably the bloodiest of all. The peasant rebellion in 1524–1525 was crushed by the Imperial troops of the Holy Roman emperor, who slaughtered peasants by the tens of thousands. Over 100,000 persons probably were killed in Germany alone.

These revolts are mentioned here to illustrate the fact that fundamental changes in the economic and political structure of a social system are often achieved only after traumatic and violent social conflict. Any economic sys-

tem generates a class or classes whose privileges are dependent on the continuation of that system. Quite naturally, these classes go to great lengths to resist change and to protect their positions. The feudal noblity fought a savage rearguard action against the emerging capitalist market system, but the forces of change ultimately swept them aside. Although the important changes were brought about by aspiring merchants and minor noblemen, the peasants were the pathetic victims of the consequent social upheavals. Ironically, they were usually struggling to protect the status quo.

OTHER FORCES IN THE TRANSITION TO CAPITALISM

The early sixteenth century is a watershed in European history. It vaguely marks the dividing line between the old, decaying feudal order and the rising capitalist system. After 1500, important social and economic changes began to occur with increasing frequency, each reinforcing the other and together having the cumulative effect of ushering in the system of capitalism. The population of western Europe, which had been relatively stagnant for a century and a half, increased by nearly one-third in the sixteenth century and stood at about 70 million in 1600.

The increase in population was accompanied by the *enclosure movement*, which had begun in England as carly as the thirteenth century. The feudal nobility, in ever-increasing need of cash, fenced off, or enclosed, lands that had formerly been used for communal grazing. Enclosed lands were used to graze sheep to satisfy the booming English wool and textile industries' demand for wool. The sheep brought good prices, and a minimal amount of labor was needed to herd them.

The enclosure movement reached its peak in the late fifteenth and sixteenth centuries, when in some areas as many as three-fourths to nine-tenths of the tenants were forced out of the countryside and into the cities to try to support themselves. The enclosures and the increasing population further destroyed the remaining feudal ties, creating a large new labor force—a labor force without land, without any tools or instruments of production, and with only labor power to sell. This migration to the cities meant more labor for the capitalist industries, more men for the armies and navies, more men to colonize new lands, and more potential consumers, or buyers of products.

Another important source of change was the intellectual awakening of the sixteenth century, which fostered scientific progress that was promptly put to practical use in navigation. The telescope and the compass enabled men to navigate much more accurately for much greater distances. Hence the "age of exploration." Within a short period, Europeans had charted sea routes to India, Africa, and the Americas. These discoveries had a twofold importance. First, they resulted in a rapid and large flow of precious metals into Europe, and second, they ushered in a period of colonization.

Between 1300 and 1500, European gold and silver production had stagnated. The rapidly expanding capitalist trade and the extension of the market system into city and countryside had led to an acute shortage of money. Because money consisted primarily of gold and silver coin, the need for these metals was critical. Beginning around 1450, this situation was alleviated somewhat when the Portuguese began extracting metals from the African Gold Coast, but the general shortage continued until the middle of the sixteenth century. After that date there occurred such a large inflow of gold and silver from the Americas that Europe experienced the most rapid and long-lasting inflation in history.

During the sixteenth century prices rose in Europe between 150 and 400 percent, depending on the country or region chosen. Prices of manufactured goods rose much more rapidly than either rents or wages. In fact, the disparity between prices and wages continued until late in the seventeenth century. This meant that the landlord class (or feudal nobility) and the working class both suffered, because their income rose less rapidly than their expenses. The capitalist class was the great beneficiary of the price revolution. They received larger and larger profits as they paid lower real wages and bought materials that appreciated greatly as they held them as inventories.

These larger profits were accumulated as capital. *Capital* refers to the materials that are necessary for production, trade, and commerce. It consists of all tools, equipment, factories, raw materials and goods in process, means of transporting goods, and money. The essence of the capitalist system is the existence of a class of capitalists who own the capital stock. It is by virtue of their ownership of this capital that they derive their profits. These profits are then plowed back, or used to augment the capital stock. The further accumulation of capital leads to more profits, which leads to more accumulation, and the system continues in an upward spiral.

The term *capitalism* describes this system of profit-seeking and accumulation very well. Capital is the source of profits and hence the source of further accumulation of capital. But this chicken-egg process had to have a beginning. The substantial initial accumulation, or *primitive accumulation*, of capital took place in the period under consideration. The four most important sources of the initial accumulation of capital were (1) the rapidly growing volume of trade and commerce, (2) the putting-out system of industry, (3) the enclosure movement, and (4) the great price inflation. There were several other sources of initial accumulations, some of which were somewhat less respectable and often forgotten—for example, colonial plunder, piracy, and the slave trade.

During the sixteenth and seventeenth centuries the putting-out system was extended until it was common in most types of manufacturing. Although this was not yet the modern type of factory production, the system's increased degree of specialization led to significant increases in productivity. Technical improvements in shipbuilding and navigation also lowered transportation costs. Thus during this period capitalist production and trade and commerce thrived and grew very rapidly. The new capitalist class (or middle class or bourgeoisie) slowly but inexorably replaced the nobility as the class that dominated the economic and social system.

2.4 *The Rise of the Bourgeoisie*

The capitalist class, having stripped away the restrictions of feudalism and having created a working class, was able to achieve tremendous advances in the development of the material forces of production. There are few paeans so eloquently appreciative of capitalism's accomplishments as the following reading from Karl Marx and Friedrich Engels' *Communist Manifesto* of 1848. The bourgeoisie dominates an ever-increasing proportion of social activity and draws into itself an ever-increasing proportion of the globe. In the process it not only creates a proletariat, but it also constantly expands that proletariat and begins to draw it together. The dynamic of capitalism contains an internal contradiction between (1) the increasing centralization of the means of production under continuing private control, on the one hand, and (2) the increasingly social character of production, on the other.

> The following is excerpted from *The Communist Manifesto* by KARL MARX and FRIEDRICH ENGELS (first published in 1848).

The history of all hiterto existing society is the history of class struggles.

Freeman and slave, patrician and plebeian, lord and serf, guild-master and journeyman, in a word; oppressor and oppressed, stood in constant opposition to one another, carried on an uninterrupted, now hidden, now open fight, a fight that each time ended, either in a revolutionary re-constitution of society at large, or in the common ruin of the contending classes.

In the early epochs of history, we find almost everywhere a complicated arrangement of society into various orders, a manifold graduation of social rank. In ancient Rome we have patricians, knights, plebeians, slaves; in the Middle Ages, feudal lords, vassals, guild-masters, journeymen, apprentices, serfs; in almost all of these classes, again, subordinate gradations.

The modern bourgeois society that has sprouted from the ruins of feudal society, has not done away with class antagonisms. It has but established new classes, new conditions of oppression, new forms of struggle in place of the old ones.

Our epoch, the epoch of the bourgeoisie, possesses, however, this distinctive feature; it has simplified the class antagonisms. Society as a whole is more and more splitting up into two great hostile camps, into two great classes directly facing cach other: Bourgeoisie and Proletariat.

From the serfs of the Middle Ages sprang

the chartered burghers of the earliest towns. From these burgesses the first elements of the bourgeoisie were developed.

The discovery of America, the rounding of the Cape, opened up fresh ground for the rising bourgeoisie. The East-Indian and Chinese markets, the colonization of America, trade with the colonies, the increase in the means of exchange and in commodities, generally, gave to commerce, to navigation, to industry, an impulse never before known, and thereby, to the revolutionary element in the tottering feudal society, a rapid development.

The feudal system of industry, under which industrial production was monopolized by closed guilds, now no longer sufficed for the growing wants of the markets. The manufacturing system took its place. The guild-masters were pushed on one side by the manufacturing middle-class; division of labor between the different corporate guilds vanished in the face of division of labor in each single workshop.

Meantime the markets kept ever growing, the demand, ever rising. Even manufacturing no longer sufficed. Thereupon, steam and machinery revolutionized industrial production. The place of manufacture was taken by the giant, Modern Industry, the place of the industrial middle-class, by industrial millionaires, the leaders of whole industrial armies, the modern bourgeoisie.

Modern Industry has established the world-market, for which the discovery of America paved the way. This market has given an immense development to commerce, to navigation, to communication by land. This development has, in its turn, reacted on the extension of industry; and in proportion as industry, commerce, navigation, railways extended in the same proportion the bourgeoisie developed, increased its capital, and pushed into the background every class handed down from the Middle Ages.

We see, therefore, how the modern bourgeoisie is itself the product of a long course of development, of a series of revolutions in the modes of production and of exchange.

Each step in the development of the bourgeoisie was accompanied by a corresponding political advance of that class. An oppressed class under the sway of the feudal nobility, an armed and self-governing association in the medieval commune, here independent urban republic (as in Italy and Germany), there taxable "third estate" of the monarchy (as in France), afterwards, in the period of manufacturing proper, serving either the semi-feudal or the absolute monarchy as a counterpoise against the nobility, and in fact, cornerstone of the great monarchies in general, the bourgeoisie has at last, since the establishment of Modern Industry and of the world-market, conquered for itself, in the modern representative State, exclusive political sway. The executive of the modern State is but a committee for managing the common affairs of the whole bourgeoisie.

The bourgeoisie, historically, has played a most revolutionary part.

The bourgeoisie, wherever it has got the upper hand, has put an end to all feudal, patriarchal, idyllic relations. It has pitilessly torn asunder the motley feudal ties that bound man to his "natural superiors," and has left remaining no other nexus between man and man than naked self-interest, than callous "cash payment." It has drowned the most heavenly ecstasies of religious fervor, of chivalrous enthusiasm, of philistine sentimentalism, in the icy water of egotistical calculation. It has resolved personal worth into exchange value, and in place of the numberless indefeasible chartered freedoms, has set up that single, unconscionable freedom—Free Trade. In one word, for exploitation, veiled by religious and political illusions, it has substituted naked, shameless, direct, brutal exploitation.

The bourgeoisie has stripped of its halo every occupation hitherto honored and looked up to with reverent awe. It has converted the physician, the lawyer, the priest, the poet, the man of science, into its paid wage-laborers.

The bourgeoisie has torn away from the family its sentimental veil, and has reduced the family relation to a mere money relation.

The bourgeoisie has disclosed how it came to pass that the brutal display of vigor in the Middle Ages, which Reactionists so much admire, found its fitting complement in the most slothful indolence. It has been the first to show what man's activity can bring about. It has accomplished wonders far surpassing Egyptian pyramids, Roman aqueducts, and Gothic cathedrals; it has conducted expeditions that put in the shade all former Exoduses of nations and crusades.

The bourgeoisie cannot exist without constantly revolutionizing the instruments of production, and thereby the relations of production, and with them the whole relations of society. Conservation of the old modes of production in unaltered form, was, on the contrary, the first condition of existence for all earlier industrial classes. Constant revolutionizing of production, uninterrupted disturbance of all social conditions, everlasting uncertainty and agitation distinguish the bourgeois epoch from all earlier ones. All fixed, fast-frozen relations, with their train of ancient and venerable prejudices and opinions, are swept away, all newly-formed ones become antiquated before they can ossify. All that is solid melts into air, all that is holy is profaned, and man is at last compelled to face with sober senses, his real conditions of life, and his relations with his kind.

The need of a constantly expanding market for its products chases the bourgeoisie over the whole surface of the globe. It must nestle everywhere, settle everywhere, establish connections everywhere.

The bourgeoisie has through its exploitation of the world-market given a cosmopolitan character to production and consumption in every country. To the great chagrin of Reactionists, it has drawn from under the feet of industry the national ground on which it stood. All old-established national industries have been destroyed or are daily being destroyed. They are dislodged by new industries, whose introduction becomes a life and death question for all civilized nations, by industries that no longer work up indigenous raw material, but raw material drawn from the remotest zones; industries whose products are consumed, not only at home, but in every quarter of the globe. In place of the old wants, satisfied by the productions of the country, we find new wants, requiring for their satisfaction the products of distant lands and climes. In place of the old local and national seclusion and self-sufficiency, we have intercourse in every direction, universal interdependence of nations. And as in material, so also in intellectual production. The intellectual creations of individual nations become common property. National one-sidedness and narrow-mindedness become more and more impossible, and from the numerous national and local literatures there arises a world-literature.

The bourgeoisie, by the rapid improvement of all instruments of production, by the immensely facilitated means of communication, draws all, even the most barbarian, nations into civilization. The cheap prices of its commodities are the heavy artillery with which it batters down all Chinese walls, with which it forces the barbarians' intensely obstinate hatred of foreigners to capitulate. It compels all nations, on pain of extinction, to adopt the bourgeois mode of production; it compels them to introduce what it calls civilization into their midst, i.e., to become bourgeois themselves. In a word, it creates a world after its own image.

The bourgeoisie has subjected the country to the rule of the towns. It has created enormous cities, has greatly increased the urban population as compared with the rural, and has thus rescued a considerable part of the population from the idiocy of rural life. Just as it has made the country dependent on the towns, so it has made barbarian and semi-barbarian countries dependent on the civilized ones, nations of peasants on nations of bourgeois, the East on the West.

The bourgeoisie keeps more and more doing away with the scattered state of the population, of the means of production, and of property. It has agglomerated population, centralized means of production, and has concentrated property in a few hands. The necessary consequence of this was political centralization. Independent, or but loosely connected provinces, with separate interests, laws, governments and systems of taxation, became lumped together in one nation, with one government, one code of laws, one national class-interest, one frontier and one customs-tariff.

The bourgeoisie, during its rule of scarce one hundred years, has created more massive and more colossal productive forces than have all preceding generations together. Subjection of Nature's forces to man, machinery, application of chemistry to industry and agriculture, steam-navigation, railways, electric telegraphs, clearing of whole continents for cultivation, canalization of rivers, whole populations conjured out of the ground—what earlier century had even a presentiment that such productive forces slumbered in the lap of social labor?

We see then: the means of production and of exchange on whose foundations the bourgeoisie built itself up, were generated in feudal society. At a certain stage in the development of these means of production and of exchange, the conditions under which feudal society produced and exchanged, the feudal organization of agriculture and manufacturing industry, in one word, the feudal relations of property became no longer compatible with the already developed productive forces; they became so many fetters. They had to be burst asunder; they were burst asunder.

Into their places stepped free competition, accompanied by a social and political constitution adapted to it, and by the economical and political sway of the bourgeois class.

A similar movement is going on before our own eyes. Modern bourgeois society with its relations of production, of exchange and of property, a society that has conjured up such gigantic means of production and of exchange, is like the sorcerer, who is no longer able to control the power of the nether world whom he has called up by his spells. For many a decade past the history of industry and commerce is but the history of the revolt of modern productive forces against modern conditions of production, against the property relations that are the condition for the existence of the bourgeoisie and of its rule. It is enough to mention the commercial crises that by their periodical return put on trial, each time more threateningly, the existence of the entire bourgeois society. In these crises a great part not only of the existing products, but also of the previously created productive forces, are periodically destroyed. In these crises there breaks out an epidemic that, in all earlier epochs, would have seemed an absurdity—the epidemic of over-production. Society suddenly finds itself put back into a state of momentary barbarism; it appears as if a famine, a universal war of devastation had cut off the supply of every means of subsistence; industry and commerce seem to be destroyed; and why? Because there is too much civilization, too much means of subsistence, too much industry, too much commerce. The productive forces at the disposal of society no longer tend to further the development of the conditions of bourgeois property; on the contrary, they have become too powerful for these conditions, by which they are fettered, and so soon as they overcome these fetters, they bring disorder into the whole of bourgeois society, endangering the existence of bourgeois property. The conditions of bourgeois society are too narrow to comprise the wealth created by them. And how does the bourgeoisie get over these crises? On the one hand by enforced destruction of a mass of productive forces; on the other, by the conquest of new markets, and by the more thorough exploitation of the old ones.

That is to say, by paving the way for more extensive and more destructive crises, and by diminishing the means whereby crises are prevented.

The weapons with which the bourgeoisie felled feudalism to the ground are now turned against the bourgeoisie itself.

But not only has the bourgeoisie forged the weapons that bring death to itself; it has also called into existence the men who are to wield those weapons—the modern working-class—the proletarians.

In proportion as the bourgeoisie, i.e., capital, is developed, in the same proportion is the proletariat, the modern working-class, developed, a class of laborers, who live only so long as they find work, and who find work only so long as their labor increases capital. These laborers, who must sell themselves piecemeal, are a commodity, like every other article of commerce, and are consequently exposed to all the vicissitudes of competition, to all the fluctuations of the market.

Owing to the extensive use of machinery and to division of labor, the work of the proletarians has lost all individual character, and, consequently, all charm for the workman. He becomes an appendage of the machine, and it is only the most simple, most monotonous, and most easily acquired knack that is required of him. Hence, the cost of production of a workman is restricted, almost entirely, to the means of subsistence that he requires for his maintenance, and for the propagation of his race. But the price of a commodity, and also of labor, is equal to its cost of production. In proportion, therefore, as the repulsiveness of the work increases, the wage decreases. Nay more, in proportion as the use of machinery and division of labor increases, in the same proportion the burden of toil also increases, whether by prolongation of the working hours, by increase of the work enacted in a given time, or by increased speed of the machinery, etc.

Modern Industry has converted the little workshop of the patriarchal master into the great factory of the industrial capitalist. Masses of laborers, crowded into the factory, are organized like soldiers. As privates of the industrial army they are placed under the command of a perfect hierarchy of officers and sergeants. Not only are they the slaves of the bourgeois class, and of the bourgeois State, they are daily and hourly enslaved by the machine, by the over-looker, and, above all, by the individual bourgeois manufacturer himself. The more openly this despotism proclaims gain to be its end and aim, the more petty, the more hateful and the more embittering it is.

The less the skill and exertion or strength implied in manual labor, in other words, the more modern industry becomes developed, the more is the labor of men superseded by that of women. Differences of age and sex have no longer any distinctive social validity for the working-class. All are instruments of labor, more or less expensive to use, according to their age and sex.

No sooner is the exploitation of the laborer by the manufacturer so far at an end, that he receives his wages in cash, than he is set upon by the other portions of the bourgeoisie, the landlord, the shopkeeper, the pawnbroker, etc.

The low strata of the middle-class—the small tradespeople, shopkeepers, and retired tradesmen generally, the handicraftsmen and peasants—all these sink gradually into the proletariat, partly because their diminutive capital does not suffice for the scale on which Modern Industry is carried on, and is swamped in the competition with the large capitalists, partly because their specialized skill is rendered worthless by new methods of production. Thus the proletariat is recruited from all classes of the population.

The proletariat goes through various stages of development. With its birth begins its struggle with the bourgeoisie. At first the contest is carried on by individual laborers, then by the workpeople of a factory, then by the operatives of one trade, in one locality, against the individual bourgeois who directly exploits them. They direct their attacks not against the bourgeois conditions of production, but against the instruments of production themselves; they destroy imported wares that compete with their labor, they smash to pieces machinery, they set factories ablaze, they seek to restore by force the vanished status of the workman of the Middle Ages.

At this stage the laborers still form an incoherent mass scattered over the whole country, and broken up by their mutual competition. If anywhere they unite to form more compact bodies, this is not yet the conse- quence of their own active union, but of the union of bourgeoisie, which class, in order to attain its own political ends, is compelled to set the whole proletariat in motion, and is moreover yet, for a time, able to do so. At this stage, therefore, the proletarians do not fight their enemies, but the enemies of their enemies, the remnants of absolute monarchy, the landowners, the non-industrial bour- geoisie, the petty bourgeoisie. Thus the whole historical movement is concentrated in the hands of the bourgeoisie; every victory so obtained is a victory for the bourgeoisie.

2.5 *Capitalism and the Evolution of the Family*

Before the rise of industrial capitalism, most productive activity was cen- tered within the household unit. In the towns as well as in the countryside, women engaged in a substantial amount of material production in the home, while shouldering the principal responsibility for rearing children and maintaining the home. In feudal society a sexual division of labor in repro- duction was thus already well developed. Children learned methods of production within the family unit, engaged themselves in production, and were integrated directly into the world of work.

With the development of capitalism, independent family producers split progressively into two classes, propertied capitalists and propertyless wage- workers. Production was increasingly removed from the home and con- centrated in factories, where workers labored under the direct supervision of capitalists. This process of the separation of production from the home is a relatively recent phenomenon in human history. It is characteristic of the capitalist era.

The new system of social production profoundly transformed the process of social reproduction and the ideal of family life. Whereas previously men and women were both engaged in production, now this interdependence was much reduced: men became engaged primarily in the system of production, and women in the system of reproduction. The first industries to develop in a factory setting were textiles; women and children who earlier had done most of the spinning, weaving, sewing, etc. within the home made up the bulk of the early factory labor force in these industries. But as capitalist industrialization progressed, few new industries were open to women. As a result, most women lost their previous connection to production and their social role became exclusively one of reproduction—mothering and main- taining the adult male labor force. In the following reading Eli Zaretsky describes this historical process, showing how the separation of production from reproduction changed the family, as the female housewife and the male wage-worker became the two characteristic workers of capitalist society.

More recently, women have begun to be reintegrated into production, this time not in the home but rather as wage-workers. The family's evolution illustrates a point made earlier by John Gurley about historical materialism: changes in the material reality of production profoundly affect the actual evolution of the family and ideas about the family. We shall investigate the evolution of the sexual division of labor in greater detail in Chapter 9.

THE EARLY BOURGEOIS FAMILY IN ENGLAND

The prevalent form of family life in England before the rise of industry in the eighteenth and nineteenth centuries was that of an economically independent, commodity-producing unit. Often referred to as the "patriarchal" family, it survives today only among the petit bourgeoisie. It originated between the disintegration of feudalism in the fourteenth century and the rise of capitalism in the sixteenth. During this period peasant families extricated themselves from feudal ties to become tenants or (far less often) landowners. In feudal society separate households were a subordinate part of a larger enterprise, generally the manor.

. . .

On the basis of small-scale commodity production a new form of the family developed in the early bourgeois period. The household of a property-owning family in seventeenth-century England was a complicated economic enterprise that included not only children and relatives but servants, apprentices, and journeymen from different social classes. At its head was the *paterfamilias* who worked alongside his wife, children, employees, and wards. He was solely responsible for the economic and spiritual welfare of his family and represented in his person the supposed unity

and independence of the family. The domestic relations of the household were an acknowledged part of the production relations of early capitalism.

. . .

The early bourgeois family—the family as a self-contained productive unit—furnished the basis for a new ideology of the family linked with the newly emerging ideas of private property and individualism. Much of this ideology was expressed through religion, particularly Puritanism, which was an inseparable part of the early bourgeois outlook. Taken together, the changes achieved by the bourgeoisie in seventeenth-century England established a new form of the family and an ethic of family life integral to the bourgeois system of rule.

. . .

The bourgeoisie's acceptance of economic life helped encourage a new acceptance of sexuality, eating, and other noneconomic material processes of the family. The family had been scorned in medieval society as the realm of both production and sexuality. The Catholic Church, anti-sexual and savagely anti-female, had sanctioned family life only reluctantly, as the alternative to damnation, and had forbidden it to the clergy. The right of the clergy to marry had been a basic issue during the Reformation. In seventeenth-century England, Puritanism, with its acceptance of the life of material necessity, embraced the the married state and exalted the family as part of the natural (i.e., God-given) order of productive and spiritual activity. Sexuality and emotional expression were encouraged, so long as they occurred within marriage. The Puritans condemned only "unnatural" forms of sexuality such as the profligacy practiced at the court, and homosexuality, which they viewed with particular horror. They argued that emotional and sexual expression must be "weaned"—held within the bounds of nature and not carried to artificial excess.

. . .

These changes [accompanied] a new conception of human nature, that of possessive individualism. The bourgeoisie condemned the fixed stratification of medieval society as "artificial" and viewed competitiveness based upon economic self-interest as the natural basis of society. As market relations developed, the identification of the individual with a fixed social position began to give way to a commitment to the "individual" (i.e., the individual family) who would rise or fall on the basis of independent efforts. The family came to be seen as a competitive economic unit apart from, and later even opposed to, the rest of society. In the seventeenth century competitiveness and acquisitiveness were still restricted by the corporate ideals of mercantilism; by the eighteenth century they were generally encouraged.

The bourgeois acceptance of a certain degree of selfishness and aggression as part of human nature gave rise to a search for new principles of social order. While it was the vehicle of private ambition, the family was hierarchically organized and strictly disciplined. It forced the "natural" materialism of its members to take a socially acceptable form. The early bourgeoisie understood the family to be the basic unit of the social order—"a little church, a little state"—and the lowest rung in the ladder of social authority. They conceived of society as composed not of individuals but of families, each an indissoluble cell. If they spoke of "individual

rights," it was because of the sovereignty of paternal power.

. . .

Taken together, these developments shaped a new ideal of family life. Marriage was coming to be understood as a partnership based upon common love and labor; [a man's] wife was a companion or "helpmeet." The early bourgeois family gave rise to a new set of expectations based upon the couple's common destiny—not only love but mutual affection and respect, trust, fidelity, and premarital chastity. As in medieval society, children were quickly integrated into the adult order, but it was understood that when grown they would marry according to their own desires, although listening to their parents' counsel. In keeping with the high value placed upon both productive labor to expand the family's fortune and the weaning of one's emotions over time, maturity and old age were idealized. The symbol of the wise and self-disciplined grandfather now replaced, for a time, the more traditional image of the dotard.

The bourgeois familial ideal obscured two contradictions that emerged in the course of capitalist development: the oppression of women and the family's subordination to class relations. The rise of the bourgeoisie entailed a simultaneous advance and retrogression in the position of women. In the economic life of medieval England women were closer to equality with men than they later were under capitalism. For example, women participated as equals in many guilds in the fourteenth century. With the rise of capitalism they were excluded and, in general, economic opportunities for women not in families—such as spinsters or widows—declined. On the other hand women were given a much higher status within the family. For the Puritans, women's domestic labor was a "calling," a special vocation comparable to the crafts or trades of their husbands. Like their husbands, women did God's work.

. . .

Hence, women were encouraged to think

of themselves almost as independent persons at the same time that they were imprisoned within the family. During the English Revolution the question of female equality was debated politically for the first time. Within many sects women played leading roles as preachers and organizers. (This was particularly true in sects that downgraded the importance of learning for salvation, since women were so little educated.) These stirrings of women's equality reached a level in the seventeenth century sufficient to call forth a counter-movement among preachers and others that stressed female subordination within the family. One argument made was that the family was the economic property of the husband, and that married women owned nothing in their own right.

So long as the family was considered the "natural" or God-given basis of society, the issue of women's equality could not emerge on a large scale. The bourgeois view that the family (rather than individuals or classes) was the basic unit of society reinforced the deeply rooted traditions of male supremacy. And this view persisted as long as the family was a basic unit of social production. The issue of women's equality was largely muted until the late eighteenth and nineteenth centuries when the rise of industry finally destroyed the bourgeois ideal of the family as an independent productive unit.

That ideal had always been ideological, obscuring the class differences among the supposedly "independent" producers of seventeenth-century England. According to the bourgeoisie, "private property" defined the family as an independent unit, guaranteed its political freedoms, and provided a new justification for the rule of the father. By "private property" the seventeenth-century bourgeoisie meant both one's own labor power (i.e., "property in one's person"), and the land or tools one employed. This obscured the fact that labor alone could never make one an "independent" producer: farmers required land, implements, and stock; weavers required materials and the use of a

loom. Hence as capitalism developed, "private property" split—into capital on one hand, and labor power on the other.

In the seventeenth and eighteenth centuries this split took the form of "domestic industry" —the family worked as a unit but in direct dependence on the capitalist class. Weavers, for example, were dependent upon merchant clothiers who supplied their wool, monopolized new technical inventions such as the knitting frame, finished the production of cloth by hiring workers, and served as intermediaries between the weaving family and the shopkeepers who sold their cloth. Only the ownership of land bestowed a measure of independence upon the artisan family. Domestic industry preserved the "unity" but not the "independence" of the original bourgeois ideal.

· · ·

DECLINE OF THE BOURGEOIS FAMILY

Once families were brought together in a common workshop, they were no longer supervised by the father but by the master. They no longer worked at their own rhythm, but according to the systematic labor discipline required by a coordinated division of labor. . . . These changes in the organization of production led to the formation of a new ideology of the family. Earlier the bourgeoisie had portrayed the family as the progressive center of individualism, but as industrial production destroyed the basis of the early bourgeois family, the family came to be either scorned as a backward institution or nostalgically romanticized. In either case it was contrasted to "society," the system of social production and administration.

· · ·

Reflecting this separation, the belief in separate "spheres" for men and women came to dominate the ideology of the family in the epoch of industrial capitalism. As the family was now idealized, so was the familial role of women. According to one of the domestic manuals that began to flourish in the 1830s and '40s, "that fierce conflict of worldly interests, by which men are so deeply occupied, [compels them] to stifle their best feelings."[1] Men, according to Ruskin, are "feeble in sympathy."[2] But women, by contrast, whose "everyday duties are most divine because they are most human," nurture within the family the "human" values crushed by "modern life." Earlier, the feudal aristocracy had idealized women for their delicate beauty. In the eighteenth century the bourgeoisie had stressed their role as practical and intelligent housewives. Now the dominant image of women was that of the mother who, freed from domestic labor by the abundance of servants could devote herself wholly to her child.

[1]S. Ellis, *The Daughters of England* (London, 1845), pp. 22–23, quoted in J. A. and Olive Banks, *Feminism and Family Planning in Victorian England* (New York, 1964, 1972), p. 59; see also p. 22.

[2]Quoted in Millett, *Sexual Politics* (New York: 1970), p. 105.

The Capitalist Mode
of Production

IN CHAPTER 2 WE DEFINED a mode of production in terms of both "forces of production" and "relations of production" and analyzed the historical emergence of the capitalist mode of production. In this chapter we shall continue our theoretical inquiry into the capitalist system by examining in greater detail the essential features of the capitalist mode of production. In so doing we shall be abstracting for the moment from many of the realities of our society, such as its complex class structure, international relations, production within the home, etc. in order to focus more clearly on the most important characteristics of the capitalist mode of production itself. We shall then, in the next parts of this book, become much more concrete and apply the theoretical analysis of the capitalist mode of production developed here to present-day capitalism in the United States.

The relations of production under capitalism define the distinguishing characteristics of a capitalist society: the basic economic structures or institutions by which the production, distribution, and consumption of goods and services are organized. These structures are "basic" in a triple sense. First, as Dobb argued in Chapter 2, the emergence of these institutions defines the *historical* period of capitalism, providing us with a historical delineation of the capitalist epoch. Second, they are basic in a *logical* sense in that they define what we mean by the capitalist mode of production. Third, they are basic in an *empirical* sense; as we argue through the rest of this book, these institutions are the

most important for understanding the nature of capitalist society.

What then, are the basic characteristics that distinguish the capitalist mode of production? First of all, the production of goods and services takes the form of production of commodities; that is, goods and services are produced for sale on a market rather than for direct use by the producer. But the prevalence of market exchange does not by itself signify the existence of a capitalist mode of production, for we could imagine a society of independent artisans and small farmers who produced for a market. Such a society, which existed for example in New England around 1600 to 1750, tends to be transitional because its relatively egalitarian class structure is unstable. Sooner or later, significant inequalities in wealth and power are bound to emerge.

Distinguishing the capitalist mode of production from the "petty commodity production" of independent market-oriented artisans and farmers, the second basic characteristic of capitalism is the existence of two classes: a class of *capitalists* who among themselves have a class monopoly over the means of production, and a class of propertyless *wage-workers* who sell their capacity to work, or labor-power, to capitalists in exchange for a wage or salary. The vast majority of people own very little or no property, aside from personal property such as their clothes, cars, homes, and household items. More precisely, most people own very little *income-earning* property, and they therefore can obtain the income they need to maintain themselves and their families only by selling their labor-power on a labor market to the highest bidder. Hence under capitalism labor-power is a commodity, subject to the fluctuations of "supply and demand" in the market for labor. The capitalist mode of production therefore presupposes both the existence of commodity production in general and the transformation of labor itself into a commodity in particular.

A third basic characteristic of the capitalist mode of production is that capitalists and not workers control the process of production itself. As part of the wage bargain, workers relinquish control over their labor during the stipulated working day and have no say in the disposition of the things the workers produce, the product. Hence workers are deprived of control over both their work activities and the work product. The decisions about what to produce, how to organize the production process, what technology to use, etc. are made by capitalists. As the forces of production develop over time, capitalists tend to organize the production process along increasingly hierarchical lines, creating many different levels of employment, from production and clerical workers on the bottom to "middle management" to high-level managers and executives. Capitalists organize production hierarchically in order to maintain their control over the production process and to further the productivity of their workers. Thus the social relations of production take hierarchical forms under capitalism.

Certain particular legal relations of ownership, or private property rules, derive from these basic characteristics of the capitalist mode of production. These rules, whose enforcement is the primary responsibility of the state, establish that the owner of a piece of property has the exclusive right to the use of that property, to enjoy the benefits from it, to consume it, to dispose of it, to sell it, and so forth. For personal items, such as household articles, these rules usually just reflect patterns of use: the "ownership" of beds or toothbrushes among people in a family only identifies the ways in which the beds or tooth-

brushes will be used. However, for *social objects*, such as factories, offices, schools, recreations areas, land in a community, and labor services, these property rules also signify and reflect relations among people in different classes. No matter how social in character "private" property may be, the vesting of ownership of society's economic apparatus in the hands of capitalists gives capitalists the legal right to control that property's use and disposition. Our legal system does not make this distinction between personal possessions and income-producing property, but the distinction is important nonetheless in understanding capitalism.

In this chapter, we shall investigate the important features of a society dominated by these capitalist relations of production: the reality of exploitation underlying legal forms of equality and freedom; the hierarchical nature of the capitalist mode of production, apparent once we leave the realm of markets and exchange and enter factories and offices to examine production and the labor process directly; the ceaseless drive to expand that is inherent in the process of capital accumulation; the cyclical economic crises of capitalism that are generated both by the basic class conflicts between capitalists and workers and by the competition among the capitalists as they attempt to *sell* the commodities they produce; and finally, the ways in which the capitalist mode of production reproduces not only capital but also labor-power through a set of reproductive institutions, such as the state, the educational system, and the family, whose purpose is to insure that the reproduction of capitalist social relations will occur.

EXPLOITATION

Unlike societies characterized by slavery and serfdom, capitalist societies such as the United States guarantee to each individual freedom and equality before the law. That means that no one is directly compelled to work for someone else or to enter into any sort of contract or exchange. On the contrary, each of us has the freedom to enter into contracts as we desire and to own property without interference. This apparent freedom and equality to carry on our private affairs has led many defenders of capitalism to laud the operations of the competitive market. As Milton Friedman has put it, with a free market everybody gains because "no exchange will take place unless both parties benefit from it";[1] otherwise they would not enter into the transaction.

How then is it possible to speak of exploitation under capitalism, of the reproduction of a class division between those who have to work for a living and those who can live, without needing to work, off the fruits of other people's labor? The answer is that although the basic transaction between capitalists and workers appears on the surface to be a voluntary contractual exchange between equals, it is in reality a coercive exchange between unequals. Workers do not have to sell their labor services to any individual capitalist, but they must work for some capitalist in order to obtain the income they need to buy the commodities necessary to maintain themselves and their families. The wage or salary income that workers receive is necessary for their immediate survival. Capitalists, with their accumulated wealth arising from ownership of the means of production, are not so immediately vulnerable. They enter as buyers into the market for labor with the great advantage of being able to wait, if necessary, until the terms are favorable to them, and being able to influence those terms with the wealth at their disposal. The result is unequal: the working class as a whole produces commodities whose total monetary value is much greater than the value of their wage and salary income. The difference is captured by the capitalist class in the form of profits, interest, and rent.

Think of the economy as a way of organizing and dividing the total labor time

[1]Milton Friedman, *Capitalism and Freedom* (Chicago: University of Chicago Press, 1963), p. 13.

available to society for the production of valuable commodities (including the production of machines, buildings, etc. that are used as inputs in the production of other commodities). Each person's income represents his or her share of that total product. Then we see that capitalists and workers receive shares of the *product* of all social labor which do not correspond to the shares of labor time actually worked, as is evident from the fact that an owner of a factory need not put in any labor time to receive a share of the product. The commodities the workers can buy with their wages and salaries embody less social labor time than they themselves put in. The basically unequal and coercive nature of the capital-labor relationship is thus obscured by the existence of markets. This explanation of the mechanism of exploitation in a competitive capitalist economy was developed by Karl Marx in his theory of surplus value.

AUTHORITARIANISM IN PRODUCTION

The lack of freedom and equality that characterizes the capitalist mode of production becomes much clearer once we leave the sphere where commodities are exchanged (i.e., markets) and investigate directly the organization of production in capitalist factories, offices, farms, and mines. In any capitalist firm the organization of production is authoritarian in that the basic decisions are made by capitalists and executed by workers. The right to participate in decision-making defines, in the political sphere, what we mean by a democracy. This basic democratic right is relinquished by workers when they sell the disposition of their labor-power to capitalists for a stipulated time period.

However, the workers are not mere pawns; they are also actors in their own right. As a result, the relationship between capitalists and workers is one of conflict. Capitalists want to get as much work as possible out of workers, to turn their potential to work, or labor-power, into maximum labor actually done. Capitalists expend a great deal of energy trying to increase the productivity of workers, using the threat of firing them, the incentives of promotions, bonuses, and so on. Workers, on the other hand, are active human beings who want to minimize the unpleasantness of the time they must spend working, and they certainly do not want to work so hard as to increase the work demanded of them; so they spend much energy trying to circumvent the aims of the capitalists. The conflict between workers and capitalists is thus one that involves not only bargaining over wage rates but also the very organization of production itself. It is out of this basic struggle that the capitalists' problem of managing labor arises; and this is a problem that gets more complex as firms get larger; organizing production on an authoritarian and increasingly hierarchical model has historically been the capitalists' solution. Despite the *appearance* of equality and freedom in the marketplace, capitalist production is premised on inequality and coercion.

ACCUMULATION OF CAPITAL AND CRISES

The reason that capitalists are in business is in order to make profits and thereby expand their capital. It is not merely a matter of greed on the part of individual capitalists, but the inexorable pressure to make profits that is created and enforced by the competitive structure of the capitalist mode of production. To meet the competition and stay in business, each individual capitalist must look continuously for ways to protect or increase profits by expanding sales, cutting costs, finding new markets and new products, etc. This in turn is likely to require an increasing *scale* of production; hence the drive to accumulate capital by reinvesting profits. The class struggle between workers and capitalists also forces capitalists to accumulate capital. When labor costs rise too high and begin to encroach on profits, capitalists must invest in new technologies that can displace workers

and they search for new areas to relocate their capital. Capitalism is thus by its very nature a system that is constantly striving to expand. As a result, capitalism spreads its geographical net and also transforms more and more areas of social life into profit-making activities.

The accumulation process can be described as a circuit or series of steps in which a capitalist starts with a certain amount of money or capital and seeks to complete the circuit with more capital. The process begins when a capitalist *invests* his money in raw materials and labor-power, and also buys or rents the tools, machines, and buildings needed in production. In the second part of the circuit, the *labor process*, the capitalist brings together the means of production and the workers who, under the direction and supervision of the capitalist and/or his managers, labor to produce commodities. This step involves the authoritarian organization of work just discussed above. To complete the circuit successfully, the commodities must then be circulated or sold on a market, for it is only when the receipts are safely in from the buyers that the capitalist will actually *realize* the profits and be able to increase his capital. The circuit can then be repeated with still greater amounts of capital involved.

The *rate* at which the accumulation of capital takes place in the economy will in general be uneven; periodically *economic crises* will break out, characterized by falling production and increased unemployment. This *cyclical* nature of capitalist expansion is due among other things to conflicts that occur between workers and capitalists in the realm of production and to a recurrent tendency for capitalists as a whole to produce more than can be sold.[2] The long-term rate at which accumulation takes place depends on the level of profits in the economy, as well as the rate at which capitalists reinvest their profits. The level of profits in turn depends on several factors: the ability of capitalists to increase

[2]We analyze the sources of economic crises in Chapter 12.

worker productivity, especially by introducing more and improved machines or other innovations in production; the amount of wage costs, as determined by a bargaining process that takes place between capitalists and workers within a given labor market environment (i.e., conditions of labor shortage or conditions of labor surplus); and the intensity with which workers work and the number of hours they work. The rate at which capitalists reinvest their profits depends upon their *expectations* of being successful in making profits in the future. All these factors are shaped by the class struggle between workers and capitalists.

SOCIAL REPRODUCTION

As a result of the accumulation of capital, capitalism reproduces itself over time on an expanded scale. The accumulation of capital means that production is taking place on a larger scale. To achieve this growth in production, capitalists on the whole need to hire more workers, even though the introduction of new technologies displaces workers in some sectors. So capitalists need to draw more and more people into the labor market as wageworkers who will work under capitalist relations of production. The result is that capitalist production reproduces not only capital but also labor and the capitalist relations of production.

The expansion of the wage-labor force, or *proletariat*, occurs as capital recreates the conditions that require more people to sell their labor-power. First of all, almost all of those people who are already workers must continue to sell their labor-power. Their wages and salaries enable them and their families to purchase the commodities they need for their material reproduction, but very few are able to save a sufficient amount out of their earnings to go into business for themselves. Second, given population growth, the number of young people who enter the labor market each year more than replaces older retiring workers. Third, as the expansion of

large-scale capital increasingly drives small capitalists (including many small farmers, merchants, and professionals) out of business, these formerly independent small capitalists are drawn into the labor market as workers. Fourth, more women enter the labor market as more areas of production are removed from the home to capitalist enterprises. Finally, immigration from other countries provides an additional important source of labor supply, particularly during periods when the demand for labor is growing rapidly. These various means of replenishing and expanding the supply of labor-power tend to meet the growing demand for labor-power by capitalists. The increasing supply insures that competition among capitalists for workers will not go so far as to upset the unequal class relationship between the capitalists and the workers.

What if the demand for workers nonetheless far outruns the growth in the supply of workers, so that the wages paid to workers rise to such an extent that they begin to cut into the profits of the capitalists? Capitalists can then respond by introducing machinery that increases the productivity of their workers and "frees" some of them for work elsewhere, and/or by reducing the rate of reinvestment of their profits, thereby throwing many people out of work and setting off an economic crisis. This crisis then recreates the conditions necessary for a new round of capital accumulation. We thus see that "the capitalist production process reproduces . . . the conditions which force the laborers to sell themselves in order to live, and enables the capitalist to purchase them in order that he may enrich himself. It is no longer a mere accident that capitalist and laborer confront each other in the market as buyer and seller."[3]

To reproduce labor-power and the capitalist relations of production, however, it is not enough to reproduce only the conditions for the sale of labor-power. Workers must be

[3]Karl Marx, *Capital*, vol. I (New York: International Publishers, 1967), p. 577.

reproduced physically and psychologically and with appropriate skills, training, and attitudes. Although the capitalist mode of production establishes a basic dynamic of reproduction on an expanding scale and expands the wage-labor force, the actual reproduction of workers is not carried out by the capitalists themselves; it occurs through certain *reproductive institutions*. The most important of these reproductive institutions are the family, the schools, and the state. The family is where most of the physical reproduction of workers takes place—women not only bear and rear children but also maintain adult workers.[4] The family, the schools, and

the state recreate the acceptance of capitalist relations of production—the family and the schools teaching subordination to authority and the state defending, with the use of force, if necessary, challenges to private property. The family and the schools provide as well the general skills and personality traits required of workers in capitalist production. These reproductive institutions, then, enable the capitalist mode of production to be reproduced.

The first reading in this chapter explores the exploitative nature of the capitalist mode of production and presents an overview of Marx's analysis of capitalism. The second reading looks at the authoritarian organization of capitalist production. The third and fourth readings discuss the logic of capitalist accumulation and the possibility of economic crises. The final two readings take up the analysis of social reproduction under capitalism.

[4]We have already noted in Chapter 2 how the family evolved as a reproductive institution with the rise of the capitalist mode of production. Here we may note as well that the family as a reproductive institution must itself be reproduced, in a process that perpetuates sexism within the capitalist mode of production. See Chapter 9.

3.1   *The Theory of Surplus Value*

The organization and allocation of the total labor time available to society for production was analyzed by Karl Marx using the concepts of value and surplus value. In the following reading John Gurley explains Marx's basic theory of how the capitalist mode of production operates, and how its surface appearances conceal and mystify its exploitative nature.

The following is excerpted from Chapter 3 of *Challengers to Capitalism: Marx, Lenin and Mao* by JOHN G. GURLEY. © 1976 by John G. Gurley. San Francisco: San Francisco Book Company, 1976. Reprinted by permission of the author and the publisher.

Marx defined capitalism as a particular, historically-determined mode of production. He analyzed this mode dialectically in terms of a growing contradiction between the productive forces and the social relations of production that would reveal itself in increasingly severe crises and evermore intense struggles between the bourgeoisie and the proletariat. Inasmuch as Marxian theory reflected the rise of the industrial working class, and served that class, it was highly crit-

ical of both the capitalist mode and its ideologists. It was also revolutionary in that it was at the same time an analysis, a prediction, and a catalyst of the coming overthrow of the bourgeoisie by the proletariat—and, hence, of bourgeois theory by Marxian theory.

Marx insisted that "capital" is not a thing but a definite social relation which belonged to a specific historical formation of society. "The means of production become capital,"

Marx wrote, "only insofar as they have become separated from the laborer and confront labor as an independent power." Means of production are capital when they have become monopolized by a certain sector of society and used by that class to produce surplus value—that is, the income of the capitalist class (generally profits, interest, and rent) that comes from the exploitation of another class. Consequently, capital, for Marx, is not only part of the forces of production but it is also a particular employment of those forces, a social relation.

Capital appears in four major forms: (1) industrial, (2) trading, (3) lending, and (4) renting. Industrial capital *produces* and *realizes* surplus value—the former in the production sphere and the latter in the circulation sphere—while the other forms *redistribute* it among the various claimants of capitalists. Capital, in the social forms of instruments of labor, raw materials, and labor-power, produces surplus value in the production sphere. Capital, in the social forms of commodities and money, realizes surplus value for the capitalist class in the sphere of circulation. Capital, in the social forms of merchants' (trading) capital, interest-bearing (lending) capital, and landed (renting) capital, distributes the surplus value among industrial, commercial, financial, and landed capitalists. Surplus value appears mainly as industrial profits, commercial profits, interest, and rent. (Major forms are shown below.)

Forms of Capital	*Surplus Value*
I. Industrial Capital	
A. Productive capital	
1. Constant capital	
a. Instruments of labor	
b. Raw materials	The Production of Surplus Value
2. Variable capital (labor-power)	
3. Surplus value (unpaid labor)	
B. Circulation capital	
1. Commodity capital	The Realization of Surplus Value
2. Money capital	

Forms of Capital	*Surplus Value*
II. Merchants' (Trading) Capital	
III. Interest-Bearing (Lending) Capital	The Redistribution of Surplus Value
IV. Landed (Renting) Capital	

The Production and Realization of Surplus Value

Marx demonstrated that surplus value is created in the production sphere. However, its realization (the sale of the commodities at their "value"—a term defined below) occurs in the sphere of circulation. Surplus value arises when a capitalist purchases labor-power (the capacity for labor) at its value, employs the labor-power in a work process that he controls, and then appropriates the commodities produced. Surplus value is the difference between the net value of these commodities and the value of labor-power itself.

The *value* of labor-power is the cost of maintaining and reproducing the worker and his [or her] family at a socially-accepted standard of living. This level, in some poor countries, may include only the bare necessities, but in others it will also include a "moral element"—what "society," in its real development, has determined to be an average standard of living for a laborer and his family.

A worker sells his labor-power—his mental and physical capabilities—to a capitalist for its value, and the capitalist uses the labor-power to obtain commodities which have a value higher than that of the labor-power purchased. Thus, the secret of surplus value is that labor-power is a source of more value than it has itself. The capitalist is able to capture the surplus value through his ownership of the means of production and his historically-established right to purchase labor-power as a commodity, to control the work process, and to claim the product as his property. This surplus value, according to Marx, is the measure of capital's exploitation of labor.

Marx used a simple model of the firm to

illustrate his concept of exploitation. The gross value of a commodity produced by a firm is the socially-necessary labor-time which is embodied in that commodity at all stages of its production. ("Socially necessary" means that the commodity is produced under the normal conditions of production with the average degree of skill and intensity prevalent at the time—and that there is a demand for it.) Marx divided the *gross value* of a commodity into three parts.

The first portion of gross value is *constant capital* (c), which is the value—the socially-necessary labor-time—of capital goods and raw materials used up in the production of a commodity. For instance, machinery is used up in the sense that it depreciates when used to produce commodities. Such items are called "constant" because they add no more value to the final product than they themselves lose in the production process. That is, workers may have been exploited when they previously produced the machines and raw materials, but the machines and raw materials themselves cannot be exploited by the capitalist when they are used to produce other commodities, for they do not produce more than their own value; only labor does that.

The second part of a commodity's gross value is *variable capital* (v). This is the value of the direct labor which is used in the production process (along with the machinery and the raw materials) *and* which is paid for. It is the value of labor-power. This is equal to the wages paid for the socially-necessary labor-time required to maintain and reproduce the worker and his family at a socially-accepted level of living. Thus, if a worker, in a 10-hour day, is able to produce enough in 6 hours to maintain and reproduce himself, this is equal to his wage and is Marx's variable capital. It is called "variable" because the use of labor-power by the capitalist results in the worker producing more value than it costs to reproduce him.

Surplus value (s), the third portion of gross value, is the unpaid amount of the direct labor—a part of the value of the commodity produced by the worker in the remaining 4 hours of the workday, which is appropriated by the capitalist in the form of surplus value. Thus, a capitalist may have variable costs equal to 6 hours of labor-time and constant costs equal to 1 hour. If the workday is 10 hours, the commodities produced in the remaining 4 hours represent the surplus value—and become, in money form, profits, interest, and rent.

The three components together make up the gross value of the product. That is, let

$$C' = \text{gross value of the product}$$
$$c = \text{constant capital}$$
$$v = \text{variable capital}$$
$$s = \text{surplus value}$$

then

$$C' = c + v + s.$$

The *net value* of the product omits the using up of the capital goods and raw materials and so is equal to $v + s$. Labor creates the full value of the net product ($v + s$) but receives only v. The capitalist, by virtue of his ownership of the means of production, is enabled to appropriate s, the surplus value.

The *rate of surplus value* (s'), or the degree of exploitation, is defined as s/v, the ratio of surplus value to variable capital. Marx also called this the ratio of surplus labor-time to necessary labor-time, the former being that portion of the working day during which the worker creates surplus value, the latter being that portion of the working day during which the worker produces enough to maintain and reproduce himself. Labor is exploited to the extent that a capitalist class appropriates privately what in fact labor produced.

Does that mean that machines and raw materials are not productive? No, they are productive: they transfer their value to the product. But they are not the creators of surplus value. Machines cannot be exploited by the capitalist. The labor that produced the machines has already been exploited by the previous capitalist who received the surplus value. The machine was then sold at its value (including the surplus value) and so cannot be exploited again at the next stage of production. At this later stage of production, the machine transfers its value, and nothing more, to the commodities. But do not machines raise the productivity of labor and so enable a capitalist to obtain larger surplus value? Machines do raise labor productivity. But, while machines enable the worker to produce more, it is only the labor that produces the surplus value. Only the workers themselves produce value for the capitalist that exceeds the value of their own labor-power. A commodity is produced by direct labor and indirect labor (machines and raw materials); direct labor creates the surplus value, and indirect labor (embodied in c) aids direct labor in so doing.

Surplus value, then, arises in the depths of the production process, not on the surface of circulation, not by capitalists buying cheap and selling dear, not by their cheating. Marx illustrated this in the following way:

$$M\text{———}C\Big\langle\begin{smallmatrix}L(v)\\[4pt]MP(c)\end{smallmatrix}\ \ldots\ldots P\ldots\ldots\ldots C'\text{———}M'$$

Circulation	Production	Circulation
Money-Capital Period	Productive-Capital Period	Commodity-Capital Period

$$C' = c + v + s$$
$$C = c + v$$

$$M' - M = \text{surplus value} = C' - C$$

Starting at the left, the capitalist uses money (M) to purchase the commodities (C) needed in the production process—that is, labor-power (L) and the means of production (MP). These purchases occur in the circulation sphere, where equal values are exchanged, in this case money capital for two "inputs" in the production process. Thus, Marx termed this part of the circulation sphere (where commodities are bought with money and sold for money) the "money-capital period." The result of the production process (...P...) is the creation of a final commodity (C'), the value of which exceeds that of C by the amount of surplus value incorporated in it. This commodity is then

sold for money ($C'\text{———}M'$), a transaction carried out in the other part of the circulation sphere, where once again equal values are exchanged—initiated this time by commodity capital, the money used to buy commodities and thus to complete the circuit. C' minus C represents surplus value, as does M' minus M. The former, however, reflects the *production* of surplus value; the latter, the *realization* of surplus value. After realizing surplus value, the capitalist repeats the process on an enlarged scale with the larger sum of money capital. This means, for instance, that he enlarges the size of his plant and produces a larger volume of commodities.

The Redistribution of Surplus Value

Surplus value includes not only the profits of the industrial capitalists whom we have just considered, but also the profits of commercial capitalists, interest of moneylenders or finance capitalists, and ground rent of landowning capitalists. Marx also noted that directors of business firms and others took shares of the surplus, too. We should further note that the state maintains its bureaucracy and protects the social relations of production with some of the surplus, in the form of taxes.

The rate of surplus value (s'), as we have seen, is equal to s/v. To measure the *rate of profit* (p'), Marx used $p' = s/(c + v)$ on the assumptions (1) that all machinery and raw materials were used up entirely, and labor-power paid for, in the one production period, (2) that capitalists advanced wages to laborers, and (3) that all surplus value was retained by industrial capitalists. Thus, $C = c + v$ is the total capital advanced, and the rate of profit is the percentage that the retained surplus value bears to it. Since the rate of profit ($s/(c + v)$) is computed on a wider base than that used for the rate of surplus value (s/v), the rate of surplus value will be greater than the rate of profit if c is positive —that is, if machinery and raw materials are utilized in production.

A third ratio defined by Marx was that of

the *organic composition of capital* (g), equal to $c/(c + v)$, which is a measure for the degree of capital intensity in production. This rate shows the extent to which a capitalist uses constant capital (c) relative to total capital $(c + v)$. The organic composition of capital tends to be high when the value of machinery and raw materials is large relative to that of direct labor. This is the case, for example, in highly automated enterprises.

The three ratios—showing the rate of exploitation or surplus value (s'), the rate of profit (p'), and the organic composition of capital (g)—can be combined in one equation: $p' = s'(1 - g)$. This indicates that if g were zero—that is, if only direct labor were used by the capitalist—then the rate of profit would be equal to the rate of exploitation. As the capitalist uses more and more machinery and raw materials relative to direct labor, g rises and the rate of profit falls relative to the rate of exploitation. That is, the rate of profit then tends to understate the extent to which capitalists are exploiting labor. Thus, even though the rate of exploitation were 40 percent, the rate of profit might be only 10 percent, if the capitalist used a lot of machinery and raw materials relative to labor (enough to make $g = \frac{3}{4}$).

By focusing on the rate of profit, businessmen and their supporters not only understate the rate of exploitation but in fact hide its true source. While surplus value results from the exploitation of direct labor, it appears as though this surplus value comes from total capital $(c + v)$, from machinery and raw materials as well as from direct labor.

Furthermore, industrial capitalists do not retain all of the surplus value. Some of it is channeled to commercial capitalists (merchants), who, using commercial or money capital, buy and sell commodities within the circulation sphere. The activities of these commercial capitalists do not directly produce surplus value—it is produced entirely in the production sphere—but indirectly they contribute to its generation by shortening the time of circulation and by expanding markets. These contributions enable industrial capitalists to produce more surplus

value with the employment of less capital. Since all capital, industrial and commercial, in perfectly competitive markets earns the same rate of profit, the industrial capitalists must transfer sufficient surplus value to the commercial capitalists to permit this equality to be achieved. This transfer takes place when the industrial capitalists sell their commodities to merchants at prices below their values, while the merchants resell the commodities to consumers at their values (plus the constant and variable capital employed by the merchants, which they must recover).

In addition to this drain from industrial capitalists' surplus value, the moneylending capitalists also get a slice. These capitalists give up the use value of money, which is its ability to produce surplus value, in return for a portion of that surplus value. The moneylending capitalists loan money to industrial capitalists (and others) at certain interest rates, which are the market prices that serve to redistribute surplus value to them. The portion of the surplus value going to moneylending capitalists is interest, while the portion remaining with industrial capitalists Marx called "profits of enterprise." Clearly, the higher the rates of interest, the higher is financial capital's share of surplus value relative to that of industrial capital. Interest rates are established by competition in the loanable funds markets, and their levels may be high or low depending on the market forces of demand and supply. As Marx saw it, there is room for much conflict between financial and industrial capitalists over relative shares of surplus value.

Finally, the agricultural capitalists, in the same way as the industrial ones, exploit labor and so obtain surplus value. In this respect, there is no distinction between these two productive sectors of the economy. This surplus value is shared with the landowning capitalists, the latter receiving it in ground rent. The total income of this landowning class includes absolute rent, which reflects monopoly gains from the private ownership of a nonreproducible resource; differential rent, which is based on two equal quantities of capital and labor employed on equal areas of land with unequal results; and an element of interest, which comprises charges for land improvements.

Consequently, productive (industrial and agricultural) capitalists do not retain all of the surplus value generated within their spheres. Some of it goes to commercial capitalists, some to financial capitalists, and some to landowning capitalists. Additionally, Marx claimed, other shares are plundered by private bureaucrats, hangers-on, and just plain swindlers. In any event, the industrial capitalists' profits (after taxes) are only a modest fraction of the total fruits of exploitation. Thus, when these profits are paraded as total income of the capitalist class, they divert attention from the other shares. Further, when these profits are related to total capital $(c + v)$ to obtain a profit rate, both the rate of exploitation (surplus value) and its source are hidden. Finally, when these industrial profits are displayed after taxes have been taken out, the role of the state in supporting the capitalist class is concealed. That is, surplus value includes much of the state's receipts and expenditures, the latter intended to strengthen the class structure and its property relations.

Marxists maintain that the rate of industrial profits after taxes, therefore, is a gross understatement of the extent to which capital exploits labor. In 1974 in the United States, for example, industrial corporate profits after taxes were about $50 billion, but total surplus value (all corporate profits, interest, and rent before taxes) approached $200 billion, or about a quarter of employee compensation (wages and salaries) before taxes. Thus, the rate of exploitation, as Marx would figure it (if prices are used instead of values), was around 25 percent, while the rate of industrial profits on stockholders' equity was only a little over 10 percent.

Values and Prices

The value of a commodity, we have seen, is the socially-necessary labor-time required to produce it. The price of a commodity, on the other hand, is this labor-time valued in terms of money—say, for example, that 100 hours of labor equal $250. This $250 is divided among constant capital (c), variable capital (v), and surplus value (s). If $c = \$150$, and the rate of exploitation is 100 percent, then $v = \$50$ and $s = \$50$ $(s/v = 100$ percent$)$. In this case, the rate of profit is 25 percent—$s/(c + v) = 50/200$. If workers are free to move from one job to another to find their best advantage, wage rates for equal work will tend to be the same in each industry. Similarly, if capital is free to move, competition will tend to equalize the profit rates. Thus, following our numerical example, each sphere of production, when competition prevails, should have a profit rate of 25 percent. This would make prices proportional to values when commodities are traded one for another, provided that the organic composition of capital, $c/(c + v)$, is the same in each sphere of production—equal to 150/200, as in our numerical example.

Now, competition *will* tend to equalize rates of profit, but there is no reason to expect organic compositions of capital (the degrees of capital intensity) to be the same from one industry to the next. Suppose that our commodity has a higher organic composition than others on the average. In that event, the profit rate for our commodity would initially be lower than the average, because, while the exploitation rates, s/v, might be the same, the profit rate, $s/(c + v)$, is lower as c rises relative to v. The price of our commodity, therefore, would have to rise above $250 in order to equalize profit rates. This is accomplished by some capital moving out of this sphere, thereby reducing the supply of the commodity and raising its price. At the other end of the scale, if some commodities are produced with especially low organic compositions of capital, their profit rates will be above average. Consequently, their prices will fall below levels suggested by their values as capital moves into these spheres to take advantage of initially higher profit rates.

Thus, when the organic composition of capital differs among industries, prices will not be proportional to values, though the two will be systematically related to each other in accordance with the structure of the organic compositions of capital. The function of prices, in this case, is to redistribute surplus value among industrial capitalists so as to equalize rates of profit. Those capitalists with low organic compositions of capital, and hence initially with excess amounts of surplus value, lose portions of their surplus to other capitalists who are in the opposite position.

Surplus value is generated in the sphere of production, but it is generated differentially, in excess here and in deficiency there, depending on the organic composition of capital. To redistribute the surplus value so as to equalize profit rates requires that prices differ from values. Marx saw this process not as a weakness but as a decided strength of his analysis: the value-analysis revealed exploitation and its manifestation in surplus value; the price-analysis revealed how the total surplus value was shared within the class of industrial capitalists, in accordance with the laws of competition. At the same time, the price system also redistributed the surplus value among the various classes of capitalists —industrial, commercial, financial, and landed—as we have already seen.

Capital Accumulation

It was Marx's contention that the production of surplus value is "the absolute law" of the capitalist mode of production, that most of this surplus value is continually reconverted into capital—called capital accumulation—and that the system reproduces the capitalist relation: "on the one side the capitalist, on the other the wage-laborer." Capitalism is inherently an expanding system, for capitalists must constantly accumulate and extend their capital in order to preserve it; they must continually expand in order to remain capitalists, for if they did not they would be destroyed by competitors; they would be consumers and not capitalists. This expansion eventually occurs on a worldwide basis, for capitalists must push their mode of production into every nook and cranny of the globe. Nevertheless, capitalists also have an urge to enjoy the consumption of their capital. The overcoming of this urge is supposed to be "abstinence," which is a bourgeois justification, according to Marx, for the private appropriation of surplus value.

Marx asserted that the general law of capitalist accumulation is that it creates *both* wealth and poverty. That is to say, capitalist accumulation has an antagonistic character in that it produces and contains a unity of opposites. "The same causes which develop the expansive power of capital," Marx wrote, "develop also the labor-power at its disposal," including the reserve army of labor (a relative surplus population), whose misery and pauperism grow in step with wealth at the other pole. Furthermore, Marx continued, capital accumulation transforms the workplace into a despotic, degrading, alienating environment, one which mutilates the laborer "into a fragment of a man" and destroys "every remnant of charm in his work." Capital accumulation produces an accumulation of wealth at one pole and an "accumulation of misery, agony of toil, slavery, ignorance, brutality, mental degradation, at the opposite pole." Poverty and misery are not capitalism's negligence but its imperative, its inevitable progenies. This is Marx's principal message about the process of capitalist accumulation.

That message today may sound "wild," and indeed in some respects Marx can now be seen as having incorrectly extrapolated conditions prevalent in his time. However, before the reader plunges in to judge the message too harshly, he should be aware of its depth. For Marx, wealth could not exist by itself, just as a capitalist class could not exist in isolation. Wealth in capitalism has no other meaning than a concentration of much of society's production (its means and its products) in relatively few hands, and there is no way for that to occur without the simultaneous creation of its opposite—poverty, the material deprivation of the many, at least in relative terms. But poverty and misery, Marx contended, must be understood not only as exploitation but as alienation as well —not only materially but also "spiritually."

The Marxian theory of alienation seeks to explain how individuals in capitalist society have lost their understanding and control of the world around them and have, in the process, been stunted and perverted into something less than full human beings. For Marx, the source of all alienation lies in the work process. Alienation means that individuals no longer have an immediate and intimate relationship to the environment; they have been specialized and sorted, made into "the most wretched of commodities," divorced from the products they produce, split into mental workers and manual workers, into town people and rural people, divided into dominant and subordinate classes, thrown into selfish competition with one another. The result of alienation is the loss of personal identity—a transference of an individual's essential powers to others and to "things," even to commodities. Alienation is the negation of productivity, the diminution of one's powers.

Marx saw human beings in capitalistic society as alienated not only from the products they create and from their own labor, but also from others and from themselves. That is, workers under capitalism lose control of their products, produce as cogs in a process they do not understand, are separated from and pitted against their fellow workers, and are deprived of their essential powers. They believe that power resides outside of themselves, in the products they have actually fashioned, and they humble, demean, and almost destroy themselves before the commodity world. In the same way, a religious person might fashion a wooden idol with his own hands, kneel before it, transfer his own powers to it, and thus reduce himself to something less than a full human being. In their manifold alienated states, people lose their inner selves and become passive; they allow themselves to be directed by outside powers that they do not control and do not want to control; they subject themselves willingly to manipulation; they have a sense of powerlessness; they cannot act effectively. Marx did

not believe that capitalism was the original cause of alienation—for it existed before that —but under capitalism alienation in all of its forms is maximized.

The proletariat shares with the bourgeoisie every aspect of this commodity-dominated world. But, Marx stated, the latter experiences it as "a sign of its own power," while the former "feels destroyed in this alienation." The bourgeoisie, for Marx, sees no need for piercing the surface of phenomena; indeed it has a special interest in not revealing what is below, and even in deceiving itself on this score. On the other hand, the proletariat, while equally baffled, has a special interest in discovering the true relations and thus in developing a revolutionary consciousness. Productive activity is the catalyst of this transformation.

The capitalist mode of production extracts surplus value from wage-labor for the class of capitalists. The surplus value is used to expand capital, a process which is inherent to this social formation, and which is reinforced by competition. The accumulation process tends to generate increasing demands for labor to work cooperatively with the expanding means of production. However, accumulation leads to *concentration* of capital, which places greater magnitudes of capital in fewer hands and at the same time raises the organic composition of capital—the capital intensity of production—thereby moderating the growing demand for labor. Accumulation is also accompanied by the *centralization* of capital, by the larger capitalists gaining what smaller capitalists lose, by the expropriation of capitalist by capitalist.

The centralization of capital is the dynamic element in the accumulation process. It is furthered by the development of the credit system, which draws together scattered money resources for the use of larger capitalists; by competition, which destroys the weak and bolsters the strong; and by economies of scale (falling average costs), which give increasing cost advantages to the already-large capitals over the smaller ones, enabling the larger capitals to beat the smaller.

If capitalist accumulation is to persist, it requires above all else an ample supply of wage-labor that is continually replenished and available for work at wage levels that ensure the further production of surplus value for the class of capitalists. It is for this reason that Marx considered the reserve army of labor to be an essential ingredient of capitalism, a relatively redundant population of laborers that would expand and contract according to the requirements of the system. As soon as the accumulation process diminishes this surplus population to the point of endangering the further production of adequate amounts of surplus value (by raising wages and other advantages of labor), a reaction sets in: accumulation lags, the introduction of labor-saving machinery is quickened, the reserve army is replenished, and the rise in wages is halted. In these ways, Marx maintained, the foundations of the capitalist system are protected from the dangers of lessened exploitation. "The law of capitalistic accumulation . . . excludes every diminution in the degree of exploitation of labor, and every rise in the price of labor, which could seriously imperil the continual reproduction, on an ever-enlarging scale, of the capitalistic relation." According to Marx, the laborer exists to satisfy the needs of capital; material wealth does not exist to satisfy the need of the laborer to develop into a complete human being.

Consequently, capitalist accumulation demands the replenishment of poverty and misery, through the reserve army, to serve its requirements. But, Marx continued, there are other ways that degradation is created by the process of accumulation. First, accumulation and capitalists' pursuit of ever-larger surplus value lead to the geographical concentration of the means of production in industrial urban centers. As Marx and Engels observed, this causes a "heaping together of the laborers, within a given space . . . therefore the swifter capitalistic accumulation, the more miserable are the dwellings of the working-people." Second, accumulation of capital tears apart the fabric protecting individual proprietors,

craftsmen, and self-sufficient producers, transforming them into a surplus of dependent wage-laborers. Third, it draws wealth and talent from outlying areas into industrial and urban centers, converting the former into backward, stagnant sub-economies; or it reduces these outlying areas to specialized suppliers of raw materials for industrial capital, thereby increasing their vulnerability to adverse developments; and it transfers wealth from these areas via the price-market mechanism. Fourth, on an international scale, the capitalist mode has augmented its capital through forceful market control of weaker areas and has drained surpluses from them into the industrial regions. By these means, wealth and poverty are created together, a unity of conflicting opposites.

HOW CAPITALISM IS MYSTIFIED

Marx alleged that capitalism presents itself on the surface of life in distorted forms—that what it is really like, within its deep recesses, is quite different from what its facial expressions suggest. These surface distortions, Marx contended, lead to illusions about the capitalist mode of production, and the illusions in turn are used by bourgeois ideologists to mystify the workings of the system. Thus, a web of mystification is spun around this mode of production, hindering a clear understanding of its true nature. We are all fooled, Marx said, by capitalism's distortions.

The Distortions of Capitalism

The capitalist mode of production turns labor-power into a commodity, in a world of commodities, to be purchased and exploited by a capital-owning class that appropriates surplus value and is compelled to extend its capital and its mode of production to all corners of the globe. Capitalist relations comprise these two classes existing as a unity of opposites: the capitalist class, owning the means of production, buying the labor-power of a dispossessed proletariat, controlling the work process, possessing the products of labor; and the proletariat, selling its labor-power as wage-labor, working in an environment of alienation, receiving only part of its product, existing to facilitate capital's self-expansion. This, Marx affirmed, is the true substratum of capitalism, its bedrock.

The surface phenomena of capitalism, on the other hand, appear in forms that often distort and falsify the true relationships of this mode of production. Indeed, it was Marx's contention that capitalism, because of its perverted forms, maximizes illusion and mystification, that its essence is more heavily covered by layers of misleading superficial phenomena than that of any previous mode of production, including slavery and feudalism. The outward appearances of capitalism diverge fantastically from its inner laws, which are thereby largely hidden from view. Direct experience, within the capitalist mode, therefore, leads to illusions in the minds of those captivated by its surface data. These illusions can be dispelled only by scientific analysis of the capitalist mode, an analysis that is made possible by the rise of the industrial proletariat (and so of its ideologists) and serves the interest of that class. Thus, both the need for and the possibility of scientific analysis arise together as capitalism develops. Such insights into the workings of the system, however, are strongly resisted by the bourgeoisie and its apologists; furthermore, capitalism makes these insights extremely difficult to comprehend. This explains the continuing coexistence of illusions and their explanation.

In a pre-capitalist, rural patriarchal mode of production, social labor is revealed directly in the social products produced for the family. The work is divided according to age, sex, abilities, and other natural conditions. The different kinds of labor are direct social functions because they are functions of the family—spinning, weaving, growing food, gathering wood, and so forth. The articles produced are family products, not commodities seeking markets, and so they are directly social prod-

ucts. The social relations among the family members appear to them as mutual personal relations, because the labor of each is consciously applied as part of the combined labor of the family. The total products of these labors are social products to be used by the family in ways decided by the members.

Now consider a mode of production that breaks up such families into individual producers, each producing independently of the others, and each producing, not products for the family, but commodities for exchange—a mode that Marx termed "the most embryonic form of bourgeois production." This mode turns social relations between persons into material relations and material relations between things into social relations. In this mode, the social character of private labor, which was obvious and direct in the family situation, is now revealed only indirectly when private products are exchanged—that is, when equal values or labor-times are exchanged. Individual producers now appear to have no relations with one another, but only with their material commodities: "Individuals exist for one another only insofar as their commodities exist." Marx means that individuals, in this mode, make contact with one another only through the exchange of their commodities. For this reason, exchange value appears to be a relation between commodities—this commodity is worth so much of that commodity—but in fact it is a relation between people, between labor-times of workers. As Marx explained:

> A social relation of production appears as something existing apart from individual human beings, and the distinctive relations into which they enter in the course of production in society appear as the specific properties of a thing—it is this perverted appearance, this prosaically real, and by no means imaginary, mystification that is characteristic of all social forms of labor positing exchange-value.

Thus, the social relations of individuals appear in the inverted form of a social relation between things. This is an actual representation of this mode of production, albeit a representation which distorts the true relation between human beings.

This distorted form is carried over to the fully-developed capitalist mode of production. In addition to it, however, the capitalist mode widens the gap further between its phenomenal appearances and its essence. Labor and the means of production, for example, are forces (factors) of production. But, in the capitalist mode, labor becomes wage-labor, a commodity, a material thing; means of production become capital, incarnated in the capitalist. Thus, living labor becomes a thing, and capital, which is dead (embodied) labor, becomes alive in the capitalist; an inversion of subject and object is accomplished.

The capitalist mode especially presents itself in ways that hide the fact that surplus value comes from the exploitation of labor within the sphere of production. Surplus value, in capitalism's fantastic forms, appears to arise in the circulation sphere or from inherent powers of capital in its various forms; its very existence is shielded by market expressions of the capitalist mode that misrepresent the real relations of production.

If these distortions of fundamental bourgeois relations are not recognized as such, but are instead believed to be the true manifestations of capitalism's inner laws, then illusions are created in the minds of those deceived. Marx believed that the surface distortions of the bourgeois mode are so forceful that most people are unable to discover capitalism's underlying mechanism and so remain confused. In fact, the capitalist mode, in its inverted phenomenal forms, generates false consciousness in both capitalists and workers. It produces both the actual surface distortions and the mental illusions about what lies beneath the surface. It is on the basis of these illusions that the mystification of capitalism arises.

The acceptance, as the real thing, of the distortion that transfers social relations from people to their products, leads to a series of illusions and fantasies. Commodities become fetishes in the same way that gods, the creation of humans, take on lives of their own, fashioning social relations among themselves and with the human world. In the "religion of everyday life," objects are endowed with life, taking on the powers relinquished by their producers, who, as a consequence, diminish and deceive themselves; the objects come to rule over man. Since "the god among commodities" is gold-money, the possession of money becomes an insatiable desire, the greed of all. This social form of wealth is transformed, under capitalism, into the private power of private persons, who are able, through the power of money, to transform their own personal incapacities into their opposites. According to Marx, "Money is the supreme good, therefore its possessor is good. . . . I am *stupid*, but money is the *real mind* of all things and how then should its possessor be stupid? Besides, he can buy talented people for himself, and is he who has power over the talented not more talented than the talented?" Money, Marx claimed, "is the common whore, the common pimp of people and nations."

The Illusions of Capitalism

If the faces of capitalism are distorted, they are powerful and convincing ones which give rise to numerous illusions about this mode of production. The perverted forms of the actual world produce conceptions in the minds of people that diverge drastically from the underlying realities.

The most important of these illusions concerns surplus value—its production, its transformation as profits among industrial capitalists via the price mechanism, its realization in the circulation sphere, and its distribution among industrial, commercial, financial, and landed capitalists.

The origin of surplus value is concealed in many ways. The wage-form, especially when workers are paid by the number of the item produced, extinguishes every trace of the division of the working day into necessary labor and surplus labor, and it therefore creates the illusion that all labor is paid labor. To add to this, wage-labor appears to be "free" labor, even though actually bound to the class of capitalists. This freedom to choose to work for any capitalist reinforces the illusion that labor is not being exploited, that the production sphere cannot be the source of surplus value. Further, industrial profits of enterprise appear to be wages of management, so that both workers and industrial capitalists appear to be rewarded for different kinds of labor, some menial and some managerial. Marx commented that this makes "the labor of exploiting and the exploited labor both appear identical as labor." He added: "Now, the wage-laborer, like the slave, must have a master who puts him to work and rules over him. And assuming the existence of this relationship of lordship and servitude, it is quite proper to compel the wage-laborer to produce his own wages and also the wages of supervision, as compensation for the labor of ruling and supervising him. . . ." The greater the antagonism between the producers and the owners, the greater the role of supervision. This reaches its peak in the slave system. This tenuous claim by "rulers and supervisors" to part of the surplus value is therefore a claim that arises from the antithesis between the laborers and the capitalists, one producing and the other owning the means of production; its antagonistic nature would vanish with the disappearance of classes. Therefore, while in one sense wages of managers are part of variable capital, not surplus value, Marx saw them as largely the latter because they reflected a class relation that would disappear in a "cooperative society of associated labor," Marx's phrase for a classless society.

The source of surplus value is further concealed when values are transformed into prices, thereby redistributing surplus value among the industrial capitalists, some of whom lose a portion of the surplus generated in their production sphere and others of whom gain some—in amounts which in competition equalize rates of profit on total capital. Thus, the average profit of any capital differs from the surplus value which that cap-

ital extracted from the laborers employed by it. This transformation process, Marx wrote, "completely conceals the true nature and origin of profit not only from the capitalist, who has a special interest in deceiving himself on this score, but also from the laborer . . . [it] serves to obscure the basis for determining value itself." Each capitalist is therefore under the illusion that his profit comes as much from prices and markets as from his own process of production, and the fact is obscured that all profits are due to the aggregate exploitation of labor by total social capital within the production sphere.

The realization of surplus value in the sphere of circulation creates the illusion that this is its source. Commodities, pregnant with surplus value, are exchanged for more money than the capitalist paid for the constant and variable capital to produce them, the difference being the surplus value itself. Such transactions produce the illusion that the mode of exchange is the dominant sphere and so the basis of the mode of production. The process of production, Marx stated, "appears merely as an unavoidable intermediate link, as a necessary evil for the sake of money-making." Money seems to be made in circulation, in buying commodities below their values and selling them above their values. Surplus value appears to originate from the acumen of capitalists, from their sharp business wits, from their abilities to cut costs, to outguess the market and beat the competition, and from their shrewdness in dealing with money, stocks and bonds, bills of exchange, and the other financial accouterments of capitalism. Marx believed that the entire process by which surplus value is produced is made especially incomprehensible in financial centers, such as London, where "the paper world" distorted everything.

Finally, the origin of surplus value is obscured by the glitter of illusions which emanate from each of its several elements. Interest, a part of surplus value, appears to arise from the inherent powers of money to increase itself, powers that are completely divorced from the production process. The illusion that money-capital has automatic self-expansion powers, occult properties, money generating money, Marx called "the mystification of capital in its most flagrant form." Interest is part of surplus value—unpaid, exploited labor—but it pretends to disavow this source in favor of the innate powers of a thing, of a thing come alive. Similarly, commercial profits appear clearly to come from clever buying and selling within the circulation sphere, and thus to be severed altogether from the productive activities of industrial capitalists. Also, rent seems to arise from the powers of the earth itself, not from social relations of production; from the land or from the presence of that personification of the land, the landlord. The landlord demands his share of the total product that land helped to create. "Just as products confront the producer as an independent force in capital and capitalists —who actually are but the personification of capital—so land becomes personified in the landlord and likewise gets on its hind legs to demand, as an independent force, its share of the product created with its help."

Land is productive but, while it adds to output, it does not "naturally" produce the social form called rent. Similarly, capital is productive but it does not "naturally" produce profit or interest. By the same reasoning, labor is productive but it does not "naturally" produce wages. Interest (profit), rent, and wages are all social forms of the class structure of society that have deep historical roots. They are all components of a total product created by work, and yet each seems to arise from a separate "thing": profit from capital goods, rent from land, and wages from labor. This illusion is played out fully when the capitalist, the owner of capital goods, claims the profit; the landlord, the owner of land, claims the rent; and the worker, the owner of labor-power, claims the wages. Each appears to receive what each is entitled to. Marx called this "the trinity formula," which is "the complete mystification of the capitalist mode of production. . . . It is an enchanted, perverted, topsy-turvy world, in which Monsieur le Capital and Madame la Terre do their ghost-walking as social characters and at the same time directly as mere things."

3.2   *The Labor Process*

The capitalist mode of production is not just a system of distribution, in which capitalists strive to increase the share of profits by reducing the share of wages; it also involves a particular way of organizing production, in which capitalists seek to increase profits by establishing a labor process that will get the most out of workers. Our analysis of capitalism must therefore investigate not only the allocation of labor time and the distribution of income but also the process whereby capitalists seek to maximize the work actually done during the time spent by workers on the job.

The lack of worker control over the labor process has consequences both for the individual worker and for the society as a whole. Individual workers face the consequences of capitalist organization every day at their jobs. Although workers are engaged in activities essential for society, they can derive little satisfaction from the process or product of their labor, for it is out of their control and they work only to earn wages. Moreover, work will be organized in ways that are most profitable for capitalists rather than most useful for the whole society. We explore these consequences in much greater detail in Chapter 7.

In the following reading, Harry Braverman analyzes the essential nature of the capitalist labor process.

The worker enters into the employment agreement because social conditions leave him or her no other way to gain a livelihood. The employer, on the other hand, is the possessor of a unit of capital which he is endeavoring to enlarge, and in order to do so he converts part of it into wages. Thus is set in motion the labor process, which, while it is in general a process for creating useful values, has now also become specifically a process for the expansion of capital, the creation of a profit. From this point on, it becomes foolhardy to view the labor process purely from a technical standpoint, as a mere mode of labor. It has become in addition a process of accumulation of capital. And, moreover, it is the latter aspect which dominates in the mind and activities of the capitalist, into whose hands the control over the labor process has passed. In everything that follows, therefore, we shall be considering the manner in which the labor process is dominated and shaped by the accumulation of capital.

Labor, like all life processes and bodily functions, is an inalienable property of the human individual. Muscle and brain cannot be separated from persons possessing them; one cannot endow another with one's own capacity for work, no matter at what price, any more than one can eat, sleep, or perform sex acts for another. Thus, in the exchange, the worker does not surrender to the capitalist his or her capacity for work. The worker retains it, and the capitalist can take advantage of the bargain only by setting the worker to work. It is of course understood that the useful effects or products of labor belong to the capitalist. But what the worker sells, and what the capitalist buys, is *not an agreed amount of labor, but the power to labor over an agreed period of time*. This inability to purchase labor, which is an inalienable bodily and mental function, and the necessity to purchase the power to perform it, is so fraught with consequences for the entire capitalist mode of production that it must be investigated more closely.

When a master employs the services of a beast of burden in his production process, he can do little more than direct into useful channels such natural abilities as strength and endurance. When he employs bees in the production of honey, silkworms in the making of silk, bacteria in the fermentation of wine, or sheep in the growing of wool, he can only turn to his own advantage the instinctual activities or biological functions of these forms of life.

.   .   .

It is implied in all such employments that the master must put up with the definite natural limitations of his servitors. Thus, in taking the *labor power* of animals, he at the same time takes their *labor*, because the two, while distinguishable in theory, are more or less identical in practice, and the most cunning contrivances can get from the labor power of the animal only minor variations of actual labor.

Human labor, on the other hand, because it is informed and directed by an understanding which has been socially and culturally developed, is capable of a vast range of productive activities. The active labor processes which reside in potential in the labor power of humans are so diverse as to type, manner of performance, etc., that for all practical purposes they may be said to be infinite, all the more so as new modes of labor can easily be invented more rapidly than they can be exploited. The capitalist finds in this infinitely malleable character of human labor the essential resource for the expansion of his capital.

It is known that human labor is able to produce more than it consumes, and this capacity for "surplus labor" is sometimes treated as a special and mystical endowment of humanity or of its labor. In reality it is nothing of the sort, but is merely a prolongation of working time beyond the point where labor has reproduced itself, or in other words brought into being its own means of subsistence or their equivalent. This time will vary with the intensity and productivity of labor, as well as with the changing requirements of "subsistence," but for any given state of these it is a definite duration. The "peculiar" capacity of labor power to produce for the capitalist after it has reproduced itself is therefore nothing but the extension of work time beyond the point where it could otherwise come to a halt. An ox too will have this capacity, and grind out more corn than it will eat if kept to the task by training and compulsion.

The distinctive capacity of human labor power is therefore not its ability to produce a surplus, but rather its intelligent and purposive character, which gives it infinite adaptability and which produces the social and cultural conditions for enlarging its own productivity, so that its surplus product may be continuously enlarged. From the point of view of the capitalist, this many-sided potentiality of humans in society is the basis upon which is built the enlargement of his capital. He therefore takes up every means of increasing the output of the labor power he has purchased when he sets it to work as labor. The means he employs may vary from the enforcement upon the worker of the longest possible working day in the early period of capitalism to the use of the most productive instruments of labor and the greatest intensity of labor, but they are always aimed at realizing from the potential inherent in labor power the greatest useful effect of labor, for it is this that will yield for him the greatest surplus and thus the greatest profit.

But if the capitalist builds upon this distinctive quality and potential of human labor power, it is also this quality, by its very indeterminacy, which places before him his greatest challenge and problem. The coin of labor has its obverse side: in purchasing labor power that can do much, he is at the same time purchasing an undefined quality and quantity. What he buys is infinite in *potential*, but in its *realization* it is limited by the subjective state of the workers, by their previous history, by the general social conditions under which they work as well as the particular conditions of the enterprise, and by the technical setting of their labor. The work actually performed will be affected by these and many other factors, including the organization of the process and the forms of supervision over it, if any.

This is all the more true since the technical features of the labor process are now dominated by the social features which the capitalist has introduced: that is to say, the new relations of production. Having been forced to sell their labor power to another, the workers also surrender their interest in the labor process, which has now been "alienated." *The labor process has become the responsibility of the capitalist.* In this setting of antagonistic relations of production, the problem of realizing the "full usefulness" of the labor power he has bought becomes exacerbated by the opposing interests of those for whose purposes the labor process is carried on, and those who, on the other side, carry it on.

Thus when the capitalist buys buildings, materials, tools, machinery, etc., he can evaluate with precision their place in the labor process. He knows that a certain portion of his outlay will be transferred to each unit of production, and his accounting practices allocate these in the form of costs or depreciation. But when he buys labor time, the outcome is far from being either so certain or so definite that it can be reckoned in this way, with precision and in advance. This is merely an expression of the fact that the portion of his capital expended on labor power is the "variable" portion, which undergoes an increase in the process of production; for him, the question is how great that increase will be.

It thus becomes essential for the capitalist that control over the labor process pass from the hands of the worker into his own. This transition presents itself in history as the *progressive alienation of the process of production* from the worker; to the capitalist, it presents itself as the problem of *management*.

Industrial capitalism begins when a significant number of workers is employed by a single capitalist. At first, the capitalist utilizes labor as it comes to him from prior forms of production, carrying on labor processes as they had been carried on before. The workers are already trained in traditional arts of industry previously practiced in feudal and guild handicraft production. Spinners, weavers, glaziers, potters, blacksmiths, tinsmiths, locksmiths, joiners, millers, bakers, etc. continue to exercise in the employ of the capitalist the productive crafts they had carried on as guild journeymen and independent artisans. These early workshops were simply agglomerations of smaller units of production, reflecting little change in traditional methods, and the work thus remained under the immediate control of the producers in whom was embodied the traditional knowledge and skills of their crafts.

Nevertheless, as soon as the producers were gathered together, the problem of management arose in rudimentary form. In the first place, functions of management were brought into being by the very practice of cooperative labor. Even an assemblage of independently practicing artisans requires coordination, if one considers the need for the provision of a workplace and the ordering of processes within it, the centralization of the supply of materials, even the most elementary scheduling of priorities and assignments, and the maintenance of records of costs, payrolls, materials, finished products, sales, credit, and the calculation of profit and loss. Second, assembly trades like shipbuilding and coach

making required the relatively sophisticated meshing of different kinds of labor, as did civil engineering works, etc. Again, it was not long before new industries arose which had little prior handicraft background, among them sugar refining, soap boiling, and distilling, while at the same time various primary processes like iron smelting, copper and brass working, and ordnance, paper and powder making, were completely transformed. All of these required conceptual and coordination functions which in capitalist industry took the form of management.

The capitalist assumed these functions as manager by virtue of his ownership of capital. Under capitalist exchange relations, the time of the workers he hired was as much his own as were the materials he supplied and the products that issued from the shop. That this was not understood from the beginning is attested by the fact that guild and apprenticeship rules and the legal restraints common to feudal and guild modes of production all persisted for a period, and had to be gradually stripped away as the capitalist consolidated his powers in society and demolished the juridical features of pre-capitalist social formations. It was partly for this reason that early manufacturing tended to gravitate to new towns which were free of guild and feudal regulations and traditions. In time, however, law and custom were reshaped to reflect the predominance of the "free" contract between buyer and seller under which the capitalist gained the virtually unrestricted power to determine the technical modes of labor.

The early phases of industrial capitalism were marked by a sustained effort on the part of the capitalist to disregard the difference between labor power and the labor that can be gotten out of it, and to buy labor in the same way he bought his raw materials: as a definite quantity of work, completed and embodied in the product. This attempt took the form of a great variety of subcontracting and "putting-out" systems. In the form of domestic labor, it was to be found in textile, clothing, metal goods (nailing and cutlery),

watchmaking, hat, wood and leather industries, where the capitalist distributed materials on a piecework basis to workers for
manufacture in their own homes, through the
medium of subcontractors and commission
agents. But even in industries where work
could not be taken home, such as coal, tin,
and copper mines, mine workers themselves,
working at the face, took contracts singly or in
gangs, either directly or through the mediation of the "butty" or subcontracting
employer of mine labor. The system persisted
even in the early factories. In cotton mills,
skilled spinners were put in charge of
machinery and engaged their own help,
usually child assistants from among their
families and acquaintances. Foremen sometimes added to their direct supervisory function the practice of taking a few machines on
their own account and hiring labor to operate
them. Pollard identifies practices of this sort
not only in mines and textile mills, but also in
carpet and lace mills, ironworks, potteries,
building and civil engineering projects,
transport, and quarrying. In the United
States, it has been pointed out, the contract
system, in which puddlers and other skilled
iron and steel craftsmen were paid by the
ton on a sliding scale pegged to market prices,
and hired their own help, was characteristic
of this industry until almost the end of the
nineteenth century.

· · ·

While all such systems involved the payment of wages by piece rates, or by subcon-
tract rates, it must not be supposed that this
in itself was their essential feature. Piece rates
in various forms are common to the present
day, and represent the conversion of time
wages into a form which attempts, with very
uneven success, to enlist the worker as a
willing accomplice in his or her own exploitation. Today, however, piece rates are combined with the systematic and detailed
control on the part of management over the
processes of work, a control which is sometimes exercised more stringently than where
time rates are employed. Rather, the early

domestic and subcontracting systems represented a transitional form, a phase during
which the capitalist had not yet assumed the
essential function of management in industrial capitalism, control over the labor process; for this reason it was incompatible with
the overall development of capitalist production, and survives only in specialized
instances.

Such methods of dealing with labor bore
the marks of the origins of industrial capitalism in mercantile capitalism, which understood the buying and selling of commodities
but not their production, and sought to treat
labor like all other commodities. It was
bound to prove inadequate, and did so very
rapidly, even though its survival was guaranteed for a time by the extreme unevenness of
the development of technology, and by the
need for technology to incessantly retrace its
own steps and recapitulate, in newer industries, the stages of its historic development.
The subcontracting and "putting out" systems were plagued by problems of irregular-
ity of production, loss of materials in transit
and through embezzlement, slowness of
manufacture, lack of uniformity and uncertainty of the quality of the product. But most
of all, they were limited by their inability to
change the processes of production. Based . . .
upon a rudimentary division of labor, the
domestic system prevented the further
development of the division of labor. While
the attempt to purchase finished labor,
instead of assuming direct control over labor
power, relieved the capitalist of the uncertainties of the latter system by fixing a definite
unit cost, at the same time it placed beyond
the reach of the capitalist much of the potential of human labor that may be made available by fixed hours, systematic control, and
the reorganization of the labor process. This
function, capitalist management soon seized
upon with an avidity that was to make up for
its earlier timidity.

The control of large bodies of workers
long antedates the bourgeois epoch. The
Pyramids, the Great Wall of China, extensive

networks of roads, aqueducts, and irrigation canals, the large buildings, arenas, monuments, cathedrals, etc., dating from antiquity and medieval times all testify to this. We find an elementary division of labor in the workshops which produced weapons for the Roman armies, and the armies of precapitalist times exhibit primitive forms of later capitalist practices. Roman workshops for metalwork, pottery, leather, glassblowing, brickmaking, and textiles, as well as large agricultural estates, brought together scores of workers under a single management. These predecessors, however, were undertaken under conditions of slave or other unfree forms of labor, stagnant technology, and the absence of the driving capitalist need to expand each unit of capital employed, and so differed markedly from capitalist management. The Pyramids were built with the surplus labor of an enslaved population, with no end in view but the greater glory of the pharaohs here and in the hereafter. Roads, aqueducts, and canals were built for their military or civilian usefulness, and not generally on a profit-making basis. State-subsidized manufactories produced arms or luxury goods and enjoyed an actual or legal monopoly and large orders from noncommercial buyers, courts, or armies. The management required in such situations remained elementary, and this was all the more true when the labor was that of slaves, and sometimes supervised by slaves as well. The capitalist, however, working with hired labor, which represents a cost for every nonproducing hour, in a setting of rapidly revolutionizing technology to which his own efforts perforce contributed, and goaded by the need to show a surplus and accumulate capital, brought into being a wholly new art of management, which even in its early manifestations was far more complete, self-conscious, painstaking, and calculating than anything that had gone before.

There were more immediate precedents for the early industrial capitalist to draw upon, in the form of mercantile enterprises, plantations, and agricultural estates. Merchant capitalism invented the Italian system of bookkeeping, with its internal checks and controls; and from merchant capital the industrial capitalist also took over the structure of branch organization subdivided among responsible managers. Agricultural estates and colonial plantations offered the experience of a well-developed supervisory routine, particularly since much early mining (and the construction works that attended it) was carried out on the agricultural estates of Great Britain under the supervision of estate agents.

Control without centralization of employment was, if not impossible, certainly very difficult, and so the precondition for management was the gathering of workers under a single roof. The first effect of such a move was to enforce upon the workers regular hours of work, in contrast to the self-imposed pace which included many interruptions, short days and holidays, and in general prevented a prolongation of the working day for the purpose of producing a surplus under then-existing technical conditions. Thus Gras writes in his *Industrial Evolution*:

> It was purely for purposes of discipline, so that the workers could be effectively controlled under the supervision of foremen. Under one roof, or within a narrow compass, they could be started to work at sunrise and kept going till sunset, barring periods for rest and refreshment. And under penalty of loss of all employment they could be kept going almost all throughout the year.[1]

Within the workshops, early management assumed a variety of harsh and despotic forms, since the creation of a "free labor force" required coercive methods to habituate the workers to their tasks and keep them working throughout the day and the year. Pollard notes that "there were few areas of the country in which modern industries, particularly the textiles, if carried on in large

[1]N. S. B. Gras, *Industrial Evolution* (1930), p. 77; pp. 11–12.

buildings, were not associated with prisons, workhouses, and orphanages. This connection is usually underrated, particularly by those historians who assume that the new works recruited free labour only." So widespread does he find this and other systems of coercion that he concludes that "the modern industrial proletariat was introduced to its role not so much by attraction or monetary reward, but by compulsion, force and fear."[2]

· · ·

In all these early efforts, the capitalists were groping toward a theory and practice of management. Having created new social relations of production, and having begun to transform the mode of production, they found themselves confronted by problems of management which were different not only in scope but also in kind from those characteristic of earlier production processes. Under the special and new relations of capitalism, which presupposed a "free labor contract," they had to extract from their employees that daily conduct which would best serve their interests, to impose their will upon their workers while operating a labor process on a voluntary contractual basis. This enterprise shared from the first the characterization which Clausewitz assigned to war; it is *movement in a resistant medium* because it involves the control of refractory masses.

The verb *to manage*, from *manus*, the Latin for hand, originally meant to train a horse in his paces, to cause him to do the exercises of the *manège*. As capitalism creates a society in which no one is presumed to consult anything but self-interest, and as the employment contract between parties sharing nothing but the inability to avoid each other becomes prevalent, management becomes a more perfected and subtle instrument. Tradition, sentiment, and pride in workmanship play an ever weaker and more erratic role, and are regarded on both sides as manifestations of a better nature which it would be folly to accommodate. Like a rider who uses reins, bridle, spurs, carrot, whip, and training from birth to impose his will, the capitalist strives, through management, to *control*. And control is indeed the central concept of all management systems, as has been recognized implicitly or explicitly by all theoreticians of management. Lyndall Urwick, the rhapsodic historian of the scientific management movement and himself a management consultant for many decades, understood the historical nature of the problem clearly:

> In the workshops of the Medieval "master," control was based on the obedience which the customs of the age required the apprentices and journeymen to give to the man whom they had contracted to serve. But in the later phase of domestic economy the industrial family unit was controlled by the clothier only in so far as it had to complete a given quantity of cloth according to a certain pattern. With the advent of the modern industrial group in large factories in urban areas, the whole process of control underwent a fundamental revolution. It was now the owner or manager of a factory, i.e., the "employer" as he came to be called, who had to secure or exact from his "employees" a level of obedience and/or co-operation which would enable him to exercise control. There was no individual interest in the success of the enterprise other than the extent to which it provided a livelihood.[3]

It was not that the new arrangement was "modern," or "large," or "urban" which created the new situation, but rather the new social relations which now frame the production process, and the antagonism between those who carry on the process and those for whose benefit it is carried on, those who manage and those who execute, those who bring to the factory their labor power, and those who undertake to extract from this labor power the maximum advantage for the capitalist.

[2]Sidney Pollard, *The Genesis of Modern Management: A Study of the Industrial Revolution in Great Britain* (Cambridge, Mass., 1965), pp. 163, 207.

[3]Lyndall Urwick and E. F. L. Brech, *The Making of Scientific Management*, vol. II (London, 1946), pp. 10–11.

3.3 *The Logic of Capital Accumulation*

The capitalist mode of production has proven to be a powerful mechanism for developing and expanding the forces of production. Despite periodic economic crises, capitalism has produced ever-greater quantities of commodities. The following essay by Richard C. Edwards shows how the basic institutions of the capitalist mode of production generate an inexorable systemic pressure to expand the scale of production.

Several qualifications should be kept in mind in this discussion of the "productivity" of the capitalist mode of production. First, the growth process described below does not necessarily apply to capitalist countries in the underdeveloped part of the worldwide capitalist system.[1] Second, every item produced for the market is counted as "productive" economic output, whether or not it increases the "standard of living"—nuclear weapons, moon rockets, and television commericials are included, for example. Many things important to the quality of life are excluded—wisdom, community, justice, the opportunity for friendship. Third, the benefits from increased production are very unequally distributed. Finally, market measures of economic output do not take account of the widespread pollution, exhaustion of natural resources, and ecological damage resulting from capitalist production. Hence, while a greater quantity of production *may* contribute to a higher "standard of living," by no means does it necessarily do so.[2]

[1]See Section 13.3 for an analysis of the consequences of capitalism for economic development in underdeveloped countries.

[2]See Chapter 11.

The following was written by RICHARD C. EDWARDS for the the first edition of this book. Copyright © 1972 by Richard C. Edwards.

The capitalist period as an historical epoch has been characterized by a rapid expansion of production in the advanced countries.[1] The material productiveness of advanced capitalist societies was noted by Marx and Engels, writing in 1848:[2]

> The bourgeoisie, during its rule of scarce one hundred years, has created more massive and more colossal productive forces than have all preceding generations together. Subjection of nature's forces to man, machinery, application of chemistry to industry and agriculture, steam navigation, railways, electric telegraphs, clearing of whole populations conjured out of the ground—what earlier century had even a presentiment that such productive forces slumbered in the lap of social labor?

If the statement seemed true in 1848, how much truer it appears from the affluent perspective of another hundred years.

The purpose of this essay is to show how the basic capitalist institutions described at the beginning of this chapter have fostered such a tremendous expansion of economic

[1]Note that we are talking only about the *advanced* countries; the *failure* to generate such growth in the outlying areas is one of the aspects of this growth in advanced countries.

[2]The quote is from *The Communist Manifesto*, excerpted in Section 2.4, p. 64.

capacity. How has capitalism led to the development of what Marx and Engels called "colossal productive forces"?

The argument presented below is divided into two parts. The first section deals with those motivations and pressures which induce capitalists to strive to expand output; we note both "internal" motivations (the capitalist's own desire to accumulate) and "market pressures" (the necessity for the capitalist to maintain a competitive market position). The second section outlines the way in which workers enter the production process under capitalism, leading to the market allocation of labor resources according to profit criteria.

THE CAPITALIST AS OWNER

The capitalist mode of production is historically unique in that it concentrates the means of production in the hands of a few people —capitalists—whose *only* role in the society is to make profits; they stand to gain personally, directly, and in large measure from the expansion of profits. Their interest in production, then, is not in the social merit or intrinsic value of what they produce, but only in their product's potential profitability.

This social justification places the capitalist in contrast to the feudal lord, the ancient slave-owner, or the eastern potentate, all of whom controlled the production process as firmly as the capitalist does today. However, these earlier dominant classes rested their ideological superiority and their right to rule on claims other than economic prowess. Some classes had religious claims (the Hebrew priests, the medieval church, "divinely" appointed kings); others had military claims (medieval lords, Roman emperors, Indian war chiefs); still others had political, cultural, or other claims. Only the capitalist class bases its claim to dominance and privilege directly on its ability to make profits by selling goods on the market.

Hence it is understandable that previous dominant classes should have had less inter-est in expanding production, and that the capitalist class, whose single rationale is making and accumulating profits, should have been the historical agent for creating growth in material production.

The fundamental characteristic of capitalist production is that it is organized, controlled, and motivated by capitalists and their firms to make profits. The capitalist firm *realizes* profits only by producing goods and selling them on the market. Firms therefore attempt to sell as much as possible at as high a price as possible. The motivation to capture profits leads the capitalist firm to produce huge quantities of goods for sale on the market if it thinks it can sell them.

The question, then, is what motivates the capitalist to strive so diligently to make and accumulate profits? First, of course, the profits which are generated in a firm *belong* to the owner-capitalist. So undoubtedly the primary motivation is simply the *personal* one: the capitalist, by increasing profits, increases his own wealth and ability to consume, expands his own power and sphere of control, and enhances his own privileges and status. In capitalist society, power and status are gained primarily through one's control over commodities, especially ownership of wealth; so the incentive to accumulate is correspondingly stronger. Furthermore, these attributes are measured *relative* to other people's situations, so the desire to expand profits (and hence increase one's wealth, power and status) continues indefinitely.

Second, we have already noted the ideological basis for capitalists' need to maximize profits. The social rationale for putting capitalists in charge (rather than, say, running firms democratically or letting communities operate local firms) is that capitalists *own* as private property the means of production, and therefore they have the *right* to determine its use.

But the efficacy of this claim for *private* control of what is after all the *social* means of production, while it rests in the first instance on the inviolability of private property, ultimately reflects a deeper ideological assertion: that the whole society benefits by granting capitalists the right to control production. Everyone benefits, the argument goes, because property-owning capitalists organize society's production efficiently. The magnitude of his profits provides the evidence demonstrating the capitalist's social usefulness; for he realizes profits only to the extent that he efficiently produces what people want and need. This reasoning thus transforms the capitalist's act of making profits for himself into a socially essential and useful act. The *raison d'être* of the capitalist is his ability to expand production for the good of all. This ideological justification reinforces the capitalists' personal stake in expanding profits.

Capitalists' personal and ideological interest in expanding profits would by itself lead us to expect a powerful dynamic within capitalism for expansion of output. But they are driven to expand profits not only because they *want* to, but also because if they are to remain capitalists, the market *forces* them to do so. Capitalists do not operate independently; they sell goods in a market and buy labor and raw materials in other markets and must therefore face the constraints of supply and demand and market competition.

The choice of technology, the need to expand production, and the organization of the work process are determined primarily by the structure of the market system, and only in small part by the particular characteristics of individual capitalists. A particularly greedy or insensitive capitalist may exacerbate the oppressive conditions of the workplace, for example, but he cannot alter the basic situation. Neither can a particularly kind and humane capitalist change matters. *Capitalists act as capitalists because, if they are to survive as capitalists, the market forces them to act that way.* For example, suppose a certain capitalist decided on his own to pay higher wages, not to introduce oppressive kinds of new technology, and to distribute the product to the community at a lower price. He would be suc-

cessful for a while, making smaller profits than other capitalists, but nonetheless remaining in business.

But sooner or later other capitalists would enter the scene. They would realize that they could make higher profits if they simply paid the market wage rate, not the higher rate that our "humane" capitalist voluntarily decided to pay. They would also realize that they could make higher profits if they were unafraid to introduce more efficient technology, which our "humane capitalist" refused to do because of the alienating characteristics of that technology. Finally, with the savings gained by paying lower wages and using more efficient technology, these new capitalists would realize that they could reduce the price even a bit further than the humane capitalist did, and still make profits. By doing so, they would underprice the "humane capitalist's" profits and drive his goods from the market.

Since he can no longer sell his products, the "humane capitalist" is now faced with a dilemma: either emulate the other capitalists, reduce wages, and introduce the new technology—in short, act as a "nonhumane" capitalist—or quit being a capitalist altogether. The conclusion is that no matter how much he might wish to act differently, if he is to remain a capitalist, he must act within the constraints set by competition in the market.[3] Marx described this process as follows:[4]

[3]Notice that only certain decisions are made by the market and that there is tremendous scope left in capitalists' hands for control of work. The capitalist decides what products to produce, who shall work for him, where and at what hours work shall be performed, when new factories shall be built, what the authority relations among the workers shall be, and so forth. The market merely places *constraints* on his options, requiring him, for example, to pay the market wage, to avoid inefficient technologies, to ignore ecological damage, etc. For an excellent historical discussion, see S. A. Marglin, "What Do Bosses Do? The Origins and Function of Hierarchy in Capitalist Production," *Review of Radical Political Economics*, July 1974.

[4]Karl Marx, *Wage Labour and Capital.*

The method of production and the means of production are constantly enlarged, revolutionized, division of labor necessarily draws after it greater division of labor, the employment of machinery greater employment of machinery, work upon a large scale work upon a still greater scale. This is the law that continually throws capitalist production out of its old ruts and compels capital to strain ever more the productive forces of labor for the very reason that it has already strained them—the law that grants it no respite, and constantly shouts in its ear, March! March! ...

No matter how powerful the means of production which a capitalist may bring into the field, competition will make their adoption general; and from the moment that they have been generally adopted; the sole result of the greater productiveness of his capital will be that he must furnish at the same price, *ten, twenty, one hundred times as much as before. But since he must find a market for, perhaps, a thousand times as much, in order to outweigh the lower selling price by the greater quantity of the sales; since now a more extensive sale is necessary not only to gain a greater profit, but also in order to replace the cost of production (the instrument of production itself grows always more costly, as we have seen), and since this more extensive sale has become a question of life and death not only for him, but also for his rivals, the old struggle must begin again, and it is all the more violent the more powerful the means of production already invented are.* The division of labor and the application of machinery will therefore take a fresh start, and upon an even greater scale.

Whatever be the power of the means of production which are employed, competition seeks to rob capital of the golden fruits of this power by reducing the price of commodities to the cost of production; in the same measure in which production is cheapened, i.e., in the same measure in which more can be produced with the same amount of labor, it compels by a law which is irresistible a still greater cheapening of production, the sale of ever greater masses of product for smaller prices. Thus the capitalist will have gained nothing more by his efforts than the obligation to furnish a greater product in the same labor time; in a word, more difficult conditions for the profitable employment of his capital. While competition, therefore, constantly pursues him with its law of the cost of production and turns against himself every weapon that he forges against his rivals, the capitalist continually seeks to get the best of competition by restlessly introducing further subdivision of labor and new machines, which, though more expensive, enable him to produce

more cheaply, instead of waiting until the new machines shall have been rendered obsolete by competition.

If we now conceive this feverish agitation as it operates in the market of the whole world, *we shall be in a position to comprehend how the growth, accumulation, and concentration of capital bring in their train an ever more detailed subdivision of labor, an ever greater improvement of old machines, and a constant application of new machines—a process which goes on uninterruptedly, with feverish haste, and upon on ever more gigantic scale.*

Thus, not only does the capitalist firm *want* to expand production and profits, it is *forced* to expand production and cut costs to *retain* profits. The firm cannot stand still. It must push on.

This pressure to keep up with the market and to maintain one's competitive position also induces firms to seek new products, entirely new markets, and new technologies. Often this search for new sources of profits is carried on within the domestic economy as new products are promoted by advertising, or old markets are entered by new firms. But since the motivation is simply realization of profits, capitalist firms have increasingly turned to the cultivation of foreign markets. So a powerful tendency towards geographic expansion and extension of market control on an international scale has likewise characterized capitalism.[5]

This dynamic competition, in addition to the more routine price competition Marx described, poses both opportunities and constant threats to all firms. According to Schumpeter:[6]

The essential point to grasp is that in dealing with capitalism we are dealing with an evolutionary process. . . . Capitalism is by nature a form or method of economic change and not only never is, but never can be stationary. And this evolutionary character of the capitalist process is not merely due to the fact that

[5]See MacEwan, Section 13.1, p. 481.

[6]Joseph Schumpeter, *Capitalism, Socialism and Democracy* (New York: Harper & Row Publishers, Inc., 1950), pp. 82–85.

economic life goes on in a social and natural environment which changes and by its change alters the data of economic action; this fact is important and these changes (wars, revolutions, and so on) often condition industrial changes, but they are not its prime movers. Nor is this evolutionary character due to a quasi-automatic increase in population and capital or to the vagaries of monetary systems of which exactly the same thing holds true. The fundamental impulse that sets and keeps the capitalist engine in motion comes from the new consumer goods, the new methods of production or transportation, the new markets, the new forms of industrial organization that capitalist enterprise creates. . . . In capitalist reality as distinguished from its textbook picture, it is not price competition or a small cost advantage which counts but the competition from the new commodity, the new technology, the new source of supply, the new type of organization (the largest-scale unit of control for instance)—competition which commands a decisive cost or quality advantage and which strikes not at the margins of the profits and the outputs of the existing firms but at their foundations and their very lives.

It is hardly necessary to point out that competition of the kind we now have in mind acts not only when in being but also when it is merely an ever-present threat. It disciplines before it attacks. The businessman feels himself to be in a competitive situation even if he is alone in his field or if, though not alone, he holds a position such that investigating government experts fail to see any effective competition between him and any other firms in the same or a neighboring field and in consequence conclude that his talk, under examination, about his competitive sorrows is all make-believe. In many cases, though not in all, this will in the long run enforce behavior very similar to the perfectly competitive pattern.

Most industries have become so concentrated that one or a few firms dominate the entire national industry. In the United States a few firms in each industry account for most of the market in automobile, steel, food processing, computers, oil, drugs, aviation, chemicals, and most other goods. In these industries collusion and price agreements among the large firms have largely eliminated price competition. But even the largest firms do not escape the market pressure for reducing costs, introducing more productive technologies, expanding one's market, in-

creasing profits, and repeating the whole cycle. Large firms face *international* competition from similarly large firms in other advanced countries. Likewise *nonprice* competition continues in both domestic and foreign markets.[7]

As we noted earlier, the firm only *realizes* profits by *selling* its products in a market. So the drive for greater profits leads inevitably to the drive to expand marketed output. In many industries, especially the more monopolistic ones, unlimited expansion of sales (and profits) may be ruled out, because demand has been satisfied as much as the profit criterion allows. However, if sales cannot be expanded, profits can nonetheless be increased by reducing costs; that is, by reducing the amount of labor and other inputs which the firm must buy. The resources released by reducing inputs are then available for production elsewhere. Likewise, if output cannot be profitably expanded in one's own market, this simply increases the incentive for the firm to enter new markets—either markets in different goods or geographically new markets. In either event, the result is the same: expanding profits directly or indirectly require and hence lead to the expansion of production.[8]

But output (and hence profits) are expanded only by reinvesting previous profits to make more profits. To this end, the firm will attempt to expand its factory or build a

[7]See Baran and Sweezy, Section 4.3, p. 134.

[8]In industries where only a few firms dominate the market, the prices are presumably set by an agreement among the firms at the level which they think will yield the greatest profits. Further expansion of sales would require reduction of the artificially high monopoly price, and if the price decline was large enough, would reduce profits. It is sometimes claimed that since in this case firms *restrict* output, the existence of monopoly refutes the tendency described in the text for capitalism to generate ever-greater output. But it should be clear that while output may be restricted in particular industries, the continuing incentive to reduce costs simply requires the expansion mechanism to operate indirectly and does not change the result.

new one, buy new and better machines, or do whatever it thinks best to increase output, capture a price advantage from its competitors, develop new markets, or invade new industries—all in the pursuit of turning its previously earned profits into more profits.

Now of course the capitalist firm will reinvest its profits only if it expects to get in return not only the amount reinvested but also a dividend, the interest on the capital, or put simply, more profits than it invested. Otherwise, there would be no reason for it to invest—it could as well put the money in a safe mattress.

Hence there is an ever-expanding volume of profits seeking opportunities for reinvestment. Every time profits are created, they must be reinvested. And reinvestment means precisely creating more output, reducing costs (thus freeing resources for employment elsewhere), and expanding profits. Then the cycle is repeated. This expanding volume of profits therefore impels the firm to look for new markets, search for new products to be produced, and create more output to sell.

This process ensures that production will become increasingly efficient or market-rationalized; i.e., the capitalists will produce whatever brings the highest market value using resources for which the capitalist had to pay the least. Hence a new technology is introduced, people are thrown out of work, transferred, etc. when the savings of inputs from the new method promises higher profits.

Both "internal" motivations and competitive market pressures drive the capitalist toward more profits. Capitalists therefore have the *motivation* to expand profits. With ownership and legal control of the means of production, they have the *power* required to institute and carry out this drive for expanded profits. Finally, their accumulated profits, their control over the social surplus, provides them with the material *resources* needed to expand production. *The capitalist has therefore gathered into his own hands all of the elements required for him, in his social role as production*

organizer, to structure and restructure the workplace to suit his drive for profits.

THE WORKER AS COMMODITY

The market in labor is an important link in this process of market-rationalizing production. The wage contract is viewed as a voluntary exchange of labor services for wages. The capitalist is then free to hire, fire, and reemploy workers at will and without regard for the social consequences. In medieval society, production was carried out with the workforce on the manor. The entire workforce—serfs, artisans, bailiffs, and lord—all shared the vicissitudes of the crops. They shared unequally, of course, the lord getting many times the portion due the serf. Yet no one was fired in bad times; each person had a claim to his "just" part of the product, and everyone had a right to participate in the tradition-determined organization of work.

In a labor market, however, the capitalist firm makes its decisions about whom to hire and how many to hire strictly on the basis of profitability. Labor is treated as a commodity like any other raw material required for production. The capitalist firm is not tied to its workers by traditional obligations, as the feudal lord was to his serf. The capitalist need not consider workers' lives or rights when choosing a work force. Hence the allocation of people among various jobs is determined by the market criterion of profitability. Each worker, as the commodity "labor," is assigned to that job where he has the highest productivity, for that employment will produce the greatest profit for the capitalist.

The size of the wage which a capitalist is willing to pay depends on how valuable a worker is to the firm—or more precisely, how much his work adds to the profits of the firm. For example, a skilled worker is more valuable than an unskilled worker. Consequently, when a skilled worker enters the labor market, capitalist firms will compete to hire him and will be willing to pay a higher wage.

Capitalists will bid against each other for workers, and will quit bidding when they perceive that the wage they pay the worker would be greater than the additional profits realized from his being hired. The winner in the bidding will be that capitalist who has organized production in the most profitable manner, hence who can offer the most "productive" (i.e., profitable) employment. Labor therefore tends to be "efficiently" allocated among various uses.

The individual worker is given tremendous incentive to obtain those skills which make him valuable to the production process. Most people own no wealth assets which could provide a large enough income to support them without working. Consequently, for survival, they must sell their labor power in the market. Since a worker's labor power will be more highly valued in the market if he has productive skills, the incentive is created for him to obtain those skills. The worker goes to school, learns vocational skills, learns to be a "respectful" and disciplined worker, and so forth, in the hopes that he can earn a higher wage.

The market allocation of labor thus directly reinforces the tendency towards expansion of output under capitalism. Greater production occurs because workers are assigned to their most productive employments and because workers themselves strive to become more productive to gain higher wages.

The major theme of this essay is perhaps best restated by Baran and Sweezy:[9]

> We have come a long way since the historical dawn of capitalist production and even since Karl Marx wrote Das Capital. Nowadays the avaricious capitalist, grasping for every penny and anxiously watching over his growing fortune, seems like a stereotype out of a nineteenth-century novel. The company man of today has a different attitude. To be sure, he likes to make as much money as he can, but he spends it freely, and the retirement benefits and other perquisites which he gets from his company enable him to take a rather casual attitude towards his personal savings. Noting the contrast between the modern businessman and his earlier counterpart, one might jump to the conclusion that the old drive has gone out of the system, that the classical picture of capitalism restlessly propelled forward by the engine of accumulation is simply inappropriate to the conditions of today.
>
> This is a superficial view. The real capitalist today is not the individual businessman but the corporation. What the businessman does in his private life, his attitude toward the getting and spending of his personal income—these are essentially irrelevant to the functioning of the system. What counts is what he does in his company life and his attitude toward the getting and spending of the company's income. And here there can be no doubt that the making and accumulating of profits hold as dominant a position today as they ever did. Over the portals of the magnificent office building of today, as on the wall of the modest counting house of a century or two ago, it would be equally appropriate to find engraved the motto: "Accumulate! Accumulate! That is Moses and the Prophets!"

[9]Baran and Sweezy, *Monopoly Capital* (Monthly Review Press, New York, 1966), pp. 43–44.

3.4 *The Circulation of Commodities*

Once the phase of capitalist production of commodities is completed, the next stage begins: the sale of those commodities for money, or the process of circulation of commodities. The act of circulation is not without problems for capitalists, as Rosa Luxemburg points out in the following reading.

In the first [stage of the analysis of capital-ism,] we are all the time at the point of pro-duction, in a factory, in a mine or in a modern agricultural undertaking, and what is said applies equally to all capitalist undertakings. We are given an individual example as the type of the whole capitalist mode of produc-tion. When we [complete this stage] we are thoroughly acquainted with the daily crea-tion of profit and with the whole mechanism of exploitation in all its details. Before us lie piles of commodities of all sorts still damp with the sweat of the workers as they come from the factories, and in all of them we can clearly discern that part of their value which results from the unpaid labour of the workers and which belongs just as equitably to the capitalist as the whole commodity. The root of capitalist exploitation is laid bare before our eyes.

However, at this stage the capitalist has his harvest by no means safely in the barn. The fruit of exploitation is present, but it is still in a form unsuitable for appropriation. So long as the fruit of exploitation takes the form of piled-up commodities the capitalist can derive but little pleasure from the pro-cess. He is not the slave-owner of the classical Græco-Roman world, or the feudal lord of the Middle Ages, who ground the faces of the working people merely to satisfy their craving for luxury and to maintain an im-posing retinue. In order to maintain him-self and his family "in a manner befitting his social station" the capitalist must have his riches in hard cash, and this is also necessary if he is to increase his capital ceaselessly. To this end therefore he must sell the commod-ities produced by the wage-workers together with the surplus-value contained in them. The commodities must leave the factory and the warehouse and be thrown on to the market. The capitalist follows his commod-ities from his warehouse and from his office into the stock exchange and into the shops, and . . . we follow the capitalist.

The second stage in the life of the capitalist is spent in the sphere of commodity exchange, and here he meets with a number of diffi-culties. In his own factory the capitalist is undisputed master, and strict organization and discipline prevail there, but on the com-modity market complete anarchy prevails under the name of free competition. On the commodity market no one bothers about his neighbour and no one bothers about the whole, but for all that it is precisely here that the capitalist feels his dependence on the others and on society as a whole.

The capitalist must keep abreast of his competitors. Should he take more time than absolutely necessary in selling his commod-ities, should he fail to provide himself with sufficient money to purchase raw materials and all the other things he needs at the right moment in order to prevent his factory coming to a standstill for lack of supplies, should he fail to invest promptly and profit-ably the money he receives for the sale of his commodities, he is bound to fall behind in one way or the other. The devil takes the hindmost, and the individual capitalist who fails to ensure that his business is managed as effectively in the constant exchange between the factory and the commodity market as it is in the factory itself will not succeed in obtaining the normal rate of profit no matter how zealously he may exploit his workers. A part of his "well-earned" profit will be lost somewhere on the way and will not find its way into his pocket.

However, this alone is not enough. The capitalist can accumulate riches only if he produces commodities, i.e. articles for use.

Further, he must produce precisely those kinds and sorts of commodities which society needs, and he must produce them in just the quantities required, otherwise his commodities will remain unsold and the surplus-value contained in them will be lost. How can the individual capitalist control all these factors? There is no one to tell him what commodities society needs and how many of them it needs, for the simple reason that no one knows. We are living in a planless, anarchic society, and each individual capitalist is in the same position. Nevertheless, out of this chaos, out of this confusion, a whole must result which will permit the individual business of the capitalist to prosper and at the same time satisfy the needs of society and permit its continued existence as a social organism.

To be more exact, out of the anarchic confusion of the commodity market must develop the possibility of the ceaseless circular movement of individual capital, the possibility of producing, selling, purchasing raw materials, etc., and producing again, whereby capital constantly changes from its money form into its commodity form and back again. These stages must dovetail accurately: money must be in reserve to utilize every favourable market opportunity for the purchase of raw materials, etc., and to meet the current expenses of production, and the money which comes flowing back as the commodities are sold must be given an opportunity of immediate utilization again. The individual capitalists, who are apparently quite independent of each other, now join together in fact and form a great brotherhood, and thanks to the credit system and the banks they continually advance each other the money they need and take up the available money so that the uninterrupted progress of production and the sale of commodities is ensured both for the individual capitalist and for society as a whole. . . . The credit system is a necessary part of capitalist life, the connecting link between two phases of capital, in production and on the commodity market,

and between the apparently arbitrary movements of individual capital.

And then the permanent circulation of production and consumption in society as a whole must be kept in movement in the confusion of individual capitals, and this must be done in such a fashion that the necessary conditions of capitalist production are assured: the production of the means of production, the maintenance of the working class and the progressive enrichment of the capitalist class, i.e. the increasing accumulation and activity of all the capital of society. . . .

[A] whole is developed from the innumerable deviating movements of individual capital; [but] this movement of the whole vacillates between the surplus of the boom years and the collapse of the crisis years, [and] is wrenched back again and again into correct proportions only to swing out of them again immediately. [Out] of all this there develops in ever more powerful dimensions that which is only a means for present-day society, its own maintenance and economic progress, and that which is its end, the progressive accumulation of capital. . . .

But even with this the capitalist has not completely traversed the thorny path before him, for although profit has been turned and is being turned in increasing measure into money, the great problem now arises of how to distribute the booty. Many different groups of capitalists put forward their demands. Apart from the employer there is the merchant, the loan capitalist and the landowner. Each of these has done his share to make possible the exploitation of the wage-worker and the sale of the commodities produced by the latter, and each now demands his share of the profit. This distribution of profit is a much more complicated affair than it might appear to be on the surface, for even amongst the employers themselves big differences exist, according to the type of undertaking, in the profits obtained, so to speak, fresh from the factory.

In one branch of production commodities

are produced and sold quickly, and capital plus the normal addition returns to the undertaking in a short space of time. Under such circumstances business and profits are made rapidly. In other branches of production capital is held fast in production for years and yields profit only after a long time. In some branches of production the employer must invest the greater part of his capital in lifeless means of production, in buildings, expensive machinery, etc., i.e. in things which yield no profit on their own account no matter how necessary they may be for profit-making. In other branches of production the employer need invest very little of his capital in such things and can use the greater part of it for the employment of workers, each of whom represents the industrious goose that lays the golden egg for the capitalist.

Thus in the process of profit-making big differences develop as between the individual capitalists, and in the eyes of bourgeois society these differences represent a much more urgent "injustice" than the peculiar "exchange" which takes place between the capitalist and the worker. The problem is to come to some arrangement which will ensure a "just" division of the spoils, whereby each capitalist gets "his share", and what is more, it is a problem which has to be solved without any conscious and systematic plan, because distribution in present-day society is as anarchic as production.

Afterword

The problem that Luxemburg raises in the last paragraph of this reading—namely, how is the total pool of capitalists' profits divided up among the individual capitalists, was addressed by John Gurley in Section 3.1. As Gurley pointed out, some part of the total surplus value is appropriated by banks and landowners in the form of interest and rent, the exact share being determined primarily by the relative strength of these different capitalist groups. The remaining surplus value—i.e., total profits—is then divided among individual capitalists by a competitive market mechanism. The profit rate on capital tends to be equalized across different sectors of the economy because differences in profit rates will cause capitalists to move their capital from low-profit to high-profit sectors.

3.5   Reproduction and the Capitalist State

As we have seen in this chapter, the capitalist mode of production is marked by fundamental conflicts between capitalists and workers. The continued reproduction of the capitalist mode of production requires that these conflicts do not seriously threaten existing class relationships. The first and most basic line of defense for existing class relationships is the enforcement of the existing set of private property relations. As Paul Sweezy argues in the following reading, this is the primary function of the capitalist state. Since the legal system lumps together personal possessions with income-producing property, one may get the impression that the state is acting on behalf of everybody when it defends private property. In fact, as Sweezy explains, the state is really acting on behalf of the dominant capitalist class.

The following is excerpted from *The Theory of Capitalist Development*, by PAUL M. SWEEZY (New York: Monthly Review Press, 1942), Chapter XIII. Copyright © 1942 by Paul M. Sweezy. Reprinted by permission of Monthly Review Press.

There is a tendency on the part of modern liberal theorists to interpret the state as an institution established in the interests of society as a whole for the purpose of mediating and reconciling the antagonisms to which social existence inevitably gives rise. This is a theory which avoids the pitfalls of political metaphysics and which serves to integrate in a tolerably satisfactory fashion a considerable body of observed fact. It contains, however, one basic shortcoming, the recognition of which leads to a theory essentially Marxian in its orientation. A critique of what may be called the class-mediation conception of the state is, therefore, perhaps the best way of introducing the Marxian theory.

The class-mediation theory assumes, usually implicitly, that the underlying class structure, or what comes to the same thing, the system of property relations is an immutable datum, in this respect like the order of nature itself. It then proceeds to ask what arrangements the various classes will make to get along with each other, and finds that an institution for mediating their conflicting interests is the logical and necessary answer. To this institution, powers for maintaining order and settling quarrels are granted. In the real world what is called the state is identified as the counterpart of this theoretical construction.

The weakness of this theory is not difficult to discover. It lies in the assumption of an immutable and, so to speak, self-maintaining class structure of society. The superficiality of this assumption is indicated by the most cursory study of history. The fact is that many forms of property relations with their concomitant class structures have come and gone in the past, and there is no reason to assume that they will not continue to do so in the future. The class structure of society is no part of the natural order of things; it is the product of past social development, and it will change in the course of future social development.

Once this is recognized it becomes clear that the liberal theory goes wrong in the manner in which it initially poses the problem. We cannot ask: Given a certain class structure, how will the various classes, with their divergent and often conflicting interests, manage to get along together? We must ask: How did a particular class structure come into being and by what means is its continued existence guaranteed? As soon as an attempt is made to answer this question, it appears that the state has a function in society which is prior to and more fundamental than any which present-day liberals attribute to it. Let us examine this more closely.

A given set of property relations serves to define and demarcate the class structure of society. From any set of property relations one class or classes (the owners) reap material advantages; other classes (the owned and the non-owners) suffer material disadvantages. A special institution capable and willing to use force to whatever degree is required is an essential to the maintenance of such a set of property relations. Investigation shows that the state possesses this characteristic to the fullest degree, and that no other institution is or can be allowed to compete with it in this respect. This is usually expressed by saying that the state, and the state alone, exercises sovereignty over all those subject to its jurisdiction. It is, therefore, not difficult to identify the state as the guarantor of a given set of property relations.

If now we ask where the state comes from, the answer is that it is the product of a long and arduous struggle in which the class which occupies what is for the time the key positions in the process of production gets the upper hand over its rivals and fashions a state which will enforce that set of property relations which is in its own interest. In other words any particular state is the child of the class or classes in society which benefit from the particular set of property relations which it is the state's obligation to enforce. A moment's reflection will carry the conviction that it could hardly be otherwise. As soon as we have dropped the historically untenable assumption that the class structure of society is in some way natural or self-enforcing, it is clear that any other outcome would lack the prerequisites of stability. If the disadvantaged classes were in possession of state power, they would attempt to use it to establish a social order more favorable to their own interests, while a sharing of state power among the various classes would merely shift the locale of conflict to the state itself.

That such conflicts within the state, corresponding to fundamental class struggles outside, have taken place in certain transitional historical periods is not denied. During those long periods, however, when a certain social order enjoys a relatively continuous and stable existence, the state power must be monopolized by the class or classes which are the chief beneficiaries.

As against the class-mediation theory of the state, we have here the underlying idea of what has been called the class-domination theory. The former takes the existence of a certain class structure for granted and sees in the state an institution for reconciling the conflicting interests of the various classes; the latter, on the other hand, recognizes that classes are the product of historical development and sees in the state an instrument in the hands of the ruling classes for enforcing and guaranteeing the stability of the class itself.

It is important to realize that, so far as capitalist society is concerned, "class domi-

nation" and "the protection of private property" are virtually synonymous expressions. Hence when we say with Engels that the highest purpose of the state is the protection of private property, we are also saying that the state is an instrument of class domination. This is doubtless insufficiently realized by critics of the Marxian theory who tend to see in the notion of class domination something darker and more sinister than "mere" protection of private property. In other words they tend to look upon class domination as something reprehensible and the protection of private property as something meritorious. Consequently, it does not occur to them to identify the two ideas. Frequently, no doubt, this is because they have in mind not capitalist property, but rather private property as it would be in a simple commodity-producing society where each producer owns and works with his own means of production. Under such conditions there are no classes at all and hence no class domination. Under capitalist relations, however, property has an altogether different significance, and its protection is easily shown to be identical with the preservation of class dominance. Capitalist private property does not consist in things—things exist independently of their ownership—but in a social relation between people. Property confers upon its owners freedom from labor and the disposal over the labor of others, and this is the essence of all social domination whatever form it may assume. It follows that the protection of property is fundamentally the assurance of social domination to owners over nonowners. And this, in turn, is precisely what is meant by class domination, which it is the primary function of the state to uphold.

The recognition that the defense of private property is the first duty of the state is the decisive factor in determining the attitude of genuine Marxist socialism towards the state. "The theory of the Communists," Marx and Engels wrote in the *Communist Manifesto*, "can be summed up in the single sentence: Abolition of private property." Since the state is first and foremost the protector of private property, it follows that the realization of this end cannot be achieved without a head-on collision between the forces of socialism and the state power.

3.6   *Reproduction of Labor Power: The Family*

The capitalist mode of production, as we have seen, not only continually expands and reproduces capital but also expands and reproduces the working class. This expanded reproduction of capital and labor occurs in part without external regulation: the flow of surplus value and the reinvestment of a part of this revenue expands capital, while the flow of wages and salaries to workers provides part of the means for labor to reproduce itself. An additional portion of labor's reproduction is provided by the wageless labor of the working class itself. This wageless labor is done primarily by women doing housework and child care, and reflects the ability of sexism also to reproduce itself within the capitalist mode of production.[1]

But more than material commodities and additional labor time is required for the reproduction of workers who will be suitable for capitalist production. A particular type of "socialization" is needed; this socialization is carried on largely in the family and the schools, but also by the media and various cultural institutions. In the following reading Peggy Morton examines how the family operates as one of these reproductive institutions.

[1]See Chapter 9.

The following is excerpted from "A Woman's Work is Never Done" by PEGGY MORTON. From *Leviathan*, 2, No. 1 (March 1970). Reprinted by permission of the author.

There has been a great deal of debate over the past few years about the function of the family in capitalist society. Discussion has generally focused on the role of the family as the primary unit of socialization; the family is the basic unit in which authoritarian personality structures are formed, particularly the development of authoritarian relationships between parents and children and between men and women: the family is necessary to the maintenance of sexual repression in that sexuality is allowed legitimate expression only in marriage; through the family men can give vent to feelings of frustration, anger and resentment that are the products of alienated labor, and can act out the powerlessness which they experience in work by dominating the other members of the family; and within the family little girls learn what is expected of them and how they should act.

. . .

[How has] the family developed in different stages of capitalism as the requirements for the maintenance and production of labor power change? The essence of the position I want to argue in this paper is as follows. . . . The family is a unit whose function is the *maintenance of and reproduction of labor power*, i.e., that the structure of the family is determined by the needs of the economic system, at any given time, for a certain kind of labor power. . . .

By "reproduction of labor power" we

mean simply that the task of the family is to maintain the present work force and provide the next generation of workers, fitted with the skills and values necessary for them to be productive members of the work force. When we talk about the evolution of the family under capitalism, we have to understand both the changes in the family among the proletariat, and the changes that come from the increasing proletarianization of the labor force, and the urbanization of the society.

The pre-capitalist family functioned (as does the farm family in capitalist society) as an integrated economic unit; men, women and children took part in production work in the fields, the cottage industry and production for the use of the family. There was a division of labor between men and women, but a division within an integrated unit. There was much brutality in the old system (the oppression of women, harsh ideas about child-raising, and a culture that reflected the limitations of peasant life) but the family also served as a structure for the expression and fulfillment of simple human emotional needs.

THE FAMILY IN THE FIRST STAGES OF CAPITALISM

For those who became the urban proletariat, this was all ruthlessly swept away with the coming of factories. The function of the family was reduced to the most primitive level; instead of skilled artisans, the factories required only a steady flow of workers with little or no training, who learned what they needed on the job, and who could easily be replaced. Numbers were all that mattered and the conditions under which people lived were irrelevant to the needs of capital. The labor of women and children took on a new importance.

The result was a drastic increase in the exploitation of child labor (in Britain, in the period 1780–1840). Even small children worked 12–18 hour days, death from over-

work was common, and despite a series of Factory Acts which made provisions for the education of child labourers, the education was almost always mythical—when teachers were provided, they themselves were often illiterate. The report on Public Health, London, 1864, documents that in industrial districts, infant mortality was as high as one death in four in the first year of life, as compared to one in ten in non-industrial districts. As many as half the children died in the first five years of life in the industrial slums—not because of a lack of medical knowledge but because of the conditions under which the urban proletariat were forced to live. Girls who had worked in the mills since early childhood had a characteristic deformation of the pelvic bones which made for difficult births; women worked until the last week of pregnancy and would return to the mills soon after giving birth for fear of losing their jobs; children were left with those too young or too old to work, were given opiates to quiet them, and often died from malnutrition resulting from the absence of the mother and the lack of suitable food.

> *On what foundation is the present family, the bourgeois family, based? On capital, or private gain. In its completely developed form this family exists only among the bourgeoisie. But this state of things finds its complement in the practical absence of the family among the proletarians, and in public prostitution. . . . The bourgeois clap-trap about the family and education, about the hallowed correlation of parent and child, become all the more disgusting, the more, by the action of Modern Industry, all family ties among the proletarians are torn asunder and their children transformed into simple articles of commerce and instruments of labour.* (The Communist Manifesto)

The need of capitalism in the stage of primitive accumulation of capital for a steady flow of cheap and unskilled labor primarily determined the structure of the family. In contrast, the prevailing ideology was used in turn to prepare the working class for the new drudgery. The repressive Victorian morality, brought to the working class through the

Wesleyan sects, clamped down harder on the freedom of women, and perpetrated the ideology of hard work and discipline. The Victorian concept of the family was both a reflection of the bourgeois family, based on private property, and an ideal representing a status to which the proletarian would like to rise.

Colonized nations within imperialist nations have experienced this destruction of the family almost permanently. During slavery, the black family was systematically broken up and destroyed. Because black people have been used as a reserve army of unskilled labor, there has been no need for a family structure that would ensure that the children received education and skills. And direct oppression and repression (racism) eliminated the need for more subtle social control through the socialization process in the family. Often the women were the breadwinners because they were the only ones who could find jobs, and when there were no jobs the welfare system further discouraged the maintenance of the family by making it more difficult to get welfare if the man was around. The bourgeois family has never existed for the black colony; instead children were seen not as individual property but as belonging to the whole community.

For white North Americans, the family developed differently for those who first settled the continent and for industrial workers. "Frontier life" required the family in an even stronger form than in Europe, because all members of the family had to function as a production unit in the backbreaking work of clearing land, ploughing and harvesting. At the same time, the need for co-operation between family units meant that a strong community developed. For industrial workers, conditions were similar to those of Europe in the early stages of capitalism, i.e., the family system was weakened by the employment of all members of the family in the mines and the mills.

The evolution of the family is affected both by the proletarianization of the work force

engaged in agriculture and resulting urbanization, and by changes in the kind of labor power required which changed the form of the family among the proletariat itself.

The constant need of each capitalist to increase the productivity of his enterprise in order to remain competitive was secured both by increasing the level of exploitation of the workers and by the continual introduction of new, more complex and more efficient machinery. Thus a new kind of worker was required as the production process became more complex—workers who could read instructions and blueprints, equipped with skills that required considerable training. As the need for skilled labor increases the labor of women and children tends to be replaced by that of men—workers involve a capital investment and therefore it makes more sense to employ those who can work steadily throughout their lives.

At the same time, the growth of trade unions and the increasing revolutionary consciousness of the working class forced the ruling class to meet some of their demands or face full-scale revolt. The rise in material standards of living accommodated both the need to restrain militancy, to provide a standard of living that would allow for the education of children as skilled workers, and the need for consumers to provide new markets for the goods produced. The abolition of child labor and the introduction of compulsory education were compelled by the need for a skilled labor force.

REPRODUCTION OF LABOR POWER IN ADVANCED CAPITALISM

The transformation in the costs of educating and training the new generation of workers is fundamental to the changes that have taken place and are still taking place in the family structure. A fundamental law of capitalism is the need for constant expansion. Automation is required for the survival of the system. Workers are needed who are not only highly skilled but who have been trained to learn new skills. Profits depend more and more on the efficient organization of work and on the "self-discipline" of the workers rather than simply on speed-ups and other direct forms of increasing the exploitation of the workers. The family is therefore important both to shoulder the burden of the costs of education, and to carry out the repressive socialization of children. The family must raise children who have internalized hierarchical social relations, who will discipline themselves and work efficiently without constant supervision. The family also serves to repress the natural sexuality of its members —an essential process if people are to work at jobs which turn them into machines for eight or more hours a day. Women are responsible for implementing most of this socialization.

MONOPOLY CAPITALISM IN THE UNITED STATES

Capital Accumulation and the Capitalist Class

IN PART II OF THIS BOOK we presented a theory of the capitalist mode of production and of capitalism as a type of society. In Part III, we will investigate monopoly capitalism in the United States, so the material contained in these chapters is both more narrowly focused and more concrete than what has gone before.

In contrast to the general and theoretical approach taken in Part II, here we concentrate on the present phase of capitalism, which has been termed *monopoly capitalism*.[1] Monopoly capitalism developed out of the preceding stage of capitalism ("competitive capitalism") with the emergence in the advanced capitalist countries of huge agglomerations of capital. These immense concentrations took various forms as corporations, trusts, cartels, financial groups, conglomerates, and multinationals. Our emphasis here is on the significance of the shift from competitive to monopoly capitalism for understanding our society.

The rise of these large units of capital in no way altered the basic "laws of motion" of capitalism—its tendency toward expansion and accumulation, its cyclical and crisis-plagued progress, its reproduction of opposing social classes, and so on. These fundamental impulses characterize monopoly capitalism as well as earlier stages of capitalism. But the existence of large concentrations of capital does affect the relative strengths of the forces within capitalism, and thereby also influences the way in which capitalist society develops. Most importantly, in the sphere of circulation, the activities of these giants have transcended and transformed competitive markets, and in the sphere of production, they have reorganized the labor process. And in their relations with the state and with smaller capitalists, the large capitalists have emerged dominant.

Our analysis in this Part, then, considers capitalism in its latest stage in which capital has become highly concentrated and centralized; we investigate this development and its consequences for capital accumulation, for the labor process, for the formation of classes, and for the state. We confine our attention to the evolution of capitalism in the United States; in Chapters 12 and 13 we again pick up the perspective of capitalism as a worldwide system which we established in Part II.

In this chapter we analyze the accumulation process in monopoly capitalism and its relation to the U.S. capitalist class. We trace the evolution and growth of corporations as institutional mechanisms for accumulation and reinvestment, the demise of competition and the rise of monopoly, the difficulty capitalists as a group have in finding sufficient markets for their goods, and finally the impact of accumulation on the formation and reproduction of capitalists as a class.

---

[1]Unless specifically noted, "monopoly" and "monopolistic" are used throughout this book to refer to both monopoly and oligopoly situations (i.e., markets in which sellers have considerable discretionary market power) and not just to single-seller markets.

CORPORATIONS IN THE ACCUMULATION PROCESS

The conditions under which capital accumulation occurs have in some ways changed greatly since the nineteenth century. Then, production typically took place in small family businesses. But the period since the turn of the century has been characterized by the rise of giant corporations—firms like General Motors, IBM, AT&T, General Electric, and so on. The necessary complement to their growth, less apparent to us now because they no longer exist, was the failure of millions of unsuccessful smaller firms. In most major industries, a few huge firms by themselves account for the bulk of economic activity. The large corporations as a group dominate the American economy and are rapidly expanding, alongside giant European and Japanese firms, in the world capitalist economy. This increase in the size of firms and the increasing power of the surviving giants is a systematic consequence of the capitalist accumulation process.

In place of the individual capitalist tycoons who dominated the nineteenth century, in our own time big corporations reign supreme as the chief "capital-accumulators." As Paul Baran and Paul Sweezy have pointed out,

> The real capitalist today is not the individual businessman but the corporation. . . . The giant corporation of today is an engine for maximizing profits and accumulating capital to at least as great an extent as the individual enterprise of an earlier period. But it is not merely an enlarged and institutionalized version of the personal capitalist. There are major differences between these types of business enterprise, and at least two of them are of key importance to a general theory of monopoly capitalism: the corporation has a longer time horizon than the individual capitalist, and it is a more rational calculator.[2]

Even the giant corporations themselves sometimes turn out to be but building blocks in still more colossal units of capital. Bankers

[2]Paul Baran and Paul Sweezy, *Monopoly Capital* (New York: Monthly Review Press, 1966) p. 47.

and other capitalists operating through financial institutions are often able to gain control over several corporations, creating a "financial group." In these cases the resources centralized into one still privately owned "interest" are truly fantastic.

At the same time that successful corporations have grown large, they have succeeded in eliminating much of the competition they had earlier faced in the markets for their commodities. For example, General Motors, Ford, and Chrysler were able to drive Studebaker, Packard, Kaiser, and hundreds of other firms out of the automobile business. The result is a situation in which the predominant market structure is not competitive but rather monopolistic—or what might more accurately be described as monopolistically competitive: that is, competition continues, but it is competition only among the few remaining giant firms and it is restricted to certain forms of competitive behavior.

Declining competition in product markets creates a greater chance for large firms to achieve higher profit rates than they would otherwise have. If firms can use their monopoly power to raise prices higher than would have existed if the industry had been competitive, they can earn "monopoly profits." Large firms are thus likely to have not only larger profits than smaller firms, but profits that are more than proportionately larger. These higher profit *rates* then become the basis for the large firms' more rapid growth, and the disparity between them and smaller firms increases.

The declining competition in product markets also has implications beyond the particular industries involved. A firm in any industry may find new customers either because industrywide demand grows or because the firm is able to lure buyers away from other firms. Where many firms populate an industry, each firm tries to grow not only as the industry's market grows but perhaps more importantly, given the market, by underpricing other firms. Because each firm is a small part of a large market, it assumes that its behavior will have little effect on the

TABLE 4-A NATIONAL INCOME AND EMPLOYEES BY SECTOR, 1974

	Value Added During Production, in Billions of Dollars	Percent of National Income	Millions of Workers	Percent of Total Workers
Monopolistic industries	$ 453	40%	29	33%
Competitive industries	362	32	34	39
Industries not classified	139	12	5	6
Government	178	16	14	16
Unemployed	–	–	5	6
	$1,132	100%	87	100%

SOURCES: Industries classified according to William Shepherd, *Market Power and Economic Welfare* (New York: Random House, 1970), Appendix 14; data calculated from *Statistical Abstract of the United States* (Washington, D.C.: U.S. Government Printing Office, 1975), pp. 343, 357–58, 387.

overall market; in this case, the market itself determines the outcome. But where only a few firms co-exist in an industry, they all realize that a price war would likely result in lower prices and profits for everyone. In part this obvious interdependence among firms reinforces for each firm the incentive to advertise in order to boost demand for the industry's product; in part it increases the pressure for each firm to advertise so as to defend or expand its sales relative to the other firms.

Monopolistic competition thereby circumscribes the role of the market in establishing the price and simultaneously introduces new costs (the costs of an expanded sales effort) into the firm's operations. More importantly, monopolistic competition typically limits each firm's growth to its share of the growth in the industry's overall market. While these firms are thereby inhibited from expanding rapidly in their own industries, their high profits impel them to seek new areas for profitable reinvestment. The result is a strong impulse on the part of large firms to enter different industries, to develop new products, and to invade foreign markets.[3]

Nonetheless, while big business dominates American production, it does not exhaust it. Typically each industry contains, along with a few large, expanding firms, some small, eco-

nomically insecure firms which survive only in a subservient role to the big firms. Suppliers of parts to the big automobile manufacturers and makers of specialty tools for industry are typical cases of small firms dependent on large ones. Small, competitive firms also retain their importance in wholesale and retail trade, in the provision of most services, in agriculture, and in certain other industries. Since smaller firms usually cannot afford large amounts of capital per worker, productivity in the competitive sector lags behind the monopoly sector. As a result, competitive firms are more important in the economy as employers than would be suggested by their percentage of total production. Table 4-A gives a rough estimate of the relative sizes of the two sectors. Our analysis of the accumulation process in present-day United States must also include, then, an understanding of the relations *between* big and small business.

American corporations must also operate in the context of the world economy. During most of the post–World War II period these firms have been able to expand in their overseas markets rapidly while facing little threat to their home markets from foreign producers. Foreign profits became an increasingly important part of U.S. corporate earnings. But beginning with the invasion of Volkswagens and Japanese transitor radios in the late 1950s, large European and Japanese corporations have not only competed vigorously for their home markets but have increasingly

[3]This point is further developed in MacEwan, Section 13.1, p. 481.

challenged American firms in U.S. markets. In textiles, chemicals, oil, steel, autos, and countless other products foreign capitalists have either greatly increased their exports to the U.S. or have gone a step further and opened up production facilities in the U.S. Especially since the early 1970s this rising international competition has tended to diminish the market power of domestic monopolistic corporations in the U.S. at the same time that the multinationals—both American and foreign—have increased their market power in the world economy.

CAPITALISTS AND THE ACCUMULATION PROCESS

While large corporations have become the chief institutional mechanisms for accumulation in monopoly capitalism, behind them stand people—the owners. These are the people who benefit from corporate activities, and it is to them that we now turn our attention. After all, corporations and markets are merely ways of organizing particular social relationships, and these relationships ultimately exist between people, not institutions. For example, the accumulation process results in the payment of wages, profits, rent, and so on, thereby laying the basis for the different levels of consumption that are available to various classes in society.

Moreover, an emphasis on institutions obscures the fact that from time to time continued accumulation requires that more conscious and coordinated action be taken. For example, the Great Depression made "business as usual" impossible, and to resuscitate the system, the functions of government had to be greatly expanded; in the 1930s major reforms necessary for continued accumulation emerged (in part) out of collective action by capitalists. Similarly, in the opening decades of this century an emerging anti-capitalist movement among workers challenged the system itself; to defend capitalism, employers worked out a coordinated policy stressing repression, union-busting, and welfare policies. More recently, the partial nationalization of the railroads reflects a third case in which collective action was required, that is, where the interests of individual railroad capitalists had to yield to those of the capitalist class as a whole.

In all these cases, the normal operations of corporations and markets was seen as insufficient to reproduce the conditions for accumulation. Instead, capitalists as a group took more coordinated action in defense of their shared interests; that is, they acted as a *class*, defending their class interests.

On the other hand, as we shall see in the next chapter, accumulation has reduced most other people in society to wage-labor (employee) status. The capitalist class has thereby created a far larger class, antagonistic in its interests and potentially more powerful as an adversary. In Chapter 6 we will investigate the clash of these conflicting classes.

4.1   *The Evolution of the Corporation*

In every stage of capitalism there have been some small, some medium-sized, and some large firms. Moreover, there are always more small firms than big ones; in the United States in 1972, there were nearly 13 million firms, but only about 3,000 of these had assets in excess of $100 million.[1]

On the other hand, the kind of firm in which the bulk of economic activity occurs—the "representative" firm—has changed over time. In the nine-

[1]*Statistical Abstract of the United States*, 1975, pp. 490, 497.

teenth century, most production took place in quite small firms—what in the following reading are termed "Marshallian" firms (after the famous economist Alfred Marshall, who made this type of firm the basic unit of his theory). But with the transition to monopoly capitalism, the giant corporation has come to dominate the U.S. economy. Small firms have either been relegated to a strictly subsidiary role as "satellites" to big firms (e.g., auto parts suppliers at the mercy of the big auto companies) or continue only in relatively unimportant or stagnant industries.

In the following reading Stephen Hymer traces the evolution of the representative firm from its beginnings as a small workshop to its current status as an international corporation.

This reading is excerpted from "The Multinational Corporation and the Law of Uneven Development" by STEPHEN HYMER. From *Economics and World Order*, edited by Jagdish Bhagwati. Copyright © 1972 by the Macmillan Company. Reprinted by permission of the Macmillan Company.

Since the beginning of the Industrial Revolution, there has been a tendency for the representative firm to increase in size from the *workshop* to the *factory* to the *national corporation* to the *multidivisional corporation* and now to the *multinational corporation*. This growth has been qualitative as well as quantitative. With each step business enterprise acquired a more complex administrative structure to coordinate its activities and a larger brain to plan for its survival and growth. . . . This essay traces the evolution of the corporation, stressing the development of a hierarchical system of authority and control.

· · ·

THE MARSHALLIAN FIRM AND THE MARKET ECONOMY

Giant organizations are nothing new in international trade. They were a characteristic form of the mercantilist period when large joint-stock companies, e.g., The Hudson's Bay Co., The Royal African Co., The East India Co., to name the major English merchant firms, organized long-distance trade with America, Africa and Asia. But neither these firms, nor the large mining and plantation enterprises in the production sector, were the forerunners of the multinational corporation. They were like dinosaurs, large in bulk, but small in brain, feeding on the lush vegetation of the new worlds (the planters and miners in America were literally *Tyrannosaurus rex*).

The merchants, planters and miners laid the groundwork for the Industrial Revolution, but the driving force came from the small-scale capitalist enterprises in manufacturing, operating at first in the interstices of the feudalist economic structure, but gradually emerging into the open and finally gaining predominance. It is in the small workshops, organized by the newly emerging capitalist class, that the forerunners of the modern corporation are to be found.

The strength of this new form of business enterprise lay in its power and ability to reap the benefits of division of labor. Without the capitalist, economic activity was individualistic, small-scale, scattered and unproductive. But a man with capital, i.e., with sufficient funds to buy raw materials and advance wages, could gather a number of people into a single shop and obtain as his reward the increased productivity that resulted from specialization and cooperation. The reinvestment of these profits led to a steady increase in the size of capital, making further division of labor possible, and creating an opportunity for using machinery in production. A phenomenal increase in productivity and production resulted from this process, and entirely new dimensions of human existence were opened. The growth of capital revolutionized the entire world and, figuratively speaking, even battered down the Great Walls of China.

The hallmarks of the new system were *the market* and *the factory*, representing the two different methods of coordinating the division of labor. In the factory, entrepreneurs consciously plan and organize cooperation, and the relationships are hierarchical and authoritarian; in the market, coordination is achieved through a decentralized, unconscious, competitive process.

To understand the significance of this distinction, the new system should be compared to the structure it replaced. In the pre-capitalist system of production, the division of labor was hierarchically structured at the *macro* level, i.e., for society as a whole, but unconsciously structured at the *micro* level, i.e., the actual process of production. Society as a whole was partitioned into various castes, classes and guilds, on a rigid and authoritarian basis so that political and social stability could be maintained and adequate numbers assured for each industry and occupation. Within each sphere of production, however, individuals by and large were independent and their activities only loosely coordinated, if at all. In essence, a guild was composed of a large number of similar individuals, each performing the same task in roughly the same way with little cooperation or division of labor. This type of organization could produce high standards of quality and workmanship but was limited quantitatively to low levels of output per head.

The capitalist system of production turned this structure on its head. The macro system became unconsciously structured, while the micro system became hierarchically structured. The market emerged as a self-regulating coordinator of business units as restrictions on capital markets and labor mobility were removed. (Of course the state remained above the market as a conscious coordinator

to maintain the system and ensure the growth of capital.) At the micro level, that is, the level of production, labor was gathered under the authority of the entrepreneur capitalist.

Marshall, like Marx, stressed that the internal division of labor within the factory, between those who planned and those who worked (between "undertakers" and laborers), was "the chief fact in the form of modern civilization, the 'kernel' of the modern economic problem."[1] Marx, however, stressed the authoritarian and unequal nature of this relationship based on the coercive power of property and its anti-social characteristics. He focused on the irony that concentration of wealth in the hands of a few and its ruthless use were necessary historically to demonstrate the value of cooperation and the social nature of production.[2]

. . .

THE CORPORATE ECONOMY

The evolution of business enterprise from the small workshop (Adam Smith's pin factory) to the Marshallian family firm represented only the first step in the development of business organization. As total capital accumulated, the size of the individual concentrations composing it increased continuously, and the vertical division of labor grew accordingly.

It is best to study the evolution of the corporate form in the United States environment, where it has reached its highest stage. In the 1870s, the United States industrial structure consisted largely of Marshallian type, single-function firms, scattered over the country. Business firms were typically tightly controlled by a single entrepreneur or small family group who, as it were, saw everything, knew everything, and decided everything. By

[1]Alfred Marshall, *Principles of Economics*, 8th ed. (London: Macmillan, 1920), p. 75.

[2]Karl Marx, *Capital*, vol. I (Moscow: Foreign Language Publishing House, 1961), p. 356.

the early twentieth century, the rapid growth of the economy and the great merger movement had consolidated many small enterprises into large national corporations engaged in many functions over many regions. To meet this new strategy of continent-wide, vertically integrated production and marketing, a new administrative structure evolved. The family firm, tightly controlled by a few men in close touch with all its aspects, gave way to the administrative pyramid of the corporation. Capital obtained new powers and new horizons. The domain of conscious coordination widened, and that of market-directed division of labor contracted.

According to Chandler[3] the railroad, which played so important a role in creating the national market, also offered a model for new forms of business organization. The need to administer geographically dispersed operations led railway companies to create an administrative structure which distinguished field offices from head offices. The field offices managed local operations; the head office supervised the field offices. According to Chandler and Redlich, this distinction is important because "it implies that the executive responsible for a firm's affairs had, for the first time, to supervise the work of other executives."[4]

This first step towards increased vertical division of labor within the management function was quickly copied by the recently formed national corporations, which faced the same problems of coordinating widely scattered plants. Business developed an organ system of administration, and the modern corporation was born. The functions of business administration were subdivided into *departments* (organs)—finance, personnel, purchasing, engineering, and sales—to deal with capital, labor, purchasing, manufactur-

ing, etc. This horizontal division of labor opened up new possibilities for rationalizing production and for incorporating the advances of physical and social sciences into economic activity on a systematic basis. At the same time a brain and nervous system, i.e., a vertical system of control, had to be devised to connect and coordinate departments. This was a major advance in decision-making capabilities. It meant that a special group, the Head Office, was created whose particular function was to coordinate, appraise, and plan for the survival and growth of the organism as a whole. The organization became conscious of itself as organization and gained a certain measure of control over its own evolution and development.

The corporation soon underwent further evolution. To understand this next step we must briefly discuss the development of the United States market. At the risk of great oversimplification we might say that by the first decade of the twentieth century, the problem of production had essentially been solved. By the end of the nineteenth century, scientists and engineers had developed most of the inventions needed for mass producing at low cost nearly all the main items of basic consumption. In the language of systems analysis, the problem became one of putting together the available components in an organized fashion. The national corporation provided *one* organizational solution, and by the 1920s it had demonstrated its great power to increase material production.

· · ·

[But] the uneven growth of per capita income [that characterized economic development under capitalism] implied unbalanced growth and the need on the part of business to adapt to a constantly changing composition of output. Firms in the producers' goods sectors had continuously to innovate labor-saving machinery because the capital/output ratio was increasing steadily. In the consumption goods sector, firms had to continuously introduce new products since, according to Engel's Law, people do not generally consume proportionately more of

[3]Alfred D. Chandler, *Strategy and Structure* (New York: Doubleday & Co., 1961).

[4]Alfred D. Chandler and Fritz Redlich, "Recent Developments in American Business Administration and Their Conceptualization," *Business History Review*, Spring, 1961, pp. 103–28.

the same things as they get richer, but rather reallocate their consumption away from old goods and towards new goods. This non-proportional growth of demand implied that goods would tend to go through a life-cycle, growing rapidly when they were first introduced and more slowly later. If a particular firm were tied to only one product, its growth rate would follow this same life-cycle pattern and would eventually slow down and perhaps even come to a halt. If the corporation was to grow steadily at a rapid rate, it had continuously to introduce new products.

Thus, product development and marketing replaced production as a dominant problem of business enterprise. To meet the challenge of a constantly changing market, business enterprise evolved the multidivisional structure. The new form was originated by General Motors and DuPont shortly after World War I, followed by a few others during the 1920s and 1930s, and was widely adopted by most of the giant U.S. corporations in the great boom following World War II. As with the previous stages, evolution involved a process of both differentiation and integration. Corporations were decentralized into several *divisions*, each concerned with one product line and organized with its own head office. At a higher level, a *general office* was created to coordinate the divisions and to plan for the enterprise as a whole.

The new corporate form has great flexibility. Because of its decentralized structure, a multidivisional corporation can enter a new market by adding a new division while leaving the old divisions undisturbed. (And to a lesser extent it can leave the market by dropping a division without disturbing the rest of its structure.) It can also create competing product-lines in the same industry, thus increasing its market share while maintaining the illusion of competition. Most important of all, because it has a cortex specializing in strategy, it can plan on a much wider scale than before and allocate capital with more precision.

The modern corporation is a far cry from the small workshop, or even from the Marshallian firm. The Marshallian capitalist ruled his factory from an office on the second floor. At the turn of the century, the president of a large national corporation was lodged in a higher building, perhaps on the seventh floor, with greater perspective and power. In today's giant corporation, managers rule from the top of skyscrapers; on a clear day, they can almost see the world.

U.S. corporations began to move to foreign countries almost as soon as they had completed their continent-wide integration. For one thing, their new administrative structure and great financial strength gave them the power to go abroad. In becoming national firms, U.S. corporations learned how to become international. Also, their large size and oligopolistic position gave them an incentive. Direct investment became a new weapon in their arsenal of oligopolistic rivalry. Instead of joining a cartel (prohibited under U.S. law), they invested in foreign customers, suppliers and competitors. For example, some firms found they were oligopolistic buyers of raw materials produced in foreign countries and feared a monopolization of the sources of supply. By investing directly in foreign producing enterprises, they could gain the security implicit in control over their raw material requirements. Other firms invested abroad to control marketing outlets and thus maximize quasi rents on their technological discoveries and differentiated products. Some went abroad simply to forestall competition.

The first wave of U.S. direct foreign capital investment occurred around the turn of the century, followed by a second wave during the 1920s. The outward migration slowed down during the depression but resumed after World War II and soon accelerated rapidly. Between 1950 and 1969, direct foreign investment by U.S. firms expanded at a rate of about 10 percent per annum. At this rate it would double in less than 10 years, and even at a much slower rate of growth, foreign operations will reach enormous proportions over the next 30 years.

Several important factors account for this rush of foreign investment in the 1950s and the 1960s. First, the large size of the U.S. corporations and their new multidivisional structure gave them wider horizons and a global outlook. Secondly, technological developments in communications created a new awareness of the global challenge and threatened established institutions by opening up new sources of competition. For reasons noted above, business enterprises were the first to recognize the potentialities and dangers of the new environment and to take active steps to cope with it.

A third factor in the outward migration of U.S. capital was the rapid growth of Europe and Japan. This, combined with the slow growth of the United States economy in the 1950s, threatened the dominant position of American corporations. Firms confined to the U.S. market found themselves falling behind in the competitive race and losing ground to European and Japanese firms, which were growing rapidly because of the expansion of their markets. Thus, in the late 1950s, United States corporations faced a serious "non-American" challenge. Their answer was an outward thrust to establish sales production and bases in foreign territories. This strategy was possible in Europe, since governments there provided an open door for United States investment, but was blocked in Japan, where the government adopted a highly restrictive policy. To a large extent, United States business was thus able to redress the imbalances caused by the Common Market, but Japan remained a source of tension to oligopoly equilibrium.

What about the future? The present trend indicates further multinationalization of all giant firms, European as well as American. In the first place, European firms, partly as a reaction to the United States penetration of their markets, and partly as a natural result of their own growth, have begun to invest abroad on an expanded scale and will probably continue to do so in the future, and even to enter the United States market. This process is already well underway and may be expected to accelerate as time goes on. The reaction of United States business will most likely be to meet foreign investment at home with more foreign investment abroad. They, too, will scramble for market positions in underdeveloped countries and attempt to get an even larger share of the European market, as a reaction to European investment in the United States. Since they are large and powerful, they will on balance succeed in maintaining their relative standing in the world as a whole—as their losses in some markets are offset by gains in others.

4.2 The Centralization of Capital

Larger firms have generally been able to produce commodities at lower cost than smaller firms, and indeed this advantage has often been a cause for their growth. In part these "economies of scale" no doubt reflect more efficient technologies: as more is produced, the firm can institute a greater division of labor; it can have machines designed for more specific uses; it can profitably introduce techniques such as moving assembly lines. Probably more importantly, size yields economies of scale in market transactions as well: the larger firm can demand lower prices when buying raw materials in volume; it can better predict and coordinate production and demand; it can usually obtain credit more cheaply; it can better exploit the possibilities for "vertical integration," where it buys up sources of essential raw material supplies or gains control of the distribution and retailing network; and so on. These advantages reduce the per-unit costs of production and permit the firm profitably to underprice smaller competitors. Eventually the higher-priced producers are driven out of the market.

As accumulation proceeds, the growth of some firms and the parallel demise of many more tends to create the conditions for monopolistic market structure. Historically, as surviving firms grew larger and progressed from the workshop to the factory and then to the national corporation, they grew so big that in each industry just a few of them could produce enough to satisfy the entire national market.

But the internal growth of the firm was not the only way capitalists attained the advantages of size. They also combined or merged their firms. In some cases inefficient-sized plants were shut down. In more cases, the new combinations took advantage of their size to exploit market economies of scale. Even in cases in which no economies of scale were realized, the benefits of monopoly power could be. Where previously, with many small firms, there had been many capitalists to include in the "deal," now it was possible for just a few large capitalists to organize pricing for the entire industry. Instead of competition driving prices (and profits) down, monopoly power could maintain or even raise prices (and profits).

The following reading by Douglas Dowd describes the great merger movements that have characterized U.S. business history. As Dowd argues, mergers were an important means by which the giant corporations with their monopoly power were created.

Until about 1860, the corporate form of business was largely confined to transportation and finance. With few exceptions, the emergence of corporations in manufacturing awaited the new, large-scale technology that emerged and spread after the Civil War.

From 1873 until the mid-1890's the entire industrial capitalist world underwent what was then called "The Great Depression." Unlike the Great Depression of the 1930's, the most prominent feature of the earlier period was pressure on profits, rather than massive unemployment. That pressure was due to the steady and dramatic lowering of prices through the period, which was in turn the result of great increases in efficiency, combined with the inability to cut off domestic or foreign competition in the context of relatively free trade and relatively competitive market structures.

Consequently, that same period saw the first general attempts to control price competition through one form of business reorganization or another. "Gentlemen's agree-

ments" not to cut prices, profit pools, and trusts (all of which maintained the separate identity of the member corporations) were all tried; but the form which won out was the merger. The process in which mergers occurred is called the "combination movement." By the late 1890's, mergers or combinations (in which many firms were combined under one ownership and identity) became the rule; the years between 1897 and 1905 witnessed their first spectacular rush. During these years, over 5300 industrial firms came under the control, finally, of 318 corporations, the most advanced and powerful firms in the economy.

The turn-of-the-century wave of mergers was seen as spectacular, until subsequent waves surpassed it. As Figure 4-A shows, a higher peak was reached in the 1920's; then, after what has been called a "ripple" in the 1940's, the largest wave of all began, which continues with force to this day. Economists have speculated as to what conditions are associated with increasing or decreasing mer-

Figure 4-A Acquisitions of Manufacturing and Mining Companies 1895–1972.

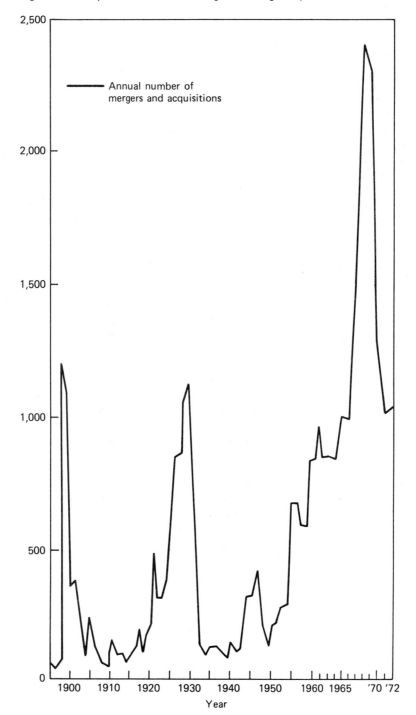

ger activity. The evidence of the past seventy years or so suggests that the only period in which the *rate* of merger activity declines is that of depression; the impulse toward bigness and power is otherwise persistent.

The first waves of mergers were an outcome of the combination of expanding technology and businesses' aims of avoiding competition and of making profits. Technology then led to centralization of production facilities in a given location (for example, steel in Pittsburgh). Since World War II, however, technological development has led to decentralization of productive facilities geographically; at the same time the *control* over those facilities has become ever more centralized, spreading not simply over one industry but many different industries. Let us examine the process more closely.

Initially, mergers took place in each industry as it began to employ modern, large-scale technology. Sometimes the process was more like warfare than business in the late 19th century.[1] Mergers spread from transportation to manufacturing, to utilities and finance, to mining and construction and trade; by now mergers are the dynamic mode in all significant business, including entertainment, hotels and even agriculture, long considered the final preserve of effective competition.

The patterns of the merger movements are striking; most striking of all is the tidal wave that began during World War II and reached its historic peak in 1968–1969. Figures 4-A and 4-B reveal not only the recent upsurge in mergers but the domination of those mergers by the largest 200 corporations and the increasing size of the transactions. As *Fortune* points out, "from 1964 through 1966, there were 293 mergers in which the acquired companies had assets of more than $10 million; in the final three years of the decade there were

530. The average size of the transactions, $38 million in the first period, rose to $64 million during the second. In the peak year of 1968 the nation's top 200 industrial firms acquired a total of 94 large companies, with aggregate assets of more than $8 billion."[2]

Throughout all this merger activity there have been several subprocesses. At first, mergers were in one industry, where all the merging firms produced much the same product. These are called *horizontal* mergers, where competitors in a given industry come under the ownership and control of one company (for example, one steel company buying out another). While those mergers continued, another form, *vertical* mergers, began to appear, especially in the 1920's, in which a company buys out its suppliers and/or its customers (for example, Ford gaining its own steel facilities; U.S. Steel buying out coal mines and a bridge-building company).

Horizontal mergers lead to concentration of power in a given industry, and to *oligopoly*: a few dominant sellers in an industry. Vertical mergers strengthen the hand of already large firms, while also creating higher barriers to entry by new firms. Around forty years ago another form of merger began to attract attention, as it does even more so today: the *conglomerate*, where the firms acquired by a corporation are only distantly related, if at all, to the industry of the acquiring firm. In the vast merger movement since 1950 all these forms—vertical, horizontal, and conglomerate—have been operating, with the conglomerate form taking the prizes for drama. The drama became especially vivid in the 1960's, with "the new conglomerates."

The expansion of the "new conglomerates" was dominated by eight companies: ITT, Gulf & Western, Ling-Temco-Vought, Tenneco, White Consolidated, Teledyne, Occidental Petroleum, and Litton Industries. "Each of these companies made acquisitions during the 1960's totaling more than a half-billion dollars; for six the asset value was over

---

[1]Tactics ranging from outright gun battles (in the fight to control the Erie Railroad, for example) to the most relentless financial "terrorism" (in Rockefeller's successful steps toward monopoly in oil) are related and detailed in Matthew Josephson, *The Robber Barons* (New York: Harcourt Brace Jovanovich, 1934), for the period 1861–1901.

[2]*Fortune*, April 1973, from which the charts are also derived.

Figure 4-B Big Acquisitions 1963–1972.

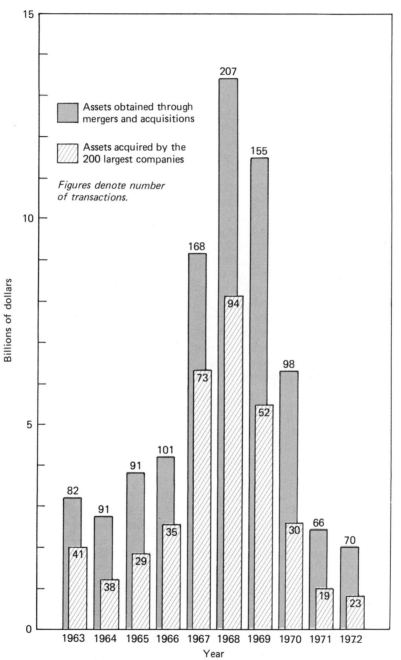

a billion dollars."[3] Of the various important aspects of this movement, one worth noting is that it has sped up the process of bringing traditionally "small business" industries— for instance, food processing, non-electrical machinery, and textiles—under the control of giant corporations.

The early merger movements, whether horizontal or vertical in origin, led to the *concentration* of economic power within the affected industries. When we add the conglomerate mergers to the earlier movement we come to an additional characteristic: *centralization*.

. . .

There is no mystery as to the size or the identity of America's giant corporations. *Fortune* annually publishes its "Fortune 500" and "Second 500," showing assets, sales, employees, income, profits, etc., of the largest industrial corporations; their data in turn are derived from a multitude of governmental and private sources, all open to the public eye.

. . .

Let us now look at some representative facts concerning the concentration and centralization of control over productive assets, sales, profits, employment and the like:[4]

The 500 largest industrial (manufacturing and mining) corporations in 1972 controlled 65 percent of the *sales* of all industrial companies, 75 percent of their total *profits*, and 75 percent of total industrial *employment*.

The 1000 largest industrial corporations in 1972 controlled about 72 percent of industrial *sales*, about 80 percent of industrial *profits*, and about 84 percent of industrial *employment*; that is, the "Second 500" account for 6.5 percent of sales, 6 percent of profits and about 9 percent of industrial jobs—a fraction of the business done

[3] John M. Blair, *Economic Concentration: Structure, Behavior and Public Policy* (New York: Harcourt Brace Jovanovich, 1972), p. 285.

[4] The data are familiar, and may be found in many economics textbooks. These are drawn primarily from Blair and Reid, both cited above, from Robert T. Averitt, *The Dual Economy* (New York: Norton, 1968), and from *Fortune*, May, 1971, May, 1972, and May-June, 1973.

by the top 500, and that leaves very little indeed for the remaining hundreds of thousands of industrial companies.

The industrial corporation with the greatest *assets* is EXXON (formerly Standard Oil of New Jersey); in 1972 its assets were $21.5 *billion*. The company with the smallest assets of the top 500 in 1972 was Varian Associates, with $188 *million*. EXXON's sales in 1972 were $20 *billion*; Varian's, $203 *million*.

The top 500 industrial companies had *sales* of $558 billion in 1972; GNP—the total money value of all goods and services at their final stage—was $1,152 billion. Total sales of the Second 500 were about $59 billion. The top ten corporations (GM, EXXON, Ford, GE, IBM, Mobil Oil, Chrysler, Texaco, ITT, and Western Electric) had sales of $133 billion. That is, the top 500 corporations controlled just under half of the entire GNP; the top *ten* corporations more than 10 percent of GNP (and about 24 percent of the top 500 and more than twice the sales of the Second 500). The top 50 of the 500 did 47 percent of the business of the 500. In short, the concentration of the economy is continued within the top 500, where the bulk of power is centralized in the hands of a small percentage.

The *assets* of the top 500 industrial corporations in 1972 were $486 billion; of the second 500, about $46 billion. The assets of the top ten companies were $109 billion, more than twice that of the Second 500.

In 1972, GM was first in sales of the top 500, with $30.4 billion—2.6 percent of GNP for one company.

The *profits* of the largest ten corporations (industrial and non-industrial)—AT&T, GM, EXXON, IBM, Texaco, Ford, Gulf Oil, Sears Roebuck, Mobil Oil, and Standard Oil of California—were $10.3 billion *after* taxes, in 1971. The two largest—AT&T and GM— made $2.2 and $1.9 billion, respectively. Total corporate profits in 1971 were just under $50 billion after taxes. That is, the ten top corporations gained over 20 percent of *all* corporate profits in 1971.

Between 1970 and 1971, the *sales* of the top 500 industrials rose by 8.4 percent. GM, increasing its sales by $9.5 billion that year, by itself accounted for 24 percent of the sales increase of the 500, and it accounted for 76 percent of the net income increase of the 500. Adding in Ford and Chrysler brings the figure up to 89 percent of the net income increase of the top 500. Auto sales and profits increased even more spectacularly in 1972 and 1973, as sales of cars rose to recordbreaking levels (about 12 million in 1973).

Between 1969 and 1972, the top 500 increased their sales by about $113 billion; but they hired 137,000 fewer workers in 1972 than in 1969.

Appendix to 4.2 (by the editors)

Table 4-B and Figures 4-C, 4-D, and 4-E present some further evidence on the role of the giant corporation in the U.S. economy. Table 4-B lists the

TABLE 4-B THE LARGEST INDUSTRIAL FIRMS, 1974
(in millions of dollars)

	Sales	Profits	Assets
Exxon	$ 42,061	$ 3,142	$ 31,332
GM	31,550	950	20,468
Ford Motors	23,621	361	14,174
Texaco	23,256	1,586	17,176
Mobil Oil	18,929	1,048	14,074
Standard Oil of Calif.	17,191	970	11,640
Gulf Oil	16,458	1,065	12,503
General Electric	13,413	608	9,369
IBM	12,675	1,838	14,027
ITT	11,154	451	10,697
Chrysler	10,971	52	6,733
U.S. Steel	9,186	634	7,718
Standard Oil (Ind.)	9,085	970	8,916
Shell Oil	7,634	621	6,129
Western Electric	7,382	311	5,240
Continental Oil	7,041	328	4,673
E.I. duPont de Nemours	6,910	404	5,980
Atlantic Richfield	6,740	474	6,152
Westinghouse Electric	6,466	28	4,302
Occidental Petroleum	5,719	281	3,326
Bethlehem Steel	5,381	342	4,513
Union Carbide	5,320	530	4,883
Goodyear Tire & Rubber	5,256	158	4,242
Tenneco	5,002	322	6,402
Phillips Petroleum	4,981	402	4,028
TOTAL (top 25)	313,382	17,879	238,697
(top 100)	539,084	28,844	403,406
Top 100 as percent of total economy	39.0[a]	33.9	56.6

[a]Corporate sales as percent of GNP.

SOURCES: *Fortune*, "The Fortune Directory of the 500 Largest U.S. Industrial Corporations," (Chicago: Time, Inc., 1975).

Survey of Current Business, Current Business Statistics, U.S. Department of Commerce, Social and Economic Statistics Administration, Bureau of Economic Analysis, U.S. GPO, October 1975.

Figure 4-C   Percent of Final Sales, Profits, and Employment Accounted for by 500 Largest Industrial Corporations

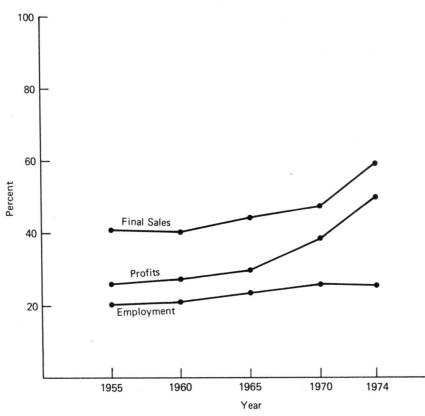

NOTE: Sales as percent of final sales (sales of top 500 include intermediate and foreign sales); profits as percent of all non-financial corporate profits; employment as percent of civilian labor force.

SOURCES: *Fortune*, "The Fortune Directory of the 500 Largest U.S. Industrial Corporations" July 1956, July 1961, May 1966, May 1971, May, 1974.

   Survey of Current Business, U.S. Department of Commerce, October 1975 and 1973 Business Statistics Supplement.

25 largest industrial corporations and their sales, profits, and assets; the bottom two rows in the table show data for the largest 100 firms. Note that these are the largest *industrial* (mining and manufacturing) firms only; for example, the biggest company of all, American Telephone and Telegraph, which itself employs nearly 1 percent of the entire U.S. labor force, is not listed, although its manufacturing subsidiary, Western Electric, independently ranks as the fifteenth largest firm in Table 4-B.

   Figures 4-C and 4-D chart the rising importance of big firms in the U.S. -

Figure 4-D   Percent of All Manufacturing Assets Held by Top Manufacturing Corporations

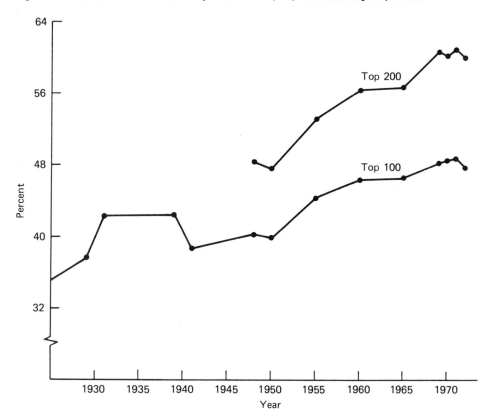

SOURCE: U.S. Bureau of the Census, *Statistical Abstract of the United States, 1975* (Washington, D.C.; U.S. Government Printing Office), p. 502 and Cabinet Committee on Price Stability, *Studies by the Staff* (Washington, D.C.; U.S. Government Printing Office, 1969), pp. 45–49.

economy as a whole. Figure 4-E shows, for several selected industries, the controlling position of the few big producers. Note that the sales and employment of large firms, when expressed as a percentage of the total economy's sales and employment, tend to be overstated: their sales are overstated because intermediate *and* final sales are included for corporations but just final sales for the economy; employment is overstated because in some cases firms report both domestic and foreign employment whereas only domestic employees are included in the economy figures. (These problems do not affect the profits data.) The percentages reported nonetheless provide a useful basis for comparison, and the trends are likely to be valid since we have no reason to believe that the data limitations affect different years differently.

Figure 4-E Percent of Total Production Accounted for by Leading Firms

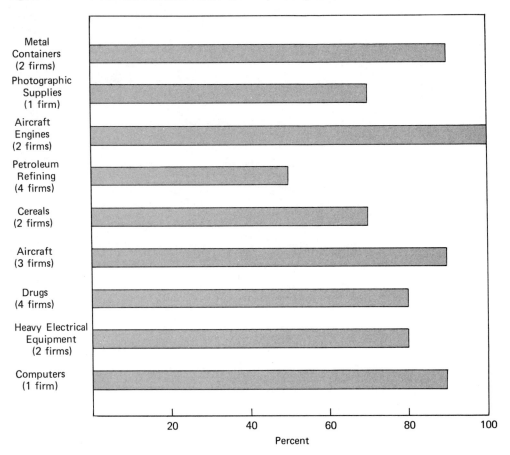

SOURCE: William D. Shepherd, *Market Power and Economic Welfare* (New York: Random House, 1970), pp. 152–54.

4.3 *Competition among Monopoly Capitalists*

The giant corporations' rise to industrial dominance has transformed the nature of competition and the role of markets. We now turn to the question of the relations among large firms (relations we have characterized as "monopolistic competition") and to the impact of these relations on the accumulation process. In the following essay Paul Baran and Paul Sweezy argue that while price competition has been largely eliminated, other forms of competition continue.

Monopoly capitalism is a system made up of giant corporations. This is not to say that there are no other elements in the system or that it is useful to study monopoly capitalism by abstracting from everything except giant corporations. It is both more realistic and more enlightening to proceed from the outset by including, alongside the corporate-monopoly sector, a more or less extensive smaller-business sector, the reason being that smaller business enters in many ways into the calculations and strategies of Big Business. To abstract from smaller business would be to exclude from the field of investigation some of the determinants of Big Business behavior.

One must, however, be careful not to fall into the trap of assuming that Big Business and smaller business are qualitatively equal or of coordinate importance for the *modus operandi* of the system. The dominant element, the prime mover, is Big Business organized in giant corporations. These corporations are profit maximizers and capital accumulators. They are managed by company men whose fortunes are identified with the corporations' success or failure.

. . .

Overall, monopoly capitalism is as unplanned as its competitive predecessor. The big corporations relate to each other, to consumers, to labor, to smaller business primarily through the market. The way the system works is still the unintended outcome of the self-regarding actions of the numerous units that compose it. And since market relations are essentially price relations, the study of monopoly capitalism, like that of competitive capitalism, must begin with the workings of the price mechanism.

The crucial difference between the two is well known and can be summed up in the proposition that under competitive capitalism the individual enterprise is a "price taker," while under monopoly capitalism the big corporation is a "price maker."

. . .

When we say that giant corporations are price makers, we mean that they can and do choose what prices to charge for their products. There are of course limits to their freedom of choice: above and below certain prices it would be preferable to discontinue production altogether. But typically the range of choice is wide. What determines which prices will be charged within this range?

The typical giant corporation . . . is one of several corporations producing commodities which are more or less adequate substitutes for each other. When one of them varies its price, the effect will immediately be felt by the others. If firm A lowers its price, some new demand may be tapped, but the main effect will be to attract customers away from firms B, C, and D. The latter, not willing to give up their business to A, will retaliate by lowering their prices, perhaps even undercutting A. While A's original move was made in the expectation of increasing its profit, the net result may be to leave all the firms in a worse position.

Under these circumstances it is impossible for a single corporation, even if it has the fullest information about the demand for the products of the industry as a whole and about its own costs, to tell what price would maximize its profits. What it can sell depends not only on its own price but also on the prices charged by its rivals, and these it cannot know in advance. A firm may thus make ever so careful an estimate of the profit-maximizing price, but in the absence of knowledge about rivals' reactions it will be right only by accident. A wrong guess about rivals' reactions would throw the whole calculation off and necessitate readjustments which in turn would provoke further moves by rivals, and so on, the whole process quite possibly degenerating into mutually destructive price warfare.

Unstable market situations of this sort were very common in the earlier phases of monopoly capitalism, and still occur from time to time, but they are not typical of present-day monopoly capitalism. And clearly they are anathema to the big corporations with their penchant for looking ahead, planning carefully, and betting only on the sure thing. To avoid such situations therefore becomes the first concern of corporate policy, the *sine qua non* of orderly and profitable business operations,

This objective is achieved by the simple expedient of banning price cutting as a legitimate weapon of economic warfare. Naturally this has not happened all at once or as a conscious decision. Like other powerful taboos, that against price cutting has grown up gradually out of long and often bitter experience, and it derives its strength from the fact that it serves the interests of powerful forces in society. As long as it is accepted and observed, the dangerous uncertainties are removed from the rationalized pursuit of maximum profits.

With price competition banned, sellers of a given commodity or of close substitutes have an interest in seeing that the price or prices established are such as to maximize the profits of the group as a whole. They may fight over the division of these profits—a subject to which we return presently—but none can wish that the total to be fought over should be smaller rather than larger. This is the decisive fact in determining the price policies and strategies of the typical large corporation. . . .

If maximization of the profits of the group constitutes the content of the pricing process under monopoly capitalism, its form can differ widely according to specific historical and legal conditions. In some countries, sellers are permitted or even encouraged to get together for the purpose of coordinating their policies. Resulting arrangements can vary all the way from tight cartels regulating both prices and outputs (a close approach to the pure monopoly case) to informal agreements to abide by certain price schedules (as exemplified by the famous "Gary dinners" in the American steel industry in the early years of the century). In the United States, where for historical reasons the ideology of competition has remained strong in spite of the facts of monopolization, antitrust laws effectively pre-

vent such open collusion among sellers. Secret collusion is undoubtedly common, but it has its drawbacks and risks, and can hardly be described as the norm toward which a typical oligopolistic industry tends. That norm, it seems clear, is a kind of tacit collusion which reaches its most developed form in what is known as "price leadership."

As defined by Burns, "price leadership exists when the price at which most of the units in an industry offer to sell is determined by adopting the price announced by one of their number."[1] The leader is normally the largest and most powerful firm in the industry —such as U.S. Steel or General Motors—and the others accept its dominant role not only because it profits them to do so but also because they know that if it should come to price warfare the leader would be able to stand the gaff better than they could.

Price leadership in this strict sense is only the leading species of a much larger genus. In the cigarette industry, for example, the big companies take turns in initiating price changes; and in the petroleum industry different companies take the lead in different regional markets and to a certain extent at different times. So long as some fairly regular pattern is maintained such cases may be described as modified forms of price leadership. But there are many other situations in which no such regularity is discernible: which firm initiates price changes seems to be arbitrary. This does not mean that the essential ingredient of tacit collusion is absent. The initiating firm may simply be announcing to the rest of the industry, "We think the time has come to raise (or lower) price in the interest of all of us." If the others agree, they will follow. If they do not, they will stand pat, and the firm that made the first move will rescind its initial price change. It is this willingness to rescind if an initial change is not followed which distinguishes the tacit-collusion situation from a price-war situation. So long as all firms accept this convention—and

[1]Arthur R. Burns, *The Decline of Competition: A Study of the Evolution of American Industry*, New York, 1936, p. 76.

it is really nothing but a corollary of the ban on price competition—it becomes relatively easy for the group as a whole to feel its way toward the price which maximizes the industry's profit. What is required is simply that the initiator of change should act with the group interest as well as its own interest in mind and that the others should be ready to signal their agreement or disagreement by following or standing pat. If these conditions are satisfied, we can safely assume that the price established at any time is a reasonable approximation to the theoretical monopoly price.

What differentiates this case from the strict price leadership case is that there all the firms are in effect committed in advance to accept the judgment of one of their number, while here they all make up their minds each time a change is in question. To borrow an analogy from politics, we might say that in the one case we have a "dictatorship" and in the other a "democracy." But the purpose in both cases is the same—to maximize the profits of the group as a whole. The "dictatorships" of course tend to occur in those industries where one firm is much bigger and stronger than the others, like steel and autos; while the "democracies" are likely to be industries in which the dominant firms are more nearly equal in size and strength.

A qualification of the foregoing analysis seems called for. In the "pure" monopoly case, prices move upward or downward with equal ease, in response to changing conditions, depending entirely on whether a hike or a cut will improve the profit position. In oligopoly this is no longer quite the case. If one seller raises his price, this cannot possibly be interpreted as an aggressive move. The worst that can happen to him is that the others will stand pat and he will have to rescind (or accept a smaller share of the market). In the case of a price cut, on the other hand, there is always the possibility that aggression is intended, that the cutter is trying to increase his share of the market by violating the taboo on price competition. If rivals do interpret the initial move in this

way, a price war with losses to all may result. Hence everyone concerned is likely to be more circumspect about lowering than raising prices. Under oligopoly, in other words, prices tend to be stickier on the downward side than on the upward side, and this fact introduces a significant upward bias into the general price level in a monopoly capitalist economy. There is truth in *Business Week's* dictum that in the United States today the price system is one that "works only one way—up."[2]

One further qualification: while price competition is normally taboo in oligopolistic situations, this does not mean that it is totally excluded or that it never plays an important role. Any company or group of companies that believes it can permanently benefit from aggressive price tactics will not hesitate to use them. Such a situation is particularly likely to arise in a new industry where all firms are jockeying for position and no reasonably stable pattern of market sharing has yet taken shape (all industries, of course, have to go through this phase). In these circumstances, lower-cost producers may sacrifice immediately attainable profits to the goal of increasing their share of the market. Higher-cost producers, unable to stand the pace, may be forced into mergers on unfavorable terms or squeezed out of the market altogether. In this fashion, the industry goes through a shake-down process at the end of which a certain number of firms have firmly entrenched themselves and demonstrated their capacity to survive a tough struggle. When this stage is reached, the remaining firms find that aggressive price tactics no longer promise long-run benefits to offset short-term sacrifices. They therefore follow the example of older industries in abandoning price as a competitive weapon and developing a system of tacit collusion that is suited to their new circumstances.

· · ·

The abandonment of price competition does not mean the end of all competition:

2*Business Week*, June 15, 1957.

it takes new forms and rages on with ever increasing intensity. Most of these new forms of competition come under the heading of what we call the sales effort. . . .

There are, it seems to us, two aspects of non-price competition which are of decisive importance here. The first has to do with what may be called the dynamics of market sharing. The second has to do with the particular form which the sales effort assumes in the producer goods industries.

To begin with, the firm with lower costs and higher profits enjoys a variety of advantages over higher-cost rivals in the struggle for market shares. . . . The firm with the lowest costs holds the whip hand; it can afford to be aggressive even to the point of threatening, and in the limiting case precipitating, a price war. It can get away with tactics (special discounts, favorable credit terms, etc.) which if adopted by a weak firm would provoke retaliation. It can afford the advertising, research, development of new product varieties, extra services, and so on, which are the usual means of fighting for market shares and which tend to yield results in proportion to the amounts spent on them. Other less tangible factors are involved which tend to elude the economist's net but which play an important part in the business world. The lower-cost, higher-profit company acquires a special reputation which enables it to attract and hold customers, bid promising executive personnel away from rival firms, and recruit the ablest graduates of engineering and business schools. For all these reasons, there is a strong positive incentive for the large corporation in an oligopolistic industry not only to seek continuously to cut its costs but to do so faster than its rivals.

There is an additional reason, in our judgment as important as it is neglected, why a tendency for costs of production to fall is endemic to the entire monopoly capitalist economy, even including those areas which if left to themselves would stagnate technologically. It stems from the exigencies of non-price competition in the producer goods industries. Here, as in industries producing consumer goods, sellers must be forever seeking to put something new on the market. But they are not dealing with buyers whose primary interest is the latest fashion or keeping up with the Joneses. They are dealing with sophisticated buyers whose concern is to increase profits. Hence the new products offered to the prospective buyers must be designed to help them increase their profits, which in general means to help them reduce their costs. If the manufacturer can convince his customers that his new instrument or material or machine will save them money, the sale will follow almost automatically.

Probably the clearest example of the cost-reducing effects of the innovating activity of manufacturers of producer goods is to be found in agriculture. As Galbraith has pointed out, "there would be little technical development and not much progress in agriculture were it not for government-supported research supplemented by the research of the corporations which devise and sell products to the farmer."[3] No doubt, as this statement implies, government research has been the main factor behind the spectacular reduction in agricultural costs during the last two decades, but the sales-hungry manufacturers of farm machinery, fertilizers, pesticides, etc., have also played an important part in the process. Similarly, producers of machine tools, computers and computer systems, business machines, automatic control equipment, loading and transfer machinery, new plastics and metal alloys, and a thousand and one other kinds of producer goods are busy developing new products which will enable their customers—comprising literally the entire business world—to produce more cheaply and hence to make more profits. In a word: producers of producer goods make more profits by helping others to make more profits. The process is self-reinforcing and cumulative, and goes far toward explaining the extraordinarily rapid advance of technology and labor productivity which charac-

[3]J. K. Galbraith, *American Capitalism*, Boston, 1952, pp. 95–96.

terizes the developed monopoly capitalist economy.

. . .

The whole motivation of cost reduction is to increase profits, and the monopolistic structure of markets enables the corporations to appropriate the lion's share of the fruits of increasing productivity directly in the form of higher profits.

. . .

Price competition has largely receded as a means of attracting buyers, and has yielded to new ways of sales promotion: advertising, variation of the products' appearance and packaging, "planned obsolescence," model changes, credit schemes, and the like.

. . .

Advertising expenditures in the American economy have experienced a truly spectacular rise. A century ago, before the wave of concentration and trustification which ushered in the monopolistic phase of capitalism, advertising played very little part in the process of distribution of products and the influencing of consumer attitudes and habits. Such advertising as did exist was carried on mainly by retailers, and even they did not attempt to promote distinctive brands or labeled articles. The manufacturers themselves had not yet begun to exploit advertising as a means of securing ultimate consumer demand for their products. By the 1890's, however, both the volume and the tone of advertising changed. Expenditures on advertising in 1890 amounted to $360 million, some seven times more than in 1867. By 1929, this figure had been multiplied by nearly 10, reaching $3,426 million.

Thus as monopoly capitalism reached maturity, advertising entered "the state of persuasion, as distinct from proclamation or iteration."

Accordingly, the advertising business has grown astronomically, with its expansion and success being continually promoted by the growing monopolization of the economy and by the effectiveness of the media which have been pressed into its service—especially radio, and now above all television. Total spending on advertising media rose to $10.3 billion in

1957, and amounted to over [$26.5] billion in [1974]. Outlays on market research, public relations, commercial design, and similar services carried out by advertising agencies and other specialized firms add more billions. And this does not include the costs of market research, advertising work, designing, etc., carried on within the producing corporations themselves.

This truly fantastic outpouring of resources does not reflect some frivolous irrationality in corporate managements or some peculiar predilection of the American people for singing commercials, garish billboards, and magazines and newspapers flooded with advertising copy. What has actually happened is that advertising has turned into an indispensable tool for a large sector of corporate business. Competitively employed, it has become an integral part of the corporations' profit maximization policy and serves at the same time as a formidable wall protecting monopolistic positions. Although advertising at first appeared to corporate managements as a deplorable cost to be held down as much as possible, before long it turned into what one advertising agency has rightly called "a must for survival" for many a corporate enterprise.

. . .

The strategy of the advertiser is to hammer into the heads of people the unquestioned desirability, indeed the imperative necessity, of owning the newest product that comes on the market. For this strategy to work, however, producers have to pour on the market a steady stream of "new" products, with none daring to lag behind for fear his customers will turn to his rivals for their newness.

Genuinely new or different products, however, are not easy to come by, even in our age of rapid scientific and technological advance. Hence much of the newness with which the consumer is systematically bombarded is either fraudulent or related trivially and in many cases even negatively to the function and serviceability of the product.

It is entirely different with the second kind of newness. Here we have to do with products

which are indeed new in design and appearance but which serve essentially the same
purposes as old products they are intended to
replace. The extent of the difference can vary
all the way from a simple change in packaging to the far-reaching and enormously expensive annual changes in automobile models.

· · ·

The emergence of a condition in which the
sales and production efforts interpenetrate to
such an extent as to become virtually indistinguishable entails a profound change in
what constitutes socially necessary costs of
production as well as in the nature of the
social product itself. In the competitive
model, given all the assumptions upon which
it rests, only the minimum costs of production
(as determined by prevailing technology),
combined with the minimum costs of packaging, transportation, and distribution (as
called for by existing customs), could be
recognized by the market—and by economic

theory—as socially necessary costs of purvey-
ing a product to its buyer.

· · ·

Matters are very different under the reign
of oligopoly and monopoly. Veblen, who was
the first economist to recognize and analyze
many aspects of monopoly capitalism, put his
finger on the crucial point at a relatively
early stage:

> *The producers have been giving continually more
> attention to the salability of their product, so that
> much of what appears on the books as production-cost
> should properly be charged to the production of salable
> appearances. The distinction between workmanship
> and salesmanship has been blurred in this way, until
> it will doubtless hold true now that the shop-cost of
> many articles produced for the market is mainly
> chargeable to the production of salable appearances,
> ordinarily meretricious.*[4]

[4]Thorstein Veblen, *Absentee Ownership and Business Enterprise in Recent Times*, New York, 1923, p. 300.

Afterword (by the editors)

Does a more monopolistic market structure tend to enhance or inhibit the
accumulation of capital? The answer to this question involves a great many
considerations, a few of which will be explored here. In particular, we shall
first consider this question at the microeconomic level; i.e., are monopolistic
firms more profitable than competitive firms and hence better able to invest
and accumulate capital? Then we will consider the question at the macroeconomic level; i.e., what is the impact of monopoly on accumulation in
the economy as a whole? We will further explore this second question in
Chapter 12.

The erosion of competition has equipped the monopoly corporations with
greatly enhanced power compared to competitive firms. One significant
power big firms enjoy is the ability to raise prices beyond what would exist
under competitive conditions. Since increasing the price of commodities by
itself generally entails no additional costs, higher prices mean higher profits.

At this point we might ask: What prevents the big firms from using their
power to raise their prices *indefinitely*? After all, if high prices are good, are
not higher prices always better? Indeed, they are, *as long as those higher prices
actually result in sales.* But higher prices might reduce the firm's sales, and this
limits the extent to which monopoly firms can raise prices. Customers may
not be able or willing to pay the higher prices, so firms must balance the
extra profits gained on each unit sold as a consequence of higher price against
the loss in profits from selling fewer units of the good.

Moreover, if monopoly firms raise their prices too high, other large corporations may try to enter the market to capture some of the high profits.

Indeed, the firm can raise its prices only to a level that will be still sufficiently unremunerative for other firms so as not to attract them. This level may be relatively high, especially where large amounts of capital are required to join the industry or where other barriers exist to inhibit firms from entering the market. Nonetheless, the firm's prices must remain within the limits imposed by these considerations.

Two factors not mentioned by Baran and Sweezy further limit the ability of monopoly firms to raise prices. One is competition from foreign firms. As European and Japanese capitalists seek out new markets, they upset old, established pricing policies and agreements on market sharing. They may attempt to establish market positions precisely by reintroducing price competition. Another factor is product substitutability: if steel firms raise prices too high, for example, their customers may try to substitute aluminum, glass, or plastic for steel. As all these limitations show, monopoly power is relative; the ability of firms to raise prices depends on their degree of monopoly power.

Let us next investigate the monopoly firms' costs. The large scale of most monopolistic corporations often permits them to reduce per-unit costs compared to smaller firms. Large corporations are able to reduce costs both because they are more rational calculators of profit opportunities (using sophisticated market research, cost accounting, etc.) and because their longer time horizons permit them to engage in extremely long-run planning. In part these economies result from being able to employ technologies that are more efficient when larger quantities are produced. More significantly, the large firm can realize savings from volume buying, manipulation of product markets, better coordination of production and demand, vertical integration, and other market economies of scale.

But monopolistic competition may also bring into play new or additional costs. The most important of these is the cost of expanded sales efforts: advertising, redesigning products for fashion or style, market research, sales staff, and so on. Each firm finds these costs necessary when all firms in an industry agree to avoid price competition, since with prices fixed, expanding sales is the only way to increase revenues. If any one firm did not engage in such advertising, it would lose its share of the market.

Whether or not monopolistic competition results in higher profits depends on the interplay of these forces. Prices are likely to be higher than if purely competitive conditions obtained, resulting in higher per-sale revenues but perhaps somewhat reduced sales. Whether costs are higher or lower depends on (1) the ability of the large firm to reduce costs—i.e., whether new costs outweigh economies of scale—and (2) given the large firm's ability to reduce costs, the extent to which it desires or is forced to do so. On the first point, Baran and Sweezy argue that despite the rising costs of the sales efforts, technical change in the capital goods industry plus the corporation's own efforts will lead to a persistent possibility for total per-unit costs to fall. On the second point, while monopoly firms may have less incentive to reduce costs because they are not so hard-pressed by competition, Baran and Sweezy argue that the "dynamics of market sharing" will reinforce the firms' resolve to cut costs wherever possible. We might note that this pressure is likely to be most strongly felt during times of business depression and crisis.

If we look at what has actually happened, the data suggest that on bal-

Figure 4-F   The Relation Between Corporate Asset Size and Rate of Return

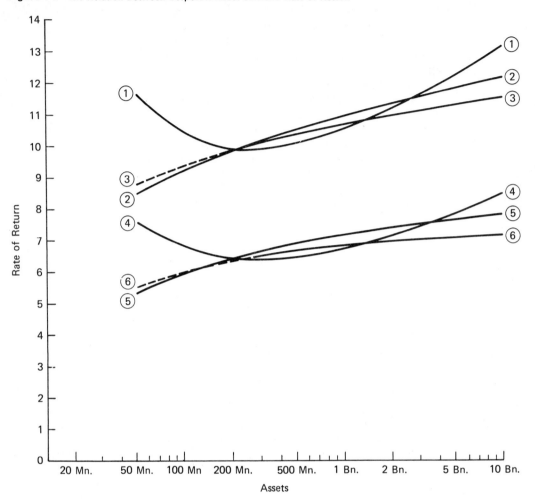

NOTE: Each line in graph represents an estimate based on a different regression equation.
SOURCE: Marshall Hall and Leonard Weiss, "Firm Size and Profitability," *Review of Economics and Statistics*, August 1967, p. 326.

ance monopoly-sector firms have earned persistently higher profit rates than other firms. First, large firms seem to have earned higher profit rates than have smaller ones, even though the business cycle caused the profit rates of all firms to fluctuate. Figure 4-F presents the results of one study relating corporate size and profitability; six different estimates (represented by the six lines on the graph) show the positive relation between size and profitability.[1] The same study reported (as other studies have) that the profits of big firms tend to be less risky as well, in the sense that there is less variability than in smaller-firm profits. Second, profits tend to be higher in industries

[1]See also William Shepherd, *Market Power and Economic Welfare* (New York: 1970), pp. 187–88.

Figure 4-G   The Relation Between Monopoly Power and Rate of Return

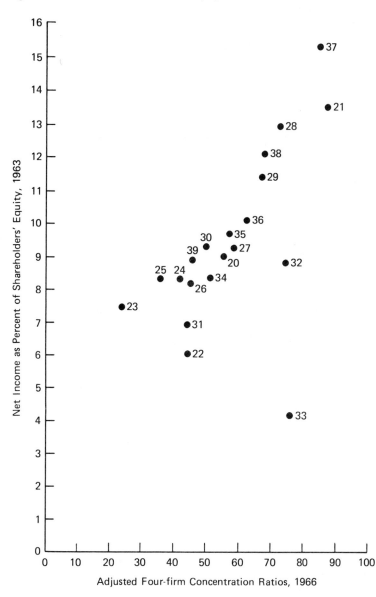

NOTE: Each dot represents one two-digit SIC industry.
SOURCE: William Shepherd, *Market Power and Economic Welfare* (New York; Random House, 1970), p. 191.

where one or a few firms account for the bulk of the industry's sales than in more competitive industries; Figure 4-G illustrates this relation.[2] Profits are

[2]Many studies have replicated this result; for a review, see L. Weiss, "Quantitative Studies in Industrial Organization," in M. Intriligator, *Frontiers in Quantitative Economics* (Amsterdam: North Holland Publishing, 1971).

particularly high where "barriers to entry" prevent outside firms from easily entering the market.[3] Finally, a third set of studies points out that the correlation between concentration and higher profits exists only for *large* firms (see Table 4-C). Apparently it is only the combination of size *and* market power characteristic of monopoly-sector firms which insures higher profit rates.[4]

TABLE 4-C CORRELATIONS BETWEEN RATE OF RETURN[a] AND CONCENTRATION, BY ASSET SIZE OF FIRMS, 1969 AND 1970 DATA

Asset Size ($ thousands)	Correlation Coefficients
Small Firms	
Under 10	−.09
10–25	−.10
25–50	−.40
50–100	.00
100–250	−.14
250–500	−.23
500–1,000	−.09
1,000–2,500	−.07
2,500–5,000	−.27
5,000–10,000	.00
10,000–25,000	−.06
25,000–35,000	−.05
Large Firms	
35,000–50,000	+.20
50,000–100,000	+.05
Over 100,000	+.24

[a]Profit before taxes and interest ÷ total assets.

SOURCE: Harold Demsetz, *The Market Concentration Doctrine* (Washington, D.C.: American Enterprise Institute, 1973).

Does a more monopolistic market structure tend to enhance or inhibit the accumulation of capital? We can now give, for the microeconomic level, a fairly definite answer: monopoly increases accumulation. Monopoly-sector firms on average are more profitable than competitive-sector firms, and hence better able to accumulate.

One final implication: under competitive conditions, the rate of profit on all units of capital will tend to be the same. Inequalities will be evened out by the flow of capital from low-profit to high-profit industries. In monopoly capitalism, however, barriers to entry prevent capital from flowing into the monopolistic industries, which as we have seen will ordinarily be the areas of higher profits. Monopoly capitalism introduces the likelihood of different

[3]See Joe S. Bain, *Industrial Organization* (New York: 1968).

[4]H. Demsetz, *The Market Concentration Doctrine* (Washington, D.C.: American Enterprise Institute, 1973).

rates of profit, then, not only between sectors but also between industries within the monopoly sector.

Let us now return to the question, to be considered in broader context in Chapter 12, of the effect of monopolistic competition on the general level of economic activity and on capital accumulation in the society as a whole.

To answer this question we must raise another first: Will there be sufficient demand for the output of the economy to employ both the means of production and the labor force at their full or near-full capacity? Or will the level of "aggregate demand" be insufficient, resulting in idle factories and unemployed workers? If the former is true, boom conditions will result, profits will be high, and accumulation will tend to proceed rapidly. If the latter holds, depression conditions will emerge, accumulation will be slow, and "stagnation" will result.

Capitalists sell various types of output. They sell consumption goods to consumers, capital goods to investors (other capitalists), military hardware and other items to government, and exports to foreign buyers. Despite increasing world trade, exports remain a relatively small part of the U.S. national economy and are largely offset by imports anyway; we can safely ignore them as a major source of sales and employment. Sales to governments are considerably larger, and we shall consider them in a moment.

Consumption goods are by far the largest category of aggregate sales, and the level of consumer buying is an important determinant of the level of economic activity. Nonetheless, consumers by and large spend most of their incomes (primarily wages), so consumer spending tends itself to be determined by the level of economic activity. Therefore, while consumer spending is one of the elements that affects whether stagnation occurs or not, it is not an important *independent cause* of prosperity or depression.

Investment, on the other hand, *is* a significant and relatively independent determinant of the level of economic activity. As capitalists earn profits, whether or not they reinvest their income becomes crucial.[5] If they do, the demand for investment goods will increase; rising demand will lead to more employment and higher wages; and rising wage incomes will tend to increase consumer spending, producing relatively full employment and high output. If capitalists do not reinvest their profits, demand for investment goods will fall, wage incomes will tend to sink, consumers will have less income to spend on consumer goods, output will fall, and stagnation will result. Hence, the rate of investment in the economy plays a critical role in determining the overall level of economic activity.

Capitalists choose to reinvest or not depending on how profitable potential investments appear to be. If there is a strong likelihood of large profits, they will be eager to reinvest; if future profits seem meager, they will be more reluctant to do so.

The question of the impact of monopoly on aggregate accumulation and on the overall level of economic activity can now be rephrased as follows:

[5]We ignore here capitalists' consumption out of profits (which would have the same effect as reinvestment) on the grounds that it is neither very large nor very volatile compared to other components in aggregate demand.

Does monopolistic competition tend to reduce the capitalist's incentive to invest? If it does, monopoly will tend to lead to stagnation.

Paul Baran among others has argued that monopolistic competition reduces the incentive for each firm to reinvest in its own industry.[6] Baran suggested two arguments. First, competitive firms are often compelled to invest in new technology while monopolistic forms can choose when to invest. Every competitive firm *must* invest in any newly-discovered device or technique which reduces the cost of production, even if its pre-existing machines are not yet worn out; if it doesn't invest, its competitors will invest and will be able to underprice and drive out of business the noninvesting firm. But monopolistic firms are not threatened by such competition, so they can include other considerations in deciding whether or when to invest in new technologies. For example, although new machines might reduce costs, existing machines may have considerable life left; monopolistic firms might decide to work their old machines until they wear out before buying new ones. Or, they might delay buying new ones because they expect further improvements shortly and want to wait for even more advanced technology. Thus, for a variety of reasons investment in monopolistic industries might be slower (and in any given period, less) than in competitive industries.

Secondly, Baran suggested that many new investments are feasible or profitable only if production is expanded. But in a monopolistic industry, extra output can be sold only if the industry's market expands or if the investing firm captures the customers of the other giant firms in the industry. The former rarely offers much opportunity, and the latter may provoke a ruinous fight. Thus monopolistic firms tend to be less willing to invest in new output-expanding technology than competitive firms.

Moreover, market barriers-to-entry restrict the profitability of investment in other monopolistic industries. The possibilities for new investment outlets are increasingly limited to the competitive industries; but these industries, suffering the continuing invasion by monopolistic firms, are themselves shrinking. Other things being equal, the result is a tendency within capitalism toward growing stagnation.

Note that this argument considers long-run trends in monopoly capitalism. The economy actually rides the roller-coaster of the business cycle, in which boom years alternate with ones of bust. But the argument implies that aside from these *cyclical* ups and downs, there exists a long-term *secular* trend toward stagnation. In any short period this long-term movement may be offset by the prosperity of the cyclical boom, but over the longer period, the secular forces will reassert themselves.

The actual experience of the economy—whether stagnation occurs or not —depends on factors other than the negative impact of monopoly on the incentive to invest. Technical change, product innovation, the appearance of new industries, investment in foreign markets, etc. would tend to offset the impact of monopoly. Most importantly, if private consumption and investment should prove insufficient to avoid depression, public expenditures may take up the slack. Indeed, such "Keynesian spending" has assumed increas-

[6]Paul Baran, *The Political Economy of Growth* (New York: Monthly Review Press, 1957), Chapter 3.

ing proportions in monopoly capitalism, especially since the 1930s.[7] Nevertheless, the transition to monopoly capitalism greatly intensified the pressures toward stagnation.

[7]But as we note below, both international competition and the interests of individual capitalists increasingly place constraints on the government's ability to pump up the economy. On the role of government spending, see below, Sections 6.2 and 11.2 and Chapter 12.

4.4   *Finance Capital and Corporate Control*

The creation of the large corporation was only one step in the continuing concentration and centralization of capital. A concurrent but more advanced step was the growth of finance capital, the extension of financial control over corporations, and the emergence of financial groups.

Banks, insurance companies, savings and loan associations, credit bureaus, and the like are financial institutions: they take in money to hold for deposit, investment, and transfer. In the normal course of their business, these institutions come to control great amounts of financial assets, such as stocks, bonds, mortgages, deposits, promissory notes, etc. The capitalists who own financial-sector businesses thus have available to them resources for investment far beyond their own capital. When they invest these resources in other, nonfinancial corporations, the financiers become industrial capitalists as well, and this fusion of bank capital with industrial capital is termed *finance capital*. When finance capitalists have sufficient investment in (or other influence over) a corporation to determine its policies, they exercise *financial control* over the corporation. Finally, a *financial group* is simply the combination of financial institutions and associated corporations which are under the sway of one or a few capitalists.

For capitalists, the purpose of engaging in business is the production of profits, not of particular commodities. Whether profits are achieved in one industry or another is immaterial. It is not surprising, then, that accumulation should progressively lead successful capitalists to identify their interests with profit-making per se rather than with particular industries. In part this interest is reflected in the "conglomerate" firm—that is, a corporation that engages in many, typically unrelated lines of business.

The rise of finance capital reflects this same trend. First, finance capital has permitted the most important groups in the capitalist class to diversify their interests and thereby create a mechanism for accumulation that is divorced from the constraints of profit-making in particular industries. For example, the Rockefeller fortunes, originally amassed in oil refining, now form the basis for the Chase Manhattan financial group. Through the holdings of this group, the Rockefeller interests have been spread out through oil companies, airlines, mining, and countless other industries. Finance capital tends to accelerate, then, the identification of leading capitalists with the entire capitalist system. In this way, finance capital increases the common interests shared within the capitalist class.

Second, financial control permits leading capitalists to collect profits without being directly concerned with the extraction of surplus value. The day-to-day and even year-to-year management of corporations can be left to suitably highly paid managers, who simply "represent the stockholder interest." Corporate owners disappear into the background, and the need to earn an "adequate" profit rate appears to outsiders as an immutable constraint imposed by impersonal capital market forces. Thus the capitalists' interests are metamorphosed into corporate imperatives without capitalist intervention.

Third, financial control obviously increases the possibility for centralization of capital far beyond what would be apparent from looking at corporations alone. For example, a financial group might well try to coordinate the policies of all the corporations it controlled so as to maximize the profits of the entire group. Such control further erodes the role of competition within the economy. To understand how much of the American economy is controlled by large capitalists we would need to know the extent of financial control.

Finally, as the legally mandated trustees of union pension funds, financial institutions hold the collective savings of workers. Finance capital thereby provides a means for capitalists to draw upon resources otherwise beyond their control and in excess of accumulated profits. The resources so controlled further increase their power.

In the following reading, David Kotz traces the rise of finance capital and provides some indication of its current significance.

The competitive stage of capitalism gave way to monopoly capitalism in the United States during the late nineteenth and early twentieth century. This transformation entailed a process of concentration of economic power, as a small number of productive enterprises came to dominate economic activity.

Alongside the growing enterprise concentration we find a process of concentration of power taking place within that part of the population which owns and controls business enterprises—the capitalist class. A segment of the capitalist class emerges—the monopoly capitalists—that owns and controls the large, monopolistic enterprises. Monopoly profits provide the basis for accumulating great personal fortunes; a number of monopoly capitalists today have personal or quasi-personal wealth in excess of one billion dollars —the Rockefellers, duPonts, Mellons, Gettys, and others. Medium and small capitalists may earn a comfortable income and even become quite rich; but they remain distinctly subordinate to the monopoly capitalists, who dominate the economy and determine its direction.

A full understanding of monopoly capitalism requires that we develop a clear picture of this dominant class of monopoly capitalists. What is the internal structure of the monopoly capitalist class? What is the precise relationship between the monopoly capitalists and the corporate institutions through which they carry out their economic functions?

There are two main opposing views of the relationship between the monopoly capitalist class and the large corporations in the

United States. The Financial Control Thesis holds that bankers are the most important controlling force over the large manufacturing, mining, transportation, utility, and distributive trade corporations (called "nonfinancial" corporations). Thus, bankers are seen as the leading section of the monopoly capitalists. According to this view, large corporations belong to one or another "financial group," each of which consists of a number of large nonfinancial corporations centered around one or a few banks and other financial institutions, with the latter serving as coordinating and control centers for the group.

The second view is the Managerial Thesis. This view holds that as stockholdings in large corporations have become increasingly dispersed over time, the stockholders have lost their power. It is alleged that the high profits of the modern large corporation free it from dependence on external sources of capital, undermining the power of bankers. According to this view, control is thus transferred into the hands of each corporation's top managers. These managers ordinarily rise up through the ranks of the corporation, and do not own a significant proportion of the corporation's stock; yet, they obtain the power to keep themselves in office and to name their own successors. According to this view, the top managers of large nonfinancial corporations have become the leading section of the monopoly capitalist class.

These two theses have divergent implications for our understanding of monopoly capitalism. Probably most important are the implications for concentration of power. According to the Managerial Thesis, large corporations act independently of one another. This contrasts with the Financial Control View that large corporations are part of still larger grouping—financial groups. Thus, the Financial Control Thesis implies a substantially greater degree of concentration of power than does the Managerial Thesis. As we shall see, the Financial Control Thesis leads one to expect more monopolistic collusion among firms and a more rapid process of centralization of capital through

mergers than would be predicted by the Managerial Thesis.

Some proponents of the Managerial Thesis do not think the top corporate managers are capitalists at all. Instead, they are supposed to be a new class of "professional managers" who have displaced the capitalists as the ruling class of modern capitalism. Some claim that this development has ended the corporation's single-minded pursuit of profits. The top managers are held to act, not as agents of the stockholders, but as "social trustees" who balance the interests of stockholders, employees, consumers, and the general public. The result is a "socially responsible corporation" and an end to the irrationality and class conflict of "old-style" capitalism.[1]

The Managerial Thesis is very widely believed, particularly among orthodox social scientists. However, recent evidence has provided strong support for the Financial Control Thesis. Before presenting this evidence, it will be helpful to look at the historical evolution of corporate control in the United States. This is necessary to fully understand the situation today, since the nature of control over the modern large corporation is the product of a century of struggle between contending groups within the capitalist class.

THE EVOLUTION OF CORPORATE CONTROL

At the close of the Civil War, the U.S. economy was one of small, local enterprises. The railroads had already adopted the corporate form of organization, but most were still local corporations, owning no more than a few hundred miles of track. An individual or small group normally exercised control over these railroad companies through ownership of a majority of the stock.

The decades that followed the Civil War witnessed a rapid extension of the railroad

---

[1]For the classic statement of this view, see Carl Kaysen, "The Social Significance of the Modern Corporation," *American Economic Review*, May 1957.

system of the U.S. Between 1865 and 1893 total rail mileage grew more than fivefold. The rapid increase in rail mileage was accompanied by the consolidation of small, local railroad corporations into great systems. During the 1880s nearly two-thirds of the railroad companies in the U.S. were absorbed by the remaining third.

The growth and consolidation of the railroads required more capital than the railroad entrepreneurs could supply themselves. They turned to investment banks for capital. Investment banks are institutions that raise capital for corporations by purchasing new bonds, stock, or other long-term securities issued by the corporation, and then reselling the securities to the ultimate purchasers.[2] In the 1880s the leading investment banks, which were located in New York City, came to acquire some influence over the railroads, as the latter became increasingly dependent on the investment banks for capital.

The growing power of the New York investment banks was partly based on their control over access to European capital. A substantial portion of the capital used to build the U.S. railroads in the nineteenth century came from European, and particularly British, capitalists. To sell bonds to British capitalists, the railroad entrepreneurs usually had to go through J. P. Morgan's investment bank; for selling bonds in Germany, Kuhn, Loeb and Company was the dominant investment bank. The New York investment banks followed the practice of not competing for one another's traditional corporate clients, which further magnified the bankers' power.

At first the investment bankers were satisfied to leave the running of the railroad companies to the enterpreneurs. However, the unrestrained competitive behavior of the railroad entrepreneurs caused problems for the bankers. The railroads built parallel routes, often creating more rail capacity than the demand could support. Frequent rate-cutting wars resulted, with losses to all parties. Attempts to form price-fixing pools were generally short-lived. The leading railroad entrepreneurs were hard-headed, individualistic capitalists who were ill-suited for cooperation with one another.

While a railroad enterpreneur might hope to gain by undercutting his rivals, the leading investment bankers, who supplied capital to many competing railroads, preferred cooperation. In the late 1880s J. P. Morgan pressured the major railroad entrepreneurs to establish cartel agreements with one another, to "avoid wasteful rivalry."[3] Those agreements also failed. The matter was finally resolved when the Panic of 1893 and the ensuing depression caused most of the large railroads, weakened by decades of rate-wars and overbuilding, to go into receivership. This allowed J. P. Morgan and Kuhn, Loeb and Company, as representatives of the bondholders, to take direct control of the railroads. They used their power to further consolidate the railroads and to establish the cooperative, monopolistic practices which the railroad entrepreneurs had resisted.

Banker Control over Manufacturing Companies

Stimulated by the improving transportation system and the discovery of new technologies in the late nineteenth century, entrepreneurs built growing companies in steel, petroleum, meat-packing, electrical machinery, farm machinery, and other manufacturing industries. The problems of cutthroat competition and unsuccessful pooling attempts plagued the industrial entrepreneurs as they had the railroads. The industrialists succeeded in limiting competition by mergers in a few industries, such as petroleum and tobacco. But competition generally prevailed until the 1890s when the leading investment bankers turned their attention to the newly incorporated manufacturing companies.

---

[2]An investment bank may also aid in the raising of capital by agreeing to purchase at a fixed price any securities that the issuing corporation is unable to sell after a certain date.

[3]Lewis Corey, *House of Morgan* (New York: 1930), p. 172.

The investment bankers fostered and financed mergers among the major competing firms in one industry after another. Entrepreneurs who resisted the combination movement, such as Andrew Carnegie, were pressured into selling out; some who went along with it and accepted banker leadership obtained management positions in the new "trusts," as they were popularly called. Between 1898 and 1903 thousands of firms took part in the "Great Merger Movement." J. P. Morgan put together many of today's well-known companies at that time, including U.S. Steel and International Harvester.

One study found that seventy-eight of the trusts formed during the Great Merger Movement obtained half or more of the market for their product. J. P. Morgan usually named the directors of the trusts he created and exerted influence to encourage collusive behavior among the trusts. The rise of banker control had greatly increased the degree of monopoly power in the manufacturing sector. The bankers benefited not only from the huge "promoter's profits" received for financing the great mergers; they also received the chance to share in the long-term profits that growing monopoly power promised to the corporations and their financial backers.

By the opening decades of this century, several distinct financial groups had emerged as the dominant forces in the economy. As explained above, a financial group is a closely associated group of financial institutions (investment banks, commercial banks, life insurance companies) and nonfinancial corporations, with the financial institutions serving as the group's control center. The Morgan group was based on the alliance between J. P. Morgan and Company and the First National Bank of New York, the latter a commercial bank. It included the three largest life insurance companies, American Telephone and Telegraph, and several dozen railroad and manufacturing companies.[4]

[4]For a detailed description of the major financial groups in 1912, see U.S. Congress, House Banking and Currency Committee, *Report of the Committee Appointed Pursuant to H.R. 429 and 574 to Investigate the Concentration of Money and Credit*, 62nd Congress, 2nd Session, 1913.

The second most powerful financial group was formed from the great wealth accumulated by John D. Rockefeller's Standard Oil Company. Standard Oil was so profitable that not only was it able to remain free of banker control, but, through an alliance with James Stillman of the National City Bank of New York, it formed a financial group that rivaled the Morgan group. The Rockefeller-Stillman group controlled numerous manufacturing and railroad companies, including Amalgamated Copper (predecessor of Anaconda Copper) and the Union Pacific Railroad.

Other important financial groups were the Mellon group, based in Pittsburgh, and the Kuhn, Loeb and Company group. Some entrepreneurs were able to function independently of the great financial groups, particularly in new industries. Henry Ford is a good example; the Ford Motor Company never borrowed from New York banks while Ford, Sr., was in charge. However, the leading bankers had won control over most of the major nonfinancial corporations.

Decline of Financial Control

Between the death of J. P. Morgan, Sr., in 1915 and the start of the Great Depression in 1929, financial control increased in some areas and declined in others. The dominant individuals who had personified banker control passed away, but the structure they had established remained. The New York financial groups extended their control over another sector of the economy in the 1920s: power utilities. Before the 1920s electric and gas utilities had been largely local companies. In the early 1920s they began to grow rapidly and issue a high volume of bonds. The leading investment banks used the device of the holding company to establish control over them. By 1929 ten great public utility holding company systems did about three-fourths of the electric light and power business in the U.S. The Morgan group controlled the two largest; only one remained free of Wall Street control.

On the other hand, new centers of power

arose in competition with New York City during the 1920s. In Cleveland, Chicago, and San Francisco financial institutions entered into competition for power with the Wall Street bankers. Some entrepreneurs built giant corporations outside the control of the bankers; the duPonts, for example, bought control of General Motors during the close of World War I and turned it into the leading automobile manufacturer.

More importantly, during the Great Depression and World War II, the power of the major bankers appears to have been substantially weakened. Control over the supply of external capital had been the source of the bankers' power. During the entire course of the severely depressed 1930s, large corporations used very little external finance, since depreciation allowances were generally sufficient to finance firm's reduced levels of operations. Thousands of investment banks and commercial banks went out of business. The largest ones survived but found they had little role to play in financing industry. When prosperity returned during World War II, the government provided most of the capital for expansion of industry.

Public demands to break up the "Money Trust," together with lobbying by Chicago and Cleveland investment banks hoping to loosen the New York banks' domination of the financing of major corporations, contributed to the adoption of New Deal laws and administrative actions that further eroded the bankers' power. Among the most important were the Banking Act of 1933, which separated investment from commercial banking, and regulations controlling the sale of utility and railroad securities.

It was during this period that the Managerial Thesis arose and became influential. Proponents of this view showed that stockholdings in many large corporations were becoming increasingly dispersed. After the entrepreneurial founders of many large corporations died, their stockholdings were divided up among numerous heirs, who were often interested only in securing income from the fortune, not in exercising control. Thus, the power associated with stockholdings was seen as declining. If financial control were also receding, the logical conclusion was that the managers of each corporation would step into the power vaccuum and assume ultimate control.

Resurgence of Financial Control

With the end of World War II came a resurgence of the power of financial institutions. The sharp decline in use of external finance during the 1930s turned out to be a temporary phenomenon; after World War II corporations resumed normal use of external finance. Nonfinancial corporations obtained between 40 and 45 percent of their total funds from external sources during 1946–52 and 1964–72, as they had in 1900–10. A sample of large manufacturing companies received 34 percent of total funds from external sources during 1949–54, compared to 30 percent in 1900–10.[5]

However, in the post–World War II period the major basis of the power of financial institutions has shifted from control over the financing process to control over the stock of large corporations. A major reason for this shift lies in the extremely rapid growth of commercial bank trust departments since 1945. Through their trust departments, commercial banks invest and manage money for individuals and institutions. For decades wealthy capitalists have placed their fortunes in bank-managed trusts, to escape taxation and to avoid dissipation of the fortune through the spending habits of heirs. In many cases the big block of stock that the founder of a corporation has passed on to his descendants has remained intact in a bank trust

---

[5]John Lintner, "The Financing of Corporations," in E. Mason, ed., *The Corporation in Modern Society* (New York: 1969), p. 180; S. Creamer, S. Dobrovolski, and I. Borenstein, *Capital in Manufacturing and Mining* (Princeton, N.J.: 1960), pp. 192–93; and the *Economic Report of the President* (Washington, D.C.: U.S. Government Printing Office, 1974), p. 339.

department. Numerous heirs receive the income from the stock, but in many cases the bank obtains the right to vote the stock. Thus, dispersion of individual stock ownership has not always resulted in dispersal of the power associated with the original block of stock.

Pension funds are the second major source of bank trust department assets. After World War II unions won the right to bargain with their employers over pension plans, and as a result the assets of private pension funds grew from under $2 billion in 1945 to $157 billion in 1972. Banks manage most private pension funds, investing them largely in corporate stock and usually holding full voting rights over the stock purchased.

Thus, increased tax rates for the wealthy combined with the insecurity that workers face regarding retirement have placed a huge amount of corporate stock in the hands of the leading banks. By 1972 bank trust departments held 25 percent of all corporate stock in the U.S.[6] The ten largest bank trust departments hold well over one-third of total bank trust department assets. A study based on post–World War II trends projected that financial institutions' holdings of corporate stock (excluding personal trust funds) would reach 55 percent of all corporate stock by the year 2000.[7]

FINANCIAL CONTROL TODAY

To what extent have the post–World War II trends discussed above enabled bankers to regain the dominant position in the economy they had occupied in the 1920s? In an attempt to assess the prevalence of financial control over large nonfinancial corporations today, I have done a study of control over large nonfinancial corporations in the U.S. for 1967–69. The sample consisted of

[6] *Trusts and Estates*, March 1974, p. 145.

[7] See Robert Soldofsky, *Institutional Ownership of Common Stock: 1900–2000* (Ann Arbor, Mich.: 1971), p. 209.

the 200 largest nonfinancial corporations, ranked by value of total assets at year-end 1969.[8] The study took advantage of previously unavailable data on bank trust department stockholdings that were made public by two government reports in 1968 and 1971.[9]

I define control as "the power to determine the broad policies guilding a corporation." This is distinguished from "managing" a corporation, by which I mean the activities of directing and administering a business. Control, then, is the power to determine how, and toward what ends, a corporation is managed. A controlling group may actively exercise its power by directly serving in top management positions, by selecting the management, or by pressuring the management. On the other hand, if the management of a corporation sticks to the policies favored by the controlling group, the latter may have no reason to intervene for long periods of time.

Table 4-D presents the overall results of the study. A majority (55 percent) of the 200 largest non-financial corporations were found to be controlled by either financial institutions, individual stockholders, or both. We found 39 percent of the sample under financial control—almost twice as many as were under owner control. Management control, as estimated by the no-suspected-or-confirmed-center-of-control category, covered

[8] There were some departures from strict asset ranking, the most important one involving the treatment of utilities. A sample based on asset rankings includes a far greater percent of utilities than samples based on other size criteria, such as sales or value added, because utilities are so capital-intensive. To avoid making the composition of the sample too dependent on the size criterion chosen, I have included only the ten largest utilities in our sample. For other criteria used in this study, see Appendix, p. 157.

[9] These studies are U.S. House Banking and Currency Committee, Subcommittee on Domestic Finance, *Commercial Banks and their Trust Activities*, 90th Congress, 2nd Session, 1968; and U.S. Securities and Exchange Commission, *Institutional Investor Study Report*, House Document 92-64, referred to the House Committee on Interstate and Foreign Commerce, 1971.

TABLE 4-D SUMMARY OF CONTROL OVER THE 200 LARGEST NONFINANCIAL CORPORATIONS, 1967–69

Control category	Number of companies	Percent of companies
Financial control	78	39.0
Owner control	43	21.5
Financial or owner control*	110	55.0
Miscellaneous**	5	2.5
No identified center of control	85	42.5
No suspected or confirmed center of control	61	30.5

*There is overlap between the categories financial control and owner control, with financial institutions and individual stockholders sharing control over 11 corporations. Hence, the figure for "financial or owner control" is less than the sum of those two categories.

**The miscellaneous category includes control by a foreign corporation and control by a self-administered fund.

TABLE 4-E NUMBER AND ASSETS OF CORPORATIONS IN THE TOP 200 CONTROLLED BY THE LEADING FINANCIAL INSTITUTIONS, 1967–69

Controller	Number of companies controlled	Assets of companies controlled ($ millions)
Chase group	21	29,966
Morgan group	15	22,417
First National Bank, Chicago	6	10,953
Mellon group	5	14,278
Lehman-Goldman, Sachs group	5	7,262
Kuhn, Loeb & Company	3	8,930
First National City Bank, New York	3	6,198
Cleveland Trust Company	3	3,383

30.5 percent of the sample. Other widely cited studies of corporate control in recent decades have found management control to be overwhelmingly prevalent largely because they left out the category of financial control.[10] By contrast, our study finds financial control to be the most frequent type of control over large nonfinancial corporations.

As Table 4-E indicates, the most powerful financial institutions are descended from the leading financial groups of the 1920s. However, some changes in relative strength have occurred since that time. The Chase group now is significantly stronger than the Morgan group, no doubt a result of the rapid growth of the oil industry since the 1920s. The Morgan group never obtained a significant position in that industry. Today the Chase group has concentrated in transportation—airlines and railroads—while the Morgan group is heavily involved in computer and office machinery companies. The Mellon

group, First National Bank of Chicago, and Cleveland Trust Company are all largely involved in heavy industry, while the Lehman-Goldman, Sachs group specializes in light industry and retail trade. The continuing primacy of New York bankers is indicated by the finding that over two-thirds of the corporations under financial control were controlled by New York financial institutions. Commercial banks have clearly replaced investment banks as the dominant financial institutions. In the two leading financial groups, commercial banks—Chase Manhattan and Morgan Guarantee Trust—are the central institutions.[11]

I found owner control to be most common among the smallest corporations in our sample. Among the smallest 40 corporations in our sample, it was more common than financial control. By contrast, financial control was most prevalent among the middle-sized companies within the top 200. The very

[10]For example, see Robert Larner, "Ownership and Control of the 200 Largest Nonfinancial Corporations," *American Economic Review*, September, 1966. Larner found 84.5 percent of the 200 largest nonfinancial corporations to be management-controlled and 15.5 percent owner-controlled in 1963.

[11]Associated with this development is today's primary role of stockholding as a basis of financial control. Of the 78 nonfinancial corporations under financial control, the control relationship was based on stockholding alone in 48 instances, a capital supplier relationship alone in 22 instances, and a combination of the two in 7 instances.

largest corporations are so large that, in most cases, not even the Morgan or Chase group can hold a sufficiently large amount of stock, or supply a sufficiently large amount of debt capital, to obtain control. In many cases, the largest corporations had representatives of several leading financial groups on their boards. It appears that control over the largest corporations may often be shared among several financial groups and institutions.

My major conclusion is that financial control has again become the most important type of control over large corporations. Furthermore, the amount of stock controlled by commercial banks is growing rapidly. If this trend continues, we can expect financial control to become still more widespread in the future. We now turn to the question of the economic and political significance of financial control today.

THE CONSEQUENCES OF FINANCIAL CONTROL

This historical sketch showed that in the past banker control has been associated with the growth of monopoly power. Bankers have encouraged growing economic concentration through mergers, and they have encouraged cooperative behavior among competitors. Of course, the drive for profits prevents cooperation from completely replacing competition under monopoly capitalism. But banker power has strengthened the tendency toward collusion in many industries.

The significant and growing power of bankers today is an important force for collusion and against competition. The leading financial institutions control many competing, or potentially competing, companies. We found the Morgan group in control of three major paper companies and five major office machinery producers. The Chase group controlled two aircraft manufacturing companies and two chemical companies in the top 200. In each case the controlling financial institutions have an interest in encouraging monopolistic cooperation. A recent anti-trust suit

uncovered an example of such "encouragement." In 1970 the Department of Justice charged a major bank, Cleveland Trust Company, with using its trust department stockholdings in four machine tool companies to promote monopolistic practices among them.[12]

The implications of banker control for monopoly power are less certain when rival financial groups control major corporations in the same industry. For example, two leading copper producers, Anaconda and Kennecott, are controlled by the Chase and Morgan groups, respectively. The historical evidence suggests that, under normal circumstances, the bankers would encourage collusive behavior in such instances. However, it is possible that rivalry between financial groups may sometimes spill over into competitive behavior among the corporations they control.

There is substantial evidence that financial institutions played an important role in the third great merger movement in U.S. history during the 1960s. For example, a House Judiciary Committee investigation found that the Chase Manhattan Bank facilitated and encouraged the acquisition program of Gulf and Western Industries during the 1960s.[13] Chase benefited from the relationship in many ways, including obtaining the financial services business of corporations taken over by Gulf and Western. The investment bank Lazard, Freres and Company played a similar role in ITT's merger program. In both of the above cases, we found the corporation to be controlled by the financial institution involved.

Financial control may affect the behavior of firms not only toward competitors or potential merger partners but also toward potential customers or suppliers. For example, during the early 1930s representatives of

---

[12]This anti-trust suit is still unsettled, as of this writing.

[13]U.S. Congress, House Judiciary Committee, *Investigation of Conglomerate Corporations*, Staff Report of the Antitrust Subcommittee, 92nd Congress, 1st Session, 1971.

the Morgan group enlisted the aid of AT&T to help out Morgan-controlled Kennecott Copper. With copper prices tumbling under the impact of the Depression, an AT&T economist advised the board to hold up copper purchases until copper prices fell further. Instead, under Morgan pressure, AT&T stepped up its purchases of copper to help support the price.

Today each major group of financial institutions controls companies that have potential buyer-seller relationships to one another. For example, Chase controls three airlines and two aircraft companies. This raises the question: To what extent do bankers today encourage buyer-seller relationships in such cases or influence the terms of such relationships? Such influence would imply that a primitive form of planning, based on the interests of the financial group as a whole, is replacing pure market relationships in which each firm follows its own self-interest. The growth of such nonmarket relationships could discourage new entry into supplier industries, thereby reducing competition. Further empirical research is needed in this subject to determine the extent of such banker practices.

These findings challenge the view that a new class of corporate managers has replaced the capitalists as the ruling class of modern capitalism and the related view that corporate managers are now the leading section of the monopoly capitalist class. As the power of individual stockholders has declined, the power of bankers has increased, preventing corporate managers from outgrowing their subordinate role. The bankers are stockholders in, and creditors of, the major corporations; as such, their interest is in the long-run profits of the corporation. That profits remain the central aim of the modern corporation is evident to anyone who studies big business behavior: the continuing power of bankers helps explain why profits retain their central role.

Although bankers are the leading section of the monopoly capitalist class, managers do have a certain amount of independent author-

ity in those corporations that are under management control. Such corporations have no single financial institution or individual stockholder in control. This may allow the management to ignore the *particular* interests of one or another major stockholder or creditor in certain matters of company policy.[14] However, this independence would not permit the management to violate the *common* interests of big stockholders and major creditors. Those common interests include the corporate pursuit of the maximum possible profits. Any corporate management that openly moved against the common interests of big stockholders and major creditors would provoke an overwhelmingly powerful coalition against itself. Any top corporate manager who decided that his company would become socially responsible at the expense of profits would be likely to find himself looking for a new job.

The extent of financial control that we have found among large corporations implies that economic power is even more centralized than the usual concentration ratios suggest. The Chase group alone controlled just over 10 percent of the 200 largest nonfinancial corporations in the late 1960s. The leading bankers have the power to determine or influence the allocation of capital over a significant portion of the economy, and to influence many other aspects of corporate behavior as well.

It is not surprising that the most powerful capitalists have, over time, chosen to operate primarily through banks. Any particular nonfinancial corporation may decline in the long run under the impact of changing technologies and new products. A bank, on the other hand, is tied to no particular industry in the long run. Through a bank, a capitalist can shift his main sphere of investment over time.

A further reason why banks tend to become centers of control under monopoly capitalism is that a capitalist who operates through a

---

[14]For example, the management may be able to resist a request from a banker to purchase an input product from a company linked to the banker.

bank obtains access to other people's capital. The great commercial banks tap the capital not only of much of the capitalist class, in the form of big checking accounts and personal trust funds, but also of a portion of the wealth of independent professionals and the working class, in the form of small checking accounts and pension funds. The Rockefellers and Mellons thus can control corporate empires of far greater worth than their own personal fortunes.

Appendix to 4.4

In answering the question: Who controls each corporation? I used three basic control categories: financial control, owner control, and management control. The criteria used for classifying a corporation according to type of control were quite long and detailed. In brief, a corporation was classified under financial control if one of the following two criteria was met: (1) a financial institution held 5 percent or more of the voting stock; (2) a financial institution was the leading supplier of debt capital to a corporation that used a substantial amount of external capital *and* the financial institution had strong representation on the corporation's board of directors. These criteria embody the two bases of financial control that have been important historically—the supplying of external capital and the holding of stock.[1]

The wording of the above criteria for financial control treats the individual financial institution as the agent of financial control. The historical record shows that in the past banker power has been based on alliances among financial institutions. I found that in the 1960s there continued to exist some well-defined groups of financial insti-

tutions, consisting of financial institutions that had close ties and worked closely together. The most important were the Chase group, the Morgan group, the Mellon group, and the Lehman-Goldman, Sachs group.

The Chase group includes Chase Manhattan Bank, Chemical Bank, Metropolitan Life Insurance Company, and Equitable Life Assurance Society. It is descended from the Rockefeller group of the 1920s; David Rockefeller, grandson of John D. Rockefeller, is chairman of Chase Manhattan. The Morgan group includes Morgan Guaranty Trust, Bankers Trust, Prudential Life, Morgan Stanley and Company, and Smith Barney and Company. The latter two institutions are investment banks. The Pittsburgh-based Mellon group includes Mellon National Bank and the First Boston Corporation, the latter an investment bank. The Lehman-Goldman, Sachs group consists of Lehman Brothers and Goldman, Sachs and Company, both New York investment banks. In applying my criteria for financial control to the sample of 200 corporations, I treated each of these four groups of financial institutions as a single financial institution for control purposes.

I classify a corporation as being under owner control if an individual, or a small group of related individuals, holds 5 percent or more of the corporation's voting stock. If no financial institution or individual stockholder is found to be in control based on our criteria, I classify the corporation under "no identified center of control."

A corporation with no identified center of control may be controlled by its own management. However, owing to limitations on the quantity and quality of the data available for determining control, some corporations in my residual category of no identified center of control are probably actually under financial or owner control. Thus, my results for financial control and owner control probably understate the actual frequency of those types of control. This is acceptable insofar as our

[1]The rationale for the 5 percent stockholding percentage rule is that it is a sufficiently large share to provide the nucleus for a successful proxy fight, should the management choose to seriously violate the stockholding group's wishes. The power associated with a capital supplier relationship, however, is more dependent on circumstances; no fixed percentage can be cited. When strong representation of the financial institution on the corporation's board accompanies the capital supplier relationship, I take the board representation as an indication that the capital supplier relationship does confer controlling power on the financial institution. By strong representation I mean two representatives of the financial institution on the corporation's board, or one representative who is on a key board committee. By a "representative" of a financial institution, I mean an officer of the financial institution or someone else who we determine to be representing the interests of the financial institution on the corporation's board.

aim is to get minimum estimates of the prevalence of financial and owner control. However, if we want a similar minimum-estimate-of-management control, the no-identified-center-of-control category is unsuitable; it is more likely to give a *maximum* estimate of management control. To get a measure of management control more comparable to our financial and owner control categories, I have deducted from the no-indentified-center-of-control category those corporations for which I found a substantial amount of evidence of financial or owner control, but not enough evidence to satisfy the criteria for financial or owner control. This smaller residual category is called "no suspected or confirmed center of control"; I use it as a measure of management control.

4.5 *Competitive Capital and Monopoly Capital*

As we have seen, large corporations have come to dominate the economy, but they have not entirely swallowed it up. Small businesses, and associated with them a diminishing but still significant class of small-business owners, remain an important feature of the American business landscape.

In these parts of the economy the conditions under which accumulation occurs are somewhat different. One important difference involves technical change. In the competitive sector, technological changes that reduce the costs of production tend, through competition, to get widely introduced and then to result in product price declines. In this case the users of the product obtain most of the benefit from the discovery or invention. In the monopoly sector, when technical change occurs, the monopoly power of large corporations permits them to maintain prices. In this case the new technique results in higher profits, since prices have been maintained while costs were reduced.

To understand the dynamics of accumulation, we must investigate the specific conditions existing in each sector, and then attempt to understand how they interact. This is what James O'Connor does in the following reading.[1]

As O'Connor points out, the monopolistic firms are more significant than their percentages of employment or sales might suggest because they are the most *dynamic* sector. The huge, concentrated profits of monopoly corporations, when reinvested, create enormous change—change in the technologies used in production, change in the type of products offered for sale, change in where jobs are available and what skills they require, change in what markets big firms operate in, and so on. Competitive firms, having smaller and more scattered profits to reinvest, tend to be more stagnant, surviving in those markets left by the big firms. Moreover, many competitive firms are totally dependent on monopolistic firms, either as chief suppliers or as chief customers. Hence the development of the economy as a whole is much more heavily influenced by the investment decisions of the monopoly corporations than by those of the competitive firms.

Finally, the higher profit *rate* in monopoly firms speeds up the process of

---

[1]In the book from which this reading is taken, O'Connor treats the state as a third sector. The public sector accounts for over 20 percent of total purchases of goods and services but only 16 percent of total employment. We defer consideration of the public sector until Chapter 6.

centralization of capital. Monopoly firms have more than proportionately larger earnings to reinvest (as well as greater access to credit from finance capitalists), producing unequal growth in the two sectors. Because they accumulate more rapidly, monopoly firms tend to expand into remaining competitive industries, and the monopoly sector as a whole grows at the expense of the competitive sector.

Production and distribution in the private sector fall into two subgroups: competitive industries organized by small business and monopolistic industries organized by large-scale capital.

THE COMPETITIVE SECTOR

In the competitive sector the physical capital-to-labor ratio and output per worker, or productivity, are low, and growth of production depends less on physical capital investment and technical progress than on growth of employment. Production is typically small scale, and markets are normally local or regional in scope. Familiar examples include restaurants, drug and grocery stores, service stations, and other branches of trade; garages, appliance repair shops, and other services; clothing and accessories, commercial displays, and other manufacturing industries. Competitive industries employ roughly one-third of the U.S. labor force, with the largest proportion in services and distribution.

What is the significance of low ratios of capital to labor and low productivity? First, competitive sector wages are relatively low, and second, there is a tendency toward overcrowding because it is relatively easy to set up business. Further, many competitive industries produce for (or sell in) markets that are seasonal, subject to sudden change in fashion or style, or otherwise irregular or unstable. Small businessmen whose product markets are irregular have little opportunity to stabilize production and employment. Nor is there much incentive to do so even when the opportunity arises: they have invested very little capital per worker and thus business losses from excess physical capacity and time in set-up and shut-down operations are relatively small.

Unstable and irregular product markets and unstable and irregular labor markets go together in competitive industries. Employment in the competitive sector tends to be relatively low paid and casual, temporary, or seasonal. Workers who want and are unable to find full-time, year-round, well-paid work in the monopolistic or state sectors will accept employment in the competitive sector on almost any terms. In the United States the chief examples are black and other minority workers who are cut off from "mainstream" opportunities by racism and discrimination, women who are excluded by sexism from good jobs and good pay, and older workers who are retired involuntarily from high-wage industries (which dictate most compulsory retirement rules). The supply of labor in competitive industries is further inflated by workers (e.g., married women, students, retired workers) who want, and will accept lower wages to obtain, irregular work; they make up about one-half of the nonagricultural labor force working less than thirty-five hours weekly. It has been estimated that about 45 percent of the U.S. work force is "peripheral," or marginal, either by choice or necessity.

The labor movement in the competitive

sector is relatively underdeveloped, in part because the social characteristics of the work force, the multitude of firms in a particular industry, and the small-scale, localized nature of production obstruct the organization of strong unions. Further, highly competitive product markets, rapid business turnover, and small profit margins make it costly for employers to recognize unions. Thus it is not unusual for union negotiators to sign "sweetheart" contracts, and established unions often are unable to influence wage rates significantly. There are partial or full exceptions—for example, the foundry industry, with about 5000 small plants, where the trend is toward industry-wide bargaining; and branches of the garment industry concentrated in a few square blocks of mid-Manhattan, where unions and contractors have enormous influence in local and state government, and which employ skilled workers.

Still, the dominant feature of the competitive sector is that workers are condemned to relative material impoverishment. In 1968, over 10 million workers earned less than $1.60 per hour, including 3.5 million paid less than $1.00 per hour. Two-thirds of these workers were employed in retail trade and service industries, and more than one-tenth were employed in agriculture, forestry, and fishing—all highly competitive and relatively low-wage industries.

Working conditions in competitive industries tend to be poor and unemployment and underemployment high. Normally, workers do not earn enough to save for times of unemployment, indebtedness, sickness, or death. Weak or corrupt labor organizations do not secure adequate company-paid health, retirement, and other fringe benefits.

Historically, incomes have been supplemented in this sector by subsistence production, extended family systems, and community-help programs (e.g., "mom and pop" grocery stores, small-scale manufacturing and related facilities which provide employment for family members independent of their productivity, subsistence farming, arti-

san labor, "taking in the neighbor's wash," etc.). However, in modern capitalism the increasing "proletarianization" (or increase in percent of workforce with nothing to sell but labor power) of the entire population, the decline in subsistence and artisan production, and the weakening and destruction of traditional community bonds increasingly compel workers to look to the state for means of subsistence. Thus they are condemned to be full or partial dependents of the state, the recipients of income supplements in the form of public hospital services and health care, subsidized housing, welfare and relief, old age assistance, food stamps, transportation subsidies, and the like.

THE MONOPOLY SECTOR

At one time most if not all industries now in the monopoly sector were organized along competitive lines. The process of monopolization involved a rapid growth in the physical capital-to-labor ratio and output per worker (physical productivity). Today, the growth of production depends less on growth of employment than on increases in physical capital per worker and technical progress. Production is typically large scale and markets are normally national or international in scope—for example, capital goods such as steel, copper, aluminum, and electrical equipment; consumer goods such as automobiles, appliances, soap products, and various food products; transportation industries such as railroads, airlines, and branches of shipping. About one-third of the U.S. work force is employed in monopolistic industries, the largest proportion in manufacturing and mining.

Wages are relatively high, even in the smaller "fringe" firms that coexist with the giants in some monopoly industries. However, low-seniority workers and many in unskilled and semi-skilled jobs are frequently little better off than their counterparts in competitive industries. For example, steelworkers with less than two years' service are ineligible for supplementary unemployment benefits, and a 1971 Equal Employment Opportunity Commission report condemned "Ma Bell" for confining women workers to "the most stifling and repetitive (and low-paid) jobs."

Barriers to the entry of new capital in monopoly industries (e.g., state regulatory agencies, high capital requirements, high overhead costs, advertising and brand loyalty, and product differentiation) create relatively stable industrial structures. Moreover, the large amounts of fixed capital invested per worker compel management to regularize production and employment to avoid losses attributable to unused productive capacity. The complexity of modern technology and work processes and the enormous task of coordinating disparate elements in the production process also compel management to minimize arbitrary or unexpected elements in production and distribution. Planning is extended downward to insure the availability of raw materials and other supplies at stable prices and upward into wholesale and retail operations in order to control demand.

For these reasons, the demand for labor is relatively stable and work is available on a full-time, year-round basis. There are two broad layers of workers in the monopoly sector (in addition to the bottom layer mentioned previously): (1) blue-collar production, maintenance, and similar workers and (2) a so-called middle class of white-collar, technical, administrative workers (the great majority white adult males, excluding women who hold typing, filing, and other unskilled and semiskilled white-collar jobs). The typical competitive firm is small and its technology is less complex; thus the demand for bureaucratic-administrative and technical-scientific workers in this sector is relatively low.

The social makeup of the work force, the relatively inelastic demand for labor, and the physical and geographic concentration of production units facilitate the growth of powerful labor unions in monopolistic industries. And monopolistic product markets, stable industrial structures, and large profit margins make it comparatively inexpensive for corporations to recognize unions. Thus since the 1930s and early 1940s, when workers in most monopolistic industries forced employers to recognize and bargain with their unions, the labor movement in this sector has been relatively well developed.

· · ·

WAGE AND PRICE DETERMINATION

Competitive sector wages, prices, and profits are determined chiefly by market forces. The essence of the competitive market mechanism is the process by which productivity increases are transformed into higher standards of living via changes in prices and profits. Assume, for example, that a group of farmers introduces hybrid corn that doubles land yields and hence (ignoring other costs) reduces costs by one-half. Clearly, given the market price of corn, they will make a profit over and above the usual margin in the industry. Three consequences are likely: first, the innovating farmers will be tempted to expand production to make even greater profits; second, other corn farmers will be compelled to introduce the hybrid, or risk being driven out of business; third, farmers growing other crops will be tempted to plant corn. In any (or all) of these events, total corn production and supply increase, and more corn is sold, but at lower prices. With demand constant, the expansion of supply will drive down prices and sooner or later eliminate the original larger-than-normal profit margins. The final effect is that the consumer (i.e., society as a whole) benefits from the innovation and cost reductions in the form of lower prices for things needed for survival.

If consumers buy the entire crop for immediate use, there is a direct link between the technical innovation (hybrid corn) and a higher material standard of life (lower prices). If manufacturers buy the corn to process it, the effect on material well-being is indirect: Fresh corn prices fall, pushing down production costs in the canneries, thus increasing profits in this branch of industry. In turn, a mechanism similar to the one just described is touched off. Cannery owners will expand production to take advantage of higher profit margins, and other businessmen will enter the corn-canning industry to make a higher return on their capital. The effect will be to increase the supply of processed corn, lower prices, eliminate excessive profits, and indirectly spread the gains from technical progress to society.

To summarize: All other things being equal, prices in competitive industries fall more or less in proportion to increases in productivity. The gains from technical progress are not monopolized by any one group of capitalists and workers in the form of permanently higher prices, profits, and wages, but rather are distributed more or less evenly among the population as a whole. "The basic principle of the market system," Joan Robinson writes, summarizing the whole issue, "is that the benefits of progress are passed on to the community as a whole, not bottled up in the industries where they happen to arise."[1]

If prices are determined by productivity in the competitive sector, what determines wages? Total demand in the economy as a whole. Upward surges of competitive-sector money wages are attributable to inflation, not to technical progress and improvements in productivity. During periods of high labor demand and general inflation, wages in unorganized industries (mainly competitive industries) increase faster than wages in organized industries (mainly monopoly industries). During periods of sluggish labor demand, union-nonunion wage differentials shift in favor of organized workers.

In the monopoly sector market forces are not the main determinants of wages, prices, and profits. Monopolistic corporations have substantial market power. Prices are administered, and in comparative terms price movements are sealed off from market forces. Most corporations operate on the basis of an after-

tax profit target (normally between 10 and 15 percent). If labor costs rise, monopolistic corporations will attempt to protect planned profit targets by increasing prices. Assuming that labor productivity remains unchanged, money wages are thus the main determinants of monopoly sector prices.

What forces determine the level of money wages? The process of wage determination in the monopoly sector will be simplified in order to highlight its essential features. First assume that the economy is expanding. In an economic boom the demand for labor increases (as well as demand for nearly everything else) in both competitive and monopoly sectors.

The supply of labor available to competitive industries is relatively inelastic and hence a sizable increase in demand will raise wages in this sector. If businessmen fail to raise wages they will not be able to attract enough workers to expand production and fill orders, nor will they be able to retain some workers already employed in competitive industry. Workers in the competitive sector (and the unemployed, as well) will seek employment in the generally more desirable monopoly sectors. Will monopoly capital be forced to offer higher wages to attract the workers it requires to expand production in the short run and meet the higher level of demand? Except during periods of extreme boom (e.g., the peak years of the Korean War), the supply of labor available to monopoly capital is relatively elastic. Thus it can attract all the workers it needs from the competitive sector at the going wage rate. Put another way, monopoly capital is able to draw on the pool of underemployed competitive sector labor (or the "invisible" reserve army of the unemployed).

Although the market forces tending to drive up monopoly sector wages normally are relatively weak, the political forces at work are very powerful. In a nutshell, during a boom the production relations alter in favor of labor. Profit margins grow at precisely the same time that unemployment falls, and union bargaining strength is enhanced at the same time that there is a larger surplus (prof-

[1] Joan Robinson, *Economics: An Awkward Corner* (New York: 1968), p. 14.

its) to bargain over. In the last analysis it is the collective power of organized labor that wrests higher wages from monopolistic corporations, not the normal forces of supply and demand.

What are the specific principles governing the administration of wages in monopoly industries? First, labor productivity; second, cost of living. Again the process will be simplified in order to focus on basic elements. The sequence of wage changes starts in monopoly sector industries in which productivity is advancing most rapidly. Unions bargain for wage increases at least commensurate with productivity increases. Subsequently, unions representing workers in other monopolistic industries seek wage increases as great as those won by their brethren in the high-productivity industries. This is called *pattern bargaining*. One of its results is that average wages tend to rise somewhat faster than average productivity (and of course, considerably faster than productivity throughout the economy).

Several empirical studies support these theses. According to one of the most thorough, "productivity gains are more likely to go to the workers the more unionized and concentrated [i.e., monopolized] the industry, although the union elasticity carries the greater weight."[2] Another scholar concludes that wage increases in one monopoly sector industry spill over to others.[3] However, pattern bargaining and uniformity of wage increases do not "trickle down" into the competitive sector. "Changes in the union-nonunion [wage] differential," Livernash writes, summing up available evidence, "and changes in relative earnings among industries do not support the existence of strong pattern influences operating broadly across industry lines throughout the economy as a whole."[4]

The final result of the process of admin-

istered prices and wages, productivity wage increases, and pattern bargaining is that many or most gains from productivity increases arising from technical progress (and other factors such as scale of production and degree of capacity utilization) are not distributed evenly throughout the population, but rather are "bottled up" in the monopoly sector by corporations and organized labor. One side-effect is the drift toward permanent inflation—that is, the continuous upward movement of wages and prices. In effect, the classic competitive market mechanism breaks down and the dominant production relations (monopoly capital and organized labor), not impersonal market forces, determine the allocation of economic resources, the wage structure and distribution of income within the working class and capitalist class.

At this point, an anomaly in the political economy of modern America must be emphasized. The determination of wages and prices in the competitive sector was analyzed without reference to the actual production or power relationships because wages and prices in these industries are determined by market forces—that is, they are determined independently of the intentions of businessmen and workers. For example, as indicated above, capitalists attempting to increase profits by expanding production lower prices and thus reduce all capitalists' profits—clearly an unintended effect.

Comparatively speaking, the situation is different in the monopoly sector: Production is planned and wages and prices are administered. Because there is more conscious human control over income and income distribution, market theory per se can throw only a limited light on the determinants of wages, prices, and profits. Precisely because wages are relatively insensitive to changes in the demand for labor and because productivity gains tend to be monopolized, we must look behind the market categories and discover the historical, social, and political forces shaping wages, prices, and income distribution.

This excursion into history begins at the close of World War II. The inseparable link

[2]Sara Behman, "Wage Changes, Institutions, and Relative Factor Prices in Manufacturing," *Review of Economics and Statistics*, 51 (August 1969), p. 236.

[3]E. Robert Livernash, "Wages and Benefits," in *A Review of Industrial Relations Research*, pp. 110–12.

[4]Livernash, "Wages and Benefits," p. 100.

between productivity and cost of living and wages in the monopoly sector and the bifurcation of wage-price determination in the monopoly and competitive sectors is rooted in an agreement imposed on organized labor during the last half of the 1940s. At the end of the war the large industrial unions entered into permanent collective bargaining relationships (for the first time under normal conditions) with large corporations that exercised monopolistic control over prices. The unions could win higher wages in two ways. The first was to demand higher wages at the expense of profits. However, because the corporations controlled prices, they could (and can) easily raise prices and pass on wage increases not "justified" by rising productivity to consumers—and thus protect their profit margins. The unions could have countered this move only by adopting a working-class perspective (in contrast to an industrial-union perspective) and agitating politically for a return to price controls without a revival of wage controls. Obviously, such a course would have been unrealistic in the context of early cold war America.

The alternative for the industrial unions was to demand that the workers share in the benefits accruing from increased productivity. In theory, two courses were available to union leaders. First, they could try to force the monopolistic corporations to lower prices when increased productivity led to lower production costs. Thus the benefits of technical progress would have been distributed more or less evenly among all consumers. But the unions recognized that they had (and have) no control over prices and chose the second course: They demanded that wages increase with productivity (and demanded cost-of-living wage adjustments, as well), with the inevitable (and clearly unintended) effect of bifurcating the working class still further. Competitive sector workers suffered. On the one hand, their wages were (and are) relatively low; on the other, they had (and have) to buy at relatively high monopolistic prices.

Needless to say, big business did not begin to grant annual wage increases, cost-of-living adjustments, additional fringe benefits, and so on without a quid pro quo. In return for wage scales pegged to productivity plus, the unions agreed not only to abstain from fighting mechanization but also to collaborate actively when major innovations required large-scale reorganization of the work process. There have been exceptions, mainly in declining industries such as railroading where featherbedding has been a major issue. From the standpoint of monopoly capital the main function of unions was (and is) to inhibit disruptive, spontaneous rank-and-file activity (e.g., wildcat strikes and slowdowns) and to maintain labor discipline in general. In other words, unions were (and are) the guarantors of "managerial prerogatives." Union leaders have long recognized that demands for both increased wages and more control over production are contradictory because wage demands are based on rising productivity which requires that management be free to fire redundant workers. At times, union leaders have been hard pressed to maintain labor discipline, especially over the issue of labor-saving technological changes. As will be seen, the number of jobs (and employed workers) in the monopoly sector tends to rise slowly, in some cases to decrease absolutely. Hence unions are one agent of technical progress and rational (in terms of profits) laborpower planning by monopoly capital.

THE EXPANSION OF THE MONOPOLY SECTOR

. . . [There is a] tendency for monopoly capital to take over and dominate competitive capital. The extensive (as contrasted with intensive) character of monopoly capital growth not only generates more unemployment in competitive industries (surplus labor) but also liquidates large numbers of small businessmen (surplus capitalists). Consider U.S. agricultural production, for example. Farming is increasingly dominated by large-scale capital employing modern technology. Thus farm output expanded by 45 percent between 1950 and 1965, whereas farm employment (workers and owners) fell by 45 percent. In the mid-1960s, almost 30 percent of the farm population (3.9 million people; an unknown number were previously farm owners) and over 23 percent of the rural nonfarm population (almost 10 million people) lived in poverty. This high incidence of poverty is attributable more to unemployment (unemployment and underemployment rates in the mid-1960s were about 20 and 40 percent, respectively) and the displacement of the small farm operator than to low wages.

The take-over by monopoly capital of traditional competitive industries such as agriculture, construction, trade, and services, together with the long-run expansion of labor supply, tends to depress profits of competitive capital. Profits also are depressed when small business must compete with large-scale capital and when a superabundance of cheap labor encourages the setting up of small business, and thus produces "overcrowding" in the competitive sector. Moreover, the relative decline in wages in competitive industries that have resisted union organization tends to keep prices down, and under certain circumstances can decrease profits. Finally, because of the economically depressed condition of competitive industries, small businessmen and farmers (as well as workers) are forced to depend more and more on the state for material survival, indirectly in the form of fair-trade laws and similar protective legislation, directly in the form of loan guarantees, farm subsidies, and similar programs.

4.6   *The Capitalist Class*

This chapter has focused on capital accumulation and the rise of the giant corporations. Because capitalists organize production through such firms, the behavior of these firms, taken together and understood as a system, is relevant for analyzing the workings of the American economy. Now, however, it is time to turn our attention to the capitalists who own these firms and to the class that benefits from this system.

A class is a group of people sharing a common position in the mode of production.[1] Workers have in common the condition that they must sell their labor-power to "earn" their "living." Similarly, capitalists share a common situation: they own capital, which they lend or use to purchase the labor-power of workers (and other things required in production) in order to produce and sell commodities and realize profits; their income thus accrues in the form of profits and interest.

Included in this category of "capitalists" are individuals as different in their situations as small businesses are different from big business: some capitalists employ few workers, face great competition, have insecure business prospects, and achieve relatively modest profits, while at the other extreme exist the Rockellers, the Mellons, and the Fords. Numerically, the capitalist class is small—only 10 percent or less of the population could in any sense be categorized as capitalists. Yet in terms of their ownership of wealth, this small group is very important: in 1962 the richest 6.7 percent of the population owned 56.3 percent of all wealth in the country, and their control of corporate assets was even higher: 77.7 percent.[2]

[1]See introduction to Chapter 2.
[2]See below, Tables 5-A and 8-D.

Associated with the rise of monopoly capitalism was the emergence within the capitalist class of a tiny segment of super-rich capitalists. (For the most notable examples, see Table 4-F). In 1969, 1 percent of the population owned more than half of all corporate stock.[3] One study has estimated that the extraction of monopoly profits since the turn of the century has benefitted this group almost exclusively, allowing it to more than double its share of wealth compared to what its share would have been if no monopoly profits had existed.[4] But a large part of the profits from monopoly capitalism have probably been concentrated in an even tinier, more privileged group, the few thousand super-rich families. Although data on their combined holdings are almost entirely lacking, estimates of the personal fortunes of some of the most prominent members suggest their immense wealth (see Table 4-F).

TABLE 4-F THE SUPER-RICH AND THEIR WEALTH, 1967

Name	Source of Wealth	Age
$1–1.5 Billion		
J. Paul Getty	Getty Oil/Inheritor	75
Howard Hughes	Hughes Tool, Hughes Aircraft, etc.	62
$500 Million–$1 Billion		
H. L. Hunt	Oil	79
Dr. Edwin Land	Polaroid	58
Daniel K. Ludwig	Shipping	70
Ailsa Mellon Bruce	Rentier/Inheritor	66
Paul Mellon	Director, Mellon Bank/Inheritor	60
Richard King Mellon	Alcoa/Inheritor	68
$300–500 Million		
N. Bunker Hunt	Oil/Inheritor	42
John D. MacArthur	Insurance	71
William L. McKnight	Minnesota Mining and Manufacturing	80
Charles S. Mott	General Motors	92
R. E. (Bob) Smith	Oil, Real Estate	73
$200–300 Million		
Howard F. Ahmanson	Oil, Savings and Loan	61
Charles Allen, Jr.	Investment Banking	65
Mrs. W. Van Allen Clark, Sr. (Edna McConnell)	Avon Products/Inheritor	80
John T. Dorrance	Campbell Soup/Inheritor	49
Mrs. Alfred I. Du Pont	Company Director/Inheritor	84
Charles W. Engelhard, Jr.	Mining and Metal	51
Sherman M. Fairchild	Fairchild Camera/IBM	72
Leon Hess	Hess Oil and Chemical	54
William R. Hewlett	Hewlett-Packard	54

[3] J. D. Smith and S. D. Franklin, "The Concentration of Personal Wealth, 1922–1969," *American Economic Review* (May 1974), Table 1, p. 166.

[4] W. Comanor and R. Smiley, "Monopoly and the Distribution of Wealth," *Quarterly Journal of Economics*, 1975.

TABLE 4-F (CONTINUED)

Name	Source of Wealth	Age
David Packard	Hewlett-Packard	55
Amory Houghton	Corning Glass/Inheritor	68
Joseph P. Kennedy	Market Operator	79
Eli Lilly	Eli Lilly & Company	83
Forrest E. Mars	Mars Candy	64
Samuel I. Newhouse	Newspapers	73
Marjorie Merriweather Post	General Foods/Inheritor	81
Mrs. Jean Mauze	Rentier/Inheritor	64
(Abby Rockefeller)		
David Rockefeller	Banker/Inheritor	52
John D. Rockefeller III	Inheritor	62
Laurance Rockefeller	Inheritor	57
Nelson Rockefeller	Governor/Inheritor	59
Winthrop Rockefeller	Governor/Inheritor	56
Cordelia Scaife May	Rentier/Inheritor	39
Richard Mellon Scaife	Rentier/Inheritor	35
DeWitt Wallace	*Reader's Digest*	78
Mrs. Charles Payson	Inheritor	65
(Joan Whitney)		
John Hay Whitney	Inheritor	63
$150–200 Million		
James S. Abercrombie	Oil/Iron	76
William Benton	*Encyclopaedia Britannica*	68
Jacob Blaustein	Standard Oil (Indiana)	75
Chester Carlson	Inventor of Xerography	62
Edward J. Daly	World Airways	45
Clarence Dillon	Banking	85
Doris Duke	Rentier/Inheritor	55
Lammot du Pont Copeland	Inheritor	62
Henry B. du Pont	Inheritor	69
Benson Ford	Ford/Inheritor	48
Mrs. W. Buhl Ford II	Ford/Inheritor	44
(Josephine Ford)		
William C. Ford	Ford/Inheritor	43
Helen Clay Frick	Steel/Inheritor	79
William T. Grant	Variety Stores	91
Bob Hope	Comedian	64
Arthur A. Houghton, Jr.	Corning Glass/Inheritor	61
J. Seward Johnson	Johnson & Johnson	72
Peter Kiewit	Construction	77
Allan P. Kirby	Inheritor	75
J. S. McDonnell, Jr.	Aircraft/Inheritor	69
Mrs. Lester J. Norris	Inheritor	65
(Dellora F. Angell)		
E. Claiborne Robins	Drugs	57
W. Clement Stone	Insurance	65
Mrs. Arthur Hays Sulzberger	Publishing/Inheritor	75
S. Mark Taper	First Financial Corp.	66
Robert W. Woodruff	Coca Cola/Inheritor	78

SOURCE: "The Richest of the Rich," *Fortune* (May 1968), 156.

The super-rich capitalists associated with the giant corporations constitute the most privileged and politically powerful part of the capitalist
class. Through their control of the large corporations, they command vast
economic, political, legal, and ideological resources. Since they have the
most far-flung interests, they are the most likely to perceive the needs of
capitalism as a system and to act upon that perception.

The ability of the big capitalists to reproduce and extend capitalist relations of production depends in part on the support of other groups in society.
Small capitalists, landlords, and other property-owning or affluent classes
are the large capitalists' most important allies, since they share many of the
same interests (especially vis-à-vis workers).

On the other hand, differences in the economic situations of small capitalists and big business leaders allow for differences of interests and perceptions. In particular, as Paul Sweezy articulates in the following reading,
those capitalists who control the monopoly corporations constitute a segment of the capitalist class whose interest and perspectives are national in
scope; Sweezy terms them the "national ruling class." These capitalists
(and the headquarters of their corporations) tend to be concentrated in the
largest cities, especially New York, Chicago, Dallas, Los Angeles, Atlanta,
and a few other major financial centers. On the other hand, small capitalists,
that much larger group which owns the small and medium-sized firms of the
competitive sector, tend to be scattered throughout large cities and small
towns.

With the rise of the national corporations to economic primacy, the
national capitalists have increasingly come to assume leading political and
ideological positions within the capitalist class.

The United States is a capitalist society,
the purest capitalist society that ever existed.
It has no feudal hangovers to complicate the
class system. Independent producers (working with their own means of production but
without hired labor) there are, but both
economically and socially they constitute a
relatively unimportant feature of the American system. What do we expect the class
structure of such a pure capitalist society to
be?

Clearly, the two decisive classes are defined
by the very nature of capitalism: the owners
of the means of production (the capitalist
class), and the wage laborers who set the

means of production in motion (the working
class). There is no doubt about the existence
or importance of these two classes in America.
Taken together they can be said to constitute
the foundation of the American class system.

The foundation of a building, however, is
not the whole building; nor does the American economic system contain only capitalists
and workers. For one thing, as we have already noted, there are independent producers
(artisans and small farmers), and to these we
should add small shopkeepers and providers
of services (for example, the proprietors of
local gas stations). These people make up the
lower middle class, or *petite bourgeoisie*, in the

original sense of the term. For another thing, there are a variety of types which stand somewhere between the capitalists and the workers and cannot easily be classified with either: government and business bureaucrats, professionals, teachers, journalists, advertising men, and so on. These are often, and not inappropriately, called the new middle classes —"new" because of their spectacular growth, both absolutely and relatively to other classes, in the last seventy-five years or so. Finally, there are what are usually called declassed elements—bums, gamblers, thugs, prostitutes, and the like—who are not recognized in the official statistics but who nevertheless play an important role in capitalist society, especially in its political life.

Viewing the matter from a primarily economic angle, then, we could say that the American class structure consists of capitalists, lower middle class in the classical sense, new middle classes, workers, and declassed elements. There is no doubt, however, that this is not a strictly accurate description of the actual living social classes which we observe about us. If we apply the criterion of intermarriageability as a test of social class membership, we shall often find that people who from an economic standpoint belong to the new middle classes are actually on the same social level as the larger capitalists; that smaller capitalists are socially indistinguishable from a large proportion of the new middle classes; and that the working class includes without very much social distinction those who perform certain generally comparable kinds of labor, whether it be with their own means of production or with means of production belonging to others.

These considerations lead us to the following conclusion: the social classes which we observe about us are not *identical* with the economic classes of capitalist society. They are rather *modifications* of the latter. This is, I believe, an important point. If we keep it firmly in mind we shall be able to appreciate the decisive role of the economic factor in the structure and behavior of social classes while

at the same time avoiding an overmechanical (and hence false) economic determinism.

. . .

What we need is a scheme which both highlights the fundamental economic conditioning of the social-class system and at the same time is flexible enough to encompass the anomalies and irregularities which actually characterize it.

The starting point must surely be the recognition that two social classes, at bottom shaped by the very nature of capitalism, determine the form and content of the system as a whole. I prefer to call these classes the ruling class and the working class. The core of the ruling class is made up of big capitalists (or, more generally, big property owners, though the distinction is not very important since most large aggregates of property have the form of capital in this country today). There are numerous fringes to the ruling class, including smaller property owners, government and business executives (in so far as they are not big owners in their own right), professionals, and so on: we shall have more to say on this subject later. The core of the working class is made up of wage laborers who have no productive property of their own. Here again there are fringes, including, especially, independent craftsmen and petty traders.

The fringes of the ruling class do not reach to the fringes of the working class. Between the two there is a wide social space which is occupied by what we can hardly avoid calling the middle class. We should not forget, however, that the middle class is much more heterogeneous than either the ruling class or the working class. It has no solid core, and it shades off irregularly (and differently in different localities) into the fringes of the class above it and the class below it. Indeed we might say that the middle class consists of a collection of fringes, and that its social cohesion is largely due to the existence in all of its elements of a desire to be in the ruling class above it and to avoid being in the working class below it.

This generalized description of the social-class structure seems to me to have many merits and no fatal defects. The terminology calls attention to the chief functions of the basic classes and indicates clearly enough the relative positions of the three classes in the social hierarchy. More important, the use of the fringe concept enables us to face frankly the *fact* that the dividing lines in American society are not sharply drawn, and that even the borderlands are irregular and unstable. This fact is often seized upon to "prove" that there are *no* classes in America. It cannot be banished or hidden by the use of an elaborate multiclass scheme . . . for the simple reason that such a scheme, however well it may seem to apply to some situations, breaks down when applied to others. What we must have is a scheme which takes full account of the fact in question without at the same time obscuring the fundamental outlines and character of the class system itself.

I shall next try to show that, at least as concerns the ruling class, the scheme proposed above does satisfy these requirements. Every community study shows clearly the existence of an upper social crust which is based on wealth. The nucleus is always the "old families" which have transmitted and usually augmented their fortunes from one generation to the next. Around this nucleus are grouped the *nouveaux riches*, the solidly established lawyers and doctors, the more successful of the social climbers and sycophants, and people whose family connections are better than their bank accounts. Taken all together, these are the people who comprise what is called "society." Except in very large cities, the whole community is aware of their existence and knows that they constitute a more or less well-defined "upper class."

So much is obvious. Certain other things, however, are not so obvious. It is not obvious, for example, that these local "upper classes" are in fact merely sections of a national upper class, nor that this national upper class is in fact the national ruling class. What we shall have to concentrate on therefore are two points: first, the structure of the national

ruling class; and second, how the ruling class rules.

The Structure of the National Ruling Class

That the local upper crusts are merely sections of a national class (also of an international class, but that is beyond the scope of the present article) follows from the way they freely mix and intermarry. The facts in this regard are well known to any reasonably attentive observer of American life, and no attempt at documentation is called for here. . . .

The national ruling class, however, is not merely a collection of interrelated local upper crusts, all on a par with each other. It is rather a hierarchy of upper crusts which has a fairly definite organizational structure, including lines of authority from leaders to followers. It is here that serious study of the ruling class is most obviously lacking, and also most urgently needed. I shall confine myself to a few hints and suggestions, some of which may turn out on closer investigation to be mistaken or at any rate out of proportion.

Generally speaking, the sections of the national ruling class are hierarchically organized with hundreds of towns at the bottom of the pyramid and a handful of very large cities at the top. Very small communities can be counted out: normally the wealth and standing of their leading citizens is no more than enough to gain them entry into the middle class when they go to the city. Even towns as large as five or ten thousand may have only a few representatives in good standing in the national ruling class. You can always tell such a representative. Typically, he is a man "of independent means"; he went to a good college; he has connections and spends considerable time in the state capital and/or the nearest big city; he takes his family for part of the year to a resort where it can enjoy the company of its social equals. And, most important of all, he is a person of unquestioned prestige and authority in his own community: he is, so to speak, a local lieutenant of the ruling class.

Cities, of course, have more—I should also judge proportionately more—national ruling-class members. And as a rule those who live in smaller cities look up to and seek guidance from and actually follow those who live in larger cities. Certain of these larger cities have in turn acquired the position of what we might call regional capitals (San Francisco, Chicago, Cleveland, Boston, and so on): the lines of authority in the given region run to and end in the capital. The relation which exists among these regional capitals is a very important subject which deserves careful study. There was a time in our national history when it would probably have been true to say that the sections of the ruling class in the regional capitals looked up to and sought guidance from and actually followed the New York section, and to a considerable extent this may still be the case. At any rate this is the kernel of truth in the Wall Street theory. My own guess, for what it is worth, is that economic and political changes in the last thirty years (especially changes in the structure and functions of the banking system and the expansion of the economic role of the state) have reduced the relative importance of New York to a marked degree, and that today it is more accurate to describe New York as *primus inter pares* rather than as the undisputed leader of all the rest.

The ruling-class hierarchy is not based solely on personal or family relations among the members of the ruling class. On the contrary, it is bulwarked and buttressed by a massive network of institutional relations. Of paramount importance in this connection are the corporate giants with divisions, branches, and subsidiaries reaching out to all corners of the country. The American Telephone and Telegraph Company, with headquarters in New York and regional subsidiaries covering forty-eight states, is in itself a powerful force welding the unity of the American ruling class; and it is merely the best-developed example of its kind. Formerly, a very large proportion of these busi-

ness empires were centered in New York, and it was this more than anything else that gave that city a unique position. Today that proportion is much reduced, and cities like Pittsburgh, Cleveland, Detroit, Chicago, and San Francisco play a relatively more prominent part than they used to. In addition to corporations, an integrating role in the ruling class is performed by businessmen's organizations like the National Association of Manufacturers, the Chambers of Commerce, the Rotary and other so-called service clubs; by colleges and their alumni associations; by churches and women's clubs; by scores of fashionable winter and summer resorts (not all located in this country); and by a myriad other institutions too numerous even to attempt to list. (It will be noted that I have not mentioned the two great political parties in this connection. The reason is not that they don't to some extent play the part of an integrator of the ruling class: they do, and in a variety of ways. But their main function is quite different, namely, to provide the channels through which the ruling class manipulates and controls the lower classes. Compared to this function, their role *within* the ruling class is of quite secondary significance.)

Finally, we should note the key part played by the press in unifying and organizing the ruling class. To be sure, not all organs of the press figure here: the great majority, like the political parties, are instruments for controlling the lower classes. But the more solid kind of newspaper (of which the *New York Times* is, of course, the prototype), the so-called quality magazines, the business and technical journals, the high-priced newsletters and dopesheets—all of these are designed primarily for the ruling class and are tremendously important in guiding and shaping its thinking. This does not mean that they in some way make up or determine the *content* of ruling-class ideas—this content is basically determined by what I may call the class situation (about which more will be said presently)—but it does mean that they standardize and propagate the ideas in such a way that the entire ruling class lives on a nearly uniform intellectual diet.

All of the formal and informal, the personal and institutional ties that bind the ruling class together have a twofold character: on the one hand they are transmission belts and channels of communication; and on the other hand they are themselves molders of ideas and values and behavior norms—let us say for short, of ruling-class ideology. And here we have to note another mechanism of the greatest importance, the mechanism by which the class passes its ideology on from one generation to the next. The key parts of this mechanism are the family and the educational system. Ruling-class families are jealous protectors and indoctrinators of ruling-class ideology; the public school system faithfully reflects it and even, contrary to popular beliefs, fosters class distinctions; and private preparatory schools and colleges finish the job of dividing the ruling-class young from their compatriots. (In this connection, we must not be confused by the fact that a considerable number of lower-class families succeed in getting their sons and daughters into the private preparatory schools and colleges. This is merely a method by which the ruling class recruits the most capable elements of the lower classes into its service and often into its ranks. It is probably the most important such method in the United States today, having replaced the older method by which the abler lower-class young people worked their way directly up in the business world.)

How the Ruling Class Rules

Let us now turn, very briefly, to the question of how or in what sense the ruling class can be said to rule. This is a question which can easily lead to much mystification, but I think it can also be dealt with in a perfectly simple, straightforward way.

The question has two aspects, economic and political. The ruling class rules the economy in the sense that its members either directly occupy the positions in the economy where the key decisions are made or, if they don't occupy these positions themselves, they hire and fire those who do. The ruling class rules the government (using the term as a shorthand expression for all levels of government) in the sense that its members either directly occupy the key positions (largely true in the higher judiciary and the more honorific legislative jobs, increasingly true in the higher administrative jobs), or they finance and thus indirectly control the political parties which are responsible for staffing and managing the routine business of government. In short, the ruling class rules through its members who (1) do the job themselves, (2) hire and fire those who do, or (3) pay for the upkeep of political machines to do the job for them. That this rule through the members of the class is in fact *class rule* does not require to be separately demonstrated: it follows from the nature and structure of the class as we have already analyzed them.

This analysis of the way the ruling class rules is, of course, sketchy and oversimplified. I think nevertheless that it will stand up provided we can meet one objection, namely, that if the ruling class really ruled it would not [make concessions, e.g., permit unions or tax corporations.]

A full answer, I think, would require a careful examination of the nature and limits of political power, something which obviously cannot be undertaken here. But the main point is clearly indicated in the following passage from Lincoln Steffens's *Autobiography.* The passage concludes a chapter entitled "Wall Street Again":

> It is a very common error to think of sovereignty as absolute. Rasputin, a sovereign in Russia, made that mistake; many kings have made it and so lost their power to premiers and ministers who represented the "vested interests" of powerful classes, groups, and individuals. A dictator is never absolute. Nothing is absolute. A political boss concentrates in himself and personifies a very "wise" adjustment of the grafts upon which his throne is established. He must know these, reckon their power, and bring them all to the support of his power, which is, therefore, representative and

limited. Mussolini, in our day, had to "deal with"
the Church of Rome. A business boss has to yield to the
powerful men who support him. The Southern Pacific
Railroad had to "let the city grafters get theirs." The
big bankers had to let the life insurance officers and
employees get theirs. J. P. Morgan should have known
what he soon found out, that he could not lick Diamond
Jim Brady. Under a dictatorship nobody is free, not
even the dictator; sovereign power is as representative
as a democracy. It's all a matter of what is represented
by His Majesty on the throne. In short, what I got out
of my second period in Wall Street was this perception
that everything I looked into in organized society was
really a dictatorship, in this sense, that it was an
organization of the privileged for the control of
privileges, of the sources of privilege and of the thoughts
and acts of the unprivileged; and that neither the pri-
vileged nor the unprivileged, neither the bosses nor the
bossed, understood this or meant it.

There is, I think, more sound political
science packed into that one paragraph than
you will find in the whole of an average textbook. And it clearly contains the fundamental answer to the contention that the
upper class doesn't rule because it has to put
up with many things it doesn't like. Obviously the ruling class has to make concessions and compromises to keep the people,
and especially the working class, in a condition of sufficient ignorance and contentment
to accept the system as a whole. In other
words, the ruling class operates within a
definite framework, more or less restricted
according to circumstances, which it can
ignore only at the peril of losing its power
altogether—and, along with its power, its
wealth and privileges.

. . .

One final problem remains, that of divisions and conflicts within the ruling class. We
are now in a position to see this problem in
its proper setting and proportions. Aside from
more or less accidental rivalries and feuds,
the divisions within the ruling class are of
several kinds: regional (based on economic
differences and buttressed by historical traditions and memories—the North-South division is the clearest example of this kind);
industrial (for example, coal capitalists vs. oil
capitalists); corporate (for example, General
Motors vs. Ford); dynastic (for example Du
Ponts vs. Mellons); political (Republicans vs.
Democrats); and ideological (reactionaries
vs. liberals). These divisions cut across and
mutually condition one another, and the
dividing lines are irregular and shifting. These
factors introduce elements of indeterminacy
and instability into the behavior of the ruling
class and make of capitalist politics something
more than a mere puppet show staged for the
benefit (and obfuscation) of the man in the
street. But we must not exaggerate the depth
of the divisions inside the ruling class: capitalists can and do fight among themselves to
further individual or group interests, and they
differ over the best way of coping with the
problems which arise from the class position;
but overshadowing all these divisions is their
common interest in preserving and strengthening a system which guarantees their wealth
and privileges. In the event of a real threat to
the system, there are no longer class differences—only class traitors, and they are few
and far between.

CHAPTER 5

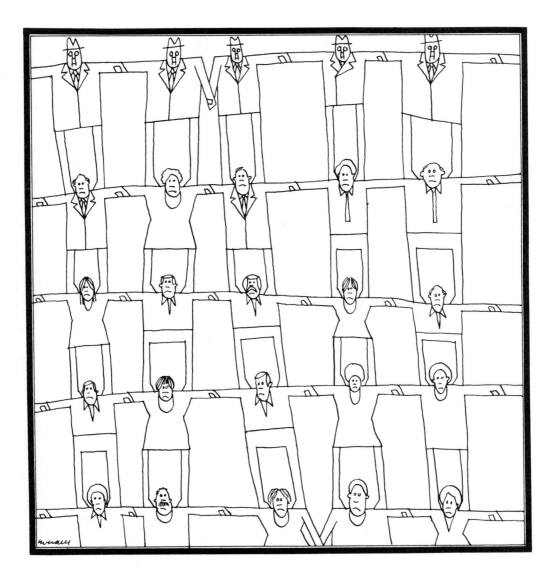

Wage-Labor
and the Working Class

IN THE LAST CHAPTER we saw how the small family-operated enterprises of the early nineteenth century have given way to the giant multinational corporations and banks that dominate American capitalism today. The tremendous concentration, centralization, and expansion of capital that has characterized the era of monopoly capitalism has simultaneously generated a major expansion of wage-labor and the working class, and significantly changed the conditions of U.S. workers. In this chapter we will investigate the development of the working class in the period of monopoly capitalism. We will look at the evolution of the wage-labor force, the continuing transformation of the labor process, the diversity of the working class, the struggles by workers to form unions and other organizations to advance their interests, and the role that labor unions have played in monopoly capitalism.

THE GROWTH OF WAGE-LABOR

During the last century there has been a significant decline in the number of small property-holders—farmers, merchants, independent professionals, and small businesspeople—in the United States. At the same time there has been an equally significant growth in the number of people who must and do sell their labor-power for a wage or salary, and who thereby surrender control over their labor-power, their authority over their work process, and their right to the final product. This group of people, whom we call wage-workers, includes not only blue-collar factory workers paid on an hourly basis but also many white-collar and service employees in offices, hospitals, schools, restaurants, government agencies, and so on. The expansion of wage-labor (and the simultaneous diminution of the old middle strata) is one of the most striking and important features of monopoly capitalist development in the United States.

The evolution of the class structure results directly from the requirements of the capitalist accumulation process. As capitalists seek to expand their surplus value, they must employ more workers to produce that surplus value. This tendency to require more wage-labor is reinforced by the victories of hard-fought labor struggles to limit the legal length of the working day, to restrict the use of child labor, to set minimum health and safety conditions, and to otherwise limit exploitation of workers. In addition to employing more wage-workers, capitalists have also expanded surplus value by using their economic power to appropriate and incorporate into capitalist production noncapitalist activities that are capable of producing a surplus, by increasing the productivity of their workers and by expanding their efforts to sell the commodities produced. The growth in the demand for wage-labor and the progressive elimination of noncapitalist producers have each contributed to the expansion of the working class in the United States. The growth of worker productivity and the sales effort by capitalists have involved substantial changes in the nature of work in capitalist enterprises.

The supply of wage-labor in the United States has been expanded from several different sources. These include the natural growth of the population, immigration from foreign countries, and the recruitment of people previously outside the sphere of capitalist production. Generally, only a small percentage of workers are able to accumulate sufficient savings to go successfully into business on their own. The natural growth of the population and increases in years of life expectancy then expands the numbers of wage-workers more than enough to compensate for the increase in the age at which people leave school and the reduction in the average retirement age. This source of expansion has been supplemented through most of U.S. history by successive groups of foreign immigrants, most recently from Mexico, Asia, and the Caribbean. (The recent decline in the birth rate within the United States has increased the importance of foreign sources of labor supply.) Finally, as large capitalists have replaced independent producers in the home, on the farm, and in the small store and workshop, they have set "free" new sources of labor supply for capitalist production. This category includes women who had formerly worked only in the home, and such people as displaced farmers and small capitalists. After World War II, for example, capital-intensive farming by agribusiness corporations displaced millions of farm people, who were then absorbed on urban payrolls. As the remaining number of people engaged in farming dwindled by the 1960s and 1970s, an increasing number of women joined the wage labor force.

In addition to increasing the employment of wage-labor, capitalists have expanded surplus value by increasing the productivity of that labor. In the monopoly capitalist period, this growth in the productivity of labor has been impressive; it has derived from several sources. The most important sources are the systematic reorganization by capitalists of the labor process itself, increases in

the general skills and training of workers, increased mechanization as more capital goods are used in production, advances in the technology of production, the reallocation of labor from low-productivity to high-productivity industries, and the reduction in unit costs achieved by producing on a larger scale. All told, the rate of increase of worker productivity (or output per worker) in the United States has been estimated to be about 3 percent per year during the twentieth century.

Of course, this increase in productivity would not result in increased surplus value for capitalists if workers were able to capture the full benefits of their increased capacity to produce goods and services. On the other hand, any reduction in real wages paid by capitalists would increase surplus value even if productivity did not rise. In general, the movement of wages depends upon a number of factors: the degree of competition among capitalists for wage-workers, the success of capitalists in expanding the supply of labor, the cost of reproducing workers, and a bargaining power struggle between capitalists and workers over wages, the outcome of which depends on the factors just mentioned and the degree of organization and militancy on each side. As it has turned out, the growth in the real wage rate in the long run has just about matched the increase in worker productivity, leaving both capitalists and workers with the same share of total income they each previously received, while increasing the absolute amount of profit for capitalists and wages for workers.

ABSTRACT LABOR, HIERARCHY, AND SYSTEMS OF CONTROL

The expansion of surplus value through the continual revolutionizing of the labor process itself has produced far-reaching changes in the way that work is organized in modern capitalist enterprises. The skilled craftsperson of an earlier era has increasingly been replaced by a mass-production worker who carries out only a small number of repetitive operations. The earlier artisans had specific knowledge and skills that were applied to a specific product in a self-controlled labor process. The modern capitalist firm, seeking to minimize its costs and to extract more work from its workers, organizes the labor process so as to standardize and routinize as much as possible the tasks and motions of workers, to render these workers into "interchangeable parts" abstracted from the specific product or process of production.

The result is the creation of what Marx called the "abstract worker," with the progressive removal of control and knowledge of the production process from the workers themselves to their "managers." As a consequence, although workers today have more years of general schooling than ever before, only a small proportion of many workers' skills are utilized in capitalist production. The process of breaking down tasks, of systematizing and rationalizing the labor process, goes on constantly, and extends today not only throughout production jobs in manufacturing, construction, and transportation but also to services and much white-collar work.

At the same time that much artisan work has become degraded, new skilled and unskilled occupations are also being created and expanded. The skilled jobs have much less routinized work and are often associated with new products or new technologies. A cycle then sets in, as capitalists attempt to expand and appropriate surplus value produced in these jobs by reorganizing the labor process, breaking down the tasks, and again initiating a process of routinization and abstraction of labor. In some instances this process may not be very practicable, as when the product and therefore the labor process is not easily standardized (e.g., for repair services, gourmet restaurants, or in many aspects of medical and legal practice). In these cases the creation of abstract labor is much less marked, and the prevalence of thousands of small entrepreneurs is very noticeable.

As capitalist firms have grown larger and more complex in their organizational structure, they have systematized and made more sophisticated the organizational techniques they use to control the labor process. In place of just a boss and a few managers or supervisors who personally oversee the production process, exercising arbitrary and discretionary power over workers, the modern giant corporations have added a bureaucratic system of rules, sanctions, incentives, formal grievance procedures, hiring, promotion, and firing policies, etc. This more formally structured organization of the labor process institutionalizes the exercise of capitalist power within the firm, making it seem less arbitrary and personal, and more fair and rational.

The bureaucratic hierarchy at the workplace is often presented as a necessary product of advanced technology, unavoidable in a complex industrial society. In fact, the content and hierarchical arrangement of most jobs has very little to do with the nature of the technological processes being used. The hierarchy must be seen primarily as a *system of control*, instituted to stratify workers, to get them to compete against each other, and thereby to elicit more work from them. The very successes of workers' struggles to limit their employers' power by organizing unions and developing solidarity among themselves has posed for capitalists the problem of finding new means of controlling workers, since the traditional means—such as firing rebellious workers and bringing in a reserve army of labor—could no longer work as well. One solution has been the institution of hierarchical job structures.

DIVISIONS AND UNIONS AMONG WORKERS

In addition to the hierarchical system of control at the workplace, continuing differences in working conditions between monopoly and competitive capitalist firms have provided a material basis for persistent divisions in the working class in the United States. Small competitive firms, often on the edge of survival, cannot afford the same wage rates, pensions, and health plans, or promises of long job tenure and promotion as large monopolistic corporations. Often these differences correspond to divisions between unionized and nonunionized workers and add to existing racial, sexual, and ethnic differences among workers. Other important sources of divisions are between "abstract workers" and the remaining craft workers, such as plumbers and carpenters who belong to their own separate craft unions; and divisions between workers employed directly by capitalists and those paid by the state out of tax revenues. These divisions produce a working class that is still diversified in both its objective conditions and its subjective consciousness.

What role do labor unions play as workers' organizations in the period of monopoly capitalism? As we have already indicated, the struggles of workers against capitalists arise from the antagonistic nature of the relationship between capitalist and workers in the capitalist mode of production. The rights that many (but by no means all) American workers have today to organize collectively, to form unions, and to require employers to recognize those unions as the legitimate bargaining agents of the workers, are rights wrested from capitalists in major labor struggles, particularly in the 1930s. Many capitalists actively resisted those organizing efforts, and militancy and active struggle on the part of workers was necessary to gain some minimal rights at the workplace.

Despite this history of struggle, the post–World War II role of the labor unions has been much more conservative. The once radical stance of many unions was curbed in the years after World War II as left-wing militant unionists were expelled from unions and legislation limiting unions' right to strike was passed by the federal government. More importantly, the economic prosperity of the postwar era provided an opportunity for capitalists to come to a more or less implicit accommodation with the nonradical leaders of the organized labor unions. The basis of this "social contract" between capital and labor was that capital would accept the legiti-

macy of the unions and be willing to negotiate real wage increases in line with increases in labor productivity, while unions would limit their demands to such wage increases and discipline their own members who violated labor-management negotiated contracts.

Capitalists have thus tended to channel unions into "economism," the concentration on negotiable quantitative wage demands, with less emphasis placed on qualitative demands relating to working conditions, particularly issues of control. This arrangement promoted stability in the workforce, permitted greater scope for long-range corporate planning, and co-opted the radical anti-capitalist thrust of unionism. Liberal capitalists believed that these benefits would far outweigh the costs of granting wage increases and relinquishing some managerial prerogatives.

By the 1970s, however, the "social contract" showed signs of becoming frayed. A fundamental problem was the much reduced ability of U.S. capitalism to provide increasing real wages to its workers, thereby undermining the labor unions bureaucrats' source of allegiance from many union members. There were other long-festering problems that were equally troublesome. As the unions became more bureaucratized and institutionalized as a formal feature of a labor-management system, a growing tension developed between ordinary workers—i.e., the rank and file—and the union bureaucrats. Workers resorted to all sorts of informal and extra-union methods to defend their interests, frequently forming dissident caucuses within unions and engaging in "wildcat" strikes that were not sanctioned by the union bureaucracy. These new forms of workers' struggles reflect the continuing guerrilla war between labor and capital and the underlying class conflicts.

The first two readings in this chapter explore the expansion of wage-labor and the evolution of the labor process in monopoly capitalism. The methods used by capitalists to control workers and the internal structure of the U.S. working class are discussed in the next two readings. The final two readings examine the role of labor unions in monopoly capitalism and illustrate how workers actively fight back against capital.

5.1 The Development of the Wage-Labor Force

The structure of the labor force has undergone profound changes since the early days of capitalism in the United States. In the following reading Michael Reich documents the changing occupational structure of the American population and the changing character of the labor force. The proportion of wage- and salary-workers in the labor force has steadily and markedly increased since the American Revolution, and in recent decades white-collar workers have become more important than blue-collar workers as a proportion of wage- and salary-earners. Although the latter trend might suggest that the proletarian character of the labor force is weakening, Reich argues that the nature of much modern white-collar work is increasingly indistinguishable from blue-collar work and no less proletarian. Despite the changing conditions of work, most workers have no choice but to sell their labor power in the marketplace and to surrender control over their own work.

Capitalism comes into full being when a large number of propertyless individuals come to a labor market to sell their labor-power to a much smaller number of propertied capitalists; these capitalists combine the means of production they own with the labor-power they purchase and direct the production of commodities which they sell on a market. When the United States began its existence as an independent nation in 1776 it was not yet by these criteria a fully developed capitalist society. There was, to be sure, production of goods that were sold as commodities and also significant class inequalities; wealth was concentrated among a small number of large landowners, slaveholders, and urban merchants. But about four-fifths of the nonslave labor force were themselves property-owners and professionals—farmers, merchants, traders, artisans, small manufacturers, lawyers, ministers, and doctors—who derived their income from their own property and labor.[1] Of those who did hire themselves out as workers, many raised their own food on small plots of land and also carried on their own business, as blacksmiths, tailors, carpenters, etc.[2] Most of the population lived in rural areas; in 1810, 80 percent of the labor force worked in agriculture.

This society of wealthy merchants, independent commodity-producers, slaveholders, and slaves became dramatically transformed in the succeeding two centuries as a capitalist class structure developed in the United States. In the early nineteenth century, capitalist relations of production began first in the manufacturing of textiles, with a labor supply recruited initially from the surrounding agri-

[1]Slaves totaled 20 percent of the population. An extended examination of the class structure in this period is contained in Jackson T. Main, *The Social Structure of Revolutionary America* (Princeton, N.J.: Princeton University Press, 1965).

[2]Ibid., p. 271.

cultural population but subsequently expanded mainly by European immigration. By 1890, after slavery was abolished and as the United States was rapidly industrializing, only one-third of the adult workforce was classified by the census-takers in the category of "independent enterprisers."

With the further advance of large-scale industry and the emergence of monopoly capitalism in the twentieth century, the proportion of small independent producers continued to decline, as did even the absolute number of petty manufacturers and merchants, shopkeepers, small-scale family farms, and artisans. By 1974 more than 80 percent of all adults in the labor force were nonmanagerial wage and salary employees, sellers of their labor-power on a labor market.[3] This

[3]I have excluded salaried managers from the proletariat because many of them supervise large numbers of workers and are highly paid executives who have more in common with capitalist owners. Some of these "managers," however, are low-level administrators, as the quotation on p. 182 from Braverman indicates.

process of proletarianization, or transformation of the labor force into mere sellers of labor-power, is summarized statistically in Table 5-A.

This growth of the wage and salary proletariat is even more remarkable when one examines the transformed role of women and blacks in the economy. Although women have always participated significantly in home production and in agriculture, the growth of capitalism in the twentieth century has dramatically increased in the proportion of women who work outside the home as wage and salary-earners, many of them on a full-time and year-round basis. In 1890, only 18 percent of adult women worked at paid jobs outside the home. Most of these women were single, under 25, and tended to leave employment when they married; most older women were married and worked primarily at home. By contrast, in 1974 45 percent of adult women were in the paid labor force, most of them wage and salary employees; and over 40 percent of married women living with

TABLE 5-A THE PROLETARIANIZATION OF THE U.S. LABOR FORCE[a]

Year	Percent Wage and Salaried Employees[b]	Percent Self-Employed[c]	Percent Salaried Managers and Administrators	Total
1780[d]	20.0	80.0	—	100.0
1880	62.0	36.9	1.1	100.0
1890	65.0	33.9	1.2	100.0
1900	67.9	30.8	1.3	100.0
1910	71.9	26.3	1.8	100.0
1920	72.9	23.5	2.6	100.0
1930	76.8	20.3	2.9	100.0
1939	78.2	18.8	3.0	100.0
1950	77.7	17.9	4.4	100.0
1960	80.6	14.1	5.3	100.0
1969	83.6	9.2	7.2	100.0
1974	83.0	8.2	8.8	100.0

Notes: [a]Defined as all income recipients who participate directly in economic activity; unpaid family workers have been excluded. [b]Excluding salaried managers and administrators. [c]Business entrepreneurs, professional practicioners, farmers, and other property owners. [d]Figures for 1780 are rough estimates. Slaves, who comprised one-fifth of the population, are excluded; white indentured servants are included in the wage and salaried employees category.

SOURCES: Data for 1780 from Jackson T. Main, *The Social Structure of Revolutionary America* (Princeton, N.J.: Princeton University Press, 1965), pp. 270–77. Data for 1880–1939 from Spurgeon Bell, *Productivity, Wages and National Income* (Washington, D.C.: Bookings Institution, 1940), p. 10. Data for 1950–1969 computed from U.S. Dept. of Labor, *Man-power Report of the President*, various years; and U.S. Dept. of Commerce, Bureau of the Census. *Census of Population*, 1950 and 1960, and *Current Population Reports*, Series P-60, various years.

their husbands and nearly half of all mothers with children under 18 were active members of the paid labor force in 1974.[4] As these data suggest, women are in the wage labor force on a more permanent basis: if past trends continue, women born in 1960 will spend an average of twenty years of their life as wage- or salary-workers.[5]

The most dramatic transformation of working status has occurred among blacks. After the Civil War some ex-slaves became artisans, some became wage-earners in urban areas or on reorganized plantations, and a few obtained land of their own to farm. But most ex-slaves eked out an existence as farm tenants or sharecroppers, dependent on the white landlord for credit, tools, work animals, and feed. Beginning about the turn of the century, however, and particularly since 1940, blacks have left agriculture and sharecropping in large numbers and joined the wage and salary proletariat. By 1970, less than 20 percent of blacks were living in rural areas, and over 97 percent of employed blacks were working outside agriculture, almost all as nonmanagerial wage- and salary-workers.[6]

Most wage and salary employees in the United States are dependent on their jobs for their livelihood; few have alternative sources of substantial income or control over productive assets. A 1962 survey (see Table 5-B) indicated that, apart from a car, a house, household possessions, and a small ($500 or less) savings account and pension fund, 45 percent of all households owned absolutely no income-producing assets (stocks, bonds, bank accounts, real estate, etc.), while an additional 40 percent of households owned income-producing assets of $10,000 or less

(assuming a rate of return of 8 percent, an asset worth $10,000 would bring in $800 per year in income). By contrast, 1 percent of all adults own over three-quarters of the corporate stock and the corporate bonds in America.[7]

TABLE 5-B THE DISTRIBUTION OF INCOME-PRODUCING ASSETS* DECEMBER 31, 1962

Size of Portfolio (in dollars)	Number of Consumer Units (millions)	Percent of Consumer Units
0	11.8	20.4
1–500	14.5	24.9
500–2,000	10.2	17.7
2,000–5,000	7.4	12.8
5,000–10,000	4.9	8.9
10,000–25,000	5.2	9.0
25,000–50,000	2.1	3.6
50,000 and above	1.8	3.1
Total	57.9	100.0

*Bank accounts, stocks and bonds of all types, real estate, mortgage assets, etc.

SOURCE: Dorothy Projector and Gertrude Weiss, *Survey of Financial Characteristics of Consumers*, Washington, D.C., Federal Reserve Board, 1966, Table A-36 p. 15. Percentages may not add to total because of rounding.

In short, the United States has become a nation of wage and salary employees who have virtually no access to income from property or control over the production process, and whose economic welfare is determined by the vicissitudes of the labor market. The process by which capitalist development progressively reduces more adults to the status of seller of labor-power has taken place in all capitalist countries; for example, data for France and Germany also indicate a steadily increasing proportion of wage- and salary-earners.[8]

At the same time, the old capitalist class has also been changing. While the traditional

[4]U.S. Bureau of the Census, *Historical Statistics of the United States, from Colonial Times to 1957* (Washington, D.C.: U.S. Govt. Printing Office, 1960); Howard Hayghe, "Marital and Family Characteristics of the Labor Force, March 1974," *Monthly Labor Review*, January 1975.

[5]V. Perella, "Women and the Labor Force," *Monthly Labor Review* (February 1968), p. 2.

[6]U.S. Department of Commerce, Census Buseau, *Census of Population, 1970*.

[7]See Robert J. Lampman, *The Share of Top Wealth-Holders in National Wealth* (Princeton, N.J.: Princeton University Press, 1962), Table 97, p. 209. See also Ackerman and Zimbalist, Section 8.1 p. 297.

[8]Data for France and Germany are reported in E. Mandel, *Marxist Economic Theory* (New York: Monthly Review Press, 1968), pp. 164–65.

image of a leisure class of rentiers who live by clipping coupons of stocks and bonds was never very accurate, it has become particularly obsolete under modern capitalism. More common today is the large capital-owner who also participates in production, for a high salary, as director, manager, trustee, or executive. A large proportion of high-level managers and executives in the largest corporations and banking institutions have substantial personal holdings in the stocks and bonds of those companies.[9]

With the increasing complexity of modern corporate organizations and bureaucracies, managers have become increasingly numer-

[9]See Robert J. Larner, "The Effect of Management-Control on the Profits of Large Corporations," in Maurice Zeitlin, ed., *American Society, Inc.* (Chicago: Markham Publishing Co., 1970).

ous (see Table 5-C). As Harry Braverman has pointed out, however, the Census Bureau's classification of managers can be quite misleading. The 6.5 million persons classified as "managers, administrators and proprietors, except farm" in 1970 "included perhaps a million managers of retail and service outlets, and as much as much as another million self-employed petty proprietors in these same fields. It included buyers and purchasing agents, officials and administrators at the various levels of government, school administration, hospitals and other such institutions; postmasters and mail superintendents; ships' officers, pilots, and pursers; building managers and superintendents; railroad conductors; union officials; and funeral directors. Since such categories consume almost half of the entire classification, it is clear without

TABLE 5-C THE CHANGING OCCUPATIONAL STRUCTURE OF THE LABOR FORCE

Occupational Group	1910	1940	1960	1972[a]	1980[a, b]	1985[a, b]
Managers, Administrators, and						
Proprietors (except farm)	6.6%	7.3%	8.5%	9.8%	10.5%	10.3%
White-Collar Workers	14.7	23.8	33.8	38.0	41.0	42.6
Professional & technical	4.7	7.5	11.4	14.0	15.7	16.8
Clerical	5.3	9.6	15.0	17.4	18.7	19.4
Sales	4.7	6.7	7.4	6.6	6.6	6.4
Blue-Collar Workers	38.2	39.8	39.5	35.0	33.1	32.3
Craft workers &						
supervisors	11.6	12.0	14.3	13.2	12.8	12.8
Operatives	14.6	18.4	19.7	16.6	15.6	15.1
Nonfarm laborers	12.0	9.4	5.5	5.2	4.7	4.4
Service Workers	9.6	11.8	11.7	13.4	13.3	13.2
Private household workers						
(e.g., maids)	5.0	4.7	2.8	1.8	1.3	1.1
Other services	4.6	7.1	8.9	11.6	12.0	12.1
Agriculture	30.9	17.4	6.3	3.8	2.1	1.6
Farmers & farm managers	16.5	10.4	3.9	2.2	—	—
Farm laborers	14.4	7.0	2.4	1.6	—	—
TOTAL[c]	100.0	100.0	100.0	100.0	100.0	100.0

Notes: [a]Data for 1972, 1980, and 1985 refer to employed persons only. [b]Projections. [c]Individual items are rounded separately and therefore may not add up to totals.

SOURCES: Data for 1910–1940 from U.S. Dept. of Commerce, Bureau of the Census, *Historical Statistics of the United States, Colonial Times to 1957*, Table D 72-122; data for 1960 from U.S. Dept. of Commerce, Bureau of the Census, *U.S. Census of Population, 1960*, Table 201; data for 1972–1985 from Neal Rosenthal, "The United States Economy in 1985: Projected Change in Occupations," *Monthly Labor Review* (December 1973), Table 2, p. 19.

further analysis of the rest that the managerial stratum of true operating executives of the corporate world is quite a small group."[10]

THE STRUCTURE OF THE PROLETARIAT

The growth of capitalist production on a large scale and the extension of capitalist production into new areas has led to significant structural changes within the wage and salary labor force. Along with a growing hierarchy in the production process, a pyramidal social structure has developed as white-collar workers, many of whom occupy intermediate positions in the occupational structure, have grown in number. C. Wright Mills was fond of referring to such workers as the *new middle class* since, unlike the small farmers and shopkeepers of the old middle class, most of these white-collar workers do not own property, which is significant in the production process. In what follows we trace the changing composition of the labor force and indicate how the character of white-collar jobs is being transformed.

The importance in the economy of blue-collar labor in industry (mining, manufacturing, and construction) increased continuously in the United States until about the 1930s, as industry displaced the family farm and the farm laborer. Since the 1930s, however, white-collar and service employment have replaced industrial blue-collar employment as the most rapidly expanding occupations in the economy. The proportion of nonmanagerial white-collar workers in the labor force grew from about 6.7 percent in 1870 to 24 percent in 1940 and 38 percent in 1972. By contrast, blue-collar employees in mining, manufacturing, and construction accounted for 37 percent of the total labor force in 1940 and have remained near this proportion since. At the same time, the proportion of service workers (excluding maids and other private household workers) in the labor force has grown from less than 5 percent in 1910 to 12 percent today (see Table 5-C).

These long-run changes in the occupational structure reflect (1) advances in the technology of production, (2) changes associated with the growth of corporate bureaucracies, and (3) shifts in the sectoral composition of goods and services produced in the economy.

1. With technical improvements related primarily to mechanization and automation, fewer industrial workers are needed to produce increasing quantities of output. For example, in manufacturing, total output increased 178 percent between 1950 and 1973, with only an 18 percent increase in production workers; in mining, output increased 67 percent in the same period, while blue-collar production employment declined by 41 percent.[11]

2. In the same period, white-collar nonproduction employment increased by 70 percent in manufacturing and by more than 60 percent in mining. As Stephen Hymer has pointed out, modern corporate enterprises have become increasingly complex in their organizational structure.[12] The modern giant corporation has far-flung sales and distribution networks and specialized divisions for research and development, product design and styling, cost accounting, personnel management, sales, marketing, finance, and overall corporate coordination. As a result, more white-collar workers—managerial, professional, technical, clerical, and sales—are needed. Research and development activities have become particularly important in many military-related sectors in American industry. These high-technology industries, such as electronics, telecommunications, and missile guidance systems, employ large numbers of scientists, engineers, designers, and technicians. Thus, white-collar workers are becoming an increasing proportion of the total labor force within the manufacturing sector of the

[10]Harry Braverman, *Labor and Monopoly Capital* (New York: Monthly Review Press, 1974), p. 259.

[11]*Statistical Abstract of the United States, 1974.* (Washington, D.C.: U.S. Government Printing Office, 1975.)

[12]See Hymer, Section 4.1, p. 120.

economy (see Table 5-D). We can expect this trend to continue; nonmanagerial white-collar workers comprised less than 10 percent of employment in manufacturing in 1899, 20 percent of total manufacturing employment in 1952, and 27 percent in 1975.[13]

TABLE 5-D SELECTED WHITE-COLLAR OCCUPATIONS AS A PERCENT OF TOTAL MANUFACTURING EMPLOYMENT

	1940	1952	1963	1975
Professional and Technical	3.0	5.3	9.3	11.2
Clerical	14.1	11.8	12.2	12.2
Sales		2.8	3.3	3.6
Total	17.1	19.9	24.8	27.0

SOURCE: U.S. Census of Population, 1940; Bureau of Labor Statistics Bulletin 1599; unpublished BLS data presented in E. Kassalow, "White Collar Unionism in the United States," in A. Sturmthal, Ed., *White Collar Trade Unions* (Urbana: University of Illinois Press, 1966), p. 318.

3. The changes in the sectoral composition of goods and services produced in the economy have also contributed to the growth of white-collar and service employment. The service sectors—wholesale and retail trade; finance, insurance, and real estate; professional, business, and personal and repair services; institutions (private hospitals, universities, foundations, etc.); and government —become increasingly important at higher levels of gross national product. These service sectors tend to employ a high percentage of white-collar workers.

On the other hand, many workers in the service occupations—such as restaurant labor, laundry and dry-cleaning workers, chambermaids, janitors, nursing aides, porters, barbers and hairdressers, and guards and police officers—fill positions that are by no means traditional white-collar office jobs. The same could be said of workers in automobile or machine repair shops, who are classified *occupationally* as blue-collar workers, but classified *industrially* in service industries. Overall, the *rate* of increase in employment in service *occupations* has matched the increase in white-collar occupations.

A large proportion of the increased employment in the service sector is concentrated in increased state and local government employment in education, health, and local public administration. For example, "the *increase* in employment in the field of education between 1950 and 1960 was greater than the total number employed in the steel, copper, and aluminum industries in either year. The *increase* in employment in the field of health between 1950 and 1960 was greater than the total number employed in automobile manufacturing in either year."[14]

THE NATURE OF WHITE-COLLAR EMPLOYMENT

As the number of white-collar jobs has grown, the character of these jobs has been transformed. First, the greatest increases (in absolute numbers) in white-collar jobs have occurred in the low-level clerical and sales categories. Second, the growth of bureaucracies and the increasing importance of machinery of various types in modern offices —copying machines, new varieties of dictating equipment, improved typewriters, key punch machines, and other accessories to electronic data and word processing—have made much work in the modern office resemble factory and assembly-line labor. The work of a telephone operator or of a secretary in a typing pool is similar in many ways to the work of a machine operator in a textile factory. Hierarchy, barriers to advancement, extreme specialization, and lack of control more and more characterize many white-collar jobs. Several recent national surveys have pointed to increasing job dissatisfaction

[13]The 1899 estimate is cited in Eli Chinoy, *Automobile Workers and the American Dream*, (Boston: Beacon Press, 1963) p. 5; 1972 and 1975 figures are from Bureau of Labor Statistics Bulletin 1599.

[14]Victor Fuchs, *The Service Economy* (New York: National Bureau of Economic Research, 1968), p. 1.

among white-collar workers as a result of such changes.[15]

Furthermore, the independent status of many once elite professional white-collar jobs has been steadily eroded. Scientists, engineers, architects, teachers, nurses, university professors, technicians, etc. find that they work in ever-larger organizations in which the content of their jobs, as well as their working conditions, are more narrowly defined and set down from above. In recent years many professional and technical white-collar workers have become subject to layoffs, a long-time hallmark of blue-collar employment.

Even doctors and lawyers have not escaped some loss of independence. For example, an increasing percentage of all doctors are employed on a salary basis in the large, urban, often university-connected hospitals, clinics, and research institutes. Fewer lawyers are engaged primarily in their own practice; many now work for large law firms or are employed directly by corporations and governments on an annual salary basis.

Finally, the salaries of white-collar workers have not risen as fast as those of blue-collar workers. In 1890, white-collar workers received on the average about double the average wage of the blue-collar manufactur-

ing worker.[16] Today most white-collar clerical and sales workers earn less than many blue-collar workers. While female clerical and sales workers receive the lowest pay, the average income of male clerical and sales workers alone is below the average income of skilled blue-collar workers.

The relative position on the income scale of professional white-collar workers has also fallen. For example, in 1904 high school teachers in large cities earned nearly three times the wage of an average manufacturing production worker.[17] Today, high school teachers earn only about 50 percent more than the average manufacturing wage earner.

In short, the expansion of the wage-labor force has occurred simultaneously with a breaking down of the old sharp distinctions between blue-collar, white-collar, and service work. Although important differences among workers still remain, as we shall see later in this chapter, there is no doubt that an increasing proportion of the total labor force falls into the category that we call the working class.

[16]In 1890, average annual earnings for clerical workers in manufacturing and steam railroads were $848, compared to $439 for blue-collar wage-earners in manufacturing; see *Historical Statistics*, p. 92. In 1969, the average weekly pay of clerical workers was $105, compared to $130 for blue-collar production workers.

[15]For a summary of some recent studies, see "Work in America," Section 7.1, p. 268, and the references cited therein.

[17]P. G. Keat, "Long-Run Changes in the Occupational Wage Structure," *Journal of Political Economy*, vol. 58, no. 6 (December 1960).

5.2   *The Creation of Abstract Labor*

When Henry Ford hit upon the idea of using a moving conveyor belt as the basis for assembly-line production of automobiles, he created what has become the symbol of capitalist work organization: the assembly-line worker. The basic principles underlying Ford's innovation had already been formulated by Frederick Taylor, an industrial engineer who systematically and in great detail investigated the labor process in industry so as to reorganize it along capitalist lines. "Taylorism," as Harry Braverman describes it in the following reading, called for the reconceptualization of labor as a series of simple motions executed by workers who were to be treated as interchangeable parts. Workers were not visualized as individuals having concrete skills or qualities, but as *abstract labor*. Braverman shows how this process of de-skilling labor has extended beyond production workers in industry to offices, retailing, and the service sector as well.[1]

[1]See also Chapter 7 for further analysis of the organization of work under capitalism.

The following is excerpted from *Labor and Monopoly Capital*, by HARRY BRAVER-MAN. Copyright © 1974 by Harry Braverman. Reprinted by permission of Monthly Review Press.

The stages of management control over labor before Taylor had included, progressively: the gathering together of the workers in a workshop and the dictation of the length of the working day; the supervision of workers to ensure diligent, intense, or uninterrupted application; the enforcement of rules against distractions (talking, smoking, leaving the workplace, etc.) that were thought to interfere with application; the setting of production minimums; etc. A worker is under management control when subjected to these rules, or to any of their extensions and variations. But Taylor raised the concept of control to an entirely new plane when he asserted as an *absolute necessity for adequate management the dictation to the worker of the precise manner in which work is to be performed.* That management had the right to "control" labor was generally assumed before Taylor, but in practice this right usually meant only the general setting of tasks, with little direct interference in the worker's mode of performing them. Taylor's contribution was to overturn this practice and replace it by its opposite. Management, he insisted, could be only a limited and frustrated undertaking so long as it left to the worker any decision about the work. His "system" was simply a means for management to achieve control of the actual mode of performance of every labor activity, from the simplest to the most complicated. To this end, he pioneered a far greater revolution in the division of labor than any that had gone before.

. . . .

Since the principles upon which it is based

are fundamental to all advanced work design or industrial engineering today, it is important to examine them in detail. And since Taylor has been virtually alone in giving clear expression to principles which are seldom now publicly acknowledged, it is best to examine them with the aid of Taylor's own forthright formulations.

FIRST PRINCIPLE

"The managers assume . . . the burden of gathering together all of the traditional knowledge which in the past has been possessed by the workmen and then of classifying, tabulating, and reducing this knowledge to rules, laws, and formulae. . . ."[1] No task is either so simple or so complex that it may not be studied with the object of collecting in the hands of management at least as much information as is known by the worker who performs it regularly, and very likely more. This brings to an end the situation in which "Employers derive their knowledge of how much of a given class of work can be done in a day from either their own experience, which has frequently grown hazy with age, from casual and unsystematic observation of their men, or at best from records which are kept, showing the quickest time in which each job has been done."[2] It enables management to discover and enforce those speedier

[1]Frederick W. Taylor, *The Principles of Scientific Management* (New York, 1967), p. 36.

[2]Ibid., p. 22.

methods and shortcuts which workers themselves, in the practice of their trades or tasks, learn or improvise, and use at their own discretion only. Such an experimental approach also brings into being new methods such as can be devised only through the means of systematic study.

This first principle we may call the *dissociation of the labor process from the skills of the workers*. The labor process is to be rendered independent of craft, tradition, and the workers' knowledge. Henceforth it is to depend not at all upon the abilities of workers, but entirely upon the practices of management.

SECOND PRINCIPLE

"All possible brain work should be removed from the shop and centered in the planning or laying-out department. . . ."[3] Since this is the key to scientific management, as Taylor well understood, he was especially emphatic on this point and it is important to examine the principle thoroughly.

In the human, as we have seen, the essential feature that makes for a labor capacity superior to that of the animal is the combination of execution with a conception of the thing to be done. But as human labor becomes a social rather than an individual phenomenon, it is possible—unlike in the instance of animals where the motive force, instinct, is inseparable from action—to divorce conception from execution. This dehumanization of the labor process, in which workers are reduced almost to the level of labor in its animal form, while purposeless and unthinkable in the case of the self-organized and self-motivated social labor of a community of producers, becomes crucial for the management of purchased labor. For if the workers' execution is guided by their own conception, it is not possible, as we have seen, to enforce upon them either the methodological efficiency or the working

pace desired by capital. The capitalist therefore learns from the start to take advantage of this aspect of human labor power, and to break the unity of the labor process.

This should be called the principle of the *separation of conception from execution*, rather than by its more common name of the separation of mental and manual labor (even though it is similar to the latter, and in practice often identical). This is because mental labor, labor done primarily in the brain, is also subjected to the same principle of separation of conception from execution: mental labor is first separated from manual labor and, as we shall see, is then itself subdivided rigorously according to the same rule.

. . .

THIRD PRINCIPLE

The essential idea of "the ordinary types of management," Taylor said, "is that each workman has become more skilled in his own trade than it is possible for any one in the management to be, and that, therefore, the details of how the work shall best be done must be left to him." But, by contrast: "Perhaps the most prominent single element in modern scientific management is the task idea. The work of every workman is fully planned out by the management at least one day in advance, and each man receives in most cases complete written instructions, describing in detail the task which he is to accomplish, as well as the means to be used in doing the work. . . . This task specifies not only what is to be done, but how it is to be done and the exact time allowed for doing it. . . . Scientific management consists very largely in preparing for and carrying out these tasks."[4]

. . .

The essential element is the systematic pre-planning and pre-calculation of all elements of the labor process, which now no longer exists as a process in the imagination

[3]Frederick W. Taylor, *Shop Management* (New York, 1903), pp. 98–99.

[4]*Principles of Scientific Management*, pp. 63–69.

of the worker but only as a process in the imagination of a special management staff. Thus, if the first principle is the gathering and development of knowledge of labor processes, and the second is the concentration of this knowledge as the exclusive province of management—together with its essential converse, the absence of such knowledge among the workers—then the third is the *use of this monopoly over knowledge to control each step of the labor process and its mode of execution.*

As capitalist industrial, office, and market practices developed in accordance with this principle, it eventually became part of accepted routine and custom, all the more so as the increasingly scientific character of most processes, which grew in complexity while the worker was not allowed to partake of this growth, made it ever more difficult for the workers to understand the processes in which they functioned.

· · ·

Modern management came into being on the basis of these principles. It arose as theoretical construct and as systematic practice, moreover, in the very period during which the transformation of labor from processes based on skill to processes based upon science was attaining its most rapid tempo. Its role was to render conscious and systematic, the formerly unconscious tendency of capitalist production. It was to ensure that as craft declined, the worker would sink to the level of general and undifferentiated labor power, adaptable to a large range of simple tasks, while as science grew, it would be concentrated in the hands of management.

· · ·

The transformation of working humanity into a "labor force," a "factor of production," an instrument of capital, is an incessant and unending process. The condition is repugnant to the victims, whether their pay is high or low, because it violates human conditions of work; and since the workers are not destroyed as human beings but are simply utilized in inhuman ways, their critical, intelligent, conceptual faculties, no matter how deadened or diminished, always remain in some degree

a threat to capital. Moreover, the capitalist mode of production is continually extended to new areas of work, including those freshly created by technological advances and the shift of capital to new industries. It is, in addition, continually being refined and perfected, so that its pressure upon the workers is unceasing. At the same time, the habituation of workers to the capitalist mode of production must be renewed with each generation, all the more so as the generations which grow up under capitalism are not formed within the matrix of work life, but are plunged into work from the outside, so to speak, after a prolonged period of adolescence during which they are held in reserve. The necessity for adjusting the worker to work in its capitalist form, for overcoming natural resistance intensified by swiftly changing technology, antagonistic social relations, and the succession of the generations, does not therefore end with the "scientific organization of labor," but becomes a permanent feature of capitalist society.

· · ·

The first comprehensive conveyor assembly line will suffice as an indication that the wrenching of the workers out of their prior conditions and their adjustment to the forms of work engineered by capital is a fundamental process in which the principal roles are played not by manipulation or cajolery but by socioeconomic conditions and forces.

In 1903, when the Ford Motor Company was founded, building automobiles was a task reserved for craftsmen who had received their training in the bicycle and carriage shops of Michigan and Ohio, then the centers of those industries. "Final assembly, for example," writes Eli Chinoy, "had originally been a highly skilled job. Each car was put together in one spot by a number of all-around mechanics." By 1908, when Ford launched the Model T, procedures had been changed somewhat, but the changes were slight compared with what was soon to come.

· · ·

The demand for the Model T was so great that special engineering talent was engaged to revise the production methods of the company. The key element of the new organization of labor was the endless conveyor chain upon which car assemblies were carried past fixed stations where men performed simple operations as they passed. This system was first put into operation for various subassemblies, beginning around the same time that the Model T was launched, and developed through the next half-dozen years until it culminated in January 1914 with the inauguration of the first endless-chain conveyor for final assembly at Ford's Highland Park plant. Within three months, the assembly time for the Model T had been reduced to one-tenth the time formerly needed, and by 1925 an organization had been created which produced almost as many cars in a single day as had been produced, early in the history of the Model T, in an entire year.

The quickening rate of production in this case depended not only upon the change in the organization of labor, but upon the control which management, at a single stroke, attained over the pace of assembly, so that it could now double and triple the rate at which operations had to be performed and thus subject its workers to an extraordinary intensity of labor.

. . .

In management's eyes as well as in the practice it dictates, the more labor is governed by classified motions which extend across the boundaries of trades and occupations, the more it dissolves its concrete forms into the general types of work motions. This mechanical exercise of human faculties according to motion types which are studied independently of the particular kind of work being done, brings to life the Marxist conception of "abstract labor." We see that this abstraction from the concrete forms of labor—the simple "expenditure of human labor in general," in Marx's phrase—which Marx employed as a means of clarifying the value of commodities (according to the share of such general human labor they embodied), is not something that exists only in the pages of the first chapter of *Capital*, but exists as well in the mind of the

capitalist, the manager, the industrial engineer. It is precisely their effort and métier to visualize labor not as a total human endeavor, but to abstract from all its concrete qualities in order to comprehend it as universal and endlessly repeated motions, the sum of which, when merged with the other things that capital buys—machines, materials, etc.—results in the production of a larger sum of capital than that which was "invested" at the outset of the process. Labor in the form of standardized motion patterns is labor used as an interchangeable part, and in this form comes ever closer to corresponding, in life, to the abstraction employed by Marx in analysis of the capitalist mode of production.

. . .

In pursuit of this "solution," industry, trade, and offices rationalize, mechanize, innovate, and revolutionize the labor process to a truly astonishing degree. The methods used are as various as the resources of science itself. And since these resources are so vast, where they cannot accomplish a large saving of labor by a revolution in production they achieve the same effect by a degradation of the product.

The construction industry, for example, divides its efforts between the destruction of sound buildings and their replacement with shoddy structures whose total life span will not equal the useful life remaining to the demolished buildings. This industry, which because of the nature of its processes is still largely in the era of hand craftsmanship supplemented by powered hand tools, the lowest level of mechanization, makes continual and determined efforts to climb out of this disadvantageous position. It favors new materials, especially plastics, painting and plastering with spray guns (a single spray plasterer keeps a number of workers busy smoothing), and the pre-assembly of as many elements as possible on a factory basis (a carpenter can install six to ten prefabricated door assemblies, pre-hung in the frames with hardware already in place, in the time it takes to hang a single door by conventional methods; and in the process becomes a doorhanger and ceases to be a carpenter). The trend of dwelling construction is best exemplified by the rapidly growing "mobile home" segment of the industry. The "mobile home" is a mass-produced factory product; of the three parties involved—the workers, the manufacturers, and the residents—only the middle one has any advantage to show from the transaction. Yet mobile homes are spreading over the landscape triumphantly, and one may easily predict for them a still greater future because of the high degree of "efficiency" with which they allocate labor and capital.

A quarter-century ago, Siegfried Giedion described the transformation of the crusty, wholesome loaf of bread into a "product" with the "resiliency of a rubber sponge."[5] But the production process for the manufacture of this bread is a triumph of the factory arts. Continuous mixing, reduction of brew fermentation time, dough which is metered, extruded, divided, and panned to the accuracy of a gram in the pound, conveyorized baking and automatic depanning, cooling, slicing, wrapping, and labelling have effectively rid the bakery of the troublesome and unprofitable arts of the baker, and have replaced the baker himself with engineers on the one hand and factory operatives on the other. The speed with which the operation is conducted is a marvel of efficiency, and, apart from its effects on the worker, if only it were not necessary for the people to consume the "product" the whole thing could be considered a resounding success.

. . .

In the manufacture of wearing apparel, every aspect of the production process is being energetically attacked. Since this is an industry which is characterized by the existence of many shops, most of them relatively small, a great many are still in the stage of traditional "rationalization," breaking down operations into a large number of smaller and simpler steps. At the same time these steps are being speeded up by the introduction of

a variety of devices, chiefly attachments to sewing machines such as needle positioners, automatic thread cutters, pleaters, and hemmers. The use of two- or three-layer bonded materials, which eliminate separate linings, and synthetic fabrics, which may be processed by novel methods such as the electronic fusing of seams in place of sewing, opens up new vistas for cheapening and transforming mass-produced clothing. Advanced production methods are copied from sheetmetal and boiler-shop techniques: die-cutting to replace hand cutting, pattern-grading equipment which produces different size copies of a master pattern, etc. There is a photoline tracer which guides a sewing head along the path of a pattern placed in a control unit. Improving on this, a photoelectric control is used to guide a sewing head along the edge of the fabric. In these latter innovations we see the manner in which science and technology apply similar principles to dissimilar processes, since the same control principles may be applied to complex contours, whether on steel or cloth.

. . .

Despite the variety of means used in all the innovations we have been describing, their unifying feature is the same as that which we noted at the outset of this discussion: the progressive elimination of the control functions of the worker, insofar as possible, and their transfer to a device which is controlled, again insofar as possible, by management from outside the direct process.

. . .

The picture of mechanization and skill cannot be completed without reference to those industries where mechanization has made the process so automatic that the worker takes virtually no physical part in it whatsoever. This theoretical ideal can be but seldom realized, and most plants considered "automatic" still require a great deal of direct labor of all sorts. But in the chemical industry it very often comes closer to realization than elsewhere, because of the nature of the continuous processes employed and the possiblity of moving the entire product-in-

[5]Siegfried Giedion, *Mechanization Takes Command* (New York, 1948), p. 198.

preparation within enclosed vessels and piping. Thus the chemical operator is singled out, time and again, as the outstanding beneficiary of "automation," and the praises of this job are sung in countless variations. The work of the chemical operator is generally clean, and it has to do with "reading instruments" and "keeping charts." These characteristics already endear him to all middle-class observers, who readily confuse them with skill, technical knowledge, etc. Yet few have stopped to think whether it is harder to learn to read a dial than to tell time. Even Blauner, who selected this work as his example of the tendency of modern industry to bring the total process of production back within the ken of the worker, admits that chemical operators need know nothing about chemical processes.[6] He cites one oil refinery personnel executive who has placed a limit on the IQ's of workers hired for operating jobs, another who calls them "only watchmen," and reports this outburst by a chemical operator:

> *It takes skill to be an operator. Maybe you've heard of this job-evaluation program that's been going on. Well, our supervisor thinks there's not much skill in our work. The way he described our jobs for the job-evaluation program, it's like he thinks you could train a bunch of chimps and they could do the job. He thinks we're a bunch of idiots. That has caused unhappy feelings.*[7]

$\cdot$ $\cdot$ $\cdot$

The enormous and continuous growth in demand for engineers has created a new mass occupation. On the one hand, this has, along with other new professions such as accounting, given a place to those thrust out of the old middle class by the relative decline of the petty entrepreneurial occupations in trade and other erstwhile arenas of small business. But on the other hand, having become a mass occupation engineering has begun to exhibit, even if faintly, some of the characteristics of other mass employments: rationalization and division of labor, simplification of duties,

application of mechanization, a downward drift in relative pay, some unemployment, and some unionization.

In a study done for the National Bureau of Economic Research, *The Demand and Supply of Scientific Personnel*, David M. Blank and George J. Stigler point out that "in the United States since 1890: demand has grown quite rapidly but supply has grown even more rapidly so salaries have drifted downward relative to those for the entire working population." Their index of the ratio of median engineering salaries to those of the full time manufacturing wage earner shows that, if the 1929 ratio is taken as 100, by 1954 the ratio was only 66.6.[8]

The engineer's job is chiefly one of design, but even design, where a project has grown large enough, may be subjected to the traditional rules of the division of labor.

$\cdot$ $\cdot$ $\cdot$

These methods are being applied to stress analysis for the intricate patterns of flush rivets in aircraft, to bridge design, hospital planning, and other engineering problems. Apart from the labor-saving aspects of the technique, it alters the occupational composition in the same manner as does numerical control. Since such techniques are used in accord with the management-favored division of labor, they replace engineers and draftsmen with data-entry clerks and machine operators, and further intensify the concentration of conceptual and design knowledge. Thus the very process which brought into being a mass engineering profession is being applied to that profession itself when it has grown to a large size, is occupied with duties which may be routinized, and when the advance of solid-state electronic technology makes it feasible to do so.

$\cdot$ $\cdot$ $\cdot$

A mass of clerical workers has come into existence whose work embraces all that was formerly handled on an informal basis in the shop itself, or on a minimal basis in the small

[6]Robert Blauner, *Alienation and Freedom* (Chicago, 1964), pp. 144–45.

[7]Ibid., p. 158, 160.

[8]David M. Blank and George J. Stigler, *The Demand and Supply of Scientific Personnel* (New York, 1957), p. 21, 25.

shop offices of the past. Since management now carries on the production process from its desktops, conducting on paper a parallel process that follows and anticipates everything that happens in production itself, an enormous mass of recordkeeping and calculation comes into being. Materials, work in progress, finished inventory, labor, machinery, are subjected to meticulous time and cost accounting. Each step is detailed, recorded, and controlled from afar, and worked up into reports that offer a cross-sectional picture at a given moment, often on a daily basis, of the physical processes of production, maintenance, shipment, storage, etc. This work is attended by armies of clerks, data-processing equipment, and an office management dedicated to its accomplishment.

· · ·

The rationalization of most office work and the replacement of the all-around clerical worker by the subdivided detail worker proceeds easily because of the nature of the process itself. In the first place, clerical operations are conducted almost entirely on paper, and paper is far easier than industrial products to rearrange, move from station to station, combine and recombine according to the needs of the process, etc. Second and more important, much of the "raw material" of clerical work is numerical in form, and so the process may itself be structured according to the rules of mathematics, an advantage which the managers of physical production processes often strive after but can seldom achieve. As flows subject to mathematical rules, clerical processes can be checked at various points by mathematical controls. Thus, contrary to the past opinion of many that office work was unlike factory work in that its complexities rendered it more difficult to rationalize, it proved easier to do so once the volume of work grew large enough and once a search for methods of rationalization was seriously undertaken.

· · ·

The incidence of developed skill, knowledge, and authority in the labor processes of society is naturally very small [among service workers] . . . and can be found only in that small layer of housekeepers and stewards who have the function of superintending institutional labor, and among the tiny number of cooks who practice the art on the chef level. Those who supervise labor in institutions correspond to the foremen who supervise factory labor, or to lower-level managers having the same function in every labor process. Chefs and cooks of superior grades, the highest skill of the service category, offer an instructive instance of the manner in which an ancient and valuable craft is being destroyed even in its last stronghold, luxury and gourmet cooking. The technological means employed in this case is that of food freezing, including its more recent forms, flash freezing and drying at sub-zero temperatures, and cryogenic freezing at temperatures at least 300 degrees below zero. In such processes, cell walls are destroyed and texture and flavor damaged.

· · ·

So far as retail trade is concerned, it is worth noting that although the "skills" of store operations have long since been disassembled and in all decisive respects vested in management, a revolution is now being prepared which will make of retail workers, by and large, something closer to factory operatives than anyone had ever imagined possible. In retail food trading, for example, the demand for the all-around grocery clerk, fruiterer and vegetable dealer, dairyman, butcher, and so forth has long ago been replaced by a labor configuration in the supermarkets which calls for truck unloaders, shelf stockers, checkout clerks, meat wrappers, and meatcutters; of these, only the last retain any semblance of skill, and none require any general knowledge of retail trade. The use of mechanical equipment for the shelving, display, and sale of commodities has thus far remained in a primitive state, in part because of the ready availability of low-cost labor and in part because of the nature of the process itself. With the perfecting of a number of computerized semi-automatic checkout systems, however, an increasing number of national chains in retail trade—in other fields as well as in food marketing—have committed themselves to replacing their present cash-register systems with new systems that, they estimate, will almost double the number of customers handled by each checkout clerk in a given time. The system will require affixing to each item a tag or label which carries the proper stock number (a universal ten-digit code has been adopted by the food industry) and perhaps a price, printed in characters which may be recognized by an optical scanner. Thus the clerk will simply pass the item over the scanner (or hold a scanner lens to the tag), and the register will transmit the operation to a computer which can either supply the price or check it against the current price list. The effects of this system on inventory control, quick and general price changes, and sales reporting to a central point require no comment. But the checkout counter then adopts as its own the assembly line or factory pace in its most complete form. The "production" of each register can be controlled from a single central station and laggards noted for future action; and, since no knowledge of prices is required, the production speed of a checkout clerk can be pegged at the highest level within a few hours after that clerk has begun the job, instead of the few weeks of learning time that are now allowed. Of course, the slowest operation will then become that of bagging, and various mechanical systems which will eliminate the separate "bagger" and enable the checkout clerk to sweep the item over the optical scanner and into the bag with a single motion are being devised and tested.

The trend to automatic filling stations, where the customer, in return for a small saving, fills his or her own tank while the transaction is monitored on a screen in the station is also worth mentioning, if only for the manner in which it combines a displacement of labor with a shift from male to female labor; the new gasoline station attendants are generally "girls," who, as everyone knows, offer a further saving to the thrifty employer.

As a quick glance at the list of service occupations will make apparent, the bulk of the work is concentrated in two areas: cleaning and building care, and kitchen work and food service. Female workers outnumber male, as in retail sales work. Training prerequisites for most of these occupations are minimal, a job ladder leading upward is virtually nonexistent, and unemployment rates are higher than average. In this occupational category are found the housekeeping jobs of a society of concentrated life and labor that masses workers and residents in multiple-dwelling units, giant office blocks, and immense factory units, and which thus develops extraordinary requirements for cleaning, caretaking, and catering. We see here the obverse face of the heralded "service economy," which is supposed to free workers from the tyranny of industry, call into existence a "higher order" of educated labor, and transform the condition of the average man. When this picture is drawn by enthusiastic publicists and press agents of capitalism (with or without advanced degrees in sociology and economics), it is given a semblance of reality by reference to professional occupations. When numbers are required to lend mass to the conception, the categories of clerical, sales, and service workers are called upon. But these workers are not asked to show their diplomas, their pay stubs, or their labor processes.

5.3 Systems of Control in the Labor Process

In the previous reading we saw how capitalists have introduced and made use of *technology* to control their workforce as productivity is increased; as a consequence, many jobs have become routinized and deskilled. At the same time, capitalists have expanded the organizational techniques they use to control their workforces, and the *social relations* of jobs have consequently become more elaborate and complex. In the following reading, Richard C. Edwards examines capitalists' use of bureaucratic methods to control workers in monopoly capitalist firms, and he contrasts this system of control with that used in small competitive businesses.

The conditions of work in capitalist enterprises have changed as capitalism itself has changed. In both cases, evolution has not overturned the fundamental relations that exist between capitalist and worker. But just as capitalism has proceeded from a competitive to a monopoly phase, so also have the organization of workers in production and the circumstances of their employment passed from one developmental stage to another. Big corporations have seized the opportunity inherent in their command of immense resources to develop new ways of motivating, controlling, disciplining, and reproducing their workforces.

During the nineteenth century much production was still carried on by skilled craftsmen, who established their own working conditions, protected the quality of their products, and limited access to their industry through craft rules, customs, apprenticeships, and the like. But as power-driven machinery and large-scale production developed, craft production was increasingly replaced by production based on unskilled and semi-skilled workers. Production itself, as well as the sale of commodities, was organized by capitalists.

In the capitalist firms of the nineteenth century, the organization of work relied on the direct and personal exercise of power by the capitalist or, in larger firms, by the capitalist's top managers. As bosses, they ruled the roost in obvious ways: they personally supervised the production process, intervening where necessary to discipline or dismiss or exhort or reward workers to facilitate production and increase output. Few rules and no grievance procedures existed to restrain their power, and their actions tended to be arbitrary and harsh. Those outside the factory gates—the "reserve army of the unemployed"—stood as ready replacements for any workers who rebelled against such tyrannical power.

In the twentieth century, however, the largest corporations have moved away from the nineteenth-century organization of work. Each worker still faces the threat of being fired and thereby losing his or her income, and each worker is of course ruled over by a supervisor. The fundamental relations have not changed. But corporations have devised much more subtle and sophisticated ways of both motivating and controlling workers, and the conditions facing workers today cannot in general be understood as merely an extension of nineteenth-century organization. A new stage has been entered. The present organization of work and the current structure of labor markets must be understood as having emerged out of the general process of capitalist development, including the long struggles by workers to organize, build solidarity among themselves, and curb their employers' power over them.

The results of this unfolding development are visible in the evolution of both *labor markets* and the *labor process*. Labor markets are the mechanisms through which the kinds of jobs, the wages paid, and the degree of job security available to any worker are determined. The labor process refers to production itself and the conditions under which human labor is used to produce goods and services. Within the firm, the relations between capitalists and workers take the specific form of a *system of control*; that is, the wage structure, promotion and firing policies, sanctions, incentives, delegation of authority, and other means by which capitalists exercise power in order to transform the labor power they have purchased into labor actually done.

I distinguish below between two essentially different systems of control: (1) By using what I term "hierarchical control," capitalists exercise power openly, arbitrarily, and personally (or through hired bosses who act in much the same way). Hierarchical control formed the organizational basis for nineteenth-century firms and continues today in the small enterprises of the competitive sector. (2) "Bureaucratic control," in which the exercise of power, still hierarchical in form, is institutionalized in the very structure of the firm and is thus made impersonal, provides the rationale for the organization of the workplace in big corporations today.[1] These are not the only systems of control possible ("technical control"—machine pacing, assembly-line production, etc.—is another), but they have been the most important historically.

In the labor market, the relations between capitalists and workers take the form of demanders and suppliers of the commodity "labor power." But the bargain exchanging wages for labor power is influenced by a great many factors, among the most important of which is the relative degree of solidarity or division among workers. An important source of the divisions among workers is the differences in their work situations which have grown out of industrial dualism.

In what follows, I outline the principal changes in work organization and labor market structure that have accompanied the rise of monopoly capitalism. My discussion must be understood as limited essentially to the organization of work in corporations of the economy's monopoly sector. Workers in the competitive sector, as well as most of the large

corporation's foreign employees, continue to face older, more direct, less institutionalized forms of control.

FROM HIERARCHICAL CONTROL TO BUREAUCRATIC CONTROL

Bureaucratic control had its roots in the dramatic economic transition which occurred in the United States between roughly 1890 and 1920. The transition from competitive to monopoly capitalism created contradictions between the firm's traditional structure and organization and its new scale and economic status. It was out of this contradiction that emerged the present form of its internal relations. In particular, a series of changes in the scale and technique of production and in the economic position of large firms combined to undermine the prevailing system of control within the firm—that system of open, arbitrary, highly visible, direct command-rule by superiors over subordinates that I termed "hierarchical control."

Hierarchical control required personal supervision. But expansion implied increasing separation of those most motivated to supervise properly (the owners and high-level managers) from the actual production activities. The expansion of each (surviving) firm's production required ever-proliferating layers of intervening—and less reliable—supervisors. The top-echelon managers were further separated from contact by the type of expansion. Since expansion often occurred by merger of competing companies, the new giants tended to be multi-plant concerns: the scattered production facilities of the previously independent companies became linked, not through geographical proximity, but rather through the administrative and supervisory apparatus. "Headquarters," rather than being divided among separate offices adjoining the dispersed plants, was centralized in the financial districts, away from all plants.

Increasing industrial concentration forced firms to concentrate more carefully on long-range planning, market manipulation, adver-

[1]In some cases (e.g., along the U.S.-Mexico border) big firms may choose to use hierarchical control.

tising, and other aspects of the sales effort, as opposed to production itself. But the actual work activities of these increasingly important administrative and other non-production operations were more complex, subtle, and less standardized than production tasks. The new tasks tended to diminish the possibility of easy, unambiguous, and quickly available evaluation of a worker's performance; these new jobs came into conflict with "close supervision," the day-to-day relation through which the authority of hierarchical control was effected.

Finally, the principal sanction in hierarchical control—frequent threats of and often massive use of firings and layoffs—was undermined by the increasingly high cost of the response which it provoked. As unions during this period threatened to achieve more comprehensive (e.g., industry-wide and cross-craft) organization, unionization and worker militancy among production workers increasingly meant that firing workers to maintain discipline resulted in long and costly strikes.

Thus capitalists found that for both the rapidly expanding white-collar staff and for the more organized blue-collar workers, they could no longer rely solely on mass dismissals and the "reserve army of the unemployed." While their power to fire recalcitrant workers remained the ultimate sanction on which their power was based, they needed alternative and more subtle control mechanisms.

These developments were most acutely felt in the emerging "core" firms of monopoly capitalism, which because of their vast size and rapid growth, found that control from the top through the mechanisms of simple hierarchy was most attenuated and difficult. On the other hand, it was precisely these firms which could benefit most from new internal structures. They had the resources to experiment with new organizational forms. They had sufficient power to withstand short-run disruptions. They began from an entrenched, stable economic position which allowed them to experiment with new forms and then to institute and capture the benefits from the procedures they devised.

Increasingly after the turn of the century, capitalists became aware of the need for *systematically* and *consciously* designing the organizational structure to meet this requirement of institutionalized control. Frederick Taylor and his scientific management disciples spread one part of the gospel, that of time and motion studies and the technical details of "human engineering." Alfred Chandler describes the continual experimentation in organizational forms at the higher corporate levels which managers at General Motors, Standard Oil (N.J.), duPont, and Sears, Roebuck carried out.[2] Industrial psychology and personnel management grew from tiny beginnings at the turn of the century to central features of big corporations within two or three decades. As David Montgomery notes, the Employment Managers Association, formed by 50 corporate officials in 1911, gathered 900 members at its 1918 convention.[3] Corporations gave support to the establishment of business schools, and Harvard's, started in 1908, was soon followed by Princeton, Stanford, and elsewhere. F. B. Miller and M. A. Coghill, in introducing their historical review of industrial psychology literature, noted that

> Our findings led us to decide that the major facets of modern personnel administration . . . existed, at least in embryo, by [1923]. . . . The fundamentals of personnel work were being practiced in representative firms, preached in five or six standard texts, and celebrated periodically in conventions of specialized practitioner associations.[4]

The new system of control, devised both as part of the corporation's response to the general worker threat to capitalist hegemony and as a specific strategy to ameliorate the crisis

[2]Alfred Chandler, *Strategy and Structure* (Cambridge: M.I.T. Press, 1962).

[3]David Montgomery, "Immigrant Workers and Scientific Management," Conference of Eleutherian Mills Historical Library, 1973 (mimeo).

[4]F. B. Miller and M. A. Coghill, *The Historical Sources of Personnel Work* (Ithaca, N.Y.: N.Y. State School of Industrial and Labor Relations, 1961).

of control in the firm, was bureaucratic control. The defining feature of bureaucratic control was the institutionalization of hierarchical power. "Rule of law"—the firm's law —replaced "rule by supervisor command" both in the organization and direction or work tasks and in the exercise of the firm's power to enforce compliance. Work activities became defined and directed by a set of work criteria—the rules, procedures, and expectations governing particular jobs. Thus for the individual worker, his or her job tended to be defined more by formalized work criteria attached to the job (or more precisely, by the interpretation given to those criteria by his or her supervisor and higher levels of supervision) rather than by specific orders, directions, and whims of the supervisor. Moreover, it is against those criteria that the worker's performance came to be measured. Both written and unwritten requirements were included in the criteria, but the essential characteristic was that the worker was able to ascertain them and that they were highly stable. The firm no longer altered the worker's tasks and responsibilities by having the supervisor tell the worker to do something different; rather, it "created a new job" or "redefined the job." From these criteria derived the "customary law" notions of "equity" or "just cause" in firing, promotions, and job assignments.

The top-echelon management retained their control over the enterprise through their ability to determine the rules, set the criteria, establish the structure, and enforce compliance. For the latter concern, enforcing compliance, bureaucratic organization again marked a departure from hierarchical control. In hierarchical control, power was vested in individuals and exercised arbitrarily according to their discretion, but with bureaucratic control power became institutionalized by vesting it in official positions or roles and permitting its exercise only according to prescribed rules, procedures, and expectations; rules governing the exercise of power were elements of the work criteria defining supervisor's jobs. Since there were formally established criteria for evaluating

the exercise of power, it also was made accountable to top-down control.

The work activities could never be completely specified by job criteria in advance, and the "rule of law" could never completely replace the "rule by command" in an hierarchical enterprise. Some situations or problems always arose which had to be handled in an *ad hoc.* particularistic way, and so supervisors could never be content merely to evaluate and never instigate. The shift to bureaucratic control must therefore be seen as a shift toward *relatively* greater dependence on institutionalized power, and bureaucratic control came to exist alongside and was reinforced by elements of hierarchical control. Bureaucratic control became, then the predominant system of control, giving shape and logic to the firm's organization, although not completely eliminating elements of hierarchical control.

The imposition of bureaucratic control in the monopoly firm had four specific consequences for the social relations of the firm:

a. The power relations of hierarchical authority were made invisible, submerged and embedded in the structure and organization of the firm rather than visible and openly manifest in personal, arbitrary power.

b. Bureaucratic control, because of its emphasis on *formal* structure and status distinctions, made it possible to differentiate jobs more finely. Organizational as well as technical (i.e., production) aspects of jobs defined their status. Each job appeared more unique and individualized by its particular position in the finely graded hierarchical order, by the job criteria which specified work activities, and by distinct status, power, responsibilities, and so on. Elements of the social organization of the firm which differentiated between jobs were emphasized, while those which created commonality diminished.

c. Bureaucratic control, by altering the social context of jobs, changed as well the kinds of worker characteristics which firms rewarded. "Good" workers in these jobs must be capable of some self-direction and initiative, since it is not feasible to give workers specific instructions for every situation that may arise. To function adequately, such workers must *internalize* the values, outlook, and goals of the firm, especially when the job depends significantly on cognitive processes. For example, consider what is involved in responding to a business letter, or taking purchasing orders from customers, or making out voucher payments, or interviewing prospective new personnel. If the employee is to do his job properly, he must put himself in the position of the firm (that is, assume the firm's values, criteria, and goals), and then interpret what from that perspective would be the appropriate response. But since the firm's goals reflect the capitalist's interests, not the worker's own interests, bureaucratic organization encounters a problem of worker motivation.

The fundamental problem of motivation results from alienated labor: where the workers have no control over work activities or the product of their labor, they can be motivated to work only by the external reward of wages, including the threat of having no income. This source of motivation continues in bureaucratic firms. But bureaucratic organization, by requiring greater reliance on the worker's internalization of the firm's (i.e., the capitalist's) goals, exacerbates the motivation problem.

Both the firm's rewards (higher pay, status, promotions) and penalties (threats of being fired, demotions, actual dismissal) are geared to the quality of an individual's work performance. But the internal social relations of bureaucratic firms—the fine degree of stratification, the multiple levels of authority and subordinacy, the isolation from participation in overall decision-making, and especially the need for workers to internalize the firm's values—require much of the worker. Attaining the firm's rewards and avoiding its penalties—that is, being successful in a bureaucratic firm—requires a particular cluster of behavioral or personality characteristics: workers must be "disciplined" and their behavior predictable; they must respect the authority of those higher in the hierarchy; they must be ablt to assume the firm's values

and outlook; they must divorce their motivation from the intrinsic content of the work and instead must value highly the external reward of wages. Workers are "successful" to the extent that they incorporate these characteristics.

d. The role of the supervisor was transformed from that of active instigator, director, and overseer of work activities to that of monitor and evaluator of the worker's performance—the superior now judged the subordinate's work according to the work criteria. Moreover, the supervisor's own work—his use of sanctions, for example—became subject to much greater evaluation and control from above.

The first two changes tended to erode the bases for common worker opposition. Increasingly, the individual worker came to face an impersonal and massive organization more or less alone. In general, the work environment became less conductive to unions and strike or other opposition activities. In those bureaucratized industries where unions remained (or were subsequently organized) more and more the unions accepted the organization of work and directed their energies towards non-control issues (wages, fringe benefits, procedures for promotion, hiring, and firing). Even where unions turned their attention to the work activities themselves, their efforts were mainly defensive, directed toward making the job criteria more explicit and openly articulated; while this tended to undermine the authority of arbitrary foremen, it strengthened the legitimacy of the overall structure. As the common basis of work experience declined, so did the possibility for united worker action concerning control over work.

BUREAUCRATIC CONTROL AND LABOR MARKETS

While the imposition of bureaucratic control had an impact on the characteristics which monopoly capitalist firms sought and rewarded in their workers, its particular relevance for the operation of labor markets lay in the exaggerated importance which its structure and incentives imparted to *stability* charactersitics in worker behavior.

The elimination of arbitrary, unpredictable, and random supervisory power and its replacement by more systematic, "rational," and institutionalized power made the firm's system of rewards and sanctions more conductive to attaining predictable behavior. That is, it tended to elicit an acceptance of the firm's power as authority and reinforce a *stable orientation to that authority*, by which I mean having "appropriate" attitudes and behavior towards the enterprise's power structure and those delegated by the enterprise to exercise power. Bureaucratic power was embedded in the organizational structure of the enterprise, and was more hidden from view because its nature was institutional rather than personal. Power could be exercised only in accord with established criteria and procedures. Bureaucratic rules allowed the supervisor to appear to detach his or her own feeling from his or her "responsibility" as supervisor. Established work criteria provided a substitute for the personal repetition of orders by the supervisor, so that the supervisor needed to intervene less often and power was seemingly less often appealed to. The existence of work criteria permitted supervisors several levels higher to evaluate both workers and their supervisors, so irregular or unpredictable behavior on the part of *supervisors* was minimized. Finally, bureaucratic rules made the use of punishment seem more legitimate by making them appear as "company policy"; moreover, the rules established a kind of "conspicuous bargaining point" such that a supervisor who simply chose to be less harsh than the rules was judged "permissive" or lenient. In these ways, then bureaucratic control rationalized the enterprise's power by making its application more predictable and stable, and hence bureaucratic control evoked more stable and predictable behavior from workers; that is, bureaucratic control tended to legitimize the firm's exercise of power, and translate it into authority.

The worker characteristics which are rewarded under bureaucratic control also have an impact on the firm's desire to reward employment stability and tenure. Consider the problem the firm has when hiring a worker who is new to that firm. The employer cannot easily determine whether or not this worker has those behavior traits which employers find important in their workers. Despite millions of dollars and forty years of research, no psychological test exists which (a) can be given to new workers (b) predicts job success reasonably well and (c) is relatively inexpensive. So personnel managers use psychological tests that admittedly predict very little; they fall back on educational credentials as screening devices, on the (not unwarranted by imprecise) assumption that diligence at work depends on the same characteristics as success in schooling; they rely heavily on recommendations from previous employers and on the workers's work record, though it is usually difficult to evaluate the context of previous work experience. So *mainly*, the firm can only learn whether a worker has the appropriate traits through a long process of actual experience with the worker on the job, and to do so it must keep workers sufficiently long to make its assessment.

Bureaucratic control fostered employment stability by creating career ladders and instituting rewards for tenure and seniority within the firm; that is, by creating what economists call "internal labor markets." Internal labor markets may be distinguished from the more general labor process of other day-by-day operations within the enterprise, since the former are specific, usually contrived mechanisms by which job vacancies are filled. For example, job bidding systems, regularized promotion procedures requiring periodic supervisors' evaluations, customs restricting job access to apprentices or assistants, and "management development" programs all constitute internal market mechanisms. The jobs filled through the operation of internal markets are restricted to the firm's existing workforce and thus, with regard to these jobs, internal markets determine the conditions on which the enterprise's workers can renegotiate the terms of their wage bargains.

Career ladders and explicit rules governing promotion were simply an extension of the bureaucratic method of organizing work by explicit rules and procedures. Promotion, as one reward, became integrated with the enterprise's system of sanctions and incentives and harnessed to its goals. That promotion and job tenure should become important in bureaucratic control is not surprising, since bureaucratic control was an explicit attempt to move away from harsh negative sanctions (frequent firings, quick and arbitrary foreman control) and toward positive incentives (promotion, some job secutiry). Finally, it should be noted that a system rewarding seniority and employment stability for the enterprise's workers in general could only occur where the firm itself had a stable basis—that is, in the solidly entrenched monopoly capitalist firms.

Thus bureaucratic control increased the rewards to those workers who demonstrated stability, both in the everyday behavior at the job and in the length of time they stayed at a job. These are the characteristics which dominate the operation of internal labor markets. For an individual worker, mobility in the internal market depends upon the firm s assessment of his or her job performance and work behavior as revealed in that job. Stability in work performance, stable orientation to authority, and employment stability are central elements in this evaluation. This finding concerning the derived demand for labor is consistent with the large firm's consolidation of power and its attempt to achieve stability throughout its operations, and it issues directly from its imposition of bureaucratic control.

Internal job allocations, like the filling of jobs in the economy at large, do not all follow the common pattern outlined above. There are always exceptions. Not all internal jobs are filled through the market—as when, for example, workers are able to switch jobs through personal contacts or other particularistic factors. Some job allocations do not involve promotion, but rather are lateral movements, which may occur for reasons different from those outlined above. Criteria other than supervisors' recommendations may sometimes be primary—competitive exams for some jobs, seniority points, licenses, or union cards for others. Yet to the extent that a general pattern characterizes internal markets, it follows bureaucratic lines.

5.4 *Divisions in the Labor Force*

Although the number of wage and salary employees has grown dramatically and an increasing proportion of occupations have become more proletarian in character, the working class in the United States has remained heterogeneous and divided against itself. In the following reading Richard C. Edwards, Michael Reich and David M. Gordon, attribute these divisions in the labor force to differences created or exacerbated by monopoly capitalist development.[1]

[1]See Chapters 8 to 10 for more on inequality, sexism, and racism in the United States.

The following is excerpted from RICHARD C. EDWARDS, MICHAEL REICH and DAVID M. GORDON, *Labor Market Segmentation* (Lexington, Mass.: D.C. Heath, 1975). Reprinted by permission D.C. Heath.

This essay is concerned with a major characteristic of twentieth-century U.S. capitalism: persistent and important *objective* divisions among American workers. We will sketch an argument that the redivision of labor in the period of monopoly capitalism has resulted not in a unified and homogeneous working class, as many had expected, but in segmentation of the labor process and of labor markets,[1] and therefore a divided working class. These divisions in the American working class can best be understood by tracing their evolution through the course of development of American capitalism.

Our argument can be summarized in four major historical propositions:

1. During the development of competitive capitalism in the nineteenth century, the creation and extension of a wage-labor system and wage-labor class were associated with a progressive homogenization of working conditions in the capitalist sector of the economy and a homogenization of labor markets. As production increasingly took the form of commodity production for profit, labor power itself increasingly became a commodity, and growing numbers of Americans sold their labor power in exchange for a wage of salary. The elimination of earlier precapitalist modes of production, the expansion of the competitive capitalist sector, and the evolution of factory production all pointed toward the homogenization of labor. The factory system eliminated many skilled crafts, creating large pools of operative jobs; mass production and greater mechanization forged standardized work requirements; larger establishments drew greater numbers of workers into common working environments. These developments laid the basis for the increasingly militant, class-conscious, anticapitalist labor

movement that appeared toward the end of the century.

2. Between roughly 1890 and 1920 the American economy experienced a critical transition. In this system of monopoly capitalism, the giant oligopolistic corporations that dominated the economy coexisted with a surviving peripheral competitive capitalist sector. The two sectors developed according to quite different laws of motion.

3. A consequence of the dualistic industrial structure was a corollary dualism in labor markets. This dualism constituted a clear *reversal* of those forces which, during the nineteenth century, had led to increasingly common, or shared, work experiences. In particular, the large oligopolistic corporations instituted a new system of labor management that was bureaucratic in form and emphasized the differentiation of jobs, rather than their homogenization. Although proletarianization continued, jobs in the capitalist sector became increasingly dissimilar, and labor markets became increasingly segmented. While these markets reflect (are a natural corollary of) divisions in the labor process, they have also institutionalized those divisions and hence perpetuated them.

4. The dualistic industrial and labor market structures have interacted with preexisting divisions by race and by sex to produce enduring divisions which are likewise rooted in objective economic structures. Segmentation of working conditions and of labor markets thus created the objective basis for the fragmented working-class politics of the twentieth century.

In what follows, we shall elaborate briefly our third and fourth propositions, beginning with the changes wrought by the transition to monopoly capitalism.

MONOPOLY CAPITALISM AND THE REDIVISION OF LABOR

The captains of the new monopoly capitalist era, released from short-run competitive pressures and in search of long-run stability, turned to the capture of strategic control over

---

[1]The *labor market* consists of those institutions which mediate, effect, or determine the purchase and sale of labor power; the *labor process* consists of the organization and conditioning of the activity of production itself, i.e., the consumption of labor power by the capitalist. Segmentation occurs when the labor market or labor process is divided into separate submarkets or subprocesses, or segments, distinguished by different characteristics, behavioral rules, and working conditions.

product and factor markets. Their new concerns were the creation and exploitation of monopolistic control, rather than the allocational calculus of short-run profit maximization.

The new needs of monopoly capitalism for control were threatened by the tremendous upsurge in labor conflict, already apparent as early as the 1870s, and reaching new levels of militancy around the turn of the century. As the work force became increasingly homogeneous and proletarian in character, the labor movement gained in strength and militancy. Large corporations were aware of the potentially revolutionary character of these movements. For example, John Commons notes that the employers' "mass offensive" on unions between 1903 and 1908 was more of an ideological crusade than a matter of specific demands. As James Weinstein has argued, the formation of the National Civic Federation (NCF), a group dominated by large "progressive" capitalists, was another explicit manifestation of the fundamental crises facing the capitalist class during this period.

To meet these threats, employers turned to strategies designed to divide and conquer the work force. The central thrust of the new strategies was to break down the increasingly unified worker interests that grew out of both the proletarianization of work and the concentration of workers in urban areas. As exhibited in several aspects of these large firms' operations, this effort aimed to divide the labor force into various segments so that the actual experiences of workers would be different and the basis of their common opposition to capitalists would be undermined.

The first element in the new strategy involved the internal relations of the firm. The tremendous growth in the size of monopoly capitalist work forces, along with the demise of craft-governed production, necessitated a change in the authority relations upon which control in the firm rested. Efforts toward change in this area included Taylorism and Scientific Management, the establishment of personnel departments, experimentation with different organizational structures, the use of industrial psychologists, "human relations experts," and others to devise appropriate "motivating" incentives, and so forth. From this effort emerged the intensification of hierarchical control, particularly the "bureaucratic form" of modern corporations. In the steel industry, for example, a whole new system of stratified jobs was introduced shortly after the formation of U.S. Steel. The effect of bureaucratization was to establish a rigidly graded hierarchy of jobs and power by which "top-down" authority could be exercised.

The restructuring of the internal relations of the firm exacerbated labor market segmentation through the creation of "internal labor markets." Job ladders were created, with definite "entry-level" jobs and patterns of promotion. Workers who were not employed in these "career" jobs—for example, those who were black or female, or who lacked the qualifications for particular entry-level jobs—were excluded from access to that entire job ladder. In response, unions often sought to gain freedom from the arbitrary discretionary power of supervisors by demanding a seniority criterion for promotion. In such cases, the union essentially took over some of the management of the internal labor process, agreeing to help allocate workers and discipline recalcitrants, obtaining in return some reduction in the arbitrary treatment of workers by management.

An important example of the effects of such policies can be seen in the evolution of employee benefits. Firms had initially attempted to raise the cost to workers of leaving individual companies (but not the cost of entering) by restricting certain benefits to continued employment in that company. Part of this strategy was "welfare capitalism" which emerged from the NCF in particular, and achieved most pronounced form in the advanced industries. At Ford, for example, education for the workers' children, credit, and other benefits were dependent on the workers' continued employment by the firm and therefore tied the worker more securely to the firm. For these workers, the loss of one's job meant a complete disruption in all aspects of the family's life. Likewise, seniority benefits were lost when workers switched companies. The net effect of these new policies was an intensification of barriers between structured and unstructured labor processes.

At the same time that firms were structuring their internal labor processes, they undertook similar efforts to divide the groups they faced in external markets. Employers quite consciously exploited race, ethnic, and sex antagonisms in order to undercut unionism and to break strikes. In numerous instances during the consolidation of monopoly capitalism, employers manipulated the mechanisms of labor supply in order to import blacks as strikebreakers, and racial hostility was stirred up to deflect class conflicts into race conflicts. For example, during the steel strike of 1919, some 30,000 to 40,000 blacks were imported as strikebreakers in a matter of a few weeks. Similarly, employers frequently transformed jobs into "female jobs" in order to render those jobs less susceptible to unionization.

Employers also consciously manipulated ethnic antagonisms to achieve segmentation. They often hired groups from rival nationalities in the same plant or in different plants. During labor unrest the companies sent spies and rumor mongers to each camp, stirring up fears, hatred, and antagonisms of other groups. The strategy was most successful when many immigrant groups spoke little English.

The manipulation of ethnic differences was, however, subject to two grave limitations as a tool in the strategy of "divide and conquer." First, increasing English literacy among immigrants allowed them to communicate more directly with each other; second, mass immigration ended in 1924. Corporations then looked to other segmentations of more lasting significance.

Employers also tried to weaken the union movement by favoring the conservative "business-oriented" craft unions against the newer "social-oriented" industrial unions. An ideology of corporate liberalism toward labor was articulated around the turn of the century in the NCF. Corporate liberalism recognized the potential gains of legitimizing some unions but not others; the NCF worked jointly with the craft-dominated American Federation of Labor to undermine the more militant industrial unions, the Socialist party, and the Industrial Workers of the World (IWW).

As the period progressed, employers also turned to a relatively new divisive means, the use of educational "credentials." For the first time, educational credentials were used to routinize skill requirements for jobs. Employers played an active role in molding educational institutions to serve these channeling functions. The new requirements helped maintain the somewhat artificial distinctions between factory workers and those in routinized office jobs and helped generate some strong divisions within the office between semiskilled white-collar workers and their more highly skilled office mates.

The rise of giant corporations and the emergence of a monopolistic core in the economy accentuated forces that stimulated and reinforced segmentation. As different firms and industries grew at different rates, a dichotomization of industrial structure developed. The larger, more capital-intensive firms were generally sheltered by barriers to entry; enjoyed technological, market power, and financial economies of scale; and generated higher rates of profit and growth than their smaller, labor-intensive competitive counterparts. However, it did not turn out that the monopolistic core firms were wholly to swallow up the competitive periphery firms.

Given their large capital investments, the large monopolistic corporations required stable market demand and stable planning horizons in order to ensure that their investments would not go unutilized. Where demand could be stabilized, large corporations developed concentrated market power. Where demand was cyclical, seasonal, or otherwise unstable, it was difficult for a monopolistic environment for production to develop. These industries (textiles and leather goods are prime examples) retained a generally competitive structure. Moreover, even in the concentrated industries, production of certain products was subcontracted or "exported" to small, more competitive and less capital-intensive firms on the industrial periphery.

Along with the dualism in the industrial structure, there developed a corresponding dualism of working environments, wages, and mobility patterns. Monopoly corporations, with more stable production and sales, developed job structures and internal relations reflecting that stability. For example, the bureaucratization of work rewarded and elicited stable work habits in employees. In peripheral firms, where product demand was unstable, jobs tended to be marked also by instability; therefore, workers in the secondary labor market experienced higher turnover rates. The result was the dichotomization of the urban labor market into "primary" and "secondary" sectors.

In addition, as the primary labor market has itself developed, a division has emerged between an "independent primary" and a "subordinate primary" segment. The independent primary sector includes many professional, managerial, and technical jobs, where professional standards tend to govern work performance, and employees are often free of specific instruction and authority. Independent primary workers tend to acquire *general* skills through formal education, and to apply those skills to variable individual situations they encounter in their work. They tend to internalize the formal objectives of their organizations and often experience substantial job mobility.

The subordinate primary segment includes many semiskilled, primary sector blue-collar and white-collar jobs that generally involve routinized, repetitive tasks, specific supervision, and formalized work rules. Most subordinate primary workers acquire specific job skills on the job, rarely learning generalized skills. Given corporate rules and union provisions, blue-collar workers in particular are more likely to remain within a single firm or within a single industry.

RACE AND SEX AND THE REDIVISION OF LABOR

Our fourth proposition is that dualistic industrial and labor-market structures interacted with preexisting differences by race and sex to produce persistent objective differences along these dimensions.

During the period of transition to monopoly capitalism, blacks still remained largely in the rural South. As late as World War I the only industries to which blacks had gained access were those which had imported black workers for strikebreaking purposes. Blacks made greater inroads into manufacturing during World War I and the 1920s, with the demand caused by the war and then the closing of foreign immigration, but they were concentrated in the least skilled and least desirable jobs. In both the steel and auto industries, for example, the large employers began systematically to segregate blacks into unskilled manufacturing jobs as a way of dividing the work force and reinforcing structured divisions within the firm's job hierarchies.

The more recent patterns of economic life for blacks developed during and after World War II. Many blacks came north during the labor shortages of the war and the subsequent mechanization of agriculture, and found themselves in segregated and isolated urban ghettos. In that context, black employment began to be dominated increasingly by three kinds of jobs: (1) low-wage jobs in the secondary market, mainly in peripheral industries; (2) some jobs in the primary labor market, largely in the core industries into which blacks had already gained access before World War II; and (3) jobs in the rapidly expanding service sectors, most of them in the secondary labor market.

The factors affecting patterns of female employment were different, though related. Although the first textile mills relied chiefly on female and child labor (women accounted for over half of the textile factory labor force in the 1840s), women workers never moved out of the clothing industries into any other manufacturing industries in significant numbers. In 1870, 70 percent of non-farm-working women were domestic servants, and another 24 percent worked in textiles and apparel. Most of the working women were young and unmarried; as late as 1890 less than 2 percent of married white women were counted in the labor force.

During the period of transition to monopoly capitalism, 1890 to 1920, the exclusion of women from nonhome production began to break down further. The growth in demand for labor generally, the particular expansion of demand for office workers—an occupation experiencing feminization in this period— and the growth of demand for teachers provided positions which were filled by women. On the other hand, the segreagation of women in manufacturing continued, and their employment in that sector did not grow as rapidly. In part because of the protective legislation of the period, women continued to be excluded from the better-paying manufacturing jobs, particularly in the capital-goods sectors.

After 1920, the number of women workers increased even more rapidly than during the transitional period. After stagnating during the 1920s and 1930s, female labor force participation rates virtually doubled between 1940 and 1970, as married women with children entered the labor force in large numbers.

The patterns of female employment that emerged after 1920 reflected both the patterns already established during the transitional period and the continuing influence of segmentation within the labor process and labor markets. First, the continued dramatic expansion of clerical work and the channeling of women in the lower-level clerical occupations were a major development in this period. Second, the equally dramatic increase in the number of service jobs in the economy, particularly in health and education, also resulted in large increases in female employment. But again a sexual stratification emerged, so that the top of the occupational hierarchies in both schools and hospitals was dominated by men. Finally, employers in the secondary labor market in peripheral manufacturing industries, in retail trade, and in some services turned increasingly to female employees. These three categories—clerical occupations, health and educational occupations, and employment in peripheral manufacturing industries and retail trade—dominate female employment today.

5.5   *Labor Unions and the Working Class*

Although the first workers' organizations in the United States were formed before 1800 (Philadelphia printers conducted a strike in 1786), as late as 1933 less than 3 million workers—about 5 percent of the total labor force— were organized into unions.[1] These unions were predominantly structured along craft lines—i.e., only skilled craftsmen were eligible for membership. Very few semi-skilled or unskilled workers, and few blacks, belonged to these craft unions.

Before the 1930s, ethnic and racial antagonisms, an open frontier, and above all, organized employer resistance (often violent and repressive and backed by the military and police power of the state) combined in blocking

[1]For data on unionization cited in this and the following paragraphs, see U.S. Department of Labor, B.L.S. Bulletin, *Directory of National Unions and Employee Associations* (Washington, D.C.: U.S. Government Printing Office, 1973).

numerous attempts to organize industry-wide unions. But during the decade of the Thirties, industrial unionism became a mass movement: 4 million workers, many of them semi-skilled or unskilled, were organized into the Congress of Industrial Organization (CIO) between 1934 and 1938 alone. The movement reached a crescendo in the massive sit-down strikes of 1936–1937, when tens of thousands of workers successfully occupied factories, often for weeks, until their unions were recognized as legitimate bargaining agents by the employers. The CIO solidified its success during World War II when it organized an additional 4 million workers into unions. By 1947, union membership had reached 14.8 million, or about 24 percent of the total labor force, and about 34 percent of the nonfarm labor force.

Over 19 million American workers were members of labor unions in 1972. About half of all blue-collar workers are members of unions and 70 percent of all union members are in mining, manufacturing, construction, and transportation. By contrast, a much smaller percentage of service and white-collar workers are unionized. Thus the decline in blue-collar production employment and the rise of white-collar and service occupations have led to a decline in the proportion of the nonfarm labor force that is unionized: 34 percent in 1947 versus 27 percent in 1972.

The degree of unionization varies considerably by industry, region, sex, and race. While approximately half of all manufacturing workers are organized, the proportion unionized is even higher in the more concentrated and heavy industries, reaching 89 percent in primary metals (steel, copper, etc.), 80 percent in rubber, and 90 percent in transportation equipment (automobiles, aircraft, etc.). Many of the remaining unorganized workers in these industries are in the smaller scattered plants. As for regional differences, union organization tends to be less extensive in the South. Women and blacks are underrepresented in the unions: about 22 percent of union members are women, although they comprise 30 percent of the labor force; similarly, blacks comprise only 11 percent of all union members, although they are one-fifth of the highly organized blue-collar occupations. Recently, unions have grown rapidly among white-collar public employees—clerks, teachers, social workers, etc.

What has been the impact of the unions? To what extent have the unions modified traditional employer control over the process of production and the conditions surrounding the workers' sale of their labor-power? We have already offered a brief answer in the introduction to this chapter. Stanley Aronowitz addresses these questions further in the following reading.

The following is excerpted from *False Promises: The Shaping of American Working Class Consciousness*, by STANLEY ARONOWITZ. © 1973 by Stanley Aronowitz. Used with permission of McGraw-Hill Book Company.

The unions are no longer in a position of leadership in workers' struggles; they are running desperately to catch up to their own membership. There are few instances in which the union heads have actually given militant voice to rank-and-file sentiment. In many cases, union sanctions for walkouts have followed the workers' own action. In others, the leadership has attempted to thwart membership initiative and, having failed, has supported a strike publicly while sabotaging it behind the scenes. For the most part, the national bureaucracies of the unions have sided with employers in trying to impose labor peace upon a rebellious membership. What is remarkable is that the rebellion has been largely successful despite enormous odds.

The unions are afraid to oppose the rank and file directly. Their opposition has taken the form of attempting to channel the broad range of rank-and-file grievances into bargaining demands which center, in the main, on wages and benefits, while the huge backlog of grievances on issues having to do with working conditions remains unsolved. Rank-and-file militancy has occurred precisely because of the refusal of the unions to address themselves to the issues of speedup, health and safety, plant removal, increased workloads, technological change, and arbitrary discharges of union militants.

Wages have, of course, also been an enormously important factor in accounting for the rash of strikes. Since 1967, workers have suffered a pronounced deterioration in living standards. Despite substantial increases in many current settlements, real wages for the whole working class have declined annually, for there are few contracts which provide for cost-of-living increases in addition to the negotiated settlements. Even where C-o-L clauses have been incorporated into the contracts, there is usually a ceiling on the amount of increase to which the company is obligated. In many contracts, the first-year increase is equal to the cost of living increase as tabulated by the Bureau of Labor Statistics for the previous year. But the second- and third-year increases are usually not as great and during these years workers' real wages are diminished significantly.

Long-term contracts, which have become standard in American industry, have robbed the rank and file of considerable power to deal with their problems within the framework of collective bargaining. Workers have been forced to act outside of approved procedures because instinctively they know that the unions has become an inadequate tool

to conduct struggles, even where they have not yet perceived the union as an outright opponent to their interests.

For most workers, the trade union still remains the elementary organ of defense of their immediate economic interests. Despite the despicable performance of labor movement leadership during the past thirty years, and especially in the last two decades, blue- and white-collar workers regard their unions as their only weapons against the deterioration of working conditions and the rampant inflation responsible for recent declines in real wages.

In part, trade unions retain their legitimacy because no alternative to them exists. In part, workers join unions because the unions give the appearance of advancing workers' interests, since they must do so to some extent to gain their support. A national union bureaucracy can betray the workers' elementary demands for a considerable period of time without generating open opposition among the rank and file. Even when workers are aware of the close ties that exist between the union leaders and the employers, rebellion remains a difficult task for several crucial reasons.

First, in many cases, the union bureaucracy is far removed from the shop floor because membership is scattered over many plants or even industries. In unions like the United Steelworkers, only half the 1.2 million members are employed in the basic steel sector of the industry. The rest of the membership spans the nonferrous metals industry, steel fabricating plants, stoneworking, can companies, and even a few coal mines. Most of the membership is in large multiplant corporations that have successfully decentralized their operations so that no single plant or cluster of factories in a single geographic region is capable of affecting production decisively. The problem of diffusion is complicated by the recent trend of U.S. corporations to expand their manufacturing operations abroad rather than within this country. In these circumstances, many workers, unable to communicate with workers in other plants of the same corporation since the union has centralized communications channels, feel powerless to improve their own conditions.

Second, the structure of collective bargaining enables the national union to transfer responsibility to the local leadership for failures of the union contract on working conditions issues, while claiming credit for substantial improvements in wages and benefits. This practice has been notable in the Auto Workers, the Rubber Workers, and others that have national contracts with large corporations.

Although the last decade has been studded with examples of rank-and-file uprisings against the least responsible of the labor bureaucrats, in nearly all cases, the new group of elected leaders has merely reproduced the conditions of the old regime. In the steel, rubber, electrical, government workers and other important unions one can observe some differences in sensitivity to the rank and file among the newer leaders. They are more willing to conduct strike struggles and their political sophistication is greater. But these unions can hardly be called radical nor have they made sharp breaks from the predominant policies of the labor movement in the contemporary era.

.   .   .

If the trade union remains an elementary organ of struggle, it has also evolved into a force for integrating the workers into the corporate capitalist system. Inherent in the modern labor contract is the means both to insure some benefit to the workers and to provide a stable, disciplined labor force to the employer. The union assumes obligations as well as wins rights in the collective bargaining agreement.

Under contemporary monopolistic capitalism, these obligations include: (1) the promise not to strike, except under specific conditions, or at the termination of the contract, (2) a bureaucratic and hierarchical grievance procedure consisting of many steps during which the control over the grievance is systematically removed from the shop floor and from workers' control, (3) a system of management prerogatives wherein the union agrees to cede to the employer "the operation of the employer's facilities and the direction of the working forces, including the right to hire, suspend, or discharge for good cause and . . . to relieve employees from duties due to lack of work," and (4) a "checkoff" of union dues as an automatic deduction from the workers' paychecks.

The last provision, incorporated into 98 percent of union contracts, treats union dues as another tax on workers' wages. It is a major barrier to close relations between union leaders and the rank and file. Workers have come to regard the checkoff as another insurance premium. Since they enjoy little participation in union affairs, except when they have an individual grievance or around contract time, the paying of dues in this manner —designed originally to protect the union's financial resources—has removed a major point of contact between workers and their full-time representatives. This procedure is in sharp contrast to former times when the shop steward or business agent was obliged to collect dues by hand. In that period, the dues collection process, however cumbersome for the officials, provided an opportunity for workers to voice their complaints as well as a block against the encroachment of bureaucracy.

The modern labor agreement is the principal instrument of the class collaboration between the trade unions and the corporations. It mirrors the bureaucratic and hierarchical structure of modern industry and the state. Its provisions are enforced not merely by law, but by the joint efforts of corporate and trade union bureaucracies. Even the most enlightened trade union leader cannot fail to play his part as an element in the mechanisms of domination over workers' rights to spontaneously struggle against speedup or *de facto* wage cuts, either in the form of a shift in the work process or by inflationary price increases.

The role of collective bargaining today is to provide a rigid institutional framework for the conduct of the class struggle. This struggle at the point of production has become regulated in the same way as have electric and telephone rates, prices of basic commodities, and foreign trade. The regulatory procedure in labor relations includes government intervention into collective bargaining, the routinization of all conflict between labor and the employer on the shop floor, and the placing of equal responsibility for observing plant rules upon management and the union.

The objective of this procedure is to control labor costs as a stable factor of production in order to permit rational investment decisions by the large corporations. The long-term contract insures that labor costs will be a known factor. It guarantees labor peace for a specified period of time. The agreement enables employers to avoid the disruption characteristic of stormier periods of labor history when workers' struggles were much more spontaneous, albeit more difficult.

An important element in the labor contract is that most of the day-to-day issues expressing the conflict between worker and employer over the basic question of the division of profit are not subject to strikes. In the automobile and electrical agreements as well as a few others, the union has the right to strike over speedup, safety issues, or a few other major questions. In the main, however, most complaints about working conditions and work assignments are adjusted in the final step of the grievance procedure by an "impartial" arbitrator selected by both the union and management. Even in industries where the strike weapon is a permitted option, the union leaders usually put severe pressure on the rank and file to choose the arbitration route since strikes disrupt the good relations between the union bureaucracy and management—good relations which are valued highly by liberal corporate officials and union leaders alike.

With few exceptions, particularly in textile and electrical corporations, employers regard labor leaders as their allies against the ignorant and undisciplined rank and file. This confidence has been built up over the past thirty-five years of industrial collective bargaining.

The trade unions have become an appendage of the corporations because they have taken their place as a vital institution in the corporate capitalist complex. If union leaders are compelled to sanction and often give at least verbal support to worker demands, it is most often because the union is a political institution whose membership selects officials. However, almost universally the democratic foundations of the trade unions have been undermined.

The left understood that the old craft unions were essentially purveyors of labor power, controlling both the supply of skilled labor and its price. The most extreme expression of their monopoly was the terror and violence practiced by craft union leadership against the rank and file. Since the old unions were defined narrowly by their economic functions and by their conservative ideology, the assumption of the Socialists and Communists who helped build industrial unions which included the huge mass of unskilled and semiskilled workers was that these organizations would express broader political and social interests, if not radical ideologies.

On the whole, despite corruption and bureaucratic resistance to the exercise of membership control, many unions in the United States have retained the forms but not the content of democracy. It is possible to remove union leaders and replace them, but it is not possible to transcend the institutional constraints of trade unionism itself.

Trade unions have fallen victim to the same disease as the broader electoral and legislative system. Just as the major power over the state has shifted from the legislative to the executive branch of government, power over union affairs has shifted from the rank and file to the corporate leaders, the trade union officials, and the government. Trade unions are regulated by the state both in their relations with employers and in their internal operations. Moreover, the problems of union leadership have been transformed from political and social issues to the routines of contract administration and internal bureaucratic procedures, such as union finances. The union leader is a business executive. His accountability is not limited to the membership—it is extended to government agencies, arbitrators, courts of law, and other institutions which play a large role in regulating the union's operations.

The contradictory role of trade unions is played out at every contract negotiation in major industries. Over the past several years the chasm between the leadership and membership has never been more exposed. . . . In contract bargaining the rank and file has veto power, but no means of initiative. In the first place, many major industries have agreements which are negotiated at the national level. There is room for local bargaining over specific shop issues, but the main lines of economic settlements are determined by full-time officials of the company and the union. One reason for this concentration of power is the alleged technical nature of collective bargaining in the modern era. Not only leaders and representatives of the local membership sit on the union's side of the bargaining table, but lawyers, insurance and pension experts, and sometimes even management consultants as well; the rank-and-file committees tend to be relegated to advisory or window-dressing functions or simply play the role of bystander. The product of the charade that is characteristic of much of collective bargaining today is a mammoth document which reads more like a corporate contract or a mortgage agreement than anything else. In fact, it is a bill of sale.

The needs of the membership only partially justify the specialization of functions within the trade unions. Insurance and pension plans do require a certain expertise, but the overall guidance of the direction of worker-employer relationships has been centralized

as a means of preventing the direct intervention of the rank and file. More, the domination of specialists within the collective bargaining process signals the removal of this process from the day-to-day concerns of the workers. The special language of the contract, its bulk and its purely administrative character put its interpretation beyond the grasp of the rank and file and help perpetuate the centrality of the professional expert in the union hierarchy.

In this connection, it is no accident that the elected union official has only limited power within the collective bargaining ritual (and, in a special sense, within the union itself). Few national union leaders make decisions either in direct consultation with the membership or with fellow elected officials. It is the hired expert who holds increased power in union affairs and who acts as a buffer for the union official between the corporate hierarchy and the restive rank and file. As in other institutions, experts have been used to rationalize the conservatism of the leadership in technical and legal terms, leaving officials free to remain politically viable by supporting the sentiments expressed by the membership while, at the same time, rejecting their proposed actions. The importance of the experts has grown with the legalization of collective bargaining, especially the management of labor conflict by the courts and the legislatures, with legislation, and restraining orders limiting strikes, picketing, and other traditional working class weapons. In industries considered public utilities, such as the railroads, a strike is almost always countered by a court order enjoining the workers from taking direct action on the grounds that such action constitutes a violation of the national interest. The lawyer has become a key power broker between the workers, their unions, and the government. He is considered an indispensable operative in contemporary labor relations.

Some unions have promoted their house counsels from staff to officers. The secretary-treasurer of the Amalgamaled Clothing

Workers of America was formerly general counsel; its president began his career as counsel for the Detroit Joint Board of the union. The president of the United Packing-house Workers was also its counsel for many years. But even without holding executive office the labor lawyer is placed in a position of both influence and ultimately of power within the organization by the increasing volume of government regulation of all types of trade union affairs. The same tendency can be observed within corporations where, together with financial experts, attorneys are replacing production men as the new men of power.

During the past decade in the auto, steel, rubber and other basic manufacturing industries, the critical issues of working class struggle have been those related to control over the workplace. The tremendous shifts in plant location, work methods, job definitions and other problems associated with investment in new equipment, expansion, and the changing requirements of skills to operate new means of production, have found the union bureaucracies unprepared. The reasons for trade union impotence at the workplace go beyond ideology. They are built into the sinews of the collective bargaining process.

Many important industries have national contracts covering most monetary issues, including wages. In the electrical, auto, and steel industries, negotiations are conducted with individual companies, but in reality there is "pattern" bargaining. A single major producer is chosen by the union and corporations to determine wage and fringe benefit settlement for the rest of the industry. All other negotiations stall until the central settlement is reached.

National union leadership always poses wage demands as the most important negotiating issues. Problems such as technological changes, work assignments, job classifications, and pace of work are usually negotiated at the local level after the economic package has been settled. And by the time the local negotiations begin—often conducted between rank-and-file leaders and middle managers—the national union has lost interest in the contract. Its entire orientation is toward the narrowly defined "economic" side of the bargaining. Although many agreements stipulate that resumption of work will not take place before the resolution of local issues, the international representatives and top leaders of the union put enormous pressure on the membership to settle these issues as quickly as possible. It is at the plant level that most sellouts take place. The local feels abandoned, but resentment is diverted to the failure of the shop leadership rather than that of the top bureaucracy, because the national union has "delivered the goods" on wages and benefits.

For example, after every national auto settlement, a myriad of local walkouts are called over workplace issues. These strikes are short-lived and usually unsuccessful. In the main, in struggles against speedup, young workers and Blacks are the spearhead. The impatience of the bureaucracy with this undisciplined action is usually expressed in long harangues to local leaders and the rank and file by international representatives who are employees of the national union. When persuasion fails, the rebellious local is sometimes put into receivership and an administrator is sent from the head office to take it over until order is restored.

. . .

Despite the conservative ideology of labor leaders and legal constraints upon them, rank-and-file pressure today is occasionally able to force unions to lead the fight against employer efforts to transfer to the working class the burdens of recessions or the dislocations of the labor force that occur during periods of technological change.

A recent illustration was provided by the 1969 national General Electric strike. The conjunction of inflation, deteriorating working conditions, and the arrogant bargaining posture of the company produced the first unified strike in the electrical industry in twenty-three years. It does not matter that the leaders of the AFL-CIO unions representing most of the workers wanted neither the strike nor unity with the independent United Electrical Workers. Rank-and-file pressure within the largest AFL-CIO union in the industry, the International Union of Electrican Workers, was sufficient to threaten the hegemony of the leadership and reverse the timid collective bargaining strategies of past contract negotiations. Repeatedly rejecting offers by the unions for arbitration of outstanding issues, GE attempted to win a clearcut victory in order to break the emerging solidarity of the workers and set a pattern for other industries. Its objective was a return to the old divide-and-conquer practice of a separate agreement with each union, but for a time it had little success in encouraging back-to-work movements.

Yet it would be a mistake to infer from the GE experience that temporary trade union militancy in response to employer opposition signals an end to class collaboration or the institutional constraints of collective bargaining on workers' autonomy. In fact, the GE strike points sharply to the persistence and dominance of these constraints. The call by the unions for arbitration and acceptance of the intervention of "neutral" political figures such as Senator Javits in a fact-finding investigation was an indication that the leadership lacked confidence in the ability of the workers to win their own struggle and sought to end the strike as soon as possible. The trade union movement, particularly the AFL-CIO with its tremendous financial resources and 13 million member, could not effectively mobilize support for the boycott that had been called by AFL-CIO President George Meany to supplement the electrical workers' own efforts.

The weakness of the strike was not a lack of willingness to fight on the part of workers. Despite the past sellouts, and the paternalism and anti-Communism used for years to split their ranks, GE workers exhibited tremendous courage and a capacity for organized struggle

in defending their living standards. But, locked within the apparatus of bureaucratic unionism, the workers were unable to broaden the struggle beyond the quantitative economic terms framed by the leadership. The strike was settled on the basis of agreement on wages and the cost-of-living clause—with all other demands referred to arbitration and discussion.

. . .

The trade union structure has become less able to solve elementary defensive problems. Higher wages for organized workers since the end of World War II have been purchased at a high price. One result of the close ties between unions and corporations has been the enormous freedom enjoyed by capital in transferring the wage increases granted to workers in the shop to the shoulders of workers as consumers. Wage increases have been granted with relative ease under these circumstances in the largest corporations and the most monopolized industrial sectors.

Equally significant has been the gradual increase of constraints in the collective bargaining agreement on the workers' freedom to oppose management's imposition of higher production norms, labor-saving technologies, and policies of plant dispersal. (The last left millions of textile, steel, auto, shoe, and other workers stranded in the forties and fifties.) The bureaucratization of grievance procedures has robbed shop stewards of their power to deal with management on the shop floor. The inability of workers to change their working conditions through the union has had two results: workers limit their union loyalty to the narrow context of wage struggles, and they go outside the union to solve their basic problems in the plant. Thus the wildcat strike has become a protest not only against the brutality of industrial management, but also against the limits imposed by unionism. The conditions pertaining to the role of trade unions during the rise of industrial capitalism in the United States no longer apply in the monopoly epoch.

5.6   Counter-Planning by Workers

As capitalists attempt to control the activities of workers in the labor process, the workers fight back in various ways, developing means to counteract managements' desires. Bill Watson describes some of these methods of workers' active resistance in the following reading, based on his own personal experience in an automobile plant.

The following is excerpted from "Counter-Planning on the Shop Floor," by BILL WATSON. From *Radical America*, vol. 5, no. 3, May–June 1971. Reprinted by permission of *Radical America*.

There is planning [by management] and counter-planning [by workers] in the plant because there is clearly a situation of dual power. A regular phenomenon in the daily reality of the plant is the substitution of entirely-different plans for carrying out particular jobs in place of the rational plans organized by management.

On the very-casual level, these substitutions involve, for example, a complete alternative break system of workers whereby they create large chunks of free time for each other on a regular basis. This plan involves a voluntary rotation of alternately working long stretches and taking off long stretches. Jobs are illegally traded off, and men relieve each other for long periods to accomplish this. The smuggling of men through different areas of the plant to work with friends is yet another regular activity requiring no small amount of organization.

The substitution of alternative systems of executing work has its counterpart in areas of the plant which have become, strictly speaking, off limits to non-workers; they are havens of the plant where men are not subject to external regulation. Usually they are bathrooms, most of which are built next to the ceiling with openings onto the roof. Chaise longues, lawn chairs, cots, and the like have been smuggled into most of them. Sweepers, who move around the plant, frequently keep tabs on what is called "john time"; the men

line up an hour here or there when they can take a turn in the fresh air of the roof or space out on a cot in one of the ripped-out stalls. The "off-limits" character of these areas is solid, as was demonstrated when a foreman, looking for a worker who had illegally arranged to leave his job, went into one of the workers' bathrooms. Reportedly he walked up the stairs into the room, and within seconds was knocked out the door, down the stairs, and onto his back on the floor. That particular incident involved two foremen and several workers and ended with the hospitalization of two participants with broken ribs and bruises.

· · ·

[Another example is the "shutdown."]
The shutdown is radically different from the strike; its focus is on the actual working day. It is not, as popularly thought, a rare conflict. It is regular occurrence, and, depending on the time of year, even an hourly occurrence. The time lost from these shutdowns poses a real threat to capital through both increased costs and loss of output. Most of these shutdowns are the result of planned sabotage by workers in certain areas, and often of plant-wide organization.

The shutdown is nothing more than a device for controlling the rationalization of time by curtailing overtime planned by management. It is a regular device in the hot summer months. Sabotage is also exerted to shut down the process to gain extra time before lunch and, in some areas, to lengthen group breaks or allow friends to break at the same time. In the especially-hot months of June and July, when the temperature rises to 115 degrees in the plant and remains there for hours, such sabotage is used to gain free time to sit with friends in front of a fan or simply away from the machinery.

A plant-wide rotating sabotage program was planned in the summer to gain free time. At one meeting workers counted off numbers from 1 to 50 or more. Reportedly similar meetings took place in other areas. Each man took a period of about 20 minutes during the next two weeks, and when his period arrived he did something to sabotage the production process in his area, hopefully shutting down the entire line. No sooner would the management wheel in a crew to repair or correct the problem area than it would go off in another key area. Thus the entire plant usually sat out anywhere from 5 to 20 minutes of each hour for a number of weeks due to either a stopped line or a line passing by with no units on it. The techniques for this sabotage are many and varied, going well beyond my understanding in most areas.

The "sabotage of the rationalization of time" is not some foolery of men. In its own context it appears as nothing more than the forcing of more free time into existence; any worker would tell you as much. Yet as an activity which counteracts capital's prerogative of ordering labor's time, it is a profound organized effort by labor to undermine its own existence as "abstract labor power."

. . .

During a model change-over, the management had scheduled an inventory which was to last six weeks. They held at work more than 50 men who otherwise would have been laid off with 90% of their pay. The immediate reaction to this was the self-organization of workers, who attempted to take the upper hand and finish the inventory in three or four days so they could have the remaining time off. Several men were trained in the

elementary use of the counting scales while the hi-lo truck drivers set up an informal school to teach other men to use their vehicles. Others worked directly with experienced stock chasers and were soon running down part numbers and taking inventory of the counted stock. In several other ways the established plan of ranking and job classification was circumvented in order to slice through the required working time.

The response to this was peculiarly harsh. Management forced it to a halt, claiming that the legitimate channels of authority, training, and communication had been violated. Being certified as a truck driver, for example, required that a worker have a certain amount of seniority and complete a company training program. There was a great deal of heated exchange and conflict, but to no avail. Management was really determined to stop the workers from organizing their own work, even when it meant that the work would be finished quicker and, with the men quickly laid off, less would be advanced in wages.

The threat which this unleashing of energy in an alternative plan of action presented to the authority of the bureaucracy was evidently quite great. Management took a stand, and, with only a limited number of men involved in a non-production activity, retained its power to plan that particular event. For six weeks, then, the "rational" plan of work was executed—which meant that the labor force was watched over and directed in an orderly fashion by foremen and various other agents of social control. The work which men want to do together takes four days—at most a six-day week; the work which is forced on them in the same amount, is monotonously dragged out for six weeks, with all the rational breaks and lunch periods which are deemed necessary for the laborers.

. . .

The co-existence of two distinct sets of relations, two modes of work, and two power structures in the plant is evident to the worker who becomes part of any of the main plant areas. But that co-existence is the object of constant turmoil and strife; it is hardly an equilibrium when considered over time. It is a struggle of losing and gaining ground. The attempt to assert an alternative plan of action on the part of workers is a constant threat to management.

·   ·   ·

We end, then more or less on the note on which we began: stressing a new social form of working-class struggle. The few examples here have been a mere glimpse of that form and hardly entitle us to fully comprehend it. But we can see that as a form it is applied to the actual working day itself and to the issues of planning and control which, in my view, make it distinctly post-unionism as a practice.

The use of sabotage as a method of struggling for control will increase as this form of struggle develops further, but this is merely the apparatus of movement. A crucial point to focus on is the differentiation of this new form of struggle from its former organization: mass unionism.

Within these new independent forms of workers' organization lies a foundation of social relations at the point of production which can potentially come forward to seize power in a crisis situation and give new direction to the society. . . . The gradual emergence of this new mode of production out of the old, "like a thief in the night" advances relatively unnoticed.

Class Conflict
and the State

THIS CHAPTER ANALYZES THE RELATIONSHIP between class conflict and the state. For the United States during the period of monopoly capitalism, we investigate both the state's role in class struggle and the impact of class forces on the evolution of government.

Conflict in capitalist society results most fundamentally from antagonism between the interests of the capitalist class and those of the working class.[1] On one side stands the capitalist class, seeking to maintain its position and privileges. To do so, capitalists must ensure the continuation of the chief prerequisite of their existence, capitalist social organization itself: markets, property relations, and capitalist control over the means of production. Capitalists survive as a class only if from generation to generation they can *reproduce* capitalist social relations and hence capitalist society. More immediately, capitalists also have a collective interest in attempting to create conditions favorable to profits and their ability to *accumulate*. Each firm's profits depend to some extent on environmental conditions which it shares with other firms (e.g., the aggregate level of economic activity and the tax rate on profits). Capitalists have a class interest in seeing that conditions are favorable to accumulation. Their most serious concern is the degree of organization and militancy of the working class.

On the other side stand the workers. Within individual firms, workers resist the conditions that produce high profits, since those same conditions typically tend to reduce workers to a more degraded, dependent, and insecure status. Other things being equal, each firm can make higher profits when its own workers earn lower wages and when its workers, afraid of losing their jobs, cannot challenge the power of bosses. The

---

[1]The class nature of social conflict is quite apparent when workers clash with their employers over conditions at the workplace: the level of wages, the pace of work, job safety, or control over production decisions. Here capitalists directly confront workers. So too class interests are visible when, e.g., union organizing is met with restrictive labor legislation or when national economic policy to regulate the level of unemployment or set the tax rate on profits is established. Here as well classes have directly opposing interests.

Class antagonisms are less obvious but equally fundamental to other forms of conflict. Capitalists (as sellers) and workers (as consumers) struggle in the marketplace—and increasingly through government agencies—over the price, safety, and quality of consumer goods and services. In their communities workers (as residents) resist capitalist efforts to raise rents or to introduce "commercial development" (which may erode home property values); they oppose the pollution from neighboring plants and regressive taxation which restricts the quality and character of schooling available to their children. In the realm of electoral politics, groups based in the working class have opposed sending their taxes and sons to protect the foreign investments of U.S. corporations, and they push for improved health care, more jobs, and unemployment benefits. Although not always identified as class battles, these conflicts as well derive fundamentally from class differences.

In some cases conflict may cut across class lines, pitting multiclass interest groups against each other; however, as we argue in this chapter, such conflict tends to be less important than class-rooted conflict.

labor movement at large, by effectively challenging work rules and, during periods of prosperity, by demanding higher wages, tends to undermine the social conditions that produce high profits. Similarly, working-class groups oppose capitalists when capitalists try to increase their profits by reducing the taxes they pay, by cheapening the products they sell, by ignoring the costs of pollution or the dangers from unsafe technology, or by exacerbating racial and other differences among their workers. As workers struggle to defend and improve their living conditions, in all these areas, they are naturally led to oppose capitalist interests.

The struggles of working people to improve their situations are crucial for defending their wages and living standards and for extracting from capitalists important reforms —for example, unemployment compensation and the social security system. During most periods these efforts to defend their interests are carried on through less-than-classwide groups—through individual unions, consumer groups, minority organizations, environmental groups, veterans' associations, feminist groups, student organizations, tax-reform associations, blue-collar groups, welfare rights groups, etc.[2] These groups attempt to combat particular symptoms or manifestations of class oppression.

Workers' struggles do not automatically threaten capitalism itself. While each working-class group poses a threat to some capitalist interests, collectively their very diversity undermines their challenge to the system, by creating the possibility for capitalists to play off some groups against others.

Social conflict, then, though it derives most fundamentally from the class divisions of society, rarely takes the form of an actual confrontation between classes. Such a confrontation inherently involves the possibility of revolution, and "normally" the power of the capitalist class is sufficient to forestall

such challenges. But separate struggles may be transformed into class confrontation during periods when the contradictions within capitalism are most intense; that is, when the systemic origins of the various manifestations of class oppression are clearest.

Because of their class origins, challenges to individual capitalists are closely related to challenges to capitalists as a class. Sometimes capitalists respond to these challenges individually. At other times they act more collectively, through organizations such as the National Association of Manufacturers, chambers of commerce, employers' organizations, industry or trade associations, and the major foundations. But in general capitalists have responded collectively to class conflict through the mechanism of the state.[3]

In this chapter we analyze the role of the state in this process of class conflict. First, however, we must consider how the capitalist class is able to dominate the activities of the state.[4]

CAPITALIST RULE OF DEMOCRATIC GOVERNMENT

The organization of the present state grew out of the struggle between capitalists and the feudal aristocracy.[5] As capitalist property relations replaced feudal relations, the feudal bases for the legitimacy of state power (the hereditary rights of nobility and monarchy) were replaced by a capitalist (especially *laissez-faire*) foundation. The state, reflecting

[2]There are of course many other so-called "interest groups" which represent capitalist rather than working-class interests and attempt to promote particular interests within the capitalist class.

[3]The state is the agent or institution in society which has the legitimate monopoly on the use of violence. That is, the state can pass laws that people either must follow or suffer the consequences of punishment, and the state can call upon police, the military, etc. to force people to obey the law. Coercion and even violence to enforce compliance with laws is "legal": a policeman who shoots a bank robber faces no punishment, whereas a bank robber who shoots a policeman does. Power and force are the essential underpinnings of the state.

[4]See Domhoff, Section 6.4, p. 242, and Edwards and Reich, Section 6.5, p. 252.

[5]See Hunt, Section 2.3, p. 54.

the interests of the new dominant class, came to take the form of a separate "public sector" or government. Still, the form of the state, whether authoritarian or democratic, was not settled.

In the advanced capitalist countries, the state came to be democratic in form, while in the undeveloped capitalist nations the state tends to be authoritarian. Yet in each case the state has acted primarily in behalf of capitalists.[6] Here we investigate the role of the state in the advanced countries, especially the United States, and ask the question: how was it possible for capitalists, who constituted an insignificant minority of the voting public, to get the state to act in their behalf?

The democratic organization of the state inherently creates a potential source of serious challenge to the capitalist class's rule. The extent to which this potential threat can be transformed into an actual challenge is limited, however, by the larger capitalist context in which the democratic state operates.

In three distinct but mutually reinforcing ways this context strengthens the capitalist class's grip on state power. First, the capitalist organization of the economy means that state activities that impede the accumulation process will create economic problems in society. Most importantly, as long as the primary responsibility for organizing production and distribution remains with the capitalist class, the state must carry out policies acceptable to capitalists. If policies are pursued which cause the profitability of new investments to decline substantially, capitalists go "on strike" by refusing to invest any further, thereby precipitating a general economic crisis. In the absence of a major and imminent alternative to capitalism, the state (no matter what party or person has been elected to power) can resolve the crisis only by taking back its anticapitalist policies. These restrictions on what the state can do derive from the capitalists'

domination of the system of production and are independent of their voting strength.[7]

Second, the capitalist class can draw upon its vast financial resources to manipulate the electoral process, and the efforts by capitalists directly to control state policies lead the modern state to be much less democratic in practice than in theory. The American political system incorporates persistent and pervasive anti-democratic practices: capitalist domination of election financing, bureaucratic government decision-making, "checks and balances" to reduce government accountability to the people, corporate corruption and bribery of officials, discriminatory administration of justice, unequal access to the media, unequal lobbying efforts, etc. These "abuses" of democracy in practice greatly enhance the capitalist class's power.

Third, the wider capitalist context within which the state operates provides a powerful ideology supporting capitalist rule. This ideology inhibits challengers to the capitalist class from mounting an attack on the state's commitment to defend private property. The capitalist class, through its control over the media, its influence in school curricula, and its control over other "ideological resources," attempts to prevent anti-capitalist or socialist ideas from being accepted by large parts of the population. The capitalist class's ability to perpetuate capitalism through the "consent of the governed" thus depends crucially on the strength of capitalist ideology: the hegemony of this ideology acts to forestall challenges to capitalist property relations.

In large part this ideology is powerful because capitalist interests are served by formal equality in the political system. For example, the Constitution requires that the state, regardless of which groups are "in power" at the moment, enforce contracts and defend private property. Even if its actions are applied equally to all citizens (an ideal frequently violated in practice), the state's defense of property will necessarily perpetu-

[6]See Weisskopf, Section 13.3, p. 499 for a discussion of the state in the third world; for the advanced countries, see the following three sections in this chapter.

[7]See Edwards and Reich, Section 6.5, p. 252.

ate capitalism—that is, the state will wind up acting in behalf of those with the most property to protect.[8] The state in this sense acts as umpire to enforce a set of rules—the laws surrounding property rights—which in principle and to a considerable extent in fact are applied equally to everyone but, nonetheless, systematically benefit capitalists. Just as in the economic sphere where equal exchange among unequally endowed individuals permits capitalists to exploit workers, so in the political sphere, where the law presupposes the rights of private property, "equality before the law" works to the benefit of capitalists.

The state's activity, including its use of force against particular working-class movements or communities, thus achieves widespread legitimacy because, *acting within the context of capitalist property relations*, the state appears to be (and often is) fair-minded and neutral in the antagonistic relationship between classes. The state guarantees legal rights to people in all economic classes; all citizens have equal rights to the protection of their persons and equal freedom to dispose of their property as they choose; in elections and juries, each citizen has one vote. The state thus appears to be "above" class or other divisions, representing instead the "public" or "national" interest.

But if capitalists have used democratic forms to perpetuate their privileges, their commitment to democracy ends at the point where genuine popular rule threatens property relations. As demonstrated by the Palmer Raids of 1919–1920, or the illegal suppression of the Black Panthers, or the decades-long unconstitutional and violent FBI and CIA campaigns against American socialists, or alternatively, the subversion of the democratically elected government of Chile in 1973, capitalists abandon democracy when "national security" or "the free world" or

"the free enterprise system"—that is, capitalist property relations—are at stake. In these cases capitalist ideology has failed to prevent serious challenges to capitalists' rule from appearing, and capitalists, like other dominant classes before them, have demonstrated that they were not willing to give up their privileges without a fight.

Because (democratic) governments must operate within a larger capitalist context, and because the class relations of capitalist society greatly limit what those governments can do, the state is properly referred to as a "capitalist" state, successor to the "feudal" state, despite its democratic form.

THE FUNCTIONS OF THE STATE: REPRODUCTION AND ACCUMULATION

The highest priority of capitalists operating through the state, as Paul Sweezy has noted, is the defense of capitalist property relations.[9] This role of the state in perpetuating capitalism we can identify as its *reproduction function*. In the United States, the government's efforts to maintain the system have taken various forms, depending on circumstances. The most extensive activities have involved legitimation, or fostering capitalist ideology. In part, the state legitimates capitalist rule through "fair-handed" administration of (property-based) laws and through the (largely illusory) appearance of democratic control of government; the state has taken a more direct hand as well in fostering capitalist ideology through schooling, direct propaganda, the media, the sponsorship of research, campaigns to purge "communist" influences from libraries and motion pictures, etc. But the state's efforts to perpetuate the system have also taken on a variety of forms in addition to legitimation. In particular, the state has violently repressed anti-capitalist threats, as in the attacks on strikers during

[8]This is the point of Anatole France's famous remark that "the law in its majesty prohibits both the rich man and the beggar from sleeping under the bridge."

[9]See Sweezy, Section 3.5, p. 108.

and after World War I and the suppression of the Black Panthers in the late 1960s. The state has also been used by capitalists to grant reforms and concessions to undermine growing dissent, as during the "New Deal" era of the 1930s and the "War on Poverty" of the 1960s.

A second important role of the state is its *accumulation function*. Although in general the state does not itself accumulate capital, its activities directly aid private accumulation. State revenues and expenditures have contributed to accumulation. To provide benefits either to particular groups of capitalists or to the class as a whole, the state has granted subsidies (in the form of tax credits, direct payments, or favorable "regulation") to countless industries, paid for costly research programs, supported vocational training and other educational efforts to develop the labor force, and so on. To counteract stagnation, the state has undertaken massive military expenditures and other spending programs which increase aggregate demand. Laws and administrative policies have also aided accumulation. To ensure an adequate labor supply, the state has placed restrictions on welfare, minimum-wage, and unemployment compensation to prevent these programs from interfering with the replenishment of the reserve army of the unemployed. To restrain trade-union power, the Taft–Hartley Act and other labor laws have outlawed certain union activities and weakened workers vis-à-vis their employers. These state activities have been directly aimed at assisting accumulation.

But capitalist society is not a harmonious world. The capitalist state, attempting to carry out its dual functions, has continuously faced conflict. One historically important source of conflict has resulted from the accumulation needs of one group of capitalists coming into opposition with the class's need to reproduce the system. For example, the Vietnam War directly benefited the capitalists who profited from war spending; these capitalists came into conflict with other capitalists who perceived the anti-war movement

as a growing threat to capitalism itself. Similarly, at the turn of the century the profits of the newly formed "trusts" brought finance capitalists into conflict with other members of the capitalist class who feared both individual ruin and the rising tide of anti-business opposition.

As conflict emerged among capitalists seeking to shape state policies to serve their class needs, the state developed a certain *relative autonomy* from the influence of individual capitalists. Conflicts within the class have blocked efforts by particular factions of capitalists to dominate governmental policies, and capitalist influence on the state has come to serve the more collective interests of the class. For example, for reproduction capitalists have understood that the state must appear to act in behalf of the public interest; for accumulation, some autonomy is needed to resolve conflicts among competing capitalists or groups of capitalists.[10] Capitalist domination of the state must therefore be understood as class domination (based on the constraints imposed on the state by its capitalist context and operating through the whole range of capitalists' associations, "interest groups," and political parties) rather than as control by particular individuals.

In attempting to carry out its dual functions the capitalist state has faced a second source of conflict. The working class and other dispossessed groups have from time to time directly opposed the state, creating a class confrontation. Even short of such conflict, however, workers' opposition creates a contradiction between those state activities needed for reproduction and those required for accumulation. In the late 1960s and early 1970s, an era of riots and protest, increasing public services were conceded in order to de-fuse dissent; these concessions in combina-

[10]This relative autonomy is perhaps most clearly seen in the efforts to identify long-run collective interests of the capitalist class in the area of foreign policy; see MacEwan, Section 13.1, p. 481.

tion with Vietnam War expenses enlarged the state budget and enhanced the bargaining strength of workers. Intensifying international competition, on the other hand, pushed capitalists to demand lower taxes and cheaper unit labor costs in order to maintain their profit rates. This conflict contributed to creating the economic crisis of the 1970s.[11] The crisis was rendered more severe because previous working-class struggles, particularly those in the 1930s and 1940s in trade unions, political parties, and, at times, openly anticapitalist organizations, had the effect of restricting the policy alternatives available to the state. For example, during the depression of the 1970s, in part because of the power of organized labor, the disastrously high unemployment which the state had permitted in the 1930s was no longer a viable option for the state. Instead the state was forced to institute haphazard policies of wage and price controls, the extension of government planning, etc.

Thus, not only has the state been a crucial element in class relations, thereby affecting the course of class struggle, but class struggle in turn has shaped and stimulated the evolution of the state. Such conflict is not the only factor influencing the state's development: later in the chapter we argue, for example, that the continuing concentration and centralization of capital has also placed new demands upon the state. Yet even here class conflict has played a part: the government's increased intervention in the economy was due in part to the struggle between corporate capitalists and small businessmen and in part to the effort by workers to establish industrial unions in response to the rise of giant corporations. Thus, the state itself is subject to a development process, being transformed at the same time that it is used to suppress opposition to the system.

We turn now to an historical sketch of the relation between class conflict and the evolution of government in the United States.

[11]See Chapter 12, p. 427.

CLASS CONFLICT AND THE EARLY EVOLUTION OF THE AMERICAN STATE

The earliest form of the state in North America was merely an extension of European imperial government. In the English colonies, colonial government grew out of the royal charters and other legal relations emanating from the British state. Local governors and other officials enforced decrees promulgated by the British cabinet or crown. Colonial laws were primarily those received from the British common law or passed by Parliament. And taxes, trade regulations, immigration policies, and the like were primarily designed to foster British trade and economic dominance and to enrich the crown treasury.

The growing economic importance of the colonies tended to create conflicts between British imperial needs and the interests of colonial merchants, manufacturers, planters, and others. For example, trade laws required colonial imports from the European continent to pass through London—the British entrepôt. Other laws called for all colonial exports to be transported in British ships and for some exports destined for European consumption to be marketed through England. While such laws ensured that British merchants would control colonial commerce, they simultaneously placed a fetter on the colonial economy: they prevented development of an internal market, and merchants desiring to participate in worldwide trade and planters wanting to sell tobacco in non-British markets were excluded from these profits. And in order both to capture the benefits from land speculation and to make Indian allies useful in its imperial rivalry with France, British policy placed restrictions on the settling of western lands; these limits produced resentment among poorer farmers eager to escape the coast and exploit the rich interior farmlands.

Such restrictions led ultimately to the American Revolution, which established the

United States as an independent nation. The achievement of independence had the important effect of freeing an incipient American capitalism from the fetters of British imperial policy. It established the necessary conditions for the development of an indigenous American capitalist class, just as the British capitalists' successful struggle against the feudal state led to the expansion of British capitalism.

In part, the independence struggle awakened new and liberating forces within American society. Several of the new state constitutions abandoned British precedent by dropping property qualifications for the franchise and by providing civil rights and personal liberties previously lacking—though these gains were still restricted to white males. A large segment of the richest colonists (the Loyalists) departed, while poorer groups such as farmers and artisans formed political groups and actively engaged in political life. Ideas of social equality and popular rule, best expressed in Tom Paine's writings, gained widespread currency.

But the new state that emerged from this period reflected more the interests of the coalition of dominant classes upon which the society continued to be based: the Southern slave-owning planters and Northern merchants, landowners, and manufacturers. The new constitution accepted slavery, placed restrictions on who could vote, strictly limited the powers of the federal government, protected property, insulated executive and judicial power from the "passions" of the people, and so forth.[12] Thus, the U.S. Constitution, while a product of more than capitalist interests, was effectively shaped by the property-owning elements of the population.

Between the Revolution and the Civil War, the American state made a long transition from its pre-Revolution colonial status to a more fully capitalist form. During this period the national government was controlled by an alliance of Southern planters and Northern merchants and industrial capitalists; the representatives of Western farming and land interests acted as junior partners. The coalition was based on a common need to defend property, yet the alliance was by no means solid. These groups' antagonistic interests intensified as the nineteenth century proceeded. The inability of any group to dominate the national government meant that no group was willing to grant it broad powers, with the result that it remained relatively weak.

Nonetheless, the state even during this period played a crucial role in establishing the conditions necessary for capitalist production. First, it actively aided the process of primary accumulation. The national government's purchases and extension of territorial rights to the West proved to be the first "goldmine" for land speculators, promoters, and developers. The military campaigns to dispossess Indians of their traditional homelands reproduced in more genocidal fashion the eviction of serfs from manors in Europe. The concentration of assets was more directly aided by subsidies, in the form of cash grants, exclusive franchise rights, and land grants, for canals, roads, and railroads; by the establishment of a National Bank and other credit institutions to mobilize profits from the Southern cotton trade, foreign commerce, etc.; and by state governments' bond issues and other efforts to accumulate funds.[13]

[12]The legislative branch was partially isolated as well: senators were originally elected by state legislatures rather than directly by voters; appointed judges and selection of the president through the electoral college were similar restraints.

[13]Primary accumulation took a different path in the U.S. than in Europe, where it simultaneously concentrated assets and "freed" the peasants for wage labor. In the U.S., the growth of capitalist production continued to be hindered by the deficiency of the wage-labor pool, a problem that was solved only by the massive Irish immigrations of the 1840s and subsequent immigrations. In this area, the state appears to have taken little action, except inadvertently: the construction of canals and roads to the West and the resulting movement of foodstuffs to the East ruined many New England farmers. While in general the farmers did not enter the factories, their financial straits encouraged their daughters to. The famous "Yankee farm girls" constituted the first large labor supply for the textile mills.

Second, the new state also carried out its reproduction function, suppressing challenges to its authority and to property rights in general. George Washington's suppression of the "Whiskey Rebellion"—a protest by Pennsylvania farmers against new whiskey taxes— was an early example; but state and national governments also dissipated or suppressed other challenges: the New York tenant farmers' refusal to pay rents to landlords, the Massachusetts revolt known as Shays' Rebellion, slaves' resistance to their bondage, artisans' attempts to organize trade unions, and textile workers' strikes for better conditions.

The governing alliance increasingly came apart over two issues: that of tariffs, which were designed by industrialists to protect them from foreign competition in the American markets, but which raised the cotton planters' and Western farmers' costs; and the extension of slavery to new areas, demanded by planters to secure their continuing economic and political position. The final break in the alliance came with the Civil War, in which the increasingly powerful Northern bourgeoisie asserted its dominance and smashed the Southern slavocracy as a contender for power.

The American state emerged from the Civil War firmly in capitalist hands. With the end of Reconstruction in 1877, the radical Republicans were purged from positions of power and white Southern property-owners were readmitted to the governing alliance. Now, however, they were junior partners, representatives of a "New South" cleared of pre-capitalist obstacles and open to capitalist penetration. Elsewhere, massive Western land grants to railroad promoters hastened the primary accumulation process. Increasingly in the Northern industrial areas, state governments and eventually the national government began intervening on the side of employers to suppress militant workers. Most importantly, the state during this period simply allowed the expansion of capitalist production to proceed on its own momentum.

THE AMERICAN STATE IN MONOPOLY CAPITALISM

The readings in this chapter investigate the role and activities of government in the United States in this century, during the era of monopoly capitalism. During this period the state has continued to be guided by the dual needs of reproduction and accumulation. But the structure of capitalism and the needs of capitalists have changed, and so also have the demands upon and the programs of the state.

The most significant change is the vastly expanded role of the state. In part, new state activities have emerged in direct response to capitalists' demands. Capitalists have increasingly sought to have the state stimulate, regulate, and coordinate the accumulation process as production has become increasingly social in character. Government planning and administration are needed to develop and operate transportation systems, to train the labor force, to regulate the international monetary system, etc.

At the same time small capitalists have continued to decline as a class while the working class has grown both numerically and as an organized economic and political power. In part this increased power has meant that the working class has been able to gain more access to the state and to obtain some reforms. Thus in part new activities have been forced upon the state by workers' demands: the social dislocation created by the Great Depression required the state to assume responsibility for the stability of the macro-economy; the working class's fight for some economic security required the state to undertake social security, welfare, medicare, and other income maintenance programs.

Such new demands upon the state have propelled it and the political system into a position that is central to both the long-term reproduction and the day-to-day functioning of American capitalism. For example, ensuring long-run energy supplies and assessing long-run capital needs have increasingly become subjects for governmental planning; wage bargaining and product pricing for the major industries increasingly involve governmental supervision; the macro tradeoffs between inflation and unemployment increasingly become issues of state policy; the access to jobs and seniority rights for minority and female workers increasingly become matters for the courts and public commissions. In all these ways, the accumulation process in monopoly capitalism has become increasingly *politicized*, and as a consequence, class conflict has increasingly tended to take place around state policies and to occur through the institutions of the state.

6.1 *Soldiers and Strikers: Class Repression as State Policy*

Class conflict takes many forms, but the sharpest struggles have frequently occurred during industrial strikes. Indeed, American history is peppered with massive, often bloody battles between workers and capitalists: the B&O strike (railroads, 1877), Homestead (steel, 1892), Pullman (rail cars, 1894), Cripple Creek (coal, 1903), Lawrence (textiles, 1912), Ludlow (coal, 1914), U.S. Steel and the Seattle general strike (1919), Gastonia (textiles, 1929), the sit-downs (rubber, autos, and electic industry, 1930s), and GE, GM, and the great post-war strike wave (1946). In the present period farmworkers, state and municipal workers, hospital employees, clerical workers, southern textile employees, and others continue this tradition of struggle.

Throughout this history the state has frequently used physical force to suppress capitalists' working-class opponents. In this reading, Vincent Pinto traces the history of police and military intervention in several labor struggles. The instances he describes are illustrative of a much more extensive pattern of government actions in behalf of employers. Often these interventions have merely enforced statutes (or court injunctions) which favored employers' interests, because of capitalists' control over the political system; the postal strike of 1970, for example, was declared illegal under the provisions of the Taft–Hartley Act. In other cases, as at Cripple Creek, official actions were clearly illegal, yet such niceties did not prevent public officials from smashing labor militance. In still other cases (the IWW in the early 1900s and the Black Panthers in the 1960s) legal harassment and false arrests, even though eventually overturned, nonetheless crippled the organizations by tying up their resources and immobilizing their leadership. In all these ways, the state has employed legal, extralegal, and illegal violence to curb working-class resistance.

This reading is excerpted from *Soldiers and Strikers: Counterinsurgency on the Labor Front, 1877–1970* by Vincent Pinto (1972). Reprinted by permission of United Front Press. Available from Banner Press, Chicago, Illinois.

The history of common people in America is one of struggle and insurrection based in the labor movement and extending in time from about the close of the Civil War to World War II. Not all of our grandparents accepted the poverty of their lot meekly. They fought back, at first in thousands and then in millions and left as their legacy the only institution in the country created by the working class: the labor unions.

On the whole, labor unions are now safely tucked away inside the system, another bureaucracy with which the worker must come to terms. By acting as the gatekeepers to every significant blue collar job, union bosses have entrenched themselves as political powers in the land. In exchange for "labor cooperation" they accept social legislation piecemeal from Congress and wage increases from corporations which are taken right back again by war taxes and profits. Now that the government is trying to blame unions for inflation, labor is rediscovering some old antagonisms.

. . .

But there was a time when a lot more was expected from unions, when the rank and file and many of its leaders were in a life and death struggle and were of a mind to seize the means for a decent living.

The right of workers to organize was not even recognized by law until 1935. Up until that time the courts could, and frequently did, declare unions "illegal conspiracies" and jail anyone they could get their hands on. The laws and powers of the state were wholly on the side of the owners.

Despite the forces arrayed against them the workers did win victories. The victories came because the workers at times were able to make a greater show of power. It was open warfare, and everyone recognized it as such.

The following recounts briefly some of the most famous and inglorious battles in our nation's history, instances in which uniformed American troops were used to smash strikes or break up labor demonstrations. These examples show us that armies exist for more than just fighting other armies. They also show that Vietnam [was] not a new war, but a type of war which the state and the people who control it have fought before: a war in which an insurgent civilian population is the target and the suppression of the people the only objective.

THE RAILROAD STRIKE OF 1877

It began on the B&O line near Martinsburg, West Virginia, on July 16. The firemen and brakemen quit first. Of all the back-breaking jobs, theirs were the worst. The immediate cause was a pay cut, but another in a long series of pay cuts which workers all over the country had been suffering in the wake of a depression that began in 1873.

Business was bad so unemployment was high, and resentful people roamed around in gloom. The average weekly wage for up to eighty hours' work on the railroads was $5 to $10, and that was good money. Then the B&O and other major lines gave out the news: anybody making more than a dollar a day would take home 10 percent less from now on. Since labor was getting plentiful it was also getting cheaper, and railroad bosses together decided to adjust to the change in value.

The workers, of course, saw it differently, and they too combined for concerted action. On the morning of the 16th of July a force of 1,200 brakemen and firemen seized the depot at Martinsburg and stopped all freight traffic. That was the spark. With nothing but local leadership, a spontaneous workers' insurrection erupted during the rest of July in 14 of the 38 states. The cities of Baltimore, Pittsburgh and Chicago passed out from under the powers of government, and for a time were governed by tinsmiths and mill hands—until the soldiers came.

When news spread about what the railroaders had done at Martinsburg, miners came down from the hills and black workers off the farms to help out. The mayor tried to head things off by arresting what leaders he could find, but this only focused attention on the town jail. When the workers prepared to storm it, he ordered the prisoners released. Governor Matthews then decided to restore calm with a portion of the West Virginia state militia, but the troops only fraternized and joked with the workers. State power was slipping away as fast as the strike was growing, and the Governor telegraphed the President for federal troops.

In the following few days the strike spread to every major railroad center in the East and Midwest. Led by the railway workers, employees in other industries struck for higher pay, and the unemployed also joined the struggle.

In Baltimore, two regiments of troops were called out for use against strikers outside the city. A crowd of several thousand of the city's workers tried to prevent them from boarding trains, and twelve were killed.

In Pittsburgh, even some businessmen favored the strike. The Pennsylvania Railroad, they felt, had been charging them outrageous freight rates. The sheriff of Pittsburgh lost control of the situation and the local militia were called out, but they, too, went over to the workers' side.

From all over the country, reports were telegraphed to Washington that the state militias were unreliable. President Hayes was kept informed by the Army's Signal Service.

The militia garrison at Philadelphia was called on to remedy the situation in Pittsburgh. When they arrived they found the city in the hands of the workers. The depot had been burned to the ground, and the freight yards were a shambles. Twenty-six workers were killed as the troops were driven into a roundhouse and held captive all night.

At Reading, Pennsylvania, the militia shot down more than a dozen strikers.

The Governor wired the President that Pennsylvania was in a state of "domestic insurrection" which he could not control, and warned that if action were not taken soon the whole country would be in "anarchy and revolution." Certainly the nervous clatter of telegraph keys all around the country made such doom-saying credible; Red flags were decorating the Bowery in New York City; in Kansas City there was a general strike; in St. Louis there were preparations for one. The atmosphere in Philadelphia, Buffalo, Cincinnati, Indianapolis was described as "menacing." From far-off San Francisco

came reports that the town was being run by workers. General Phil Sheridan had already been recalled from putting down Sioux Indians and his cavalry was thrown against workers in Chicago. In Indiana, future President Benjamin Harrison was leading the militia personally.

President Rutherford B. Hayes and his Administration have vanished from history almost without a trace. On this occasion, however, he and his cabinet were called upon to make their mark. On Tuesday, July 24, the cabinet met to consider the use of federal troops—the first time ever against strikers. The Secretary of the Navy wanted to send some gunboats to New York "to clear the streets around the Custom House," but the Secretary of the Treasury told him the streets were too crooked in that part of the city.

The Navy stayed home, but the Army was called out. Sheridan was ordered to go to Chicago with his cavalry. On Wednesday federal troops were ordered to open up communication with Pittsburgh. Two-thirds of all United States troops in the Military District of the Atlantic were sent to Pennsylvania alone. Six companies of the 23rd U.S. Infantry arrived at Union Depot in St. Louis after being side-tracked for awhile by strikers at Sedalia, Mo., but their bayonets could not prevent a socialist-led general strike from developing. At Albany, New York, General Carr said he would, regardless of bloodshed, open the blockade on the New York Central; and the next day he did. Eventually, with the overwhelming force of the military, local authorities were able to restore their control. The cost was high in human lives, but the established government, knocked off balance, had reasserted itself. By August all pockets of resistance had been cleared out.

In the wake of the insurrection, authorities had a new appreciation of the worker. They recruited larger numbers for the military, built fortress-like armories in the middle of large cities, and developed a service of secret detectives to spy on the activities of labor unions.

Many men lost their jobs as a result of that summer's strike; the railroads blacklisted anyone who had struck, and others were sent to jail. Whole families migrated to places where chances for a new life seemed better.

During the next two decades the bitter struggles of the workers continued. In 1885, General Sherman, then head of the army, predicted that "there will soon come an armed contest between capital and labor. They will oppose each other not with words and arguments and ballots, but with shot and shell, gunpowder and cannon. The better classes are tired of the insane howlings of the lower strata, and they mean to stop them."

ACTION—REACTION

In the 1930's the labor movement in the United States made spectacular gains, advancing during a depression decade, when labor was cheap and plentiful, and working people felt even more the need to organize to survive. Not since 1910 and before had collective action of the workers been so persistent and widespread.

Though many of the nation's mines and railroads had been organized for years, and though much craft work was done under contract, most industrial production, especially in the giant basic industries of steel, auto, and rubber, was still on the so-called "American Plan," that is, not unionized. This was in part due to the single-minded life-long policy of the bureaucrats within the American Federation of Labor who stubbornly clung to "trade unionism, pure and simple," confining themselves to organizing only the better-paid craft workers. The rest, the unskilled blanket stiffs and mill hands, were ignored.

Many, including Socialists and Communists, within the AFL agitated to include these workers within the ranks of organized labor, eventually forming, in late 1935, the independent CIO (Committee for Industrial Organization, later called the Congress of Industrial

Organizations). One labor historian wrote of this event: "It was as if the entire history of the American labor movement had been only a mere introduction to the great crusade that was the CIO. . . . It was a revolutionary, apocalyptic time. What generations had battled in vain to accomplish was accomplished now in a matter of weeks or days. The impossible was achieved daily. Of a sudden, or so it seemed, labor could not lose."

Strikes, show-downs, sabotage, and mass picketing were daily events as the CIO swept the country like a summer storm. Then a new tactic, the sit-down was used with success by the rubber workers of Akron, Ohio in January, 1936. But it was not until almost a year later, when national attention was focused on Flint, Michigan, that the sit-down strike became a fine-edged weapon in the hands of the United Automobile Workers. The National Guard was called out in this strike, too, but although there were several pitched battles between strikers and troops, a Governor sympathetic to the workers held the troops in check. After occupying the plants for forty-five days the workers won recognition for their union from General Motors.

It was one of the first big break-throughs in big industry. The United Electrical, Radio and Machine Workers swept through the General Electric, Westinghouse and Philco plants signing up workers for the CIO. In the summer of 1936 the UE won a hard-fought strike at the RCA plant in Camden, New Jersey. National Guard troops were used in 1938 against the UE employees in the Maytag plant at Newton, Iowa, where a 10 percent wage cut was being resisted.

The CIO grew from 1,000,000 members in 1936 to over 4,000,000 in 1940. The entire labor movement advanced in this period, taking advantage of the policies of Franklin D. Roosevelt, who saw it in the interest of government and business to make some compromises and concessions to labor.

During the Second World War organized labor rallied behind the effort to defeat fascism. It pledged itself to a "no strike" policy and voluntarily abandoned double pay for Sunday and holiday work, even though the war economy soon produced a 29 percent increase in the cost of living. In 1943 Congress limited union wage increases to 15 percent. Some small, short-lived local strikes broke out as a result, and the press treated them with extreme hostility. One large strike did take place, however. The United Mine Workers called a halt to work in April, 1943 under the leadership of John L. Lewis, who felt that Congressional wage controls required the working man to make sacrifices of a type not required of the businessman. The Federal Government seized the mines, and Lewis was forced to bargain a partial victory with the Secretary of the Interior, Harold Ickes.

LABOR'S POST-WAR STRUGGLES

The specter of the military on the labor scene appeared again after 1945, when labor initiated a large number of strikes to regain the purchasing power lost during the war.

In 1946, during a national railroad strike, President Truman seized the affected lines. He went before Congress to ask for emergency power to break strikes in any industry controlled by the Government. These powers included a provision to draft strikers into the Army and then put them back to work, and imprisonment of union officers. The rail strike was settled minutes before the President delivered his message, but the House passed the measure anyway. As the strike's effects faded, so did support for the bill, and it was allowed to die.

Repressive labor legislation did pass the Congress, however, in the form of the infamous Taft-Hartley Act of 1947. Although passed by Congress, this act was drawn up by the National Association of Manufacturers. It was business's gun to take back what labor had won in the past 30 years. It's intent was to cripple the growing power of working people and their unions.

Provisions of the Taft-Hartley Act re-

instituted injunctions, gave courts the power to fine for alleged violations. It established a sixty day cooling off period in which strikes could not be declared. It outlawed mass picketing . . . denied trade unions the right to contribute to political campaigns. It abolished the closed shop (where all workers had to be in the union) . . . It authorized employer interference in attempts of his employees to organize a union. It prohibited secondary boycotts. It authorized and encouraged the passage of state anti-union, "right to work" laws.

The Taft-Hartley Act gave business another weapon against labor, and several more justifications for the government to intervene directly on the side of business to crush strikes, including military intervention.

.   .   .

POSTAL STRIKE—1970

When the postal workers went on strike in 1970 they violated Taft-Hartley, which outlawed strikes by Federal employees.

It was the first postal strike in the history of the United States, and there was an air of insubordination about it; Not only was the law against it, but so was the opinion of most of the unions' national leadership. Nevertheless, the first picket line appeared shortly after midnight Tuesday morning, March 17, on the 45th Street side of the Grand Central Post Office in New York City.

The nation's 600,000 postal workers were divided into seven different unions, and Branch 36 of the Letter Carriers, which set up the first picket line, was one of the more militant locals among a group of unions not especially militant. The postal employees had been bargaining with the government since September, 1969, and now came word that the Nixon Administration wanted to postpone a pay raise another half-year, and make it conditional on Congressional approval of a semi-private postal corporation. The starting salary for a carrier was $6,100 a year and after 21 years of service rose to only $8,442.

It was no wonder, said the union, that 7 percent of the postal workers in New York City were on welfare.

By Wednesday night it was clear the strike was going to be a big one. Members of the Manhattan and Bronx Postal Union, representing 25,000 clerks and handlers, held a stormy meeting in the Statler Hilton Hotel and demanded that their officials call a sympathy strike with the carriers. Amid shouts of "Strike! Strike! Strike!" union members took over the speaker's platform and forced the local's president to flee through the kitchen.

Most mail in New York City had come to a standstill earlier in the day, and the Government put an embargo on letters and packages destined for the financial capital. Officials of the Stock Exchange, banks, insurance companies and department stores publicly wrung their hands over what a long strike would mean.

According to the United States Code, each striking worker could be fined up to a thousand dollars or sent to prison up to one year, or both, but it was not clear at this time how hard a line the government was going to take against the strike.

Over Wednesday night and into Thursday other cities began walking out, first in the suburbs of New York, then Akron, Ohio, St. Paul, Minnesota, Buffalo, Philadelphia, New Haven and others. It was a ragged action, not well coordinated or nationally led because the unions' top officers didn't want it. Three hundred local officials were summoned to union headquarters in Washington to attempt to get things back under control. They met privately on Thursday and on Friday negotiated a deal with the government: Union leaders would urge the men to go back to work armed with a promise from the government to take up their grievances "shortly." The rank and file met this with a chorus of boos, and promptly Chicago, Denver, Pittsburgh, Cleveland and every other major city outside the South walked out, too.

Saturday had the air of a crisis about it.

Story after story filled the media about what hardship, real and imagined, the strike was causing. In Washington, there were some unusual Saturday comings and goings reported at the Pentagon involving the National Guard commander. When on the same day the President said, "On Monday, I will meet my obligation to see to it that the mails go through," rumors that troops would be used seemed confirmed.

By Sunday it was obvious the national union officials could not get the men back. James Rademacher, national president of the Letter Carriers, asked the Post Office Department to investigate his contention that radical agitators from SDS had infiltrated the union. Though this remark made headlines it did not strike a responsive chord in the rank and file, who continued to blast Rademacher from the steps of the General Post Office in New York City, and within range of TV network microphones.

Monday the strike reached full steam, with 300,000 estimated participants. Then the President went on a national television hookup and struck a law-and-order stance: "What is at issue [he said] is the survival of a government based upon law." A national emergency existed by his own proclamation and, by further proclamation, certain National Guard and Reserve units of all services were mustered for duty in New York. "New York City is where the current illegal stoppages began. It is where the mail has been halted the longest." He might have added that New York was the center of most of the resistance, also.

By nightfall, busses and truck loads of troops began arriving in the city from Fort Dix and McGuire AFB in New Jersey, and other locations. There was some grumbling among the soldiers about strikebreaking, but mostly there was indifference. The biggest concern was over possible violence, because they were unarmed.

"You've heard of the Boston messacre and the My Lai massacre," a 22-year-old soldier told a reporter as he bedded down at Fort Hamilton in Brooklyn, "tomorrow you're going to see the New York mail massacre. It's going to be a farce. I'm a medic. I don't know a thing about the Post Office Department. Nobody knows what they're supposed to do."

The Pentagon called it Operation Graphic Hand. What it came down to for the soldier was to sort each letter on the first three digits of the zip code. There were reports of sabotage, that some soldiers were deliberately tossing letters into the wrong slots, but this was never confirmed. The striking postal employees, many of them ex-servicemen, were not especially hostile to the troops, who were thought of as conscripted labor rather than willing strikebreakers.

But Washington's action did have its designed effect. Ever since the President's announcement morale among the strikers had been slipping fast. Though the workers in New York put up a brave front at first, there was the threat of still more troops and reports that strikers in other cities were returning to the job. Only a small proportion of the total volume of backed-up mail was moving, but every official was acting as if the strike were over.

By Wednesday, the strike everywhere had crumbled, though pockets of resistance continued in New York for the rest of the week. The last troops were withdrawn from the city on Monday, March 30.

6.2 Corporate Liberalism and the Monopoly Capitalist State

Although officially sanctioned violence suppresses challengers in the short run, as the preceding reading suggested, it is an extreme act which in the longer term may *expose* class relations and *foster* more opposition. Consequently, the more secure and forward-looking segments of the capitalist class have often advocated state programs involving accommodation, reform, and ideological efforts to legitimize the state and capitalist society.

The "Progressive Era"—those critical opening decades of this century when the economy moved from its competitive to its monopolistic phase— was one of the periods during which such policies were most vigorously promoted. In the following reading James Weinstein argues that although the reforms of this period were originally inspired by "those at or near the bottom of the American social structure," the actual policies instituted were shaped by capitalists associated with the large corporations. The aim of these capitalists, in addition to deflecting dissent, was to reshape the state so that it could more appropriately respond to the new needs of the emerging monopoly sector. It is revealing that this campaign was carried forward by the agents of monopoly capital, sometimes even against the interests and over the protests of smaller capitalists, for it was during this period that the corporate capitalists achieved a dominant position within the capitalist class.

Just as the rise of competitive capitalism produced a *laissez-faire* ideology, so the evolution to monopoly capitalism resulted in a more interventionist state. The sources and rationale for this change have been obscured, as Weinstein notes, by a historical confusion about the meaning of the term "liberalism." In both periods, the rising group has advocated its reforms under the "liberal" banner and has been opposed by the "conservative" defenders of the status quo. Both early capitalists proclaiming *laissez faire* against pre-capitalist restrictions and, in turn, corporate capitalists advocating an expanded state against *laissez-faire* proscriptions did so as "liberals." The current distinction between "conservatives" and "liberals" continues to reflect in part the dichotomy between the relatively more parochial and backward-looking capitalist elements based in the competitive sector and the more economically secure, "progressive," and forward-looking capitalists in the corporate sector.

The following is excerpted from the introduction to *The Corporate Ideal and the Liberal State* by JAMES WEINSTEIN. Copyright © 1968 by James Weinstein. Reprinted by permission of Beacon Press.

[My] two main theses . . . run counter to prevailing popular opinion and to the opinion of most historians. The first is that the political ideology now dominant in the United States, and the broad programmatic outlines of the liberal state (known by such names as the New Freedom, the New Deal, the New Frontier, and the Great Society) had been worked out and, in part, tried out by the end of the First World War. The second is that the ideal of a liberal corporate social order was formulated and developed under the aegis and supervision of those who then, as now, enjoyed ideological and political hegemony in the United States: the more sophisticated leaders of America's largest corporations and financial institutions.

This position is not based upon a conspiracy theory of history, but it does posit a conscious and successful effort to guide and control the economic and social policies of federal, state, and municipal governments by various business groupings in their own long-range interest as they perceived it. Businessmen were not always, or even normally, the first to advocate reforms or regulation in the common interest. The original impetus for many reforms came from those at or near the bottom of the American social structure, from those who benefited least from the rapid increase in the productivity of the industrial plant of the United States and from expansion at home and abroad. But in the current century, particularly on the federal level, few reforms were enacted without the tacit

approval, if not the guidance, of the large corporate interests. And, much more important, businessmen were able to harness to their own ends the desire of intellectuals and middle-class reformers to bring together "thoughtful men of all classes" in "a vanguard for the building of the good community."[1] These ends were the stabilization, rationalization, and continued expansion of the existing political economy, and, subsumed under that, the circumscription of the Socialist movement with its ill-formed, but nevertheless dangerous ideas for an alternative form of social organization.

There are two essential aspects of the liberal state as it developed in the Progressive Era, one tightly and sometimes indistinguishably intertwined with the other, but both clearly different. The first was the need of many of the largest corporations to have the government (usually the federal government) intervene in economic matters to protect against irresponsible business conduct and to assure stability in marketing and financial affairs. . . .

The second was the replacement of the ideological concepts of laissez faire, or the Darwinian survival of the fittest, by an ideal of a responsible social order in which all classes could look forward to some form of recognition and sharing in the benefits of an

[1]Sidney Kaplan, "Social Engineers as Saviours: Effects of World War I on Some American Liberals," *The Journal of the History of Ideas*, XVII (June, 1956), 347.

ever-expanding economy. Such a corporate order was, of course, to be based on what banker V. Everitt Macy called "the industrial and commercial structure which is the indispensable shelter of us all."[2]

The key word in the new corporate vision of society was responsibility, although the word meant different things to different groups of men. To most middle-class social reformers and social workers—men such as Frank P. Walsh of Kansas City, or Judge Ben B. Lindsey of Denver, or Walter Weyl of the *New Republic*, or Jane Addams of Hull House, responsibility meant, first of all, the responsibility of society to individual Americans or to underprivileged social classes. To the corporation executives it meant above all, the responsibility of all classes to maintain and increase the efficiency of the existing social order. Of course some middle-class reformers, like *New Republic* editor Herbert Croly, understood that progressive democracy was "designed" to serve as a counterpoise to the threat of working class revolution."[3] But even for them the promotion of reform was not an act of cynicism: they simply sought a way to be immediately effective, to have real influence. Their purpose was not only to serve as defenders of the social system, but also to improve the human condition. In the most profound sense they failed, and badly; yet they were a good deal more than simply lackeys of the capitalist class.

The confusion over what liberalism means and who liberals are is deep-seated in American society. In large part this is because of the change in the nature of liberalism from the individualism of laissez faire in the nineteenth century to the social control of corporate liberalism in the twentieth. Because the new liberalism of the Progressive Era put its emphasis on cooperation and social responsibility, as opposed to unrestrained "ruthless"

competition, so long associated with businessmen in the age of the Robber Baron, many believed then, and more believe now, that liberalism was in its essence anti big business. Corporation leaders have encouraged this belief. False consciousness of the nature of American liberalism has been one of the most powerful ideological weapons that American capitalism has had in maintaining its hegemony. An intellectual tradition has grown up among liberal ideologues that embodies this false consciousness. Arthur M. Schlesinger, Jr., intellectual in residence of the Kennedys, for example, writes that "liberalism in America has been ordinarily the movement on the part of the other sections of society to restrain the power of the business community."[4] Consistent with this assertion is the popular image of movements for regulation and social reform—the Pure Food and Drug Act, the Federal Trade Commission, workmen's compensation, social security, unemployment insurance, the poverty program—as victories of "the people" over "the interests." In one sense this is true. Even so, Schlesinger's pronouncement is misleading. It is not only historically inaccurate, but serves the interests of the large corporations by masking the manner in which they have exercised control over American politics in this century.

Both in its nineteenth and twentieth century forms, liberalism has been the political ideology of the rising, and then dominant, business groups. Changes in articulated principles have been the result of changing needs of the most dynamic and rapidly growing forms of enterprise. Thus in the days of Andrew Jackson, liberalism's main thrust was against monopoly (and Arthur Schlesinger tells us this meant it was anti-business). But more recent scholarship has shown that it was the new business class, made up of individual small entrepreneurs (as well as threatened and declining farmers and artisans), that fought state chartered monopoly.

[2]Speech to the 17th Annual Meeting of the National Civic Federation, January 22, 1917, Box 187, National Civic Federation papers, New York Public Library.

[3]Kaplan, "Social Engineers," pp. 354–55.

[4]Arthur M. Schlesinger, Jr., *The Age of Jackson* (Boston: Little, Brown, 1946), p. 505.

Rising entrepreneurs struggled to free business enterprise of the outmoded restrictions of special incorporation and banking laws and to end what was then an overly centralized control of credit. Their laissez faire rhetoric in opposition to "unnatural" or artificial privilege was that of the common man, but their achievements—general incorporation and free banking laws, the spread of public education and popular suffrage— created the conditions for unfettered competition and rapid industrial growth. Half a century later that competition and industrial expansion had led to the development of new forms of monopoly, grown so powerful that a relative handful of merged corporations came to dominate the American political economy. Thereafter, liberalism became the movement for state intervention to supervise corporate activity, rather than a movement for the removal of state control over private enterprise.

To achieve conditions suitable for free competition during the Age of Jackson, the rising entrepreneurs and their political representatives had to believe in, and promote, ideals of equality of opportunity, class mobility, and noninterference by the government with individual initiative (although, even then, government subsidy of such necessary common services as railroads and canals was encouraged where private capital was inadequate to do the job). At the turn of the century the new trust magnates also pressed for reform in accordance with their new political, economic, and legal needs. The nature of the ideals and the needs in the two periods were different. In the first, the principles of competition and individual efficiency underlay many proposed reforms; in the second, cooperation and *social* efficiency were increasingly important. But in each case the rising businessmen—or, at least, many of them—helped promote reforms. In both instances, business leaders sponsored institutional adjustment to their needs, and supported political ideologies that appealed to large numbers of people of different social classes in order to gain, and retain, popular support for their entrepreneurial activity. In the Progressive Era, and ever since, corporation leaders did this by adapting to their own ends the ideals of middle-class social reformers, social workers, and socialists.

My main concern . . . is not with the social reformers, men and women who might be called ordinary liberals. Instead I . . . focus on those business leaders (and their various political and academic ideologues) who saw liberalism as a means of securing the existing social order. They succeeded because their ideology and their political economy alone was comprehensive. Radical critics of the new centralized and manipulated system of social control were disarmed and absorbed by the corporate liberals who allowed potential opponents to participate, even if not as equals, in a process of adjustment, concession, and amelioration that seemed to promise a gradual advance toward the good society for all citizens. In a formal democracy, success lay in evolving a social vision that could be shared by most articulate people outside the business community. Corporate liberalism evolved such a vision. More than that, it appealed to leaders of different social groupings and classes by granting them status and influence as spokesmen for their constituents on the condition only that they defend the framework of the existing social order.

As it developed, the new liberalism incorporated the concepts of social engineering and social efficiency that grew up alongside of industrial engineering and efficiency. The corollary was a disparagement of "irresponsible" individualism and localism. On the municipal level, as Samuel P. Hays has observed, the drama of business-led reform lay in competition between two systems of decision-making. One was based upon ward representation and traditional ideas of grassroots involvement in the political process; the other, growing out of the rationalization of social life made possible by scientific and technological developments, required expert analysis and worked more smoothly if decisions flowed from fewer and smaller centers outward toward the rest of society. The same competition went on at the federal level, although formal changes in the political structure were more difficult to make and, therefore, less extensive. In general, however, the Progressive Era witnessed rapid strides toward centralization and a decline in importance of those institutions which were based upon local representation, most obviously in the decline of Congress and the increasing importance of the executive branch in the shaping of policy and in the initiation of legislation. As Hays concludes, this development constituted an accommodation of forces outside the business community to political trends within business and professional life.[5] . . .

In short, . . . liberalism in the Progressive Era—and since—was the product, consciously created, of the leaders of the giant corporations and financial institutions that emerged astride American society in the last years of the nineteenth century and the early years of the twentieth.

[5]Samuel Hays, "The Politics of Reform in Municipal Government in the Progressive Era," *Pacific Northwest Quarterly*, LV, 4 (October, 1964), 168–69.

6.3   *The Expanding Role of the State*

The transition to monopoly capitalism produced a vastly greater role for government than under competitive capitalism. As James O'Connor argues in the next reading, this increasing role of the state resulted in part from the increasingly social character of production.

The state's new and more extensive activities serve the capitalist needs of reproduction and accumulation within the changed economic and social context. As O'Connor notes, larger state expenditures for military forces, welfare, social security, pollution control, etc. are required to stabilize the capitalist social order, both at home and abroad. While some of these costs of reproducing capitalist society may also contribute to accumulation, others constitute a drag on it. The state budget also expands to finance programs aimed directly at fostering accumulation: highway construction, basic research to develop new technologies, job training, subsidies to maintain essential rail service, etc. The result is a growing public sector, both at the federal and at the state and local levels.

The following is excerpted from "The Fiscal Crisis of the State" by JAMES O'CONNOR. From *Socialist Revolution* 1, Nos. 1 and 2 (Jan./Feb. and March/April 1970). Reprinted by permission of *Socialist Revolution*.

In general, the state budget continuously expands owing to the intensification of economic integration. Social production has advanced so rapidly and along so many fronts that it has pressed hard upon and finally spilled over the boundaries of immediate private property relations. [The result is] a higher and more general form of social integration rendered necessary by the advanced character of social production.

. . .

I

The first major category of [state] expenditures consists of facilities which are valuable to a specific industry, or group of related industries. These are projects which are useful to specific interests and whose financial needs are so large that they exceed the resources of the interests affected. They also consist of projects in which the financial outcome is subject to so much uncertainty that they exceed the risk-taking propensities of the interests involved. Finally, these are projects which realize external economies and economies of large-scale production for the particular industries.

. . .

[One] important state investment serving the interests of specific industries [is] highway expenditures.[1] Domestic economic growth since World War II has been led by automobile production and suburban residential construction, which requires an enormous network of complementary highways, roads, and ancillary facilities. Rejecting public transportation, on the one hand, and toll highways, on the other, the state has "socialized intercity highway systems paid for by the taxpaper—not without great encouragement from the rubber, petroleum, and auto industries.[2]

. . .

II

The second major determinant of state expenditures stems from the immediate economic interests of corporate capital as a whole. The budgetary expression of these interests takes many forms—economic infrastructure investments, expenditures on education, general business subsidies, credit guarantees and insurance, social consumption, and so on. In the United States, most of these forms appeared or developed fully only in the twentieth century, although in Europe [these governmental responsibilities] emerged in an earlier period—in France, during the First Empire, generalized state promotion buoyed the private economy; in Germany, state economic policy received great impetus from political unification and war; in Italy, laissez-faire principles did not prevent the state from actively financing and promoting accumulation in the major spheres of heavy industry; and everywhere liberal notions of small, balanced budgets and indirect taxation came face to face with the fiscal realities of wartime economies.

In the United States, the budget remained small throughout the nineteenth century; transportation investments were chiefly private, and natural resource, conservation, public health, education and related outlays were insignificant. The state served the economic needs of capital as a whole mainly in non-fiscal ways—land tenure, monetary, immigration, tariff, and patent policies all "represented and strengthened the particular legal framework within which private business was organized."[3] State subsidies to capital as a whole were confined to the State government and local levels and were largely the product of mercantile, rather than industrial capital, impulses.[4]

In the twentieth century, however, corporate capital . . . rooted in the development of the productive forces and the concentration and centralization of capital [has produced new needs.] More specifically, the rapid advance of technology has increased the pace of general economic change, the risk of capital investments, and the amount of uncontrollable overhead costs. Further, capital equipment is subject to more rapid obsolescence, and there exists a longer lead time before the typical investment is in full operation and thus is able to pay for itself. The development of the production relations

[1]Weapon expenditures fall partly into this category, but since their ultimate determinant lies elsewhere, discussion of military spending is postponed until later.

[2]Payntz Taylor, *Outlook for the Railroads*, New York, 1960, p. 91.

[3]Henry W. Broude, "The Role of the State in American Economic Development, 1820–1890," in Harry N. Scheiber, Ed., *United States Economic History: Selected Readings*, New York, 1964.

[4]Louis Hartz, *Economic Policy and Democratic Thought: Pennsylvania, 1776–1860*, Cambridge, Mass., 1948, pp. 290–91.

has also compelled corporate capital to employ state power in its economic interests as a whole, and socialize production costs. . . .

The most expensive economic needs of corporate capital as a whole are the costs of research, development of new products, new production processes, and so on, and, above all, the costs of training and retraining the labor force, in particular, technical, administrative, and non-manual workers. Preliminary to an investigation of the process of the socialization of these costs, a brief review of the relationships between technology, on the one hand, and the production relations, on the other, is required.

The forces of production include available land, constant capital, labor skills, methods of work organization, and last but not least, technology, which is a part of, but not totally identified with, the social productive forces. The advance of technology, the uses of technology, and its distribution between the various branches of the economy are all determined in the last analysis by the relations of production. The transformation from a labor-using to a labor-saving technology in mid-nineteenth century Europe was ultimately caused by the disappearance of opportunities for industrial capitalists to recruit labor "extensively" from the artisan and peasant classes at the given wage rate. During the last half of the nineteenth century, the established industrial proletariat faced less competition, their organizations were strengthened, and they were better able to win wage advances. Thus, it was the class struggle that compelled capital to introduce labor-saving innovations.

Despite the rapid advance of technology during the first half of the twentieth century, until World War II the industrial corporations trained the largest part of their labor force, excluding basic skills such as literacy. In the context of the further technological possibilities latent in the scientific discoveries of the nineteenth and twentieth centuries, this was a profoundly irrational mode of social organization.

The reason is that knowledge, unlike other forms of capital, cannot be monopolized by one or a few industrial-finance interests. Capital-as-knowledge resides in the skills and abilities of the working class itself. In the context of a free labor market—that is, in the absence of a feudal-like industrial state which prohibits labor mobility, a flat impossibility in the capitalist mode of production—no one industrial-finance interest can afford to train its own labor force or channel profits into the requisite amount of research and development. The reason is that, apart from the patent system, there is absolutely no guarantee that their "investments" will not seek employment in other corporations or industries. The cost of losing trained manpower is especially high in those industries which employ technical workers with skills which are specific to a particular industrial process.

World War II provided the opportunity to rationalize the entire organization of technology in the United States. As Dobb writes, "a modern war is of such a kind as to require all-out mobilization of economic resources, rapidly executed decisions about transfer of labor and productive equipment, and the growth of war industry, which ordinary market-mechanisms would be powerless to achieve. Consequently, it occasions a considerable growth of state[-directed] capitalism. . . ."[5] The intervention of the state through government grants to finance research programs, develop new technical processes, and construct new facilities and the forced mobilization of resources converted production to a more social process. The division of labor and specialization of work functions intensified, industrial plants were diversified, the technical requirements of employment became more complex, and, in some cases, more advanced. The end result was a startling acceleration of technology.

At the end of the war, corporate capital

[5]Maurice Dobb, *Capitalism Yesterday and Today*, New York, 1962, p. 75.

was once again faced with the necessity of financing its own research and training its own technical work force. The continued rationalization of the work process required new forms of social integration which would enable social production to advance still further. The first step was the introduction of the GI Bill, which socialized the costs of training (including the living expenses of labor trainees) and eventually helped to create a labor force which could exploit the stockpile of technology created during the war. The second step was the creation of a vast system of lower and higher technical education at the local and state level, the transformation of private universities into Federal universities through research grants, and the creation of a system to exploit technology in a systematic, organized way which included not only the education system, but also the foundations, private research organizations, the Pentagon, and countless other Federal government agencies. This system required enormous capital outlays, a large expansion of teaching and administrative personnel, an upgrading of teachers at all levels, together with programs of specialized teaching training, scholarships, libraries—in short, vast new burdens on the state budget. In turn, this reorganization of the labor process, and, in particular, the free availability of masses of technical-scientific workers, made possible the rapid acceleration of technology. With the new, rationalized social organization of technology and the labor process completed, technical knowledge became the main form of labor power and capital. There occurred a decline in the relative importance of living labor, and an increase in the importance of dead labor in the production process. Thus, statistical studies, beginning in the mid-1950's and multiplying rapidly since then, indicate that the growth of aggregate production is caused increasingly less by an expansion in labor "inputs" and the stock of physical assets, and more by upgrading labor skills, improve-

ments in the quality of physical assets, and better organization of work. One famous study demonstrated that increased education accounted for over three-fifths of the growth of output per manhour in the United States from 1929–1957.[6]

. . .

The uncontrolled expansion of production by corporate capital as a whole creates still another fiscal burden on the state in the form of outlays required to meet the *social costs of private production* (as contrasted with the socialization of private costs of production, which we have discussed above). Motor transportation is an important source of social costs in the consumption of oxygen, the production of crop- and animal-destroying smog, the pollution of rivers and oceans by lead additives to gasoline, the construction of freeways that foul the land, and the generation of urban sprawl. These costs do not enter into the accounts of the automobile industry, which is compelled to minimize its own costs and maximize production and sales. Corporate capital is unwilling to treat toxic chemical waste or to develop substitute sources of energy for fossil-fuels that pollute the air. (There are exceptions to this general rule. In Pittsburgh, for example, the Mellon interests reduced air pollution produced by its steel mills in order to preserve the values of its downtown real estate.) And corporate farming—the production of agricultural commodities for exchange alone—generates still more social costs by minimizing crop losses (and thus costs) through the unlimited use of DDT and other chemicals that are harmful to crops, animals, water purity, and human life itself.

By and large, private capital refuses to bear the costs of reducing or eliminating air and water pollution, lowering highway and air accidents, easing traffic jams, preserving forests, wilderness areas, and wildlife sanc-

[6]E. F. Denison, *The Sources of Economic Growth in the U.S. and the Alternatives Before Us*, New York, 1962, p. 148.

tuaries, and conserving the soils. In the past these costs were largely ignored. Today, owing to the increasingly social character of production, these costs are damaging not only the ecological structure, but also profitable accumulation itself, particularly in real estate, recreation, agriculture, and other branches of the economy in which land, water, and air are valuable resources to capital. The portion of the state budget devoted to reducing social costs has therefore begun to mount. In the future, the automobile industry can be expected to receive large-scale subsidies to help finance the transition to the electric or fuel-cell car. Capital as a whole will receive more subsidies in the form of new public transportation systems. Subsidies to public utilities to finance the transition to solar, nuclear, or sea energy will expand. Corporate farmers will insist on being "compensated" for crop losses arising from bans on the use of DDT and other harmful chemicals. And more Federal funds will be poured into the states to help regulate outdoor advertising, alleviate conditions in recreational areas, finance the costs of land purchase or condemnation, and landscaping and roadside development, and otherwise meet the costs of "aesthetic pollution."

. . .

III

The third major category of state expenditures consists of the expenses of stabilizing the world capitalist social order: the costs of creating a safe political environment for profitable investment and trade. These expenditures include the costs of politically containing the proletariat at home and abroad, the costs of keeping small-scale, local, and regional capital at home, safely within the ruling corporate liberal consensus, and the costs of maintaining the comprador ruling classes abroad.

These political expenses take the form of income transfers and direct or indirect subsidies, and are attributable fundamentally to the unplanned and anarchic character of capitalist development. Unrestrained capital accumulation and technological change create three broad, related economic and social imbalances. First, capitalist development forces great stresses and strains on local and regional economies; second, capitalist growth generates imbalances between various industries and sectors of the economy; third, accumulation and technical change reproduce inequalities in the distribution of wealth and income and generate poverty. The imbalances—described by Eric Hobsbawm as "the rhythm of social disruption"—not only are integral to capitalist development, but also are considered by the ruling class to be a sign of "healthy growth and change." What is more, the forces of the marketplace, far from ameliorating the imbalances, in fact magnify them by the multiplier effects of changes in demand on production. The decline of coal mining in Appalachia, for example, compelled other businesses and able-bodied workers to abandon the region, reinforcing tendencies toward economic stagnation and social impoverishment.

These imbalances are present in both the competitive and monopoly phases of capitalism. Both systems are unplanned and anarchic as a whole. But monopoly capitalism is different from competitive capitalism in two fundamental respects that explain why political subsidies are budgetary phenomena mainly associated with monopoly capitalism.

First, an economy dominated by giant corporations operating in oligopolistic industries tends to be more unstable and to generate more inequalities than a competitive economy. The source of both instability and inequality is oligopolistic price-fixing, since the interplay of supply and demand that clears specific commodity markets is no longer present. Shortages and surpluses of individual commodities now manifest themselves in the form of social imbalances. In addition, the national (and, increasingly, the international) character of markets means that economic and social instability and imbalances are no longer confined to a particular region, industry, or occupation, but rather tend to spread through the economy as a whole. Finally, Federal government policies for economic stability and growth soften the effects of economic recessions, lead to the survival of inefficient businesses, and hence, in the long-run to the need for more subsidies.

The second difference between competitive and monopoly capitalism concerns the way in which economic and social imbalances are perceived by capital and wage-labor. In a regime of competitive capitalism, businessmen exercise relatively little control over prices, production and distribution. Unemployment, regional underdevelopment, and industrial bankruptcy appear to be "natural" concomitants of "free markets." Moreover, the level and structure of wages are determined competitively, individual capitals are not able to develop and implement a wage policy, and, thus, the impact of wage changes on the volume and composition of production, the deployment of technology, and unemployment, appear to be the consequence of impersonal forces beyond human control. Because imbalances of all kinds are accepted by capital as natural and even desirable, and because the ideology of capital is the ruling ideology, the inevitability and permanence of imbalances and transitory crises tend to be accepted by society as a whole.

With the evolution of monopoly capitalism and the growth of the proletariat as a whole, this fatalistic attitude undergoes profound changes. Business enterprise gradually develops economic and political techniques of production and market control. Gradually, oligopolistic corporations adopt what Baran and Sweezy have termed a "live-and-let-live attitude" toward each other. In this setting,

the imbalances generated by capitalist development begin to be attributed to the conscious policies of large corporations and big unions, rather than to the impersonal forces of the market. Corporate capital, small-scale capital, and the working class alike begin to fix responsibility for the specific policies on particular human agents. Only in this context can the proletariat, local and regional capital, and the comprador classes be contained and accommodated by corporate capital.

The political containment of the proletariat requires the expense of maintaining corporate liberal ideological hegemony, and, where that fails, the cost of physically repressing populations in revolt. In the first category are the expenses of medicare, unemployment, old age, and other social insurance, a portion of education expenditures, the welfare budget, the anti-poverty programs, non-military "foreign aid," and the administrative costs of maintaining corporate liberalism at home and the imperialist system abroad—the expenses incurred by the National Labor Relations Board, Office of Economic Opportunity, Agency for International Development, and similar organizations. The rising flow of these expenditures has two major tributaries.

In point of time, the first is the development of the corporate liberal political consensus between large-scale capital and organized labor. Through the 19th century, private charity remained the chief form of economic relief for unemployed, retired, and physically disabled workers, even though some state and local governments occasionally allocated funds for unemployed workers in times of severe crisis. It was not until the eve of the 20th century that state and local governments introduced regular relief and pension programs. Until the Great Depression, however, welfare programs organized by the corporations themselves were more significant than government programs. Economic prosperity and the extension of "welfare capitalism" throughout the 1920s made it unnecessary for the Federal government to make funds available (in the form of loans to the state) for economic relief until 1932.[7]

The onset of the Great Depression, the labor struggles that ensued, and the need to consolidate the corporate liberal consensus in order to contain these struggles, all led finally to state guarantees of high levels of employment, wage advances in line with productivity increases, and a standard of health, education, and welfare commensurate with the need to maintain labor's reproductive powers and the hegemony of the corporate liberal labor unions over the masses of industrial workers.

. . .

The second tributary runs parallel with, but runs faster and stronger than, the first, and flows from the same source—the development of modern technology. Corporate capital at home and abroad increasingly employs a capital-intensive technology, despite a surplus of unskilled labor, partly because of relative capital abundance in the advanced economies, and partly because of the ready supply of technical-administrative labor power. From the standpoint of large-scale capital, it is more rational to combine in production technical labor power with capital-intensive technology than to combine unskilled or semi-skilled labor power with labor-intensive technology. As we have seen, the fundamental reason is that many of the costs of training technical labor power are met by taxation falling on the working class as a whole.

Advanced capitalism thus creates a large and growing stratum of untrained, unskilled white, black and other Third-World workers that strictly speaking is not part of the industrial proletariat. The relative size of this stratum does not regulate the level of wages,

because unskilled labor power does not compete with technical labor power in the context of capital-intensive technology. This stratum is not produced by economic recession and depression, but by prosperity; it does not constitute a reserve army of the unemployed for the economy as a whole. Unemployed, under-employed, and employed in menial jobs in declining sectors of the private economy (e.g., household servants), these workers increasingly depend on the state. "Make-work" state employment, health, welfare, and housing programs, and new agencies charged with the task of exercising social control (to substitute for the social discipline afforded by the wages system itself) proliferate. The expansion of the welfare rolls accompanies the expansion of employment. For the first time in history, the ruling class is beginning to recognize that welfare expenditures cannot be temporary expedients but rather must be permanent features of the political economy: that poverty is integral to the capitalist system.

. . .

The second major cost of politically containing the proletariat at home and abroad (including the proletariat in the socialist world) consists of police and military expenditures required to suppress sections of the world proletariat in revolt. These expenditures place the single greatest drain on the state budget. A full analysis of these expenditures would require detailed development of the theory of imperialism, which cannot be undertaken here.[8]

. . .

IV

In the preceding sections, we have attempted to analyze state expenditures in terms of the development of the forces and relations of production. We have seen that the increas-

---

[7]James Weinstein, *The Corporate Ideal in the Liberal State* (Boston: Beacon Press, 1968), p. 22.

[8]See Chapter 13, p. 471 (Editors' note).

ingly social character of production requires the organization and distribution of production by the state. In effect, neo-capitalism fuses the "base" and "superstructure"—the economic and political systems—and thus places an enormous fiscal burden on the state budget.

.   .   .

6.4 Capitalist Control of the State

Our analysis of the state implies that the capitalist class benefits most from state activities. But we do not mean to suggest that all state activities benefit only the capitalist class. There are times when all classes may benefit from particular state actions; for example, medical research or community immunization programs may improve everyone's health possibilities.[1] Moreover, other programs (medicare, welfare) have clearly resulted from the demands and serve the needs of groups other than capitalists.[2] What we are asserting is that the capitalist state operates to regulate the society in such a way as to serve the capitalist class interest in maintaining capitalism as a system. As the most privileged class under capitalism, capitalists are the ones who benefit most from the continuation of the system.

But this analysis of the state raises the question: How are capitalists, admittedly a small minority of the population, able to get the state to serve their interests? This is an especially important question where (as in the United States) the people who run the state are chosen in democratic elections. How, then, does the capitalist class control the state? We turn to this question in the next two readings.

The so-called "pluralist" theories of the state deny that capitalists are able to dominate state policy. The pluralists begin with the observation that there are many factions or "interest groups" in society that influence state decisions. For example, the two major political parties and occasionally minor ones compete for positions of power in the institutions of the state; also active are industry associations, church groups, taxpayer groups, public interest organizations, labor unions and many others. These groups lobby, contribute money, and otherwise try to influence decision-making. The pluralists conclude that historically no single group has been able to domi-

---

[1]Even here, class dimensions enter: for example, the bias of medical research toward investigation of cures for rare diseases rather than prevention of common ones (e.g., work-related hazards) disproportionately benefits rich people who typically are not subject to workplace health hazards and can afford the exotic cures to less common maladies.

[2]Again the simple analysis must be qualified: welfare programs provide income to the poor, but they do so in such a demeaning way and in a manner that incurs such hostility from working people (for example, through exaggerated stories of "welfare chiselers") that they also help control the poor. Hence even here the particular manner of meeting others' needs and demands reflects capitalists' power.

nate the state, nor, given the cross-cutting membership of these groups, are they likely to be able to do so in the future.

As William Domhoff shows in the next reading, pluralist theories are fundamentally wrong. Domhoff challenges the basic premise of the pluralist argument by investigating the role of the capitalist class (or, to use Domhoff's phrase, "ruling" class) in the formation of state policy.

The following is excerpted from "State and Ruling Class in Corporate America" by WILLIAM DOMHOFF, *Insurgent Sociologist*, vol. 4, no. 3 (Spring, 1974). Copyright © 1974 by *Insurgent Sociologist*. Reprinted by permission of the author.

On top of the gradually-merging social layers of blue and white collar workers in the United States, there is a very small social upper class which comprises at most 1% of the population and has a very different life style from the rest of us. Members of this privileged class, according to sociological studies, live in secluded neighborhoods and well-guarded apartment complexes, send their children to private schools, announce their teenage daughters to the world by means of debutante teas and debutante balls, collect expensive art and antiques, play backgammon and dominoes at their exclusive clubs, and travel all around the world on their numerous vacations and junkets.

There is also in America, an extremely distorted distribution of wealth and income. Throughout the twentieth century, the top 1% or so of wealthholders have owned 25–30% of all wealth and 55–65% of the wealth that really counts, corporate stock in major businesses and banks. But even that is not the whole story, for a mere .1% have at least 19% of all the wealth in the country—190 times as much as they would have if everyone had an equal share. As for income, well, the maldistribution is not quite as bad. But one recent study argues that if income from capital gains is included, the top 1.5% of wealthholders receive 24% of yearly national income. And, as all studies on matters of wealth and income are quick to point out, these estimates are conservative.

It is not hard for most of us to imagine that the social upper class uncovered in sociological research is made up of the top wealthholders revealed in wealth and income studies. However, it is not necessary to rely on our imaginations, for it is possible to do empirical studies linking the one group to the other. The first systematic studies along this line were reported by sociologist E. Digby Baltzell, but there have been others since.

In most countries, and in most times past in our own country, it would be taken for granted that an upper class with a highly disproportionate amount of wealth and income is a ruling class with domination over the government. How else, it would have been argued, could a tiny group possess so much if it didn't have its hooks into government? But not so in the United States of today. This nation is different, we are assured. It has no social classes, at least not in the traditional European sense, and anyhow there is social mobility—new millionaires are created daily. Besides, many different groups, including organized labor, organized farmers, consumers, and experts, have a hand in political decisions—at least since the New Deal. There is no such thing as a ruling class in America.

In this paper I am going to suggest that in fact a ruling class does dominate this country, a suggestion which not only flies in the face of prevailing academic wisdom, but raises problems for political activists as well. To support this suggestion, I will describe four processes through which the wealthy few who are the ruling class dominate government. Let me begin by defining two terms, "ruling class" and "power elite." By a ruling class, I mean a clearly demarcated social upper class which

a. has a disproportionate amount of wealth and income:

b. generally fares better than other social groups on a variety of well-being statistics ranging from infant mortality rates to educational attainments to feelings of happiness to health and longevity;

c. controls the major economic institutions of the country; and

d. dominates the governmental processes of the country.

By a power elite I mean the "operating arm" or "leadership group" or "establishment" of the ruling class. This power elite is made up of active, working members of the upper class and high-level employees in institutions controlled by members of the upper class.

Both of these concepts, I contend, are important in a careful conceptualization of how America is ruled. The distinction between ruling class and power elite allows us to deal with the everyday observation, which is also the first objection raised by critics of ruling-class theory, that some members of the ruling class are not involved in ruling, and that some rulers are not members of the upper class. Which is no problem at all, in reality. There always have been many members of ruling classes who spent most of their time playing polo, riding to hounds, or leading a worldwide social life. And there always have been carefully-groomed and carefully-selected employees, such as Dean Rusk of the Rockefeller Foundation, Robert McNamara of Ford Motor Company, Henry Kissinger of the Council on Foreign Relations, and Herb Stein of the Committee for Economic Development, who have been placed in positions of importance in government.

Now, many other criticisms have been raised about ruling-class theory, and many different kinds of evidence have been put forth to deal with these criticisms. One typical criticism is that the ruling class is never specified in a way that it can be studied empirically. But this argument can be met by reputational, positional, and statistical studies which show that certain social registers, blue books, prep schools, and exclusive clubs are good indicators of upper-class standing.

Another usual comment is that there is no reason to believe the alleged ruling class is "cohesive" or "class conscious," a criticism which can be countered by pointing to systematic evidence on interregional private school attendance, overlapping club memberships, interlocking corporate directorships, and nationwide attendance at annual upper-class retreats like the Bohemian Grove and the Ranchero Visitadores.

Then there is the assertion that members of the upper class have lost control of corporations and banks to middle-class managers and technocrats, which flies in the face of facts on corporate ownership, on the social backgrounds of corporate directors, and on the motives and goals of corporate managers.

Perhaps the most important criticism, however, is that championed by political scientists, who say proponents of ruling-class theory do not spell out the mechanisms by which the ruling class supposedly dominates government. Not content to infer power from such indicators as wealth and well-being statistics, they want the case for governmental domination by a ruling class demonstrated in its own right, without appeal to statistics on wealth, income, health, and happiness.

My first attempt to satisfy the political science fraternity on this score was to show that members of the power elite hold important governmental positions, especially in the executive branch of the federal government, which I assume everyone now agrees is the most important part of American government. But critics were not satisfied by a sociology-of-leadership approach, which infers "power" to be present when a disproportionate number of people from a given class, ethnic, racial, or religious group appear in positions of responsibility in a given institution.

      .   .   .

Such critics often argue that members of the power elite may not act in the interests of the ruling class while in governmental positions. Instead, they may act in the "national interest," a claim that probably strikes many people as a little empty when they contemplate oil industry tax favors, subsidies to corporations and rich farmers, defense contract overruns, loans to failing corporations, and the general social science finding that most human beings rarely if ever transcend their class, religious and/or ethnic background in viewing the world.

      .   .   .

I have a new way of thinking about the problem of ruling class and government that may put things in a new light. Simply put, I think there are four general processes through which economically and politically active members of the ruling class, operating as the leaders of the power elite, involve themselves in government at all levels. I call these four processes:

1. the special-interest process, which has to do with the various means utilized by wealthy individuals, specific corporations, and specific sectors of the economy to satisfy their narrow, short-run needs;

2. the policy-planning process, which has to do with the development and implementation of general policies that are important to the interests of the ruling class as a whole;

3. the candidate-selection process, which has to do with the ways in which members of the ruling class insure that they have "access" to the politicians who are elected to office; and

4. the ideology process, which has to do with the formation, dissemination, and enforcement of attitudes and assumptions which permit the continued existence of policies and politicians favorable to the wealth, income, status, and privileges of members of the ruling class.

Let me now turn to each of these processes to show their role in ruling class domination

of the government. Although my focus will be on the federal government in Washington, I believe the general schema can be applied, with slight modifications, to state and local governments.

The special-interest process, as noted, comprises the several means by which specific individuals, corporations, or business sectors get the tax breaks, favors, subsidies, and procedural rulings which are beneficial to their short-run interests. This is the world of lobbyists, Washington super-lawyers, trade associations, and advisory committees to governmental departments and agencies. This is the process most often described by journalists and social scientists in their exposés and case studies concerning Congressional committees, regulatory agencies, and governmental departments. This process also has been the target of the excellent investigations by Ralph Nader and his colleagues.

      .   .   .

The information in these [and other similar] studies might seem on its face to be impressive evidence for ruling-class theory. After all, it shows that members of the ruling class are able to realize their will on innumerable issues of concern to them. They can gain tax breaks, receive subsidies, subvert safety laws, and dominate regulatory agencies, among other things. However, in the eyes of most political scientists this is not adequate evidence, for it does not show that the various "interests" are "coordinated" in their efforts. Moreover, it does not show directly that they dominate policy on "big issues," or that they control either of the political parties.

In order to deal with this argument it is necessary to consider next the policy-formation process, the process by which policy on "large issues" is formulated, for it is in the policy process that the various special interests join together to forge general policies which will benefit them as a whole. The central units in the policy network are such organizations as the Council on Foreign Relations, the Committee for Economic Development, the Business Council, the American Assembly, and the National Municipal

League, which are best categorized as policy-planning and consensus-seeking organizations of the power elite. I will not repeat here the information on the financing and leadership of these organizations which shows beyond a doubt that they are underwritten and directed by the same upper-class men who control the major corporations, banks, foundations, and law firms. More important for our purpose is what goes on in the off-the-record meetings of these organizations.

The policy-planning organizations bring together, in groups large and small, members of the power elite from all over the country to discuss general problems—e.g., overseas aid, the use of nuclear weapons, tax problems, or the population question. They provide a setting in which differences on various issues can be thrashed out and the opinions of various experts can be heard. In addition to the group settings, these organizations also encourage general dialogue within the power elite by means of luncheon and dinner speeches, special written reports, and position statements in journals and books.

It was in groups such as these that the framework for a capital-labor detente was worked out at the turn of the century, that the bill for a Federal Trade Commission was drafted, that the plans for social security were created, that the ideas behind the Marshall Plan were developed, that national goals for the 1960's were projected, and the "population problem" was invented.

·   ·   ·

Let me summarize the policy-planning network by means of the diagram on the next-page, and list some of the most important functions of [the policy-making organizations].

1. They provide a setting wherein members of the power elite can familiarize themselves with general issues.
2. They provide a setting where conflicts within the power elite can be discussed and compromised.
3. They provide a setting wherein members of

the power elite can hear the ideas and findings of their hired experts.

4. They provide a "training ground" for new leadership within the ruling class. It is in these organizations that big businessmen can determine which of their peers are best suited for service in the government.

5. They provide a framework for commissioned studies by experts on important issues.

6. Through such avenues as books, journals, policy statements, press releases and speakers, they can greatly influence the "climate of opinion" both in Washington and the country at large.

There are several points for political scientists and other critics of ruling-class theory to consider in contemplating the policy-planning network. First, it provides evidence that businessmen, bankers, and lawyers concern themselves with more than their specific business interests. Second, it shows that leaders from various sectors of the economy do get together to discuss the problems of the system as a whole. Third, it suggests that members of the power elite who are appointed to government are equipped with a general issue-orientation gained from power-elite organizations that are explicitly policy oriented. Fourth, it reveals that the upper-middle-class experts thought by some to be our real rulers are in fact busily dispensing their advice to those who hire them.

If I am right that members of the ruling class gain their narrow interests through the well-known devices of the special-interest process and their general interests through the little-studied policy-planning process, then the question immediately arises: how is all this possible when we have a government elected by the people? Shouldn't we expect elected officials to have policy views of their own that generally reflect the wishes of the voters who sent them to office? There is certainly one group of political scientists who believe this to be the case—they have developed a detailed argument to suggest that the deep-seated political ambitions of individuals

THE POWER ELITE POLICY-MAKING PROCESS

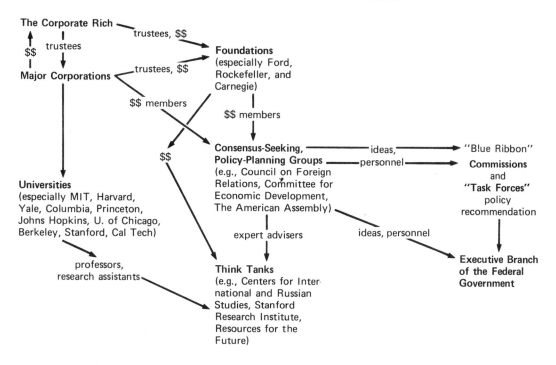

and parties lead them to take the policy stands which will get them a majority of the vote, thereby insuring that the policy views of politicians will reflect more or less the views of the people.

To answer questions about our elected officials, we must examine the political parties and the candidates they nominate. When it comes to the parties, political scientists have suggested that a fully developed political party fulfills four functions: (1) integrating conflicting regional, ethnic, and class identifications; (2) selecting candidates to fill offices; (3) political education; and (4) policy making. In the United States, however, the parties have little or nothing to do with political education or policy making: "Particularly in our own century," writes political scientist Walter Dean Burnham, "American political parties have been largely restricted in functional scope to the realm of the constituent [integrative function]

and to the tasks of filling political offices."[1] Another observer, the executive director of the National Committee for an Effective Congress, puts the matter even more strongly:

> *For all intents and purposes, the Democratic and Republican parties don't exist. There are only individuals [candidates] and professionals [consultants, pollsters, media advisers].*[2]

It is because American politics is restricted largely to office-filling functions that I prefer to talk about the candidate-selection process rather than the political process. The term political process gives the impression that more is going on in our electoral system than

[1]Walter Dean Burnham, "Party Systems and the Political Process," p. 279. In *The American Party Systems*, William Chambers and Walter Dean Burnham, eds. (Oxford University Press, 1967).

[2]John S. Saloma III and Frederick H. Sontag, *Parties* (Alfred A. Knopf, 1972), p. 295.

is really the case. And it is precisely because the candidate-selection process is so individualistic and issueless that it can be in good part dominated by means of campaign contributions from members of the ruling class. In the guise of fat cats, the same men who direct corporations and take part in the policy groups play a central role in the careers of most politicians who advance beyond the local or state legislature level in states of any size and consequence. To quote again from Walter Dean Burnham: "Recruitment of elective elites remains closely associated, especially for the more important offices and in the larger states, with the candidates' wealth or access to large campaign contributions."[3]

The fat cats, of course, are by and large hard to distinguish in their socio-economic outlook whatever their political party. Indeed, most corporations, banks, and law firms try to have personnel who are important donors to both parties. Then too, many of the fattest cats of the opposing parties join together as leaders of such policy-planning groups as the Council on Foreign Relations and Committee for Economic Development. For example, in 1968 there were 144 members of the Council on Foreign Relations who gave $500 or more to the Republicans, 56 who contributed $500 or more to the Democrats. One hundred twenty-six members of the National Council of the Foreign Policy Association donated sums of $500 or more to Republicans, 71 gave to Democrats. At the Committee for Economic Development, there were 95 Republican donors and 16 Democratic donors. Although well-connected in both parties, we can see a power elite preference for the Republican Party, at least in 1968. There is one other difference among fat cats worth nothing—Southern and Jewish members of the upper class are more likely to be Democrats than are their WASPy counterparts.[4]

What kind of politicians emerge from this individualistically-oriented electoral politics that has to curry favor with large contributors? The answer is available from several studies. Politicians are first of all people from the higher levels of the social ladder: "The wealthiest one-fifth of the American families contribute about nine of every ten of the elite of the political economy."[5] They are secondly, at least among those who wish to go beyond local and state politics, quite ambitious men who are constantly striving for bigger and better things. They are thirdly people who are by and large without strong ideological inclinations; the exceptions to this statement are well known precisely because they are so unusual. Finally, with the exception of the local level, where businessmen are most likely to sit on city councils, they are in good part lawyers, an occupational grouping that by training and career needs produces ideal go-betweens and compromisers. The result of the candidate selection process, in short, is (1) men who know how to go along to get along, and (2) men who have few strong policy positions of their own, and are thus open to the suggestions put forth to them by the fat cats and experts who have been legitimated as serious leaders within the framework of the policy-planning network.

When we consider the interaction between the policy process and the political process, it is not surprising that there is a considerable continuity of policy between Republican and Democratic administrations. As columnist Joseph Kraft wrote about the Council on Foreign Relations, "the Council plays a special part in helping to bridge the gap between the two parties, affording unofficially a measure of continuity when the guard changes in Washington."[6] Nor is it surprising that Hubert Humphrey would reveal in early 1973 that he had asked Henry Kissin-

---

[3]Burnham, op. cit., p. 277.

[4]G. William Domhoff, *Fat Cats and Democrats* (Prentice-Hall, 1972), for the information in this paragraph.

[5]Kenneth Prewitt and Alan Stone, *The Ruling Elites* (Harper & Row, 1973), p. 137.

[6]Joseph Kraft, "School for Statesmen," *Harper's Magazine*, July, 1958, p. 68.

ger before the election in 1968 to serve as *his* foreign policy adviser should he win the Presidency. But David Halberstam's *The Best and The Brightest* best reveals the degree to which politicians defer to representatives of the policy process. After winning an election based upon "new frontiers" and non-existent missile gaps, President-elect John F. Kennedy called in Republican Robert Lovett, a Wall Street financier who hadn't even voted for him, and asked him for his advice as to whom should be appointed to important government positions. Kennedy did this because he only knew mere politicians, not the kind of "serious men" who were expert enough to run a government:

> *He had spent the last five years, he said ruefully, running for office, and he did not know any real public officials, people to run a government, serious men. The only ones he knew, he admitted, were politicians, and if this seemed a denigration of his own kind, it was not altogether displeasing to the older man. Politicians did need men to serve, to run the government.*[7]

Among Lovett's suggestions were Dean Rusk of the Rockefeller Foundation, Robert McNamara of Ford Motor Company, and Douglas Dillon of Dillon, Read, who, as we all know, ended up as Kennedy's choices to head the state, defense, and treasury departments.

So politics in America has little to do with issues and public policy. It is an exercise in image-building, name-calling, and rumor mongering, a kind of carnival or psychological safety valve. Thus, a Richard M. Nixon can unctuously claim he is dealing with the issues in the 1972 campaign, when in fact even the *Wall Street Journal* has to admit that all he does is wave the flag and accuse people who disagree with him of being traitors.[8] And at about the same time he is pretending to discuss the issues, he can quietly tell his campaign strategists not to worry about what the platform says because "Who the hell ever read a platform?"[9]

. . .

I conclude that the notion of public policy being influenced to any great extent by the will of the people due to the competition between the two political parties is misguided. "Politics" is for selecting ambitious, relatively issueless middle- and upper-middle-class lawyers who know how to advance themselves by finding the rhetoric and the rationalizations to implement both the narrow and general policies of the bi-partisan power elite.

At this point I can hear the reader protesting that there is more to American politics than this. And so there is. I admit there are serious-minded liberals who fight the good fight on many issues, ecologically-oriented politicians who remain true to their cause, and honest people of every political stripe who are not beholden to any wealthy people. But there are not enough of them, for there is also a seniority system dominated by ruling class-oriented politicians who have a way of keeping the insurgents off the important committees and out of the centers of power. There is in addition a Southern Democratic delegation which retains its stranglehold on Congress despite all the claims of the mid-Sixties that its star was about to fade. Then there are the machine Democrats who aid the Southerners in crucial ways even while they maintain a liberal voting record. And finally, there are the myriad lobbyists and lawyers who are constantly pressuring those who would resist the blandishments of the power elite. As former Congressman Abner Mikva once said, the system has a way of grinding you down:

> *The biggest single disappointment to a new man is the intransigence of the system. You talk to people and they say, "You're absolutely right, something ought to be done about this." And yet, somehow, we go right*

[7]David Halberstam, *The Best and The Brightest* (Random House, 1972), p. 4.

[8]James P. Gannon, "Is GOP Campaign Rhetoric Too Hot?," *Wall Street Journal*, Sept. 8, 1972, p. 8.

[9]"Republicans: Cloth-Coat Convention," *Newsweek*, August 7, 1972 p. 23.

on ducking the hard issues. We slide off the necessary confrontations. This place has a way of grinding you down.[10]

In short, even though there is more to American politics than fat cats and their political friends, the "more" cannot win other than headlines, delays, and an occasional battle. The candidate-selection process produces too many politicians who are friendly to the wealthy few.

Contemplation of the ways in which the special-interest, policy-planning, and candidate-selection processes operate brings us to the $64 question: why do we, the general public, acquiesce in this state of affairs? Why is it, as Marx warned, that the ruling ideas of any age are the ideas of the ruling class? Why does the ruling class have what the Italian Marxist Antonio Gramsci called "ideological hegemony," by which he meant that "the system's real strength does not lie in the violence of the ruling class or the coercive power of its state apparatus, but in the acceptance by the ruled of a "conception of the world" which belongs to the rulers?"[11] Unfortunately, no one has given an adequate answer to these interrelated questions. Such an answer would involve insights from a variety of disciplines including history, anthropology, and psychology as well as political science and sociology, and would quickly lead to age-old problems concerning the origins of the state and the general nature of the relationship between leaders and led.

However, at the sociological level which concerns me in this paper, we certainly can see that members of the ruling class work very hard at helping us to accept their view of the world. Indeed, we can be sure from past experience that they will stop at nothing —despite their protestations of "democracy" and "liberalism"—to get their views across.

[10]Robert Sherrill, "92nd Congress: Eulogy and Evasion," *The Nation*, February 15, 1971.

[11]Giuseppe Fiori, *Antonio Gramsci: Life of a Revolutionary* (NLB, London, 1970), p. 238.

Through the ideology process, they create, disseminate, and enforce a set of attitudes and "values" that tells us this is, for all its defects, the best of all possible worlds. At the fount of this process are the same foundations and policy-planning groups which operate in the policy process. For in addition to providing policy suggestions to government, these policy-planning organizations also provide the new rationales which make the policies acceptable to the general public. Thus, in the case of the ideology process we must link these organizations not to the government, as in the policy process, but to a dissemination network which includes middle-class discussion groups, public relations firms, corporate-financed advertising councils, special university and foundation programs, books, speeches, and various efforts through the mass media.

The dissemination apparatus is most readily apparent in the all-important area of foreign policy. Perhaps most critical here is the Foreign Policy Association and its affiliate, the World Affairs Council. Tightly interlocked with the Council on Foreign Relations, the Foreign Policy Association provides literature and discussion groups for the "attentive public" of upper-middle-class professionals, academics, and students. For local elites, the Council on Foreign Relations sponsors Committees on Foreign Relations in over 30 cities around the country. These committees meet about once a month during the nonsummer months to hear speakers provided by the Council on Foreign Relations or the government. The aim of this program is to provide local elites with information and legitimacy so they may function as "opinion leaders" on foreign policy issues. In addition to the Foreign Policy Association and the Committees on Foreign Relations, there are numerous foreign affairs institutes at major universities which provide students and the general public with the perspectives of the power elite on foreign policy. Then too, political leaders often play an intermediary role

THE FLOW OF FOREIGN POLICY IDEOLOGY
TO THE GENERAL PUBLIC:
POLITICAL LEADERS PLAY AN INTERMEDIARY ROLE

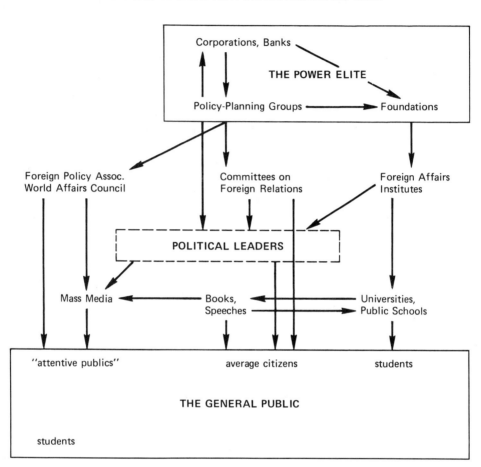

in carrying foreign policy positions to the general public.

The enforcement of the ideological consensus if carried out in a multitude of ways that include pressure, intimidation and violence as well as the more gentle methods of persuasion and monetary inducement. Those who are outspoken in their challenge to one or another of the main tenets of the American ideology may be passed over for promotions, left out of junkets, or fired from their jobs. They may be excluded from groups or criticized in the mass media. If they get too far outside the consensus, they are enmeshed in the governmental law enforcement apparatus which is shaped in the policy-formation process with a special assist from the ruling-class dominated American Bar Association and its affiliated institutes and committees. But I do not think we need spend much time considering the bitter details of ideology enforcement, for they are all too fresh in our minds after years of struggle over civil liberties and the war in Southeast Asia.

6.5 *Party Politics and Class Conflict*

Government in capitalist society is not class-neutral. As Domhoff has argued in the previous reading, the notion of class-neutrality is belied by the class origins of those who have political influence and resources, by the class orientations of most high officials, and by the class bias of formal and informal mechanisms for making public policy. These political "facts of life" contradict the pluralist view that there are many within-class and cross-class special-interest groups, equally and freely competing for policy influence and public power, and that class represents only one basis (out of many) on which such interest groups form. Instead it appears that special-interest politics represent only part of the political process, and interest groups tend in any case disproportionately to represent capitalist rather than other interests.

Yet we must go further to understand how a numerically insignificant capitalist class can dominate a nominally democratic state. In the following reading Richard Edwards and Michael Reich begin by noting the important pro-capitalist constraints that capitalist organization of the economy places upon any government.

Edwards and Reich go on to investigate the operation and evolution of the American system of party politics. Their analysis emphasizes the class character of capitalist society, including the dominant position of the capitalist class, and they interpret the history of party politics as the history of class struggle in the political sphere. The electoral system produces the public acquiescence to (if not outright support of) state policy, but, they argue, voting and elections also create an important arena for class struggle.

This essay was written by RICHARD C. EDWARDS and MICHAEL REICH for this book. Copyright © 1978 by Richard C. Edwards and Michael Reich. We thank John Judis for letting us draw on his unpublished notes in this article.

Do democratic governments in capitalist countries represent the people or do they instead reflect the *class* nature of those societies. Both Marx and Lenin identified the state unequivocally with the capitalist class; in Marx's (and Engels') words:

The bourgeoisie has at last, since the establishment of modern industry and of the world market, conquered for itself, in the modern representative state, exclusive political sway. The executive of the modern state is but a committee for managing the common affairs of the whole buorgeoisie.[1]

Both stressed the capitalist use of the state as a "special repressive force" against working class and peasant insurgency.[2] In many third-world countries—for instance, Chile, Iran, or Indonesia—the capitalist class relies principally on force and terror to retain the support (or acquiescence) of other classes.

But the U.S. state has functioned largely through the consent of the governed rather than through recourse to its repressive apparatus. And the political process in the United States—the struggle that determines government policies and officials—is formally democratic and includes participation by wage-workers, farmers, and small businesspeople as well as large capitalists. Is it then valid to describe the U.S. state as "but a committee

[1] Karl Marx and Frederick Engels, *The Communist Manifesto*.

[2] See Vladimir Lenin, *State and Revolution, Selected Works*, vol. 2, (Moscow: 1960).

for managing the common affairs of the whole bourgeoisie"?

Our intention here is to answer this question by examining the operation and evolution of American party politics. We argue that, while capitalists have historically dominated the American government, changes in capitalism itself have made their control both more crucial and more uncertain. The most important challenge to capitalists' domination of the state comes from the political power of the working class.

Our argument proceeds as follows. First, we review how the capitalist economy imposes objective constraints on the state, regardless of what party gets elected or who the high government officials are. This context biases the political system in favor of capitalists and constitutes the most fundamental source of the capitalists' power over the state. Second, we look at how the two major political parties operate. Capitalists have dominated both parties, and Democratic and Republican programs can be seen as alternative strategies for advancing capitalist interests. On the other hand, working class groups in this century have been able to gain some significant leverage in the Democratic Party. As a result, certain reforms have been won that extend democracy and that present capitalist rule with a potentially serious challenge. Third, we argue that in response to this growing challenge capitalists have sought to restructure the state so that, while its democratic form is maintained, its democratic content is reduced. In the present period, the operation of the state reflects a growing conflict between capitalism and democracy.

I. CAPITALIST CONSTRAINTS ON THE STATE

We begin by examining the economic context in which state policies are fashioned. This context—that is, capitalist relations of production—places severe constraints upon what the state can and cannot do. Investment decisions and the production of goods and services (and therefore also the level of economic activity and the number of jobs in the economy) are determined primarily by capitalists seeking to make profits. Consequently, the state cannot execute public policies that lower substantially the rate of capitalists' profit without jeopardizing the "health" of the economy. For example, if the state taxes profits too much or allows unions too much power, capitalists will reduce their investments. Similarly, state policies that undermine the work incentive, redistribute income and wealth, or otherwise interfere with the capitalist mode of production create economic problems. Even the prospect of such policies in the future is enough to erode "business confidence," send the stock market down, and encourage the outflow of funds eroding the national currency's exchange rate. When lowered profit prospects affect enough investors, reduced investment produces an economic downturn, a balance of payments problem, and a fiscal crisis for the state.

Hence, state policies are constrained by the imperatives of the capitalist economy *regardless of who runs the state or what their intentions may be*. Even if a pro–working-class government is elected, its power to make changes is fundamentally constrained to the extent that capitalists control investment.[3] The capitalist class is thus able to achieve without direct control a relative dominance over the "democratic" state simply because that state exists in the larger context of capitalist society.

In the United States, because capitalists dominate the political process, the state typically tends to promote capitalists' interests.

The concept of capitalist dominance over the state must be qualified in two important ways. First, the state must operate for the

[3]In many advanced capitalist countries today much investment is undertaken by the state. This fact is not by itself evidence that the capitalist class has "lost control" of that investment; see O'Connor, Section 6.3, p. 235. On the other hand, the growth of this state investment may ease the constraints on a pro–working-class government.

general capitalist interest, but not necessarily for the interest of any individual capitalist. Since capitalists compete with each other for profits, state policies that are in the common interest of the whole capitalist class may actually conflict with particular interests of specific capitalists. For example, an individual capitalist may wish to see a tariff for his product erected against foreign competition. Most capitalists, however, benefit from access to overseas markets, and a specific tariff may bring retaliation by foreign governments against U.S. exports. In this case, for the state to pursue capitalists' classwide interests it must oppose certain capitalists' particular interests. Thus, the state operates with some autonomy from the pressures of individual capitalists.[4]

Indeed, since capitalists are busy making their individual profits, they do not always have a classwide outlook of their interests. While the capitalist class agrees on fundamental issues of property, it is often divided on others—such as foreign policy and welfare and labor legislation. Their divisions may be expressed in public political struggle, or a consensus may be built through the policy formation process.[5] In either case it is the state that executes the policies that best fit the capitalists' classwide interests. The state may even see that a certain policy is in the long-term common interests of capital before many capitalists so perceive it. This was the case, for example, when Keynesians pushed the idea of state deficit spending to stimulate the economy—a policy the capitalist class later came to support.

Second, the capitalist class's dominance over the state is relative rather than absolute. In recent decades, government policies in advanced capitalist nations have been increasingly subject to another important influence: the working class, which has grown not only numerically but also in its organiza-

tional strength and political clout. In the United States the political influence of organized labor unions and federations of unions, particularly in the Democratic Party, has restricted the range of options available to the state. For example, the state cannot attempt to reduce inflation by creating the extremely high levels of unemployment that existed in the 1930s. Thus, by seeking to implement programs in their interests, labor unions, black groups, organizations of poor people, etc. push the state in directions that are often opposite to those desired by capitalists. So while capitalists dominate the state, they are not unopposed and their control is far from complete. We now turn to the contradictions that are created by these pressures.

II. THE EXTENSION OF DEMOCRACY

From the capitalists' standpoint, the electoral process serves to legitimize their control, yet it also threatens it. In the long run, the state's effectiveness in legitimizing capitalist dominance depends upon the state *appearing* neutral in the class struggle. Hence, it must be open to all interests and politics. This can and does lead to a parade of special interests, representing parts of the working class as well as parts of the capitalist class. These special interests often threaten policies important for capital accumulation. Another and more serious problem is that the electoral system provides an opening for a working-class movement to contest for the right to govern. Given universal suffrage in a society in which the working class far outnumbers capitalists, the capitalist class must take this potential threat seriously.

The early ruling classes were aware of the potential contradictions of representative government. They were concerned with creating a balanced coalition of various propertied interests (Southern slaveholders and Northern merchants and manufacturers). They established forms of government that allowed only for indirect representation of the (relatively)

---

[4]This perspective explains the often expressed grumblings of business against state policy and helps us avoid the mistaken conclusion that the state is acting in a generally anticapitalist manner.

[5]See Domhoff, Section 6.4, p. 242.

propertyless workers, small farmers, and artisans.[6] The president was to be chosen by an electoral college. Senators were originally elected by legislative houses. In many states, only white male property-owners could participate in electing these legislators. An elaborate system of checks and balances among the judicial, legislative, and executive branches was designed to prevent propertyless groups or any single section of the propertied classes from running roughshod over the others. In this way, the Founding Fathers insulated the chief public offices from worker and farmer control and balanced competing propertied interests.

The present American electoral system, which allows for universal adult suffrage and direct election of senators, was only achieved through the struggles of women, small farmers, workers, and blacks and other minorities. Like the economic reforms won by the working class, these democratic reforms have created new opportunities for previously excluded groups to influence state policy.

Capitalists and the Political Parties

With the expanded franchise and direct election of office-holders, electoral activity came to be organized through the mechanism of political parties. Capitalists have been active in the affairs of both major parties, but in this century consistent political differences have existed between the parties. The Republican Party today represents both "moderate" corporate capitalists (the "liberal" or "Eastern establishment" wing) and small business and the more conservative and reactionary big-business elements (the party's right wing). Republican programs tend to rely more directly and immediately on repression ("law and order") to maintain capitalist rule, and Republicans see little merit in policies (e.g., welfare, mass higher education, etc.) that serve to legitimize capitalism and to co-opt working-class dissent. Instead, the Republican

Party is openly for high profits, rapid capital accumulation, and the policies that would promote them: lower business taxes, restrictions on unions, reducing those government payments to the poor which interfere with work incentives, higher unemployment to replenish the reserve supply of workers, etc.

In contrast, those big-business capitalists who favor a strategy of "corporate liberalism" operate within the Democratic Party. These capitalists are also primarily concerned about profits and accumulation. But, in contrast to the Republicans, the corporate liberal strategy to achieve accumulation makes them more favorable to reform policies: welfare, aid to education, accommodation with labor unions, maintaining low levels of unemployment through deficit spending, etc. Such reforms, although costly perhaps in the short run, may alleviate serious class conflicts that would be even more costly to capitalists.[7]

Yet the two parties tend to develop a symbiotic relationship. Republican policies to promote accumulation, such as those of the 1950s, succeed until sufficient resentment among workers gathers to necessitate reforms, including full employment, social security and welfare improvements, extension of public services, and enforcement of anti-discrimination laws. The Republican accumulation strategy thus becomes outmoded because it provokes too much dissent. Democrats are able to exploit these grievances to create a winning electoral coalition. Once in power, as in the 1960s, they begin to increase social service spending, stimulate the economy, and undertake other reforms or legitimation programs. Eventually, however, the costs of these efforts (in higher taxes, inflation, the "burden" of regulation, more militant workers,

---

[6]Slaves and Indians were to be kept in place largely through force and terror.

[7]Although their primary allegiance is to "moderate Republicanism" (i.e., some mixture of legitimation policies and repression), corporate capitalists are financially more able, and hence more willing, to support reform programs than are small capitalists, who are directly threatened by higher taxes, the costs of regulation, etc. Thus, some corporate capitalists (especially investment bankers and corporate lawyers) are Democrats.

etc.) tends to mobilize capitalists, small businesspeople, homeowners, tax-payers, and other groups into resisting further programs—that is, the Democratic accumulation strategy becomes obsolete. Once again the guard changes.

The Democratic Party's greater ability to attract working class support (see below) has tended to make it an increasingly dominant party. Especially in Congress, state legislatures, governorships, etc., the Democrats have established "permanent" majorities. As the Republican Party has declined, it has become a less effective vehicle for the "Republican" accumulation strategy. This strategy then reappears as the program of the conservative wing of the Democratic Party.

Workers and the Democratic Party

The working class is naturally more attracted to the Democratic Party, which offers some concessions and reforms, than to the Republican Party, which offers workers very little. In the twentieth century the working class has been able to use its electoral power to increase its influence within the Democratic Party. It has affected candidate selection and legislative action, and Democratic administrations have been forced to include representatives of working-class and minority interests. In some local and state races, anticapitalist working-class candidates have been able to win Democratic nominations and sometimes the election itself.

By 1900, the American working class was becoming the majority class in America. But its members were not organized politically. The American Federation of Labor (AFL), whose members primarily were skilled workers, followed pressure-group tactics, pressuring both parties and supporting neither officially. In 1901, the Socialist Party formed, and it was able to build a growing working-class constituency until the end of World War I, when it was permanently weakened by internal splits and by government repression. After World War I, the march of the work-

ing class into the Democratic Party began, first with the white urban ethnic minorities (many of whom had been Democrats earlier), and then with the industrial unions and blacks in the 1930s and 1940s. By the late 1940s, the Democratic Party had become the "party of the working class." The key event was the open support of Roosevelt by leaders of the Congress of Industrial Organizations (CIO) in 1936. (In fact, the CIO was Roosevelt's single largest campaign contributor in 1936.) Open CIO support broke the AFL tradition. It was based on an understanding of the importance of political action for the success of the industrial union's organizing drive.

In return for their organized support, Democratic officials supported legislation favored by working-class interests and appointed representatives from the labor unions and black organizations to administration positions within the federal, state, and local bureaucracies. Through these positions, labor and black representatives were able to fight on behalf of their respective interests within administrations.

But while the Democratic Party is the party of the working class, it is not a working-class party. As we indicate below, capitalist interests hold key positions of power in the party through their financial role. The party's programs and candidates come out of a complex process of maneuver and compromise that involves interests of small and large capitalists as well as working-class interests. And the dominant ideology and practice within the Democratic Party sees labor and business as interest groups, whose contending claims it seeks to balance, rather than as conflicting classes. As a consequence, the party has successfully transformed potentially autonomous working-class power into a subordinated interest group. While the results express working-class interests, they also express the predominance of capitalist interests within the party. In this sense, the Democratic Party, like the state itself, is an arena of class struggle. Compared to the Republican Party, it is a much more favorable arena of struggle for the working class, and that is why working-class groups flocked into it in the 1930s. But it expresses nonetheless the relative dominance of the American capitalist class over other contenders for political power.

During the 1930s, the growing working-class movement demanded and finally obtained unemployment compensation, social security, welfare programs, public housing, and government support for collective bargaining. Without this pressure, the government would never have acted. But the final results of the legislation only emerged after intense struggles among capitalists and between capital and labor, and they ultimately reflected the predominance of capital interests. Social security, for instance, was largely financed through workers' incomes; capitalist pressure was able to eliminate the redistributive aspects of the proposals for social security that were supported by many working people. The Wagner Act of 1935, putting unions and collective bargaining on a legal basis, was passed over considerable opposition from capitalists who saw labor unionism as a threat to their rates of profit and eventually to their control over the means of production.

But over the next twenty years, capitalists were able to blunt the impact of labor unionism. The anti-capitalist elements were driven out of the labor movement and McCarthyist repression was used to decimate the Left. For most of the postwar period, monopoly corporations were able to grant wage increases while maintaining or increasing their rates of profit. And labor leaders themselves were brought into a political consensus around capitalist goals in a pro-capitalist and anti-communist Cold War liberalism that was centered in the Democratic Party. Although the party has struggled against some sections of the capitalist class and small business, it has never opposed the entire capitalist class on any important issue.

So the Democratic Party itself tends to mirror the contradictions of the entire electoral system. Possibilities exist for working-class victories, including important reforms.

The larger context in which politics occurs, however, tends both to restrict the nature of reforms and to limit the probability of their being enacted. Moreover, capitalists have attempted to retain control of the state by restructuring the political system.

III. THE ATTACK ON DEMOCRACY

As the public electoral process has been opened up, the capitalist class has moved to prevent working class and small business interests from taking full advantage of their new opportunities. First, capitalists have tried to limit the effect of the electoral process on state policy by isolating decision-making in governmental bodies that are far removed from democratic accountability. Second, capitalists have sought to control the parties themselves through financial means and through their control over the media and the ideological apparatus. Finally, they have attempted, when necessary, to destroy third parties and to preserve the present two-party system.

Like other capitalist measures, these actions were not taken consciously by a united capitalist class, but instead were instituted by fractions of that class acting in concert with politicians who shared their interests. But their net effect was to limit, at least temporarily, the challenge posed by the democratic reforms of the electoral system.

Isolating "Democratic" Government from the People

Throughout the twentieth century power has been shifted from elected and hence democratically-accountable government institutions to appointed, non-accountable bodies. As a result, party politics, citizen voting, and the entire electoral process have come to have less and less effect on government policy.

In part this shift reflects the dramatic

decline of the Congress (and state legislatures and town meetings) as real governing
bodies; more, it reflects the rapidly growing
power of the bureaucracies, "public authorities," regulatory bodies, state commissions,
the courts, "expert" or "professional" bodies,
and so on. The Congress, legislatures, and
the like are all popularly elected, of course,
while the latter groups (the bureaucracy,
courts, etc.) are appointive. Moreover, while
officials in popularly-accountable bodies tend
to serve fairly short terms (two to four years
generally, excepting the Senate), the non-
accountable agencies are run by officials
enjoying, as an additional protection from
popular will, extremely long terms (five or
seven or ten years or even life).

The most salient and crucial case of this
shift in power away from democratic accountability has emerged with the expansion of
executive power. The American president
was originally likened to a monarch. Like a
monarch, the president would be aware of
popular needs and interests, but would be accountable only to his propertied peers. He
would be able to make decisions that were
unpopular to the public at large but that were
necessary for preserving or extending capitalism. Like that of monarchs, the power of the
president was to be checked by feudal barons
in the legislative and judicial branches. Today, participation in the electoral process is
broader and presidents are elected directly by
universal suffrage. Monopoly capitalists have
become the dominant propertied interest; and
monopoly capitalism's economic contradictions demand a greater role for the federal
government in the economy. Presidents, facing popular movements and having to follow
unpopular policies but moving with capitalist
support, have created a new and greater
realm of decision-making and planning for
themselves: the national security apparatus
and the Executive Office of the President.

The purpose of creating this new realm
was to insulate an area of decision-making
and planning from popular pressure—which
in the first instance meant shielding it from
congressional influence (and since cabinet

members are partially responsible to congressional scrutiny, it meant shielding it
from even cabinet influence).[8] The expanded
power taken by the executive has consequently occurred at the expense of Congress.
There have been four significant steps on this
path in the twentieth century. In the early
decades of this century, Theodore Roosevelt
and Woodrow Wilson began framing their
own legislation and sending it to Congress
rather than leaving this initiative to Congress. In 1939, having begun to draw back
from the second phase of New Deal programs
under capitalist pressure and also having
begun to plan for war with Germany,
Franklin Roosevelt created the Executive
Office of the President. Among other things,
he moved the Bureau of the Budget from the
Treasury Department to the Executive
Offices; this meant that appointees were not
subject to congressional approval, and that
its operations were shielded from public
influence.[9]

In 1946, Harry Truman, about to launch
the Cold War in the face of possible public
resistance, made the Council of Economic
Advisors, the National Security Council, and
the Central Intelligence Agency part of the
Executive Offices. Finally, Richard Nixon
moved even more drastically to enlarge the
Executive Offices. Some of his innovations
succeeded, such as the Office of Management and Budget; others, such as the attempt
to create a domestic counterintelligence
agency within the Executive Offices, were
abandoned during the Watergate scandals.[10]

The development of capitalist-sponsored
policy formation groups, such as the Council
for Foreign Relations and the Committee for

[8]Of all federal government officials, members of the
House of Representatives, elected locally every two
years, are most likely to represent special interests—
often, the special interests of the working class and
minorities—in conflict with interests of the capitalist
class.

[9]See William E. Leuchtenberg, *Franklin D. Roosevelt and
the New Deal* (New York: 1963), pp. 327–28.

[10]See Rowland Evans, Jr., and Robert D. Novak, *Nixon
in the White House* (New York: 1972), pp. 237–41.

Economic Development, accompanied the enlargement of executive power and the creation of the Executive Office. These corporate capitalist groups have contributed both their members and their ideas to the president's executive councils.

As with the Executive Offices, so in state and local governments and in other areas of the federal government, power and decision-making have been transferred out of institutions (e.g., Congress) that are somewhat sensitive to popular opinion (even if imperfectly so) and into other institutions that retain nearly no democratic content. The National Security Council, the Federal Reserve Board, the New York Port Authority, state bureaucracies, licensing commissions, etc. have become the anti-democratic form of modern "democratic" government. In this way, the main area of state policy formation has been subject to direct capitalist influence, while it has been relatively isolated from the electoral process and from working-class pressures. This has limited the effect of the electoral process on American policy.

Controlling the Republicans and Democrats by the Purse Strings

The American political parties are decentralized coalitions of state and local parties that come together, every four years, to nominate a presidential candidate. Neither the Republicans nor the Democrats are explicitly tied to one class's interests, as is for example the British Labor Party. They are both multiclass coalitions.

The capitalist class maintains tremendous influence within the two parties largely through its major responsibility for campaign finances. The scope of these contributions has come into better focus recently with the disclosure of widespread and massive contributions by corporations directly out of their corporate coffers. Gulf Oil alone, for example, has admitted to having dispensed millions of dollars during the 1960s and 1970s.[11] These

legal and illegal contributions, often hidden in the books as "business expenses" and hence used to reduce the corporation's taxes, supplemented the vast above-board (and legal) giving by wealthy individuals. No candidate can expect to be nominated or elected without enormous contributions, especially as the scope of the campaign widens from city to nation.

Most political scientists concede that the Republican Party depends on capitalist support. It reportedly commands the allegiance of 80 to 90 percent of American capitalists. But the Democrats also depend on capitalist financing. In a study of the Democrats, William Domhoff estimates that Democratic candidates receive 45 to 65 percent of their funds from capitalist donors, while labor unions contribute at most 20 to 25 percent, "little people" about 15 percent, and racketeers, in some areas, up to 15 percent. Domhoff shows how capitalist interests are able to use their financial power to weed out overtly anti-capitalist candidates at the primary level, especially in state and federal races.[12]

Capitalist financial influence has not led to political uniformity. The Democrats remain a party more influenced by working class interests than the Republicans. But what financial influence does ensure is that the candidates of both parties fall within a generally acceptable spectrum of political views, neither too far to the left nor to the right. Given capitalist influence, neither party will nominate candidates for state or national office who oppose capitalist property relations, or who advocate, on the other side, race war or the abrogation of bourgeois democracy. When a person who has strayed too far to the left or right has gained a presidential nomination—for instance, Goldwater in 1964 or McGovern in 1972—capitalists have almost universally supported his opponent, with the result of a resounding defeat for the candidate and cries for moderation within the defeated party.

[11] *New York Times*, March 5, 1976, p. 1.

[12] See William Domhoff, *Fat Cats and Democrats* (Englewood Cliffs, N.J.: Prentice-Hall, 1972); see also David Nichols, *Financing Elections* (New York: 1974).

In 1971 and 1974, new campaign financing legislation was passed, ostensibly in order to expose and limit capitalist influence over the campaign financing process. But aside perhaps from limiting contributions to presidential campaigns, these laws do not in practice limit capitalist contributions; they only require new means of funneling them to candidates. For example, replacing the sub rosa corporate gifts is the open and systematic collection of contributions from corporate management under the (legal) rubric of corporate "political action committees." Similarly, although direct contributions to candidates are limited, wealthy individuals can undertake *independent* advertising campaigns to promote a candidate and spend any amount desired. Indeed, there is some evidence that the new rules may *increase* capitalist influence.

It would be a mistake, however, to view campaign financing as the only or even principal level of capitalist control over the political parties. In fact, a few rich individuals were *more* able to buy politicians in the nineteenth century than today. At least as important today is who the capitalist-controlled media are likely to promote as an attractive public personality—a required attribute for a candidate—and what the likely class orientation of such a person will be. Probably more important are how the two-party system defuses dissent, how the capitalist class has dealt with labor union leaders and other groups, and how serious challenges to capitalist rule are smashed.

Maintaining the Two-Party System

The American party system has evolved in such a way as to favor capitalist interests. The structure of the two-party system, with winner-take-all elections, single-member districts, and separate election of Congress and president, makes it difficult for third parties to arise that would unite the working class and small businesspeople against capitalist interests. And when third parties have arisen, capitalists, along with political allies in the

established parties, have been able to isolate them and absorb them back into the Democratic or Republican parties or repress and smash them.[13]

In some countries in Western Europe, officials are elected on a proportional system. Each party gains seats in local or national assemblies according to its proportion of the total vote. So parties that initially represent minority political positions or class interests can arise and still gain some victories on the basis of which to go forward. They can also influence the election of a head of government, who is chosen either by the majority party or, if there is no majority, by a coalition of parties.

In the United States, by contrast, election of a single representative from each district on the basis of a winner-take-all election is the universal form. In cities where proportional voting was tried, the success of anti-capitalist candidates led to vigorous attempts to go back to the winner-take-all form.[14] At the beginning of this century, capitalist reformers eliminated the ward system of voting in many cities, a system that—like the proportional one—had encouraged representation by minority interests.[15] American capitalists, aware of the importance and success of their political party system for preserving capitalist hegemony, encouraged its adoption by Germany and Japan after World War II.

This electoral system in the United States has given third parties an enormously difficult time in building a stable base of support, especially in national elections. Leaders of the Democrats and Republicans have been able to cast such parties in the role of spoilers, often by taking over one of the third party's main issues. The result is that the voters have to choose between the survival of the third party and their support for the party's issue.

[13]E. E. Schattschneider, *Party Government*, Chap. 4 (New York: 1942).

[14]Belle Zeller and Hugh A. Bone, "The Repeal of Proportional Representation in New York City," *American Political Science Review*, 42 (1948).

[15]James Weinstein, *The Corporate Ideal in the Liberal State* (Boston: 1968), Chap. 4.

This happened to the Populist Party in 1896, which lost its distinctive character when the Democrats nominated William Jennings Bryan on a "free silver" platform. In the 1948 elections, the Progressive Party saw its base of support eroded by the Democratic Party because of Truman's earlier veto of the anti-labor Taft-Hartley bill (which became law anyway). A similar fate met the right-wing American Independence Party in 1972, when Nixon and the Republican Party were able to attract many of its supporters.

Recently, these older means of restricting electoral competition to the two major parties have been supplemented by new elements. Campaign financing "reform" makes public funds available, but almost all the money goes to Republicans and Democrats under the law's restrictive formula. Similarly, although the "equal time" laws mandate equal access to TV and radio broadcast time for all serious condidates the major networks, with official connivance, regularly violate these laws. For example, the broadcast of the Carter-Ford debates evaded the law's strictures by a legal ruse: sponsorship of the debates by the League of Women Voters transformed them into "legitimate news events," which are not subject to equal time laws. Thus even as popular pressure forces Congress to pass new laws opening up access to political resources, administrative and legal fiat transforms these reforms into new barriers protecting the monopoly of the two major parties.

If a third party's issues fall largely outside the range of capitalist acceptability, then different strategies are sometimes followed. During World War I, when the Socialist Party advocated a socialist transformation of society and opposition to American participation in the war, the Party was illegally and violently suppressed and its victorious candidates barred from holding office. Similarly, the Black Panther Party was subjected to terror tactics during the late 1960s. The Socialist Worker's Party through court action was able to force the FBI to disclose that for thirty-eight years it planted undercover agents within the party to disrupt its activities, ruin its finances, embarrass its candidates, etc.[16]

Democracy in Form but Not in Content

The isolation of government from the electoral system, the capitalists' financial weight with both parties, and the sterility of the present two-party system have wrung from American government much of its democratic content. Many civil liberties and personal freedoms remain, but the basic elements of democratic government—consent of the governed and control of the government by popular majority—have been seriously eroded.

Not only have old methods of making government accountable decayed, but new ones have been avoided. For example, although referenda on important issues were technically impossible (given the difficulty in communications) when the Constitution was written, in the electronics age they are technically trivial; yet fear of what the people might decide (as, for example, on war policy during the Vietnam era) prevents this most democratic of decision-making procedures from achieving a serious hearing.

So the average citizen's participation in "democratic government" is restricted to voting once every two or four years. Yet as we have seen, even voting has had less and less influence on how the government operates. These developments have not escaped the average citizen: modern "democracy," rather than fostering participation, has reduced the public's interest in elections. Despite what was widely perceived as a very close race, roughly 70 million eligible voters refused to vote in the 1976 presidential elections—a massive non-turnout accounting for nearly half of all qualified voters.[17] When a large sample was earlier interviewed as to why they were not planning to vote, non-

[16] *New York Times*, September 15, 1976, p. 15.

[17] *New York Times*, November 4, 1976, p. 28.

voters declared that "candidates say one thing and then do another" (68 percent), "it doesn't make any difference who is elected" (55 percent), and "all candidates seem pretty much the same" (50 percent).[18] Although such attitudes are much deplored by defenders of the system, these citizens seem to understand their own increasing power-lessness.

IV. MONOPOLY CAPITALISM, THE STATE, AND CLASS CONFLICT

The state's activities have grown enormously in the period of monopoly capitalism. This growth has been caused in part by the persis-tent tendency for production to become more social in nature. In order to regulate the movement of the economy as a whole, the state has undertaken macroeconomic plan-ning. Similarly, the state has taken on new responsibilities for planning transportation systems, energy development, training of the labor force, reorganizing the international monetary system, and so on.

The struggle of working-class groups to improve their living standards has been a second cause of the growth in state activities. The reform struggles of the 1930s produced federal responsibility for social security, regu-lation of labor relations, unemployment com-pensation, etc. These struggles were extended in the 1960s and 1970s to obtain federal anti-discrimination statutes, state expenditures for education, pollution control, Medicare and

[18] *Newsweek*, September 13, 1976, p. 16.

Medicaid, legalization of collective bargain-ing rights for some state workers, health and safety regulations at workplaces, and product safety. Thus, the state has become more im-mediately and directly involved in the accu-mulation process.

For capitalists, this increasing intervention of the state in the economy makes control over state policies more crucial. How the state regulates industries, sets taxes, conducts macroeconomic policy, buys military hard-ware, etc. has an increasing impact on prof-its. The problem this creates for capitalists, as we have seen, is that their control over the state is far from complete. It is certainly less complete than their control over the means of production, and it becomes more uncertain with the continuing demise of small prop-ertied interests and the expansion of an enfranchised working class.

At the same time, because of the growth of state activities, the working class must also struggle over state policy to defend or advance its interests. Class struggle occurs not only in relation to individual employers, but more and more spills over into the political arena itself. This struggle includes, though is not limited to, elections and party politics.

We have seen how capitalists have respond-ed to democratic political reforms by seeking to limit democracy. The struggle to extend democracy consequently has become increas-ingly a struggle against capitalists and against the structural constraints that capitalist rela-tions of production place upon the state. The struggle to extend democracy has become more than ever a struggle against the capital-ist mode of production.

PART IV

CLASS STRUCTURE
AND
EXPLOITATION

Alienation

ASKED IF HE LIKED HIS JOB, one of John Updike's characters replied, "Hell, it wouldn't be a job if I liked it." After reading Elinor Langer's description of her job with the telephone company,[1] one can appreciate that reply. But why do most jobs seem so onerous? Is this inevitable in any modern industrial society? Or does it have something to do with the capitalist mode of production? This chapter seeks to answer these questions by investigating the way in which work is organized and jobs are shaped in a capitalist society.

The stultifying character of factory work has been a major theme in descriptions of capitalist societies since the rise of industrial capitalism. Adam Smith, considered the founder of modern (bourgeois) economics, wrote in 1776 that "in the progress of the division of labor, the employment of the far greater part of those who live by labor . . . comes to be confined to a few very simple operations. . . . But the understandings of the greater part of men are necessarily formed by their ordinary employments. . . [A man so employed] generally becomes as stupid and ignorant as it is possible for a human creature to become."[2]

But it is Karl Marx who is rightly associated with the most penetrating descriptions and analyses of the condition of labor under capitalism. In his *Economic and Philosophical Manuscripts of 1844*, Marx introduced the concept of alienation to analyze the situation of workers in a capitalist enterprise.[3] For Marx, alienation does not describe a subjective feeling on the part of workers; rather, it refers to an objective situation in which they find themselves under the capitalist mode of production.

Today we tend to think of alienation as a psychological state of mind involving elements of dissatisfaction with the world and isolation from others. An alienated worker doesn't like his or her job; an alienated student can't get along with his or her teachers; an alienated person is simply "turned off" by the society in which he or she lives. In this way we use the term "alienation" in its subjective sense to describe something that people experience and feel. It is important to distinguish clearly between this *subjective* concept of alienation and the *objective* concept which Marx used in his analysis of capitalism. In its objective sense, alienation means powerlessness or lack of control; a person is alienated from something (e.g., a job) if he or she has no control over it. Clearly, an objective situation of alienation can give rise to a subjective feeling of alienation; but it need not necessarily do so.

Marx characterized workers under capi-

[1]Langer, Section 1.1, p. 4.

[2]Adam Smith, *The Wealth of Nations* (New York: Modern Library, 1937), p. 734.

[3]The discussion of Marx's concept of alienation in the following paragraphs is based on the section on "Alienated Labor" in Marx's *Economic and Philosophical Manuscripts*, published in *Karl Marx Early Writings*, trans. and ed. T. B. Bottomore (New York: McGraw-Hill, 1963), pp. 120–134.

talism as "alienated labor" because their position as a class in the social relations of production is subject to three kinds of objective alienation. First, workers are alienated from the *product* of their work. Because the capitalist owns the means of production and the output of the production process, workers have no control over what is produced and how it is used. Second, workers are alienated from the *process* of work. It is the capitalist (and/or his hired managers) who determine how the process of production takes place and what the worker must do during his or her working hours. Finally, workers are alienated from their "species being"—that is, from their own essence as human beings. Here Marx reasons from the premise that the distinguishing feature of human life is that work is undertaken not just in order to permit physical survival (as in the case of animals); most importantly, work is undertaken as a purposefully creative act that gives meaning to life. Under capitalism, work becomes essentially a means for maintaining the worker's physical existence and it ceases to be in any relevant sense a life-fulfilling activity. Thus workers are alienated from themselves because they have no control over their own humanness—i.e., their potential for creative work.

To understand the way in which objective alienation is bound up with the capitalist mode of production, one need only compare the position of a worker in a capitalist enterprise (e.g., a textile mill worker) with that of an independent craftsperson (e.g., a handloom weaver). The mill worker has no influence on what kind of cloth is produced, nor on how it is produced, nor on when it is produced; indeed, he or she may never even see the final product and has no reason to take any interest in it. On the other hand, the weaver makes many decisions about the production of his or her fabric and can take pride in the final product. For the mill worker the only reason to work is to earn a wage on which to live. The weaver must also work for a living, but the weaver's greater degree of control over the work product and process generates opportunities for creativity and fulfilment

that give the work a very different and more fundamentally human character.

Although the contrast between textile mill workers and handloom weavers was a very important one in the nineteenth century, during Marx's lifetime, such examples may seem somewhat irrelevant in the late twentieth century. One might well question whether Marx's characterization of alienated labor still applies to contemporary advanced capitalist societies. And one might ask whether there exist alternative, nonalienated forms of labor that are feasible in a modern industrial society.

We will show in the first reading in this chapter that there is a great deal of job dissatisfaction in the United States today. Alienation among workers has become a frequent subject of newspaper reports, magazine articles, and books. But this refers to alienation in its subjective sense. Does alienation in Marx's objective sense exist too, and is it responsible for the subjective alienation we hear so much about?

We will argue in this chapter that most of the American working class is indeed alienated in the Marxist sense, in spite of all of the technological change that has taken place during more than a century of capital accumulation. We will also seek to show that it is this objective state of alienation that is responsible for much of the dissatisfaction with work that we observe in the United States. Since the objective alienation of workers is inherent in capitalist social relations of production, it follows that the subjective alienation of workers can be attributed in large part to our capitalist institutions. As long as work is organized along capitalist lines, dissatisfaction with work is bound to be a continuing problem.

Job dissatisfaction is not only a serious concern in its own right; it often has even more serious consequences. Tedious and unrewarding work threatens both the physical and the mental health of the worker.[4] Alcoholism and drug addiction are not uncommon responses

[4]For a more thorough discussion of this issue, see the Report of the Special Task Force to the Secretary of Health, Education and Welfare, *Work in America* (Cambridge: M.I.T. Press, 1973), chap. 3.

to working conditions in American factories. Even more common is the general state of passivity outside the workplace. The effects of a deadening job carry over into the home and community life of the workers, resulting in a subjective feeling of alienation not only from work but from family, community, and the society at large.

Moreover, the objective situation of alienation at the workplace also has deleterious consequences for other spheres of life. The worker who is denied participation and control over the work situation is unlikely to be able to participate effectively in community or national decision making, even if there are formal opportunities to do so. This is because effective participation in decision making requires certain skills (keeping oneself informed, understanding the issues, presenting one's viewpoint clearly and forcefully) and certain attitudes (a motivation to participate, and the self-confidence to do so) which a worker shut off from decision-making at work has little opportunity to develop. In other words, participatory democracy at the workplace appears to be an essential prerequisite for meaningful democracy in community and national affairs.[5]

For all the problems associated with alienated labor, the question remains: Is there any alternative? Many people believe that alienated labor (in both senses) is not merely characteristic of capitalist social relations but is inextricably rooted in the nature of complex technology in a modern industrial society. In this "technologically determinist" view, alienated labor is necessary for the efficient operation of large-scale modern enterprises, and such enterprises are in turn necessary to maintain a high and growing standard of living. The experience of the Soviet Union, where workers appear to be just as alienated as in the United States, is often cited to support the technologically determinist view of alienation.

We believe that alienation is *not* the inevitable product of technological advance. We will argue in the second reading in this chapter that the character of technological change itself has been shaped by capitalists in their own interest; what appears as the inevitably alienating nature of work in a modern enterprise is in fact largely the result of deliberate choice by the dominant capitalist class. This implies that alternative social relations of production might well give rise to different forms of technological change and work organization. In particular, we would expect that a society controlled by the working class in its collective interest would develop nonalienated forms of labor, thereby minimizing alienation in its subjective as well as its objective sense. It is of course unrealistic to imagine a nation of craftspeople in the United States today. But worker control of even large-scale and complex modern enterprises can generate opportunities for pride and fulfilment arising out of participation in a common endeavor whose social purpose is understood and valued by the whole community. Thus, we believe that truly democratic control of the workplace can go a long way to reduce alienation and all of its harmful consequences.

But is this likely to happen in the United States? Even if there are more desirable forms of work organization than the authoritarian and alienating structure imposed by capitalists, what prospects are there for any real change in the current situation? We address this critical question in the last reading of the chapter. Like so many aspects of our capitalist society, the organization of work is not stable: it gives rise to certain contradictions which are likely to intensify over time. For example, increasing worker consciousness of alienation and dissatisfaction with work may well lead to reduced motivation and initiative, higher absenteeism, production slowdowns, and even sabotage, all of which threaten the profitability of the enterprise for the capitalist. Such contradictions in turn offer opportunities for significant change, provided that workers can organize effectively to challenge some of the basic elements of capitalist control over the workplace.

[5]This point is very persuasively developed in Carole Pateman, *Participation and Democratic Theory* (London: Cambridge University Press, 1970).

One final note: it should be apparent from the discussion that our analysis of the capitalist enterprise applies not only to privately owned firms but also to state-run enterprises insofar as these are organized along authoritarian and hierarchical lines. For some purposes the distinction between private and public ownership is in itself significant—e.g., for a discussion of the distribution of income. But for the questions raised in this chapter, it is the distinction between authoritarian and democratic forms of work organization that is paramount. Authoritarian enterprises are found in both the private and public sector of capitalist societies and also in the public sector of many "state socialist" societies such as the Soviet Union. Truly democratic enterprises are much rarer in the contemporary world, but, in certain ways, producers' cooperatives in the United States, the kibbutzim of Israel, the worker-managed enterprises of Yugoslavia, and the agricultural communes of China come close to the democratic ideal. We will explore further the organization of work under participatory socialism in Chapter 14.

7.1 *Work in America*

Increasing evidence of worker discontent in the United States in the late 1960s—manifested in rising absenteeism, frequent strikes, etc.—led to growing concern among businesspeople and government officials that the prosperity of the capitalist economy might be threatened. One result of this official concern was the commissioning in 1971 of 'a special task force to prepare a report to the secretary of Health, Education and Welfare on "Work in America," focusing on the qualitative aspects of the work experience and the problem of job dissatisfaction. Like so many such commissioned reports, this one served primarily as a substitute for government action to meet real grievances, and its recommendations have been largely ignored. But like other such reports, it does provide a large amount of useful information documenting serious social problems.

This reading is excerpted from the report of the task force; it discusses the growth of worker dissatisfaction in the United States and attempts to identify some of its causes and consequences.

The reading is excerpted from the Report of the Special Task Force to the Secretary of Health, Education and Welfare, *Work in America* (Cambridge: M.I.T. Press, 1973).

A recent survey . . . was undertaken by the Survey Research Center, University of Michigan, with support from the Department of Labor. This unique and monumental study . . . is based on a representative sample of 1,533 American workers at all occupational levels. When these workers were asked how important they regarded some 25 aspects of work, they ranked in order of importance:

1. Interesting work
2. Enough help and equipment to get the job done
3. Enough information to get the job done
4. Enough authority to get the job done
5. Good pay
6. Opportunity to develop special abilities
7. Job security
8. Seeing the results of one's work.

What the workers want most, as more than 100 studies in the past 20 years show, is to become masters of their immediate environments and to feel that their work and they themselves are important—the twin ingredients of self-esteem. Workers recognize that some of the dirty jobs can be transformed only into the merely tolerable, but the most oppressive features of work are felt to be avoidable: constant supervision and coercion, lack of variety, monotony, meaningless tasks, and isolation. An increasing number of workers want more autonomy in tackling their tasks, greater opportunity for increasing their skills, rewards that are directly connected to the intrinsic aspects of work, and greater participation in the design of work and the formulation of their tasks.

WHO IS DISSATISFIED?

When we cite the growing problem in the country of job dissatisfaction . . ., are we talking about 5% or 50% of the workers in the country? It is clear that classically alienating jobs (such as on the assembly-line) that allow the worker no control over the conditions of work and that seriously affect his mental and physical functioning off the job probably comprise less than 2% of the jobs in America. But a growing number of white-collar jobs have much in common with the jobs of auto-workers and steelworkers. Indeed, discontent with the intrinsic factors of work has spread even to those with managerial status. It is, however, almost as difficult to measure these feelings of discontent about work as it is to measure such other basic feelings as pride, love, or hate. Most of the leading experts on work in America have expressed disappointment over the unsophisticated techniques commonly used to measure work dissatisfaction.

The Gallup poll, for example, asks only "Is your work satisfying?" It is not surprising that they get from 80% to 90% positive responses (but even this crude measure shows a steady decrease in satisfaction over the last decade). When a similar question was asked of auto and assembly-line workers, 60% reported that their jobs were "interesting." Does this mean that such high percentages of blue-collar workers *are really satisfied* with their jobs? Most researchers say no. Since a substantial portion of blue-collar workers (1) report being satisfied with their jobs *but also indicate they wish to change them* and (2) report they would continue working even if they didn't have to *but only to fill time*, then this can only mean that these workers accept the necessity of work but expect little satisfaction from their specific jobs.

Those workers who report that they are "satisfied" are really saying that they are not "dissatisfied" . . ., i.e., their pay and security are satisfactory, but this does not necessarily mean that their work is intrinsically rewarding. This distinction is illustrated by an interview sociologist George Strauss held with a blue-collar worker on a routine job. This worker told Strauss, in a rather offhand way, "I got a pretty good job." "What makes it such a good job?" Strauss responded. The worker answered:

> *Don't get me wrong. I didn't say it is a* good *job. It's an O.K. job—about as good a job as a guy like me might expect. The foreman leaves me alone and it pays well. But I would never call it a good job. It doesn't amount to much, but it's not bad.*[1]

Robert Kahn suggests that the direct question of satisfaction strikes too closely to one's self-esteem to be answered simply:

> *For most workers it is a choice between no work connection (usually with severe attendant economic penalties and a conspicuous lack of meaningful alternative activities) and a work connection which is burdened with negative qualities (routine, compulsory scheduling, dependency, etc.). In these circumstances, the individual has no difficulty with the choice; he chooses work, pronounces himself moderately satisfied, and tells us more only if the questions become more searching. Then we learn that he can order jobs clearly*

[1] George Strauss, "Is There a Blue Collar Revolt Against Work?," 1972.

in terms of their status or desirability, wants his son to be employed differently from himself, and, if given a choice, would seek a different occupation.[2]

More sophisticated measures of job satisfaction designed to probe the specific components of a job offer great contradictions to simple "Are you satisfied?" surveys. When it asked about specific working conditions, the Michigan survey found that great numbers of "satisfied" workers had major dissatisfactions with such factors as the quality of supervision and the chance to grow on a job. A 1970–71 survey of white, male, blue-collar workers found that less than one-half claimed that they were satisfied with their jobs most of the time. The proportion of positive responses varied according to the amount of variety, autonomy, and meaningful responsibility their jobs provided.

· · ·

SOURCES OF DISSATISFACTION

Based on what we know about the attitudes of workers toward their jobs, we can identify the following two factors as being major sources of job dissatisfaction: the anachronism of Taylorism and diminishing opportunities to be one's own boss.

The Anachronism of Taylorism

Frederick Winslow Taylor, father of time and motion studies and author of *Principles of Scientific Management*, propagated a view of efficiency which, until recently, was markedly successful—so long as "success" was measured in terms of unit costs and output. Under his tutelage, work tasks were greatly simplified, fragmented, compartmentalized, and placed under continuous supervision. The worker's rewards depended on doing as he was told and increasing his output. Taylor's advice

resulted in major, sometimes spectacular, increases in productivity.

Several events have occurred to make Taylorism anachronistic. Primarily, the workforce has changed considerably since his principles were instituted in the first quarter of this century. From a workforce with an average educational attainment of less than junior high school, containing a large contingent of immigrants of rural and peasant origin and resigned to cyclical unemployment, the workforce is now largely native-born, with more than a high school education on the average, and affluence-minded. And, traditional values that depended on authoritarian assertion alone for their survival have been challenged.

Simplified tasks for those who are not simple-minded, close supervision by those whose legitimacy rests only on a hierarchical structure, and jobs that have nothing but money to offer in an affluent age are simply rejected. For many of the new workers, the monotony of work and scale of organization and their inability to control the pace and style of work are cause for a resentment which they, unlike older workers, do not repress.

Attempts to reduce the harmful effects of Taylorism over the last two generations have not got at the nub of the problem. For example, the "human relations" school attempts to offset Taylor's primacy of the machine with "tender, loving care" for workers.[3] This school (which has many adherents in personnel offices today) ignores the technological and production factors involved in a business. This approach concentrates on the enterprise as a social system—the workers are to be treated better, but their jobs remain the same. Neither the satisfaction of workers nor their productivity is likely to improve greatly from the human relations approach. Alternatives to Taylorism, therefore, must arise from the assumption that it is insufficient to adjust either people to technology or technology to people. It is necessary to consider both the

[2]Robert Kahn, "The Meaning of Work: Interpretation and Proposals for Measurement," 1972.

[3]Robert Kahn, "The Work Module," 1972.

social needs of the workers and the task to be performed. This viewpoint challenges much of what passes as efficiency in our industrial society.

Many industrial engineers feel that gains in productivity will come about mainly through the introduction of new technology. They feel that tapping the latent productivity of workers is a relatively unimportant part of the whole question of productivity. This is the attitude that was behind the construction of the General Motors auto plant in Lordstown, Ohio, the newest and most "efficient" auto plant in America. Early in 1972, workers there went out on strike over the pace of the line and the robot-like tasks that they were asked to perform. This event highlights the role of the human element in productivity: What does the employer gain by having a "perfectly efficient" assembly-line if his workers are out on strike because of the oppressive and dehumanized experience of working on the "perfect" line? As the costs of absenteeism, wildcat strikes, turnover, and industrial sabotage become an increasingly significant part of the cost of doing business, it is becoming clear that the current concept of industrial efficiency conveniently but mistakenly ignores the social half of the equation.

It should be noted that Taylorism and a misplaced conception of efficiency is not restricted to assembly-lines or, for that matter, to the manufacturing sector of the economy. The service sector is not exempt. For example, in the medical care industry, the phenomenal growth in employment over the past decade or so has occurred largely in lower-level occupations. This growth has been accompanied by an attempt to increase the efficiency of the upper-level occupations through the delegation of tasks down the ladder of skills. This undoubtedly results in a greater efficiency in the utilization of manpower, but it rigidifies tasks, reduces the range of skills utilized by most of the occupations, increases routinization, and opens the door to job dissatisfaction for a new generation of highly educated workers.

As we have seen, satisfying jobs are most often those that incorporate factors found in high-status jobs—autonomy, working on a "whole" problem, participation in decision making. But as Ivar Berg and others have noted, as a result of countless public and private policies and decisions that determine our occupational structure, growth in occupational opportunities has occurred largely in middle and lower levels. The automation revolution that was to increase the demand for skilled workers (while decreasing the need for humans to do the worst jobs of society) has not occurred. What we *have* been able to do is to create such jobs as teacher aides, medical technicians, and computer keypunch operators—not jobs with "professional" characteristics. Undoubtedly, these jobs have opened opportunities for many who would otherwise have had no chance to advance beyond much lower-skilled positions. But it is illusory to believe that technology is opening new high-level jobs that are replacing low-level jobs. Most new jobs offer little in the way of "career" mobility—lab technicians do not advance along a path and become doctors.

Diminishing Opportunities to Be One's Own Boss

Our economic, political, and cultural system has fostered the notion of independence and autonomy, a part of which is the belief that a hardworking person, even if he has little capital, can always make a go of it in business for himself. Or, to put it another way, if things get too bad in a dependent work situation, it has been felt that the individual could always strike out on his own.

This element of the American Dream is rapidly becoming myth, and disappearing with it is the possibility of realizing the character traits of independence and autonomy by going into business for oneself. The trend of the past 70 years or more, and particularly in recent years, has been a decrease in small independent enterprises and self-employment, and an increase in the domination of large corporations and government in the work-force. In the middle of the 19th century, less than half of all employed people were wage and salary workers.[4] By 1950 it was 80%, and by 1970, 90%. Self-employed persons dropped from 18% in 1950 to 9% in 1970.

    ·   ·   ·

The trend is toward large corporations and bureaucracies which typically organize work in such a way as to minimize the independence of the workers and maximize control and predictability for the organization. Characterologically, the hierarchical organization requires workers to follow orders, which calls for submissive traits, while the selection of managers calls for authoritarian and controlling traits. With the shift from manufacturing to services—employment has gone from about 50–50 in 1950 to 62–38 in favor of services in 1970—the tyranny of the machine is perhaps being replaced by the tyranny of the bureaucracy.

    Yet, the more democratic and self-affirmative an individual is, the less he will stand for boring, dehumanized, and authoritarian work. Under such conditions, the workers either protest or give in, at some cost to their psychological well-being. Anger that does not erupt may be frozen into schizoid depressed characters who escape into general alienation, drugs, and fantasies. More typically, dissatisfying working environments result in the condition known as alienation.

> *Alienation exists when workers are unable to control their immediate work processes, to develop a sense of purpose and function which connects their jobs to the over-all organization of production, to belong to integrated industrial communities, and when they fail to become involved in the activity of work as a mode of personal self-expression.*[5]

    ·   ·   ·

[4]The figures in this section are from Michael Maccoby and Katherine Terzi, "Work and the American Character," 1972.

[5]Robert Blauner, *Alienation and Freedom*, 1964.

BLUE-COLLAR BLUES

    ·   ·   ·

Work problems spill over from the factory into other activities of life: one frustrated assembly-line worker will displace his job-generated aggression on family, neighbors, and strangers, while a fellow worker comes home so fatigued from his day's work that all he can do is collapse and watch television. The difference in reactions may only be a function of their ages, as this Studs Terkel interview with a steelworker illustrates:

> You're at the tavern. About an hour or so?
> *Yeah. When I was single, I used to go into hill-billy bars, get in a lot of brawls. . . .*
> Why did you get in those brawls?
> *Just to explode. I just wanted to explode. . . .*
> You play with the kids . . . ?
> *. . . When I come home, know what I do for the first 20 minutes? Fake it. I put on a smile. I don't feel like it. I got a kid three-and-a-half years old. Sometimes she says, Daddy, where've you been? And I say, work. I could've told her I'd been in Disneyland. What's work to a three-year-old? I feel bad, I can't take it out on the kid. Kids are born innocent of everything but birth. You don't take it out on the wife either. This is why you go to the tavern. You want to release it there rather than do it at home. What does an actor do when he's got a bad movie? I got a bad movie every day.*[6]

    ·   ·   ·

Blue-collar discontent is exacerbated by distinctions between blue-collar and white-collar privileges on the job. For example, the blue-collar worker must punch time clocks, making it difficult for him to arrange his work schedule to manage such personal chores as visiting the doctor, getting his car repaired, and visiting the school to discuss his children's problems. More basically, 27% of all workers have no paid vacations, 40% have no sick leave, and perhaps 70% will never receive a private pension check (even though large

[6]Studs Terkel, "A Steelworker Speaks," *Dissent*, Winter 1972.

percentages may be employed in firms with pension plans).[7] Virtually all of those workers who are without these benefits are found among the ranks of non-professionals.

A problem related to management privileges is the general feeling among workers that their bosses abuse their disciplinary prerogatives, and that their unions do not challenge such "abuses." They often claim that work rules, particularly in the auto industry, are similar to military discipline. Some younger, more educated workers are even beginning to question the constitutionality of punishment at work without due process.

· · ·

Perhaps the most consistent complaint reported to our task force has been the failure of bosses to listen to workers who wish to propose better ways of doing their jobs. Workers feel that their bosses demonstrate little respect for their intelligence. Supervisors are said to feel that the workers are incapable of thinking creatively about their jobs.

In summary, the cause of the blue-collar blues is not bigotry, the demand for more money, or a changing work ethic. An autoworker explains the real genesis of the blues:

> If you were in a plant you'd see—everybody thinks that General Motors workers have it easy, but it's not that easy. Some jobs you go home after eight hours and you're tired, your back is sore and you're sweatin'. All the jobs ain't that easy. We make good money; yeah, the money is real good out there, but that ain't all of it—cause there's really a lot of bad jobs out there.

· · · ·

WHITE-COLLAR WOES

The auto industry is the *locus classicus* of dissatisfying work; the assembly-line, its quintessential embodiment. But what is striking is the extent to which the dissatisfaction of the assembly-line and blue-collar worker is mirrored in white-collar and even managerial positions. The office today, where work is segmented and authoritarian, is often a factory. For a growing number of jobs, there is little to distinguish them but the color of the worker's collar: computer keypunch operations and typing pools share much in common with the automobile assembly-line.

Secretaries, clerks, and bureaucrats were once grateful for having been spared the dehumanization of the factory. White-collar jobs were rare; they had higher status than blue-collar jobs. But today the clerk, and not the operative on the assembly-line, is the typical American worker, and such positions offer little in the way of prestige. Furthermore, the size of the organizations that employ the bulk of office workers has grown, imparting to the clerical worker the same impersonality that the blue-collar worker experiences in the factory. The organization acknowledges the presence of the worker only when he makes a mistake or fails to follow a rule, whether in factory or bureaucracy, whether under public or private control.

· · ·

Traditionally, lower-level white-collar jobs in both government and industry were held by high school graduates. Today, an increasing number of these jobs go to those who have attended college. But the demand for higher academic credentials has not increased the prestige, status, pay, or difficulty of the job. For example, the average weekly pay for clerical workers in 1969 was $105.00 per week, while blue-collar production workers were taking home an average of $130.00 per week.[8] It is not surprising, then, that the Survey of Working Conditions found much of the greatest work dissatisfaction in the country among young, well-educated workers who were in low-paying, dull, routine, and fractionated clerical positions. Other signs of

[7]The figures are from Basil Whiting, "The Suddenly Remembered American," 1971, and the *Wall Street Journal*, December 3, 1971, p. 4.

[8]All figures in this section are from Judson Gooding, "The Fraying White Collar," 1970.

discontent among this group include turnover rates as high as 30% annually and a 46% increase in white-collar union numbership between 1958 and 1968. A 1969 study of 25,000 white-collar employees in eighty-eight major companies showed a decline in the percentage of positive responses concerning several key factors of job satisfaction since 1965. For example, there was a 34% decline in the belief that their company would act to do something about their individual problems. These changing attitudes (and the failure of employers to react constructively to them) may be affecting the productivity of these workers: a survey conducted by a group of management consultants of a cross section of office employees found that they were producing at only 55% of their potential. Among the reasons cited for this was boredom with repetitive jobs.

Loyalty to employer was once high among this group of workers who felt that they shared much in common with their bosses—collar color, tasks, place of work. Today, many white-collar workers have lost personal touch with decision makers, and, consequently, they feel estranged from the goals of the organiza-tions in which they work. Management has exacerbated this problem by viewing white-collar workers as expendable: because their productivity is hard to measure and their functions often non-essential, they are seen as the easiest place to "cut fat" during low points in the business cycle. Today, low-level white-collar workers are more likely to be sacrificed for the sake of short-term profitabil-ity than are blue-collar workers.

· · ·

CONCLUSION

Albert Camus wrote that "without work all life goes rotten. But when work is soulless, life stifles and dies." Our analysis of work in America leads to much the same conclusion: Because work is central to the lives of so many Americans, either the absence of work or employment in meaningless work is creating an increasingly intolerable situation. The hu-man costs of this state of affairs are mani-fested in worker alienation, alcoholism, drug addiction, and other symptoms of poor men-tal health.

7.2 *Capitalism and Alienation*

Worker alienation is now widely recognized as a serious problem in the United States and, indeed, in all advanced capitalist societies. There remains considerable confusion, however, about what is meant by the term "aliena-tion." And there is much disagreement about its causes.

In this section Herbert Gintis and Samuel Bowles seek to clarify the con-cept of alienation and the relationship between capitalism and alienation. Part I (drawn from an article by Gintis) analyzes the meaning of alienation, making the important distinction between its subjective and its objective sense. Part II (drawn from an article by Bowles and Gintis) makes a powerful case that the roots of alienated labor lie in the social relations of capitalist production rather than in the nature of technology itself.

Part I of the following is excerpted from an essay written by HERBERT GINTIS for the first edition of this book. Copyright © 1972 by Herbert Gintis. Printed

Part I:
The Meaning of Alienation

THE EXPERIENCE OF ALIENATION

As Robert Blauner explains in his book *Alienation and Freedom*,[1] the worker experiences alienation from work in the form of powerlessness, meaninglessness, isolation, and self-estrangement. He or she is *powerless* because bureaucratic organization is ruled from the top, through lines of hierarchical authority treating the worker as just another piece of machinery, more or less delicate and subject to breakdown, to be directed and dominated.

Work seems *meaningless* because it is divided into numberless fragmented tasks, and the worker has some expertise over only one of these tasks; consequently, his contribution to the final product is minimal, impersonal, and standardized. Work also seems meaningless because most workers realize only too well the limited extent to which their activities contribute to perceived social welfare. If he produces steel, his factory pollutes atmosphere and streams. If he makes automobiles, his product congests, smogs, kills, and, finally, after thirty months of "service," falls apart. If he processes cost accounts or his secretary types the corporation's plan to avoid paying taxes, they know their work is unrelated to satisfying anyone's real needs. If he sells insurance, he understands that his success depends only on his relative cunning and talent in duping his customer.

Moreover, the worker is supremely and uniquely *isolated* in work: fragmentation of tasks precludes true solidarity and cooperation; hierarchical authority lines effectively pit workers on different "levels" against one another; and since workers do not come together to determine through their social interaction the important decisions governing production, no true work community develops. Lastly, the powerless, meaningless, and isolated position of the worker leads him to treat work merely as an *instrument*, as a *means* toward the end of material security, rather than an end in itself. But work is so important to a person's self-definition and self-concept, that he then comes to view *himself* as an instrument, as a means, to some ulterior end. Hence develops his *self-estrangement*.

That a person may be self-estranged—alienated from himself, his essence, and his psyche—has been characterized as the focal point of the industrial worker's self-concept, be he blue-collar or white-collar. As Erich Fromm notes:[2]

> *[A person] does not experience himself as an active agent, as the bearer of human powers. He is alienated from these powers, his aim is to sell himself successfully on the market. His sense of self does not stem from his activity as a loving and thinking individual, but from his socio-economic role. . . . He experiences himself not as a man, with love, fear, convictions, doubts, but as that abstraction, alienated from his real nature, which fulfills a certain function in the social system. His sense of value depends on his success: on whether he can make more of himself than he started out with, whether he is a success. His body, his mind, and his soul are his capital, and his task in life is to invest it favorably, to make a profit of himself. Human qualities like friendliness, courtesy, kindness, are transformed into commodities, into assets of the "personality package" conducive to a higher price on the personality market.*

[1]Robert Blauner, *Alienation and Freedom* (Chicago: University of Chicago Press, 1964), especially Chapter 1.

[2]Erich Fromm, *The Sane Society* (New York: Rinehart and Winston, Inc., 1955), p. 142.

A PROBLEM POSED

That capitalist society is alienating is a central element in the radical critique of capitalism, and the term has even attained general public acknowledgement—bemoaned by politicians everywhere, trotted out as a catch-all explanation of "youth unrest" by television commentators, and generally seen by youth themselves as characterizing their own condition. But exactly what alienation *is*, and the nature of its *causes*, remains shrouded in uncertainty and confusion.

The difficulty surrounding the concept of alienation arises from the fact that it comprises both subjective, psychological elements and objective, social elements. Before the rise of the New Left in the decade of the 1960s, alienation was treated as a purely subjective phenomenon, essentially independent of the structure of society. In the Silent Decades following World War II, alienation was proposed as a part of the "human condition" by noted French philosophers, among whom Sartre, Camus, and Beckett are the most widely read in the U.S. We personally encounter the phenomenon on this subjective level, and we respond most immediately to its manifestations in our own lives, in the Beatles' "Nowhere Man," Nichols' *The Graduate*, and Phillip Roth's *Portnoy's Complaint*. Yet the sources of alienation inhere in the social system itself. Alienation as a general phenomenon coincides with the rise of capitalism.

We now see the treatment of alienation as an element of human nature as merely symptomatic of the political quiescence of the Silent Decades. Indeed, the very *appearance* of the concept of alienation coincides with the breakdown of feudal society and the rise of capitalism, in the works of Hegel and Marx, and the literary works of Kafka and Dostoevsky.

Yet the growing awareness of the social basis of alienation—an awareness of quite recent vintage—still fails to achieve the proper analytical depth. This is due in part to the particular *form* in which this awareness is couched. Alienation is seen to arise directly from the nature of technology in "modern industrial society" and, hence, to remain independent of any particular set of economic institutions. This view is reinforced through our understanding of the historical development of capitalism's main competitor, state socialism in the Soviet Union and Eastern Europe. So-called "socialist man" seems to differ little from his capitalist counterpart, and so-called "socialist society" seems little better equipped to avoid the problems of Alienated Man and Alienated Woman than its avowed adversary.

This paper will try to show not only that alienation is a social rather than a psychological problem at its root but that it results from the structure of technology only in the most immediate and superficial sense, because the form that technological development takes is itself strongly influenced by the structure of economic institutions and their day-to-day operations. If capitalist and [state] socialist economies experience these same problems, it is due to some essential similarities of their basic economic institutions.

AN ANALYSIS

The root meaning of the verb "to alienate" is "to render alien" or, more concretely, "to separate from" (e.g., "She alienated my husband's affections" means "She separated my husband's affections from me"). We can use this root meaning to motivate a social definition of alienation: when your pocket is picked, you are "alienated" from your wallet; similarly, when the structure of society denies you access to life-giving and personally rewarding activities and relationships, you are alienated from your life. Alienation, on the subjective level, means that elements of personal and social life that should be meaningful and integral, become meaningless, fragmented, out of reach, and—if one has an existentialist bent—absurd. The alienated individual is powerless to control central aspects of his life, just as he cannot "control" the wallet snatched from him.

Alienation appears on many levels. Most of these can be explained in terms of *social roles*. A social role is a "slot" that people fit into, carrying with it characteristic duties and obligations, and defined by what other people expect of the person in that role. These expectations become institutionalized, so the same behavior is expected of any individual who occupies a particular role. For example, take the role of foreman. A foreman, no matter what particular individual happens to occupy the position, is expected to supervise his workers, remain somewhat aloof and above them, and in general be more responsive than are the workers to the company's interests in getting the work done. Butcher, baker, worker, soldier, capitalist, lover, husband, community member—all these are social roles.

The nature of these roles and their availability to the individual are quite as important as the distribution of material goods and power in assessing the value of a social system. Alienation occurs because the roles open to individuals do not satisfy their immediate needs in terms of their interpersonal activities in family, community, and work, and their requirements for healthy personal psychic development. Thus, we center on the role concept to emphasize the inherently *social* nature of alienation. To be alienated is to be separated in concrete and specific ways from "things" important to well-being; however, these "things" are not physical objects or natural resources but are types of collaboration with others, with society, and with nature. These "things" are social roles.

The structure of roles at a point in time, and the way they change and develop over time, depends on criteria and priorities laid down by basic social and economic institutions. . . . [A] lienation arises when the social criteria determining the structure and development of important social roles are *essentially independent of individual needs*. These conditions are precisely what occur under capitalism: the social roles involving participation in work process and community (and to a lesser extent family life) develop in accordance with market criteria and are essentially independent of individual needs. The result is alienation.

· · ·

ALIENATION OF WORK PROCESS

To illustrate the alienating consequences of capitalist institutions, consider the organization of work activities. An individual's work is of utmost importance for his personal life. Work directly engages nearly half of one's active life and is potentially the single major outlet for initiative, creativity, and craft. Moreover, work roles are basic and formative in individual personality development. But are these considerations reflected in the actual social decisions determining the structure of work roles? For instance, is the factory worker's welfare considered when the capitalist decides to produce automobiles by routine and monotonous assembly line operations? Are the secretary's needs considered when she is reduced to the full-time subservient role of typing, stenography, and stamp licking? The structure of work roles is essentially determined by a set of basic economic institutions that operate on quite different criteria. The market in labor means that the worker sells his services to the capitalist firm and essentially agrees to relinquish total control over his work activities, thus leaving the determination of work roles to those who control capital and technology. Both technology and work roles are essentially determined by the dictates of profit maximization or output maximization and maintenance of hierarchy.

Control of work activities through alienating institutions has implications on both subjective and objective levels. Subjectively, workers mostly experience their work activities as "alien"—as opposing rather than contributing to their personal well-being and psychic growth. This is understandable in that their own needs were peripheral in the decision process determining the nature of work roles—their work activities have been snatched from them.

Objectively, alienating control leads to predictable consequences. In the early stages of the Industrial Revolution, this control resulted in work activities that were brutal, unhealthy, boring and repetitive, and required long hours. More recently, it has taken the form of bureaucratic organization of production, where individual work roles are so fragmented and formalized that the worker finds his initiative and autonomy totally muffled by and subordinated to a mass of regulations and "operating procedures." Also, hierarchical stratification of workers along lines of status and authority subjugates some workers to the personal control of others, subjects all workers to the control of managers and capitalists, and precludes cooperation and equality as a condition of production. Hence, bureaucratic organization and hierarchical control are the concrete modern manifestations of the worker's alienation from his [or her] work activities.

Part II: The Source of Alienation

MARKETS, TECHNOLOGY, AND ALIENATED WORK

Few readers will question [the alienated character] of work in the corporate capitalist economy. But have we correctly identified capitalism as the source of the problem? If the historical development of the structure and content of jobs is responsive to the wills and needs of workers to the extent feasible, given the technological alternatives, our indictment of capitalism must be tempered; for in this case alienated labor would assume the status of a condition of humankind, an externally imposed technological imperative.

What are the determinants of jobs in U.S.

capitalism? The private ownership of the means of production and the operation of the market in labor, or more broadly the social relations of capitalist production, act to place the determination of the organization of production—and hence the content of the job—in the hands of a small group of employers, while compelling most individuals to relinquish disposition over their productive activities to these employers in return for a wage or salary. Moreover, employers determine the content of work-activities, as well as the direction of technological and organizational innovation, according to criteria manifestly tangential if not inimical to the concerns of workers: profitability and the maintenance of the employers' own elevated economic positions. Lastly, the product of labor is not owned by the worker; nor does the worker have a voice in determining what commodities the enterprise will produce.

The *prima facie* case, that the roots of alienated labor lie in the social relations of capitalist production, is thus quite strong. The needs and wishes of workers will be embodied in employers' decisions only to the extent that they further the latter's goals. The social relations of the corporate capitalist enterprise are organized to reflect the interests of capitalists and directors, to whom all other groups are subservient and even pitted against one another. However, the issue is really considerably more complex. For workers can express their needs, not directly through control within the enterprise, but indirectly through their personal discretion as to which jobs they will or will not accept. Indeed, the standard argument in liberal economic theory is an attempt to prove the following assertion. When firms maximize profits, and when labor and all other factors of production are bought and sold on markets where prices and wages are determined by supply and demand, then the structure of jobs will reflect workers' preferences, subject only to the availability of natural resources and known technologies of production. Thus the sphere of work is integrated, in the sense that workers essentially choose their job structures within the limits imposed by nature and the level of scientific knowledge.

Let us consider the argument in more detail. Suppose that workers are faced with a job structure characterized by repressive and routine jobs subject to hierarchical authority, and they decide they would prefer more satisfying work. How do they express this preference? Clearly by offering their services at a lower wage or salary to an employer who provides the kind of work they desire. Thus some enterprising employer will note that he can obtain cheaper labor than his competitors if he provides these jobs, and will look around for a production technique compatible with them, the (ostensibly lower) efficiency of which is more then counterbalanced by the lower wage bill. If he discovers such a profitable organizational or technical alternative, then the workers will get the jobs they prefer and his competitors will be forced to adopt the same production technique in order to hold their workers. So the story goes.

In this view, if jobs are unrewarding it must be due to either the nature of technology or the preference of workers for higher incomes as opposed to desirable jobs. The desirability of jobs is reflected in the wage at which the worker is willing to accept the job, or what economists call the supply price of labor. Indeed, most of us, in deciding our life's work, make some trade-offs between income and job desirability. The employer does have some incentive to make work attractive, hence lowering his labor costs. But does this mechanism render work responsive to the needs or wills of workers? We believe not.

First, there is ample evidence, to be reviewed shortly, that even within the confines of existing technologies work could be organized so as to be more productive and more satisfying to workers. That these opportunities exist and are resisted by employers points to the unresponsiveness of job structure and content to worker needs. Second, technology itself is not the result of the inexorable and unidimensional advance of knowledge. Rather, it reflects the monopolization of control over new investment and effective control over technical information by capitalists and their representatives. The history of technology thus represents an accumulation of past choices made for the most part by and in the interests of employers. Hence even the limits of present technologies cannot be exempted from analysis. We must ask, "Was the process determining the path of technological change responsive to the needs of workers?" Lastly, there is ample evidence that the choices made by workers facing a trade-off between higher incomes and more participatory workplaces (or other work objectives) are systematically biased by the compulsory forms of socialization—especially schooling—imposed on young people.

We conclude that work is a social phenomenon which under capitalism follows a logic of its own, apart from the wills of the mass of individuals affected by it. Thus alienated labor is a condition of capitalist society. It is neither a psychological condition of workers nor a product of modern "mass-production technology."

That the hierarchical division of labor is not necessarily efficient contradicts many deeply held, but empirically unsubstantiated, opinions. We shall discuss three of these. The first such opinion is that the productivity of capitalist enterprise and its victory over traditional work-forms during the Industrial Revolution demonstrate the unique compatibility of the hierarchical division of labor with advanced technology. The second opinion is that the fragmentation and routinization of jobs leads, in itself, to increased productivity, despite its deleterious effect on worker satisfaction. The third, and most important, is that no other known form of work organization is more productive than the hierarchical division of labor. We believe all three are incorrect.

Rather we believe that the success of the factory system in the early stages of the Industrial Revolution was due primarily to the tapping of cheap labor supplies, the extension of the hours of work, and the forced increase in the pace of work; that job fragmentation is a means of reducing the solidarity and power of workers; and that democratic participation in production tends to increase productivity.

The inability of new technologies to account for the emergence of the capitalist factory system in Great Britain has been documented by Stephen Marglin[3] ... He argues that the success of the capitalist production unit must be attributed to its efficacy as a means of economic and social control. First, if all workers could perform all tasks, their knowledge of the production process would allow them to band together and go into production for themselves. In the guild system this was prevented by legal restrictions—the guild-masters had control over the number of new masters admitted, and all production had to be under the direction of a legal guild-approved master. In "free enterprise" this form of control was interdicted.

Second, even within the capitalist firm, the boss's control depended on the lack of control of each worker. To allow all workers the capacity to deal knowledgeably and powerfully with all parts of the production process both increases their sense of control and autonomy and undercuts the boss's legitimacy as the coordinator of production. Yet it is this legitimacy which maintains his position of financial controller and intermediary between direct producers and consumers. Job enlargement and democratic worker control would soon threaten the political stability of the firm. That this policy of "divide and conquer" through task-fragmentation was central in the minds of bosses is amply illustrated in Marglin's cited essay.

But if early factories used technologies apparently similar to the contemporary work-er-controlled operations, why were the former able to undersell and eventually displace their more traditional competitors? To what was the increase in per capita productivity in the early Industrial Revolution due? The answer seems to lie in the system of hierarchical control as a direct means of increasing the employers' power over workers. Having all workers under one roof allowed the capitalist to increase drastically the length of the work week. Instead of making his or her own work-leisure choice, the worker was forced to accept a 12- or 15-hour work day, or have no work at all. Since all workers were paid more or less subsistence wages independent of the length of the work-day, the factory system drastically reduced labor costs. Moreover, the system of direct supervision in the factory allowed the capitalist to increase the pace of work and the exertion of the worker. Lastly, the factory system used pools of pauper, female, and child labor at much lower cost than that of able-bodied men.

As a result, the capitalist was able to pay generally higher weekly wages to the male labor force, while reducing the cost of output and appropriating huge profits. It was their greater capacity to accumulate capital, to reinvest and expand, which tipped the balance in favor of capitalist enterprise. But this was due to increased exertion of labor, not to the technical efficiency of the factory system. This situation forced the independent producers to increase their own work-day to meet their subsistence needs, given the falling prices of their product. In this way these producers maintained their position alongside the factory for over a quarter century.

Eventually, however, the factory system did win out on technical grounds. The reasons are interesting in light of our discussion of technological determinism. First, because only the capitalist producers had the financial resources to invest heavily in new machinery, inventors sought to meet their needs. They thus geared their innovations to types compatible with the social relations of factory production. Second, because of the large

[3]Stephen Marglin, "What Do Bosses Do? The Origins and Functions of Hierarchy in Capitalist Production," *The Review of Radical Political Economics*, Vol. 6, No. 2 (Summer 1974).

number of independent producers, it would have been impossible for them to protect patent rights, whereas the large size of the capitalist firm provided a stable and conspicuous market for the inventor. Third, most inventors aimed at allying with capitalist partners and going into production for themselves. All these factors lend to the pattern of technical innovation a strong bias toward the hierarchical, fragmented production relations of the capitalist firm.

The tremendous pace of technological change in the nineteenth century was of course a major factor in the success of the capitalist class and in the rapid international expansion of capitalism. And the development of new techniques, as well as the pressure for product standardization and rigid production scheduling, no doubt brought about changes in the social relations of production. Yet, our analysis, which draws heavily on Stephen Marglin's "What Do Bosses Do?" indicates that the division of labor and the power relations of the capitalist enterprise cannot be explained by technological necessity. In a path-breaking study of the development of the U.S. steel industry, Katherine Stone has documented that the social organization of work did not arise from technological necessity at all, but from the needs of management to *control* the process of production.[4] In the period from 1890 to 1910, steel came of age in the United States. Spurred by the merger activities of Andrew Carnegie, U.S. Steel became the world's first billion-dollar corporation, which, by 1901, controlled 80 percent of the U.S. market. This phenomenal growth, which involved large-scale introduction of new techniques and machine processes in production, was securely founded on the hierarchical division of labor. Yet the evidence clearly shows that the new social relations of steel production were *not* technologically determined.

Prior to 1890, steel production was characterized by a great degree of worker control over production. The group of skilled workers contracted with management, receiving a price per ton of steel based on a sliding scale which reflected the current market price. The skilled workers then hired other workers ("unskilled") whom they paid out of their pockets, and agreed on a division of receipts among themselves. Because of their knowledge and control of the work process, and through the power of their union (the Amalgamated Association of Iron, Steel and Tin Workers), the skilled workers had veto power over any management-proposed changes in the work process, including technical innovation.

This situation posed a crucial dilemma for the early steel magnates: How could technical innovation be introduced without the benefits accruing to the workers themselves? Clearly only by breaking the power of workers to control the process of production. In 1892, Henry Clay Frick was called on to do the job. Workers were locked out of the Homestead Mill, Pinkerton men were called in to enforce company decisions, and a "non-union shop" was declared. The Amalgamated Steel Workers Union was smashed, hierarchical procedures instituted, innovation proceeded apace, and the future of a high-growth and high-profit steel industry was assured. As David Brody concludes: "In the two decades after 1890, the furnace worker's productivity tripled in exchange for an income rise of one half; the steel worker's output doubled in exchange for an income rise of one fifth. . . . The accomplishment was possible only with a labor force powerless to oppose the decisions of the steel men."[5]

Here we have a clear case of profit rather than efficiency determining the social division of labor. But once centralized control is imposed, it does seem to follow that efficiency dictates fragmented and routinized jobs. Indeed, this is the converse of a general pro-

[4]Katherine Stone, "The Origins of Job Structures in the Steel Industry," *The Review of Radical Political Economics*, Vol. 6, No. 2 (Summer 1974).

[5]David Brody, *The Steel Workers in America: The Non-Union Era* (New York: Harper & Row, 1970).

position deduced from many laboratory experiments in organizational efficiency. Vroom has summed up the results of these laboratory exercises in his masterful survey of experimental literature in industrial social psychology. The evidence indicates, he writes, that "decentralized structures have an advantage for tasks which are difficult, complex, or unusual, while centralized structures are more effective for those which are simple and routinized."[6] Turning this proposition around, we find that, given that the corporate unit is based on centralized control, the most efficient technologies will be those involving routinized, dull, and repetitive tasks. In a decentralized environment, the reverse would be true. This shows that the common opinion as to the superior productivity of fragmentation, as based on the observed operation of centralized corporate enterprise, entails a false inference from the facts.

Finally, the opinion that there is no known organizational technique superior to hierarchical control, seems also to be controverted by the extensive evidence on the efficiency of worker participation. The results of dozens of studies indicate that when workers are given control over decisions and goal-setting, productivity rises dramatically. The recent HEW study, *Work in America*, records 34 cases of the reorganization of production toward greater worker participation which simultaneously raised productivity and worker satisfaction.[7] Also Blumberg concludes:

> There is scarcely a study in the entire literature which fails to demonstrate that satisfaction in work is enhanced or ... productivity increases accrue from a genuine increase in workers' decision-making power. Findings of such consistency, I submit, are rare in

social research ... the participative worker is an involved worker, for his job becomes an extension of himself and by his decisions he is creating his work, modifying and regulating it.[8]

But such instances of even moderate worker control are instituted only in marginal areas and in isolated firms fighting for survival. When the crisis is over, there is usually a return to "normal operating procedure." The threat of workers' escalating their demand for control is simply too great, and the usurpation of the prerogatives of hierarchical authority is quickly quashed. Efficiency in the broader sense is subordinated to the needs of bureaucratic control.

The lower productivity of the hierarchical division of labor must be ascribed directly to worker alienation. In a situation where workers lack control over both the process and product of their productive activities, their major preoccupation is to protect themselves from the arbitrary dictates of management. Their concern for the efficiency goals of management is at best perfunctory, and usually these goals are actively opposed as contrary to their interests. Significantly, many unions oppose current work reorganization schemes—even those allowing token worker participation—because workers have little defense against being displaced by productivity increases, and do not stand to share in whatever profit increases result. But this should not be allowed to obscure the fact that workers normally harbor a tremendous "reserve power" of effectiveness and inventiveness, awaiting only the proper conditions of control and integration to be liberated. The burden of proof has shifted markedly to those who contend that hierarchical forms of production are the necessary price of ever-increasing affluence. Work is for the most part "meaningless" and repressive not because of the nature of technology and the

[6]Victor H. Vroom, "Industrial Social Psychology," in G. Lindsey and E. Aaronsen (eds.), *The Handbook of Social Psychology* (Reading, Mass.: Addison-Wesley, 1969), p. 242.

[7]*Work in America*, Report of a Special Task Force to the Secretary of Health, Education and Welfare (Cambridge, Mass.: M.I.T. Press, 1973).

[8]Paul Blumberg, *Industrial Democracy* (New York: Schocken Books, 1969), p. 123.

division of labor, but because of the nature of the class structure and the social relations of production.

. . .

CONCLUSION

To locate the source of alienated labor in the social relations of capitalist production, and to understand the roots of these social relations in the class structure of society, is of fundamental importance. For social relations can be changed, and such changes in the past have been the major historical markers of progress toward civilization.

We propose a goal for the transformation of work, i.e., work as an *integrated process* wherein the dialectic relating our social being to our social becoming is strengthened rather than fragmented through the structure of the production unit. Integrated work means that jobs develop over time in keeping with our needs, to limits imposed by productive technology—a technology which, through demo-cratic control, itself moves toward liberated embodied forms. The various experiments in worker control—however limited their extent—show the viability of this vision.

A thoroughgoing industrial democracy must be a cornerstone of a socialist program in the contemporary capitalist world. Yet control over the immediate work process by producers themselves, essential as it may be in the revolutionizing of society, is certainly no panacea, and may have little meaning if isolated from other fundamental issues. Workers' control, by itself, does not provide answers to questions such as: What will be produced, how much power will individual productive units have in allocating resources, where will production be located, where will people live, what will be the approach to leisure and culture, the role of work and creativity? If our ultimate aim is human liberation, we must tackle much more than the workplace, and our analysis of alienated work must be part of a more general program of socialist transformation.

7.3 *Contradictions of the Labor Process in Monopoly Capitalism*

At the end of the last reading, Gintis and Bowles held out a vision of an integrated work process based on democratic control of the workplace and more general socialist transformation. But what are the prospects that current worker dissatisfaction can lead to such fundamental change? This is the principal question addressed by Howard Wachtel in the final reading of this chapter.

Wachtel first analyzes the sources of recent demands for worker control of enterprises in the United States by focusing on certain contradictions in the labor process that arise in the monopolistic stage of capitalist development. He then goes on to examine various possible responses to these contradictions by workers and by capitalists. Whether the existing contradictions can be resolved by capitalists in a manner that protects their basic interests, or whether the contradictions will give rise to a struggle by workers that successfully challenges these capitalist interests, depends to a large extent on whether a strong and radical working class movement can be developed out of the currently unorganized and diffuse opposition to the *status quo*.

The following is excerpted from "Class Consciousness and Stratification in the Labor Process" by HOWARD WACHTEL. From *The Review of Radical Political Economics*, 6, No. 1 (Spring 1974). Reprinted by permission of the author.

There appear to be two dominant contradictions involving the working class today. One involves the comparative decline in material insecurity from previous generations of workers and the consequent reorientation of working class demands, especially but not exclusively among young workers, from issues of wages and old age security to issues of worker control. The other involves a contradiction within bureaucracy and hierarchically stratified jobs, also converging toward a demand for worker control. As the labor process becomes more stratified in monopoly capitalism, supervision and hierarchy proliferate. And at some point resistance by workers to the proliferation of supervision and hierarchy manifests itself in action by workers at the point of production—some spontaneous, some organized—to resist the consequences of the stratification in the labor process. This contradiction in the labor process itself, when coupled with the decline in the disciplining effect of material insecurity, forms the basis for an analysis of current development among workers in the United States.

.   .   .

These contradictions derive from the logical functioning of monopoly capitalism, especially from the transformation from modern industry to monopoly capitalism. . . . First, the tendency for surplus value to rise, coupled with the economic gains won by workers (especially in the depression and ensuing world war years), has enabled the working class to capture a share of this rising surplus value. Second, though business cycles have by no means been expurgated, their severity has been muted. Young workers (under 35) lack the socialization of the severe hardships of the depressions and consequently respond less docilely to threats of firings than do some of their older counterparts. These economic gains, it is important to note, have also been won in part by the trade union movement which capitalized on the crisis of capitalism of the 1930's. Thus, the growth of trade unions, which for a while muted militant worker discontent, have themselves contributed to the creation of the conditions which have led to new contradictions and new working class demands.

To understand the qualitative dimension of these new working class demands, we must look at the work situation, especially at the contradiction in the process of labor force stratification, which historically has been an important weapon in the hands of capitalists and managers, used to weaken the strength of working class movements. The commodity fetishism of markets in capitalism is now joined in bureacratic economic organization by an "office fetishism"—"an aspect of exploitative relations. . . hidden behind the office," having the effect of creating "a mystification of the activities of office-holders."[1] But the internal logic of the functioning of bureacracy contains its own inherent contradiction:

> *A completely bureacratized organization would require that the number of rules be almost as great as the number of concrete decisions. Since this is impossible and the number of rules is much smaller, an important element of imprecision and unpredictability creeps into the organization. To cope with this defect, those in authority tend to multiply rules, whose sheer number and increasing inconsistency with each other have a strong negative effect on those who are required to observe these rules, and this drives them to inactivity.*[2]

The intersection of these two contradictions—the decline in the work disciplining

[1]Branko Horvat, *An Essay on Yugoslav Society* (New York: International Arts and Sciences Press, 1969), pp. 11, 13.

[2]*Ibid.*, p. 16.

aspect of economic insecurity and the proliferation of hierarchy, work rules, and work supervision—becomes manifested in the type of worker uprisings typified by Lordstown[3] (where the average age of the workers was under 25) and is revealed in the decline in the rate of increase of worker productivity that took place in the late 1960's.

The issue of worker productivity is a central one for capitalism, involving the basic production relation that determines the distribution of the rewards of net output at the point of production. It is particularly important for the profitability of the firm, faced as they have been recently with substantial international competition. In the late 1960's and early 1970's we have heard a great deal about the "productivity crisis." Between 1968 and 1969 the percent change in productivity was barely positive (officially stated at 0.4%), down from the meager productivity increases of 2.9% and 2.1% in the two previous years. Between 1969 and 1970 it was not much higher (only 1.0%) but thereafter has risen sharply to 3.6% and, most recently between 1971 and 1972, to 4.2%. These figures are important because the one short-term weapon that capital has is to speed up the production process thereby increasing labor productivity. This speed-up coincided during this period with the maturation of the two contradictions isolated for investigation here. To speed up requires more supervisory personnel to discipline workers into their new rate of work. Superimposed upon a declining willingness of workers newly integrated into this wage labor system, the imposition of increased hierarchy and supervision to increase labor productivity led to the Lordstown-type worker uprising.

Another quantitative indicator of developments in the labor process is unit labor costs which are a combination of the amount of

compensation a worker receives each hour and the amount of output the worker can produce each hour (labor productivity). Between 1959 and 1965 unit labor costs in manufacturing actually *declined by* 3.2%— that is, it cost the employer some 3.2% less to produce each unit of output in 1965 than it did in 1959. This is caused by a combination of comparatively large increases in productivity and low increases in wages. But between 1966 and 1972 unit labor costs *increased* by 23.3%—that is, it cost the employer over 23% more to produce each unit in 1972 than it did in 1966. Though wage increases are part of the reason for this sharp increase in unit labor costs, the slowing down of productivity increases plays an equally important role.

The combination of sluggish productivity increases coupled with the failure of speedups to increase productivity via the traditional weapon of increased stratification and supervision, led to real concern during this period. Especially important were the data showing the United States with the lowest rate of productivity increase between 1965 and 1972 among all its major trading competitors. This led to the formation of so-called "Productivity Councils" and a rash of studies proclaiming the decline of the "work ethic."

Summing up these concerns for industry and reflecting a no-compromise attitude about worker control, Joseph E. Godfrey, General Manager of the (in) famous General Motors Assembly Division, remarked: "Within reason and without endangering their health, if we can occupy a man for 60 minutes we've got that right." Marx could not have described the struggle over work time and the "ownership" of a worker's labor power better! Godfrey goes on to reveal another critical point about workers productivity. The year-to-year changes in productivity involve primarily rearrangement of the existing technology by speed-ups rather than the introduction of fancy new machines: "A typical example would be to rearrange a

---

[3]An important strike in 1972 involving a highly stratified and automated GM Vega factory and young workers drawn from rural and semi-rural towns.

man's work area so that he no longer has to walk to get needed parts but can simply reach for them. With the time saved, the worker might be asked to put on an additional part." James Roche, chairman of the board of GM, put the matter more succinctly, in his *Christmas Message* to GM's 794,000 employees:

> *The company did not seek extra effort beyond a "fair day's work," but did expect increased output per man hour from better equipment and methods and most importantly by the* cooperation of labor. (*emphasis added*)[4]

. . .

Judson Gooding, an editor of *Fortune* and chronicler for the advanced segment of management on these issues, reports that the quit rate at Ford was 18% in 1969, reaching a height of 25% in some plants. And absenteeism doubled at Ford and GM between 1960 and 1970, amounting to an average of 5% reaching a high of 10% on Fridays and Mondays. In response, "Some GM plants, groping for a solution, have even tried rewarding regular attendance with Green Stamps, or initialed glasses that over the months . . . form a set." But as a GM official commented, "If they won't come in for $30.50 a day, they won't come in for monogrammed glasses."[5] Work quality, as well, has suffered:

> *At one Ford assembly plant, the manager . . . had to keep 160 repairmen busy fixing defects on brand-new cars just off the assembly line a few feet away, where 840 men labored imperfectly to assemble those same cars.*[6]

. . .

Thus the contradiction in the labor process is complete: worker discontent, manifested in absenteeism, turnover of jobs, sabotage, and decline in productivity, derives from the hierarchy and irrationality of bureacratic management (the absence of worker control) which exacerbates the tendency toward the decline in worker productivity due to the proliferation of inconsistent work rules and the proliferation of supervisory personnel. But capitalists respond in the system's most logical fashion by trying to increase worker productivity through speed-ups, enforced by even more rules and more supervisory personnel.[7] Lacking the previous strength of the disciplining threat of firings, young workers (especially) resist and respond with militant wildcat strikes such as Lordstown and with more passive forms of resistance such as absenteeism, turnover, slowdowns, sabotage, and poor work quality.

In short, the rise in material security for workers won by trade unions out of the growing surplus value and the stratification of workers by capitalists as a response to this worker organization (and ultimately legitimized by trade unions) have been the instruments for the creation of new work situations and "new workers" which have now created new contradictions. Without employing a dialectical methodology, the authors of the government-sponsored report, *Work in America*, concluded (dialectically) that: "It may be argued that the very success of industry and organized labor in meeting the basic needs of workers has unintentionally spurred demands for esteemable and fulfilling jobs."[8] The manifest response of the relevant parties to these contradictions will be examined in the next section of this paper.

---

[7]This is the initial response of capital and the one most consistent with the basic production (and therefore) power relations of capitalism. However, if these speed-up schemes are resisted by workers, a dialectic then arises in which capital proclaims the inherent "inhumaneness" of speed-ups and responds with "human relations" or "job enrichment" schemes. We return to this point later.

[8]*Work in America*, Report of a Special Task Force to the Secretary of Health, Education and Welfare (Cambridge, Mass.: M.I.T. Press, 1973), p. 12.

---

[4]Judson Gooding, *The Job Revolution* (New York: Walker and Company 1972), pp. 69–70.

[5]*Ibid.*, p. 12.

[6]*Ibid.*, p. 18.

WORKER AND CORPORATE RESPONSES TO CONTRADICTIONS IN THE LABOR PROCESS

The decline in labor productivity and the concern among corporate leaders with the decline in work discipline (labelled the decline in the "work ethic") have recently led to governmental and foundation financial support for studies on "what ails the blue-collar worker," culminating with the introduction of legislation (S.736) in the U.S. Senate by Senator Kennedy and 18 of his colleagues which provides for "research for solutions to the problem of alienation among American workers and to provide for pilot projects and provide technical assistance to find ways to deal with that problem. . . . ."

Though the statistical survey results of these various studies are interesting, we should be cautious in reading too much political significance into them, and we must be careful in interpreting their results in relation to the question of class consciousness. In general, these studies report widespread work dissatisfaction among all occupations, income levels ages, races, and sexes. However, the intensity of dissatisfaction on all dimensions is greater among young workers (under 30). The most dissatisfied group of workers in the Sheppard-Herrick study[9] are black workers under age 30, followed by workers under age 30 who have some college education, and women workers under age 30. And these tendencies are fairly constant over all income groups among young workers up to $10,000 per year. Of the issues that concern young workers, job control—including job rotation, quality of work, worker participation—are more important than wage and security issues. Herrick and Quinn[10] ranked

job characteristics most closely associated with job satisfaction and found that of the top ten characteristics, only one could be considered a wage or security issue (greater paid vacation), the remaining characteristics being associated with job control.

The report of the U.S. Department of Health, Education and Welfare, *Work in America*, reached similar conclusions with regard to the higher level of dissatisfaction among young workers. They attribute this to the following: (1) young people have higher expectations as a result of their higher education; (2) the greater material security of young people "makes them less tolerant of unrewarding jobs"; (3) "All authority in our society is being challenged"; (4) "Many former students are demanding what they achieved in part on their campuses . . . —a voice in setting the goals of the organization"; and (5) "young blue-collar workers, who have grown up in an environment in which equality is called for in all institutions are demanding the same rights . . . as university graduates." Summing up the present failures of the human relations school of management (in which workers are treated better without changing the jobs or who controls them), the HEW report concludes:

> Simplified tasks for those who are not simple-minded, close supervision by those whose legitimacy rests only on a hierarchical structure, and jobs that have nothing but money to offer in an affluent age are simply rejected. For many of the new workers, the monotony of work and scale of organization and their inability to control the pace and style of work are cause for a resentment which they, unlike older workers, do not repress.[11]

In sum, two themes emerge from all the studies: first, that job satisfaction is more closely associated with job control rather than wage and security issues; and second, that workers (especially young workers) see job dissatisfaction firmly rooted in hierar-

[9]See Harold L. Sheppard and Neal Q. Herrick, *Where Have All the Robots Gone?* (New York: The Free Press, 1972).

[10]Neal Q. Herrick and Robert P. Quinn, "Who's Unhappy?" *Manpower* (January 1972), p. 22.

[11]*Work in America*, p. 18. [Ed. note—See Section 7.1, p. 268.]

chically stratified work situations. Both of these findings are consistent with our previous discussion of contradictions among the working class in monopoly capitalism today. Further, we find that the most dissatisfied groups—young blacks, young women, and young workers with some college education—contain workers who are entering into *new* social relations of production or are entering social relations of production far below their expectations and the expectations that society's ideology fosters. This is much the same as petty commodity producers becoming wage-laborers and entering into new social relations of production, with the consequent radicalization of those workers in the period Marx was analyzing.

· · ·

The "stick" of more hierarchy, supervision and stratification in work in order to increase productivity by enforcing a speed-up are not the only devices which capital has tried when faced with work discipline problems. They have some "carrots" in their bag of tricks as well. Earlier in this century, as a response to the workers' opposition to the excesses of Taylorism, a "human relations" school of management flourished in which the idea was to make the jobs more pleasant while not altering the control over the production process. Today, complementing these human relations experiments, are experiments in workers' participation, frequently called "job enrichment" schemes. But the central question is *Who is getting rich from job enrichment?* . . .

There is little question in the minds of capitalists and their managers that job enrichment of the workers' participation sort is good business (especially in view of the fact that the old hierarchical system became bad business). The job enrichment "movement" has been receiving increasing attention in the popular press. An article in *Reader's Digest*[12] proclaims: "Worker alienation

means low morale and productivity." And "Employers are realizing that people are capable of doing far more than their jobs either require or allow. . . ." HEW reports on dozens of profitable experiments in various forms of workers' participation.

· · ·

Such experiments in workers' participation as we are witnessing today are not new in our history, and they usually arise in response to a crisis in the old form of production caused by worker resistance. Blumberg[13] reports on dozens of experiments earlier in this century with workers' participation schemes. In nearly all instances these schemes where introduced during a period of crisis in the production process and were eliminated once the crisis had been overcome and because workers started (gradually) to wrest more and more control from management. Almost without exception, these schemes of workers' participation produced sustained increases in rates of productivity change. . . .

This returns us to a principal contradiction of capitalist production, namely the contradiction between the progressive development of the means of production being retarded by the less progressive social relations of production, rooted, as they are, in property relations. In the present context, there is ample evidence that the forces of production (productivity) are retarded by the relations of production (the hierarchical structure of stratified jobs). Workers are manifesting an antagonistic response to hierarchically stratified work relations. Moreover, a more profound inhibition to the further expansion of the means of production arises under capitalist social relations of production—namely the retardation of technical innovation by workers who stand to lose (individually) rather than benefit from technical innovation since they do not control the distribution of the fruits of technical innovation.

[12]Trevor Armbrister, "Beating Those Blue-Collar Blues," *Reader's Digest* (April 1973), pp. 231–240.

[13]Paul Blumberg, *Industrial Democracy* (New York: Schocken Books, 1969), chapter 5.

What we are witnessing is an attempt to mediate this contradiction, reducing its antagonistic edge, by restructuring work (perhaps temporarily, perhaps permanently), by altering *slightly* the control of the production process. History has shown that such timid steps towards socialist *form* without socialist *substance* are less likely to be successful in contrast to their success under socialism. If left solely within the bounds of capitalism, such changes in work will constitute a most important reform, but a reform within capitalism nonetheless. But the question is: can you be a little bit socialist or have a little bit of workers' control? Or does a dialectic arise in which workers are propelled by their experiences towards higher and higher demands for the elimination of capitalists and managers as a class once workers realize that it is they who are most central to production and the managers who are an artifact of capitalist hierarchical control and work stratification and who become superfluous once stratification and hierarchy in work are eliminated?

In short, the social organization of the enterprise must reproduce a workers' consciousness consistent with the capitalist relations of production embodied in work hierarchy and job stratification. A "noncapitalist" social organization of the enterprise—embodied in job rotation, worker participation in decisions, reduced hierarchy and stratification—may erode the very worker consciousness required to reproduce the capitalist relations of production. If this should happen, then one can expect increased militancy within the working class at the point of production reflecting a challenge to the decision-making hegemony of capitalists and their managers.

Several caveats about this analysis are warranted. First, we do not know if the same level of dissatisfaction (and its distribution among workers) is unique to the present working class or whether it was common to other generations too. It is fairly widely accepted that trade union leaders in the past,

as well as today, have negotiated away job control demands of rank-and-file workers in exchange for wage and security concessions. Second, we do not know what political form (if any) these discontents will take. If they remain rooted in economic concerns, then the politicization needed for class consciousness will not arise.

The political direction of workers in response to current contradictions is still uncharted, though rank-and-file caucuses are certainly one significant development. We have already seen how one giant monopoly capitalist company (GM) has responded to the situation and how GM workers have responded to GM. But not all corporate elites respond by increasing the intensity of labor and the number of supervisory personnel. Gooding, HEW and Sheppard-Herrick detail many experiments with job enrichment and worker participation designed to mute this new form of worker discontent. Gooding is quite explicit when it comes to the reasons for responding creatively:

> It would seem preferable by far to introduce the improvements in work conditions before they are demanded, at the pace and time chosen by management, rather than being forced to make radical changes, under union pressure, at times not of management's choosing. . . . . The choice comes down to moving with the exigencies of the times—not mollycoddling but accomodating the demands of people for more control over their environments—or existing in a grim atmosphere of discontent or active hatred.[14]

On the other side, trade union officials, with few exceptions, have not been responsive to these new worker demands. Sheppard and Herrick asked employers and union officials whether they believed workers are "very or somewhat satisfied with their opportunity to do interesting and enjoyable work." In contrast to the low proportions of workers who thought they do interesting work, 85 percent of employers and 58 percent of union officials thought workers were satisfied with their

[14]Gooding, *The Job Revolution*, pp. 15, 17.

work conditions. Typical of the union reaction is that of Frank Pollara, assistant research director of the AFL-CIO:

> *Motivation, as I understand it, is an abstract concept that has very little relevance, very little pertinence, very little meaning for the industrial world today.*[15]

Other union leaders, notably Irving Bluestone of the UAW, have responded in a more progressive fashion:

> *A departure from the miniaturization of the job embraces the idea of bringing the democratic institution of society into the work place. Participatory management at all levels, worker decision-making, broader distribution of authority, increasing rather than diminishing responsibility and accountability are combined with the engineering of more interesting jobs, with the opportunity to exercise a meaningful measure of autonomy and to utilize more varied skills.*[16]

In sum, with the relative decline in material insecurity among workers today compared to the previous generation of workers, workers are now concentrating on nonwage demands of the job control sort. Coupled with the proliferation of work stratification, the relative decline in material insecurity has led to intensified job dissatisfaction, manifested in sporadic outbursts which cripple production and an overall decline in labor productivity. Initially, capital responds with a larger dose of the same medicine, namely increased work supervision, hierarchy and work speed-ups. But part of the problem is caused by the very character of the labor process under monopoly capitalism which is characterized by work speed-up, hierarchy and supervision. So the medicine of monopoly capitalism merely feeds the disease. Failing these remedies, some of the more advanced segments of the monopoly capitalist managers suddenly discover the innate virtues of job enrichment and worker participation. The important question for radicals,

beyond an understanding of this dynamic in the labor process, is whether a taste of worker participation offered by corporate managers to ride out the immediate crisis can be contained, or whether once put into practice, workers' participation develops a dynamic of its own which leads to more radical working class demands for an embryonic form of socialism appropriate to the character of advanced monopoly capitalist economies.

The critical political questions facing radicals touch on an issue beyond the scope of this paper—namely, the transition to socialism in advanced monopoly capitalist countries. The critical questions are as follows:

1. Will the new contradictions in the labor process outlined in this paper generate a politicization of workers, creating a working class consciousness which enables workers to unify themselves politically, thereby transcending the disunifying elements of stratification?

2. If workers do become politicized, then will they develop a radical or reformist class consciousness?

3. Can workers begin to define their own radical ideology and political programs, within their own organizations, transcending their day-to-day work situation in order to see their problems as *systemic* rather than personal?

Answers to these three questions will portend crucial political developments over the next decade.

Along all these dimensions, the contradictions will, no doubt, become more severe as international competition places increased "productivity pressure" on domestic production. The first (and most logical) response by capitalists will follow the lines suggested by the theory developed earlier, namely speed-ups and the intensification of the use of labor. To discipline workers, we can expect even more unemployment created [by the capitalist state].[17] But these developments are

---

[15]Quoted in *ibid.*, p. 179.

[16]Irving Bluestone, "Democratizing the Workplace" (mimeo, June 22, 1972).

[17][Ed. note—See chapter 12, and especially Crotty and Rapping, Section 12.4, p. 461, for an analysis of the employment objectives of a capitalist state.]

secondary in the sense that they are external forces which impinge upon a set of contradictions (and exacerbate them) which are already inherent in the production process under monopoly capitalism. And the new dimension added by monopoly capitalism to the traditional contradictions of competitive capitalism inheres in the labor stratification process. Combined with a relative decline in material insecurity won from earlier working class struggles, the disciplining force of alienated work is now less powerful. However, the outcome of these contradictions in terms of a politicized working class must await the actual practice which radicals and others engage in over the next years as well as the outcome of the challenge from radical rank-and-file caucuses which have been mounted in trade unions against their established leadership.

CHAPTER 8

Inequality

CAPITALISM HAS GENERATED a tremendous increase in the productive capacity of the capitalist economies of North America, Western Europe, Japan, Australia, and New Zealand. Yet this tremendous growth in the forces of production has been accompanied by vast inequalities in the distribution of the fruits of that production. The disparity in income and wealth between the industrialized nations at the center of the world capitalist system and the underdeveloped areas on the periphery has been increasing continously since the early days of colonial plunder. Moreover, *within* each capitalist nation tremendous fortunes co-exist with indescribable poverty in spite of the growth of the modern "welfare state." And while inequalities in income and wealth reveal the primary dimension of inequality in a capitalist society, they also give rise to further inequalities—in power, political influence, occupational status, and privilege —which exist alongside and reinforce the inequalities in income and wealth.

It is no historical accident that great inequalities have always characterized capitalism. Quite the contrary: a significant degree of income inequality is inherent in the capitalist mode of production. The generation of an unequal distribution of income can be traced directly to the operation of the basic capitalist institutions described in Chapter 3.

THE NECESSITY OF INCOME INEQUALITY

The most fundamental characteristic of the distribution of income under capitalism is that it is tied directly to the production process. The only legitimate claims to income arise from possession of "factors of production" that are used to produce goods and services.[1] Factors of production can be divided into two basic categories: labor-power and the (physical) means of production. Labor-power includes all of the productive capacities of human beings, from the most elementary manual ability to the most sophisticated technical skills. The means of production include all forms of property devoted to productive purposes: land, natural resources, buildings, plant and equipment, etc. The income received by any individual depends on how much labor-power and/or means of production he or she possesses, and on how highly the factors are valued in the relevant market.

People who sell their own labor-power receive *labor income* in the form of wages or salaries; the amount of such income an individual receives depends on wage or salary rates established in the labor market. Although the nature of the work varies enormously from one job to another, people must do some work in order to receive labor income. People who own means of production are in a position to receive *property income*

[1]There are other sources of income from which some people do receive a limited amount of income in capitalist societies—e.g., welfare agencies, gifts, prizes, crime, etc. However, such sources are always treated as exceptions to the normal capitalist rules of the game— exceptions that arise from unusually distressing or pathological circumstances.

without doing any work. People may own means of production directly (e.g., by owning a piece of land or a building) or indirectly (e.g., by owning stock that represents some fraction of the assets of a corporation). In either case, such ownership entitles the owner to a share of the surplus value that is realized when the means of production are combined with labor-power to produce output that is sold on the market. This surplus value is received as property income in the form of profits, interest, or rent.

The class structure of a capitalist society is reflected in the sources of people's incomes. Capitalists are those whose primary source of income is ownership of means of production. Capitalists may (and usually do) also hold jobs that provide them with labor income, but they are still capitalists as long as their property income is substantial enough to enable them to live without working if they chose to do so. Workers are those who own little or no means of production and who depend therefore on labor income for their livelihood. Some people—such as small-scale family farmers, independent professionals, and small business proprietors—receive income that represents a return on both their own labor-power and some means of production that they possess. It may be difficult to determine what proportion of their income is attributable to labor and what proportion is attributable to property. But with the continuing development of the capitalist mode of production such "intermediate" classes of people become less and less significant as a proportion of the total population.[2] Most of the income generated in an advanced capitalist economy can be identified clearly as labor income or property income, and most people can be classified unambiguously as workers or capitalists.

The most basic source of income inequality in a capitalist society is the vastly unequal distribution of property income that results from the capitalist-class monopoly of the means of production. Under capitalism a small minority of the population (the capitalists) own most of the means of production and a large majority (the workers) own virtually nothing productive other than their own labor-power.[3] Since income from property is dependent on ownership of property, this concentration in ownership of the means of production results in a corresponding concentration in property income. In fact, it is generally true that the rate of return to productive property increases with the size of the property owned; thus the degree of inequality in the distribution of property income tends to be even greater than the degree of inequality in the distribution of property ownership.[4]

In advanced capitalist societies property income typically accounts for roughly 25 to 30 percent of total national income.[5] Even if labor income were distributed equally among the entire population, the large inequality in the distribution of property income would lead to a highly unequal distribution of total income. In fact, however, capitalism requires an unequal distribution of labor income as well as property income.

A high degree of inequality in the distribution of labor income arises necessarily from the alienated character of labor in a capitalist enterprise. Since workers under capitalism are deprived of control over the process and product of their work, they will rarely be motivated to work by intrinsic aspects of the work process or by any sense of dedication to the enterprise, the community, or the society as a whole. As long as work itself is perceived as a burden to be endured rather than a creative or a socially rewarding endeavor, workers must be motivated to work by extrinsic re-

[2]See Reich, Section 5.1, p. 179, for a discussion of long-term changes in the class structure of the United States.

[3]See Table 8-D, p. 300, for estimates of the distribution of ownership of the means of production (income-producing wealth) in the United States.

[4]See the afterword to Section 4.3, p. 140, for evidence that larger units of productive property tend to gain higher rates of return than smaller units.

[5]For evidence on this point, see Simon Kuznets, *Modern Economic Growth* (New Haven: Yale University Press, 1966), pp. 167–86.

wards such as income with which they can purchase material goods and services. For the same reasons people in a capitalist society generally require a monetary incentive such as a wage increase or a promotion to a higher-paying job in order to be induced to acquire new skills and increase their productive abilities through education, job training, etc.

In principle, nonmonetary status rewards could substitute for income rewards and provide an extrinsic psychic rather than material motivation for work. But capitalist ideology (promoted by powerful ideological institutions such as schools, the media, etc.) places so high a value on monetary success that significant status can rarely be achieved independently of income. Hence, status rewards unrelated to monetary success cannot be expected to play a significant motivational role under capitalism. Instead, material gain incentives are generally necessary to encourage the development of productive attributes and to call forth the energies of workers who do not control the work process.

In order for a material gain incentive system to operate effectively, there must be a highly differentiated hierarchy of jobs with correspondingly differentiated levels of pay. This is not to suggest that *no* work would be done in a capitalist society in the absence of significant labor income differentials. The point is rather that the capitalist mode of production, because it depends on alienated labor, is characterized by a serious conflict between income equality on the one hand and economic efficiency on the other. A high degree of income equality could be attained in a capitalist society only at a very high cost in productive efficiency. In order to remain economically viable, the capitalist mode of production therefore requires significant inequalities in the distribution of labor income.

If people with high property incomes received low labor incomes, and vice versa, then the inequality in the distribution of labor would offset to some extent the inequality in the distribution of property incomes. It is quite evident, however, that in the real world of capitalism the opposite is true. Inequalities

in labor income tend to reinforce inequalities in property income because one form of income can be used to generate the other. Capitalists with substantial property income can use it to help themselves (and their children) enhance their labor skills and command higher salaries for their labor-power. Similarly, the relatively few privileged workers who manage to reach high-paying jobs can afford to invest some of their labor income in the acquisition of productive property. On the opposite end of the scale, those people with no property income find it much more difficult to raise their labor income, and vice versa.

For the reasons discussed in the preceding paragraphs, we can conclude that a substantial degree of inequality in the distribution of overall income is inherent in the nature of capitalist institutions. This means that only a complete transformation of the mode of production could eliminate income inequality in currently capitalist societies. Such a transformation would not only have to eliminate private ownership of the means of production; it would also have to develop a new system of work organization that did not rely on individual material gain incentives to motivate people to work.

THE DEGREE OF INCOME INEQUALITY

While a significant amount of inequality is inevitable, the actual degree of income inequality in any given capitalist society will depend on a number of variable factors. Particularly significant is the division of total income between property income and labor income, respectively. Property income is much more highly concentrated than labor income, since only a small minority of people own significant quantities of income-producing property while most people earn some amount of labor income. Moreover, there are limits beyond which salaries do not rise (even automobile executives and sports superstars in the United States today do not get salaries as high as a million dollars a year), while there are no limits to the amount of income-producing property that a person can own. Therefore, the higher the share of property income in total national income, the more unequal the overall distribution of income is likely to be.

One of the most important determinants of the share of property income is the state of the class struggle between capitalists and workers. As long as capitalists maintain control of the means of production, they can assure that property income will persist, for they can pose the very real threat of withholding their property from production if they do not receive some income for it. However the share of property income in total income is variable within a certain range; it is likely to increase when workers as a class are weak and to fall when workers are strong.[6] Capitalists obviously have a class interest in weakening the bargaining power of workers. One way in which they attempt to do this is by fostering antagonisms within the working class which undermine the potential for working class unity. Indeed, a differentiated hierarchy of jobs (described earlier as essential for a material gain incentive system) is often developed by capitalists to a much greater degree than is functionally necessary because it helps to weaken workers' bargaining power by segmenting the labor force.[7] But capitalists do not always succeed in dominating workers in such ways; there are circumstances in which workers are able to improve their bargaining power and increase their share of total income. Unless the resulting income gains are concentrated in a relatively privileged segment of the labor force, they will lead to a more equal overall distribution of income.

The exercise of economic and political power can affect the overall distribution of income in other ways as well. Without necessarily changing the relative shares of prop-

erty and labor income, powerful classes or groups of people can use their power to change the distribution of property income or labor income in their own favor. We have seen in Chapter 4 how the capital accumulation process tends to increase the concentration of ownership of means of production in the hands of the wealthy, as large companies jointly monopolize industries and increase their own profits. Similarly, people with relatively good educational backgrounds are generally able to assure themselves (and their children) of better opportunities to increase their earnings than people from less privileged classes. And in Chapters 9 and 10 we will see how discrimination against women and blacks reduces their income-earning capacity relative to men and whites.

Finally, the state plays an extremely important role in determining the final outcome of the income distributional process. This is not only because the pattern of government taxation and transfers affects the level of disposable income available to each individual. The government also profoundly affects the pre–tax-and-transfer income of individuals by its expenditure patterns (which firms and industries it chooses to purchase goods and services from), its subsidies (which industries are favored), its regulatory policies (what rates airlines, utilities, etc. can charge), its macroeconomic policies (what will be the rate of unemployment and inflation), its attitude toward the wage bargaining process (under what circumstances will strikes be tolerated), and—in general—its enforcement of the legal rules of the game under which the capitalist economy operates. Thus the current distribution of income depends to a considerable extent on the ability of different classes and groups to get the government to act on their behalf.

We have seen in Chapter 6 that wealthy capitalists are clearly in the strongest position to shape government policy. But there are also circumstances in which poorer groups may be able to mobilize enough power in the political arena to improve their economic position. On the one hand, organized workers

[6]See Crotty and Rapping, Section 12.4, p. 461, for an analysis of the relationship between property and labor income shares and the strength of the working class in the United States.

[7]See Edwards, Reich, and Gordon, Section 5.4, p. 200.

may develop enough strengh to use orthodox political methods (electing pro-labor representatives, etc.) to force the state to take some actions in their favor. On the other hand, various oppressed groups with little access to orthodox channels of power may take to the street in protest demonstrations, riots, etc., forcing the state to ameliorate their condition in the interest of preserving the stability of the society as a whole. Whatever the reasons for it, however, such income redistribution in favor of the poor would have to stop far short of equality because of the systemic capitalist need for an unequal distribution of income.

In the three readings in this chapter we will turn from these theoretical considerations to examine some of the salient facts about the generation and reproduction of inequality in our own society. The first reading documents the persistence of inequalities in the distribution of income and wealth in the United States. The second examines a major government program designed to help the poor— the welfare system—and investigates why it has had so little effect on the overall distribution of income. The last reading shifts the focus from the *structure* of inequality to the *dynamics* of inequality; it analyzes why the American educational system, ostensibly an important means of equalizing opportunity,

has in fact served primarily to perpetuate inequality by transmitting it from one generation to the next.

The persistence of inequality in the United States is clearly an important element in our critique of American capitalism. Whether it is also likely to give rise to contradictions that could threaten the future viability of the system is not clear. In the past, mounting protests by impoverished groups have often been warded off by judicious redistributional policies on the part of the government; for example, Franklin Roosevelt's New Deal policies helped to alleviate the problems of the poor and unemployed in 1930s. More generally, the long-run growth of total income in the United States has made it possible for the *absolute* level of income of the poor to increase even without any change in their *relative* position in the overall distribution. These same processes may continue to contain protests against income inequality in the future. But as we shall see in Section 11.1, there is reason to believe that the long-run rate of growth of total income in the United States will slow down, and this could seriously exacerbate the tensions arising from the persistent inequalities we discuss in this and the following two chapters.

8.1   *Capitalism and Inequality in the United States*

In the following reading Frank Ackerman and Andrew Zimbalist present detailed information on the distribution of income and wealth in the United States. The importance of property ownership as a source of income inequality emerges clearly from their presentation, as does the role of government in maintaining the overall pattern of inequality.

In this essay we first document the extent of income and wealth inequality in the United States; we then consider the effect of

taxes and government spending on the distribution of income and wealth; and, finally, we relate the observed inequalities in the

TABLE 8-A DISTRIBUTION OF BEFORE-TAX FAMILY INCOME

	1974	1969	1964	1960	1956	1950	1947
Poorest fifth	5.4%	5.6%	5.2%	4.9%	5.0%	4.5%	5.0%
Second fifth	12.0	12.3	12.0	12.0	12.4	12.0	11.8
Middle fifth	17.6	17.6	17.7	17.6	17.8	17.4	17.0
Fourth fifth	24.1	23.4	24.0	23.6	23.7	23.5	23.1
Richest fifth	41.0	41.0	41.1	42.0	41.2	42.6	43.0
Richest 5%	15.3	14.7	15.7	16.8	16.3	17.0	17.2

SOURCE: U.S. Census Bureau, *Current Population Reports*, Series P-60, No. 75, p. 26 and No. 99, p. 8.

TABLE 8-B DISTRIBUTION OF BEFORE-TAX INCOME AMONG UNRELATED
INDIVIDUALS

	1974	1964	1947
Poorest fifth	3.4%	2.4%	1.9%
Second fifth	7.7	7.1	5.8
Middle fifth	13.7	12.8	11.9
Fourth fifth	24.3	24.5	21.4
Richest fifth	50.9	53.1	59.1
Richest 5%	21.0	22.6	33.3

SOURCE: U.S. Census Bureau, *Current Population Reports*, Series P-60, No. 52, p. 7, and No. 99, p. 8.

United States to the class structure of the capitalist mode of production.

THE DISTRIBUTION OF INCOME AND WEALTH

Income

The best measure of ability to purchase goods and services is after-tax income. However, appropriate data exist only for the distribution of before-tax income, so we must look at that first and consider the tax structure separately. A good way to illustrate the income distribution is to rank the population by income and measure the percentage of total personal income received by the highest-income fifth of the population, the next fifth, and so on. The more income going to the top fifth and the less going to the bottom fifth, the more unequal is the distribution of income.

The Census Bureau collects income statistics separately for families of two or more people and for "unrelated individuals" not living in family units. In 1974, there were 190 million people living in families and 19 mil-

lion "unrelated individuals."[1] Tables 8-A and 8-B present the distribution of income for both groups.

Table 8-A shows that since World War II the poorest 20 percent of all families have consistently received less than 6 percent of total family income, while the richest 20 percent have gotten over 40 percent. In 1974, the top 5 percent of all families received over 15 percent of total family income, or nearly three times as much as the entire bottom 20 percent.[2]

[1]U.S. Census Bureau, *Current Population Reports*, Series P-60, No. 99, pp. 1, 19.

[2]In 1974, the dollar incomes corresponding to the income groups shown in Tables 1 and 2 were as follows:

Bottom Income in:	Families	Unrelated Individuals
Poorest fifth	0	0
Second fifth	$ 6,500	$ 2,095
Middle fifth	$10,722	$ 3,300
Fourth fifth	$14,916	$ 5,636
Richest fifth	$20,445	$ 9,296
Richest 5%	$31,948	$15,658

SOURCE: Ibid, p. 8.

The income of individuals who don't live in families (Table 8-B) is more unequally distributed than that of families: in 1974 the top fifth got 51 percent of income among unrelated individuals, compared to 41 percent among families. But while the family distribution is quite stable over time, the individual distribution has been growing more equal. Between 1947 and 1974 the share of the top fifth dropped from 59 to 51 percent of individual income, with the gain distributed over all four other fifths. This is probably due to the rise of social security and private pension payments to retired people, who often do not live in family units. (In 1974, only 14 percent of family heads were 65 or older, compared to 34 percent of unrelated individuals, and 40 percent of the bottom four-fifths of unrelated individuals. So increased income for retired people should affect the unrelated individuals' distribution far more than the family distribution.)[3]

The growth in income equality among individuals is not likely to continue. The gains associated with large numbers of people starting to receive social security or pensions cannot be repeated because social security coverage is already widespread, and private pensions are no longer expanding rapidly. Furthermore, both social security and most private pension plans are running out of money[4] and may not be able to keep up their present levels of payments; the immediate prospects are for less, not more, real income transfers to retired people.

Tables 8-A and 8-B are based on the Census Bureau's definition of personal money income, which includes government and other transfers to individuals (unemployment insurance, welfare, social security, pensions, etc.) but excludes capital gains (that is, the increase in the value of assets such as corporate stocks). Because one-half of capital gains are tax-exempt, stockholders generally prefer

capital gains to dividends; corporations systematically retain earnings rather than pay them out in dividends, so capital gains are a customary source of income for many rich people. A complete picture of income distribution should include capital gains.

Table 8-C presents a rough adjustment of the share of the top 20 percent of families to include estimated capital gains.[5] When capital gains are included, even the slight apparent decline in the income share of the top fifth of families vanishes. We conclude therefore that when capital gains are included, the distribution of family income has not essentially changed since World War II. (A similar adjustment in unrelated individual income would reduce but not eliminate the drop in the top fifth's share.)

TABLE 8-C CAPITAL GAINS AND THE TOP FIFTH'S SHARE OF FAMILY INCOME

Year	Share of Top Fifth Without Capital Gains	Total Reported Net Capital Gains	Share of Top Fifth with Capital Gains
	(all figures are percent of total family income)		
1947	43.0	2.2%	44.2%
1950	42.6%	2.6	44.1
1956	41.2	2.8	42.8
1960	42.0	2.6	43.5
1964	41.1	3.2	43.1
1969	41.0	3.9	43.2
1972	42.1	3.3	44.0

SOURCE: *Survey of Current Business*, February 1975; the most recent data available is for 1972.

Wealth

Income distribution is only part of the picture of the distribution of economic welfare.

[3]Ibid., p. 9.

[4]See, for instance, *Dollars & Sense*, No. 8 (Summer 1975), p. 16, and No. 9 (Sept. 1975), pp. 4–5. We thank Janet Corpus and Regina O'Grady for help in researching pension funds and social security.

[5]See Edward C. Budd, *American Economic Review* (May 1970); John Gorman, *Survey of Current Business* (May 1970); John Hinrichs, *Survey of Current Business* (February 1975). Reported capital gains are twice as great as taxable capital gains, since federal laws consider only half of long-term capital gains as taxable income; data on taxable capital gains are in Gorman and Hinrichs. We are assuming that all capital gains are long-term and go to the richest 20 percent (which is approximately true) and that capital gains bear the same proportion to family as to individual income.

TABLE 8-D DISTRIBUTION OF WEALTH, 1962

	Households		Total Wealth		% Wealth Income-Producing[a]	IncomeProducing Wealth[a]	
Wealth Size	%	Cum. %	%	Cum. %		%	Cum. %
Negative	1.7	1.7	—	—	—	—	—
Zero	8.1	9.8	—	—	—	—	—
$0–1,000	15.5	25.3	0.3	0.3	8	—[b]	—[b]
$1–5,000	18.6	43.9	2.4	2.7	10	0.4	0.4
$5–10,000	15.7	59.6	5.5	8.2	16	1.6	2.0
$10–25,000	23.0	82.6	17.6	25.8	23	7.1	9.1
$25–50,000	10.7	93.3	17.9	43.7	42	13.2	22.3
$50–100,000	4.3	97.6	14.1	57.8	62	15.4	37.7
$100–200,000	1.2	98.8	7.6	65.4	66	8.8	46.5
$200–500,000	0.9	99.7	12.9	78.3	83	18.8	65.3
$500,000+	0.3	100.0	21.7	100.0	91	34.7	100.0

[a]All assets other than homes, automobiles, and non-interest-bearing accounts.
[b]Negligible quantity.
SOURCE: Dorothy Projector and Gertrude Weiss, *Survey of Financial Characteristics of Consumers* (Federal Reserve Board, 1966), various tables.

Two people with the same incomes but with different amounts of wealth are certainly not in the same position economically. We must consider, therefore, the distribution of wealth as well as income.

A person's wealth includes all of the property (or "assets") the person owns. It is important to distinguish between two major types of wealth: (1) income-producing wealth, such as stocks, bonds, and real estate other than one's own home; and (2) property held for personal use, such as cars, homes, and checking account deposits. Property for personal use is relatively widely distributed throughout the population, corresponding in predictable ways to the income distribution (richer families are more likely to own their homes and to have a second car). And it has little direct effect on the distribution of income and power in the economy.

Income-producing wealth, on the other hand, is quite tightly concentrated in the hands of a small minority. Because it produces income, it reinforces the position of this group at the top of the income distribution. And because ownership of stocks, one of the major forms of income-producing wealth, brings with it ownership of corporations, the minority of top wealth-holders have tremendous power over the workings of the economy.[6] Our examination of wealth, then, must focus particularly on corporate stocks and other forms of income-producing wealth.

A 1966 survey of over 2500 households provides useful data on the distribution of wealth.[7] Table 8-D presents some of its major findings. In 1962, households with under $200,000 of wealth, 98.8 percent of all households, owned only 65.4 percent of all wealth, and only 46.5 percent of income-producing wealth. Households with over $200,000 in wealth, only 1.2 percent of all households, owned the rest—one-third of all wealth and one-half of income-producing wealth.

Corporate stock is even more concentrated than other forms of income-producing wealth. The same study found that in 1962 the wealthiest 1 percent of the population owned

[6]The very rich, as a group if not as individuals, own and control major corporations. For a review of recent debates on this subject, see Edward S. Herman, "Do Bankers Control Corporations?", *Monthly Review*, June 1973.

[7]Dorothy S. Projector and Gertrude Weiss, *Survey of Financial Characteristics of Consumers*, (Federal Reserve Board, 1966).

31 percent of personally owned corporate stock; the top 5 percent owned 83 percent and the top 20 percent owned 96 percent.[8]

It is difficult to judge changes in the distribution of wealth over time, since the data are much more fragmentary than for income distribution. There have been some studies of time trends in the proportion of total personal wealth held by the wealthiest people at the top of the distribution, and the results of these studies are presented in Table 8-E. According to the figures in the table, the shares of both the top 1 percent and the top 1/2 percent of all wealth-holders have decreased between 1922 and 1969. Virtually all of the change, however, appears to have occurred between 1939 and 1945 (i.e., during World War II). From 1922 to 1939, and from 1945 to 1969, there have been fluctuations but no significant trends one way or the other. Just as in the case of the distribution of income, there is no evidence for growing equality in the distribution of personal wealth since 1945.

TABLE 8-E CONCENTRATION OF WEALTH, 1922–1969

| | Percent of Total Wealth Held by | |
Year	Top 1/2% of Wealth-Holders	Top 1% of Wealth-Holders
1922	29.8	31.6
1929	32.4	36.3
1933	25.2	28.3
1939	28.0	30.6
1945	20.9	23.3
1949	19.3	20.8
1953	22.0	27.5
1958	21.7	26.9
1962	21.6	27.4
1965	23.7	29.2
1969	19.9	24.9

SOURCE: 1922–1949: Robert J. Lampman, *The Share of Top Wealth-Holders in National Wealth, 1922–1956* (Princeton, N.J.: Princeton University Press, 1962), Table 97, p. 209; 1953–1969: J. D. Smith and S. D. Franklin, "The Concentration of Personal Wealth, 1922–1969," *American Economic Review*, (May 1974), Table 1, p. 166.

[8]Ibid., pp. 110–14, 151.

Personally owned wealth does not tell the whole story. Wealth is also held by pension funds and by trusts and estates. All of these are usually managed by bank trust departments, which held $187 billion in stocks, or 19.1 percent of the outstanding shares, in 1968.[9] Trusts and estates are established by rich people, while pensions will eventually benefit workers. However, pensions are usually managed and controlled by banks or other financial institutions, so their wealth is not a source of power or current income for workers in the same sense that personal wealth is a source of power to capitalists.

To the extreme concentration of personally owned wealth, therefore, we must add the control by banks of another big chunk of institutionally owned wealth.

A View from the Bottom

Extensive poverty accompanies the great concentration of income and wealth. The most common estimates of poverty, published by the Social Security Administration (SSA), define it as an income below $5,038 for a nonfarm family of four in 1974 (with different income cutoffs for different family sizes and residences). In 1974, 24.3 million people, or 12 percent of the population, were living in poverty by these criteria. The SSA allows food expenditures of $1.15 per person per day, and assumes that food makes up one-third of the total household budget. We reject poverty lines in the neighborhood of $5,000, and thus most poverty figures published by government agencies, as implausibly low.

A more reasonable definition of poverty is the Bureau of Labor Statistics (BLS) subsistence budget for 1967. It totals $8,673 (in

[9]About half was in pension funds and half in personal trusts and estates; see Edna Ehrlich, "The Functions and Investment Policies of Personal Trust Departments —Part II," *Federal Reserve Bank of New York, Monthly Review*, January 1973, p. 15; Raymond Goldsmith, *Institutional Investors and Corporate Stock*, National Bureau of Economic Research, 1973, p. 316. We thank David Gold for these references.

1974 dollars) for an urban family of four. The BLS calculates its budget on a much more detailed, and reasonable, basis than the SSA budget. It assumes that of the $8,673, taxes and social security take $1,029, leaving $7,644 after tax. Food, assumed to cost less than $1.76 per person per day (this requires very careful shopping and cooking and no meals away from home), takes $2,425 for the year. The BLS assumes rent, heat, and utilities for an inexpensive five-room, one-bath apartment to be under $132 per month. House furnishings and household expenditures add another $441. Clothing and personal care together total $1,029 for the family or $257 per person. Transportation, assumed to be by an eight-year-old used car except in cities with good public transportation, costs $660. Medical care and medical insurance for the whole family costs $698 (less than the cost of many family medical insurance plans or of a one-week stay in a hospital). Only $1,030 remains for other expenses.

Most people would agree that a family living on the BLS subsistence budget would feel quite poor, always worrying about making ends meet and constantly threatened with financial disaster in the event of an unexpected illness or job layoff. In 1974, 29 percent of families in the U.S. had incomes lower than $8,673.[10]

TAXATION AND GOVERNMENT SPENDING

Taxation

How do taxes affect the distribution of income? To answer this question we first examine specific taxes and then present evidence on their overall impact.

[10]There are more families with fewer than four people than with more than four, so using the four-person family cutoff point overstates the percentage of families living beneath the BLS budget. However, we use this figure because a breakdown of family incomes by family size is not yet available for 1974. Source: U.S. Census Bureau, *Current Population Report*, Series P-60, No. 99, p. 7.

Table 8-F displays the major sources of government revenue at all levels (federal, state, and local combined). The largest is the individual income tax, almost all collected at the federal level. It is widely believed that the federal income tax is a progressive tax, taking a greater percentage of income from the rich than from the poor, and thereby equalizing the distribution of income. But this view is mistaken; the federal income tax has little, if any, redistributive effect.

TABLE 8-F TOTAL GOVERNMENT REVENUE, BY SOURCE (billions of dollars)

	1973	1965	1950
TOTAL	426.2	202.6	66.7
Individual income taxes	121.2	52.9	16.5
Insurance trust payments[a]	76.7	26.5	5.5
Sales, excise, customs taxes	55.5	29.4	12.1
Property taxes	45.3	22.6	7.3
Corporation income taxes	41.6	27.4	11.1
Estate and gift taxes	6.3	3.5	0.9
All other[b]	79.6	40.3	13.3

[a]Primarily social security; also includes government employee pension payments, unemployment taxes, and similar programs.

[b]Includes minor taxes, license fees, public utility and state liquor store income, and borrowing.

SOURCE: U.S. Census Bureau, *Statistical Abstract of the U.S.*, *1975*, pp. 252–53; *1966*, p. 418; and *1952*, p. 358.

It is important to distinguish between the nominal and effective rates of taxation. Nominal income tax rates are progressive, taking more from the rich than from the poor. But because of loopholes that benefit the rich more than the poor (such as taxation of only 50 percent of capital gains, tax-free interest on municipal and state bonds, tax breaks for homeowners but not tenants, income splitting, etc.), the effective rates are nearly proportional. Table 8-G shows that in 1962 the share of the top fifth was only 1.8 percent lower and the share of the bottom fifth 0.3 percent higher after tax than before tax. Possibly because they are so embarrassing, the federal government has stopped publishing such figures.

TABLE 8-G INCOME DISTRIBUTION BEFORE AND AFTER THE FEDERAL INCOME TAX, 1962

	Poorest Fifth	Second Fifth	Middle Fifth	Fourth Fifth	Richest Fifth	Richest 5%
Before tax	4.6%	10.9%	16.3%	22.7%	45.5%	19.6%
After tax	4.9	11.5	16.8	23.1	43.7	17.7

SOURCE: Edward C. Budd, *Inequality and Poverty*, (New York: W. W. Norton, 1967), pp. xiii, vi.

The second most important source of government revenue is insurance trust payments, primarily the social security tax. In 1975, all wage and salary income up to $14,100 was taxed at the rate of 5.85 percent.[11] Wage and salary income above $14,100, and all unearned income, were not touched by social security. This means someone making $5,000 a year, for instance, paid 5.85 percent of $5,000, or $292.50, while an executive with a $50,000 salary paid 5.85 percent only on his first $14,100, amounting to $824.85, or 1.65 percent of his total salary. And a landlord with no salary but $50,000 income from rents didn't pay a cent into social security.

While the federal income tax is nearly proportional in impact, the social security tax is clearly regressive, taking a higher percentage from the poor than from the rich. More than half of all taxpayers give more each year to the Social Security Administration than they do to the Internal Revenue Service.[12]

Sales taxes and similar charges are the third largest source of government income. Of the $55.5 billion collected in 1973, gasoline, alcohol, and tobacco taxes accounted for $25.1 billion, and general state and local sales taxes made up most of the rest.[13] Sales taxes are based only on what you spend, not on your entire income; since richer people save a higher percentage of their income and spend a lower percentage, they pay a lower percentage of income in sales taxes than do poor people. In particular, lower-income people undoubtedly spend a higher percentage of their income on the most heavily taxed goods—gasoline, alcohol, and tobacco —than do higher-income people.

Property taxes, the fourth largest form of government revenue, are also regressive. Landlords pass on property taxes to tenants in higher rents; and the richer you are, the less of your income you spend on rent. Similarly, if you are a homeowner, the richer you are, the smaller the proportion of your income you are likely to spend on home expenses and property tax.

Corporation income taxes, fifth in importance, have been growing more slowly than other taxes. In 1950 they accounted for 17 percent of all taxes; by 1973 they were only 10 percent. In theory, they are progressive: the *nominal* rates are 22 percent on the first $25,000 of a corporation's income; 26 percent for corporate income between $25,000 and $50,000; and 48 percent above $50,000. However, because of numerous loopholes, the *effective* tax rates are considerably below this. For instance, in 1969 the effective tax rate on the 100 largest U.S. corporations was only 26.9 percent, and the leading oil companies paid a meager 5.8 percent.[14]

At least three major loopholes reduce corporate taxes. First, industry is allowed to claim accelerated depreciation, which means padding the tax deductions for the costs of plants and machinery. Second, the investment tax credit enables companies to deduct 10 percent of the value of new investment from their tax payment (this is in addition to their normal depreciation deductions). Third,

[11]From time to time the taxable income limit and the tax rate are raised, but as long as the basic procedure remains the same, the social security tax remains highly regressive.

[12]William K. Tabb, "Income Shares and Recovery," *The Nation*, October, 4, 1975, p. 301.

[13]U.S. Census Bureau, *Statistical Abstract of the United States, 1975*, p. 255.

[14]Charles A. Vanik, "Corporate Federal Tax Payments and Federal Subsidies to Corporations," *Hearings Before the Joint Committee*, 92nd Congress, 2nd session, July 19–21, 1972.

U.S.-based multinational corporations can take advantage of the foreign tax credit that allows them to subtract from U.S. taxes an amount equal to foreign taxes paid on income returned to the U.S. In addition, other write-off provisions and accounting manipulations are possible to further reduce the corporate tax burden. It is also important to point out that corporate taxes are often paid indirectly by the consumer in the form of higher prices.

Taxes on wealth—estate and gift taxes—constitute less than 2 percent of government revenue, and have very little impact on the distribution of wealth. Trust funds allow the estate tax to be skipped from one generation to the next. An estate left to a spouse is taxed at one-half the normal rate. Gift taxes can be avoided or greatly minimized by parcelling out gifts over several years or over several recipients. One recent study calculated the effective wealth tax rate for individuals with net worth over $500,000 to be a trifling one-half of one percent.[15]

When all taxes are considered together, there is little, if any, difference in the distribution of before- and after-tax income. A 1974 Brookings Institution study attempted to calculate the impact of the overall tax structure on the distribution of family income in 1966.[16] Such calculations depend on certain assumptions about the extent to which businesses and landlords pass on taxes to consumers. Table 8-H reports the findings of this study for the "most progressive" and "least progressive" assumptions regarding the incidence of various taxes.

Under the "most progressive" assumptions the after-tax distribution results in the poorest fifth having 0.4 percent more income than before taxes, while the richest fifth's share is reduced by 2 percent. Under the "least progressive" assumptions there is basically no change between the before- and after-tax distributions of income.

[15]James Wetzler, *Studies on the American Distribution of Wealth*, Ph.D. thesis, Harvard University, 1973, p. 60.

[16]Joseph Pechman and Benjamin Okner, *Who Bears the Tax Burden?* (Washington, D.C.: The Brookings Institution, 1974).

TABLE 8-H ADJUSTED FAMILY INCOME BEFORE AND AFTER ALL TAXES, 1966

Fifths of All Families	Most Progressive Assumption		Least Progressive Assumption	
	Before Tax	After Tax	Before Tax	After Tax
Poorest 20%	3.9%	4.3%	4.0%	4.1%
Second 20%	10.0	10.3	10.2	10.1
Third 20%	16.3	16.4	16.7	16.3
Fourth 20%	22.0	23.3	22.6	23.2
Richest 20%	47.7	45.7	46.6	46.3

SOURCE: Joseph Pechman and Benjamin Okner, *Who Bears the Tax Burden?* (Washington, D.C.: The Brookings Institution, 1974), p. 56.

Government Spending

If taxes don't improve the income distribution, what about government spending? It's not much help either. The effect of government spending is largely to preserve the society's basic institutions that generated the inequality in the first place.

Table 8-I summarizes the components of government spending (federal, state, and local combined). The largest single item is the military budget. It goes in large part to cost-plus contractors. Profits are guaranteed and the capital-intensive nature of military production assures that wage payments are a small portion of total costs. The same applies to space and technology outlays. And a major function of military and diplomatic activity is to maintain U.S. control and profitable investment opportunities for U.S. corporations in as much of the world as possible. Military and space spending, one-fifth of government spending in 1973, seem to benefit the rich, not the poor.

Interest on debt is paid to owners of government bonds, who are usually very wealthy. Since over half of the government's debt was borrowed during World War II and the peak Vietnam War spending years, it may also be considered an indirect cost of war.[17]

Police departments protect the property of businesses and affluent homes, while provid-

[17]*Dollars & Sense*, No. 5 (March 1975), p. 10.

TABLE 8-I TOTAL GOVERNMENT SPENDING,
BY FUNCTION (billions of dollars)

	1973	1965	1950
TOTAL	432.6	205.6	70.3
Military, State Department	79.6	55.8	18.4
Space program and technology	3.3	5.1	0.0
Interest on debt	25.1	11.4	4.9
Police	7.3	2.8	0.9
Natural resources	16.4	11.0	5.0
Highways	19.2	12.3	3.9
Postal Service	9.6	5.3	2.3
Fire protection, sanitation, and sewage	8.1	3.7	1.3
Housing and urban renewal	7.3	2.2	0.6
Education	75.7	29.6	9.6
Social security	56.4	16.6	0.7
Public employee pensions	10.4	3.5	0.6
Health and hospitals	18.7	7.7	2.8
Public welfare	27.0	6.4	3.0
Unemployment compensation	4.2	2.4	2.0
Veterans' benefits[a]	7.4	4.2	3.3
Local parks and recreation	2.6	1.1	0.3
All other[b]	52.3	24.6	11.0

[a]Excluding some benefits included in other categories.
[b]General administration, public utilities and liquor stores, and miscellaneous.

SOURCE: U.S. Census Bureau, *Statistical Abstract of the United States, 1975*, p. 253.

ing zero or negative benefits to poor neighborhoods. Natural resource spending is ambiguous in impact, but benefits many particular industries. Highways and the Postal Service are used at times by almost everyone, but disproportionately benefit business: automobile manufacturers, trucking firms, and related companies in the case of highways; nearly all advertisers in the case of the Postal Service.

Fire protection, sanitation, and sewers seem neutral in distributional impact. Housing and urban renewal may at times provide housing for the poor but more frequently have subsidized private construction companies, and destroyed existing low-income neighborhoods to "renew" them for new business use.

The programs mentioned so far, amounting to two-fifths of government spending in

1973, have a fairly clearly neutral or regressive effect on income distribution. The situation is more complex in the remaining cases, roughly speaking the "health education and welfare" programs.

Education is the only budget category in Table 9 rivaling the military in size. It is often viewed as a great equalizer, allowing the poor to "get ahead." Yet, as many critics have shown,[18] the educational system usually tracks people into jobs corresponding in status to their parents' jobs, and provides differentially greater opportunities to get ahead for those who already started ahead. While education provides an orderly channel for the upward mobility of some low-income individuals, there is little evidence that it raises the relative position of low-income people as a group.

Social security and pension payments have been a rapidly growing part of government spending, rising from 2 percent of the total in 1950 to 15 percent in 1973. As mentioned above, they are probably among the causes of the one observed instance of growing equality—the distribution of income of unrelated individuals. They are also, however, one of the areas most threatened with cutbacks in the next few years, because the funds from which they are paid are being rapidly depleted.

The remaining areas of health and welfare spending—health and hospitals, public welfare, unemployment compensation, and veterans' benefits—all surely provide greater benefit to the poor than to the rich. Like social security, many of these programs emerged from periods of crisis and popular struggle, from the 1930s to the present. But they are very partial victories: public hospitals and public welfare, for instance, provide notoriously inadequate services under degrading and insulting conditions.[19]

[18]See Bowles, Section 8.3, p. 315, for an analysis of how and why the U.S. educational system does not promote greater equality.

[19]See Edwards, Section 8.2, p. 307, for a detailed analysis of the limited distributional impact of welfare programs.

It is extremely difficult, if not impossible, to assess precisely the overall distributive effects of all types of government spending. The programs of clearly greater benefit to the poor than to the rich amounted to less than 30 percent of government spending in 1973 (social security, pensions, health and hospitals, welfare, unemployment compensation, veterans' benefits), and over half of that amount was in social security and pensions. Over the years, as government spending has accounted for a larger and larger share of GNP, the distribution of family income (covering 90 percent of the population) has not become more equal. It seems likely, therefore, that government spending serves not to redistribute resources to the poor but to maintain the existing unequal distribution of resources and the capitalist institutions that generate it.

CLASS AND INCOME DISTRIBUTION

There are many sources of income inequality in the United States. Race, sex, education, and regional differences all affect the distribution of income. The primary source of high incomes, however, is ownership of income-producing property. At the very top of the income pyramid are the big capitalists, supported primarily by their stocks and bonds. Just below the top there is a concentration of small businesspeople, whose income arises both from their property and their labor. The rest of the people (roughly 80 percent) live mainly on wages and salaries, pensions, or welfare.

Table 8-J presents data from federal income tax returns on the sources of income by income bracket in 1973. We define "small business" income to include rent and income from unincorporated businesses and professions, farms, partnerships, and small business corporations. "Capitalist" income includes dividends, capital gains, and interest. Small business and capitalist income each amount to only 8 percent of all income, but they are concentrated in the hands of upper-income groups.

Taxpayers who reported under $25,000 in net taxable income, the vast majority, got 89 percent of their income from wages and salaries, and only 6 percent from capitalist sources (including interest on savings accounts). At higher income levels, the share of wages and salaries falls steadily and that of capitalist income rises. Small business income is of greatest relative importance in the $50,000 to $100,000 bracket, but even there it is not the major form of income; above $100,000 it fades rapidly. The 3,500 taxpayers reporting over $500,000 in net taxable income (they averaged over a million dollars each) got three-quarters of their incomes from dividends, capital gains and interest, and only one-tenth from salaries.

Moreover, the Internal Revenue Service data used in Table 8-J are biased to minimize

TABLE 8-J INCOME BY SOURCE, 1973

Size of Taxable Income ($)	Number of Tax Returns (thousands)	Total Income ($ billion)	Wages and Salaries	Small Business (% of total income)	Capitalist
All Sizes	80,693	827.1	83	8	8
0–25,000	76,469	651.3	89	5	6
25–50,000	3,502	112.3	71	17	11
50–100,000	597	39.4	49	29	20
100–500,000	122	20.5	35	22	40
500,000 and up	3.5	3.6	10	6	75

SOURCE: U.S. Internal Revenue Service, *Statistics of Income 1973: Individual Income Tax Returns*, Table 4. Some minor sources of income, included in total income, are not shown separately.

the significance of property for the rich. Much of capitalist income, including all interest on state and municipal bonds, is tax-exempt and therefore not included in these figures. Exaggerated depreciation and depletion allowances are common. Tax-exempt charitable donations can be padded and overstated. True income figures, therefore, would show even greater concentrations of capitalist income in the hands of the very rich.

The argument that property ownership is a primary source of income inequality gains further support from a comparison of income distribution in capitalist and state socialist countries. An exhaustive study of international patterns of inequality found that out of seventy-two countries for which comparable data were available, the four Soviet-bloc countries in the sample (East Germany, Czechoslovakia, Poland, and Hungary) had the four most equal income distributions.[20] Even the relatively egalitarian capitalist countries (New Zealand, Canada, the Scandinavian countries) had income distributions substantially more unequal than those of the four Soviet-bloc countries. Another study found that in 1960 the ratio of the average income of the highest 10 percent of income earners to that of the lowest 10 percent was roughly 5 to 1 in the Soviet Union and 30 to 1 in the United States.[21] Such differences can be attributed to the absence of property income as well as the absence of unemployment in state socialist countries.

CONCLUSION

In this paper we have documented the extent of income and wealth inequality in the United States. The basic pattern of inequality has scarcely changed in the last thirty years, and appears to be unaltered by government taxation and spending policies. At the upper end of the distribution, property income accruing to the capitalist class is the primary source of inequality. The evidence available from international comparisons suggests that socialism leads to much more equality.

[20]Jerry Lee Cromwell, *Income Inequalities, Discrimination and Uneven Capitalist Development*, Ph.D. thesis, Harvard University, 1974, pp. 234–37, 279–87.

[21]Murray Yanowitch, "The Soviet Income Revolution," reprinted in M. Bornstein and D. R. Fusfeld, eds., *The Soviet Economy* (Homewood, Ill.: Richard Irwin, 1966), p. 237. The presence of many free services (e.g., education, medicine) and many state-subsidized goods and services (e.g., house rent, transportation, basic food items) makes the actual distribution of income yet more equal in the Soviet-bloc countries than these figures would indicate.

8.2   *Who Fares Well in the Welfare State?*

In the last reading, Ackerman and Zimbalist showed that the overall redistributive impact of government taxation and expenditure in the United States is minimal. But are there not specific programs that significantly redistribute income? The one government program supposed to be devoted exclusively to the poor is the welfare system. In this reading, Richard C. Edwards *defines* the welfare system as all those programs specifically designed to benefit the poor. Since the welfare system has expanded enormously in the past few decades, one would surely expect it to have had a significant equalizing impact. Yet a careful look at the facts suggest that even in this particular case such a conclusion is not justified.

The following essay was written by Richard C. Edwards for this book. Copyright © 1972, 1978 by Richard C. Edwards.

Income inequality in the United States has diminished only slightly over the last several decades, and it actually increased in the early 1970s. Aggregate income data reveal that no significant progress toward more equality has been achieved since World War II, and in particular the poorest fifth of the population continues to receive the same small proportion of total income, less than 6 percent, which they received decades ago.[1]

These decades also witnessed the creation and growth of manifold public assistance and other anti-poverty programs. These programs —the "welfare system"—have often been perceived as a powerful force for greater equality; instead they have had a miniscule impact on the distribution of income in the United States.

The failure of the welfare system to make any meaningful reduction in inequality should not be surprising. As in other areas, in the field of income distribution the state's policies must operate within severe limits. These limits derive from the capitalist organization of production: most generally, *an extensive welfare system would undermine the incentive to work*. The availability of income from sources other than the sale of labor-power would permit people to avoid wage-labor. Just as the recipients of stock dividends often choose not to work, so too might others if welfare benefits, unemployment compensation, etc. were adequate and readily available. After all, capitalist ideology glorifies the pursuit of self-interest and provides little concept of social obligation. Moreover, in a system of alienated labor, individual material rewards (rather than, for example, the social necessity of production or the intrinsic rewards of the job) are the chief motivation to work; if an alternate means of livelihood were provided, large numbers of people might well quit work. "Decent" welfare benefits would thus come into serious competition with low-wage, boring, exhausting, and dangerous wage-labor.

The corollary constraints placed on state

[1]See Table 8-A, p. 298.

welfare policies are twofold. First, those able to perform wage-labor—that is, those who are not disabled or old or mothers with small children or otherwise prevented from being employed—have typically been excluded from all welfare benefits except the most short-term "emergency" relief. In times of welfare "crackdowns," these persons, however needy, have been the first ones purged from the rolls. Second, the general level of welfare benefits has been determinedly kept low, to reduce as much as possible the "attractiveness" of being on welfare. While the level of benefits has fluctuated somewhat in response to political demands by the dispossessed—in particular, the widespread and persistent compaigns in the late 1960s to increase welfare benefits resulted in slightly higher payments—these gains have always been offset by relative declines during periods of less intense political struggle or whenever welfare benefits threatened the level of inequality needed to maintain the work incentive. The pervasive efforts in the 1970s to eliminate the "chiselers" from the welfare rolls and "cut the fat" from welfare budgets reflect these conflicts.

The capitalist economy thus places restrictions on state welfare programs, whether those programs are administered by conservative Republicans or liberal Democrats. In the first part of this essay I describe the nature, size, and trends in welfare expenditures in the United States, in order to assess the impact of the welfare system. In the second part I investigate the theoretical reasons for the failure of the welfare system significantly to alter inequality in a capitalist society.

THE POVERTY OF WELFARE

Included in the "welfare system" as that term is used here are all those programs which grant either cash payments or goods and services exclusively or at least principally to poor people; eligibility must be based at least in part on the beneficiary's lack of income.[2] Table 8-K lists the major programs that are included.

TABLE 8-K EXPENDITURES UNDER THE WELFARE SYSTEM IN 1974, INCLUDING ALL FEDERAL, STATE, AND LOCAL PROGRAMS
(billions of dollars)

Category	Amount Spent State and Local	Federal
Cash payments	$ 7.0	$ 9.9
Food	–	2.9
Health	5.4	6.3
Housing	.5	3.7
Education	–	3.1
Unemployment insurance	5.0	1.7
Other[a]	3.1	3.7
	$21.0	$31.3
	Total $52.3	

[a]School lunches, aid to refugees, etc.

SOURCES: U.S. Congress, Joint Economic Committee, *Studies in Public Assistance*, paper #20; U.S. Office of Management and Budget, *The Budget of the United States Government, Fiscal Year 1976*, Appendix, pp. 415, 422; *Statistical Abstract of the United States, 1975*, p. 281.

[2]For example, general education programs are not included, since they are undertaken on the part of the *general* population and not in particular for the benefit of poor people; on the other hand, some of Title I funds, which were designated as antipoverty monies, are included. The dividing line was generously applied, however, including for example the federally financed employment service, which with good justification could as well be considered as a subsidy to employers rather than part of the welfare system. One large program sometimes thought of as part of the welfare system which we have *not* included is the social security program, since it represents no (or very little) transfer to the poor from the rest of society but rather is mainly an insurance scheme in which poor recipients as a lifetime group have paid in as much as they receive back. It is true, of course, that the social security system redistributes income over people's lifetimes, returning income during that part of their lives when their incomes are low. This does not constitute redistribution to the poor, however, since the beneficiaries have by and large paid for the benefits they receive. For a careful study which comes to this same conclusion, see Elizabeth Deran, "Income Redistribution Under Social Security," *National Tax Journal*, XIX, No. 3, p. 285. See also John Brittain, "The Real Rate of Interest on Lifetime Contributions Toward Retirement Under Social Security," in *Old-Age Income Assurance*, U.S. Congress, Joint Economic Committee, December 1967, Part iii.

While the welfare system has provided gradually increasing absolute benefits to the poor, it has *never threatened the overall structure of inequality*. First, the total expenditures on welfare programs have never been great enough to affect the income distribution significantly; since the poor help finance the welfare system through their tax payments, the redistributive impact is even less than the total expenditures would indicate. Second, the level of welfare benefits as a percentage of median family income or average weekly wages has remained constant or declined, so one cannot argue that welfare programs have contributed much to greater equality over time. These facts, which I present below, explain why a rising amount of total benefits has been entirely consistent with a nearly constant degree of income inequality.

First let us look at the aggregate impact of the welfare system. Total welfare costs in 1974 were $52.3 billion. In order to grasp the impact of that magnitude, suppose that in 1974 (with no other changes in tax or welfare laws) the government had taxed an additional $52.3 billion from the richest fifth (20 percent) of the population. At the same time, imagine that this $52.3 billion had been transferred to the poorest fifth of the population, distributed evenly among them. What would have happened? The richest fifth would still be, by far, the richest; their "reduced" incomes would still be *more than one and one-half times greater* than the *next richest* fifth. Furthermore, the poorest fifth would still be the poorest; their "expanded" incomes would still be *less than three-quarters* of the income of the *next poorest* fifth of the population.[3]

This exercise, insignificant as it would be for income redistribution, *grossly overestimates* the impact of the welfare system. This is so for three reasons. First, only some benefits

[3]This assumes that aggregate personal income, as it appears in Department of Commerce National Income Accounts, follows the income distribution which was calculated from CPS data and given in Table 8-A, p. 298.

from the programs we have included go to poor people. For example, all federal health and medical spending, except that relating to defense and medical research, have been included, yet many of these programs are not at all directed toward the poor. Second, I have ignored all of the administrative costs, boondoggles, subterfuges, etc., which accompany welfare programs in this country. Certainly even with the best intentions, much of the $52.3 billion spent on welfare on 1974 never actually reached poor people; for example, the salaries of welfare workers and the cost of most "poverty research" are included in this figure. Third, I assumed that the entire tax burden required to finance the welfare program was paid for by the richest fifth. But the welfare system is in fact paid for out of general tax revenues to which the poor contribute, so the redistributive impact is overestimated to the extent that the poor pay for their own benefits.

That welfare expenditures have not been of sufficient magnitude to threaten the overall structure of inequality becomes even more evident if we relate the total cost of the programs we have included in the welfare system to other economic magnitudes. In 1938, while the United States was recovering from the Depression, welfare expenditures amounted to 6.78 percent of total personal income. But, as Table 8-L shows, since World War II the total amount spent on welfare programs by all federal, state, and local governments has remained a roughly constant—and lower—proportion of total personal income. While welfare expenditures have been growing absolutely, they have not grown relative to other economic magnitudes: in comparison to personal income, welfare expenditures have barely maintained their position. Needless to say, the income-equalizing impact has likewise at best remained constant over time.

In order to determine the *overall* redistributive impact of the welfare system we must also consider who pays the taxes that finance welfare programs. Welfare expenditures redis-

TABLE 8-L WELFARE EXPENDITURES AS A PERCENT OF TOTAL PERSONAL INCOME

Year	All Welfare Costs (billions of $)	Total Personal Income (billions of $)	Welfare as a Percent of Personal Income
1938	$ 4.7	$ 68.6	6.78%
1950	8.8	228.5	3.86
1960	13.3	400.8	3.31
1968	26.9	685.8	3.82
1974	52.3	1150.5	4.55

SOURCE: Calculated from *Statistical Abstract*, 1940, pp. 366ff.; 1952, p. 219; 1960, p. 283; 1969, p. 275; 1975, p. 281, 386; and *The National Income and Product Accounts of the United States, 1929–1965* (Supplement to the Survey of Current Business), Dept. of Commerce, G.P.O., Washington, D.C., 1966, pp. 32–33.

tribute income to the poor only to the extent that the poor do not themselves pay for those programs.

Welfare programs are financed from both state and local tax revenues and from federal revenues. Since federal taxes are assessed approximately in proportion to income while state taxes are considerably more biased against the poor,[4] a *conservative* estimate of the poor's tax contribution toward financing the welfare system can be obtained by assuming that the $52.3 billion in 1974 was paid for out of federal taxes alone.[5] This assumption would mean that the poorest fifth would have contributed between $2.5 billion and $3.0 billion toward paying for welfare benefits, and the poorest two-fifths of the population (all of whose incomes were below $10,000) contributed over $9.0 billion. Hence any estimate of the *net* benefit to the poor from the welfare system would require our reducing welfare expenditures by between $2.5 and $9.0 billion.

[4]Joseph Pechman and Benjamin Okner, *Who Bears the Tax Burden?* (Washington, D.C.: The Brookings Institution, 1974), pp. 8–9.

[5]This assumption is used by Robert Lampman, "Transfer and Redistribution as Social Process," in Shirley Jenkins, ed., *Social Security in International Perspective* (New York: Columbia University, 1969), p. 41.

TABLE 8-M PUBLIC ASSISTANCE BENEFITS AS A PERCENT OF MEDIAN INCOME

	(1) Median Annual Income of Civilian Employed Males	(2) Average Annual Money Payment Under General Assistance Program	(3) Average General Assistance Payment as Percent of Median Income (2)/(1)	(4) Average Annual Money Payment Under Aid to Dependent Children Program	(5) Average Aid to Dependent Children Payment as Percent of Median Income (4)/(1)
1950	$ 2,831	$ 564	19.9%	$ 852	30.1%
1960	4,822	804	16.7	1,296	26.9
1968	7,080	1,128	15.9	1,920	27.1
1974	10,608	1,680	15.8	2,616	24.7

SOURCE: *Statistical Abstract*, 1969, p. 296, *Current Population Reports*, U.S. Department of Commerce, Series P-60, No. 69, April 6, 1970, p. 82; *Statistical Abstract*, 1975, pp. 304, 364.

The same point is made by examining the benefits from individual programs. Public assistance, one of the largest programs, is the program usually thought of when people mention "welfare." Suppose we express the average annual payment made to an individual under this program as a percentage of some comparable magnitude, say the median annual income of employed civilian males.[6] Then both of the public assistance categories had lower payments in 1974 than in 1950, as shown in Table 8-M. *Relative to the average income earner, the average welfare recipient suffered a decline in position.*

The same phenomenon—diminished or at best constant benefits relative to the median national income or to average wages—has occurred in other programs as well. For example, the unemployed worker, if he or she happened to be among the three-quarters of the civilian labor force who were eligible for unemployment compensation, did little better: in 1950, average weekly benefits for a worker who was unemployed were 34.4 percent of the average weekly wage in manufac-

turing. In 1960, the average unemployment benefits remained at roughly that level (35.2 percent), and by 1974 benefits had climbed to only 36.5 percent. Thus there was little change in relative benefits.[7]

[7]*Statistical Abstract*, 1975, pp. 302, 365. The worker who was fully employed at the legal minimum wage did no better: as the following table shows, the minimum wage, while rising absolutely, has not increased sufficiently to keep pace with inflation and the general rise in wages. Thus a worker "protected" by the minimum wage has suffered a decline in position relative to the average worker.

THE MINIMUM WAGE AS A PERCENT OF AVERAGE WAGES

	(1) Legal Minimum Wage[a]	(2) Average Hourly Wage in All Manufacturing	(3) Minimum Wage as Percent of Average Mfg. Wage: (1)/(2)
1940	$0.30	$0.66	45.9%
1950	0.75	1.44	52.1
1955	1.00	1.86	53.8
1960	1.00	2.26	44.2
1965	1.25	2.61	47.9
1968	1.60	3.01	53.2
1974	2.00	4.40	45.4

[a]Note: the minimum wage law in 1968 covered only 62% of the civilian labor force, some of whom were eligible only for a lower minimum wage than that given in (1); most of those not covered earn less than the minimum wage.

SOURCE: *The Fair Standards Act, 1938–1968*, U.S. Department of Labor, Wage and Hour and Public Contracts Divisions. U.S. Government Printing Office, 1968; *Statistical Abstract*, 1969, p. 228.

[6]I chose median income of employed civilian males as our index only because the data are convenient. For example, since many welfare recipients are women, it might have been more appropriate to use median income of employed civilian females. The results, however, would have been the same since the ratio of median incomes of employed civilian males to females has remained nearly constant over the time period we are considering.

Figure 8-A Welfare benefits as a percentage of average wages or income

Total welfare is shown as % of personal income; social security retirement benefits and general assistance are shown as % of median income of employed civilian males; minimum wage is shown as % of average weekly wage in manufacturing industries.

SOURCE: See text and tables above.

The same is true of the social security program. We do not include social security as part of the welfare system, since it is primarily an insurance scheme in which poor recipients as a lifetime group have paid in as much as they receive back. But popular illusions about the impact of social security makes the case illustrative nonetheless. In the category of old-age retirement benefits, for example, the average annual stipend as a percentage of the median income of civilian employed males remained constant at roughly 18 percent between 1950 and 1970; only in the early 1970s, as a consequence of stagnating wages, did the social security benefit creep over 20 percent.[8] These trends are summarized in Figure 8-A.

None of the above is meant to deny that some poor people benefit from the welfare

[8]*Statistical Abstract*, 1975, pp. 288, 364.

system or that in some absolute sense they were better provided for in 1968 or 1974 than in earlier years. Furthermore, struggles waged by groups such as the National Welfare Rights Organization to obtain rights for poor people directly improve the lives of those aided. Moreover, it is clear that continuing struggle is essential to *maintain* the gains achieved in the past.

The conclusion to the previous analysis is clear: welfare programs have not been growing relative to the rest of the economy, and in many cases they have even suffered declines. The welfare system has never threatened the overall structure of inequality in the United States. And the welfare system has operated within very narrow constraints.

Evidence from abroad suggests remarkably similar conclusions. For example, one study of the celebrated "welfare state" in Denmark revealed that although the Danish welfare system is much larger and more comprehensive than its U.S. counterpart, it has had almost no impact on the distribution of income in Denmark.[9] Another study, by the Secretariat of the Economic Commission of Europe, considered the distributional impact of the entire system of taxes and benefits in Western European countries. After noting that there was some redistributive effect for the very poor and very rich, it concluded that "the general pattern of income distribution, by size of income, for the great majority of households, is only slightly affected by government action.[10]

WHY IS WELFARE SO INEFFECTIVE?

The failure of the U.S. welfare system to generate greater equality must reflect something more fundamental than lack of political will, poor leadership, or "mistakes." Such *ad hoc* explanations would be acceptable for a short span of history. But starting at least as early as Franklin Roosevelt's New Deal, the liberals dominating national politics committed themselves to securing more income for America's poor. While we must doubt the depth of their commitment, *the immense political pressure apparently required in order to institute equalizing programs is itself testament to the strength*

of the underlying economic forces. Even the public commitment mobilized by Johnson's "War on Poverty" failed to produce any significant trend toward greater equality. Given this history, there is a *prima facie* presumption that the welfare system's failure to generate greater equality reflects a more basic characteristic of the economic system.

If we provisionally accept that the constraints within which the welfare system has worked over the past thirty years are imposed by the capitalist system, what can be said about the direct relation between those constraints and capitalism?

One of the consequences of the capitalist development process is that it destroys motivation for work other than that based on wages. In a society where individual material rewards—wages—are the main incentive to work, significant inequalities in labor earnings must exist in order to induce workers to work hard, to acquire and apply productive skills, to accept alienation at the workplace, and to acquiesce in their lack of control over productive activities.[11] Inequality is required so that "good workers" can be rewarded, "bad workers" can be punished; the incentives to "go along" and "work hard" are made clear to all. The need for inequality is most clearly manifest within bureaucratic offices, where both the incentive to rise and the *ex post* justification of hierarchical levels of authority are much strengthened by income differentials.

If the need for such inequality does not seem plausible, imagine the opposite: suppose all workers received the same wage. The standard response—"But then who would be willing to work hard?"—simply restates the case.

Inequality serves other functions as well. For example, the ideological rationale for ac-

[9]The study, *Velstand Uden Velfaerd* (Wealth without Welfare) by the economist Bent Hansen, is discussed by Jacques Hersh in " 'Welfare State' and Social Conflict," *Monthly Review*, XXII, No. 6 (November 1970), 29–41. Hersh (p. 34) quotes Hansen as concluding: "Beneath the surface of a modern welfare society, social injustice and social barriers are still thriving.... In our time, the gap between the rich and the poor is growing deeper." The statement is all the more revealing since the author is a leading member of the Social Democrats, who until recently ruled the government almost uninterruptedly since World War II.

[10]Economic Commission of Europe, *Incomes in Postwar Europe: A Study of Policies, Growth, and Distribution*, Geneva, 1967, pp. 1–15.

[11]This abstracts from the most concentrated source of inequality in capitalist society—namely, concentration of capital ownership and capital income among a tiny portion of the population.

cepting alienating work conditions—that alienating work makes possible higher consumption levels, and that higher consumption is the true path to personal fulfillment—also depends in part on the existence of inequality. An intense drive for higher consumption is more easily maintained, by advertising, for example, in an atmosphere of inequality, where a fundamental appeal can be made to the pleasure of consuming things which other people do not have.

An adequate welfare system would be even more tenuous in a capitalist society than equal wages. The welfare system provides income *without work*. The destructive impact on work incentives of an "adequate welfare income" would therefore be all the greater. The obstacle to an adequate welfare system is simply this: in a society which requires and depends on the wage incentive to force people to work, no one would work if an adequate income were available without work.

One important feature of the *current* welfare system is that it never in any fundamental way breaks the link between income and the necessity to work. It avoids doing so in several ways. First, work is almost always more remunerative than welfare.[12] Second, few benefits are available to persons in the work force: 25 percent of the poor live in families headed by *fully* employed males who earn less than the poverty income;[13] yet these families are eligible for few benefits. Most benefits go to indigent children, old people, the blind, female heads of households with small children, etc., all of whom cannot participate in the labor market. The point is not that these persons are not deserving; clearly they are. However, the chief criterion for their benefit eligibility under the present system is not that they are poor, but rather that they cannot sell their labor-power on the market.

Third, benefits available to people potentially or actually in the labor force tend to be more like wage supplements than wage substitutes. Benefits provided in the form of services (health care, training, job counseling, etc.) cannot be used to purchase the family's food, shelter, and clothing. The food stamp program is devised to insure that the stamps benefits a family only so long as the family has an alternative income with which to buy the stamps. Public housing requires people to pay rent. School meals, though subsidized, still require some money. Welfare benefits as wage supplements may marginally increase a family's standard of living, but they do not weaken the necessity to work.

A certain minimal level of welfare that does not undermine the work incentive is entirely consistent with the operation of capitalist institutions and the preservation of inequality. Unemployment compensation and employment services (counseling and referrals) help establish mobility in the labor market and therefore provide general benefits to employers as well as workers. Some expenditures for basic public health measures maintain the health and welfare of the national work force and increase its productivity. Public hospital expenditures divert the poor, when they are sick, to public hospitals, thereby freeing quality hospitals for their speciality, treating the rich.

Finally, some welfare programs are required just because extreme poverty poses a threat to the economic system. Those affected have no stake in maintaining the system and may make demands for change. The preservation of capitalism requires that poverty be alleviated, or at least that something be done about its appearance. In this sense, basic income support for persons *not* in the labor force stabilizes the system from two directions. It depoliticizes conflict and diverts poor people's demands around which they might otherwise organize to threaten the economic system. And by focusing exaggerated attention on welfare programs, it diverts the animosity

[12]See Bradley R. Schiller, "The Permanent Poor: An Inquiry into Opportunity Stratification," unpublished Ph.d. dissertation, Harvard University, 1969.

[13]Cited in Anthony Downs, "Who Are the Urban Poor" (CED Report).

and frustration of the lower-middle class downward rather than upward. Such expenditures therefore strengthen the stability of the system itself. In all of these ways, a minimal welfare system represents a good investment by capitalists in the preservation of the system and the increased productivity of its workers.

Yet while it is true that an "adequate" welfare system would (from the employers' perspective) dangerously undermine the work incentive and in this sense come into conflict with the prerequisites of capitalist production, the political forces limiting the welfare system cannot be understood simply by exclusive reference to *capitalists'* power to keep welfare costs down and eligibility requirements up. After all, antagonism toward welfare recipients has often come from the working class as well as from employer segments of the population.

Working-class opposition to welfare is not necessarily irrational or mean-spirited; in fact, *it is this wider opposition to welfare which indicates the systemic* (as opposed to conspiratorial) constraints on more generous state welfare policies. Most immediately, under current tax laws low-income people must pay a major portion of welfare costs—it was estimated above that the poorest two-fifths of the population contributes over $9

billion annually. Undoubtedly more important is the fact that liberal welfare benefits create great frustration for those who are poor but who are not eligible for benefits and who must therefore sell their labor-power to survive; a system in which some must work at alienating jobs while others get income "free" is perceived as patently unfair. If this anger is more often directed at welfare recipients than at wealthy "coupon-clippers" (who also need not work to survive), it is only because the former are more visible: they are not able to retreat to elite communities and posh resorts.

Thus capitalism itself (and not just capitalists, though they do their part) imposes real limits on state welfare policies. As long as workers accept the rationale of wage-labor and are unable to impose the costs of welfare on capitalists, they will have grounds for opposing the expansion of welfare benefits. These limits explain why the welfare system cannot be viewed as a meaningful attack on inequality. Historically, it has never played that role. From the English Poor Laws of the sixteenth century to the cutbacks of the 1970s, welfare programs have simply kept the poor from becoming *too* poor, that is, from becoming *rebelliously* poor. And an adequate welfare system would directly and fundamentally conflict with the operation of the basic capitalist institutions.

8.3   *Schooling and the Reproduction of Inequality*

In analyzing the distribution of income it is important to distinguish between equality of *income*, on the one hand, and equality of *opportunity*, on the other. Equality of income means that everyone receives the same income. Equality of opportunity means that everyone has the same chance to reach the top (or the bottom) of the prevailing income hierarchy, in the sense that a person's family background has no influence on a person's chances of economic success. Inequality of opportunity exists to the extent that economic success (or failure) is transmitted from parents to children.

We have seen that capitalist societies are characterized by a high degree of income inequality. A hierarchy of unequal incomes, based on the distinction between capitalists and workers and the hierarchical division of the labor force, is an essential feature of the capitalist mode of production. But does this inequality of income necessarily imply inequality of opportunity as well? Many defenders of the capitalist order concede that the distribution of income must be and will be unequal, but they argue that it is inequality of *opportunity* rather than inequality of *income* that really matters. This raises the question of whether it is possible to equalize opportunity within the unequal structure of a capitalist society.

One important source of unequal opportunity under capitalism is the intergenerational transmission of wealth. As long as income-producing property can be transferred from parents to children through inheritance, the children of the rich will have much greater chances of economic success than the children of the poor—if only because they can count on a steady flow of property income. It would require a drastic curtailment of the rights of inheritance to prevent such intergenerational transmission of wealth; but to interfere seriously with these rights would be as incompatible with the capitalist mode of production as to abolish private property altogether.

A second source of unequal opportunity in a capitalist society is the intergenerational transmission of the capacity to command labor income. Parents from high socioeconomic classes generally pass on to their children certain attitudes, skills, privileges, etc. which give them better opportunities for success in the labor market than children from lower classes. Some of the economic advantages that are transmitted in this way can be purchased with parents' income (e.g., a first-rate education); others are associated with parents' social status (e.g., useful contacts).

For advocates of more equal economic opportunity within the framework of a capitalist society, it is this second source of unequal opportunity that has appeared to be the most amenable to change. In particular, reformers in the United States have looked to the expansion of the *educational* system as the most promising means of providing that equality of opportunity which has long been promised to all Americans. Indeed, it has been an important part of the prevailing American ideology that the school system can and does lead to greater equality of both income and opportunity.

Yet, as Samuel Bowles argues in the following reading, the American educational system is in fact instrumental in the legitimation of income inequality and in its transmission from one generation to the next. For one of the primary functions of schools in a capitalist society is to *reproduce* the hierarchical division of labor that is such an essential feature of the capitalist mode of production.

The argument that schooling cannot be expected to reduce inequality in the United States derives additional support from some recent evidence on trends in educational attainment and labor income.[1] Since World War II,

[1] See Samuel Bowles and Herbert Gintis, *Schooling in Capitalist America* (New York: Basic Books, 1976), pp. 33–34, for documentation of this point; the data cited by Bowles and Gintis refer only to men 25 years or older, but the same general pattern no doubt applies to women as well.

the degree of inequality in years of schooling attained by Americans has been significantly reduced, as more and more students finish their high school education. Yet in the same period the distribution of labor income has actually become more unequal. So even when efforts are made to equalize access to education, the impact on the structure of economic rewards is minimal. The impact on the distribution of economic opportunity is likewise very limited, for inequality of both income and opportunity is deeply rooted in the capitalist system.

The following is excerpted from "Unequal Education and the Reproduction of the Social Division of Labor" by SAMUEL BOWLES. From *Schooling in a Corporate Society: The Political Economy of Education in America and the Alternatives Before Us*, edited by Martin Carnoy (New York: David McKay Co., 1972). Copyright © 1971 by Samuel Bowles. Reprinted by permission of the author.

The ideological defense of modern capitalist society rests heavily on the assertion that the equalizing effects of education can counter the disequalizing forces inherent in the free market system. That educational systems in capitalist societies have been highly unequal is generally admitted and widely condemned. Yet educational inequalities are taken as passing phenomena, holdovers from an earlier, less enlightened era, which are rapidly being eliminated.

The record of educational history in the U.S., and scrutiny of the present state of our colleges and schools, lend little support to this comforting optimism. Rather, the available data suggest an alternative interpretation. In what follows I will argue (1) that schools have evolved in the U.S. not as part of a pursuit of equality, but rather to meet the needs of capitalist employers for a disciplined and skilled labor force, and to provide a mechanism for social control in the interests of political stability; (2) that as the economic importance of skilled and well educated labor has grown, inequalities in the school system have become increasingly important in reproducing the class structure from one generation to the next; (3) that the U.S. school system is pervaded by class inequalities, which have shown little sign of diminishing over the last half century; and

(4) that the evidently unequal control over school boards and other decision-making bodies in education does not provide a sufficient explanation of the persistence and pervasiveness of inequalities in the school system. Although the unequal distribution of political power serves to maintain inequalities in education, their origins are to be found outside the political sphere, in the class structure itself and in the class subcultures typical of capitalist societies. Thus unequal education has its roots in the very class structure which it serves to legitimize and reproduce. Inequalities in education are a part of the web of capitalist society, and likely to persist as long as capitalism survives.

THE EVOLUTION OF CAPITALISM AND THE RISE OF MASS EDUCATION

In colonial America, and in most precapitalist societies of the past, the basic productive unit was the family. For the vast majority of male adults, work was self-directed, and was performed without direct supervision. Though constrained by poverty, ill health, the low level of technological development, and occasional interferences by the political authorities, a man had considerable leeway in choosing his working hours, what to produce, and how to produce it. While great inequalities in wealth, political power, and other aspects of status normally existed, differences in the degree of autonomy in work were relatively minor, particularly when compared with what was to come.

Transmitting the necessary productive skills to the children as they grew up proved to be a simple task, not because the work was devoid of skill, but because the quite substantial skills required were virtually unchanging from generation to generation, and because the transition to the world of work did not require that the child adapt to a wholly new set of social relationships. The child learned the concrete skills and adapted to the social relations of production through learning by doing within the family. Preparation for life in the larger community was facilitated by the child's experience with the extended family, which shaded off without distinct boundaries, through uncles and fourth cousins, into the community. Children learned early how to deal with complex relationships among adults other than their parents, and children other than their brothers and sisters.[1]

It was not required that children learn a complex set of political principles or ideologies, as political participation was limited and political authority unchallenged, at least in normal times. The only major socializing institution outside the family was the church, which sought to inculcate the accepted spiritual values and attitudes. In addition, a small number of children learned craft skills outside the family, as apprentices. The role of schools tended to be narrowly vocational, restricted to preparation of children for a career in the church or the still inconsequential state

bureaucracy. The curriculum of the few universities reflected the aristocratic penchant for conspicuous intellectual consumption.

The extension of capitalist production, and particularly the factory system, undermined the role of the family as the major unit of both socialization and production. Small peasant farmers were driven off the land or competed out of business. Cottage industry was destroyed. Ownership of the means of production became heavily concentrated in the hands of landlords and capitalists. Workers relinquished control over their labor in return for wages or salaries. Increasingly, production was carried on in large organizations in which a small management group directed the work activities of the entire labor force. The social relations of production—the authority structure, the prescribed types of behavior and response characteristic of the workplace—became increasingly distinct from those of the family.

The divorce of the worker from control over production—from control over his own labor—is particularly important in understanding the role of schooling in capitalist societies. The resulting hierarchical social division of labor—between controllers and controlled—is a crucial aspect of the class structure of capitalist societies, and will be seen to be an important barrier to the achievement of social class equality in schooling.

Rapid economic change in the capitalist period led to frequent shifts of the occupational distribution of the labor force, and constant changes in the skill requirements for jobs. The productive skills of the father were no longer adequate for the needs of the son during his lifetime. Skill training within the family became increasingly inappropriate.

And the family itself was changing. Increased geographic mobility of labor and the necessity for children to work outside the family spelled the demise of the extended family and greatly weakened even the nuclear family. Meanwhile, the authority of the church was questioned by the spread of secu-

[1]This account draws upon two important historical studies: P. Aries, *Centuries of Childhood* (New York: Random House, 1970); and B. Bailyn, *Education in the Forming of American Society* (New York: Random House, 1960).

lar rationalist thinking and the rise of powerful competing groups.

While undermining the main institutions of socialization, the rise of the capitalist system was accompanied by urbanization, labor migration, the spread of democratic ideologies, and a host of other developments which created an environment—both social and intellectual—which would ultimately challenge the political order.

An institutional crisis was at hand. The outcome, in virtually all capitalist countries, was the rise of mass education. In the U.S., the many advantages of schooling as a socialization process were quickly perceived. The early proponents of the rapid expansion of schooling argued that education could perform many of the socialization functions which earlier had been centered in the family and to a lesser extent, in the church. An ideal preparation for factory work was found in the social relations of the school: specifically, in its emphasis on discipline, punctuality, acceptance of authority outside the family, and individual accountability for one's work. The social relations of the school would replicate the social relations of the workplace, and thus help young people adapt to the social division of labor. Schools would further lead people to accept the authority of the state and its agents—the teachers—at a young age, in part by fostering the illusion of the benevolence of the government in its relations with citizens. Moreover, because schooling would ostensibly be open to all, one's position in the social division of labor could be portrayed as the result not of birth, but of one's own efforts and talents. And if the children's everyday experiences with the structure of schooling were insufficient to inculcate the correct views and attitudes, the curriculum itself would be made to embody the bourgeois ideology. Where pre-capitalist social institutions—particularly the church— remained strong or threatened the capitalist hegemony, schools sometimes served as a modernizing counter-institution.

The movement for public elementary and secondary education in the U.S. originated in the 19th century in states dominated by the burgeoning industrial capitalist class, most notably in Massachusetts. It spread rapidly to all parts of the country except the South. The fact that some working people's movements had demanded free instruction should not obscure the basically coercive nature of the extension of schooling. In many parts of the country, schools were literally imposed upon the workers.

The evolution of the economy in the 19th century gave rise to new socialization needs and continued to spur the growth of education. Agriculture continued to lose ground to manufacturing; simple manufacturing gave way to production involving complex interrelated processes; an increasing fraction of the labor force was employed in producing services rather than goods. Employers in the most rapidly growing sectors of the economy began to require more than obedience and punctuality in their workers; a change in motivational outlook was required. The new structure of production provided little built-in motivation. There were fewer jobs like farming and piece-rate work in manufacturing in which material reward was tied directly to effort. As work roles became more complicated and interrelated, the evaluation of the individual worker's performance became increasingly difficult. Employers began to look for workers who had internalized the production-related values of the firms' managers.

The continued expansion of education was pressed by many who saw schooling as a means of producing these new forms of motivation and discipline. Others, frightened by the growing labor militancy after the Civil War, found new urgency in the social control arguments popular among the proponents of education in the antebellum period.

A system of class stratification developed within this rapidly expanding educational system. Children of the social elite normally attended private schools. Because working class children tended to leave school early, the class composition of the public high schools was distinctly more elite than the public primary schools. And university education, catering mostly to the children of upper-class families, ceased to be merely training for teaching or the divinity and became important in gaining access to the pinnacles of the business world.

Around the turn of the present century, large numbers of working class and particularly immigrant children began attending high schools. At the same time, a system of class stratification developed within secondary education. The older democratic ideology of the common school—that the same curriculum should be offered to all children—gave way to the "progressive" insistence that education should be tailored to the "needs of the child." In the interests of providing an education relevant to the later life of the students, vocational schools and tracks were developed for the children of working families. The academic curriculum was preserved for those who would later have the opportunity to make use of book learning, either in college or in white-collar employment. This and other educational reforms of the progressive education movement reflected an implicit assumption of the immutability of the class structure.[2]

The frankness with which students were channeled into curriculum tracks, on the basis of their social class background, raised serious doubts concerning the "openness" of the class structure. The relation between social class and a child's chances of promotion or tracking assignments was disguised—though not mitigated much—by another "progressive" reform: "objective" educational testing. Particularly after World War I, the capitulation of the schools to business values and concepts of efficiency led to the increased use of intelligence and scholastic achievement testing as an ostensibly unbiased means of measuring the product of schooling and classifying students. The complementary growth of the guidance counseling profession allowed much of the channeling to proceed from the students' "own" well-counselled-choices, thus adding an apparent element of voluntarism to the system.

The class stratification of education during this period had proceeded hand in hand with the stratification of the labor force. As large bureaucratic corporations and public agencies employed an increasing fraction of all workers, a complicated segmentation of the labor force evolved, reflecting the hierarchical structure of the social relations of production.

The social division of labor had become a finely articulated system of work relations dominated at the top by a small group with control over work processes and a high degree of personal autonomy in their work activities, and proceeding by finely differentiated stages down the chain of bureaucratic command to workers who labored more as extensions of the machinery than as autonomous human beings.[3]

One's status, income, and personal autonomy came to depend in great measure on one's place in the hierarchy of work relations. And in turn, positions in the social division of labor came to be associated with educational credentials reflecting the number of years of schooling and the quality of education received. The increasing importance of schooling as a mechanism for allocating children to positions in the class structure, played a major part in legitimizing the structure itself.[4] But at the same time, it undermined the simple processes which in the past had preserved the position and privilege of the upper class families from generation to gen-

---

[2]See D. Cohen and M. Lazerson, "Education and the Corporate Order," *Socialist Revolution* 2, No. 3 (May/-June, 1971).

[3]See Reich, Section 5.1, p. 179.

[4]See S. Bowles, "Contradictions in U.S. Higher Education," in James H. Weaver, ed., *Modern Political Economy* (Boston: Allyn and Bacon, 1973).

eration. In short, it undermined the processes serving to reproduce the social division of labor.

In pre-capitalist societies, direct inheritance of occupational position is common. Even in the early capitalist economy, prior to the segmentation of the labor force on the basis of differential skills and education, the class structure was reproduced generation after generation simply through the inheritance of physical capital by the offspring of the capitalist class. Now that the social division of labor is differentiated by types of competence and educational credentials as well as by the ownership of capital, the problem of inheritance is not nearly as simple. The crucial complication arises because education and skills are embedded in human beings, and—unlike physical capital—these assets cannot be passed on to one's children at death. In an advanced capitalist society in which education and skills play an important role in the hierarchy of production, then, laws guaranteeing inheritance are not enough to reproduce the social division of labor from generation to generation. Skills and educational credentials must somehow be passed on within the family. It is a fundamental theme of this paper that schools play an important part in reproducing and legitimizing this modern form of class structure.

CLASS INEQUALITIES IN U.S. SCHOOLS

Unequal schooling reproduces the hierarchical social division of labor. Children whose parents occupy positions at the top of the occupational hierarchy receive more years of schooling than working class children. Both the amount and the content of their education greatly facilitate their movement into positions similar to their parents'.

Because of the relative ease of measurement, inequalities in years of schooling are particularly evident. If we define social class

standing by the income, occupation, and educational level of the parents, a child from the 90th percentile in the class distribution may expect on the average to achieve over four and a half more years of schooling than a child from the 10th percentile.[5] As can be seen in Table 8-N, social class inequalities in the number of years of schooling received arise in part because a disproportionate number of children from poorer families do not complete high school. Table 8-O indicates that these inequalities are exacerbated by social class inequalities in college attendance among those children who did graduate from high school: even among those who had graduated from high school, children of families earning less than $3,000 per year were over six times as likely *not* to attend college as were the children of families earning over $15,000.[6]

Inequalities in schooling are not simply a matter of differences in years of schooling attained. Differences in the internal structure of schools themselves and in the content of schooling reflect the differences in the social class compositions of the student bodies. The social relations of the educational process ordinarily mirror the social relations of the work roles into which most students are likely to move. Differences in rules, expected modes of behavior, and opportunities for choice are most glaring when we compare levels of schooling. Note the wide range of choice over curriculum, life style, and allocation of time afforded to college students, compared with the obedience and respect for authority expected in high school. Differentiation occurs also within each level of schooling. One needs only to compare the social relations of a junior college with those of an elite four-year college,

---

[5]The data for this calculation refer to white males who were in 1962 aged 25–34. See S. Bowles, "Schooling and Inequality from Generation to Generation," *Journal of Political Economy*, 80, No. 3 (May/June 1972).

[6]For recent evidence on these points, see U.S. Bureau of the Census, *Current Population Reports*, Series P-20, Nos. 185 and 183.

TABLE 8-N PERCENTAGE OF MALE CHILDREN AGED 16–17 ENROLLED IN PUBLIC SCHOOL, AND PERCENTAGE AT LESS THAN MODAL GRADE LEVEL, BY PARENT'S EDUCATION AND INCOME, 1960[a]

	Percent of Male Children Aged 16–17 Enrolled in Public School	*Percent of Those Enrolled Who Are Below the Modal Level*
1. Parent's education less than 8 years Family income:		
less than $3,000	66.1	47.4
$3,000–4,999	71.3	35.7
$5,000–6,999	75.5	28.3
$7,000 and over	77.1	21.8
2. Parent's education 8–11 years Family income:		
less than $3,000	78.6	25.0
$3,000–4,999	82.9	20.9
$5,000–6,999	84.9	16.9
$7,000 and over	86.1	13.0
3. Parent's education 12 years or more Family income:		
less than $3,000	89.5	13.4
$3,000–4,999	90.7	12.4
$5,000–6,999	92.1	9.7
$7,000 and over	94.2	6.9

[a]According to Bureau of the Census definitions, for 16-year-olds 9th grade or less and for 17-year-olds 10th grade or less are below the modal level. Father's education is indicated if father is present; otherwise mother's education is indicated.

SOURCE: Bureau of the Census, Census of Population, 1960, Vol. PC-(2)5A, Table 5.

or those of a working class high school with those of a wealthy suburban high school, for verification of this point.

The differential socialization patterns in schools attended by students of different social classes do not arise by accident. Rather, they stem from the fact that the educational objectives and expectations of both parents and teachers, and the responsiveness of students to various patterns of teaching and control, differ for students of different social classes.[7] Further, class inequalities in school

socialization patterns are reinforced by the inequalities in financial resources. The paucity of financial support for the education of children from working class families not only leaves more resources to be devoted to the children of those with commanding roles in the economy; it forces upon the teachers and school administrators in the working class schools a type of social relations which fairly closely mirrors that of the factory. Thus financial considerations in poorly supported working class schools militate against small intimate classes, against a multiplicity of elective courses and specialized teachers (except disciplinary personnel), and preclude the amounts of free time for the teachers and free space required for a more open, flexible educational environment. The lack of financial

[7]That working class parents seem to favor more authoritarian educational methods is perhaps a reflection of their own work experiences, which have demonstrated that submission to authority is an essential ingredient in one's ability to get and hold a steady, well-paying job.

TABLE 8-O COLLEGE ATTENDANCE IN 1967 AMONG
HIGH SCHOOL GRADUATES, BY FAMILY INCOME[a]

Family Income[b]	Percent Who Did Not Attend College
Total	53.1
under $3,000	80.2
$3,000 to $3,999	67.7
$4,000 to $5,999	63.7
$6,000 to $7,499	58.9
$7,500 to $9,999	49.0
$10,000 to $14,999	38.7
$15,000 and over	13.3

[a]Refers to individuals who were high school seniors in October 1965 and who subsequently graduated from high school. Source: U.S. Department of Commerce, Bureau of the Census, *Current Population Report*, Series P-20, No. 185, July 11, 1969, p. 6. College attendance refers to both two- and four-year institutions.

[b]Family income for 12 months preceding October 1965.

support all but requires that students be treated as raw materials on a production line; it places a high premium on obedience and punctuality; there are few opportunities for independent, creative work or individualized attention by teachers. The well-financed schools attended by the children of the rich can offer much greater opportunities for the development of the capacity for sustained independent work and the other characteristics required for adequate job performance in the upper levels of the occupational hierarchy.

While much of the inequality in U.S. education exists between schools, even within a given school different children receive different educations. Class stratification within schools is achieved through tracking, differential participation in extracurricular activities, and in the attitudes of teachers and particularly guidance personnel who expect working class children to do poorly, to terminate schooling early, and to end up in jobs similar to their parents'.[8]

[8]See P. Lauter and F. Howe, "How the School System is Rigged for Failure," *The New York Review of Books* (June 18, 1970).

Not surprisingly, the results of schooling differ greatly for children of different social classes. The differing educational objectives implicit in the social relations of schools attended by children of different social classes has already been mentioned. Less important but more easily measured are differences in scholastic achievement. If we measure the output of schooling by scores on nationally standardized achievement tests, children whose parents were themselves highly educated outperform the children of parents with less education by a wide margin. A recent study revealed, for example, that among white high school seniors, those students whose parents were in the top education decile were on the average well over three grade levels ahead of those whose parents were in the bottom decile.[9] While a good part of this discrepancy is the result of unequal treatment in school and unequal educational resources, it will be suggested below that much of it is related to differences in the early socialization and home environment of the children.

Given the great social class differences in scholastic achievement, class inequalities in college attendance are to be expected. Thus one might be tempted to argue that the data in Table 8-O are simply a reflection of unequal scholastic achievement in high school and do not reflect any *additional* social class inequalities peculiar to the process of college admission. This view is unsupported by the available data, some of which are presented in Table 8-P. Access to a college education is highly unequal, even for children of the same measured "academic ability."

The social class inequalities in our school system and the role they play in the reproduction of the social division of labor are too

[9]Calculation based on data in James S. Coleman et al., *Equality of Educational Opportunity*, Vol. II (Washington: U.S. Dept. of Health, Education & Welfare, Office of Education, 1966), and methods described in Bowles, "Schooling and Inequality from Generation to Generation."

TABLE 8-P PROBABILITY OF COLLEGE ENTRY FOR A MALE WHO HAS REACHED GRADE 11[a]

| | | Socioeconomic Quartiles[b] | | | |
| | | Low | | | High |
		1	2	3	4
	Low 1	.06	.12	.13	.26
Ability	2	.13	.15	.29	.36
Quartiles[b]	3	.25	.34	.45	.65
	High 4	.48	.70	.73	.87

[a]Based on a large sample of U.S. high school students as reported in John C. Flannagan and William W. Cooley, *Project TALENT, One-Year Follow-Up Studies*, Cooperative Research Project No. 2333, School of Education, University of Pittsburgh, 1966.

[b]The socioeconomic index is a composite measure including family income, father's occupation and education, mother's education, etc. The ability scale is a composite of tests measuring general academic aptitude.

evident to be denied. Defenders of the educational system are forced back on the assertion that things are getting better; the inequalities of the past were far worse. Yet the available historical evidence lends little support to the idea that our schools are on the road to equality of educational opportunity. For example, data from a recent U.S. Census survey reported in Table 8-Q indicate that graduation from college has become increasingly dependent on one's class background. This is true despite the fact that the probability of high school graduation is becoming increasingly equal across social classes. On balance, the available data suggest that the number of years of schooling which the average child attains depends at least as much now upon the social class standing of his father as it did fifty years ago.[10]

The argument that our "egalitarian" education compensates for inequalities generated elsewhere in the capitalist system is patently fallacious. But the discrepancy between the ideology and the reality of the U.S. school system is far greater than would appear from a passing glance at the above data. In the first place, if education is to compensate for the social class immobility due to the inheritance of wealth and privilege, education must be structured so that the poor child receives not less, not even the same, but *more* than equal benefits from education. The school must compensate for the other disadvantages which the lower-class child suffers. Thus the liberal assertion that education compensates for in-

[10]See P. M. Blau and O. D. Duncan, *The American Occupational Structure* (New York: Wiley, 1967). More recent data do not contradict the evidence of no trend towards equality. A 1967 Census survey, the most recent available, shows that among high school graduates in 1965, the probability of college attendance for those whose parents had attended college has continued to rise relative to the probability of college attendance for those whose parents has attended less than eight years of school. See U.S. Bureau of the Census, *Current Population Reports*, Series P-20, No. 185, July 11, 1969.

TABLE 8-Q AMONG SONS WHO HAD REACHED HIGH SCHOOL, PERCENTAGE WHO GRADUATED FROM COLLEGE, BY SON'S AGE AND FATHER'S LEVEL OF EDUCATION

| Son's Age in 1962 | Likely Dates of College Graduation[a] | Father's Education | | | | | | |
| | | Less Than 8 Years | Some High School | | High School Graduate | | Some College or More | |
			Percent Graduating	Ratio to < 8	Percent Graduating	Ratio to < 8	Percent Graduating	Ratio to < 8
25–34	1950–1959	07.6	17.4	2.29	25.6	3.37	51.9	6.83
35–44	1940–1949	08.6	11.9	1.38	25.3	2.94	53.9	6.27
45–54	1930–1939	07.7	09.8	1.27	15.1	1.96	36.9	4.79
55–64	1920–1929	08.9	09.8	1.10	19.2	2.16	29.8	3.35

[a]Assuming college graduation at age 22.

SOURCE: Based on U.S. Census data as reported in William G. Spady, "Educational Mobility and Access: Growth and Paradoxes," *American Journal of Sociology*, Vol. 73, No. 3 (November 1967).

equalities in inherited wealth and privilege is falsified not so much by the extent of the social class inequalities in the school system as by their very existence, or, more correctly, by the absence of compensatory inequalities.

Second, considering the problem of inequality of income at a given moment, a similar argument applies. In a capitalist economy, the increasing important of schooling in the economy will increase income inequality even in the absence of social class inequalities in quality and quantity of schooling. This is so simply because the labor force becomes differentiated by type of skill or schooling, and inequalities in labor earnings therefore contribute to total income inequality, augmenting the inequalities due to the concentration of capital. The disequalizing tendency will of course be intensified if the owners of capital also acquire a disproportionate amount of those types of education and training which confer access to high-paying jobs.

CLASS CULTURE AND CLASS POWER

The pervasive and persistent inequalities in U.S. education would seem to refute an interpretation of education which asserts its egalitarian functions. But the facts of inequality do not by themselves suggest an alternate explanation. Indeed, they pose serious problems of interpretation. If the costs of education borne by students and their families were very high, or if nepotism were rampant, or if formal segregation of pupils by social class were practiced, or educational decisions were made by a select few whom we might call the power elite, it would not be difficult to explain the continued inequalities in U.S. education. The problem of interpretation, however, is to reconcile the above empirical findings with the facts of our society as we perceive them: public and virtually tuition-free education at all levels, few legal instruments for the direct

implementation of class segregation, a limited role for "contacts" or nepotism in the achievement of high status or income, a commitment (at the rhetorical level at least) to equality of educational opportunity, and a system of control of education which if not particularly democratic, extends far beyond anything resembling a power elite. The attempt to reconcile these apparently discrepant facts leads us back to a consideration of the social division of labor, the associated class cultures, and the exercise of class power.

The social division of labor based on the hierarchical structure of production gives rise to distinct class subcultures. The values, personality traits, and expectations characteristic of each subculture are transmitted from generation to generation through class differences in family socialization and complementary differences in the type and amount of schooling ordinarily attained by children of various class positions. These class differences in schooling are maintained in large measure through the capacity of the upper class to control the basic principles of school finance, pupil evaluation, and educational objectives.

The social relations of production characteristic of advanced capitalist societies (and many socialist societies) are most clearly illustrated in the bureaucracy and hierarchy of the modern corporation.[11] Occupational roles in the capitalist economy may be grouped according to the degree of independence and control exercised by the person holding the job. There is some evidence that the personality attributes associated with the adequate performance of jobs in occupational categories defined in this broad way differ considerably, some apparently requiring independence and internal discipline, and others emphasizing such traits as obedience, predictability, and willingness to subject oneself to external controls.

These personality attributes are developed

[11]Ed. note: see Edwards, Section 5.3, p. 193.

primarily at a young age, both in the family and, to a lesser extent, in secondary socialization institutions such as schools. Because people tend to marry within their own class (in part because spouses often meet in our class segregated schools), both parents are likely to have a similar set of these fundamental personality traits. Thus children of parents occupying a given position in the occupational hierarchy grow up in homes where child-rearing methods and perhaps even the physical surroundings tend to develop personality characteristics appropriate to adequate job performance in the occupational roles of the parents. The children of managers and professionals are taught self-reliance within a broad set of constraints; the children of production line workers are taught obedience.

While this relation between parents' class position and child's personality attributes operates primarily in the home, it is reinforced by schools and other social institutions. Thus, to take an example introduced earlier, the authoritarian social relations of working class high schools complement the discipline-oriented early socialization patterns experienced by working class children. The relatively greater freedom of wealthy suburban schools extends and formalizes the early independence training characteristic of upper-class families.

The operation of the labor market translates differences in class culture into income inequalities and occupational hierarchies. The personality traits, values, and expectations characteristic of different class cultures play a major role in determining an individual's success in gaining a high income or prestigious occupation. The apparent contribution of schooling to occupational success and higher income seems to be explained primarily by the personality characteristics of those who have higher educational attainments.[12]

[12]This view is elaborated in H. Gintis, "Education, Technology, and Worker Productivity," *American Economic Association Papers & Proceedings*, May 1971.

Although the rewards to intellectual capacities are quite limited in the labor market (except for a small number of high level jobs), mental abilities are important in getting ahead in school. Grades, the probability of continuing to higher levels of schooling, and a host of other school success variables, are positively correlated with "objective" measures of intellectual capacities. Partly for this reason, one's experience in school reinforces the belief that promotion and rewards are distributed fairly. The close relationship between the amount of education attained and later occupational success thus provides a meritocratic appearance to mask the mechanisms which reproduce the class system from generation to generation.

Positions of control in the productive hierarchy tend to be associated with positions of political influence. Given the disproportionate share of political power held by the upper class and their capacity to determine the accepted patterns of behavior and procedures, to define the national interest, and in general to control the ideological and institutional context in which educational decisions are made, it is not surprising to find that resources are allocated unequally among school tracks, between schools serving different classes, and between levels of schooling. The same configuration of power results in curricula, methods of instruction, and criteria of selection and promotion which confer benefits disproportionately on the children of the upper class.

The power of the upper class exists in its capacity to define and maintain a set of rules of operation or decision criteria—"rules of the game"—which, though often seemingly innocuous and sometimes even egalitarian in their ostensible intent, have the effect of maintaining the unequal system.

The operation of two prominent examples of these "rules of the game" will serve to illustrate the point. The first important principle is that excellence in schooling should be rewarded. Given the capacity of the upper class to define excellence in terms on which upper-class children tend to excel (for example, scholastic achievement), adherence to this principle yields inegalitarian outcomes (for example, unequal access to higher education) while maintaining the appearance of fair treatment.[13] Thus the principle of rewarding excellence serves to legitimize the unequal consequences of schooling by associating success with competence. At the same time, the institution of objectively administered tests of performance serves to allow a limited amount of upward mobility among exceptional children of the lower class, thus providing further legitimation of the operations of the social system by giving some credence to the myth of widespread mobility.

The second example is the principle that elementary and secondary schooling should be financed in very large measure from local revenues. This principle is supported on the grounds that it is necessary to preserve political liberty. Given the degree of residential segregation by income level, the effect of this principle is to produce an unequal distribution of school resources among children of different classes. Towns with a large tax base can spend large sums for the education of their disproportionately upper-class children even without suffering a higher than average tax rate. Because the main resource inequalities in schooling thus exist between rather than

within school districts, and because there is no effective mechanism for redistribution of school funds among school districts, poor families lack a viable political strategy for correcting the inequality.

The above rules of the game—rewarding "excellence" and financing schools locally—illustrate the complementarity between the political and economic power of the upper class. Thus it appears that the consequences of an unequal distribution of political power among classes complement the results of class culture in maintaining an educational system which has thus far been capable of transmitting status from generation to generation, and capable in addition of political survival in the formally democratic and egalitarian environment of the contemporary United States.

THE LIMITS OF EDUCATIONAL REFORM

The role of the schools in reproducing and legitimizing the social division of labor has recently been challenged by popular egalitarian movements. At the same time, the educational system is showing signs of internal structural weakness.[14] These two developments suggest that fundamental change in the schooling process may soon be possible. Analysis of both the potential and the limits of educational change will be facilitated by drawing together and extending the strands of our argument.

. . .

I have argued that the structure of education reflects the social relations of production. For at least the past 150 years, expansion of education and changes in the forms of schooling have been responses to needs generated by the economic system. The sources of present inequality in American education were found in the mutual reinforcement of class subcul-

---

[13]Those who would defend the "reward excellence" principle on the grounds of efficient selection to ensure the most efficient use of educational resources might ask themselves this: Why should colleges admit those with the highest college entrance examination board scores? Why not the lowest, or the middle? The rational social objective of the college is to render the greatest *increment* in individual capacities ("value added" to the economist), not to produce the most illustrious graduating class ("gross output"). Yet if incremental gain is the objective, it is far from obvious that choosing from the top is the best policy. And because no one has even attempted to construct a compelling argument that choosing from the top is the policy which maximizes the increment of learning for students, we can infer that the practice is supported by considerations other than that of efficient allocation of resources in education.

[14]See Bowles, "Contradictions in U.S. Higher Education."

tures and social-class biases in the operations of the school system itself. The analysis strongly suggests that educational inequalities are rooted in the basic institutions of our economy. Reconsideration of some of the basic mechanisms of educational inequality lends support to this proposition. First, the principle of rewarding academic excellence in educational promotion and selection serves not only to legitimize the process by which the social division of labor is reproduced. It is also a basic part of the process that socializes young people to work for external rewards and encourages them to develop motivational structures fit for the alienating work of the capitalist economy. Selecting students from the bottom or the middle of the achievement scale for promotion to higher levels of schooling would go a long way toward equalizing education, but it would also jeopardize the schools' capacity to train productive and well-adjusted workers.[15] Second, the way in which local financing of schools operates to maintain educational inequality is also rooted in the capitalist economy, in this case in the existence of an unequal distribution of income, free markets in residential property, and the narrow limits of state power. It seems unwise to emphasize this aspect of the long-run problem of equality in education, however, for the inequalities in school resources resulting from the localization of finance may not be of crucial importance in maintaining inequalities in the effects of education. Moreover, a significant undermining of the principle of local finance may already be underway in response to pressures from the poorer states and school districts.

Of greater importance in the perpetuation of educational inequality are differential class subcultures. These class-based differences in personality, values, and expectations, I have argued, represent an adaptation to the different requirements of adequate work perfor-

mance at various levels in the hierarchical social relations of production. Class subcultures, then, stem from the everyday experiences of workers in the structure of production characteristic of capitalist societies.

It should be clear by this point that educational equality cannot be achieved through changes in the school system alone. Nonetheless, attempts at educational reform may move us closer to that objective if, in their failure, they lay bare the unequal nature of our school system and destroy the illusion of unimpeded mobility through education. Successful educational reforms—reducing racial or class disparities in schooling, for example— may also serve the cause of equality of education, for it seems likely that equalizing access to schooling will challenge the system either to make good its promise of rewarding educational attainment or to find ways of coping with a mass disillusionment with the great panacea.[16]

Yet, if the record of the last 150 years of educational reforms is any guide, we should not expect radical change in education to result from the efforts of those confining their attention to the schools. The political victories of past reform movements have apparently resulted in little if any effective equalization. My interpretation of the educational consequences of class culture and class power suggests that these educational reform movements failed because they sought to eliminate educational inequalities without challenging the basic institutions of capitalism.

Efforts to equalize education through changes in government policy will at best scratch the surface of inequality. For much of the inequality in American education has its

[15]Consider what would happen to the internal discipline of schools if the students' objective were to end up at the bottom of the grade distribution!

[16]The failure of the educational programs of the War on Poverty to raise significantly the incomes of the poor is documented in T. I. Ribich, *Education and Poverty* (Washington, D.C.: The Brookings Institution, 1968). In the case of blacks, dramatic increases in the level of schooling relation to whites have scarcely affected the incomes of blacks relative to whites. See R. Weiss, "The Effects Education on the Earnings of Blacks and Whites," *Review of Economics and Statistics* 52, no. 2 (May 1970), 150–59.

origin outside the limited sphere of state power, in the hierarchy of work relations and the associated differences in class culture. As long as jobs are defined so that some have power over many and others have power over none—as long as the social division of labor persists—educational inequality will be built into society in the United States.

CHAPTER 9

Sexism

BEGINNING IN THE LATE 1960s, feminism once again became a widespread social and political movement in the United States—a movement that has touched, in one way or another, almost every person in the country.[1] Earlier feminists fought for the vote, for rights to education, and for married women's rights to own property. Today, campaigns fighting discrimination against women and sexual inequality have begun to reach everywhere: the media, schools, sports, clubs, political parties, hospitals, churches, labor unions, government agencies, offices, factories, and, of course, families themselves. The feminist movement has begun to alert and to change the consciousness of women, and of men as well. It has exposed patterns and incidences of sexism that have always existed but were often ignored, patterns that women experienced but could not always label. Today, there is much more consciousness of and struggle against the reality that women do not have the same economic opportunities as men; that women still have the primary responsibility for parenting of children and for housework, whether or not they hold a paid job; that women are sexually assaulted by individual men—as in rape—and assaulted and stereotyped by male-dominated institutions—as in much advertising; that women, in other words, are subjected to a special and systematic oppression. We shall use the term sexism, or alternatively male dominance, to denote this systematic oppression of women.

[1]This introduction and the entire chapter were prepared with the major assistance of Nancy Chodorow.

From the perspective of what human relationships and human fulfillment *could* be, the system of male dominance distorts and warps interpersonal relationships for *both* sexes; it creates barriers between men and women as well as among women and among men, and it narrows the kinds of personal relationships and personal development available or allowable. For example, sexism pressures men always to appear strong and tough and not to express their feelings and emotions; men thus limit their own personal development.

Sexism does not oppress women and men equally, however. All men derive some privileges from it, and men are in many ways the agents of the oppression of women. Men are not likely to see all the ways in which women are oppressed, and they are unlikely to give up all their privileges willingly.

How can we account for the present status of women? How is that status affected by capitalism? What is the connection between the system of sexism and the capitalist system? What sorts of changes are needed to eliminate sexism from our society? In this chapter we shall take up these questions.

We begin by observing that, although there are important biological differences between the sexes, our understanding and experience of the concepts "male" and "female" are much more the product of social and cultural than of biological and physiological factors. Anthropologists, who live in and study different societies, find a wide variety of rituals, symbols and divisions of labor that serve to distinguish the sexes; these differences are so varied (and even completely opposite from one society to another) that they could not possibly emerge directly from biology. In the first reading in this chapter, Gayle Rubin provides numerous examples that illustrate this variety. It turns out that most societies, and certainly our own, go to truly astonishing lengths to differentiate males and females. Physiology does dictate that only women can bear and breast-feed infants, but the remaining aspects of parenting are all open to social arrangement. Their organization cannot be explained by biology alone. For Rubin, the "sex-gender system" is the social process that transforms the biological differences between the sexes into structured social relations of gender. All sex-gender systems, anthropologists also tell us, have hitherto included some form of gender inequality, i.e., women were subordinated to men in pre-capitalist societies, but again in varying ways and to varying degrees.

The sex-gender system that prevailed in feudal, pre-capitalist Western Europe was based primarily on the patriarchal family of the time. In feudal society lords controlled the labor of their serfs, and a set of legal relations and religious beliefs supported this arrangement. Within the family, which was the basic production unit of feudal society, another serf-type relationship held: the father controlled the labor of women and children and exercised power over the capacity of the wife to bear children. Indeed, this unequal relationship provides our definition of patriarchy. The patriarchal authority structure was also accompanied by a set of legal relations that vested most property and legal rights with the father. Marriage essentially involved the exchange of women from one patriarchal family to another, as the father "gave away" the bride. Patriarchy was a self-reproducing system that bequeathed to men control over a major component of the means of production and reproduction.

The development of petty commodity and wage-labor systems of production at first strengthened this system of patriarchy. As a result, the relative status of women declined; for example, women in the United States had

fewer property rights in the nineteenth century than they had in the eighteenth. Capitalist development at first reinforced patriarchy simply by removing many production activities from the home to factories and thereby reducing the significance of women's labor in home production. A decline in women's status followed. But to see fully why patriarchy was strengthened, we must examine the important functions that the patriarchal family served for capitalism.

Most importantly, the patriarchal family served the reproduction needs of capitalism. Capitalism involves not only the accumulation of capital, but also the reproduction of labor-power. The physical and emotional labor of maintaining wage-workers and children—cooking, keeping house, caring for children—must be somehow organized if reproduction of wage-labor is to occur. The patriarchal family that already existed by the time the capitalist mode of production had emerged provided a ready-made system for these purposes. Men could work as wage-workers in factories and leave to their wives the essential reproductive activities that continued to be carried out in the home. While young single women could expect to work for several years at wage labor outside the home, most married women could not, for reproductive work itself required many hours of labor over most of a wife's adult married life. Women who did want a career were rejecting the possibility of having a family. This alone kept many married women out of the wage labor force and confined them to the home. In the United States, for example, at the end of the nineteenth century over 95 percent of all married women stayed at home to do unpaid work in the household (the percentage was a little lower among black married women). As late as 1940 only 15 percent of married women were in the wage labor force.

As long as they had the patriarchal family to meet their needs, capitalists did not have to bother to create a new institution of social reproduction. As long as they could get immigrant men from abroad and from rural areas, capitalists did not need to draw upon married women for wage labor. At the same time, the general exclusion of married women from wage labor perpetuated their economic dependence upon men. The sexual division of labor thus simultaneously reproduced the male wage labor force for capital and the subordination of women.

Moreover, sexism is very useful to capitalists who employ women as wage-workers.[2] Women who lack the economic support of a husband and women who are in the wage labor force on only a temporary basis have always been an important source of easily exploitable labor for capitalists. Such subordinated women provide a significant portion of the marginal labor force needed by capitalists to draw upon during upswings in the business cycle and to release during downswings. And the divisions between men and women workers that result from sexism weaken labor's overall strength against capital.

Although capitalism at first reinforced patriarchy, in the longer run capitalism fundamentally undermined it. Today, it is no longer accurate to speak of the family as patriarchal in the full feudal sense of the term. But the result has not been equality for women. Instead, a system of male dominance has evolved, firmly rooted in the needs of the capitalist system. And it is still accurate to speak of the contemporary family as generally male-dominant and embodying sexual inequality.[3] We must examine both how capitalism attacked patriarchy and how capitalism is an obstacle to the further elimination of male dominance.

The attack by capitalism on patriarchy occurred on both economic and ideological levels. At the economic level, the employment of women in industry, by giving women a potential source of economic independence, tended to undermine the power of husbands and fathers over women's labor. This tendency has become stronger in the present century, and particularly since World War II.

The decline in the birth rate, the growth of mass schooling for children, the increase in life expectancy and the spread of productivity-increasing appliances within the home have reduced substantially the portion of a wife's labor time needed for social reproduction within the home. And the progressive exhaustion of reserve supplies of male immigrants and farmers has made all women and especially married women a more important source of wage labor for capitalists.

At the ideological level, bourgeois revolutions, such as in the United States in 1776 and in France in 1789, spread new ideas about the inalienable rights of individuals and the immorality of slavery. These ideals were not at first extended to women (or to slaves), but in the last half of the nineteenth century such ideas did support the struggles of feminist movements for full citizenship rights for women. Real advances were made by these movements, such as women's right to vote and to hold property when they were married. The legal inequality of women was still an issue in the 1970s, when feminists again made use of much proclaimed ideas about individual rights and the equality of individuals before the law to help win changes in laws concerning abortion, access to credit, employment, etc.

But despite the undermining of patriarchy and advances in women's rights, male dominance has survived in monopoly capitalism. Although the economic and ideological bases of patriarchy have been much dissolved, capitalist development has maintained male dominance rather than eliminating it. To see why this is, we will examine the functions that the male-dominant family and sexism serve for monopoly capitalism. This will aid us in understanding how and why sexism continues to be perpetuated by the capitalist system.

To appreciate why the male-dominant family is still functional for capitalism we must consider why much reproduction work is still located in the family. To begin with, many reproductive activities, especially the care of young children, are hard to standardize and require considerable labor time. As a result, it

[2]A statistical appendix following this introduction provides a series of tables that document trends in the position of women in the wage-labor force.

[3]In principle, families could be egalitarian, but that is generally not the case today.

is difficult for capitalist firms to compete against the unpaid labor of women available in the household. One might think that the capitalist state would provide substitutes, especially since this would free more labor for the wage labor force. This has occurred to some extent in periods of labor scarcity; for example, government child care centers were established during World War II and some income tax deductions are made available for child care expenses today. But the degree of U.S. state expenditure on such activities has so far been quite minimal, because of the endurance of sexist beliefs about motherhood, and because working women with small children have somehow been able to make their own child care arrangements, at their own expense.

The psychological factors in social reprodution have also insured the survival of the male-dominant family and made it useful to capitalism. The labor performed by women in the family is more than purely physical work. Much of it is emotional work: building and maintaining interpersonal relationships and insuring the emotional development and stability of children and men so that they can function in a capitalist society. This work is crucial for the reproduction of labor-power in capitalism, and it becomes even more important in advanced capitalism.[4] It is one of the principal functions that the modern family serves for capitalism, and it would be difficult for individual capitalists or the state to provide it so well.

At the same time, the male-dominant family is so organized as to insure its own reproduction; this point is crucial for understanding the perpetuation of sexism. As long as mothering is carried out primarily by women and not equally by men and women, little boys and girls develop emotionally in different ways. Girls tend to develop in ways that help prepare them for their future role as nurturant mothers; they sense themselves as more in personal connection with other people, and they tend to be more open to their emotions.

Boys tend to develop in ways more adapted to becoming fathers and wage-workers; they are more likely to repress their emotions and thereby be able to work responsibly and regularly at alienated labor outside the home; typically, they are engaged very little in the emotional development of children.[5] The male-dominant family thus perpetuates sexism while benefiting capitalism.

Male dominance today is also based in the sexist operation of the labor market, in a manner that also benefits capitalism. It is still true that women who are trying to support themselves and their families or who are only temporarily in the wage labor force provide an especially vulnerable and therefore exploitable labor supply for capitalists. Many of the lowest-paid jobs in the economy are filled by such women.

Since the turn of the century, women have been entering the U.S. wage labor force in very large numbers, and many women are now wage-workers on a permanent and not at all marginal basis. But women have not entered wage labor on an equal basis with men, and sexism has been perpetuated. By and large, women have entered already female occupations, such as nursing, or new occupations, such as office work, that became quickly feminized and were segmented from male jobs.[6] The effect of this sexual segregation has been to limit women's wages, to the benefit of capitalists. In turn, the lower wages

[4]See the comments along these lines in Morton, Section 3.6, p. 111.

[5]This argument is further developed in Nancy Chodorow, *Mothering: Psychoanalysis and the Social Organization of Gender* (Berkeley: University of California Press, 1978); see also Beatrice Whiting and Carolyn Pope Edwards, "A Cross-Cultural Analysis of Sex Differences in the Behavior of Children Aged Three Through Eleven," *The Journal of Social Psychology*, 91 (1973), 171–88.

[6]For more on the history of job segregation by sex, see Alice Kessler-Harris, "Stratifying by Sex: Understanding the History of Working Women," in R. Edwards, M. Reich, and D. Gordon, eds., *Labor Market Segmentation* (Lexington, Mass.: D.C. Heath, 1975), and Heidi Hartmann, "Capitalism, Patriarchy and Job Segregation by Sex," in M. Blaxall and B. Reagan, eds., *Women and the Workplace: The Implications of Occupational Segregation* (Chicago: University of Chicago Press, 1976), as well as the other essays in both of these volumes.

received by women and the continued inequality inherent in their having responsibility for child-care and housekeeping has perpetuated women's economic dependence upon men.

The long-term rise in real wages in this century has allowed more single women to subsist on their own (although at a lower standard of living than single men) but these wages are hardly sufficient for most women to support any children. The family thus continues to rest on an economic basis that is unequal for women and inherently sexist. Sexism is now based not just in the family but also, and increasingly so, in a labor market that segregates jobs unequally by sex.

The modern family, however, does not fit perfectly the needs of capitalism. Largely through the input of women's labor, the family provides primary emotional relationships and a place to escape from alienated wage labor. It therefore potentially contains an implicit critique of social relations based purely on exchange, and indicates, albeit in a sexist and distorted form, what society could be like if it were governed by criteria of human needs instead of the exchange relations of capitalism.

In recent decades women's lives have changed, and the status of women has undergone some evolution. For example, the development of contraceptive techniques and successful feminist struggles to legalize abortion have given women more control over sexuality and procreation. One of the most striking changes has been the increases in the number and proportion of married women and mothers who work at wage labor.[7] In the United States, over half of all husbands who are wage-workers have wives who are also wage-workers, and both husband and wife are now wage-workers in over a third of all husband-wife families with young children.

These wives, however, are still unequal wage-workers: the relative wages, degree of occupational segregation, and unequal responsibility of working wives for housework has remained relatively unchanged. More-

over, contradictory demands are increasingly being made upon women. Within the family itself, women face contradictions between being good mothers (active, nurturant, and caring for the welfare of their children) and being good wives (passive and submissive to their husbands seeking escape from the alienated work world). Women wage-workers are expected to be good wives, filling their household responsibilities when they come home, resuscitating their husbands for the following day, and expected to be good wage-workers without themselves receiving the same kind of support. At the same time, a society that pressures women to become mothers and provides practically no alternate child care arrangements expects these same mothers to be fulltime wage workers. These contradictions have been intensifying, producing a growing feminist consciousness, and a consciousness that sexism is currently firmly rooted in the capitalist system. The feminist struggle is a struggle against both forms of oppression.

Statistical Appendix: Women in the United States Wage Labor Force

Three major themes stand out when we look at the place of women in the U.S. wage-labor force. First, an enormous increase has taken place in the number and proportion of women who work outside the home; second, there is a marked tendency for occupations and jobs to be segregated by gender, and the degree of such segregation has not diminished over the years; and third, the increase in wage-labor participation of women has been accompanied by a *widening* income differential between men and women, with women continuing to receive lower pay than men. In the following paragraphs we examine briefly the data that exhibit these themes.

PARTICIPATION IN WAGE-LABOR

Figure 9-A and Tables 9-A and 9-B indicate, from a variety of viewpoints, the long-run trends in the numbers and proportion of wom-

[7]See the statistical appendix.

Figure 9-A Women workers in the labor force

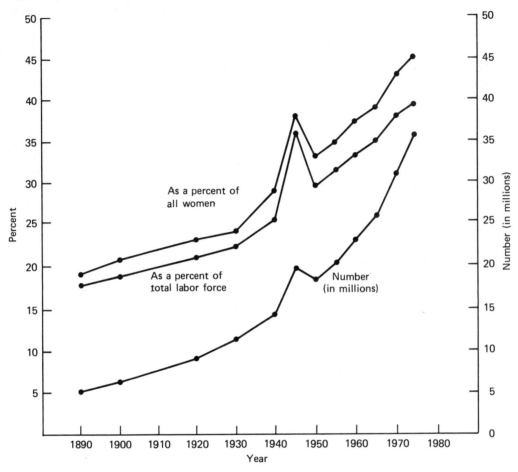

1890–1930: Persons 14 years and older in the total labor force.
1940–1974: Persons 16 years and older in the civilian labor force.
SOURCE: U.S. Department of Labor, Women's Bureau, *1975 Handbook on Women Workers*, Bulletin 297 (Washington, D.C.: U.S. Government Printing Office, 1975), Table 2.

en who are wage and salary workers. In Figure 9-A we see that the percentage of women who are wage-workers increased from 18.2 percent in 1890 to 45.0 percent in 1974.[1] In the same period women workers rose from 17 percent to 39 percent of the wage-labor force. As one might expect, such a massive

increase in the number of women workers has resulted in a substantial change in the characteristics of women entering the wage-labor force. This shift can be seen by comparing the female wage-labor force of 1890 with that of the present.

In 1890, most women workers were young

---

[1]We are using the term "wage-workers" for those who receive a wage or salary for their work and the term "wage-labor force" to refer to all those who are working for a wage or salary or presently searching for such a job. The official government statistics that we are using also count the self-employed (e.g., small business-

people, independent professionals, farmers) in the labor force category. We will ignore this group in our discussion; their importance has declined markedly in recent decades (see Reich, Section 5.1, p. 179), and the proportion of the self-employed in the labor force is much lower among women than among men.

TABLE 9-A MARITAL STATUS OF WOMEN IN THE LABOR FORCE

Year	Married: Husband Present	Never Married	Widowed Separated Divorced	All Women in Labor Force
1890	13.2%	69.2%	17.2%	100%
1940	30.3	48.5	21.2	100
1950	46.7	30.4	22.9	100
1960	52.8	23.2	24.0	100
1970	58.2	22.2	19.6	100
1974	57.7	23.3	19.0	100

SOURCES: U.S. Bureau of the Census, *Historical Statistics of the United States, Colonial Times to 1957; 1975 Handbook on Women Workers*, Table 4.

—over half were under 25—and single—70 percent had never married. Only 13 percent of all working women were married and living with their husbands. Most women workers dropped out of the wage-labor force, never to return, once they were married; in 1890 only 4.5 percent of married women (with husbands present) were wage-workers. Adult women who were not supported economically by men —women who were divorced, separated, or widowed—were more likely to be in the wage-labor force; their participation rate in 1890 was 29 percent. Black women were also more likely to be wage-workers—37.7 percent in 1890 compared to only 15.8 percent of white women.[2]

Tables 9-A and 9-B show the shifts in the marital and family status of women workers

[2]U.S. Bureau of the Census, *Historical Statistics of the United States, From Colonial Times to 1957*, p. 72.

that have taken place since 1890. Since that time the largest increase in women workers has occurred among married women with husbands present (see Table 9-A); such women now comprise three-fourths of all women workers.

In 1947, among families with both spouses present, there were 29.9 million husbands who were employed, and only 6.5 million employed wives. By 1974 the comparable figures were 39.3 million working husbands (an increase of 31 percent over 1947) and 20.4 working wives (an increase of 214 percent).[3] More recently, the increase in working women has been particularly marked among married women with children. The increase in the number of working wives has been especially rapid since World War II, as Table 9-B shows. Today, over half of all married women with school-age children are wage-workers, as are over a third of married women with preschool-age children. The highest wage-labor force participation rates today are still found among women who provide the primary economic support for their children: of mothers with children under 18 who were widowed, divorced, or separated, 62.0 percent were wage-workers in 1974.[4] The wage-labor participation rates of both white and minority-race women have increased since 1890, but

[3]U.S. Department of Labor, *Manpower Report of the President, 1974*, Table B-1; U.S. Department of Labor, Women's Bureau, *1975 Handbook on Women Workers*, Bulletin 297.

[4]*1975 Handbook on Women Workers*, Table 10.

TABLE 9-B LABOR FORCE PARTICIPATION RATES OF WOMEN, BY MARITAL AND CHILD STATUS

Year	Never Married	Married, Husband Present			Widowed Separated Divorced
		Total	With Children 6–17 Only	With Children 0–6	
1890	36.9%	4.5%	–	–	28.6%
1940	48.1	14.7	–	–	36.2
1950	50.5	23.8	28.3	11.9	37.8
1960	44.1	30.5	39.0	18.6	40.0
1970	53.0	40.8	49.2	30.3	39.1
1974	57.2	43.0	51.2	34.4	40.9

SOURCES: *Manpower Report of the President, 1975; 1975 Handbook on Women Workers; Historical Statistics of the United States.*

a greater increase has occurred among white women, so that the racial differences in participation rates are much smaller today than in 1890: 47.9 percent among minority-race women in 1974, compared to 44.5 percent among white women.[5]

The above trends indicate that women in the United States are increasingly in the wage-labor force on a permanent basis. The life cycle of women has changed, with fewer years spent in pregnancy and raising children, and more years devoted to participation in wage-labor.

Despite this increase in the participation of women in wage-labor outside the home, the amount of time that women spend working in the home is still substantial. Table 9-C shows the results of a survey of husband-wife families who kept detailed records on the time they spent on shopping, food preparation, and after-meal cleanup, care of family members, care of clothing, house, yard and car, and household management and record-keeping.

[5] *1975 Handbook on Women Workers,* Table 15: in this report minority race denotes blacks, American Indians, Japanese, Chinese, Filipinos, and Koreans.

The amount of time spent on household work varied with the number and age of children, and with whether the wife worked outside the home. The average time spent on household work ranged from 4 to 8 hours daily for women who were also wage-workers, and from 5 to 12 hours daily for those who were not. The time spent by husbands on household work was considerably less. A comparison of these results with a similar survey from the 1920s indicated that neither the proliferation of household appliances nor the increase in the number of women who are wage-workers had resulted in significantly less time spent in housework. The average working wife today puts in a 66- to 75-hour week at combined wage-labor and household jobs.

OCCUPATIONAL SEGREGATION

Despite the growth in the numbers and proportion of women in the wage-labor force, the occupational segregation between "men's work" and "women's work" that was apparent at the end of the nineteenth century has not diminished in intensity.

TABLE 9-C AVERAGE DAILY TIME SPENT ON HOUSEHOLD WORK

Number of Children	Age of Wife or Youngest Child	Nonemployed-Wife Families		Employed-Wife Families	
(1)	(2)	(3a)	(3b)	(4a)	(4b)
	Wife	*Wife*	*Husband*	*Wife*	*Husband*
	Under 25	5.1	0.9	3.5	1.4
None	25–39	5.9	1.2	3.6	1.4
	40–54	6.2	1.5	4.3	1.8
	55 and over	5.4	2.0	4.3	1.1
	Youngest Child				
	12–17	7.1	1.7	4.8	1.7
Two	6–11	7.4	1.6	5.4	1.5
	2–5	8.2	1.6	6.2	1.7
	1	8.8	1.7	6.2	3.5
	Under 1	9.5	1.5	7.7	1.6

How to read this table:
    Take, for example, a family with no children (col. 1) where the wife is between 25 and 39 years of age (col. 2 and row 2). If the wife is not employed (col. 3) she does an average of 5.9 hours per day (col. 3a) while her husband does an average of 1.2 hours per day (col. 3b). Even if the wife in this family works (col. 4) she still does 3.6 hours of housework (col. 4a) per day while her husband does an average of 1.4 hours per day (col. 4b).
SOURCE: *1975 Handbook on Women Workers:* based on a sample of 1378 families in upstate New York in 1967–68 and 1971.

The sectors that accounted in 1870 for almost all of women's wage employment were agriculture, domestic servants, and textile apparel industries: of nonfarm women wage workers in 1870, 70 percent were domestic servants, and 24 percent worked in textiles and apparel.[6] Women had always played a major role in the labor force in textiles, the first major factory-based industry to emerge in the United States, but they never moved from clothing into other manufacturing industries in significant numbers. The rapid growth of manufacturing in the nineteenth century did not lead to comparable increases in the employment of women in those industries. At the same time the decline in the importance of maids and servants and agricultural employment reduced the significance of these occupations for working women (see Table 9-D).

TABLE 9-D MAJOR OCCUPATIONAL GROUPS OF EMPLOYED WOMEN

	1900	1940	1974
Professional and technical	8.1%	12.8%	14.9%
Managers and administrators	7.3	4.5	5.2
Clerical and sales	8.2	28.8	41.7
Craft workers	1.5	1.1	1.5
Operatives	23.8	19.5	13.0
Nonfarm laborers	2.6	1.1	1.1
Service workers	35.5	29.4	21.4
Private household	28.8	18.1	3.9
Other service	6.7	11.3	17.5
Farm workers	13.1	2.8	1.2
Total	100.0	100.0	100.0

SOURCES: *Historical Statistics of the United States; 1975 Handbook on Women Workers.*

The areas in which female employment have grown most rapidly are the newly expanding occupations that have for long been seen as "women's work"; office and retail sales workers, nurses, schoolteachers, cooks, and waitresses. These occupations alone accounted for nearly two-thirds of all

[6]U.S. Bureau of the Census, *Comparative Occupational Statistics, 1870–1940.*

employed women in 1973. As Table 9-E shows, these occupations are predominantly female in composition.

TABLE 9-E PERCENTAGE FEMALE IN SELECTED OCCUPATIONS, 1973

Total labor force	38.4
Professional and technical	40.0
Computer specialists	19.5
Librarians	82.1
Physicians	12.2
Registered nurses	97.8
Teachers, college and university	27.1
Teachers, elementary school	84.5
Managers and administrators	18.4
Sales workers	41.4
Insurance agents	12.9
Sales clerks, retail trade	69.0
Clerical workers	76.6
Bookkeepers	88.3
Computer operators	40.3
Keypunch operators	90.9
Postal clerks	26.9
Secretaries	99.1
Shipping clerks	14.4
Telephone operators	95.9
Craft workers	4.1
Operatives	31.4
Sewers and stitchers	95.5
Nonfarm laborers	6.9
Service workers	63.0
Private household	98.3
Other	58.1
Farmworkers	17.0

SOURCE: *1975 Handbook on Women Workers.*

One major attribute of the occupations in which women are concentrated is that they are relatively low-paying compared to occupations that contain a very small proportion of women. This pattern extends also to the industries that employ large numbers of blue-collar women: in general, the higher the proportion of women, the lower the average wages in the industry.

This association between low wages and high concentrations of women workers is not accidental. On the one hand, the most rapidly expanding job sectors have been low-wage jobs and women have been drawn into the wage-labor force to meet the expanded demand for labor. On the other hand, the restriction of women to female-sex-typed occupations has the effect of overcrowding those occupations, holding down pay rates in them and thereby contributing to women's lower earnings.

WAGES

The trends in money income of men and women from 1947 to 1974 are shown in Table 9-F. For year-round, full-time workers, the ratio of female income to male income has fallen, from .64 in 1955 to .57 in 1974. It is often said that women's wages are lower than men's because they are more likely to move in and out of the labor force and therefore have less job experience than men. But several studies have examined earnings differences between men and women who have the same

years of job experience, age, education, hours worked per year, etc. These studies consistently find that more than half of the total earnings gap between men and women can *not* be attributed to such factors.[7]

Women received substantially lower earnings than men in the same broadly classified occupations, as Table 9-G indicates. Much of this difference is due to the fact that women and men have different jobs within these occupational groups. Of professional and technical workers in 1974, for example, about 40 percent were women. But within this group, over three-fourths of elementary schoolteachers, librarians, and nurses were

[7]See, for example, L. E. Suter and H. P. Miller, "Income Differences between Men and Career Women, *"American Journal of Sociology,* 78 (January 1973), 78 962–74. A number of such studies are summarized in I. V. Sawhill, "The Economics of Discrimination Against Women: Some New Findings," *Journal of Human Resources* 8, no. 3, (Summer 1974), 383–96.

TABLE 9-F MEDIAN TOTAL MONEY INCOME OF MALES AND FEMALES[a]

Year	All Income Recipients			% Full-Time[b]		Full-Time Workers		
	Male	Female	F/M	Male	Female	Male	Female	F/M
1947	$2230	$1027	.46	–	–	–	–	–
1950	2570	953	.37	–	–	–	–	–
1955	3358	1120	.33	63.1	31.1	$ 4246	$2734	.64
1960	4081	1262	.31	58.3	28.3	5435	3296	.60
1965	4824	1564	.32	59.8	29.3	6479	3883	.60
1970	6670	2237	.34	56.6	30.0	9184	5440	.59
1974	8379	3079	.37	55.9	30.4	12152	6957	.57

[a]Income in current prices of civilians 14 years or older.
[b]Year-round full-time workers—i.e., those working at least 35 hours per week and 50 weeks per year.
sources: U.S. Department of Commerce, Bureau of the Census, *Current Population Reports,* Series P-60, annual issues.

TABLE 9-G USUAL WEEKLY EARNINGS OF FULL-TIME MEN AND WOMEN WORKERS, 25–54 YEARS OF AGE, BY OCCUPATION, MAY 1974

	Women	Men	Ratio of Women's to Men's Earnings
Professional and technical	$189	$261	.72
Managers and administrators	165	274	.60
Sales	94	226	.42
Clerical	126	193	.65
Operatives	108	168	.64
All occupations	134	223	.60

source: Deborah P. Klein, "Women in the Labor Force: The Middle Years," U.S. Department of Labor, *Monthly Labor Review* (November 1975), p. 13.

women, while nine-tenths of engineers, doctors, and lawyers were men. This sexual segregation tends to occur as well within detailed occupational classifications. The economic consequence of this segregation is lower average wages for women than for men.

9.1   *The Social Nature of Sexism*

It is often argued that the subordinate position of women and the dominant position of men is a natural and inevitable consequence of biology. How significant are the biological differences of men and women in determining social roles? In the following reading, Gayle Rubin argues that biology is just the raw material; it is transformed by social experience and social interaction. Just as every society has a particular mode of production, so every society has what Rubin calls a sex-gender system that gives particular meaning to the concepts of "male" and "female."

The following is excerpted from "The Traffic in Women: Notes on the 'Political Economy' of Sex," by GAYLE RUBIN, from R. Reiter, ed., *Toward an Anthropology of Women.* © 1975 by Rayna R. Reiter. Reprinted by permission of Monthly Review Press.

The literature on women—both feminist and anti-feminist—is a long rumination of the question of the nature and genesis of women's oppression and social subordination. The question is not a trivial one, since the answers given it determine our visions of the future, and our evaluation of whether or not it is realistic to hope for a sexually egalitarian society. More importantly, the analysis of the causes of women's oppression forms the basis for any assessment of just what would have to be changed in order to achieve a society without gender hierarchy. Thus, if innate male aggression and dominance are at the root of female oppression, then the feminist program would logically require either the extermination of the offending sex, or else a eugenics project to modify its character. If sexism is a by-product of capitalism's relentless appetite for profit, then sexism would wither away in the advent of a successful socialist revolution. If the world historical defeat of women occurred at the hands of an armed patriarchal revolt, then it is time for Amazon guerrillas to start training in the Adirondacks.

· · ·

Gender is a socially imposed division of the sexes. It is a product of the social relations of sexuality. Kinship systems rest upon marriage. They therefore transform males and females into "men" and "women," each an incomplete half which can only find wholeness when united with the other. Men and women are, of course, different. But they are not as different as day and night, earth and sky, yin and yang, life and death. In fact, from the standpoint of nature, men and women are closer to each other than either is to anything else—for instance, mountains, kangaroos, or coconut palms. The idea that men and women are more different from one another than either is from anything else must come from somewhere other than nature. Furthermore, although there is an average difference between males and females on a variety of traits, the range of variation of those traits shows considerable overlap. There will always be some women who are taller than some men, for instance, even though men are on the average taller than women. But the idea that men and women are two mutually exclusive categories must arise out of something other than a nonexistent "natural" opposition. Far from being an expression of natural differences, exclusive gender identity is the suppression of natural similarities. It requires repression: in men, of whatever is the local version of "feminine" traits; in women, of the local definition of "masculine" traits. The division of the sexes has the effect of repressing some of the personality characteristics of virtually everyone, men and women. . . . Gender is not only an identification with one sex; it also entails that sexual desire be directed toward the other sex. The sexual division of labor is implicated in both aspects of gender—male and female it creates them, and it creates them heterosexual. The suppression of the homosexual component of human sexuality, and by corollary, the oppression of homosexuals, is therefore a product of the same system whose rules and relations oppress women.

[I call the sex/gender system] that part of social life which is the locus of the oppression of women, of sexual minorities, and of certain aspects of human personality within individuals. . . . As a preliminary definition, a "sex/gender system" is the set of arrangements by which a society transforms biological sexuality into products of human activity, and in which these transformed sexual needs are satisfied.

The purpose of this essay is to arrive at a more fully developed definition of the sex/gender system.

. . .

MARX

There is no theory which accounts for the oppression of women—in its endless variety and monotonous similarity, cross-culturally and throughout history—with anything like the explanatory power of the Marxist theory of class oppression. Therefore, it is not surprising that there have been numerous attempts to apply Marxist analysis to the question of women. There are many ways of doing this. It has been argued that women are a reserve labor force for capitalism, that women's gen-erally lower wages provide extra surplus to a capitalist employer, that women serve the ends of capitalist consumerism in their roles as administrators of family consumption, and so forth.

However, a number of articles have tried to do something much more ambitious—to locate the oppression of women in the heart of the capitalist dynamic by pointing to the relationship between housework and the reproduction of labor. . . . To do this is to place women squarely in the definition of capitalism, the process in which capital is produced by the extraction of surplus value from labor by capital.

. . .

The amount of the difference between the reproduction of labor power and its products depends . . . on the determination of what it takes to reproduce that labor power. Marx tends to make that determination on the basis of the quantity of commodities—food, clothing, housing, fuel—which would be necessary to maintain the health, life, and strength of a worker. But these commodities must be consumed before they can be sustenance, and they are not immediately in consumable form when they are purchased by the wage. Additional labor must be performed upon these things before they can be turned into people. Food must be cooked, clothes cleaned, beds made, wood chopped, etc. Housework is therefore a key element in the process of the reproduction of the laborer from whom surplus value is taken. Since it is usually women who do housework, it has been observed that it is through the reproduction of labor power that women are articulated into the surplus value nexus which is the *sine qua non* of capitalism. It can be further argued that since no wage is paid for housework, the labor of women in the home contributes to the ultimate quantity of surplus value realized by the capitalist. But to explain women's usefulness to capitalism is one thing. To argue that this usefulness explains the genesis of the oppression of women is quite another. It is precisely at this point that the analysis of capitalism ceases to explain very much about women and the oppression of women.

Women are oppressed in societies which can by no stretch of the imagination be described as capitalist. In the Amazon valley and the New Guinea highlands, women are frequently kept in their place by gang rape when the ordinary mechanisms of masculine intimidation prove insufficient. "We tame our women with the banana," said one Mundurucu man. The ethnographic record is littered with practices whose effect is to keep women "in their place"—men's cults, secret initiations, arcane male knowledge, etc. And pre-capitalist, feudal Europe was hardly a society in which there was no sexism. Capitalism has taken over, and rewired, notions of male and female which predate it by centuries. No analysis of the reproduction of labor power under capitalism can explain foot-binding, chastity belts, or any of the incredible array of Byzantine, fetishized indignities, let alone the more ordinary ones, which have been inflicted upon women in various times and places. The analysis of the reproduction of labor power does not even explain why it is usually women who do domestic work in the home, rather than men.

In this light it is interesting to return to Marx's discussion of the reproduction of labor. What is necessary to reproduce the worker is determined in part by the biological needs of the human organism, in part by the physical conditions of the place in which it lives, and in part by cultural tradition. Marx observed that beer is necessary for the reproduction of the English working class, and wine necessary for the French.

> . . . the number and extent of his [the worker's] so-called necessary wants, as also the modes of satisfying them, are themselves the product of historical development, and depend therefore to a great extent on the degree of civilization of a country, more particularly on the conditions under which, and consequently on the habits and degree of comfort in which, the class of free labourers has been formed. In contradistinction therefore to the case of other commodities, there enters into the determination of the value of labour-power a historical and moral element. . . . (my italics)

It is precisely this "historical and moral ele-

ment" which determines that a "wife" is among the necessities of a worker, that women rather than men do housework, and that capitalism is heir to a long tradition in which women do not inherit, in which women do not lead, and in which women do not talk to god. It is this "historical and moral element" which presented capitalism with a cultural heritage of forms of masculinity and femininity. It is within this "historical and moral element" that the entire domain of sex, sexuality, and sex oppression is subsumed. And the briefness of Marx's comment only serves to emphasize the vast area of social life which it covers and leaves unexamined. Only by subjecting this "historical and moral element" to analysis can the structure of sex oppression be delineated.

ENGELS

In *The Origin of the Family, Private Property, and the State*, Engels sees sex oppression as part of capitalism's heritage from prior social forms. Moreover, Engels integrates sex and sexuality into his theory of society. . . . The idea that the "relations of sexuality" can and should be distinguished from the "relations of production" is not the least of Engels' intuitions:

> According to the materialistic conception, the determining factor in history is, in the final instance, the production and reproduction of immediate life. *This again, is of a twofold character: on the one hand, the production of the means of existence, of food, clothing, and shelter and the tools necessary for that production; on the other side, the production of human beings themselves*, the propagation of the species. The social organization under which the people of a particular historical epoch and a particular country live is determined by both kinds of production: by the stage of development of labor on the one hand, and of the family on the other. . . . (my italics)

This passage indicates an important recognition—that a human group must do more than apply its activity to reshaping the natural world in order to clothe, feed, and warm itself. We usually call the system by which elements of the natural world are transformed into objects of human consumption the "economy." But the needs which are satisfied by economic activity even in the richest, Marxian sense, do not exhaust fundamental human requirements. A human group must also reproduce itself from generation to generation. The needs of sexuality and procreation must be satisfied as much as the need to eat, and one of the most obvious deductions which can be made from the data of anthropology is that these needs are hardly ever satisfied in any "natural" form, any more than are the needs for food. Hunger is hunger, but what counts as food is culturally determined and obtained. Every society has some form of organized economic activity. Sex is sex, but what counts as sex is equally culturally determined and obtained. Every society also has a sex/gender system—a set of arrangements by which the biological raw material of human sex and procreation is shaped by human, social intervention and satisfied in a conventional manner, no matter how bizarre some of the conventions may be.*

*That some of them are pretty bizarre, from our point of view, only demonstrates the point that sexuality is expressed through the intervention of culture. Some examples may be chosen from among the exotica in which anthropologists delight. Among the Banaro, marriage involves several socially sanctioned sexual partnerships. When a woman is married, she is initiated into intercourse by the sib-friend of her groom's father. After bearing a child by this man, she begins to have intercourse with her husband. She also has an institutionalized partnership with the sib-friend of her husband. A man's partners include his wife, the wife of his sib-friend, and the wife of his sib-friend's son. Multiple intercourse is a more pronounced custom among the Marind Anim. At the time of marriage, the bride has intercourse with all of the members of the groom's clan, the groom coming last. Every major festival is accompanied by a practice known as *otiv-bombari*, in which semen is collected for ritual purposes. A few women have intercourse with many men, and the resulting semen is collected in coconut-shell buckets. A Marind male is subjected to multiple homosexual intercourse during initiation. Among the Etoro, heterosexual intercourse is taboo for between 205 and 260 days a year. In much of New Guinea, men fear copulation and think that it will kill them if they engage in it without magical precautions. Usually, such ideas of feminine pollution express the subordina-

The realm of human sex, gender, and procreation has been subjected to, and changed by, relentless social activity for millennia. Sex as we know it—gender identity, sexual desire and fantasy, concepts of childhood—is itself a social product. We need to understand the relations of its production, and forget, for awhile, about food, clothing, automobiles, and transistor radios. In most Marxist tradition, and even in Engels' book, the concept of the "second aspect of material life" has tended to fade into the background, or to be incorporated into the usual notions of "material life." Engels' suggestion has never been followed up and subjected to the refinement which it needs. But he does indicate the existence and importance of the domain of social life which I want to call the sex/gender system.

.   .   .

The organization of sex and gender once had functions other than itself—it organized society. Now, it only organizes and reproduces itself. The kinds of relationships of sexuality established in the dim human past still dominate our sexual lives, our ideas about men and women, and the ways we raise our children. But they lack the functional load they once carried. One of the most conspicuous features of kinship is that it has been systematically stripped of its functions—political, economic, educational, and organizational. It has been reduced to its barest bones—*sex and gender*.

Human sexual life will always be subject to convention and human intervention. It will never be completely "natural," if only because our species is social, cultural, and articulate. The wild profusion of infantile sexuality will always be tamed. The confrontation between immature and helpless infants and the developed social life of their elders will prob-

tion of women. But symbolic systems contain internal contradictions whose logical extensions sometimes lead to inversions of the propositions on which a system is based. In New Britain, men's fear of sex is so extreme that rape appears to be feared by men rather than women. Women run after the men, who flee from them, women are the sexual aggressors, and it is bridegrooms who are reluctant.

ably always leave some residue of disturbance. But the mechanisms and aims of this process need not be largely independent of conscious choice. Cultural evolution provides us with the opportunity to seize control of the means of sexuality, reproduction, and socialization, and to make conscious decisions to liberate human sexual life from the archaic relationships which deform it. Ultimately, a thoroughgoing feminist revolution would liberate more than women. It would liberate forms of sexual expression, and it would liberate human personality from the straightjacket of gender.

9.2 *Capitalism, the Family and Personal Life*

Capitalist development has resulted in the decline of the family as a productive unit and its rise as a personal sphere, a shift that has affected significantly the status of women. In the following reading, Eli Zaretsky discussess the split that developed between socialized labor in commodity production and privatized labor by women in the home. The family became the focus of the desire for personal fulfillment; the burden of insuring this fulfillment fell mainly upon women.

The following is abridged from pages 23 through 38 and page 81 in *Capitalism, The Family and Personal Life* by ELI ZARETSKY. (Harper & Row, Publishers, Colophon Books.) Copyright © 1976 by Eli Zaretsky. By permission of Harper & Row, Publishers, Inc. and Pluto Press.

The organization of production in capitalist society is predicated upon the existence of a certain form of family life. The wage labor system (socialized production under capitalism) is sustained by the socially necessary but private labor of housewives and mothers. Child-rearing, cleaning, laundry, the maintenance of property, the preparation of food, daily health care, reproduction, etc. constitute a perpetual cycle of labor necessary to maintain life in this society. In this sense the family is an integral part of the economy under capitalism. Furthermore, the functions currently performed by housewives and mothers will be as indispensable to a socialist society as will be many of the forms of material production currently performed by wage labor. A socialist movement that anticipates its own role in organizing society must give weight to all forms of socially necessary labor, rather than only to the form (wage labor) that is dominant under capitalism.

· · ·

It is only under capitalism that material production organized as wage labor and the forms of production taking place within the family, have been separated so that the "economic" function of the family is obscured. . . . Sexuality and reproduction, like the production of food and shelter, are basic forms of "economic" or material necessity in any society. Only with the emergence of capitalism has "economic" production come to be understood as a "human" realm outside of "nature." Before capitalism, material production was understood, like sexuality and reproduction, to be "natural"—precisely what human beings shared with animals. From the viewpoint of the dominant culture in previous societies what distinguished humanity was not production but rather culture, religion, politics, or some other "higher" ideal made possible by the surplus appropriated from material production. In ancient Greece, for example, the labor of women and slaves within the household provided the material

basis upon which male citizens could participate in the "free" and "democratic" world of
the polis. Politics distinguished human life
from the animal existence of women and
slaves. Similarly, in medieval Europe, the
surplus appropriated from peasant families
supported the religious and aristocratic orders
who together defined the purpose and meaning of the entire society. The serfs toiling in
the field were understood as animals; they
became human because they had "souls"—
i.e., they participated in religion. Before capitalism the family was associated with the
"natural" processes of eating, sleeping, sexuality, and cleaning oneself, with the agonies
of birth, sickness, and death, *and* with the
unremitting necessity of toil. It is this association of the family with the most primary and
impelling material processes that has given
it its connotation of backwardness as society
advanced. Historically, the family has appeared to be in conflict with culture, freedom,
and everything that raises humanity above the
level of animal life. Certainly it is the association of women with this realm that has been
among the earliest and most persistent sources
of male supremacy and of the hatred of
women.

Capitalism, in its early development, distinguished itself from previous societies by the
high moral and spiritual value it placed upon
labor spent in goods production. This new
esteem for production, embodied in the idea
of private property and in the Protestant idea
of a "calling," led the early bourgeoisie to
place a high value upon the family since the
family was the basic unit of production. While
in feudal society the "personal" relations of
the aristocracy were often highly self-conscious and carefully regulated, the domestic
life of the masses was private and unexamined,
even by the church. Early capitalism developed a high degree of consciousness concerning the internal life of the family and a rather
elaborate set of rules and expectations that
governed family life. This led to a simultaneous advance and retrogression in the status
of women. On one hand, women were fixed
more firmly than ever within the family unit;
on the other hand, the family had a higher
status than ever before. But the feminist idea
that women in the family were outside the
economy did not yet have any basis. As in
pre-capitalist society, throughout most of
capitalist history the family has been the basic
unit of "economic" production—not the
"wage-earning" father but the household as a
whole. While there was an intense division of
labor *within* the family, based upon age, sex,
and family position, there was scarcely a
division *between* the family and the world of
commodity production, at least not until the
nineteenth century. Certainly women were
excluded from the few "public" activities
that existed—for example, military affairs.
But their sense of themselves as "outside" the
larger society was fundamentally limited by
the fact that "society" was overwhelmingly
composed of family units based upon widely
dispersed, individually owned productive
property. Similarly, women had a respected
role within the family since the domestic labor
of the household was so clearly integral to the
productive activity of the family as a whole.

But the overall tendency of capitalist development has been to socialize the basic processes of commodity production—to remove
labor from the private efforts of individual
families or villages and to centralize it in large-
scale corporate units. Capitalism is the first
society in history to socialize production on a
large scale. With the rise of industry, capitalism "split" material production between its
socialized forms (the sphere of commodity
production) and the private labor performed
predominantly by women within the home.
In this form male supremacy, which long
antedated capitalism, became an institutional
part of the capitalist system of production.

This "split" between the socialized labor of
the capitalist enterprise and the private labor
of women in the home is closely related to a
second "split"—between our "personal" lives
and our place within the social division of
labor. So long as the family was a productive
unit based upon private property, its members understood their domestic life and "personal" relations to be rooted in their mutual
labor. Since the rise of industry, however, proletarianization separated most people (or

families) from the ownership of productive property. As a result "work" and "life" were separated; proletarianization split off the outer world of alienated labor from an inner world of personal feeling. Just as capitalist development gave rise to the idea of the family as a separate realm from the economy, so it created a "separate" sphere of personal life, seemingly divorced from the mode of production.

This development was a major social advance. It is the result of the socialization of production achieved by capitalism and the consequent decline in socially necessary labor time and rise in time spent outside production. Personal relations and self-cultivation have always, throughout history, been restricted to the leisure classes and to artists, courtiers, and others who performed the rituals of conversation, sexual encounter, self-examination, and physical and mental development according to well-developed and socially shared codes of behavior. But under capitalism an ethic of personal fulfillment has become the property of the masses of people, though it has very different meanings for men and for women, and for different strata of the proletariat. Much of this search for personal meaning takes place within the family and is one reason for the persistence of the family in spite of the decline of many of its earlier functions.

The distinguishing characteristic of this search is its subjectivity—the sense of an individual, alone, outside society with no firm sense of his or her own place in a rationally ordered scheme. It takes place on a vast new social terrain known as "personal" life, whose connection to the rest of society is as veiled and obscure as is the family's connection. While in the nineteenth century the family was still being studied through such disciplines as political economy and ethics, in the twentieth century it spawned its own "sciences," most notable psychoanalysis and psychology. But psychology and psychoanalysis distort our understanding of personal life by assuming that it is governed by its own internal laws (for example, the psychosexual dynamics of the family, the "laws" of the mind or of

"interpersonal relations") rather than by the "laws" that govern society as a whole. And they encourage the idea that emotional life is formed only through the family and that the search for happiness should be limited to our "personal" relations, outside our "job" or "role" within the division of labor.

Thus, the dichotomies that women's liberation first confronted—between the "personal" and the "political," and between the "family" and the "economy"—are rooted in the structure of capitalist society. . . . The means of overcoming it is through a conception of the family as a historically formed part of the mode of production.

The rise of capitalism isolated the family from socialized production as it created a historically new sphere of personal life among the masses of people. The family now became the major space in society in which the individual self could be valued "for itself." This process, the "private" accompaniment of industrial development, cut women off from men in a drastic way and gave a new meaning to male supremacy. While housewives and mothers continued their traditional tasks of production—housework, reproduction, etc.— this labor was devalued through its isolation from the socialized production of surplus value. In addition, housewives and mothers were given new responsibility for maintaining the emotional and psychological realm of personal relations. For women within the family "work" and "life" were not separated but were collapsed into one another. The combination of these forms of labor has created the specific character of women's labor within the family in modern capitalist society.

.   .   .

This transformation gave rise to a new form of the family, one with no apparent connection to the rest of society. The production of exchange value was removed from the family and vested in large-scale, "impersonal" corporate units. But rather than destroying traditional bourgeois family life this transformation gave it a new meaning as the realm of happiness, love, and individual freedom. With the rise of corporate capitalism, the family became the major institution in society given over to the personal needs of its members. Society divided between an inner and an outer world. At one pole the individual was central and a sometimes desperate search for warmth, intimacy, and mutual support prevailed. At the other pole social relations were anonymous and coerced; the individual was reduced to an interchangeable economic unit.

This same transformation mystified and obscured the place of the housewife within capitalist production. The specific class position of the housewife under capitalism now lay in her "classlessness"—i.e., the absence of a direct relation to the capitalist class. Socialists and others understood her class position to be that of her husband, since her relation to the outside world was mediated through him. But the creation of a separate sphere of personal life among the proletariat entailed the creation of a separate class of housewives and mothers whose physical and mental labor reproduced this separate sphere. In contrast to the proletarian who worked in large socialized units and received a wage, the housewife worked alone and was unpaid. Rather than working for a corporation the housewife worked for a particular man, for herself, and for their children and relatives. Housework and child-rearing came to be seen as natural or personal functions performed in some private space outside society.

· · ·

Women and children lost the central place they had occupied in the early proletariat. Child labor was slowly eliminated and women were transformed into a marginal labor force in relation to capitalist production, with their primary loyalty to the home. The housewife emerged, alongside the proletarian—the two characteristic laborers of developed capitalist society. Her tasks extended beyond the material labor of the family to include responsibility for the "human values" which the family was thought to preserve: love, personal happiness, domestic felicity. In contrast, the working-class husband's primary responsibility was understood to be earning a wage, whether or not his wife worked. The split in

society between "personal feelings" and "economic production" was integrated with the sexual division of labor. Women were identified with emotional life, men with the struggle for existence. Under these conditions a new form of the family developed—one that understood itself to operating in apparent freedom from production, and that placed a primary emphasis on the personal relations of its members.

· · ·

CONCLUSION

As capitalism developed the productive functions performed by the family were gradually socialized. The family lost its core identity as a productive unit based upon private property. Material production within the family— the work of housewives and mothers—was devalued since it was no longer seen as integral to the production of commodities. The expansion of education as well as welfare, social work, hospitals, old age homes, and other "public" institutions further eroded the productive functions of the family. At the same time the family acquired new functions as the realm of personal life—as the primary institution in which the search for personal happiness, love, and fulfillment takes place. Reflecting the family's "separation" from commodity production, this search was understood as a "personal" matter, having little relation to the capitalist organization of society.

· · ·

Increasingly cut off from production, the contemporary family threatens to become a well of subjectivity divorced from any social meaning. Within it a world of vast psychological complexity has developed as the counterpart to the extraordinary degree of rationalization and impersonality achieved by capital in the sphere of commodity production. The individualist values generated by centuries of bourgeois development—self-consciousness, perfectionism, independence— have taken new shape through the insatiability of personal life in developed capitalist society. The internal life of the family is dominated by a search for personal fulfill- ment for which there seem to be no rules. Much of this search has been at the expense of women.

9.3   *Women: Domestic Labor and Wage-Labor*

Although wage-labor has grown to be the predominant form of organization of labor under capitalism, there remains one major area that is organized differently: housekeeping and child care. Capitalism has conquered and virtually replaced other pre-capitalist forms of organizing production, such as the self-sufficient family farm, but the amount of time spent by women in unpaid domestic labor has not significantly decreased.[1] In the following reading, Jean Gardiner explores the economic, psychological, and ideological factors that have been important in maintaining domestic labor under capitalism.

[1]See Table 9-C in the Statistical Appendix to the Introduction to this chapter, p. 338. Trends in the time spent on housework since the 1920's are examined in Joann Vanek, "Time Spent on Housework," *Scientific American* (November 1974), pp. 116–20.

The following is excerpted from "Women's Domestic Labor," by JEAN GARDINER, *New Left Review*, no. 89 (January–February 1975). Reprinted by permission of the *New Left Review*.

Many changes have occurred since the rise of capitalism affecting the role of women's domestic labour: e.g., changes in women's paid employment, decline in family size and infant mortality, inprovements in housing, the development of the welfare state, mass production of consumer products like prepared food and clothing. Furthermore, if we are to have any notion of how the current feminist movement relates to tendencies in capitalism and of how to direct our struggles, it is essential for us to understand how past changes in the role of women in the family have occurred, and to recognize that the current situation is by no means a static one.

WHY HAS DOMESTIC LABOUR BEEN MAINTAINED?

The character of domestic labour under capitalism has two important aspects. Firstly, a historical prerequisite of the capitalist mode of production was that the domestic family economy of workers ceased to be self-sufficient and self-reproducing. The capitalist mode of production could only develop once the mass of producers had been deprived of independent means of subsistence and were thus dependent on selling their labour power for a wage. Thus domestic labour lost its independent economic basis. But dependence on wages has never meant that workers' needs are in fact all satisfied through the purchase of commodities. Thus the second aspect of women's domestic labour is that at all stages of capitalist development it has played an essential although changing role in meeting workers' needs.

Therefore, capitalism developed out of feudalism through workers becoming dependent on the wage system, but has never provided totally for workers' needs through commodity production, instead retaining domestic labour to carry out an important part of the reproduction and maintenance of labour power. There are three possible reasons why this should be the case. (1) It may be more profitable in a strict economic sense from the point of view either of capital as a whole or of dominant sections of capital. (2) The socialization of all services currently performed in the home might so alter the nature of those services that they would cease to meet certain needs, especially emotional needs. (3) Any further erosion of domestic labour might undermine ideological aspects of the family (e.g., authoritarianism, sexism, individualism) which are important in maintaining working-class acceptance of capitalism. I shall look at each of these possible reasons in turn.

Economic Factors

A number of economic factors need to be taken into account in considering whether it might or might not be profitable from the point of view of capital for housework and childcare to be socialized. These can be broadly summarized within the following three categories of problems facing capitalists: (1) the overall level of wages that capitalists have to pay workers; (2) the availability of a labour force that is adequate both quantitatively and qualitatively; (3) the expansion of markets for capitalist commodities.

First let us look at the problem of wages or the value of labour power. Marx wrote that "the value of labour power is determined, as in the case of every other commodity, by the labour time necessary for the production and consequently also the reproduction of this special article."[1] ... It ... seems clear that Marx was confining his analysis of consumption in the working-class family to consumption of commodities. This is because his was an analysis of a pure capitalist mode of production, in which the only productive relations were those of wage labour working for capital. Thus I shall take the value of labour power to refer to the value of commodities purchased by the wage and consumed by the worker's

family. This gives us a definition of necessary labour or value as that portion of labour performed in commodity production which goes to workers' consumption via wages, and a definition of surplus labour or value as that portion of labour performed in commodity production which is unpaid and goes to profits for capitalist accumulation or consumption.

This implies that necessary labour is not synonymous with the labour embodied in the reproduction and maintenance of labour power once one takes account of domestic labour. To put the argument in a different way, the overall standard of living of workers is not determined just by the wage bargain between capital and labour, as it appears to be in Marx's analysis, but also by the contribution of domestic labour. Likewise the role of the state through taxation and social spending needs to be taken into account.

What this approach implies is that the value of labour power is not determined in any straightforward sense by the historically determined subsistence level of the working class. If one accepts that there is, at any given time, a historically determined subsistence level, this level can be achieved by varying the contributions to it of commodities purchased out of wages on the one hand and domestic labour performed by housewives on the other. Thus, at a given level of subsistence and a given level of technology, necessary labour may in fact be a variable.

This approach clearly has implications also for the determination of the rate of surplus value. In Marx's analysis of capital the rate of surplus value was determined by the dual struggle between wage labour and capital: (1) the labour extracted from workers in the capitalist production process; (2) the wage bargain between wage labour and capital. In fact, because of the role of domestic labour, the variability of the price level and the intervention of the state via taxation and social spending, the struggle over the surplus is also conducted at other levels, no less important from a capitalist viewpoint although considerably less organized from the point of view of labour. The contribution which

[1]Karl Marx, *Capital* Vol. I, Moscow 1961, p. 170.

domestic labour makes to surplus value is one of keeping down necessary labour to a level that is lower than the actual subsistence level of the working class. For example, it could be argued that it is cheaper for capital to pay a male worker a wage sufficient to maintain, at least partially, a wife who prepares meals for him, than to pay him a wage on which he could afford to eat regularly at restaurants. This seems intuitively to be the case, although it appears to conflict with the argument that if housework were socialized the resulting savings in labour time should substantially cheapen the process. The important point here is that the savings in labour time are only one aspect of socialization. The other is that work which as housework is not paid for as such (the wife's remuneration out of her husband's wage packet often being kept to a minimum, because it is not seen as hers by right) becomes wage work, commanding payment in accordance with what is generally expected in the labour market.

Thus very great savings in labour time are probably necessary for the socialization of housework not to entail rises in the value of labour power. (This does not, of course, imply that socialization would never occur if it did entail rises in the value of labour power, since there are a number of other factors discussed below which may influence this). It may, in fact, be the case that many of the services which have remained domestic tasks are actually not subject to major savings in labour time. For example, adequate socialized pre-school childcare requires a minimum of one adult to five children, without taking account of administrative and ancillary workers. If one compares this with the average family with its $2\frac{1}{2}$ children to one woman, one gets a rough estimate of no more than a 50 percent saving of labour.

Thus in terms simply of the overall level of wages, there appear to be pressures working against the socialization of housework and childcare from a capitalist viewpoint. However, the remaining two types of economic factor suggested above as relevant would seem to push in the opposite direction. The first of these is the availability of an adequate labour force. Pressure for socialization of housework and childcare might spring from a recognition by capital that it will be unable to recruit sufficient women workers without taking responsibility, directly or through the state, for performing some of the tasks previously carried out by women in their families. A rather different aspect of this problem is that socialization of childcare might also arise for educational reasons, i.e., from pressure to influence the quality of the labour force in the next generation.

The third related economic factor concerns adequate markets for capitalist production. Production of commodities for workers' consumption is clearly one important area of capitalist expansion. Capitalists are not always preoccupied with the need to hold down wages, since at certain periods rising wages can act as a stimulus to capitalist accumulation as a whole. During such a phase of capitalist development, therefore, socialization of housework might occur in response to capital's search for new areas of expansion. This clearly happened for example, in the fifties and sixties in Britain with the expansion of convenience foods.

If we now attempt to put together the different economic arguments related to socialization of housework, two different possible interpretations emerge. On the one hand, there may be conflicting pressures on capital as a whole, so that different pressures will dominate at different phases of capitalist development (i.e., depending on whether there is economic crisis and stagnation or expansion and rising productivity and employment). On the other hand, there may be conflicting pressures amongst capitalists, e.g., between those who require an expanding female labour force or whose profitability is related to sales of consumption goods to workers and those whose major concern is to hold down wages. (This may or may not reflect a genuine conflict of interests amongst capitalists; it may merely be perceived as a conflict by individual capitalists who are incapable of recognizing the long-term interests of capital as a whole.) However, it is important to stress that the two interpretations are not mutually exclusive, as I shall discuss more fully below.

Thus one can find economic arguments both to explain the retention of domestic labour under capitalism and to suggest the possibility of changes in its role in connection with subsequent developments in capitalism. I shall now turn briefly to the other two sets of reasons put forward as possible explanations why domestic labour has retained its importance.

Psychological Factors

The first of these concerns the nature of the services provided by domestic labour and the impossibility of producing genuine substitutes in the form of commodities. This also raises the question of the way male workers specifically benefit from women's role in the home. For an important component of the use values produced by women in the family is the direct personal relationships within the family on which they are based. It is arguable that the emotional content of many of the tasks a wife performs for her husband is as important to him as their practical purpose. Thus a man who was deprived of his wife's services, while being provided with additional wages sufficient to purchase commodity substitutes, might feel immeasurably worse off and indeed highly discontented. This is not to say that the family currently satisfies all of men's emotional needs, but rather that there are very few ways in which these needs can be satisfied outside it in capitalist society. Certainly our image of what socialism would be like does not eliminate domestic work, but rather poses it as a cooperatively shared activity rather than the sole responsibility of women.

Ideological Factors

The other possible explanation concerns the ideological role of the family. It is possible that any further erosion of domestic labour might undermine the notion of the independent family, responsible for its own survival and competing with other families towards

that end. It is also possible that socialization of pre-school childcare might reduce competitiveness, individualism and passive acceptance of authoritarianism. In addition, eliminating domestic labour further might undermine male domination, sexual divisions within the working class and women's passivity, all of which contribute to the political stability of capitalist society. However, changes in ideology occur in a highly complex way and certainly not just in response to changes in production. The whole area of ideology needs far more consideration that I can give it here.

CONFLICTING ECONOMIC PRESSURES

As was pointed out above, different economic pressures will be operating in different phases of capitalist development, and these will influence whether housework and childcare remain domestic or become socialized. This can be illustrated in the following way. In a situation of economic stagnation like the current one in Britain, when the overall rate of investment and economic growth is very low, the state will attempt to hold down wages and workers' consumption as a whole and to encourage investment and export by giving profit incentives to business. This will have the following implications with respect to the socialization of housework and childcare.

1. The state will be attempting to minimize the level of its social spending, redirecting resources as much as possible out of workers' consumption into industrial investment. Therefore, it is unlikely that the state will expand childcare facilities or other substitutes for domestic labour.

2. Although capitalists producing workers' consumption commodities will be attempting to maintain their markets, capitalists generally will be trying to hold down wages. The overall effect of this will be to reduce the profitability of the capitalists producing for workers' consumption and possibly to redirect capital into areas where state intervention or other factors are raising profitability, e.g., exports. Because of this, it is unlikely that capital will be at-

tracted during such a period into production for workers' consumption, including capitalistic socialization of housework or childcare.

3. Commodity production which represents a direct substitution for domestic labor, like convenience foods, may be an area of workers' consumption which is especially subject to decline in a period of crisis, because there will be pressure on housewives to substitute their own labour for commodities in order to stretch the wage further. It is interesting to note, for example, that in 1971, a year of very high unemployment and acceleration in the rise of food prices, convenience food sales fell by 5 percent whilst seasonal food sales rose by 4 percent, a dual reversal of long-term trends up to that point.

4. Although in a period of stagnation there may be individual areas of shortage of female labour (e.g., nurses), setting up pressures on individual employers to provide crèches [i.e., childcare centers] or other facilities, overall shortage of labour is unlikely to be a major problem because of the relatively high level of unemployment.

If we now turn to a situation of economic growth, with a high rate of investment and rapid rise in output per head accompanied by a strong balance of payments, there would be more likelihood of further socialization taking place.

1. It would be possible for both workers' consumption of commodities and state social spending to rise without reducing profitability.

2. Capital would be attracted into new areas of production for workers' consumption which rising wages would make profitable.

3. Rising wages might be a prerequisite of rapid growth, if it was necessary to win acceptance by the workers of new techniques and new ways of organizing labour on which growth might be dependent (e.g., shift work).

4. Likewise, if capital required more women to do full-time work or shift work or simply needed larger numbers of women workers, socialized childcare might be a prerequisite.

. . .

In attempting to pose an approach to the role of domestic labour, I have argued that domestic labour does not create value, on the definition of value which Marx adopted, but does nonetheless contribute to surplus value by keeping down necessary labour, or the value of labour power, to a level that is lower than the actual subsistence level of the working class. This being the case, at a time of economic crisis such as the present, when a major requirement for capital is to hold down the level of wages, domestic labour performs a vital economic function and further socialization of housework or childcare would be detrimental from a capitalist point of view. However, other pressures (e.g., the need for women wage workers or the need to expand markets for workers' consumption) might lead to further socialization of housework and childcare in a period of capitalist expansion. What I have not dealt with here are ways in which political campaigns deriving from the women's movement and labour movement could influence what might actually happen. But I hope that the analysis contributes to providing a framework within which debates about political strategy can be placed.

9.4 Woman's Consciousness, Man's World

As we have seen, sexism and capitalism reinforce each other. In the following reading, Sheila Rowbotham examines several aspects of this relationship. Rowbotham sees capitalism as having eroded much of the basis for patriarchy, or male control over the woman's productive capacity and her person. But capitalism has still maintained the subordination of women as a group, and an effective feminist movement must be anti-capitalist as well as anti-sexist.

The predicament of being born a woman in capitalism is specific. The social situation of women and the way in which we learn to be feminine is peculiar to us. Men do not share it, consequently we cannot be simply included under the general heading of "mankind." The only claim that this word has to be general comes from the dominance of men in society. As the rulers they presume to define others by their own criteria.

Women are not the same as other oppressed groups. Unlike the working class, who have no need for the capitalist under socialism, the liberation of women does not mean that men will be eliminated. Sex and class are not the same. Similarly people from oppressed races have a memory of a cultural alternative somewhere in the past. Women have only myths made by men.

We have to recognize our biological distinctness but this does not mean that we should become involved in an illusory hunt for our lost "nature." There are so many social accretions round our biology. All conceptions of female "nature" are formed in cultures dominated by men, and like all abstract ideas of human nature are invariably used to deter the oppressed from organizing effectively against that most unnatural of systems, capitalism.

The oppression of women differs too from class and race because it has not come out of capitalism and imperialism. The sexual division of labour and the possession of women by men predates capitalism. Patriarchal authority is based on male control over the woman's productive capacity, and over her person. This control existed before the development of capitalist commodity production. It belonged to a society in which the persons of human beings were owned by others. Patriarchy, however, is contradicted by the dominant mode of production in capitalism because in capitalism the owner of capital owns and controls the labour power but not the persons of his labourers.

.   .   .

In order to understand the traces of patriarchy which have persisted into the present, it is essential to see what part patriarchy played in precapitalist society. The dominance of men over women in the past was more clearly a property relation than it is now. We usually think of property as things. However, animals and people can also be possessions. The word "stock" still covers the breeding of animals and people as well as assets on the stock exchange. But women are no longer so clearly means of production owned by men. When a man married in a society in which production was only marginally beyond subsistence, he married a "yoke-fellow" whose labour was crucial if he were to prosper. Her procreative capacity was important not only because of the high infant mortality rate but also because children meant more hands to labour. The wife's role in production was much greater because although tasks were already sexually divided many more goods were produced in the household. Women who were too high up in the social scale to work with their own hands supervised household production.

The family was a collective working group. The father was its hand, but for survival the labour of wife and children was necessary. Notions of leisure were necessarily restricted in a situation of scarcity when the surplus produced was very small. Consequently, the economic and social cohesion of the family was more important than what individuals in the family might want or regard as their right. Indeed the notion that women and children had individual interests which could not be included in those of the father is a modern concept that belongs to capitalism. It would have seemed bizarre, atomistic and socially destructive in earlier times. The productive forces of capital thus made the concept of individual development possible even though it was still confined in practice to the lives of those who belonged to the dominant class.

The introduction of individual wages and the end of the ownership of people in serfdom did not dissolve the economic and social control of men over women. The man remained the head of the family unit of production and he retained control over the ownership of property through primogeniture. Both his wife's capacity to labour and her capacity to bear his children were still part of his stock in the world. Moreover, the notion that this was part of the order of things was firmly embedded in all political, religious and educational institutions.

Although capitalism temporarily strengthened the control over women by the middle- and upper-class men in the nineteenth century by removing them from production, it has tended to whittle away at the economic and ideological basis of patriarchy. As wage labour become general and the idea spread in society that it was unjust to own other people, although the exploitation of their labour power was perfectly fair, the position of the daughter and the wife appeared increasingly anomalous. Ironically, middle-class women came to the conviction that their dependence on men and the protection of patriarchal authority were intolerable precisely at a time when the separation of work from home was shattering the economic basis of patriarchy among the working class. The factories meant that the economic hold of men over women in the working-class family was weakened. Machinery meant that tasks formerly done by men could be done by women. The woman's wage packet gave her some independence. Ideologically, however, men's hold persisted among the workers and was nurtured by the male ruling class.

Subsequently by continually reducing the scope of production, by developing the separation between home and work, and by reducing the time spent in procreation, a great army of women workers has been "freed" for exploitation in the commodity sys-

tem. This integration of married women into the labour market has been especially noticeable in the advanced capitalist countries since the Second World War and testifies to the tendency for capital to seek new reserves of labour. The result in terms of women's consciousness at work is only now beginning to be felt. While the dissolution of the extended kinship networks has produced in the nuclear family a streamlined unit suitable for modern capitalism, it has forced an examination of the relationships of man to woman and parent to child.

The struggle of the early feminist movement for legal and political equality and the assumptions it has bequeathed to women now, despite the degeneration of its radical impulse, have strained the hold of patriarchy in the capitalist state, though without dislodging it. The power of the working class within capitalism and the growth of new kinds of political movements recently, particularly for black liberation, have touched the consciousness of women and brought many of us to question the domination of men over women. This has taken a political shape, in the new feminism of women's liberation.

The development of contraceptive technology in capitalism means that the idea of sexual liberation can begin to be realized. The fact that sexual pleasure now need not necessarily result in procreation means a new dimension of liberation in the relation of men and women to nature is possible. It also removes some of patriarchy's most important sanctions against rebellion. The right to determine our own sexuality, to control when or if we want to give birth, and to choose who and how we want to love are central in both women's liberation and in gay liberation. All these are most subversive to patriarchy.

However, although capitalism has itself eroded patriarchy and has brought into being movements and ideas which are both anti-capitalist and anti-patriarchal, it still maintains the subordination of women as a group. Patriarchy has continued in capitalism as an ever present prop in time of need. Although women are not literally the property of men, the continuation of female production in the family means that women have not yet even won the right to be exploited equally. The wage system is capitalism has continued to be structured according to the assumption that women's labour is worth half that of men on the market. Behind this is the idea that women are somehow owned by men who should support them. Women are thus seen as economic attachments to men, not quite as free labourers. Their wage is still seen as supplementary. If a woman has no man she is seen as a sexual failure and the inference is often that she is a slut as well. She also has to struggle to bring up a family alone, on half a man's income. This very simple economic fact about the position of women in capitalism acts as a bribe to keep women with men: it has no regard for feeling or suffering and makes a mockery of any notion of choice or control over how we live. It also means that women make up a convenient reserve army which will work at half pay and can be reabsorbed back into the family if there is unemployment.

Our sexual conditioning means that we submit more readily than men to this intolerable state of affairs. We are brought up to think not only that it is just that the private owner of capital can extract profit from the surplus we produce but also that it is legitimate for the capitalist to return to us in the form of wages about half the sum he has to pay a man. Equal pay is obviously only the beginning of an answer to this. . . . The inequality of women at work is built into the structure of capitalist production and the division of labour in industry and in the family. The equality of women to men, even the equal *exploitation* of women in capitalism, would require such fundamental changes in work and at home that it is very hard to imagine how they could be effected while capitalism survives.

Our labour in the family goes unrecognized except as an excuse to keep us out of the better jobs in industry and accuse us of absenteeism and unreliability. This separation between home and work, together with the responsibility of women for housework and child care, serves to perpetuate inequality. Women, as a group in the labour force, are badly paid and underprivileged. This is not only economically profitable to capitalism, it has proved a useful political safety valve. There are many aspects of women's consciousness which have never fully come to terms with the capitalist mode of production. There is no reason why these should not take a radical and critical form in the context of a movement for liberation but in the past they have been used against women and against the working class. It is quite handy for capitalism if wives can be persuaded to oppose their husbands on strike, or if men console themselves for their lack of control at work with the right to be master in their own home. When this happens patriarchy is earning its keep. Similarly, when men and women do not support each other at work both patriarchy and capitalism are strengthened.

Because production in the family differs from commodity production we learn to feel that it is not quite work. This undermines our resentment and makes it harder to stress that it should be eliminated as much as possible not only by technology but by new styles of living, new buildings, and new forms of social care for the young, the sick and the old.

In capitalism housework and child care are lumped together. In fact they are completely different. Housework is drudgery which is best reduced by mechanizing and socializing it, except for cookery, which can be shared. Caring for small children is important and absorbing work, which does not mean that one person should have to do it all the time. But we are taught to think there is something wrong with us if we seek any alternative. The lack of nurseries and of other facilities for children and the rigid structuring of work and the division of labour between the sexes again makes choice impossible.

Propaganda about our feminine role helps to make us accept this state of affairs. Values linger on after the social structures which conceived them. Our ideas of what is "feminine" are a strange bundle of assumptions, some of which belong to the Victorian middle class and others which simply rationalize the form patriarchy assumes in capitalism now. Either way the notion of "femininity" is a convenient means of making us believe submission is somehow natural. When we get angry we are called hysterical.

Thus, although capitalism has eroded the forms of production and property ownership which were the basis of patriarchy, it has still retained the domination of men over women in society. This domination continues to pervade economic, legal, social and sexual life.

It is not enough to struggle for particular reforms, important as these are. Unless we understand the relationship of the various elements within the structure of male-dominated capitalism, we will find the improvements we achieve are twisted against us, or serve one group at the expense of the rest. For example, the wider dissemination of contraceptive information and the weakening of guilt about our sexuality have meant a major improvement in the lives of many women. However, the removal of fear alone is not enough because relations between the sexes are based on the ownership of property, property consisting not only of the woman's labour in procreation, but also of her body. Therefore, while class, race and sex domination remain a constituent element of relations between men and women, women and women, and men and men, these relations will continue to be distorted. Sexual liberation in capitalism can thus continue to be defined by men and also continue to be competitive. The only difference between this and the old set-up is that when patriarchy was secure men measured their virility by the number of children they produced, now they can apply more suitable means of assessing masculinity in a use-and-throw-away society and simply notch up sexual conquests.

. . .

Capitalism is not based on the organization of production for people but simply on the need to secure maximum profit. It is naïve to expect that it will make exceptions of women. It is imposlible now to predict whether capitalism could accommodate itself to the complete elimination of all earlier forms of property and production and specifically to the abolition of patriarchy. But it is certain that the kind of accommodation it could make would provide no real solution for women when we are unable to labour in commodity production because we are pregnant: socially helpless people protected in capitalism are not only treated as parasites who are expected to show gratitude but are under the direct power of the bourgeois state. Also class and race cut across sexual oppression. A feminist movement which is confined to the specific oppression of women cannot, in isolation, end exploitation and imperialism.

We have to keep struggling to go beyond our own situation. This means recognizing that the emphases which have come out of women's liberation are important not only to ourselves. The capacity to bring into conscious combination the unorganizable, those who distrust one another, who have been taught to despise themselves, and the connection which comes out of our practice between work and home, personal and political, are of vital significance to other movements in advanced capitalism. Similarly, the comprehension in women's liberation of the delicate mechanism of communication between the structures of capitalist society and the most hidden part of our secret selves is too important not to become part of the general theory and practice of the Left. Women's liberation has mounted an attack on precisely those areas where socialists have been slow to resist capitalism: authoritarian social relationships, sexuality and the family. "Personal" relations within capitalism, where the labour force is reproduced, are becoming increasingly crucial in the modern organization of industry. We have to struggle for control not merely over the means of production but over the conditions of reproduction.

CHAPTER 10

Racism

A GOOD DEAL OF MEDIA PUBLICITY in recent years has given the impression that major gains are being made by racial minorities in the United States. We are told about the growth of a black middle class and the rise of black voting and political power. We hear much about anti-discrimination legislation, and "affirmative action" lawsuits to increase minority employment. The reality, however, is that racial inequality in the United States has persisted; our society is still deeply racist, as the conflicts over busing of school children in both Northern and Southern cities has clearly and tragically indicated. Why has racism persisted? Our concern in this chapter will be to analyze the nature of modern racism, and to try to understand its development and persistence within a capitalist system.

Modern racism has been defined as the "predication of decisions and policies on considerations of race for the purpose of subordinating a racial group and maintaining control over that group," or ,as "the systematized oppression of one race by another."[1] Such systematic racial oppression is not an age-old form of domination that has existed in all human societies. Racial factors played a minor role in the earlier slave systems of ancient Greece and Rome, and the casual racial prejudices and ethnocentrism that Europeans held against people of color in the fifteenth and early sixteenth centuries was qualitatively different from modern racism. Nothing like the systematic racial oppression of modern slavery existed in these societies, where it was commonly possible for people of different ethnic and racial groups to attain high social positions.

Modern racism began with the European colonization of the rest of the world and the subsequent systematic class domination of people of color. Race became a central justification of the colonial system ("the white man's burden") and the basis for the formation of classes in the colonies. In North America, the clearing away of the native "Indian" population and the enslavement of Africans for plantation labor led to the transformation of previously casual racial prejudices into a systematized and codified ideology and practice of racial subordination.[2]

Racism can take two different forms: *individual racism*, the overtly discriminatory ideas, attitudes, and practices of individual whites

[1] These definitions are presented in Stokely Carmichael and Charles Hamilton, *Black Power* (New York: Random House, 1967), and James and Grace Boggs, *Racism and the Class Struggle* (New York: Monthly Review Press, 1970).

[2] Race itself became more a social than a scientific biological category. A person with one-eighth African ancestry and seven-eighths European ancestry was considered black, while whites were required to be pure European; such logic has no scientific justification. It is estimated that over 70 percent of blacks in the United States are part-European. See Lerone Bennett, *Before the Mayflower* (Baltimore: Penguin Books, 1966), p. 273. The evolution of systematic racism in the seventeenth century is described in Winthrop Jordan, *White Over Black* (Baltimore: Penguin, 1968).

against blacks and other racial minorities;[3] and *institutional racism*, the functioning of institutions according to operating rules that may seem fair and unbiased on the surface, but result nonetheless, sometimes without conscious intent, in the subordination of blacks and other racial minorities. A substantial degree of both individual and institutional racism is evident in the United States, having permeated every sphere of social life. Blacks and other racial minorities face discrimination in employment, housing, schooling, and just about everywhere else. And racial stereotypes, cultural oppression, police harassment, etc. abound.

The effects of racism in the United States include differentials in income, occupational status, infant mortality rates, and many other measures. For example, nonwhites continue to lag far behind whites in income. Data on the relative income of nonwhites and whites (see Table 10-A) show only a small upward trend between 1945 and 1974, with median nonwhite family incomes fluctuating around an average level of about 57 percent of white family incomes. Nonwhite incomes rise relative to white incomes during years of economic boom when labor shortages reduce nonwhite unemployment and open new employment areas for nonwhites. But the gains are mostly eliminated during recessions; little permanent improvement in the relative income position of blacks and other racial minority groups has occurred since World War II.

Moreover, occupational statistics indicate that whites have maintained their relative advantage in occupational status over people of color since at least 1890. An examination of U.S. Census data from 1890 to 1960

TABLE 10-A   RATIO OF NONWHITE TO WHITE MEDIAN INCOME, UNITED STATES, 1945–74

Years	Families	Males	Females
1945	.56		
1946	.59	.61	
1947	.51	.54	
1948	.53	.54	.49
1949	.51	.49	.51
1950	.54	.54	.49
1951	.53	.55	.46
1952	.57	.55	
1953	.56	.55	.59
1954	.56	.50	.55
1955	.55	.53	.54
1956	.53	.52	.58
1957	.54	.53	.58
1958	.51	.50	.59
1959	.52	.47	.62
1960	.55	.53	.70
1961	.53	.52	.67
1962	.53	.49	.67
1963	.53	.52	.67
1964	.56	.57	.70
1965	.55	.54	.73
1966	.60	.55	.76
1967	.62	.59	.78
1968	.63	.61	.79
1969	.63	.59	.85
1970	.64	.60	.92
1971	.63	.61	.90
1972	.62	.62	.95
1973	.60	.63	.93
1974	.62	.63	.92

SOURCE: U.S. Bureau of the Census, *Income of Families and Persons in the United States*, Current Population Reports, series P-60, various years (Washington, D.C.: U.S. Government Printing Office).

showed that, although the overall occupational distribution shifted markedly during the seventy-year period, the relative concentration of black males in the lowest-paid occupations changed very little.[4] Noneconomic indices display the same pattern of racial disadvantage. For example, in 1973 the infant mortality rate was 15.8 per 1,000

[3]In addition to blacks, the other racial minorities numerous enough to be recognized and counted by the U.S. Census are Indians, Japanese, Chinese, Filipinos, Koreans, and Hawaiians. These groups together constitute the Census category "nonwhite," of which blacks account for about 90 percent. The 1970 Census also counted persons of Spanish origin (Mexican, Puerto Rican, Cuban, etc.); many of them are classified as whites.

[4]Richard B. Freeman, "Long-Term Changes in Black Labor Market Status," mimeo, 1972.

white births compared to 26.2 per 1,000 nonwhite births.[5]

There have been some areas of improvement. In recent years, blacks have been elected mayors of several large cities, and the number of blacks in managerial and professional positions has increased. And the differences between blacks and whites in schooling, while still substantial, are not as great today as in 1900. Young black males aged 25 to 29 years old in 1900 had completed a median of 3.7 years of school, compared to 8.2 years for white males in the same age group; the comparable figures in 1970 were 12.2 (black) and 12.7 (white).[6] Moreover, black women, who used to work primarily as domestic servants and farm laborers, have moved in large numbers into the same low-level clerical and nonhousehold service jobs held by many white women; as a result the income differential between black and white women has narrowed, as shown in Table 10-A.[7]

But these improvements are surprisingly small when measured against the struggles and protests of blacks, as in the Civil Rights movement in the 1950s and 1960s, and the anti-discriminatory legislation and widely publicized "affirmative action" programs of the 1970s. Racial inequality has persisted despite these efforts, and despite the tremendous transformation that has taken place in the economic role of blacks since 1930. In that year 53.8 percent of blacks lived in the rural South, most as farm laborers, tenants, or small independent farmers.[8] The rural South was the poorest area of the nation, and the area with the greatest relative income gap between whites and blacks. With the subsequent mechanization of Southern agriculture and demand for black labor in urban-centered capitalist industry and services, tens of millions of blacks moved out of the rural South. By 1970, 81.3 percent of the black population was located in urban centers, and concentrated in racial ghettos; most employed blacks today have wage-labor jobs in manufacturing, transportation, and services.[9] Since this massive migration has been toward areas of higher wages and narrower racial income differentials, the persistence of the gap between black and white incomes is quite remarkable.

The continuing income inequality indicates that the transition for blacks from a farming people to incorporation into the urban working class has occurred in ways that have reproduced rather than eliminated racism. As a result, blacks have made very little progress in overcoming racial inequality *within* many urban areas: indeed, as Table 10-B indicates, the income of nonwhites relative to whites within many major urban areas showed no improvement between the 1950 and 1970 Censuses. The inequalities of the agricultural South have been transferred to urban factories and ghettos.

Besides blacks, the other racial minorities in the United States—Chicanos, Puerto Ricans, American Indians, and people of Asian origin—also experience racism. Each of these groups has its own specific history of incorporation into the American working class; they share with blacks and each other

---

[5]U.S. Bureau of the Census, "The Social and Economic Status of the Black Population in the United States, 1974" (Washington, D.C.: U.S. Government Printing Office, 1975), p. 126.

[6]Based on U.S. Census of Population, 1940 to 1970. Figures for females are nearly identical to those for males.

[7]Much of this narrowing, however, is due to the decline in white women's earnings relative to men described in Chapter 9; also Table 10-A understates the gap between black and white women because black women are more likely to be the sole support of a family and on the average work more hours per year than white women.

Notice that the relative improvement for nonwhite women shown in column 3 of Table 10-A did not have much of an effect on the relative position of nonwhite families; this is because the rate of increase in labor-force participation has been greater among white women than nonwhite women, thus maintaining the greater income of white families.

[8]Daniel Price, *Changing Characteristics of the Negro Population* (Washington, D.C.: U.S. Government Printing Office, 1966); *1970 Census of Population.*

[9]Ibid.

the experience of having been incorporated into the lowest-paid segments of the American working class. The numbers of people of Asian and Spanish origin in the labor force has especially increased in the 1960s and 1970s, filling an ever-larger percentage of the lowest-paying jobs at the bottom of the occupational hierarchy, and in highly competitive and labor-intensive firms. Racial factors thus continue to be prominent in American life.[10]

Despite the above evidence, it is often argued that racism is an aberration in the United States, a legacy from the past that will gradually disappear in a democratic, capitalist society. Proponents of this view argue as follows: the capitalist drive to rationalize production, lower costs, and expand profits is itself a strong force for the elimination of racial discrimination. Employers are trying to maximize their profits, and in organizing their workforce they will be interested in a worker's productivity and potential contribution to profits and not in his or her skin color. The pressures from other firms competing for workers will overcome the resistance of racist employers who persist in discriminating. Similarly, purchasers of goods and services will be interested only in the product's price and its quality and not in the race of the workers who produce it. Thus, market forces, by allocating labor to its most efficient use, are themselves a strong stimulus for ending discrimination. And if market forces do not operate with sufficient speed or effectiveness, the government can be expected to pass and implement anti-discrimination legislation, create job-training and compensatory education programs, provide aid for ghetto economic development, and so on, for the purpose of hastening the

TABLE 10-B RATIO OF NONWHITE TO WHITE MALE[a] MEDIAN INCOME IN SELECTED CITIES, 1949–1969

	1949	1969	1949–1969
SMSA's in North and West			
Chicago	.714	.713	−.001
Cleveland	.702	.718	.016
Detroit	.808	.738	−.070
Los Angeles	.704	.726	.024
New York	.678	.712	.034
Philadelphia	.686	.689	.003
Pittsburgh	.729	.638	−.091
San Francisco	.712	.686	−.026
St. Louis	.632	.583	−.049
Average change			−.018
SMSA's in South			
Atlanta	.520	.531	.011
Baltimore	.630	.631	.001
Birmingham	.581	.515	−.066
Dallas	.505	.550	.045
Houston	.554	.551	−.003
Memphis	.484	.583	.099
New Orleans	.557	.507	−.050
Washington, D.C.	.627	.610	−.017
Average change			.003

[a]14 years and older.

1949 data is for the Standard Metropolitan Area (SMA); from the U.S. Census of Population, 1950, *Characteristics of the Population*, Table 185.

1969 data is for the Standard Metropolitan Statistical Area (SMSA); from the U.S. Census of Population, 1970, state volumes, Table 192.

[10]At the same time, to fill their need for cheap labor the European capitalist countries have been increasingly drawing upon foreign labor, much of it people of darker complexion and races from North Africa, Italy, Portugal, Greece, Turkey, and Yugoslavia. The racial and ethnic heterogeneity and hierarchy of the American working class has thus become reproduced in Europe as well.

eradication of racism. There has, in fact, been much U.S. governmental activity along these lines since the mid-1960s.

Why then has racism proven so difficult to eradicate in the United States? We argue in this chapter that the conventional analysis in the preceding paragraph is not correct. Racism is not an aberration; it has persisted in the United States precisely because racial oppression is consistent with the logic of class divisions under capitalism and reinforces the interests of the capitalist class as a whole. By contributing to divisions and antagonisms among the population, thereby weakening hostility to the capitalist class, and by providing to whites a convenient scapegoat for social and economic oppression that is generated by capitalism itself, racism plays an important role in *stabilizing* a capitalist society. Whatever its origins—and we should keep in mind the historical importance for Northern capitalism of the westward expansion against Indian opposition and the profits from black slavery—racism is likely to take firm root in a capitalist society. Racism is useful to capitalism; moreover, the hierarchical, materialistic, competitive, and individualistic environment of capitalism is not conducive to the elimination of racism. It is therefore unlikely that racism can be eradicated within the framework of a capitalist society.

10.1 *Institutional Racism*

Many of us are accustomed to think of racism as consisting primarily of overt discriminatory attitudes and acts by individual whites against individual blacks. But as Stokely Carmichael and Charles Hamilton point out in the following reading, racism is also to a great extent subtly embedded in the normal operation of established social institutions. Often an institution's operating rules appear fair and unbiased on the surface, but have the effect of penalizing blacks anyway. Carmichael and Hamilton analyze such *institutional* racism in terms of a colonial model and examine the operation of black colonial status in its political, economic, and social dimensions.

The following is condensed by permission of Random House, Inc. from Chapter 1 of *Black Power: The Politics of Liberation in America* by STOKELY CARMICHAEL and CHARLES V. HAMILTON. Copyright © 1967 by Stokely Carmichael and Charles V. Hamilton. Reprinted by permission of Random House, Inc., and Jonathan Cape Ltd.

What is racism? The word has represented daily reality to millions of black people for centuries, yet it is rarely defined—perhaps just because that reality has been such a commonplace. By "racism" we mean the predication of decisions and policies on considerations of race for the purpose of *subordinating* a racial group and maintaining control over that group. That has been the practice of this country toward the black man; we shall see why and how.

Racism is both overt and covert. It takes two, closely related forms: individual whites acting against individual blacks, and acts by the total white community against the black community. We call these individual racism and institutional racism. The first consists of overt acts by individuals, which cause death, injury or the violent destruction of property. This type can be recorded by television cameras; it can frequently be observed in the process of commission. The second type is less overt, far more subtle, less identifiable in terms of *specific* individuals committing the acts. But it is no less destructive of human life. The second type originates in the operation of established and respected forces in the society, and thus receives far less public condemnation than the first type.

When white terrorists bomb a black church and kill five black children, that is an act of individual racism, widely deplored by most segments of the society. But when in that same city—Birmingham, Alabama—five hundred black babies die each year because of the lack of proper food, shelter and medical facilities, and thousands more are destroyed and maimed physically, emotionally and intellectually because of conditions of poverty and discrimination in the black community, that is a function of institutional racism. When a black family moves into a home in a white neighborhood and is stoned, burned or routed out, they are victims of an overt act of individual racism which many people will condemn—at least in words. But it is institutional racism that keeps black people locked in dilapidated slum tenements, subject to the daily prey of exploitative slumlords, merchants, loan sharks and discriminatory real estate agents. The society either pretends it does not know of this latter situation, or is in fact incapable of doing anything meaningful about it. We shall examine the reasons for this in a moment.

Institutional racism relies on the active and pervasive operation of anti-black attitudes and practices. A sense of superior group position prevails: whites are "better" than blacks; therefore blacks should be subordinated to whites. This is a racist attitude and it permeates the society, on both the individual and institutional level, covertly and overtly.

"Respectable" individuals can absolve themselves from individual blame: *they* would never plant a bomb in a church; *they* would never stone a black family. But they continue to support political officials and institutions that would and do perpetuate institutionally racist policies. Thus *acts* of overt, individual racism, may not typify the society, but institutional racism does—with the support of covert, individual *attitudes* of racism.

. . .

To put it another way, there is no "American dilemma" because black people in this country form a colony, and it is not in the interest of the colonial power to liberate them. Black people are legal citizens of the United States with, for the most part, the same *legal* rights as other citizens. Yet they stand as colonial subjects in relation to the white society. Thus institutional racism has another name: colonialism.

Obviously, the analogy is not perfect. One normally associates a colony with a land and people subjected to, and physically separated from, the "Mother Country." This is not always the case, however; in South Africa and Rhodesia, black and white inhabit the same land—with blacks subordinated to whites just as in the English, French, Italian, Portuguese and Spanish colonies. It is the objective relationship which counts, not rhetoric (such as constitutions *articulating* equal rights) or geography.

The analogy is not perfect in another respect. Under classic colonialism, the colony is a source of cheaply produced raw materials (usually agricultural or mineral) which the "Mother Country" then processes into finished goods and sells at high profit—sometimes back to the colony itself. The black communities of the United States do not export anything except human labor. But is the differentiation more than a technicality? Essentially, the African colony is selling its labor; the product itself does not belong to the "subjects" because the land is not theirs. At the same time, let us look at the black people of the South: cultivating cotton at $3.00 for a ten-hour day and from that buying cotton dresses (and food and other goods) from white manufacturers. Economists might wish to argue this point endlessly; the objective relationship stands. Black people in the United States have a colonial relationship to the larger society, a relationship characterized by institutional racism. That colonial status operates in three areas—political, economic, social—which we shall discuss one by one.

POLITICAL COLONIALISM

Colonial subjects have their political decisions made for them by the colonial masters, and those decisions are handed down directly or through a process of "indirect rule." Politically, decisions which affect black lives have always been made by white people—the "white power structure."

. . .

The black community perceives the "white power structure" in very concrete terms. The man in the ghetto sees his white landlord come only to collect exorbitant rents and fail to make necessary repairs, while both know that the white-dominated city building inspection department will wink at violations or impose only slight fines. The man in the ghetto sees the white policeman on the corner brutally manhandle a black drunkard in a doorway, and at the same time accept a payoff from one of the agents of the white-controlled rackets. He sees the streets in the ghetto lined with uncollected garbage, and he knows that the powers which could send trucks in to collect that garbage are white. When they don't he knows the reason: the low political esteem in which the black community is held. He looks at the absence of a meaningful curriculum in the ghetto schools —for example, the history books that woefully overlook the historical achievements of black people—and he knows that the school board is controlled by whites. He is not about to listen to intellectual discourses on the pluralistic and fragmented nature of political power. He is faced with a "white power structure" as monolithic as Europe's colonial offices have been to African and Asian colonies.

There is another aspect of colonial politics frequently found in colonial Africa and in the United States: the process of indirect rule .... In other words, the white power structure rules the black community through local blacks who are responsive to the white leaders, the downtown, white machine, not to the black populace. These black politicians do not exercise effective power. They cannot be relied upon to make forceful demands in behalf of their black constituents, and they become no more than puppets. They put loyalty to a political party before loyalty to their constituents and thus nullify any bargaining power the black community might develop. Colonial politics causes the subject to muffle his voice while participating in the councils of the white power structure. The black man forfeits his opportunity to speak forcefully and clearly for his race, and he justifies this in terms of expediency. Thus, when one talks of a "Negro Establishment" in most places in this country, one is talking of an Establishment resting on a white power base, of handpicked blacks whom that base projects as showpieces out front. These black "leaders" are, then, only as powerful as their white kingmakers will permit them to be. This is no less true of the North than the South.

·   ·   ·

ECONOMIC COLONIALISM

The economic relationship of America's black communities to the large society also reflects their colonial status. The political power exercised over those communities goes hand in glove with the economic deprivation experienced by the black citizens.

Historically, colonies have existed for the sole purpose of enriching, in one form or another, the "colonizer"; the consequence is to maintain the economic dependency of the "colonized." All too frequently we hear of the missionary motive behind colonization: to "civilize," to "Christianize" the underdeveloped, backward peoples. But read these words of a French Colonial Secretary of State in 1923:

> What is the use of painting the truth? At the start, colonization was not an act of civilization, nor was it a desire to civilize. It was an act of force motivated by interests. An episode in the vital competition which, from man to man, from group to group, has gone on ever increasing; the people who set out to seize colonies in the distant lands were thinking primarily of themselves, and were working for their own profits, and conquering for their own power.[1]

One is immediately reminded of the bitter

[1] Albert Sarraut, French Colonial Secretary of State, speaking at the Ecole Coloniale in Paris. As quoted in Kwame Nkrumah's *Africa Must Unite* (London : Heinemann Educational Books, Ltd., 1963), p. 40

maxim voiced by many black Africans today: the missionaries came for our goods, not for our good. Indeed, the missionaries turned the Africans' eyes toward heaven, and then robbed them blind in the process. The colonies were sources from which raw materials were taken and markets to which finished products were sold. Manufacture and production were prohibited if this meant—as it usually did—competition with the "Mother Country.". Rich in natural resources, Africa did not reap the benefit of these resources herself. In the Gold Coast (now Ghana), where the cocoa crop was the largest in the world, there was not one chocolate factory.

This same economic status has been perpetrated on the black community in this country. Exploiters come into the ghetto from outside, bleed it dry, and leave it economically dependent on the larger society. As with the missionaries, these exploiters frequently come as the "friend of the Negro," pretending to offer worthwhile goods and services, when their basic motivation is personal profit and their basic impact is the maintenance of racism. Many of the social welfare agencies—public and private—frequently pretend to offer "uplift" services; in reality, they end up creating a system which dehumanizes the individual and perpetuates his dependency. Conscious or unconscious, the paternalistic attitude of many of these agencies is no different from that of many missionaries going into Africa.

· · ·

Again, as in the African colonies, the black community is sapped senseless of what economic resources it does have. Through the exploitative system of credit, people pay "a dollar down, a dollar a week" literally for years. Interest rates are astronomical, and the merchandise—of relatively poor quality in the first place—is long since worn out before the final payment. Professor David Caplovitz of Columbia University has commented in his book, *The Poor Pay More*, "The high markup on low-quality goods is thus a major device used by merchants to protect themselves against the risks of their credit business"

(p. 18). Many of the ghetto citizens, because of unsteady employment and low incomes, cannot obtain credit from more legitimate businesses; thus they must do without important items or end up being exploited. They are lured into the stores by attractive advertising displays hawking, for example, three rooms of furniture for "only $199." Once inside, the unsuspecting customer is persuaded to buy lesser furniture at a more expensive price, or he is told that the advertised items are temporarily out of stock and is shown other goods. More frequently than not, of course, all the items are overpriced.

· · ·

Out of a substandard income, the black man pays exorbitant prices for cheap goods; he must then pay more for his housing than whites. Whitney Young, Jr. of the Urban League writes in his book, *To Be Equal*: "most of Chicago's 838,000 Negroes live in a ghetto and pay about $20 more per month for housing than their white counterparts in the city" (pp. 144–45). Black people also have a much more difficult time securing a mortgage. They must resort to real estate speculators who charge interest rates up to 10 percent, whereas a FHA loan would carry only a 6 percent interest rate. As for loans to go into business, we find the same pattern as among Africans, who were prohibited or discouraged from starting commercial enterprises. "The white power structure," says Dr. Clark in *Dark Ghetto*, "has collaborated in the economic serfdom of Negroes by its reluctance to give loans and insurance to Negro business" (pp. 27–28). The Small Business Administration, for example, in the ten-year period prior to 1964, made only *seven* loans to black people.

This is why the society does nothing meaningful about institutional racism: because the black community has been the creation of, and dominated by, a combination of oppressive forces and special interests in the white community. The groups which have access to the necessary resources and the ability to effect change benefit politically and economically from the continued subordinate status of the black community. This is not to say that every single white American consciously oppresses black people. He does not need to. Institutional racism has been maintained deliberately by the power structure and through indifference, inertia and lack of courage on the part of white masses as well as petty officials. Whenever black demands for change become loud and strong, indifference is replaced by active opposition based on fear and self-interest. The line between purposeful suppression and indifference blurs. One way or another, most whites participate in economic colonialism.

. . .

SOCIAL COLONIALISM

The operation of political and economic colonialism in this country has had social repercussions which date back to slavery but did not by any means end with the Emancipation Proclamation. Perhaps the most vicious result of colonialism—in Africa and this country—was that it purposefully, maliciously and with reckless abandon relegated the black man to a subordinated, inferior status in the society. The individual was considered and treated as a lowly animal, not to be housed properly, or given adequate medical services, and by no means a decent education.

. . .

The social and psychological effects on black people of all their degrading experiences are . . . very clear. From the time black people were introduced into this country, their condition has fostered human indignity and the denial of respect. Born into this society today, black people begin to doubt themselves, their worth as human beings. Self-respect becomes almost impossible. . . .

There was the same result in Africa. And some European colonial powers—notably France and Portugal—provided the black man "a way out" of the degrading status: to become "white," or assimilated. France pursued a colonial policy aimed at producing a black French elite class, a group exposed and acculturated to French "civilization."

. . .

In a manner similar to that of the colonial powers in Africa, American society indicates avenues of escape from the ghetto for those individuals who adapt to the "mainstream." This adaptation means to disassociate oneself from the black race, its culture, community and heritage, and become immersed (dispersed is another term) in the white world. What actually happens, as Professor E. Franklin Frazier pointed out in his book, *Black Bourgeoisie*, is that the black person ceases to identify himself with black people yet is obviously unable to assimilate with whites. He becomes a "marginal man," living on the fringes of both societies in a world largely of "make believe." This black person is urged to adopt American middle-class standards and values. As with the black African who had to become a "Frenchman" in order to be accepted, so to be an American, the black man must strive to become "white." To the extent that he does, he is considered "well adjusted"—one who has "risen above the race question." These people are frequently held up by the white Establishment as living examples of the progress being made by the society in solving the race problem. Suffice it to say that precisely because they are required to denounce—overtly or covertly—their black race, *they are reinforcing racism in this country*.

In the United States, as in Africa, their "adaptation" operated to deprive the black community of its potential skills and brain power. All too frequently, these "integrated" people are used to blunt the true feelings and goals of the black masses. They are picked as "Negro leaders," and the white power structure proceeds to talk to and deal only with them. Needless to say, no fruitful, meaningful dialogue can take place under such circumstances. Those handpicked "leaders" have no viable constituency for which they can speak and act. All this is a classic formula of colonial cooptation.

. . .

10.2 *The Demand for Black Labor*

Racism first emerged full-fledged in the United States as an essential aspect of slavery. But the breakup of slavery and the triumph of the North in 1865 did not result in the end of racism. Instead, racism continued to be an important feature of American life, both in the agricultural labor systems of the post–Civil War South and in the modern era of monopoly capitalism. Throughout all these periods black labor played a central role in production, but the form of exploitation of black labor—and with it, the form that racism took—evolved with the different phases of capitalist development. In the following reading, Harold Baron analyzes this historical process and outlines how the current conditions of black people have developed.

The following is excerpted from "The Demand for Black Labor: Historical Notes on the Political Economy of Racism," by HAROLD BARON, *Radical America*, vol. 5, no. 2 (March–April 1971), pp. 1–46. © 1971 by Harold Baron. Reprinted by permission of the author and *Radical America*.

The economic base of racism would have to be subjected to intensive analysis in order to get at the heart of the oppression of black people in modern America. If we employ the language of Nineteenth Century science, we can state that the economic deployment of black people has been conditioned by the operation of two sets of historical laws: the laws of capitalist development, and the laws of national liberation. These laws were operative in the slave era as well as at present. Today the characteristic forms of economic control and exploitation of black people take place within the institutional structure of a mature state capitalist system and within the demographic frame of the metropolitan centers. The economic activities of blacks are essentially those of wage (or salary) workers for the large corporate and bureaucratic structures that dominate a mature capitalist society. Thus today racial dynamics can be particularized as the working out of the laws of the maintenance of mature state capitalism and the laws of black liberation with the metropolitan enclaves (rather than a consolidated territorial area) as a base.

This essay places major emphasis on capitalist development. While attention will be paid to aspects of national liberation, it would

be a very different essay if that were the main point of concentration. Further, in order to make the inquiry manageable, it concentrates on the key relationship of the demand for black labor.

. . .

The completeness with which race and slavery became merged in the United States is revealed by a review of the status of blacks on the eve of the Civil War. About 89% of the national black population was slave, while in the Southern states the slave proportion was 94%. The status of the small number of quasi-free Negroes was ascribed from that of the mass of their brothers in bondage. Nowhere did this group gain a secure economic position; only a few of them acquired enough property to be well off. In the countryside, by dint of hard work, a few acquired adequate farms. Most, however, survived on patches of poor soil or as rural laborers. Free blacks fared the best in Southern cities, many of them being employed as skilled artisans or tradesmen. The ability of free blacks to maintain a position in the skilled trades was dependent on the deployment of a larger number of slaves in these crafts and industrial jobs. Slave-owners provided a defense against a color bar as they protected their investment in urban slaves. However the rivalry from a growing urban white population between 1830 and 1860 forced blacks out of many of the better jobs, and in some cases out of the cities altogether. "As the black population dropped, white newcomers moved in and took over craft after craft. Occasionally to the accompaniment of violence and usually with official sanction, slave and free colored workers were shunted into the most menial and routine chores."[1]

Basic racial definitions of the slave system also gained recognition in the North, through the development of a special servile status for blacks. During the colonial era, Northern colonies imported slaves as one means of coping with a chronic labor shortage. While most blacks were employed in menial work, many were trained in skilled trades. "So long as the pecuniary interests of a slave-holding class stood back of these artisans, the protests of white mechanics had little effect. . . ." With emancipation in the North, matters changed. As Du Bois further noted concerning Philadelphia, during the first third of the Nineteenth Century, the blacks, who had composed a major portion of all artisans, were excluded from most of the skilled trades.[2] Immigrants from Europe soon found out that, although greatly exploited themselves, they could still turn racism to their advantage. The badge of whiteness permitted even the lowly to use prejudice, violence, and local political influence to push blacks down into the lowest occupations. In 1850, 75% of the black workers in New York were employed in menial or unskilled positions. Within five years the situation had deteriorated to the point at which 87.5% were in these categories.[3] Northern states did not compete with

slave states for black workers, even when labor shortages forced them to encourage the immigration of millions of Europeans. Through enforcement of fugitive slave laws and discouragement of free black immigration, through both legal and informal means, the North reinforced slavery's practical monopoly over blacks.

For the pre–Civil War period, then, we can conclude that there was no significant demand for black labor outside the slave system. The great demand for black workers came from the slave plantations. No effective counterweight to plantation slavery was presented by urban and industrial employment. As a matter of fact, in both North and South the position of the urban skilled black worker deteriorated during the generation prior to the Civil War. In the South the magnitude of cities and industries was limited by the political and cultural imperatives inherent in hegemony of the planter class. Whatever demand there was for black labor in Southern cities and industries was met essentially by adapting the forms of slavery to these conditions, not by creating an independent pressure for free blacks to work in these positions.

To a large extent the more heightened form of racism in the United States grew out of the very fact that the USA was such a thoroughgoing bourgeois society, with more bourgeois equalitarianism than any other nation around. Aside from temporary indenture, which was important only through the Revolutionary era, there were no well-institutionalized formal or legal mechanisms for fixing of status among whites. Up to the Civil War the ideal of an equalitarian yeoman society was a major socio-political factor in shaping political conditions. Therefore if the manumitted slave were not marked off by derogation of his blackness, there was no alternative but to admit him to the status of a free-born enfranchised citizen (depending on property qualifications prior to the 1830s).

Under these circumstances the planter class made race as well as slavery a designation of condition. A large free black popula-

[1]Richard Wade, *Slavery in the Cities* (New York, 1964), p. 275.

[2]W. E. B. Du Bois, *The Philadelphia Negro* (1967 Edition, New York), p. 33. See also Herman Bloch, *The Circle of Discrimination* (New York, 1969), pp. 21–26.

[3]Robert Ernst, "The Economic Status of New York Negroes, 1850–1863," reprinted in August Meier and Elliot Rudwick, ed., *The Making of Black America* (New York, 1969), Vol. 1, pp. 250–61.

tion that had full citizens' rights would have been a threat to their system. They therefore legislated limitations on the procedures for manumission and placed severe restrictions on the rights of free blacks. Low-status whites who did have citizens' rights were encouraged by the plantocracy to identify as whites and to emphasize racial distinctions so as to mark themselves off from both slave and free blacks precisely because this white group did have a legitimate place in the political process. Fear of competition from blacks, either directly or indirectly through the power of large planters, also gave the large class of non-slave-holding whites a real stake in protecting racial distinctions. In Latin America, by contrast, the remnants of feudal traditions regarding the gradations of social ranks already provided well-established lowly positions into which free Negroes or half-castes could step without posing a threat to the functional hegemony of the slave-master class. Further, given the small number of Europeans and the great labor shortage, ex-slaves provided ancillary functions, such as clearing the frontier or raising food crops, that were necessary for the overall operation of the slave system.

.   .   .

The Civil War destroyed the Southern plantocracy as a major contender for the control of national power. For a decade during Reconstruction, the freedmen struggled to establish themselves as an independent yeomanry on the lands they had worked for generations. However both South and North agreed that blacks were to be subservient workers—held in that role now by the workings of "natural" economic and social laws rather than the laws of slavery. The Compromise of 1877 was the final political blow to black Reconstruction, remanding to the dominant white Southerners the regulation of the black labor force.

Abolition of slavery did not mean substantive freedom to the black worker. He was basically confined to a racially defined agrarian labor status in which he was more exploited than any class of whites, even the landless poor. White land-owners extracted an economic surplus from the labor of blacks through a variety of arrangements, including peonage, wage labor, sharecropping, and rent tenancy. Even the black owners of land were often dependent on white patronage for access to the small plots of inferior soil to which they usually held title. Profits predicated on low wages or onerous share arrangements were often augmented by long-term indebtedness at usurious rates of interest for advances of provisions and supplies. Many a sharecropper and laborer would not realize any appreciable money income for years on end.

The methods of labor control over the black peasantry did not greatly raise net labor costs over those of the slavery era. In both eras the black masses received only enough to survive and reproduce. Pressure on profits came from falling commodity prices rather than from rising labor costs. "The keynote of the Black Belt is debt. . . ." wrote W.E.B. Du Bois at the turn of the century. "Not commercial credit, but debt in the sense of continued inability of the mass of the population to make income cover expenses."

.   .   .

Characteristically blacks were engaged on the cotton plantations, especially those with richer lands. The form of engagement was roughly divided between sharecropping, wage labor, and rental tenancy. Between 1890 and 1910 the number of black men in agriculture increased by over half a million, or 31%. During this entire period three out of five black men were employed in agriculture.

Maintaining the semi-servile status of the black labor force required the augmentation of color-caste distinctions. Southern slavery, after all, had been more than just an economic arrangement: it was a cultural system that provided a wide range of norms congruent with plantation discipline. Slave status had served as a line of demarcation throughout the society. Therefore emancipation not only changed the economic form of planter control, but also left gaps in the social superstructure that reinforced it. Under these conditions the strengthening of racialism per se in all cultural arrangements became an imperative for any hope of continuance of the planters' hegemony over Southern society. Since racism had pervaded all major facets of social and political control, much of the further elaboration of color-caste distinctions arose in the course of the Southern ruling class's struggles to keep the rest of the whites in line.

The road to the establishment of this new system of order in the South was by no means a smooth one. Abrogation of the slave system had made possible some new types of mobility among both blacks and whites, bringing about changes in the forms of inter-racial conflict and class conflict. Blacks were now able to move geographically, even in the face of continued legal and extra-legal restraints. The migration that took place was mainly a westerly one within the South. Inside the black community class mobility developed through the emergence of a small middle class. At the same time, there now opened up to poorer whites areas that had formerly been the preserve of slavery. During the pre–Civil War era no white would compete with a slave for his position on the plantation. Albeit when planters and slaveless small farmers did contend for land, as frequently occurred, the black slave was indirectly involved. With emancipation, racial rivalry for the soil became overt. Freedmen struggled to gain land, sometimes as owners but more frequently as indebted tenants. At the same time, many white smallholders, forced out from infertile and worn soil, sought many of the same lands. After the Civil War the white farmers increased in numbers at a greater rate than the blacks. By 1900, even as tenants, the whites were in the majority. Blacks moved from a non-competitive status in slavery (or perhaps better "concealed competition between the bond and the free"), . . . to a condition of overt inter-racial competition. . . .

In the social and political realms the conflicts inherent in the black peasantry's sub-jugation became intertwined with the conflicts inherent in the subordination of any potential political power in the hands of the white smallholders and landless. As things turned out, blacks were to suffer both from the control of the propertied and from the competition of the poor. The political process provided a major means by which this was carried out. "It is one of the paradoxes of Southern history," writes C. Vann Woodward, "that political democracy for the white man and racial discrimination for the black were often products of the same dynamics." The imperatives of preserving class rule supplied the basis of the paradox: "It took a lot of ritual and Jim Crow to bolster the rule of white supremacy in the bosom of a white man working for a black man's wage."[4] Functionally the poorer whites were permitted to influence the formal political process only under conditions that would not undermine the essential power and economic control of the ruling class. The execution of this strategy was completed during the defeat of the Populist movement in the 1890s by excluding the black people from politics and by heightening the color-caste distinctions through an extension of Jim Crow laws and customs. Since the black people had already been defeated through Redemption 20 years before, the moves to disfranchise black people at the turn of the century had as "the real question . . . *which whites* would be supreme." Ruling circles channeled disfranchisement to their own ends "as they saw in it an opportunity to establish in power 'the intelligence and wealth of the South' which could of course 'govern in the interests of all classes.'"[5] Many whites as well as blacks were denied the ballot, and the substantive differences expressed in the political process were delimited to a narrower range. Inter-class conflicts among whites were much displaced by inter-racial conflicts, and the hegemony of larger property interests was secured.

[4]C. Vann Woodward, *Origins of the New South* (Baton Rouge, Lousiana, 1951) p. 211.

[5]Ibid., pp. 328–30.

The agrarian designation of the black masses was reinforced by the lack of competition for their labor from other sectors of the economy. The Southern demand for factory help, except for unskilled work, was essentially a demand for white labor. The textile industry, the primary industry of the New South, was marked off as a preserve of the white worker.

. . .

The rather-considerable increase in industrial employment of blacks between 1890 and 1910 was concentrated in railroading, lumbering, and coal mining—that is, in non-factory-type operations with these three industries often located in rural areas. Lumbering and allied industries could almost have been considered an extension of agriculture, as the workers shifted back and forth from one to the other.

Outside of agriculture the vast bulk of black workers were to be found either in domestic and personal service or in unskilled menial fields that were known in the South as "Negro jobs." In the cities the growth occupations were chiefly porters, draymen, laundresses, seamstresses. However nonpropertied whites did begin to crowd into many skilled positions that had been the black man's preserve under slavery. Black mechanics and artisans, who had vastly outnumbered Southern whites as late as 1865, fought a losing battle for these jobs down to 1890, when they were able to stabilize a precarious minority position in some of the construction trades.[6]

. . .

Northern ruling classes were quick to accept those conditions in the South that stabilized the national political system and provided the raw commodities for their mills and markets. Therefore they supported the establishment of a subservient black peasantry, the regional rule of the Southern propertied interests, and the racial oppression that

made both of these things possible. The dominant Northern interests shared the ideal of the smooth kind of racial subjugation projected by the paternalistic Southern elite, but they went along with what proved necessary.

. . .

In the North itself during this period there was minimal work for blacks, even though the Northern economy was labor-starved to the extent that is promoted and absorbed a European immigration of over 15,000,000 persons. Blacks were not only shut off from the new jobs, but lost many of the jobs they had traditionally held. The Irish largely displaced them in street paving, the Slavs displaced them in brickyards, and all groups moved in on the once black stronghold of dining-room waiting.

. . .

The reasons for this displacement of black workers in the North are complex. Northern capital engaged Southern workers, both black and white, by exporting capital to the South rather than by encouraging any great migration, thus enabling itself to exploit the low wage structure of the economically backward South while avoiding any disturbance in its precarious political or economic balance. Sometimes racism would operate directly, as when the National Cash Register Company (Dayton, Ohio) laid off 300 black janitors because the management wanted to have white farm boys start at the bottom and work their way up.[7] In addition, job competition often led white workers to see blacks, rather than employers, as the enemy. At least 50 strikes, North and South, in which white workers protested the employment of blacks have been recorded for the years 1881 to 1900.[8] There was a minor counter-theme of class solidarity which existed to a certain extent in the Knights of Labor and was reaffirmed by the Industrial Workers of the World, but as the job-conscious American

[6]Charles H. Wesley, *Negro Labor in the United States, 1850–1925* (New York, 1927), p. 142; W. E. B. Du Bois, *The Negro Artisan* (Atlanta, 1902), pp. 115–20.

[7]Frank U. Quillan, *The Color Line in Ohio* (Ann Arbor, 1913), p. 138.

[8]W. E. B. Du Bois, *The Negro Artisan*, pp. 173–75.

Federation of Labor gained dominance over the union movement, racial exclusion became the operative practice, with the only major exception occurring among the United Mine Workers.[9] (It was actually more common in the South than in the North for black workers to hold a position so strong in particular industries that unions had to take them into account; in these instances they were generally organized in separate locals.) Episodes in which blacks were used as strikebreakers contributed to the unions' hostility toward blacks, but it should be added that racism seriously distorted the perceptions of white workers. Whites were used as scabs more frequently and in larger numbers, but the saliency of racial categories was able to make the minority role of blacks stand out more sharply, so that in many white workers' minds the terms "scab" and "Negro" were synonymous.[10]

WORLD WAR I TO WORLD WAR II

The new equilibrium of racial regulation that had stabilized around tenancy agriculture as the dominant force of black exploitation received its first major disturbance from the impact of World War I. A certain irony inheres in the condition that imperialism's cataclysm should begin the break-up of agrarian thralldom within the United States.

[9]Sterling Spero and Abram Harris, *The Black Worker* (New York, 1968) is still essential on this. Also see Bernard Mandel, "Samuel Gompers and the Negro Workers, 1886–1914," *Journal of Negro History* (January 1955), pp. 34–60; Herbert G. Gutman, "The Negro and the United Mine Workers of America," in Julius Jacobson, ed., *The Negro and the American Labor Movement* (New York, 1968), pp. 49–127; and the entire issue of *Labor History* (Summer 1969).

[10]William M. Tuttle, Jr., "Labor Conflict and Racial Violence: The Black Worker in Chicago, 1894–1919," *Labor History* (Summer 1969) pp. 406–32; Spero and Harris: *The Black Worker*, pp. 131–34. For a national survey on strikebreaking see Leslie Fishel, *The North and the Negro, 1865–1900* (unpublished dissertation, Harvard University, 1953), pp. 454–71.

The War's effect on black people took place through the mediation of the market-place, rather than through any shake-up of political relations. Hostilities in Europe placed limitations on American industry's usual labor supply by shutting off the flow of immigration at the very time the demand for labor was increasing sharply due to a war boom and military mobilization. Competition with the Southern plantation system for black labor became one of the major means of resolving this crisis of labor demand.

The black labor reserve in the countryside that had existed essentially as a *potential* source of the industrial proletariat now became a very *active* source. Whereas in the past this industrial reserve had not been tapped in any important way except by rural-based operations such as lumbering, with the advent of the War the industrial system as a whole began drawing on it. This new demand for black workers was to set in motion three key developments: first, the dispersion of black people out of the South into Northern urban centers; second, the formation of a distinct black proletariat in the urban centers at the very heart of the corporate-capitalist process of production; third, the break-up of tenancy agriculture in the South. World War II was to repeat the process in a magnified form and to place the stamp of irreversibility upon it.

Migration out of the countryside started in 1915 and swept up to a human tide by 1917. The major movement was to Northern cities, so that between 1910 and 1920 the black population increased in Chicago from 44,000 to 109,000; in New York from 92,000 to 152,000; in Detroit from 6,000 to 41,000; and in Philadelphia from 84,000 to 134,000. That decade there was a net increase of 322,000 in the number of Southern born blacks living in the North, exceeding the aggregate increase of the preceding 40 years. A secondary movement took place to Southern cities, especially those with shipbuilding and heavy industry.

Labor demand in such industries as steel, meat-packing, and autos was the key stimulant to black migration. The total number of wage-earners in manufacturing went from 7,000,000 in 1914 to around 9,000,000 in 1919—an increase twice that of any preceding five-year period.

· · ·

The profit-maximization imperatives of Northern capitalist firms for the first time outweighed the socio-political reasons for leaving the Southern planters' control over black labor undisturbed and without any serious competition.

· · ·

The tremendous social dislocations created by the mobilization and the wartime economic boom heightened inter-racial tensions and laid the groundwork for over 20 race riots that occurred on both sides of the Mason-Dixon Line. Careful studies of the two major race riots in Northern industrial centers (East Saint Louis in 1917 and Chicago in 1919) reveal the tremendous friction that had developed between white and black workers.[11] These hostilities were not simply an outgrowth of race prejudice, for in both cases employers had fostered competition for jobs, especially by employing blacks as strikebreakers. Conflict between working-class whites and working-class blacks was analogous in a way to the previously discussed racial competition among tenants and smallholders for land in the South. When the conflict erupted into mass violence, the dominant whites sat back and resolved the crises in a manner that assured their continued control over both groups.

· · ·

Black workers were employed on management's own terms. Sometimes these terms would involve the deliberate use of blacks to divide the work force. As a case in point, International Harvester integrated the hiring of blacks into its open-shop policies. Part of its strategy was to keep any nationality group from becoming too numerous in any one

plant lest they become cohesive in labor conflicts. The decision on hiring was left up to the individual plant superintendents, some keeping their shops lily-white, others hiring large numbers of black workers. Harvester's management was caught up in a contradiction between its need for black workers, especially in the disagreeable twine mill and foundry, and its desire to keep them below 20% at any one plant.[12]

A somewhat different approach was taken by Ford Motor Company. In the 1921 depression Henry Ford decided to maintain the black work force at the gigantic River Rouge plant in the same proportion as blacks in the total population of the Detroit area. The great majority of blacks at the River Rouge plant were employed in hot, heavy jobs in the rolling mills and foundry, but it was company policy to place a few in every major production unit and even allow a certain amount of upgrading to skilled positions. At the other Ford plants, as at the other major auto companies, black workers were confined to hard unskilled jobs. But the job concessions at Rouge became a mechanism by which Ford was able to gain considerable influence over Detroit's black community. Hiring was channeled through some preferred black ministers who agreed with Henry Ford on politics and industrial relations. Company black personnel officials were active in Republican politics and in anti-union campaigns. Ford had learned early a racial tactic that is widely employed today—that of trading concessions, relaxing economic subordination in order to increase political subordination.[13]

· · ·

In the South, where four-fifths of the nation's black population still lived at the end of the 1920s, the situation of black labor was to all appearances essentially unchanged. The number of black men engaged in Southern

[11]Elliot M. Rudwick, *Race Riot at East Saint Louis, July 2, 1917* (Carbondale, 1964); William Tuttle, *Race Riot: Chicago in the Red Summer of 1919* (New York, 1970).

[12]Robert Ozanne, *A Century of Labor-Management Relations at McCormick and International Harvester* (Madison, 1967), pp. 183–87.

[13]Bailer: "The Negro Automobile Worker," pp. 416–19; Herbert Northrup, *Organized Labor and the Negro* (New York, 1944), pp. 189–95.

industry grew during this decade only 45% as fast as the number of whites. Black workers were concentrated in stagnant or declining plants, such as sawmills, coal mines, and cigar and tobacco factories. The increased hiring of blacks in such places was chiefly a reflection of the fact that the jobs had no future and the employers were not able to attract white workers. Black employment in textiles was severely limited, as in South Carolina, where state law forbade blacks to work in the same room, use the same stairway, or even share the same factory window as white textile workers. Industry in the South, as far as black workers were concerned, still offered little competition to the dominance of agrarian tenancy.

Beneath the surface, however, significant changes were taking place in the rural South. . . . Cotton cultivation was moving westward, leaving many blacks in the Southeast without a market crop. Out in the new cotton lands in Texas and Oklahoma whites provided a much larger proportion of the tenants and sharecroppers. By 1930 a slight decrease was seen in the number of black farm operators and laborers. Later, the great depression of the 1930s accelerated this trend as the primary market for agricultural commodities collapsed and the acreage in cotton was halved. Black tenants were pushed off land in far greater proportions than whites. New Deal agricultural programs were very important in displacing sharecroppers and tenants, since they subsidized reductions in acreage. In the early government-support programs landlords tended to monopolize subsidy payments, diverting much of them out of tenants' pockets. When the regulations were changed in the tenants' favor, the landowner had an incentive to convert the tenants to wage laborers or dismiss them altogether so as to get the whole subsidy. The great depression marked the first drastic decline in the demand for black peasants since their status had been established after the Civil War.

In 1940 there were 650,000 fewer black farm operators and laborers than there had been a decade earlier—representing a one-third drop in the total. The push out of the countryside helped maintain a small net rate of migration to the North. More significantly, however, during the depression decade a high rate of black movement to the city kept on while the rate of white urbanization slackened greatly.

Although the great majority of black people remained in the rural South, we have dealt primarily with the character of the demand for black workers in the course of their becoming established directly in the urban industrial economy. This initial process was to form the matrix into which the ever-increasing numbers of black workers were to be fitted. As the size of the black population in big cities grew, "Negro jobs" became roughly institutionalized into an identifiable black sub-labor market within the larger metropolitan labor market. The culture of control that was embodied in the regulative systems which managed the black ghettos, moreover, provided an effective, although less-rigid, variation of the Jim Crow segregation that continued with hardly any change in the South. Although the economic base of black tenancy was collapsing, its reciprocal superstructure of political and social controls remained the most-powerful force shaping the place of blacks in society. The propertied and other groups that had a vested interest in the special exploitation of the black peasantry were still strong enough to maintain their hegemony over matters concerning race. At the same time, the variation of Jim Crow that existed in the North was more than simply a carry-over from the agrarian South. These ghetto controls served the class function for industrial society of politically and socially setting off that section of the proletariat that was consigned to the least-desirable employment. This racial walling off not only was accomplished by direct ruling-class actions, but also was mediated through an escalating reciprocal process in which the hostility and competition of the white working class was stimulated by the growth of the black proletariat and in return operated as an agent in shaping the new racial controls.

. . .

CURRENT CONDITIONS OF DEMAND

The changes that took place in the economic deployment of black labor in World War II were clearly an acceleration of developments that had been under way since World War I. In a process of transition, at a certain point the quantity of change becomes so great that the whole set of relationships assume an entirely different character. Such a nodal point took place during World War II, and there resulted a transformation in the characteristic relations of institutional racism from agrarian thralldom to a metropolitan ghetto system.

Within a generation, few of the concrete economic or demographic forms of the old base remained. In 1940, over three-fourths of all blacks lived in the South, close to two-thirds lived in rural areas there, and just under half were still engaged in agriculture. By 1969, almost as many blacks lived outside the South as still resided in that region, and only 4% of the black laborers remained in agriculture, as they had left the farms at a much more rapid rate than whites. Today, only about a fifth of the total black population live in the rural areas and small towns of the South.

The United States, during the Twentieth Century, has become a distinctively urban nation—or, more accurately, a metropolitan nation with its population centered in the large cities and their surrounding configurations. The first three decades of this century witnessed the rapid urbanization of whites; the next three decades saw an even more rapid urbanization of blacks. In 1940 the proportion of the country's black population living in urban areas (49%) was the same as that proportion of whites had been in 1910. Within 20 years, almost three fourths of all blacks were urban dwellers, a higher propor-

tion than the corresponding one for whites. More specifically, the black population has been relocated into the central cities of the metropolitan areas—in 1940, 34% of all blacks resided in central cities; in 1969, 55%. The larger cities were the points of greatest growth. In 1950 black people constituted one out of every eight persons in the central cities of the metropolitan areas of every size classification, and one out of every twenty in the suburbs. By 1969, black people constituted one out of every four in the central city populations of the large metropolitan areas (1,000,000 plus), and about one out of six in the medium-size metropolitan areas (250,000 to 1,000,000), while in the smaller-size metropolitan areas (below 250,000) and the suburbs the proportions remained constant. Today black communities form major cities in themselves, two with populations over 1,000,000, four between 500,000 and 1,000,000, and eight between 200,000 and 500,000.[14] Newark and Washington, D.C. already have black majorities, and several other major cities will most likely join their ranks in the next 10 years.

The displacement of blacks from Southern agriculture was only partially due to the pull of labor demand in wartime. Technological innovation, being a necessary condition of production, acted as an independent force to drive the tenants out of the cotton fields. The push off the land occurred in two phases. Initially, right after the war, the introduction of tractors and herbicides displaced the cotton hands from full-time to seasonal work at summer weeding and harvest. The now part-time workers moved from the farms to hamlets and small towns. During the 1950s mechanization of the harvest eliminated most of the black peasantry from agricultural employment and forced them to move to the larger cities for economic survival.

Elimination of the Southern black peasantry was decisive in changing the forms of racism throughout the entire region, for it

---

[14]These estimates are as of 1969. Data from the 1970 census were not available at the time of writing.

meant the disappearance of the economic foundation on which the elaborate super-structure of legal Jim Crow and segregation had originally been erected. Not only did this exploited agrarian group almost vanish, but the power of the large landholders who expropriated the surplus it had produced diminished in relation to the growing urban and industrial interests. While the civil-rights movement and the heroic efforts associated with it were necessary to break the official legality of segregation, it should be recognized that in a sense this particular form of racism was already obsolete, as its base in an exploitative system of production had drastically changed. The nature of the concessions made both by the ruling class nationally and by the newer power groups of the South can be understood only in terms of this fuller view of history.

For the United States as a whole, the most-important domestic development was the further elaboration and deepening of monopoly state capitalism. As the political economy has matured, technological and management innovation have become capital-saving as well as labor-saving. Capital accumulation declines as a proportion of the gross national product, and a mature capitalist economy enters into a post-accumulation phase of development. Under these conditions the disposal of the economic surplus becomes almost as great a problem as the accumulation of it. Corporations promote consumerism through increased sales effort, planned obsolescence, and advertising. The State meets the problem by increasing its own expenditures, especially in non-consumable military items, by providing monetary support to consumption through subsidies to the well-off, and by spending a certain amount on welfare for the working class and the poor. Markedly lower incomes would add to the surplus disposal problems and would create economic stagnation as well as risking the most-disruptive forms of class struggle.

Working-class incomes have two basic minimum levels, or floors. One is that which can be considered the level of the good trade-union contract which has to be met even by non-union firms that bid in this section of the labor market. State intervention is usually indirect in the setting of these incomes, but has grown noticeably in the last few years. The other income floor is set by direct government action via minimum-wage and welfare legislation. In the Northern industrial states where trade unions are stronger, both these income floors tend to be higher than in rural and Southern states.

Although in the mature capitalist society both economic and political imperatives exist for a certain limiting of the exploitation of the working class as a whole, each corporation still has to operate on the basis of maximizing its profits. The fostering of a section of the working class that will have to work at the jobs that are paid at rates between those of tho two income floors works to meet the needs of profit maximization. Other jobs that fall into this category are those that might pay at the collective bargaining contract level but are subject to considerable seasonal and cyclical unemployment, and those from which a high rate of production is squeezed under hard or hazardous conditions. In all the developed Western capitalist states, there exists a group of workers to fill the jobs that the more politically established sectors of the working class shun. These marginal workers generally are set apart in some way so that they lack the social or the political means of defending their interests. In Western Europe usually they are non-citizens coming from either Southern Europe or Northern Africa. In England they are colored peoples coming from various parts of the Empire. In the urban centers of the United States race serves to mark black and brown workers for filling in the undesirable slots.

Further, in the distribution of government transfer payments each class and status group strives to maximize its receipts. Therefore the powerless tend to receive a smaller proportion of these funds, and those that are delivered to them come in a manner which stigmatizes and bolsters political controls.

Specifically, in the metropolitan centers in

America, there is a racial dual labor-market structure. Side by side with the primary metropolitan job market in which firms recruit white workers and white workers seek employment, there exists a smaller secondary market in which firms recruit black workers and black workers seek jobs. In the largest metropolitan areas this secondary black market ranges from one-tenth to one-quarter of the size of the white market. For both the white and black sectors there are distinct demand and supply forces determining earnings and occupational distribution, as well as separate institutions and procedures for recruitment, hiring, training, and promotion of workers.

The distinctiveness of these two labor forces is manifested by many dimensions—by industry, by firm, by departments within firms, by occupation, and by geographical area. Within all industries, including government service, there are occupational ceilings for blacks. In a labor market like that of the Chicago metropolitan area, there are a number of small and medium-size firms in which the majority of the workers are black. However about two-thirds of the small firms and one-fifth of the medium ones hire no blacks at all. In larger firms a dual structure in the internal labor market marks off the position of the black workers along the same lines that exist in the metropolitan labor market.

A review of black employment in Chicago in 1966 finds that blacks tend to work in industries with lower wages, higher turnover, and higher unemployment. Further, they are also over-represented in the industries which exhibit sluggish growth and obviously less chance for advancement. Black men provide a third of the blue-collar workers in such industries as textiles, retail stores, primary metals, and local transportation, while in utilities, advertising, and communication they constitute less than 6%. Black women are even more concentrated in furnishing over half the blue-collar women workers in five industries—personal services, education, retail stores, hotels, and railroads.

In terms of internal labor market segregation, one of the Chicago firms best known as a fair-practice employer has a major installation located in the black community in which blacks constitute 20% of the blue-collar workers and less than 5% of the craftsmen and white-collar workers. A General Motors plant with 7500 workers is reported to have 40% black semi-skilled operatives, but only between 1% and 2% black craftsmen. A foundry firm will have one black clerk out of nearly 100 white-collar workers, while 80% of its blue-collar operators will be black.

·   ·   ·

The dual labor market operates to create an urban-based industrial labor reserve that provides a ready supply of workers in a period of labor shortage and can be politically isolated in times of relatively high unemployment. In a tight labor market the undesirable jobs that whites leave are filled out of this labor reserve so that in time more job categories are added to the black sector of the labor market. If the various forms of disguised unemployment and sub-employment are all taken into account, black unemployment rates can run as high as three or four times those of whites in specific labor markets in recession periods. The welfare and police costs of maintaining this labor reserve are high, but they are borne by the State as a whole and therefore do not enter into the profit calculations of individual firms.

This special exploitation of the black labor force also leads to direct economic gains for the various employers. Methodologically it is very difficult to measure exactly the extra surplus extracted due to wage discrimination, although in Chicago it has been estimated that unskilled black workers earn about 17% less on similar jobs than unskilled white workers of comparable quality.[15] While in a historical sense the entire differential of wage income between blacks and whites can be

[15]D. Taylor, "Discrimination and Occupational Wage Differences in the Market for Unskilled Labor," *Industrial and Labor Relations Review* (April 1968), pp. 375–90.

attributed to discrimination, the employer realizes only that which takes place in the present in terms of either lesser wage payments or greater work output. Estimates of this realized special exploitation range on the order of 10% to 20% of the total black wage and salary income.[16]

The subordinate status of the black labor market does not exist in isolation, but rather is a major part of a whole complex of institutional controls that constitute the web of urban racism.[17] This distinctive modern form of racism conforms to the 300-year-old traditions of the culture of control for the oppression of black people, but now most of the controls are located within the major metropolitan institutional networks—such as the labor market, the housing market, the political system. As the black population grew in the urban centers a distinctive new formation developed in each of these institutional areas. A black ghetto and housing market, a black labor market, a black school system, a black political system, and a black welfare system came into being—not as parts of a self-determining community, but as institutions to be controlled, manipulated, and exploited. When the black population did not serve the needs of dominant institutions by providing a wartime labor reserve, they were isolated so that they could be regulated and incapacitated.

This model of urban racism has had three major components with regard to institutional structures: (1) Within the major institutional networks that operate in the city there have developed definable black sub-sectors which operated on a subordinated basis, subject to the advantage, control, and priorities of the dominant system. (2) A pattern of mutual reinforcement takes place between the barriers that define the various black sub-sectors. (3) The controls over the lives of black men are so pervasive that they form a system analogous to colonial forms of rule.

The history of the demand for black labor in the post-war period showed the continued importance of wartime labor scarcities. The new job categories gained during World War II essentially were transferred into the black sectors of the labor market. Some war industries, like shipbuilding, of course, dropped off considerably. In reconversion and the brief 1948–1949 recession blacks lost out disproportionately on the better jobs. However the Korean War again created an intense labor shortage, making black workers once more in demand, at least until the fighting stopped. The period of slow economic growth from 1955 to the early 1960s saw a deterioration in the relative position of blacks as they experienced very high rates of unemployment and their incomes grew at a slower rate than those of whites. The civil-rights protests had generated little in the way of new demand. Only the coincidence of the rebellions of Watts, Newark, and Detroit with the escalation of the Vietnam War brought about a sharp growth in demand for black labor.

All the available evidence indicates that there has been no structural change of any significance in the deployment of black workers, most especially in private industry. Certain absolute standards of exclusion in professional, management, and sales occupations have now been removed, but the total growth in these areas has been slight except where a black clientele is serviced, as in the education and health fields. The one significant new demand in the North has been that for women clerical workers. This arises from a shortage of this particular kind of labor in the central business districts, which, being surrounded by the black community, are increasingly geographically removed from white supplies of these workers. About 90% of Chicago's black female white-collar workers work either in their own communi-

[16]For a recent estimate see Lester Thurow, *The Economy of Poverty and Discrimination* (Washington, 1969). He finds the gains due to wage discrimination were $4,600,000,000 in 1960. Advantages to white workers due to higher employment rates were $6,500,000,000.

[17]For an extended treatment of the institutionalization of racism in the metropolis see Harold Baron, "The Web of Urban Racism," in Louis Knowles and Kenneth Prewitt, eds., *Institutional Racism in America* (New York, 1969), pp. 134–76.

ties or in the central business districts, and are not employed in the rapidly growing outlying offices. In the South the whole pattern of racial regulation in the major cities is shifting over to a Northern model, so that the basic situation of black workers in Atlanta or Memphis is approaching that of the North about a decade ago.

Until the uprisings in the mid-60s, management of racial affairs was carried out either by the unvarnished maintenance of the status quo (except when black workers were needed) or by an elaborate ritual of fair practices and equal employment opportunity. The latter strategy operated as a sort of sophisticated social Darwinism to make the rules of competition for the survival of the fittest more equitable. Actually it blurred institutional realities, channeling energies and perceptions into individualized findings of fact. The black protest movement finally forced a switch to a policy of affirmative action that is supported by legal encouragement. In either case no basic structures have actually been transformed. As a review of studies on the current racial status in several industries finds: "Over the long haul, however, it is apparent that the laws of supply and demand have exercised a greater influence on the quantitative employment patterns of blacks than have the laws of the land."[18]

In the Cold War era the trade-union movement lost its innovative dynamism and became narrowly wage-oriented. Overwhelmingly, the net racial effect of the collective-bargaining agreements was to accept the given conditions in a plant. Only a very few unions, usually from the CIO, conducted any fights for the upgrading of black workers. More usual was the practice of neglecting shop grievances. Within union life itself the black officials who arose as representatives of their race were converted into justifiers of the union administration to the black workers. On the legislative and judicial fronts—that

is, away from their day-to-day base of operations—national unions supported the programs of civil-rights organizations and the fair-employment symbolism. In fact by the early 1960s the racial strategies of national trade unions and those of the most-sophisticated corporate leadership had converged.

The actions of the black community itself were destined to become the decisive political initiator, not only in its own liberation struggles but on the domestic scene in general. From World War II through the Korean War the urban black communities were engaged in digesting the improvements brought about by the end of the depression and by the wartime job gains. Both bourgeois and trade-union leadership followed the forms of the New Deal–labor coalition, but the original substance of mass struggle was no longer present.

The destabilization of the whole agrarian society in the South created the conditions for new initiatives. The Montgomery bus boycott was to re-introduce mass political action into the Cold War era. The boldness of the civil-rights movement, plus the success of national liberation movements in the Third World, galvanized the black communities in the major cities. At first the forms of the Southern struggle were to predominate in pro-integration civil-rights actions. Then youth and workers were swept into the movement and re-defined its direction toward black self-determination. The mass spontaneity in the ghetto rebellions revealed the tremendous potential of this orientation.

The ghetto systems and the dual labor markets had organized a mass black proletariat, and had concentrated it in certain key industries and plants. In the decade after World War II the most important strategic concentration of black workers was in the Chicago packing houses, where they became the majority group. United Packinghouse Workers District I was bold in battles over conditions in the plants and supplied the basic leadership for militant protest on the South Side. Even though the UPW was the most advanced of all big national unions on the

[18]Vernon M. Briggs, "The Negro in American Industry: A Review of Seven Studies," *Journal of Human Resources* (Summer 1970), pp. 371–81.

race question, a coalition of black officials and shop stewards had to wage a struggle against the leadership for substantive black control. This incipient nationalist faction was defeated in the union, and the big meat packers moved out of the city; but before it disappeared the movement indicated the potential of black-oriented working-class leadership. The Packinghouse Workers' concrete struggles contrasted sharply with the strategy of A. Philip Randolph, who set up the form of an all-black Negro American Labor Council and then subordinated its mass support to maneuvers at the top level of the AFL-CIO.

After the ghetto uprisings workers were to re-assert themselves at the point of production. Black caucuses and Concerned Workers' Committees sprang up across the country in plants and installations with large numbers of blacks. By this time the auto industry had created the largest concentration of black workers in the nation on its back-breaking production lines in Detroit. Driven by the peculiarities of the black labor market, the "big three" auto companies had developed the preconditions for the organization of the Dodge Revolutionary Union Movement (DRUM) and the League of Revolutionary Black Workers. The insertion onto this scene of a cadre that was both black-conscious and class-conscious, with a program of revolutionary struggle, forged an instrument for the militant working-class leadership of the Black Liberation Movement. The League also provides an exemplary model for proletarians among other oppressed groups, and might even be able to stimulate sections of the white working class to emerge from their narrow economistic orientation.

The ruling class is caught in its own contradictions. It needs black workers, yet the conditions of satisfying this need compel it to bring together the potential forces for the most-effective opposition to its policies, and even for a threat to its very existence. Amelioration of once-absolute exclusionary barriers does not eliminate the black work force that the whole web of urban racism defines. Even if the capitalists were willing to forego their economic and status gains from racial oppression, they could not do so without shaking up all of the intricate concessions and consensual arrangements through which the State now exercises legitimate authority. Since the ghetto institutions are deeply intertwined with the major urban systems, the American Government does not even have the option of decolonializing by ceding nominal sovereignty that the British and French empires have both exercised. The racist structures cannot be abolished without an earthquake in the heartland. Indeed, for that sophisticated gentleman, the American capitalist, the demand for black labor has become a veritable devil in the flesh.

10.3 *The Economics of Racism*

In the introduction to this chapter we pointed out that racism is often seen as an aberration in the United States. According to conventional analyses of racial discrimination, employers hurt themselves financially by discriminating against blacks since the labor supply that employers draw upon is thereby restricted. On the other hand, white workers are said to benefit since discrimination reduces the competition from blacks for the jobs and wages of white workers.

In the following reading Michael Reich undertakes a statistical test of the effects of racism in the United States. Reich criticizes the conventional explanation of racism and concludes from his analysis that racism benefits white employers and other rich whites while it hurts poor whites and white employees. Thus racism is seen as a phenomenon of *capitalist* society. Racism is useful to capitalism because it obfuscates class interests and provides a convenient psychological outlet for worker frustration, thereby reinforcing the existing class structure.

It should be stressed that Reich argues not that racism is necessary to capitalism but that capitalism nurtures racist ideologies and practices that help to stabilize the capitalist system. Racism is likely to take firm root in a capitalist society and to last as long as do capitalist institutions themselves.

The following is a revised version of "The Economics of Racism" by MICHAEL REICH. From *Problems in Political Economy: An Urban Perspective*, edited by David M. Gordon. Copyright © 1970 by Michael Reich. Reprinted by permission of the author.

In the early 1960s it seemed to many that the elimination of racism in the U.S. was proceeding without requiring a radical restructuring of the entire society. There was a growing civil rights movement, and hundreds of thousands of blacks were moving to Northern cities where discrimination was supposedly less severe than in the South. Government reports pointed to the rapid improvement in the levels of black schooling as blacks moved out of the South: in 1966 the gap between the median years of schooling of black males aged 25 to 29 and white males in the same age group had shrunk to one-quarter the size of the gap that had existed in 1960.[1]

By 1970, however, the optimism of earlier decades had vanished. Despite new civil rights laws, elaborate White House conferences, special ghetto manpower programs, the War on Poverty, and stepped-up tokenist hiring, racism and the economic exploitation of blacks has not lessened. During the past twenty-five years there has been virtually no permanent improvement in the relative economic position of blacks in America. Median black incomes have been fluctuating at a level between 47 percent and 63 percent of median white incomes, the ratio rising during

economic expansions and falling to previous low levels during recessions.[2] Segregation in schools and neighborhoods has been steadily increasing in almost all cities, and the atmosphere of distrust between blacks and whites has been intensifying. Racism, instead of disappearing, seems to be on the increase.

Besides systematically subjugating blacks so that their median income is 55 percent that of whites, racism is of profound importance for the distribution of income among white landowners, capitalists, and workers. For example, racism clearly benefits owners of housing in the ghetto where blacks have no choice but to pay higher rents there than is charged to whites for comparable housing elsewhere in the city. But more importantly, racism is a key mechanism for the stabilization of capitalism and the legitimization of inequality. We shall return to the question of who benefits from racism later, but first we shall review some of the economic means used to subjugate blacks.

THE PERVASIVENESS OF RACISM

Beginning in the first grade, blacks go to schools of inferior quality and obtain little of the basic training and skills needed in the

[1]U.S. Department of Labor, Bureau of Labor Statistics, Report No. 375, "The Social and Economic Status of Negroes in the United States, 1969," p. 50.

[2]The data refer to male incomes: see Table 10-A, p. 360.

labor market. Finding schools of little relevance, more in need of immediate income, and less able anyway to finance their way through school, the average black student still drops out at a lower grade than his white counterpart. In 1974 only 8.1 percent of blacks aged 25 to 34 were college graduates, compared to 21.0 percent of whites in the same age bracket.[3]

Exploitation really begins in earnest when the black youth enters the labor market. A black worker with the same number of years of schooling and the same scores on achievement tests as a white worker receives much less income. The black worker cannot get as good a job because the better-paying jobs are located too far from the ghetto or because he or she was turned down by racist personnel agencies and employers or because a union denied admittance or maybe because of an arrest record. Going to school after a certain point doesn't seem to increase a black person's income possibilities very much. The more educated a black person is, the greater is the disparity between his income and that of a white with the same schooling. The result: *in 1966 black college graduates earned less than white high school dropouts*.[4] And the higher the average wage or salary of an occupation, the lower the percentage of workers in that occupation who are black.

The rate of unemployment among blacks is generally twice as high as among whites.[5] Layoffs and recessions hit blacks with twice the impact they hit whites, since blacks are the "last hired, first fired." The ratio of average black to white incomes follows the business cycle closely, buffeirng white workers from some of the impact of the recession.

Blacks pay higher rents for inferior housing, higher prices in ghetto stores, higher

insurance premiums, higher interest rates in banks and lending companies, travel longer distances at greater expense to their jobs, suffer from inferior garbage collection and less access to public recreational facilities, and are assessed at higher property tax rates when they own housing. Beyond this, blacks are further harassed by police, the courts, and the prisons.

When conventional economists attempt to analyze racism they usually begin by trying to separate various forms of racial discrimination. For example, they define "pure wage discrimination" as the racial differential in wages paid to equivalent workers—that is, those with similar years and quality of schooling, skill training, previous employment experience and seniority, age, health, job attitudes, and a host of other factors. They presume that they can analyze the sources of "pure wage discrimination" without simultaneously analyzing the extent to which discrimination also affects the factors they hold constant.

But such a technique distorts reality. The various forms of discrimination are not separable in real life. Employers' hiring and promotion practices; resource allocation in city schools; the structure of transportation systems; residential segregation and housing quality; availability of decent health care; behavior of policemen and judges; foremen's prejudices; images of blacks presented in the media and the schools; price gouging in ghetto stores—these and the other forms of social and economic discrimination interact strongly with each other in determining the occupational status and annual income, and welfare, of black people. The processes are not simply additive but are mutually reinforcing. Often, a decrease in one narrow form of discrimination is accompanied by an increase in another form. Since all aspects of racism interact, an analysis of racism should incorporate all its aspects in a unified manner.

No single quantitative index could adequately measure racism in all its social, cultural, psychological, and economic dimen-

[3]U.S. Bureau of the Census, Series P-60, "Educational Attainment."

[4]U.S. Bureau of the Census, Series P-60, "Income in 1966 of Families and Persons in the United States."

[5]See, for example, U.S. Department of Labor, *Manpower Report of the President*, various years.

sions. But while racism is far more than a narrow economic phenomenon, it does have very definite economic consequences: blacks have far lower incomes than whites. The ratio of median black to median white incomes thus provides a rough, but useful, quantitative index of the economic consequences of racism for blacks. We shall use this index statistically to analyze the causes of racism's persistence in the United States. While this approach overemphasizes the economic aspects of racism, it is nevertheless an improvement over the narrower approach taken by conventional economists.

COMPETING EXPLANATIONS OF RACISM

How is the historical persistence of racism in the United States to be explained? The most prominent analysis of discrimination among economists was formulated in 1957 by Gary Becker in his book, *The Economics of Discrimination*.[6] Racism, according to Becker, is fundamentally a problem of tastes and attitudes. Whites are defined to have a "taste for discrimination" if they are willing to forfeit income in order to be associated with other whites instead of blacks. Since white employers and employees prefer not to associate with blacks, they require a monetary compensation for the psychic cost of such association. In Becker's principal model, white employers have a taste for discrimination; marginal productivity analysis is invoked to show that white employers lose while white workers gain (in monetary terms) from discrimination against blacks.

Becker does not try to explain the source of white tastes for discrimination. For him, these attitudes are determined outside of the economic system. (Racism could presumably be ended simply by changing these attitudes, perhaps by appeal to whites on moral grounds.) According to Becker's analysis,

[6]Gary Becker, *The Economics of Discrimination* (Chicago: University of Chicago Press, 1957).

employers would find the ending of racism to be in their economic self-interest, but white workers would not. The persistence of racism is thus implicitly laid at the door of white workers. Becker suggests that long-run market forces will lead to the end of discrimination anyway: less discriminatory employers, with no "psychic costs" to enter in their accounts, will be able to operate at lower costs by hiring equivalent black workers at lower wages, thus bidding up the black wage rate and/or driving the more discriminatory employers out of business.

The approach to racism argued here is entirely different. Racism is viewed as rooted in the economic system and not in "exogenously determined" attitudes. Historically, the American Empire was founded on the racist extermination of American Indians, was financed in large part by profits from slavery, and was extended by a string of interventions, beginning with the Mexican War of the 1840s, which have been at least partly justified by white supremacist ideology.

Today, by transferring white resentment toward blacks and away from capitalism, racism continues to serve the needs of the capitalist system. Although individual employers might gain by refusing to discriminate and hiring more blacks, thus raising the black wage rate, it is not true that the capitalist class as a whole would benefit if racism were eliminated and labor were more efficiently allocated without regard to skin color. We will show below that the divisiveness of racism weakens workers' strength when bargaining with employers; the economic consequences of racism are not only lower incomes for blacks but also higher incomes for the capitalist class and lower incomes for white workers. Although capitalists may not have conspired consciously to create racism, and although capitalists may not be its principal perpetuators, nevertheless racism does support the continued viability of the American capitalist system.

We have, then, two alternative approaches to the analysis of racism. The first suggests that capitalists lose and white workers gain from racism. The second predicts the opposite—capitalists gain while workers lose. The first says that racist "tastes for discrimination" are formed independently of the economic system; the second argues that racism interacts symbiotically with capitalistic economic institutions.

The very persistence of racism in the United States lends support to the second approach. So do repeated instances of employers using blacks as strikebreakers, as in the massive steel strike of 1919, and employer-instigated exacerbation of racial antagonisms during that strike and many others.[7] However, the particular virulence of racism among many blue- and white-collar workers and their families seems to refute our approach and support Becker.

SOME EMPIRICAL EVIDENCE

Which of the two models better explains reality? We have already mentioned that our approach predicts that capitalists gain and workers lose from racism, whereas the conventional Beckerian approach predicts precisely the opposite. In the latter approach racism has an equalizing effect on the white income distribution, whereas in the former racism has a disequalizing effect. The statistical relationship between the extent of racism and the degree of inequality among whites provides a simple yet clear test of the two approaches. This section describes that test and its results.

First, we need a measure of racism. The index we use, for reasons already mentioned, is the ratio of black median family income to white median family income (abbreviated as B/W). A low numerical value for this ratio indicates a high degree of racism. We

have calculated values of this racism index, using data from the 1960 Census, for each of the largest forty-eight metropolitan areas (boundaries are defined by the U.S. Census Bureau, who use the term standard metropolitan statistical areas—SMSA's). There is a great deal of variation from SMSA to SMSA in the B/W index of racism, even within the North; Southern SMSA's generally demonstrated a greater degree of racism. The statistical techniques used are based on this variation.

We also need measures of inequality among whites. Two convenient measures are: (1) the percentage share of all white income that is received by the top 1 percent of white families; and (2) the Gini coefficient of white incomes, a measure which captures inequality within as well as between social classes.[8]

Both of these inequality measures vary considerably among the SMSA's; there is also a substantial amount of variation in these within the subsample of Northern SMSA's. Therefore, it is very interesting to examine whether the pattern of variation of the inequality and racism variables can be explained by causal hypotheses. This is our first source of empirical evidence.

A systematic relationship across SMSA's between our measure of racism and either measure of white inequality does exist and is highly significant: where racism is greater, income inequality *among whites* is also greater.[9] This result is consistent with our model and is inconsistent with the predictions of Becker's model.

This evidence, however, should not be accepted too quickly. The correlations re-

[7]See, for example, David Brody, *Steelworkers in America: the Nonunion Era* (Cambridge: Harvard University Press, 1966); Herbert Gutman, "The Negro and the United Mineworkers," in *The Negro and the American Labor Movement*, ed. J. Jacobson (New York: Anchor, 1968); S. Spero and H. Harris, *The Black Worker* (New York: Atheneum, 1968), *passim*.

[8]The Gini coefficient varies between 0 and 1, with 0 indicating perfect equality and 1 indicating perfect inequality. For a more complete exposition, see H. Miller, *Income Distribution in the United States* (Washington, D.C.: U.S. Government Printing Office, 1966).

[9]For example, the correlation coefficient between the B/W measure of racism and the Gini coefficient of white incomes is $r = -.47$. A similar calculation by S. Bowles, across states instead of SMSA's, resulted in an $r = -.58$.

ported may not reflect actual causality since other independent forces may be simultaneously influencing both variables in the same way. As is the case with many other statistical analyses, the model must be expanded to control for such other factors. We know from previous inter-SMSA income distribution studies that the most important additional factors that should be introduced into our model are: (1) the industrial and occupational structure of the SMSA's; (2) the region in which the SMSA's are located; (3) the average income of the SMSA's; and (4) the proportion of the SMSA population that is black. These factors were introduced into the model by the technique of multiple regression analysis. Separate equations were estimated with the Gini index and the top 1 percent share as measures of white inequality.

All the equations showed strikingly uniform statistical results: racism as we have measured it was a significantly disequalizing force on the white income distribution, even when other factors were held constant. A 1 percent increase in the ratio of black to white median incomes (that is, a 1 percent decrease in racism) was associated with a .2 percent decrease in white inequality, as measured by the Gini coefficient. The corresponding effect on top 1 percent share of white income was two and a half times as large, indicating that most of the inequality among whites generated by racism was associated with increased income for the richest 1 percent of white families. Further statistical investigation reveals that increases in the racism variable had an insignificant effect on the share received by the poorest whites and resulted in a decrease in the income share of the whites in the middle income brackets.[10] This is true even when the Southern SMSA's are excluded.

Within our model, we can specify a number of mechanisms that further explain the

statistical finding that racism increases inequality among whites. We shall consider two mechanisms here: (1) total wages of white labor are reduced by racial antagonisms, in part because union growth and labor militancy are inhibited; (2) the supply of public services, especially in education, available to low- and middle-income whites is reduced as a result of racial antagonisms.

Wages of white labor are lessened by racism because the fear of a cheaper and underemployed black labor supply in the area is invoked by employers when labor presents its wage demands. Racial antagonisms on the shop floor deflect attention from labor grievances related to working conditions, permitting employers to cut costs. Racial divisions among labor prevent the development of united worker organizations both within the workplace and in the labor movement as a whole. As a result, union strength and union militancy will be less the greater the extent of racism. A historical example of this process is the already mentioned use of racial and ethnic divisions to destroy the solidarity of the 1919 steel strikers. By contrast, during the 1890s, black-white class solidarity greatly aided mineworkers in building militant unions among workers in Alabama, West Virginia, and other coalfield areas.[11]

The above argument and examples contradict the common belief that an exclusionary racial policy will strengthen rather than weaken the bargaining power of unions. Racial exclusion increases bargaining power only when entry into an occupation or industry can be effectively limited. Industrial-type unions are much less able to restrict entry than craft unions or organizations such as the American Medical Association. This is not to deny that much of organized labor is egregiously racist or that some skilled craft workers benefit from racism.[12] But it is

[10]A more rigorous presentation of these and other variables and the statistical results in available in Michael Reich, "Racial Discrimination and the White Income Distribution" (Unpublished Ph.D. diss., Harvard University, 1973).

[11]See footnote 7 above.

[12]See, for example, H. Hill, "The Racial Practices of Organized Labor: the Contemporary Record," in *The Negro and the American Labor Movement*, ed. J. Jacobson (New York: Anchor, 1968).

important to distinguish actual discriminatory practice from the objective economic self-interest of most union members.

The second mechanism we shall consider concerns the allocation of expenditures for public services. The most important of these services is education. Racial antagonisms dilute both the desire and the ability of poor white parents to improve educational opportunities for their children. Antagonisms between blacks and poor whites drive wedges between the two groups and reduce their ability to join in a united political movement pressing for improved and more equal education. Moreover, many poor whites recognize that however inferior their own schools, black schools are even worse. This provides some degree of satisfaction and identification with the status quo, reducing the desire of poor whites to press politically for better schools in their neighborhoods. Ghettos tend to be located near poor white neighborhoods more often than near rich white neighborhoods; racism thus reduces the potential tax base of school districts containing poor whites. Also, pressure by teachers' groups to improve all poor schools is reduced by racial antagonisms between predominantly white teaching staffs and black children and parents.[13]

The statistical validity of the above mechanisms can be tested in a causal model. The effect of racism on unionism is tested by estimating an equation in which the percentage of the SMSA labor force that is unionized is the dependent variable, with racism and the structural variables (such as the SMSA industrial structure) as the independent variables. The schooling mechanism is tested by estimating a similar equation in which the dependent variable is inequality in years of schooling completed among white males aged 25 to 29.

[13]In a similar fashion, racial antagonisms reduce the political pressure on governmental agencies to provide other public services that would have a pro-poor distributional impact. The two principal items in this category are public health services and welfare payments in the Aid to Families with Dependent Children program.

Once again, the results of this statistical test strongly confirm the hypothesis of our model. The racism variable is statistically significant in all the equations and has the predicted sign: a greater degree of racism results in lower unionization rates and greater degree of schooling inequality among whites. This empirical evidence again suggests that racism is in the economic interests of capitalists and other rich whites and against the economic interests of poor whites and white workers.

However, a full assessment of the importance of racism for capitalism would probably conclude that the primary significance of racism is not strictly economic. The simple economics of racism does not explain why many workers seem to be so vehemently racist, when racism is not in their economic self-interest. In noneconomic ways, racism helps to legitimize inequality, alienation, and powerlessness—legitimization that is necessary for the stability of the capitalist system as a whole. For example, many whites believe that welfare payments to blacks are a far more important factor in their taxes than is military spending. Through racism, poor whites come to believe that their poverty is caused by blacks who are willing to take away their jobs, and at lower wages, thus concealing the fact that a substantial amount of income inequality is inevitable in a capitalist society. Racism thus transfers the locus of whites' resentment towards blacks and away from capitalism.

Racism also provides some psychological benefits to poor and working-class whites. For example, the opportunity to participate in another's oppression compensates for one's own misery. There is a parallel here to the subjugation of women in the family: after a day of alienating labor, the tired husband can compensate by oppressing his wife. Furthermore, not being at the bottom of the heap is some solace for an unsatisfying life; this argument was successfully used by the Southern oligarchy against poor whites allied with blacks in the interracial Populist movement of the late nineteenth century.

Thus, racism is likely to take firm root in

a society that breeds an individualistic and competitive ethos. In general, blacks provide a convenient and visible scapegoat for problems that actually derive from the institutions of capitalism. As long as building a real alternative to capitalism does not seem feasible to most whites, we can expect that identifiable and vulnerable scapegoats will prove functional to the status quo. These noneconomic factors thus neatly dovetail with the economic aspects of racism discussed earlier in their mutual service to the perpetuation of capitalism.

PART

CONTRADICTIONS
OF THE
MACROECONOMY

Irrationality

THE AVERAGE AMERICAN IS FAR RICHER than the average citizen of most other countries; but are we any happier? Nearly every year the productive capacity of the U.S. economy grows larger; but does this growth improve the quality of our lives? And why, with filthy cities and crumbling housing and rising crime, does the capitalist economy leave millions of ready and willing workers out of jobs?

The vast wealth and increasing productivity of the U.S. economy are everywhere evident. Almost every year new records of industrial output are set; even serious economic crises cause only a temporary halt in the growth of real output. News reporters approvingly quote the latest figures showing higher sales of new cars, travel services, television sets, cosmetics, pain relievers, cigarettes, health care, cameras, clothes, home appliances, and other consumer products. Agricultural productivity climbs, and now the average farm worker provides food and fiber for nearly sixty consumers. World trade, a large part of which is accounted for by U.S. exports and imports, routinely expands. The energies and resources of millions of people are devoted to the invention and promotion of new products for popular consumption.

Yet there remains the nagging feeling that all this activity is simply "running in place," that the potential of the economy has not been harnessed to serve people's real needs. We observe countless examples of productive capacity and individual effort devoted to activities that add nothing to human well-being and often impede the growth of human

potentialities. In 1974, American firms spent $26 billion on advertising; drug firms alone spent over $400 million on hard-sell commercials, probably creating more "nagging pain symptoms" than their products relieved. At a time of growing inadequacy in world food supplies, Craig Claiborne, food editor for the *New York Times*, took a friend to dinner in Paris; total cost of the "meal of the century": $4,000. As diminishing energy supplies stimulated more environmentally dangerous oil exploration, GM reported record-high sales of Cadillacs; average gas mileage: 9 miles per gallon. The bankruptcy of the Penn-Central Railroad, while it marked another collapse of rail transit for the heavily populated East Coast, nonetheless proved to be a bonanza for corporate lawyers; it was estimated that their fees would run in the tens of millions of dollars. The Bufferin commercial, Mr. Claiborne's Parisian paté, the Detroit gas-guzzlers, and railroad lawsuits all use society's scarce resources and count in the annual GNP.[1]

Thus are useless activities proliferated, and frivolous wants satisfied before serious ones. Moreover, the organization of economic activity and the choice of production techniques often lead to unnecessary and irreparable

[1]*Statistical Abstract of the United States, 1975*, pp. 790, 793; *New York Times*, November 14, 1975, p. 1; U.S. Environmental Protection Agency, *1974 Gas Mileage Guide for Car Buyers; Forbes Magazine*, November 1, 1974. The paté, of course, counts negatively in the U.S. GNP, positively in the French. French visitors to Disney World increase the U.S. GNP.

damage to the environment. No one needs to be reminded of the detergents, oils, and sludge that foul our streams, rivers, and seacoasts: the "deaths" of Lakes Erie and Ontario only foreshadow the future fates of the other Great Lakes. The massive scarring of the countryside from strip-mining renders ugly and unusable what was formerly a precious natural heritage. Mountains of urban garbage, industrial trash, and the waste of radioactive power plants compound the damage. All this comes to a head in urban development that spreads mindlessly outward: between 1950 and 1975 Connecticut lost 70 percent of its farmland to "urban sprawl," while New Jersey lost nearly 40 percent.[2]

Nor is the public sector record more encouraging. The U.S. government channels billions of dollars into the production of modern weapons; by the mid-1970s, the annual defense budget had forever burst the $100 billion mark. Only forty-eight days after the $6 billion ABM missile complex in North Dakota became operational, the government decided to shut it down as obsolete.[3] More billions were poured into military aid for dictatorships around the world, from South Korea to Iran to Chile. At the same time daycare, welfare programs, food stamps, public sector jobs and wages, legal aid, education, and other programs of direct benefit to people have been trimmed for lack of funds.

These topsy-turvy social priorities are aspects of the fundamental *irrationality* of capitalist production. Capitalist production is irrational because it wastes scarce economic resources on socially unnecessary or low-priority production while failing to meet many essential needs. The extent of the mis-ordered priorities varies from one capitalist nation to another, and some mis-ordering also arises in contemporary state socialist nations. Yet there are powerful forces arising directly from capitalism which serve to divorce production priorities from social needs.

The increasing conflict between people's

needs and what capitalism produces creates growing contradictions within capitalism.

THE ORIGINS OF HUMAN NEEDS

What human beings want and need in any society is not simply god-given nor the result of "human nature"; instead, people's needs are a product of both their "fundamental needs" and their specific historical and social development. As Richard Lichtman put it,

> *Every society, in order merely to survive, must satisfy the basic subsistence needs of its members for food, shelter, clothing and human recognition. There is a level of productivity that must be achieved by any social group, for human beings have fundamental needs whose violation brings social disorganization or death. That is one half of the truth. The other is that human needs are satisfied through specific means of production that shape and alter the original needs and give rise to new needs whose satisfaction depends upon new technical instruments and new forms of social organization. Every society, therefore, in struggling to satisfy fundamental human needs, shapes these needs in distinctive ways and produces new needs which were not part of any original human nature."*[4]

Capitalist society, like all societies, shapes people's "fundamental needs" even as it satisfies them. Thus, for example, people need food. In monopoly capitalist society the need for food is met through the production of food for profit by agribusiness. But in order to earn higher profits, agribusiness firms seek to fulfill not just the simple need for sustenance. After all, they are in business not to satisfy needs but rather to earn profits. So they try to encourage consumption of foods that are *profitable*. For example, they promote foods with much sugar and cholesterol because they are sensitive to profit, not to tooth decay or fatty heart tissue. They advertise foods containing additives, on which profit margins are higher, rather than nutritionally sound foods.[5] Thus in all societies

[2] *New York Times*, February 8, 1976, section 8, p. 1.

[3] *New York Times*, November 25, 1975, p. 1.

[4] Richard Lichtman, "Capitalism and Consumption," *Socialist Revolution*, 1, No. 3 (May/June 1970), 83.

[5] See Zwerdling, Section 1.5, p. 19.

people must eat; but in capitalist society this fundamental need for food has been reshaped socially to appear as specific market demands for steroid-fed beef, nondairy creamers, oranges artificially dyed bright orange, sugar-frosted flakes, and salty or sweetened baby foods.

CAPITALIST PRODUCTION VERSUS HUMAN NEEDS

In this chapter we argue that capitalist society is irrational in the way in which it shapes old needs and creates new ones and in the way in which it provides for the satisfaction of these needs. This irrationality is seen as a fundamental characteristic of capitalist society rather than, for example, the result of inadequate knowledge, of the "facts of life" or "necessary tradeoffs," or of unfortunate "accidents"; capitalist production tends to generate such irrationalities *consistently* as part of its *normal* functioning.

Irrationality exists, for example, in the fact that capitalist society provides food products which, rather than providing nutrition, are detrimental to people's health. Food additives cause cancer, they may have disastrous genetic effects, and they appear to be linked to hyperactivity in children. Processing foods frequently eliminates nutrients, and fatty or sweet foods contribute to obesity, heart disease, and so on. People sooner or later rebel against these manipulations, as is evidenced by the popular interest in health foods, natural products, organic gardening, diets and nutrition, and consumerist efforts to ban Red Dye II, cyclamates, nitrites, and other dangerous additives. But such efforts by themselves do not solve the problem, because it derives fundamentally from the conflict between capitalist production priorities and human needs.

Firms in the food industry, and especially in recent years multinational agribusiness firms, have reorganized and developed food production on the basis of profitability and a wider market. This long historical process,

revolutionizing the way food is produced, makes it no longer possible, for example, to easily retrace society's steps to an "organic" food supply. Most small local farmers have mostly been driven out of business, so Eastern cities now depend on fruits and vegetables from Florida and California, meat from the Midwest, and so on. The truck farms have been paved over into suburbs and "industrial parks." Hence, the problem is not simply one of banning additives; it is instead the problem of reorganizing an entire food-production system that produces food far away from where it is consumed and therefore necessarily relies on taste enhancers, texturizers, preservatives, color restorers, and other additives. The food so produced is necessary to sustain life, yet eating it "may be hazardous to your health." Capitalist society, which has increased consumption levels, including the amount we eat, produces poisoned food.

What is it about the capitalist organization of production that generates these outcomes? The readings in this chapter explore this question in greater detail.[6] Here, however, we can point to the most basic source of social irrationality in capitalist production: the fact that firms produce for profit and only incidentally because the product is useful.

Production for profit means that only those social needs which appear as "dollar votes"—that is, market demands—will be met. Thus a carcinogenic additive and an "all-natural" ingredient are on an equal footing: each will be introduced into foodstuffs if and only if it is profitable, not because it improves the nutritional content of foods. Also, production for profit is biased in favor of those whose incomes afford them the greatest purchasing power. Hence the superficial wants of the rich take precedence over the basic needs of the poor.

Production for profit also establishes an exclusive concern for *private* benefits and costs while ignoring the *social* consequences of pro-

---

[6]One of the greatest of capitalism's irrationalities, its unplanned and crisis-plagued character, is the subject of Chapter 12.

duction. But as production becomes increasingly social in character, the social consequences become more important. For example, agribusiness capitalists deciding how to produce food tend to ignore the benefits that accrue to the whole society from having food with high nutritional value, because these benefits do not add to the profits of the firms. And the ecological damage and increased cancer caused by pesticide-polluted water tend to be ignored since they do not raise the firms' costs.

The terms "external economy" and "external dis-economy" have been used by economists to refer to those benefits and costs resulting from a private action that do not result in corresponding monetary gains or losses for the person or firm who took the action. External economies characterize the provision of almost all collective social services; the inadequacy of such services under capitalism can be attributed in large part to the inability of capitalists to realize profits corresponding to the social benefits provided.

Finally, production for profit creates great pressures for economic expansion, independent of the *need* for growth. But the more productive an economy becomes, the more questionable is the desirability of increasing production still further.

On the one hand, continual expansion exacerbates the problem of maintaining an ecological balance between human beings and our environment. The higher the rate of production, the faster natural resources are used up or destroyed and waste products are dumped back onto the land and into the water. Yet because capitalists continually seek new outlets for profitable reinvestment, continuous growth in productive capacity is inherent in capitalism and could not be restrained without a fundamental change in the mode of production.

On the other hand, continual expansion under capitalism gives rise to the problem of selling what is produced: how to dispose of the continually increasing surplus of production over the essential consumption requirements of the society. The problem is not a lack

of human need; the unmet needs of the poor, the unsatisfied demand for public services, etc. remain. But in order for the surplus commodities to be absorbed, it is necessary that the *market demand* for goods and services keep pace with the expanding supply.

Of course capitalists do not wait for consumers to decide what their desires are; instead, firms take an active role in stimulating consumption demand. Their most obvious activity is the tremendous sales effort, exemplified by massive advertising. But marketing considerations have also penetrated into the production sphere, and many commodities are purposely designed and constructed to go out of fashion or wear out very quickly, insuring that consumers will periodically have to buy a new model of the product. Automobiles are one of the most blatant examples of such planned obsolescence, but they are by no means atypical. In order to stimulate more sales, superflous accessories are often attached to products such as automobiles and forced upon the consumer in need of the basic good. As the readings in this chapter argue, the need to expand sales has opened the way for wasteful forms of public expenditures, a massive advertising and sales effort, and an excessive emphasis on individualistic, private consumption.[7]

The emphasis on consumption complements the alienated nature of work under capitalism. Production is eliminated as an arena for the worker's expression and self-fulfillment; the principal incentive to work is wages—external to the work process and useful only during the nonwork part of the day or week. The alienation of the worker from production thus leaves only the sphere of consumption as an arena for expressing one's individuality, asserting one's humanity, and simply escaping the debilitating effects of one's job. At work one only "earns" a living; it is at home that one "lives."

The overall preoccupation of a capitalist society with production and consumption of

[7]See Baran and Sweezy, Section 4.3, p. 134, for a discussion of the sales effort.

commodities contributes to an increasing imbalance between the satisfaction of material and nonmaterial human needs. As it produces rising quantitative levels of material consumption, capitalism sets the stage for the relatively greater urgency of nonmaterial needs and desires—needs for community, for participation, for identity, for self-expression, for affection. In part these new demands are met by new "commodities"—massage parlors offer "affection," housing developers sell "community living," psychiatrists and sensitivity-training centers release people from self-doubt for a fee. Yet in general nonmaterial needs cannot be satisfied with commodities that can be profitably marketed, so they remain unfulfilled. Nothing could be more illustrative of the fundamental irrationality of the capitalist system than the intensity with which capitalists seek to create and satisfy new material wants at the same time that other needs are both becoming more important and are ignored.

Thus the poisoning of our food grows with the profits of agribusiness; the satisfaction of our material needs is met with a more frantic sales effort; the depletion of our resources evokes not conservation but instead an intensified search for oil in the tundra; and the spoiling of our environment leads not to curbing wastes but instead to a new "growth industry" selling anti-pollution devices. Thus production becomes increasingly social in character but continues to be privately owned and controlled, and the contradictions of capitalism emerge.

In this chapter we investigate some of the ways in which capitalism causes production priorities to collide with human needs. We will argue that the process by which production decisions are made under capitalism is one that progressively separates what people need to survive and develop and what they can obtain, and therefore capitalist production becomes increasingly irrational in the most fundamental sense of the word.

11.1   *The Irrationality of Capitalist Economic Growth*

Economic growth can be defined as expanding the capacity to produce goods and services. Long-run increases in productive capacity or production itself are referred to as *secular* economic growth, to be distinguished from the more transitory increases in production that occur, for example, during the upswing of a business cycle. Secular growth establishes a rising trend line around which each succeeding business cycle fluctuates. In discussing secular growth, we abstract from the economy's short-run fluctuations and focus instead on the longer-term trend.

Economic growth, by making possible rising levels of per capita real consumption, opens the door for the elimination of people's oldest banes: poverty, insecurity, hunger, ignorance, the dehumanizing fight for survival. Growth means that society has at its disposal increased resources with which to feed, clothe, and educate itself, to insure its survival against natural disasters, to relieve its people from spending all their lives in degrading or alienating work. On the basis of these inherent potentialities, we might expect that the rapid rates of growth recorded by advanced capitalist nations represent a mighty movement for human liberation. But as Thomas E. Weiss-kopf argues in the following reading, the character of the economic growth process under capitalism severely limits its contribution to the satisfaction of real human needs. Capitalist economic growth is fundamentally irrational, and its very irrationality creates contradictions that threaten the viability of the capitalist system.

The following essay was written for this book by THOMAS E. WEISSKOPF. Copyright © 1978 by Thomas E. Weisskopf.

I. CAPITALISM AND ECONOMIC GROWTH

"Accumulate! Accumulate! That is Moses and the Prophets!" It is no accident that this is probably the most often quoted line from Marx's *Capital*, for one of the central and fundamental truths about capitalism is its inherently expansionary nature. As Marx showed in his work, and as Marxists and non-Marxists have recognized ever since, there are powerful forces operating in a capitalist system to stimulate the production of goods and services on an ever-increasing scale. The search for profits, under monopolistic as well as competitive conditions, creates irresistible pressures on capitalist firms to increase their production and their sales.[1] Firms that succeed in growing are likely to remain viable units of the capitalist economy; firms that fail to grow risk absorption by stronger firms, or extinction.

The expansionary drive of capitalist firms has led in the last few centuries to enormous growth in the quantity of goods and services produced by the world capitalist economy. By its very nature, however, the process of capitalist growth is very uneven—both geographically and intertemporally. In some countries, and in some regions within any given country, there is rapid economic growth; in other countries and regions there is slow growth or actual economic deterioration. In some periods production expands rapidly; in other periods it slows down or declines. The uneven and cyclical character of capitalist growth is analyzed in the next chapter; my attention here will be focused on the problems and contradictions involved in the overall long-run economic growth that

has characterized the U.S. economy and the world capitalist system as a whole since the emergence of the capitalist mode of production.

The available data on long-run economic growth show clearly that the advanced capitalist nations of the world have expanded enormously their productive capacity.[2] In the United States from 1865 to 1975 the rate of growth of total economic output has averaged roughly 3.5 percent per year, and the rate of growth of per capita output has averaged roughly 2 percent per year.[3] This means that total output is now almost fifty times greater, and per capita output almost ten times greater, than what it was at the end of the Civil War.

Such an impressive quantitative growth performance does not mean that the *quality* of life has shown a corresponding degree of improvement. Total output includes goods and services that contribute to people's real welfare (food, health care, etc.); but it also includes goods and services that contribute little or nothing to real welfare (weapons, advertising expenditures, etc.). The growth of total output tells us nothing about the growth of other aspects of life such as personal fulfillment or friendship, nor does it take into account the destruction of communities and the deterioration of the environment that may result from the growth process. Indeed, as I will argue below, the capitalist process of economic growth is characterized by a pervasive irrationality that seriously limits its ability to meet real human needs.

[2]See Simon Kuznets, *Modern Economic Growth* (New Haven: Yale University Press, 1966), for a thorough review of the evidence.

[3]See Simon Kuznets, *Six Lectures on Economic Growth* (New York: Free Press, 1961), Table 1; and *Statistical Abstract*, 1975, Table 617.

[1]See Edwards, Section 3.3, p. 99.

In the drive to expand the volume of production, capitalist firms and the capitalist system as a whole confront two major problems. On the one hand, they must secure the inputs and organize them so as to *produce* goods and services. This is a problem faced by people in any society engaged in production, but it is particularly acute under capitalism because of the drive to keep increasing the volume of production. On the other hand, capitalist firms must also be concerned with finding markets in which they can *sell* their increased output. This problem arises specifically because capitalism involves production for the market rather than production for use. Capitalist producers cannot be sure that they will be able to find buyers for all that they can produce; unless they do so, their profits will be reduced or turned into losses because of unsold output or unutilized productive capacity. Thus the expansionary drive of the capitalist system creates intense pressures to sell as well as to produce an expanding volume of output.

In this essay I will argue that the capitalist drive both to produce and to sell more and more goods and services is fundamentally irrational. Section II discusses the process of expanding production; section III discusses the process of expanding sales; and section IV considers some contradictions that arise in the process of capitalist economic growth.

II. THE EXPANSION OF OUTPUT

Human labor is the source of all output, for nothing can be produced without work. The amount of output produced in a society during any given period of time is a function of the amount of time that people devote to work and the productivity of their labor. In other words, total output can be expressed as the product of the total number of hours of labor time and the average amount of output produced per hour of labor time. The tremendous expansion of output that has taken place—and continues to take place—under the capitalist mode of production has involved great increases in both labor time and labor productivity. In analyzing the character of the capitalist growth process, it will be useful to examine in turn each of these sources of growth.

The amount of labor time devoted to capitalist production can be increased either by expanding the number of workers in the capitalist wage-labor force or by expanding the average number of hours worked (per day, or per year) by each worker. Throughout the history of the capitalist mode of production capitalists have sought to increase the supply of labor time in both of these ways.

In the early stages of capitalism growing capitalist firms were increasingly able to use their superior competitive strength to drive out of business petty commodity producers— small farmers, artisans, independent merchants, etc.—who then had little choice but to join the burgeoning proletariat. Once under the direct control of capitalists, they were generally obliged to work much longer hours than they would have on their own. More recently, capitalist firms have increasingly sought to increase their labor supply by bringing into the capitalist wage-labor force inhabitants of foreign countries where precapitalist modes of production remain prevalent. This has been accomplished both by importing foreign "guest" workers to work in domestic enterprises (e.g., Mediterranean workers in the industrial centers of Western Europe, and Mexican and Caribbean workers in the United States) and by investing capital in foreign countries to draw on their local supply of potential workers.

Independent producers, self-employed persons, and others have often resisted being reduced to wage-laborers. Similarly, workers have resisted increases in work hours, and the growth of worker organization and militance has enabled many workers to set limits on the length of the working day. To some degree capitalists can and have overcome this resistance by paying higher wages to increase the supply of labor. Since this reduces profits, however, capitalists have generally sought other ways to accomplish the same end. For example, the power of the capitalist state has frequently been used to weaken the position of pre-capitalist producers (at home and abroad) and to undermine their resistance to the growth of the capitalist mode of production.[4]

Increases in the productivity of labor have now become most important for growth in the relatively advanced capitalist nations. As opportunities to extend the capitalist system by bringing in new workers become more limited, capitalists have an increasing incentive to expand output by raising the productivity of the available wage-labor force.

One way to increase labor productivity is by a "speed-up"—increasing the *pace* of work so that more work is actually done in the available labor time. Capitalists may try to induce workers to work faster by paying higher wages or bonuses; alternatively, capitalists may use their power to mechanize production to force a faster work pace. Other important sources of increased labor productivity are: (2) increases in the average "quality" of labor (improvements in the productive skills or abilities of workers); (3) increases in the amount of "capital goods" (plant and equipment, etc.) utilized per worker; (4) advances in the technology of production, which enable more output to be produced with a given quantity and quality of labor and capital goods; and (5) improvement in the efficiency of the overall allocation of economic resources, through increases in the extent of the division of labor and in labor mobility.

An often ignored but increasingly important element in the process of production is the natural environment of the earth. The environment both provides raw materials and absorbs waste materials. Most of the raw materials used in producing goods and services are themselves the output of prior processes of production, but they derive originally from the earth's natural resources: land, minerals, etc. By definition, such natural resources cannot be produced; thus their

supply is ultimately limited. In practice, it is usually possible to increase the available supply of natural resources by investing in the discovery of new sources of supply or in the improvement of existing ones. Moreover, powerful nations can secure or increase supplies of natural resources from foreign territories; this has been an important source of imperialist actions. But eventually, as more and more natural resources are depleted, the finite supply of natural resources must act as a constraint on the expansion of output.

Just as production requires inputs from the earth, it returns outputs to the earth in the form of waste materials, worn-out durable goods, etc. And just as the earth's supply of inputs is ultimately limited, its capacity to absorb outputs is finite. At low levels of productive activity the unwanted by-products of production can be unloaded into nearby air, water, and land without creating any serious problem. But as the scale of production increases it becomes increasingly necessary to devote resources to careful waste disposal, recycling, etc. to avoid adverse effects on the environment and on life itself. Thus, the real cost of disposing of ultimate outputs, like the real cost of obtaining ultimate inputs, increases with economic growth and acts as a constraint upon it.

The environment is bound to come under increasing pressure in any society in which the scale of production is expanding, but under the capitalist mode of production the pressure is likely to be particularly intense. This is basically because the benefits of exploiting the environment (either as resource supplier or as waste absorber) can be captured by individual capitalist firms in the form of higher profits, while the costs of such exploitation are generally borne by the society at large. It is very difficult to make individual firms accountable for the long-run costs of natural resource depletion or the adverse environmental effects of waste disposal; hence profit-maximizing firms are generally able to ignore them. Sooner or later the society as a whole pays for these consequences—in the form of a deteriorating environment, or

---

[4]MacEwan, Section 13.1, p. 481, analyzes the critical role of the state in capitalist expansion.

higher taxes and prices to maintain it—but in the meantime individual firms enhance their own levels of output, their profits, and their competitive position vis-à-vis other firms.

In summary, the process of capitalist economic growth generates a rapidly increasing capacity to produce goods and services. At the same time, however, the process has a series of negative effects on the quality of people's lives. The capitalist effort to expand the amount of labor time devoted to production results in the destruction of pre-capitalist social systems at home and abroad and the sacrifice of leisure time for more work time. The capitalist drive for increased labor productivity leads to the acceleration of work intensity at the expense of work enjoyment, and the disruption of communities and social networks in the interest of greater labor mobility and allocational efficiency. Finally, the capitalist growth process leads to environmental deterioration in the form of growing pollution and a reckless use of land and other natural resources.

To some extent all of these negative effects are necessary concomitants of economic growth, no matter what the nature of the social system in which the growth occurs. The particular irrationality of capitalist economic growth, however, arises from the way in which capitalist institutions and the power of the capitalist class almost always cause the quantitative expansion of productive capacity to take precedence over improvements in the quality of life.

III. MARKETS FOR EXPANDING OUTPUT

If producers fail to find purchasers for their products, they will forfeit potential profits and face possible extinction in the competitive marketplace. If the capitalist economy as a whole fails to find purchasers for the aggregate supply of goods and services produced, the consequences are likewise severe. For if the aggregate demand of purchasers falls below the aggregate supply of output produced, inventories of unsold products will build up and producers will begin to curtail their production. Since producers cannot afford to go on producing more than they can sell, the capitalist economy as a whole will tend toward a situation in which the *actual* level of total output is equal to the level of aggregate demand.

There is no automatic mechanism in a capitalist economy that serves to maintain aggregate demand at a level equal to the potential level of total output, as determined by the productive capacity of the economy. Indeed, the history of capitalist development has been one of periodic failures to do so; hence the capitalist business cycle. Whatever the level of production necessary to meet people's real needs, any shortfall of actual output below potential output leads in a capitalist society to a rise in unemployment. When both one's income and one's self-respect depend on regular full-time employment, the loss of one's job can be catastrophic. High levels of unemployment can therefore lead to serious social and political tensions as well as widespread hardship.

Because of actual losses in profits, and because mass unemployment creates opposition, capitalists as a class have a general interest in avoiding substantial and prolonged shortfalls in aggregate demand of the kind that characterized the Great Depression in the 1930s. From time to time capitalists may benefit from a temporary downturn in the economy;[5] yet in the long run they need to expand aggregate demand in order to expand their own sales. The capitalist system, however, sets important constraints on the way in which aggregate demand can be increased.

There are four types of expenditure which add up to the aggregate demand for the output of a capitalist economy: domestic private consumption, domestic private investment, government purchases, and net exports—i.e., the excess of sales to foreign countries (ex-

[5]Such circumstances are described by Crotty and Rapping, Section 12.4, p. 461.

ports) over purchases from foreign countries (imports). Table 11-A shows the division of the U.S. national product among these categories of expenditure since 1929.

TABLE 11-A AGGREGATE DEMAND IN THE UNITED STATES, 1929–1974

Year	GNP $ Billion (current prices)	GNP $ Billion (1972 prices)	C	I	G	E
				(as % of GNP)		
1929	103	308	74.9	15.7	8.2	1.1
1934	65	234	78.8	5.1	15.1	0.9
1939	91	317	73.8	10.3	14.6	1.2
1944	210	547	51.5	3.4	45.9	−0.9
1949	258	491	69.0	13.7	14.9	2.4
1954	366	614	64.4	14.4	20.7	0.5
1959	487	720	63.9	16.0	20.0	0.1
1964	636	874	63.0	15.2	20.4	1.4
1969	936	1079	62.0	15.6	22.2	0.2
1974	1407	1211	63.0	15.1	21.4	0.5

GNP = gross national product.
 C = total personal consumption expenditures.
 I = gross private domestic investment.
 G = government purchases of goods and services.
 E = net exports of goods and services.

SOURCES: 1949–1974: *Economic Report of the President*, 1976, Tables B-1, B-2. 1929–1944: Ibid., 1970, Tables C-1, C-2; GNP figures in 1958 dollars converted into 1972 dollars at rate of $1 (1972) = $0.66 (1958), given in ibid., 1976, Table B-3.

Expanding exports to foreign markets would appear to be an attractive means of stimulating aggregate demand. Individual firms often seek out new markets abroad to expand their sales; this drive for foreign markets provides added fuel for imperialist actions. From the point of view of the aggregate economy, however, the growth of exports is not likely to contribute much to net demand because it will tend to be offset by a corresponding growth of imports. The sale of products abroad brings foreign currency home; this foreign currency must sooner or later be spent on imported foreign goods if it is to be of use to anyone. Increasing exports can be an important means of stimulating aggregate demand in the short run; but in the long run

it cannot substitute for a steadily growing domestic demand, especially in the United States where exports only constitute about 5 percent of the national product.

Private consumption is by far the largest of the possible sources of aggregate demand (see Table 11-A for evidence from the United States). People with relatively low incomes (e.g., wage-earners) spend virtually all their income on consumption, while people with high incomes (e.g., capitalists) tend to spend a smaller proportion of their income on consumption. If aggregate demand is too low, it is always possible in principle to increase it by redistributing income from rich people with a relatively low propensity to consume to poor people with a high propensity to consume. But this option is necessarily a limited one in a capitalist society, for a substantial degree of income inequality is essential to the operation of the capitalist mode of production.[6] More concretely, a redistribution of income in favor of the poor would tend to reduce the incentive to work in the wage-labor force and/or to increase the level of real wages received by workers. In the context of inadequate aggregate demand higher wages need not cut into profits, for they may enable total output and income to rise. But the establishment of higher wage scales will make it more difficult for capitalists to protect their profits if and when the problem of inadequate demand is alleviated. Thus redistribution of income as a method of maintaining aggregate demand is generally opposed by capitalists; and even to the extent that it occurs it may eventually become counterproductive because, by cutting into profits, it is likely to reduce the capitalist incentive to invest.

Private investment demand is quantitatively much less significant than consumption demand, but it plays a strategic role in determining the level of aggregate demand because —unlike consumption demand—it is not

[6]See the introduction to Chapter 8 for a discussion of the functional role of inequality in a capitalist society.

dependent on the level of national income itself. Most fundamentally private investment demand depends on the profit expectations of capitalists. These expectations are likely to be the more favorable the more rapidly markets are growing and the more successfully workers' wages are kept in check. Thus growth in private investment calls for growing levels of consumption as well as limits on the share of income going to workers.

To the extent that investment rather than consumption demand serves to sustain the overall level of aggregate demand in any given year, it exacerbates the problem of maintaining aggregate demand in later years. For investment serves to increase the productive capacity of the economy in future years, and aggregate demand therefore has to rise that much further in future years to reach the level of potential output.

No one knows whether private consumption plus investment demand can remain sufficiently buoyant in the long run to sustain a capitalist economy. Bourgeois economists usually assume that the appetites of consumers and investors will be continuously and sufficiently stimulated by new products and new techniques of production. However, in an increasingly affluent as well as unequal society, it may not be so easy to ensure the steady growth of private demand.

One would ordinarily expect the urgency of material consumption for consumers to diminish as their level of consumption increased beyond the minimum necessary for survival. There are still many poor people in the advanced capitalist countries;[7] yet the majority of the population can afford to consume more than a socially essential minimum, and the rich have enormous surplus purchasing power. What is to induce the more affluent to raise their demand for goods and services continually over time?

The answer lies in one of the most deeply rooted characteristics of capitalist society—

the ethos of consumerism. Consumerism derives from a fundamental tenet of capitalist ideology: the assertion that the primary requirement for individual self-fulfillment and happiness is the possession and consumption of material goods. Like all aspects of capitalist ideology, this consumerist assertion is grounded in the basic capitalist relations of production. A society based on alienated labor allows most people little opportunity for individual expression or fulfillment in production; the main outlet for creativity and satisfaction is in one's life as a consumer. Relations among people in capitalist production assume the form of relations among commodities. The resulting commodity fetishism reinforces consumerism, for it emphasizes the importance of material goods—rather than social relations—as the primary source of individual welfare.

This is not to argue that people are somehow foolish or irrational to attach so much importance to consumption. For it is not merely a matter of taste or discretion; there simply isn't much choice in a capitalist society. As Ellen Willis has observed:

> ... the profusion of commodities ... is a bribe, but like all bribes, it offers benefits—in the average American's case, a degree of physical comfort unparalleled in history. Under present conditions, people are preoccupied with consumer goods not because they are brainwashed, but because buying is the one pleasurable activity not only permitted but actively encouraged by the power structure. The pleasure of eating an ice cream cone may be minor compared to the pleasure of meaningful, autonomous work, but the former is easily available and the latter is not. A poor family would undoubtedly rather have a decent apartment than a new TV, but since they are unlikely to get the apartment, what is to be gained by not getting the TV?"[8]

Within the overall consumerist ideological framework, there are also more obvious and direct mechanisms by which individual capitalist firms stimulate the demand for their

---

[7] See Ackerman and Zimbalist, Section 8.1, p. 297, for estimates of the number of Americans living in poverty.

[8] Ellen Willis, "Consumerism and Women," *Socialist Revolution*, 1, No. 3 (May/June 1970), 70.

products. This is especially true of monopoly capitalist firms, which have greater resources to devote to the sales effort and greater need to stimulate demand artificially than competitive firms.[9] No person in the United States, nor in other advanced capitalist nations, can escape the effort of producers to induce consumers to buy their wares. Massive advertising is only the most obvious manifestation of the pervasive sales effort that characterizes the modern capitalist system. Frequent model changes, fancy packaging, planned obsolescence, contrived fads, and so on, all serve to increase private consumption demand at a considerable cost in wasted resources.[10] Irrational as it is, such stimulation of private expenditure plays a functional role in helping to promote aggregate demand in a capitalist economy.

Yet even the widespread stimulation of consumer demand may not always be sufficient to enable private demand to keep pace with the growth of productive capacity. The historical evidence for most advanced capitalist nations—the United States in particular—suggests that government purchases of goods and services have played an important role in enabling aggregate demand to match potential output. In virtually all capitalist nations the share of government purchases in aggregate demand has shown a significant long-run upward trend.[11] In the United States, the government share rose from 8 percent in 1929 to 15 percent in 1949 to

22 percent in 1969, falling back slightly to 21 percent in 1974 (see Table 11-A).[12]

Increases in government purchases do not necessarily imply equal increases in aggregate demand. To the extent that the government finances its purchases by taxing the private sector, private consumers and businesses sacrifice income and presumably cut back on private consumption and investment. But the net effect of raising government purchases and taxation by an equal amount is to raise aggregate demand, since some fraction of the private sector income taxed to finance the government purchases would have been saved rather than spent. And when the government engages in deficit spending it adds an even more powerful demand stimulus to the economy.

It is difficult to prove that increasing government purchases have been necessary to maintain aggregate demand in the advanced capitalist nations, since it is impossible to know what would have happened if they had not increased. But in the United States there has been a striking correlation between the degree of overall economic prosperity and the time trend of government purchases. Figure 11-A traces the growth of actual output and potential output, as well as several major expenditure categories, in the United States from 1929 to 1974. When actual output is below potential output, there is idle capacity, unemployment, and general economic hard times. When actual output is close to potential output, there is high capacity utilization and low unemployment. Actual output may even exceed potential

---

[9]See Baran and Sweezy, Section 4.3, p. 134.

[10]The best-documented example of waste in consumer goods is discussed in an innovative study by Fisher, Griliches, and Kaysen, "The Costs of Automobile Model Changes Since 1949," *Journal of Political Economy*, 70, No. 4 (October 1962). The authors estimate conservatively that the cost of model changes amounted to $5 billion a year over the 1956–60 period, plus a total of $7 billion in future gasoline costs. See also Paul Baran and Paul Sweezy, *Monopoly Capital* (New York: Monthly Review Press, 1966), pp. 131–38.

[11]For evidence from the period since World War II, see Ian Gough, "State Expenditure in Advanced Capitalism," *New Left Review*, No. 92 (July/August 1975), Section II.

[12]I exclude from consideration here that part of total government expenditure which takes the form of transfers of income (e.g., welfare and social security payments), because only government purchases of goods and services add directly to aggregate demand. Government transfers may add indirectly to aggregate demand to the extent that they redistribute income from people with lower propensities to consume to people with higher propensities to consume. However, as Edwards, Section 8.2, p. 307, has explained, such redistributive transfers are necessarily limited in scope in a capitalist society.

Figure 11-A Potential output and its utilization in the U.S., 1929–1975

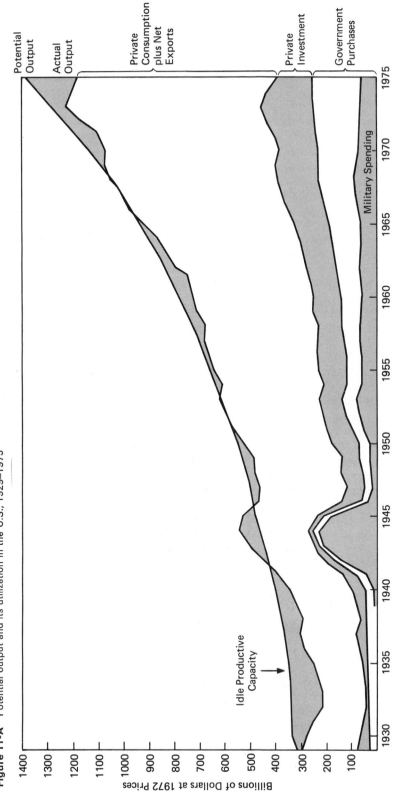

SOURCES: Annual data on actual output (GNP) in 1972 dollars were obtained as described in the sources for Table 11-A. Corresponding data on private consumption, net exports, private investment, government purchases, and military spending were calculated by multiplying the value of actual output (in 1972 dollars) by the ratios of private consumption, etc., to actual output (in current prices); these ratios were obtained form the same sources cited in Table 11-A.

Estimates of potential output are designed to reflect the level of output that an economy could achieve with reasonably full employment of the regular labor force and reasonably full utilization of plant and equipment. There is no precise way to calculate the potential output of the U.S. economy, since total productive capacity depends in part upon the intensity with which the available productive resources are used. The estimates used here are based on potential output series published in the U.S. Department of Commerce, *Long Term Economic Growth, 1860–1970* (Washington, D.C.: U.S. Government Printing Office, 1973), pp. 182–83. Series A-4 was used for 1929–1952; series A-5 was used for 1952–1970; and it was assumed that potential output increased at a rate of 4% per year from 1970 to 1975.

output (temporarily) if the labor force and the existing productive capacity are utilized more intensively then usual (e.g., during World War II).

It is readily apparent from Figure 11-A that for much of the forty-five-year period actual output in the United States remained below potential output. Only during the early 1940s, the early 1950s, and the late 1960s did actual output come close to potential output. The same time pattern is clearly reflected in the rate of unemployment plotted in Figure 11-B. From its peak level of almost 25 percent in the middle of the Great Depression, unemployment fell to its lowest levels in the early 1940s and tended to rise again thereafter except in the early 1950s and the late 1960s. Figures 11-A and 11-B also show that it is in the same three periods of relative economic prosperity that the level of government purchases (and the share of government purchases as a proportion of potential output) has risen most rapidly. Conversely, periods of depression and high unemployment have been associated with declining or at most slowly rising levels (and shares) of government purchases.

To the extent that government purchases are required to provide an adequate market for the output of advanced capitalist economies, there is no reason to expect the character of those purchases to be any more rational than the character of private expenditure in a capitalist society. Government purchases can take the form of investment (i.e., expenditure on goods and services which increase the future productive capacity of the economy) or consumption (i.e., expenditure on goods and services consumed on behalf of the people at large, or made available for public use). Insofar as government purchases take the form of investment they have the same drawback, from the point of view of aggregate demand maintenance, as private investment: they increase the future productive capacity of the economy. Thus it is in the form of consumption that government purchases can most usefully serve to make up for any possible shortage of private demand.

There are many important areas where more government consumption expenditure could do much to improve the quality of life —e.g., by providing collective consumption goods and services such as better health care, neighborhood recreational and entertainment facilities, etc. All such expenditure has the effect of raising the real incomes of the poor, who stand to gain much more by the provision of collective consumption goods and services than the rich. Poor people fight for such expenditure and sometimes even win. But from the point of view of capitalists and the capitalist economy, government expenditure on useful items of collective consumption poses the same problems as a redistribution of income to the poor: lowering the incentive to work, placing upward pressure on real wage levels, etc. Moreover, the public provision of collective consumption goods and services might well reduce the demand for privately marketed goods and services that fulfill similar needs, and thereby possibly even reduce the total demand for private sector output in the economy.

Far better, for the purpose of maintaining aggregate demand as well as private sector profitability, are government purchases of goods and services which neither increase productive capacity nor in any way meet people's real needs and raise their standard of living. Military spending is the most obvious candidate,[13] but other forms of public waste—lavish governmental facilities, expensive "prestige" projects such as a trip to the moon, etc.—serve just as well.

Different capitalist nations vary with respect to the need for government purchases to maintain aggregate demand and with respect to the forces affecting the composition of government expenditure. In the United States, military spending has clearly played a major role in sustaining aggregate demand (see Figures 11-A and 11-B). Not only has a substantial fraction of government purchases

[13]Military spending does not necessarily have to be wasteful, if it is designed to meet real rather than contrived threats and if it is undertaken efficiently.

Figure 11-B Government purchases, military spending, and unemployment in the U.S., 1929–1975

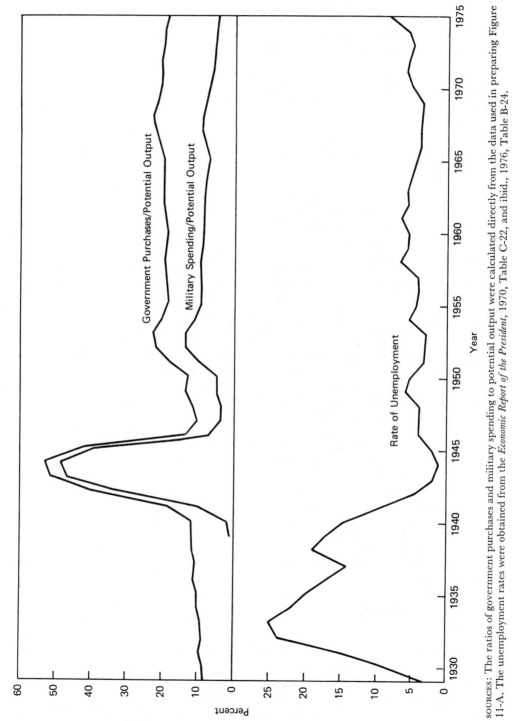

SOURCES: The ratios of government purchases and military spending to potential output were calculated directly from the data used in preparing Figure 11-A. The unemployment rates were obtained from the *Economic Report of the President*, 1970, Table C-22, and ibid., 1976, Table B-24.

been devoted to the military during the past four decades, but—even more important—it is variations in the level of military spending that have been almost wholly responsible for variations in the total level of government purchases. The rising levels of government purchases associated with the relatively prosperous periods of the early 1940s, the early 1950s, and the late 1960s have coincided precisely with stepped-up military outlays for World War II, the Korean War and the Vietnam War. The more slowly growing (or declining) levels of government purchases associated with the remaining periods of recession and depression have coincided to a large extent with stagnating or declining military outlays during peacetime.

In sum, the historical record suggests that the prosperity of the United States economy has been closely linked to military expenditure for the past forty-five years. This is clearly not the case in all advanced capitalist nations, for there are some (e.g., West Germany and Japan) in which a sustained period of prosperity since World War II has been compatible with low levels of military spending. And it may well be that in the future the American economy will not depend so much on the stimulus of militarism to maintain aggregate demand. However, the analysis of this section leads to the conclusion that the capitalist search for markets in which to sell an ever-expanding volume of goods and services is likely to lead in one way or another to wasteful patterns of production and consumption. The drive to sell, without at the same time undermining private profitability, is a powerful force contributing to the irrationality of capitalist society.

IV. CONTRADICTIONS OF CAPITALIST GROWTH

The process of capitalist economic growth involves several potential contradictions that seem likely to intensify over time. These contradictions stem from the increasing financial and social costs of maintaining a rapid rate of economic growth, and from the increas-

ingly irrational character of capitalist growth itself—its inability to meet real human needs.

Limits to Growth

Economic growth serves an important stabilizing function in a capitalist society. Capitalism is inherently unequal, and serious conflict over the division of the "economic pie" is an ever-present threat to the stability of the capitalist order and to the dominance of the capitalist class. But to the extent that the pie itself can be expanded over time, the size of each person's piece can be increased without any change in the degree of inequality, and the struggle over the division of the pie can be attenuated. Thus economic growth, by making it possible for people to look forward to higher material standards of living in the future, can help to deflect anger about all the inequities in material standards of living in the present.

In the past rapid economic growth has played this stabilizing role for capitalism, but there are increasingly serious grounds for questioning whether such growth can continue into the future. The basic problem is that the world capitalist system is now beginning to run up against physical and political limits on the availability of productive resources—limits set by the resistance of nature and the resistance of people to the expansion of capitalism.

The notion of physical limits to growth has impressed itself forcefully upon the industrialized world in the 1970s. Rising prices of raw materials and increasingly serious problems of pollution have drawn attention to the limited and exhaustible supply of many basic mineral products in the world and to the limited capacity for absorption of waste materials by the environment. These two physical constraints lead to a rise in the real cost of production, whether the cost appears in the form of higher prices for goods and services or an unmeasured (but no less real) deterioration in the quality of the environment. The short-sightedness and wastefulness with which capitalist producers deplete the environment exacerbates a problem that all growing economies must ultimately face: the need to stabilize the rate of resource use and waste disposal so as to preserve the earth's environment.

There are also growing political limits on the growth of the rich capitalist countries in general and the United States in particular. The era in which powerful capitalist nations could easily dominate most of the rest of the world, obtaining cheap labor, cheap raw materials, etc., is fast drawing to a close. With the growth of anti-imperialist resistance around the world, more and more countries are opting out of the world capitalist system in favor of some form of socialism. Moreover, even in poor countries still within the capitalist system, nationalistic governments are imposing more and more conditions on the operation of foreign capital within their borders. American capitalism in particular is running into more severe limitations on its *lebensraum* as its hegemonic position within the capitalist world is increasingly eroded.[14] The result is not a complete loss of access to raw materials, labor, and markets, but an increasingly costly and uncertain access that will take its toll on the economies of the rich capitalist nations.

The above-mentioned physical and political constraints do not necessarily mean an end to economic growth in the United States. There remain other potential sources of growth, the most important of which is technological change. Rising raw material prices, increasing scarcity of labor, etc. will create strong incentives for the development of new techniques of production appropriate to a changing pattern of resource availability. But the task is undoubtedly becoming more difficult, and the ability of the American economy to continue to "deliver the goods" on a growing scale will become more and more problematic.

An end to rapid long-run economic growth

generates two significant contradictions for a capitalist society. First, as the rate of economic growth diminishes, so does the effectiveness of its crucial stabilizing function. A future of slow growth means a future of rising conflict within the capitalist world—between nations, and between classes within nations. Inequities will become increasingly intolerable, and the struggle between labor and capital over shares of the economic pie will intensify.

Second, the very viability of the capitalist economic order may well be threatened by the need to bring economic activities into a sustainable relationship with the environment. Discussing the implications of the "ecological crisis" for a capitalist society, Robert Heilbroner has observed that

> Some economic growth is certainly compatible with a stabilized rate of resource use and disposal, for growth could take the form of the expenditure of additional labor on the improvement (aesthetic or technical) of the natural environment. . . . But there is no doubt that the main avenue of traditional capitalist accumulation would have to be considerably constrained; that net investment in mining and manufacturing would effectively cease; that the rate and kind of technological change would need to be supervised and probably greatly reduced; and that, as a consequence, the flow of profits would almost certainly fall.
>
> Is this imaginable within a capitalist setting—that is, in a nation in which the business ideology permeates the view of nearly all groups and classes and establishes the bounds of what is possible and natural, and what is not? Ordinarily I do not see how such a question could be answered in any way but negatively, for it is tantamount to asking a dominant class to acquiesce in the elimination of the very activities that sustain it.[15]

In short, the "ecological crisis" poses a threat to capitalism that appears to be ultimately irresolvable.

[15]Robert Heilbroner, "Ecological Armageddon," *The New York Review of Books*, 17, No. 8 (April 23, 1970). Heilbroner, in spite of the overwhelming persuasiveness of the argument he has just made, goes on to suggest that the "extraordinary challenge" to capitalism may be met by an "extraordinary response" that would somehow permit the retention of the capitalist setting. But this would appear to be mainly wishful thinking.

[14]See Chapter 13 for a discussion of the changing pattern of international economic relations and role of the United States in the world capitalist economy.

It remains possible that American capitalism may be able to postpone the day of reckoning, as long as technological advances succeed in offsetting the physical constraints and U.S. foreign policy succeeds in minimizing the political constraints on the growth of the American economy. But the longer the American pie does continue to grow, the more it intensifies a second kind of contradiction which arises out of the irrationality of the growth process itself.

Irrationality of Growth

In the second and third sections of this essay I have argued that capitalist economic growth is fundamentally irrational: it involves a quantitative expansion of economic output at the expense of the quality of life, and it generates wasteful patterns of production and consumption. The essence of this irrationality is a lack of balance: the capitalist system generates more and more individually marketable commodities while undermining social and nonmarketable sources of people's well-being. What makes this process potentially contradictory is that the degree of imbalance is bound to increase as capitalist growth itself continues over time.

The processes of urbanization and industrialization accompanying economic growth bring more and more people closer together (even as they remove people further and further from their natural environment). Many spheres of life necessarily become more and more *social*; individual private solutions to problems become less and less satisfactory. Thus the process of capitalist growth itself creates increasing needs for collective activities and services that simultaneously benefit large communities of people. But the capitalist system is ill-equipped to satisfy such collective needs, for they do not lend themselves to profitable marketing by private firms. Public authorities are generally called upon to meet these needs, but their ability to do so effectively is limited for reasons discussed earlier.

Just as capitalism is far more successful in delivering private goods than public services, so it can be much more successful in satisfying people's material desires than in meeting their nonmaterial needs. People's needs are obviously not limited to the material, whether individual or collective. Walter Weisskopf (drawing on the work of the psychologist, A. H. Maslow) describes a hierarchy of needs as follows:

> *Proceeding from the lower and progressing to the higher . . .: physiological needs, such as hunger; safety needs, such as the need for physical and mental security, including the need for a comprehensive "philosophy that organizes the universe and the [people] in it into a sort of satisfactorily coherent meaningful whole"; the needs for belongingness and love; the need for esteem; and the need for self-actualization. What matters is not whether this classification is correct and exhaustive, but that there is a hierarchy of needs. . . . Various needs related to different dimensions of existence have to be brought into balance, although certain physiological and quasiphysiological needs are prevalent if they are not satisfied. . . . Consequently,* need satisfaction which continuously increases the supply of means along one level and neglects needs on a different level is contrary to human well-being. *What is required is a* balanced system of need satisfaction *on various levels. (Italics in original.)*[16]

Not only does capitalist growth not provide any such balance of need satisfaction, but the nature of the growth process renders more and more difficult the satisfaction of such nonmaterial needs as those for belongingness (community), participation, love, and self-actualization. The inherently one-sided character of capitalist growth becomes contradictory because the more capitalism succeeds in delivering rising quantities of goods and services, the greater is the need for precisely those benefits that capitalism cannot provide. This growing inbalance between people's material and nonmaterial welfare is bound to lead to increasing tensions in people's lives.

Obviously, there are many people—even in the rich industrialized countries like the United States—who still suffer significant material deprivation under capitalism. It is

[16]Walter Weisskopf, "Economic Growth vs. Existential Balance," *Ethics*, 65, No. 2 (January 1965).

surely premature to suggest that the imbalances of capitalist affluence represent the primary contradiction in advanced capitalist societies. The point here is that, far from gaining increased support and stability from its ability to deliver economic growth, capitalism may well generate growing anxiety and conflict even among many of the apparent beneficiaries of the growth process. In the past economic growth has usually played a stabilizing role for capitalism, by promising a better material future for the materially deprived. But as and when material deprivation becomes less widespread, the same process of growth may turn into an increasingly destabilizing force.

11.2 Military Spending and Production for Profit

The immense military expenditures of the U.S. government—over a hundred billion dollars annually by the mid-1970s—constitute the most blatant and dangerous irrationality of capitalism. The armaments stockpiled (or used in Vietnam or elsewhere) not only represent resources wasted, but more importantly threaten to annihilate rebellious peoples around the world and ultimately destroy humanity itself.

Yet military expenditures, because they are government expenditures, are often thought to result from particular *political* circumstances rather than from the institutional structure of capitalism. The high level of U.S. military expenditures is sometimes explained in terms of the external threat to national security or in terms of the quirks of domestic politics (e.g., the alliance of a few powerful Southern congressmen with the Pentagon).

In response to these arguments, three points should be made. First, in Chapter 13 we will argue that imperialism abroad is a natural consequence of capitalism at home, and that keeping the world open for capitalist penetration requires a substantial commitment of military strength. The threat to national security used to justify a high level of military expenditure is in part a direct consequence of the American capitalist system.

Second, military expenditures help to maintain aggregate demand. The close correlation between military expenditures and economic prosperity testifies to the importance of "defense" spending in the United States.[1] While expenditures to maintain aggregate demand need not necessarily take the form of military expenditures, Michael Reich shows in the following reading that there are powerful forces in a capitalist system which favor such expenditures.

Finally, the military sector comprises the very heart of capitalist America. As Reich demonstrates, military expenditures benefit the largest and most powerful corporations, and their impact extends to many smaller companies as well. Thus, the role of "defense" spending is not to line the pockets of a few unscrupulous profiteers; instead, it is vital to the interests of many of the most powerful members of the U.S. capitalist class.

[1]See Weisskopf, Section 11.1, p. 395.

The following essay was written for this book by MICHAEL REICH. Copyright © 1978 by Michael Reich.

Since 1950 the U.S. government has spent well over a trillion dollars on the military, or about one-tenth of total economic output. Almost two-fifths of the federal budget feeds the "military-industrial complex." Nearly one-tenth of the labor force is engaged in military-related employment.

Why does this murderous and seemingly irrational allocation of resources occur? Why do we give the Pentagon $100 billion a year when so many basic social needs are ignored both in the United States and in the rest of the world? In this essay I will argue that the growth and persistence of a high level of military spending is a natural outcome in an advanced capitalist society that both suffers from the problem of inadequate private aggregate demand and plays a leading role in the preservation and expansion of the international capitalist system.

This perspective on military spending can best be understood by examining three more specific propositions:

> Beginning in 1950, if not earlier, the United States economy was insufficiently sustained by private aggregate demand; some form of government expenditure was needed to maintain expansion.
>
> The U.S. government turned to military spending to provide such expansion precisely because military spending provides the best means of stimulating the economy and simultaneously serving the interests of large corporations.
>
> Federal expenditures on social welfare programs on a scale comparable to the military budget are not a feasible substitute.

Arguments in support of these propositions would advance the view that military spending is indispensable to the *domestic* economy. They would not touch on the other half of the argument—that militarism is a natural outgrowth of the international operations of American capitalism. I have not chosen to examine the second half of the argument in detail here because others have provided ample support.[1]

[1]See MacEwan, Section 13.1, p. 481.

THE INADEQUACY OF PRIVATE DEMAND

The depression of the thirties illustrated the incredible levels of unemployment and business lethargy the system would generate if left alone. The economy did not actually recover from the depression until World War II, when massive levels of government spending in defense created sufficient demand to alleviate unemployment. Since the war, the patterns have remained. An elaborate analysis of postwar investment demand by Bert Hickman, for example, showed that sluggish growth in the American economy from 1948 to 1963 could best be explained by a *downward* trend in business fixed investment as well as a full-employment surplus in the government budget.[2] Hickman showed, in other words, that private investment was tending to decline by itself and that government *deficits* would be necessary to overcome these declines. Without the stimulus provided by government spending, economic growth in this period would have been substantially lower.

The government cannot supply this economic stimulation simply by lowering its taxes. While the economy can be stimulated for a time by reducing taxes and running larger deficits instead of increasing government expenditures, tax cuts cannot serve these purposes indefinitely. With government expenditures held constant, additional tax decreases have increasingly small effects on the economy. Eventually, taxes will reach such a low level that the stimulative effects of further decreases will be marginal.

So expenditures can and must play a role in stimulating the economy. Since 1950, military expenditures, averaging about 10 percent of GNP, have played this stimulative role. The fluctuation of military spending has been highly correlated with the cyclical pattern of the economy.[3] This is largely because military expenditures play such a

[2]Bert Hickman, *Investment Demand and U.S. Economic Growth* (Washington, D.C.: Brookings Institution, 1965).

[3]See Figure 11-A, p. 403, and Figure 11-B, p. 405.

large role in the industries that produce capital goods—the sector of the economy that is most subject to cyclical fluctuations and is most affected by secular declines in business fixed investment. In that sector, military spending plays twice as great a role as in the economy as a whole.[4] And declines in military spending have been followed by declines in overall economic growth. This has been true at least partly because those sectors most heavily involved with the military, including the aerospace, communications, and electronics industries, have been among the fastest-growing industries in the economy in the postwar period. When military spending stagnates, the most dynamic industries will stagnate too.[5]

THE ATTRACTIONS OF MILITARY SPENDING

The second proposition is that, given the necessity of some form of government expenditures, military spending provides the most convenient outlet for such expenditures. Military contracts are both easily expandable in the economy without confronting any corporate opposition and highly attractive to the firms that receive them.

Military spending is easily expandable because it adds to rather than competes with private demand. Military spending provides little competition for several reasons:

First, a convenient rationalization of the need for massive armaments expenditures exists. The ideology of anti-communism and the Cold War has been drummed into politicians and the public for thirty years and is a

powerful force behind military spending. The U.S. government's role as global policeman for capitalism has reinforced this rationale.

Second, armaments are consumed rapidly or become obsolete very quickly. In southeast Asia, vast stocks of bombers were shot down, ammunition was used up or captured, and so on. The technology of advanced weapons systems becomes obsolete as fast as defense experts can think of "improvements" over existing weapons systems (or as soon as Soviet experts do). So the demand for weaponry is a bottomless pit. Moreover, the kind of machinery required for production is highly specific to particular armaments. Each time a new weapon is needed or a new process created, much existing production machinery must be scrapped. Extensive retooling involving vast new outlays is required. Since the technologies involved tend to be highly complex and exotic, much gold-plating (or rather titanium-plating) can occur; only specialists know how superfluous a particular frill is and whether a $1 billion missile would work as well as a $2 billion missile.

Third, there is no universally accepted yardstick for measuring how much defense we have or need. The public cannot recognize waste here as it would in, say, education or public housing. How do we know when an adequate level of military security is achieved? National security managers can always claim by some criteria that what we have is not enough. Terms like "missile gaps" and "nuclear parity" and "superiority" are easily juggled. Military men always have access to new "secret intelligence reports" not available to the general public. Since few people are willing to gamble with national defense, the expertise of the managers is readily accepted. Politicians and the general public have little way of adequately questioning their judgment.

These factors help explain why military spending can expand almost indefinitely. But what creates a strong preference for military spending in the first place?

To understand the sources of this pressure, we must first examine the role of defense con-

[4]In 1958, 9.6 percent of total output in the economy was attributable to military spending, while in the metalworking industrial sectors (consisting of primary metals, nonelectrical machinery, electrical equipment and ordnance, and instruments and allied products) an unweighted average of 19.9 percent of output was attributable to military expenditures. See Table 11-D.

[5]I am not asserting here that every capitalist economy at all times must be suffering from inadequate private aggregate demand. I am asserting *only*, in this section, that the U.S. economy has been sick in this respect for the last several decades.

tractors themselves. Military contracts are highly advantageous to the firms that receive them, and we can certainly expect that those corporations will push for more.

One hundred corporations receive over two-thirds of all prime contract awards each year, and fifty corporations receive 60 percent; the list of the top one hundred contractors has exhibited very little turnover in the last twenty years.[6] Prime contract awards are concentrated among just four industries: aircraft (43 percent), electronics and telecommunications (19.3 percent), shipbuilding and repairing (10.3 percent), and ammunition (5 percent).[7] Moreover, subcontracts appear to be just as concentrated among the big firms.[8]

For these major beneficiaries of military spending, the rewards are high. Boondoggling and profiteering are endemic. Both the nature of the military "product" and the nature of the buyer-seller relationship in the military "market" foster this profiteering.

It has always been presumed that all armaments production should be carried on by private profit-seeking corporations as much as possible. Theoretically, the government, as sole buyer, would purchase from the most efficient, least-cost firms. But given the long lead times, inherent cost, and technological uncertainties in developing and producing complicated weapons systems, the government would find it difficult, to say the least, to identify in advance and reward the most efficient military contractors. In fact, of course, the Pentagon has rarely shown any interest in holding down costs or identifying efficient firms, since until recently it has not faced a real budget constraint of its own. The

reality is that contractors and the Pentagon both follow the maxim of socialized risk but private profits—in C. Wright Mills' term, "socialism for the rich."

The profit incentives in military contracts reward boondoggling and waste. The Pentagon provides without charge much of the fixed and working capital for major military contracts, underwrites and subsidizes the costs of technological research and development for firms that engage in civilian as well as military production, and negotiates (and when necessary, renegotiates) cost-plus contracts that virtually guarantee the contractors against any losses. Military spending is supposed to take place competitively, but in fact it almost never does. Any number of excuses may justify the relaxation of competitive procedures. Of the Pentagon's contract dollars, 90 percent are negotiated under such "exceptions."[9]

Because of the special relationship between the Pentagon and the defense corporations, cost overruns are permitted. Final costs average 320 percent of original cost estimates[10] The average contractor, in other words, ends up charging the government over three times the cost estimate he initially submitted to "win" the contract. And because most contracts are on a cost-plus basis, his profits go up by 300 percent as well.

Companies do not lose their privileged status if their weapons do not meet specifications or perform properly. According to one study,[11] of thirteen major aircraft and missile programs since 1955 which cost $40 billion, only four (costing $5 billion) performed at as much as 75 percent of the design specifications. Yet the companies with the poorest performance records reported the highest profits.

As a result, profits for defense work are higher than those in every industry except

---

[6]W. Baldwin, *The Structure of the Defense Market, 1955–64* (Durham: Duke University Press, 1967), p. 9.

[7]Research Analysis Corporation, "Economic Impact Analysis," in U.S. Congress, Joint Economic Committee, *Economic Effect of Vietnam Spending*, Vol. II, 1967, p. 827.

[8]M. Peck and F. Scherer, *The Weapons Acquisition Process* (Boston: Harvard Business School, 1962), pp. 150–52; and M. Weidenbaum, *The Modern Public Sector* (New York: Basic Books, 1969), p. 40.

[9]U.S. Congress, Joint Economic Committee Print, *The Economics of Military Procurement* (Washington, D.C.: U.S. Government Printing Office, 1969), p. 4.

[10]Peck and Scherer, *The Weapons Acquisition Process*.

[11]*The Economics of Military Procurement*, p. 1.

pharmaceuticals. This is obscured by the Defense Department, which sometimes releases profits computed as a percentage of sales or costs. But, in the normal business world, profits are figured as a percentage of *investment*. Defense contractors invest very little of their own money, because in most cases the government provides most of the investment and working capital needed to set up plants and machinery and to buy the necessary materials and parts. The profits when measured against investment are often huge.

Murray Weidenbaum, formerly an economist for the Boeing Company and Assistant Secretary of the Treasury, studied a sample of large defense contractors.[12] He found that in 1962 and 1963 they earned 17.5 percent on investment, compared to average civilian market earnings of 10.6 percent. And this probably understates the case. Many military contractors also sell in the civilian market. The machinery provided free by the Pentagon, the allocation of all overhead costs to military contracts, and the technological edge gained in cost-plus military contracts can be of enormous importance in increasing profits on civilian sales for firms doing some business with the Pentagon. In one of the most outrageous cases that has come to light, a tax count showed in 1962 that North American Aviation Company had realized profits of 612 percent and 802 percent on its investment in "military" contracts in two successive years.[13] With these profits and privileges, it seems clear, defense contractors have every reason to push for as much military spending as possible.

Yet the popular press sometimes conveys the view that defense firms are few—an economic enclave somehow isolated from the rest of the economy. And there is superficial evidence for the enclave view. As I noted above, fifty corporations receive 60 percent of prime

contract awards. Prime contracts are concentrated in just four industries. Subcontracts appear to be just as concentrated among the big firms.

But this enclave image is highly misleading. First, a list of the top military contractors is virtually identical with a list of all the largest and most powerful industrial corporations in America (see Table 11-B). Nathanson estimates that of the 500 largest manufacturing corporations in 1964, at least 205 were significantly involved in military contracts, either in production or in research and development.[14] Among the top 100 firms, 65 are significantly involved in the military market. As Table 11-B shows, all but four of the largest 25 industrial corporations in 1973 were among the 75 largest contractors for the Defense Department. Of these four, one is an oil company indirectly involved in military sales and two are steel companies also indirectly involved. It is difficult to think of these top corporations as constituting an "enclave."

Second, there are no self-contained enclaves in the American economy. As the study of input-output economics has revealed, the structure of American industry is highly interdependent. Focusing only on the prime contractors is like looking at only the visible part of an iceberg. This represents only the direct impact of the military budget. The indirect impact on subcontractors, on producers of intermediate goods and parts, and on suppliers of raw materials ties military spending into the heart of the economy.

Third, corporations in the civilian market have been competing to get a piece of the military action. A study of the years between 1959 and 1962 indicates that "manufacturing firms outside the defense sector purchased 137 companies in the defense sector (i.e., aircraft and parts, ships and boats, ordnance, electrical machinery, scientific instruments and computers)." By 1966, of the top 500 manufacturing firms 93 had diversified into the

[12]Murray Weidenbaum, "Arms and the American Economy," *American Economic Review* (May 1968), p. 56.

[13]R. F. Kaufman, *The War Profiteers* (Indianapolis: Bobbs-Merrill, 1970).

[14]C. Nathanson, "The Militarization of the American Economy," in D. Horowitz, ed., *Corporations and the Cold War* (New York: Monthly Review Press, 1969), p. 231.

TABLE 11-B MILITARY CONTRACTORS IN THE AMERICAN ECONOMY, 1973

Top Pentagon Contractors Fiscal Year 1974			Top Industrial Corporations 1973		
1	General Dynamics	(96)[a]	1	General Motors	(20)[b]
2	Lockheed	(44)	2	Exxon	(19)
3	McDonnell Douglas	(39)	3	Ford	(32)
4	United Aircraft	(59)	4	Chrysler	(4)
5	General Electric	(5)	5	General Electric	(5)
6	Boeing	(33)	6	Texaco	(31)
7	Litton	(47)	7	Mobil	(34)
8	Hughes Aircraft	([c])	8	IBM	(25)
9	Rockwell International	(35)	9	ITT	(28)
10	Raytheon	(103)	10	Gulf	(39)
11	Western Electric (AT&T)	(12)	11	Standard Oil (CA)	(23)
12	Grumman	(156)	12	Western Electric	(11)
13	Northrup	(228)	13	U.S. Steel	—
14	Westinghouse	(14)	14	Westinghouse	(14)
15	Textron	(83)	15	Standard Oil (Ind.)	(50)
16	Chrysler	(16)	16	Dupont	(47)
17	Sperry Rand	(62)	17	GTE	(36)
18	FMC	(90)	18	Shell	(59)
19	Exxon	(2)	19	Goodyear Tire & Rubber	(42)
20	General Motors	(1)	20	RCA	(27)
21	Honeywell	(54)	21	Continental Oil	—
22	LTV	(23)	22	International Harvester	—
23	Standard Oil (CA)	(11)	23	LTV	(22)
24	Tenneco	(29)	24	Bethlehem Steel	—
25	IBM	(8)	25	Eastman Kodak	(74)

[a]Number in parentheses indicates rank in *Fortune* list of 500 largest industrial corporations.

[b]Number in parentheses indicates rank among largest 100 Department of Defense contractors.

[c]Not included in the *Fortune* 500 list because shares are not publicly traded on a stock exchange.

SOURCES: *Fortune Magazine*, May 1974; and *Aviation Week and Space Technology*, November 25, 1974.

defense sector from a traditional nondefense base.[15]

Military spending is very important for a large number of manufacturing industries. As Table 11-C shows, about 11.5 percent of all manufacturing output as early as 1958 was attributable to military-related expenditures; the corresponding figure is 20 percent for the metalworking production sector, comprised of metals and metal products, nonelectrical machinery, electrical equipment and supplies, transportation equipment, ordnance, and instruments. The percentage of profits attri-

butable to military spending is probably even higher, given that profit rates are higher on military contracts.

Another important feature is the increasing concentration produced by military spending within industry. Almost all of military spending goes to the most concentrated industries in the economy. The standard measure of concentration in an industry is the percentage of sales accounted for by the top four firms. Industries in which four firms monopolized over 50 percent of the sales accounted for about one-quarter of all sales by manufacturing industries in 1958. But 90 percent of all military contracts go to these most concentrated indus-

[15]Ibid., pp. 215–16.

TABLE 11-C DIRECT AND INDIRECT DEPENDENCE
OF INDUSTRIAL SECTORS ON MILITARY
EXPENDITURES, 1958

Sector	Percent of Total Output Attributable to Military
1. Food and kindred products	1.6
2. Apparel and textile mill products	1.9
3. Leather products	3.1
4. Paper and allied products	7.0
5. Chemicals and allied products	5.3
6. Fuel and power	7.3
7. Rubber and rubber products	5.6
8. Lumber and wood products	3.9
9. Nonmetallic minerals and products	4.7
10. Primary metals	13.4
11. Fabricated metal products	8.0
12. Machinery, except electrical	5.2
13. Electrical equipment and supplies	20.8
14. Transportation equipment and ordnance	38.4
15. Instruments and allied products	20.0
16. Misc. manufacturing industries	2.8
17. Transportation	5.9
18. Construction	2.1
Average, metalworking industries (Sectors 10–15)	19.9
Average, all manufacturing (Sectors 1–16)	11.5
Average, (Sectors 1–18)	9.6

SOURCE: Computed from Wassily Leontief and P. B. Hoffenberg, "The Economic Impact of Disarmament," *Scientific American* (April 1961).

tries. Certainly, an expenditure program that benefits 20 of the top 25 corporations and contributes to the concentration of economic power among the corporate giants is going to enjoy a political power base that lies deep in the heart of the U.S. economy.

Military spending has also created privileged interest groups within the occupational structure—an important factor that ties to government policy many professional people, university administrators, and labor union leaders. A large number of the most highly trained people in the economy owe their jobs to defense spending. For example, nearly half of all engineers and scientists employed in private industry are at work on military or space-related projects. Many of the scientists and engineers pursuing research in the universities receive money from the Pentagon.

The military industries generally employ a highly skilled work force. A 1962 Department of Labor study of the electronics industry showed that at military-space-oriented plants 59.2 percent of employees were highly paid engineers, executives, or skilled blue-collar craftsmen. In the consumer-oriented plants of the same electronics industry, in contrast, 70.2 percent of the employees were semiskilled and unskilled blue- and white-collar workers.[16] Professional and managerial workers comprise 22 percent of all private defense-related employment, but only 15 percent of all U.S. manufacturing employment.[17] Thus, a large proportion of the people in the most educated strata, many still university-based, are tied by military spending to a vested interest in existing national priorities. A large number of blue-collar workers are engaged in military-related work. The carrot the government can dangle in front of major union leaders has been a factor in their growing conservatism and endorsement of Cold War policies.

Military spending has a regressive impact on the distribution of income within the U.S. —that is, it benefits the rich and hurts the poor. This is suggested by the higher proportion of professional and skilled workers in defense-related work. Computations by economist Wassily Leontief show that one dollar of military spending generates half as many jobs, but 20 percent more in salaries, than does one dollar of civilian spending.[18] This means that tax money extracted from the

[16]Bureau of Labor Statistics *Bulletin* (October 1963), p. 37.

[17]*Monthly Labor Review* (May 1964), p. 514.

[18]From W. Leontief and M. Hoffenberg, "The Economic Impact of Disarmament," *Scientific American*, 9 (April 1961); and Leontief et al., "The Economic Effect—Industrial and Regional—of an Arms Cut," *Review of Economics and Statistics* (August 1965).

whole population is paid out in such a way as to benefit high earners much more than low earners. Perhaps by accident, or perhaps by design, military spending is one of the mechanisms by which higher income groups use the government to prevent redistribution of income from taking place.

So military spending is easily expandable, is highly profitable, and benefits the major corporations in the economy. These factors combine to ensure that major corporations will push for military spending and that opponents will have little strength to resist its expansion. The same cannot be said for the nonmilitary sector.

THE OPPOSITION TO SOCIAL SERVICE EXPENDITURES

The last of my three major propositions was that federal spending on socially useful needs on a scale comparable to the military budget is not a feasible substitute. Social services spending is unlikely to be as profitable and expandable as is military spending. Social expenditures have never had the blank check that the military until recently has enjoyed.

Many kinds of social spending put the government in direct competition with particular industries and with the private sector as a whole. This goes against the logic of a capitalist economy. For example, government production of low-cost housing in large amounts would substantially reduce profits of private builders and landlords who own the existing housing stock. The supply of housing would be increased, and land would be taken away from private developers who want to use it for commercial gain. Similarly, building *effective* mass public transportation would compete with the automobile interests.

Any one of these interests taken by itself might not be sufficient to put insurmountable obstacles in the way of social spending. Most social service programs affect only one particular set of interests in the private economy. But there are so many forms of potential interference. Each of the vested interests is

explicitly aware of this problem and each works to help the others. They adopt a general social ideology that says that too much social spending is dangerous and that governmental noninterference is good.

Furthermore, the capitalist system as a whole is threatened by massive governmental social spending because the very necessity of private ownership and control over production is inevitably called into question. The basic assumption in any capitalist society that goods and services should be produced by private enterprise according to criteria of market profitability thus also fuels the general ideology limiting social spending. This limits the satisfaction of collective needs, such as clean air and water and esthetic city planning, that cannot be expressed in market terms as demand for individually saleable commodities.

Massive social spending also tends to upset the labor market, one of the essential institutions of a capitalist economy. Public expenditures on an adequate welfare program would make it difficult for employers to get workers. If the government provided adequate nonwage income without stigma to recipients, many workers would drop out of the labor force rather than take low-paying and unpleasant jobs. Those who stayed at jobs would be less likely to put up with demeaning working conditions. The whole basis of the capitalist labor market is that workers have no legitimate income source other than the sale of their labor power, and capitalist ideology has long made it a cardinal rule that government should not interfere with this incentive to work.[19] Powerful political forces thus operate to insure that direct income subsidization at adequate levels does not come into being.

Finally, good social services, since they have given people some security, comfort, and satisfaction—that is, have fulfilled real needs—interfere with the market in consumer goods. Corporations can only sell goods to people by playing on their unsatisfied needs and yearnings. New needs are constantly

[19]See Edwards, Section 8.2, p. 307.

being artificially created: the need for a sporty new car to enhance one's status, the need for new cosmetics to build one's sex appeal, and so on. These needs are based on people's fears, anxieties and dissatisfactions that are continually pandered to by the commercial world. But if people's needs were being more adequately fulfilled by the public sector—if they had access to adequate housing, effective transportation, good schools, and good health care—they would be much less prey to the appeals of the commercial hucksters. These forms of collective consumption would have interfered with the demand for consumer products in the private market.

Military spending is acceptable to all corporate interests. It does not interfere with existing areas for profit-making, it does not undermine the labor market, it does not challenge the class structure, and it does not produce income redistribution. Social spending does all these things and thus faces obstacles for its own expansion.

I do not mean to imply by the above analysis that a capitalist economy has not and will not provide any basic social services through government expenditures. Some social overhead investment is obviously important and necessary for the smooth functioning of any economy, and the provision of local and national public goods has always been considered a proper activity for capitalist governments. For example, expenditures on education, highways, and transportation are obviously necessary to provide workers and to get them to the point of production; such expenditures are motivated by the needs of production and only incidentally to fill human needs. In fact, most state and local government expenditures have been directed to these basic infrastructural needs.

In recent decades production has become, as Marx put it, more social in character: the economy has become much more complex, more interdependent, more urbanized, more in need of educated labor. The recent increase in state and local expenditures can be explained by these increases in the social costs of production. Expenditures for such

needs would be consistent with and are often necessary for private profitability.

Moreover, state and local expenditures are not motivated by the need to stimulate aggregate demand, for only the Federal government is concerned with maintaining aggregate demand. But nonmilitary federal purchases have barely, if at all, increased as a percentage of GNP since the thirties. Nonmilitary federal purchases of goods and services were only 2.8 percent in 1974. By contrast, nonmilitary federal purchases as a percent of GNP were 4.6 percent in 1938, 1.9 percent in 1954, and 2.4 percent in 1964.[20] Thus it cannot be said that the federal government has significantly turned to social services expenditures and away from military expenditures to meet the problem of inadequate aggregate demand.

In short, there are important obstacles to government spending for social needs. And the recent record reflects those obstacles; the government has not been spending money on those needs.

CONCLUSION

Is military spending really necessary to capitalism? I have framed the answer to this question in the following way. A capitalist economy with inadequate aggregate demand is much more likely to turn to military than social spending because military spending is more consistent with private profit and the social relations of production under capitalism. If this military outlet were blocked—by massive public opposition, for instance—it is certainly possible that a capitalist economy might be able to accommodate, transforming itself instead of committing suicide. But that kind of reasoning misses the point. Military spending is favored by corporate powers and is likely to be defended with considerable vigor. As long as there are easy profits available through military spending, capitalists will turn to them.

[20]Data from *Economic Report of the President, 1976* (Washington D.C.: U.S. Government Printing Office, 1971).

11.3 *Nature and Its Largest Parasite*

The pollution and destruction of the natural environment reflect one way in which the collective needs of society are ignored in capitalist production. Society at large has an immense stake in protecting our natural environment, but this interest is not mirrored in the mechanisms that determine production priorities. Production organized for profit ignores the environmental costs of producing goods and the environmental costs of disposing of goods; that is, these true costs to society do not help guide consumers in what to consume, nor are capitalists forced to pay for them. Production for private gain might have made sense in an earlier age characterized by open frontiers and an apparently limitless natural environment. In the present age, however, it is all too clear that we live within a closed system of limited natural and environmental resources. As a result, we must devote much greater attention to the quality of the world environment and restrain the unlimited exploitation of resources which fuels increases in the quantity of goods and services. The implications of this necessary change in orientation are profound.

In the following reading Michael Best and William Connolly explore some of the conflicts between the environment and production for profit. Best and Connolly go beyond simply pointing out that firms' profit calculations do not consider damage to the environment. Instead they provide a much more powerful analysis by investigating the conflict between social needs and the requirements for profit in the light of the vast power of monopoly corporations. This analysis shows that far from accepting the "inevitable" outcomes of market determination, corporations have actively intervened to counter, suppress, and eliminate ecologically more sound production. In part this power has been used directly to destroy technologies (mass-transit, long-haul rail freight) which, while less destructive environmentally, threatened the profitability of the corporations' investments or markets. In part this power has been used to influence the state to guarantee corporate investments; for example, national energy policy, by focusing research and development on coal and oil rather than solar or geothermal energy, has guaranteed the profitability of massive corporate holdings of coal and oil.

The importance of this analysis is that it indicates the enduring nature of the conflict between social priorities (in this case the need to preserve the environment) and production for profit. This conflict is not simply a *technical* problem susceptible of resolution through technical means.[1] Instead it reflects the profound irrationality of private control of social production.

[1]For example, bourgeois economists recommend a system of "compensatory" taxes and subsidies to make concern for the environment profitable.

The following is reprinted by permission of the publisher, from MICHAEL H. BEST and WILLIAM E. CONNOLLY: *The Politicized Economy* (Lexington, Mass.: D.C. Heath and Company, 1976).

Ecology deals with the balance between human beings and nature. The issues posed by such a relationship touch the very survival of humanity on the planet earth. We depend on nature for air to breathe, soil to grow food, water to drink and to sustain vegetation, fossil fuels to provide heat and to power the production system, metals to provide material for commodities. But if nature is our host we are its parasites. We abuse it unmercifully, robbing it of nonrenewable materials, straining its self-restorative capacities.

If some economic systems are more parasitical than others, the structural sources of that relationship must be confronted before the host collapses from the strain. The issue is particularly pertinent today. For as corporate capitalism, the ultimate eco-parasite on any measure of resource use or waste disposal, faces a new round of internal crises, ecology is apt to lose its popularity as a political issue. Such a lapse must be challenged because the current maladies of the system are partly rooted in a long-term debt to nature that is coming due.

In *The Social Costs of Private Enterprise*, published in 1950, K. William Kapp documents the

> *destructive effects of air and water pollution . . . [and] occupational diseases . . . , the competitive exploitation of both self-renewable and exhaustible natural wealth such as wildlife, petroleum and coal reserves, soil fertility and forest resources . . .; the diseconomies of the present transport system.*[1]

These social costs have gone unnoted and untended, according to Kapp, because they "do not enter into the cost calculations of private firms." Air, water, and soil pollution have so far escaped the net of the market because the environmental effects of particular economic transactions are diffused over a wide population and, to some extent, projected onto future populations. Under such

circumstances it is quite irrational for any individual producer or consumer to accept the higher costs involved in curtailing various assaults on the environment. Thus a company that purified the water used in production before disposing it into streams would add to its own costs, fail to benefit from the purified water flowing downstream, and weaken its competitive market position with respect to those companies unwilling to institute purification procedures. Since it is reasonable to assume that other companies in a market system will not voluntarily weaken their position in this way, it is irrational for any single company to choose to do so. The same logic applies to the consumer who assesses the rationality of, say, placing an emission control device on his automobile exhaust system.

Thus a range of practices which are desirable from the vantage point of the public are irrational from the vantage point of any particular consumer or producer. And a range of policies which are rational from the vantage point of individual consumers and producers are destructive of the collective interest in preserving nonrenewable productive resources and in maintaining the environment's capacity to assimilate wastes. This is the "tragedy of the commons."[2]

PRODUCT ALTERNATIVES AND CORPORATE PRIORITIES

To specify the cause of a problem is to establish as well its appropriate remedy. We think the failure to consider the social costs of resource depletion and pollution grow out of the *power* of corporations to impose their priorities on *governments* and *markets* and that those priorities, in turn, flow from structural tendencies in corporate capitalism. We will start by exploring three related areas of production and consumption: transportation, energy, and petrochemical products.

---

[1]K. William Kapp, *The Social Costs of Private Enterprise* (Cambridge: Harvard University Press, 1950), p. 229.

[2]This analysis is developed in Garret Hardin, "The Tragedy of the Commons," *Science* (1968), 1243–48.

Transportation

A national transportation system built around the private automobile, truck, and airplane uses fuel and metal resources extravagantly, imposes an enormous load on the self-purification capacities of the ecosystem, and increases the transportation costs of low income families. Assuming each vehicle to be half full, it takes ten gallons of gasoline per person to fly from Boston to New York, seven gallons per person by car, and only two gallons per person by train.[3]

If mass transit systems were introduced into our urban areas to replace commuting by automobile, 50 percent of the fuel now consumed by automobile could be saved. And since it takes six times as much fuel to haul a ton of freight from Los Angeles to New York by truck as it does by rail, it is clear that the truck imposes similar strains on the fuel resources and waste absorption capacities of the environment.[4]

Why does the United States depend on such an irrational transportation system, then, and what stops us from shifting to more rational forms? A large part of the answer to these questions emerges when we explore the emergent hegemony of the automobile corporations in the first part of the twentieth century.

During the 1920s the United States had rather extensive trolley, transit, and rail systems and there was ample potential to expand these services to meet the needs of a growing industrial population. The dissolution of these systems is not sufficiently explained through reference to a history of informed consumer choices in a competitive economy, nor is such an explanation adequate to explain the contemporary pressure against the redevelopment of rail and transit systems.

As Bradford Snell has documented in a report to the Senate Judiciary Subcommittee on Antitrust and Monopoly,[5] the competitive situation of the twenties was short-lived. During the middle twenties General Motors, often in conjunction with Standard Oil of California and Firestone Tire, launched an investment program enabling it first to control and then to dismantle the electric trolley and transit systems of 44 urban areas in 16 states. Often operating through a holding company, National City Line, the three corporations acquired electric rail systems, uprooted the tracks, and substituted diesel-powered bus systems. After acquisition and conversion, the systems were sold back to local groups, but only with a contractual clause which precluded the purchase of new equipment "using any fuel or means of propulsion other than gas."[6]

The life of a diesel bus is 28 percent shorter than that of its electric counterpart; its operating costs are 40 percent higher. Thus the typical result of the substitution of one system for the other was "higher operating costs, loss of patronage, and eventual bankruptcy."[7] General Motors pursued a similar program of acquisition and conversion with rail lines.

General Motors and its satellite companies benefited in two ways from this policy. First its profits from the sale of buses and diesel-powered locomotives are higher than from trolleys and electric trains. Second, the financial difficulties faced by these converted transportation systems encouraged consumers to buy more cars. General Motors' *incentive* to make cars and trucks the basic vehicles of American ground transportation is clear enough: Its gross revenues are 10 times greater if it sells cars rather than buses and 25 to 35 times greater if it sells trucks rather

---

[3]S. David Freeman, *Energy: The New Era* (New York: Vintage Books, 1974), p. 128.

[4]Barry Commoner, *The Closing Circle* (New York: Alfred Knopf, 1971), p. 169.

[5]*American Ground Transport: A Proposal for Reconstructuring the Automobile, Truck, Bus, and Rail Industries*, presented to the Subcommittee on Antitrust and Monopoly of the Committee of the Judiciary (U.S. Senate, Washington, D.C.: U.S. Government Printing Office, 1972).

[6]Ibid., p. 37.

[7]Ibid., p. 37.

than locomotives.[8] Its expansion into mass transportation systems thereby enhanced its ability to make cars and trucks more attractive to consumers than alternative modes of ground transportation.

Its policy of acquiring, converting, selling, and strangling mass transportation systems—in combination with the escalating pressure from the American Road Builders Association, American Trucking Association, and American Petroleum Association to launch massive state and federal highway construction programs—helped to make the truck and the automobile dominant vehicles for shipping and transportation in the country. Sandwiched between a private corporation with impressive market power over ground transportation and a governmental pressure system biased in favor of those organized corporate interests that pressed successfully for $156 billion in highway construction between 1945 and 1970, it was inevitable that mass transportation systems would eventually lose out to the "competition."

But as profitable as the operation was to the corporations involved, it was disastrous for the country. Besides the strain it imposes on our fuel resources, it has created cities crisscrossed with highways, straddled by distorted housing patterns, smothered in toxic emissions of carbon monoxide, lead, and other deadly chemical combinations from gasoline-powered vehicles.

It is absurd to argue that consumers have

chosen cars and trucks over transit and rail systems after having considered each option in the light of its comparative costs and benefits, including the costs of highway construction and the effects on the environment. But rather a few corporations with effective market power, including control over information about the effects of alternative forms, helped to eliminate one mode of transportation as a viable consumer option and thereby stimulated consumer demand for the only option available. Thereafter market control in this area was further solidified as national patterns of employment (e.g., automobile factories, oil production, highway construction) and satellite entrepreneurial activities (e.g., motels, tourist businesses) developed around this system and established a vast constituency whose immediate interests are tied to the maintenance and expansion of an ecologically irrational transportation system.

Energy

Between October 17, 1973 and January 1, 1974 Americans became thoroughly aware of the nation's dependence on foreign energy supplies. On the first date Arab nations imposed a boycott on oil to industrial nations restricting energy use by American consumers; on the second, the Arabs doubled the price of crude oil, sending consumer prices skyward.

The energy crunch, it is often asserted, converted the recession of the mid-seventies into a near depression, one which took the form of high inflation and high unemployment. But this explanation stops where it should begin. Why has the United States become so dependent on Arab oil, thereby making boycotts and price increases effective, and what do our expanding energy needs forbode for the future?

The American economy cannot sustain full employment unless it achieves a rather high rate of growth. That growth in the past has been fueled by a large and cheap supply of energy, especially oil. Thus United States oil

[8]Ibid., p. 38. General Motors did, according to findings by the Interstate Commerce Commission, make cost claims for its diesel locomotives to potential buyers that were "erroneous," "inflated," and "manifestly absurd," (Ibid., p. 41) and corporate elites knew about the dangerous levels of pollution from cars and trucks as early as 1953. Nevertheless our argument leans less on an assessment of corporate *intent* formed in the twenties to dismantle trolley and train systems, and more on the identification of *policy tendencies* that emerge when a small group of corporations dominate all forms of ground transportation, some of which are more profitable than others. Moreover, consumer tastes and preferences are not strictly given, but are subject to the influence of advertising and all the other corporate resources devoted to shaping consumer demand.

consumption increased from 2.4 to 6.4 billion barrels a year between 1950 and 1973. Between 1960 and 1972 alone, while our total energy consumption increased by 60 percent, no increase was made in our capacity to extract fuel from the earth. Instead we increasingly depended on cheap fuels from abroad. If present trends continue, that dependence will deepen:

> Before the Arab boycott we were importing one third of our oil supplies; if we return to a business as usual posture, we could well be importing one-half of our oil supplies by 1980.[9]

Moreover, the waste in our energy supply system is unbelievable. Only one-third of the oil discovered in any oil reservoir is actually lifted out. Fifty percent of the coal is left behind in deep coal mining. And conversion processes are equally wasteful. Only 20 percent of the energy potential of oil is employed in the automobile engine; 60 percent of energy potential is lost in the conversion of coal into electricity. These figures only symbolize the immense amounts of energy lost in mining, distribution, and conversion processes. Electric rates are set by public authorities, but they offer the lowest rates to the biggest users, encouraging large users to substitute electricity for less wasteful forms of energy. Electric rates are also set on a cost-plus basis, discouraging managers from seeking ways to curb costs of materials and production.

While established energy resources are being rapidly depleted or subjected to the vagaries of international politics or both, the United States government has concentrated its research and development of energy alternatives in one area: nuclear energy. That policy promises to increase our dependence on a fuel with serious storage problems for radioactive wastes and increases the likelihood that the plutonium necessary for the construction of nuclear weapons will become widely available.

[9]Freeman, Energy, p. 119.

The energy crisis of the 1970s, then, was anchored in our increasing dependence on Arab oil; that dependency in turn was rooted in the growth imperatives of corporate capitalism as well as in the wasteful patterns of consumption predicated on cheap and plentiful fuel supplies. Finally, actions of the state tended to reinforce these patterns.

What has led us to this situation? Energy policy, as we have seen, results from both market processes and state actions. But the political and economic power of the energy industry complex insures that state activities, rather than serving the public's needs, will support the interests of the corporations.

Oil companies drill and refine oil for profit. Neither the oil industry nor any other agency is charged to ensure that the supply of oil in the United States matches its oil needs. As things stand, oil companies can be stimulated to meet oil needs only by market demands or governmental incentives that make it profitable for them to expand.

The increasing market power of the multinational energy firms has tightened their grip on energy policy. One important consequence has been the decline in competition between alternative energy sources. Coal, which was a rather competitive industry, underwent a wave of mergers during the 1960s. By 1969 the thirteen largest coal producers accounted for 51 percent of coal production. Since part of the remaining coal production is in the hands of consuming companies, such as steel, this figure understates the extent of oligopoly. More importantly, the most significant mergers cut across the energy industries. In 1962 the oil industry accounted for 2 percent of coal production, but by 1969 it accounted for 25 percent. The oil companies have indeed diversified very effectively, for by 1969 the four largest firms had acquired holdings in gas, oil, shale, tar sands, and uranium. Such concentration decreases interfuel price competition and enables the oil industry to influence the type and supply of energy in its favor. As David Freeman, a student of energy resources in the United States, has concluded:

One does not have to subscribe to a conspiracy theory to observe that a shortage of energy is a situation most favorable to the energy companies. Concentration within the industry makes it less likely that any producers will scramble to enlarge supplies unless profit margins are most attractive.[10]

The energy industry complex, led by oil, matches its market power with impressive leverage over governmental officials. Its huge contributions to presidential and congressional candidates, the secret and illegal political funds held by Gulf Oil and other oil companies, its favored policy treatment including the earlier oil depletion allowance and oil import quotas, all testify to the political power of energy corporations. It would take strong leadership by the President to launch needed new programs of energy research and development into the ecologically promising areas of solar energy, geothermal power, tides, wind power, and organic wastes. But no President has been eager to take on the oil companies; to do so would be to write off immediately the electoral college votes of Texas and to unleash a well financed campaign of vilification against him. Any president who called for nationalization of energy would risk even more militant responses. The combined market and governmental power of the oil companies makes it exceedingly difficult to develop alternative energy forms *until* the energy problem itself attains crisis proportions.

Petrochemicals

The chemical revolution of the post–World War II period resulted in the systematic substitution of synthetic for organic substances in the production of innumerable commodites. Detergents replaced soap; synthetic fibres replaced cotton and wool; plastics substituted for leather, rubber, and wood; and massive infusions of synthetic fertilizers in intensive land cultivation replaced organic fertilizers tied to more extensive land use.

Barry Commoner has demonstrated that such a substitution of synthetic for organic materials is almost always incompatible with ecological imperative, for the "chemical substances . . . which are absent from biological systems are, for that reason, frequently toxic and/or nonbiodegradable."[11] Typically, too, each synthetic material requires more energy for its production than does its organic counterpart.

Again, neither sovereign voters nor sovereign consumers can be said to have chosen these materials over their organic counterparts in the light of an informed assessment of the comparative utility of each option. In agriculture, once some farmers intensified the use of synthetic fertilizers, market competition required all farmers to do so; oligopolistic soap companies found that detergents were more profitable than soap—even though wastes from the latter are far less destructive of soil and waterways; and petrochemical companies generally found the production of synthetic alternatives to be more profitable to them in the short run than the production and sale of organic materials.

In the areas of transportation, energy production and petrochemicals, then, product decisions with adverse environmental effects reflect the private priorities of corporations with massive market power. Another area where the needs of capitalist production and the environment collide is the workplace.

THE ENVIRONMENT AND THE WORKER

The work enviornment of the blue-collar worker is too often filled with deadly fumes, carcinogenic dust, high noise levels, and intense heat. Periodically a major mine disaster or a particularly harsh outbreak of cancer amongst workers handling deadly chemicals will arouse public awareness and mobilize support for reform of the work environment. But, just as typically, conditions

[10]Ibid., p. 155.

[11]Commoner, *The Closing Circle*, p. 47.

gradually return to normal as public attention shifts elsewhere. One earlier incident, exceptional in the death and injury produced, exposes strikingly this cycle of brief uproar followed by a larger period of benign neglect.

In 1930, as the Depression was deepening, workers were too weak to insist on health standards and the public was easily kept ignorant about the most oppressive conditions of work. A subsidiary of Union Carbide began a hydroelectric project in the southern part of West Virginia, diverting water from two rivers through a tunnel to be constructed near the town of Gauley Bridge. The Gauley Bridge disaster, as it came to be known when finally it became a public issue five years after the fact, involved a group of mostly black, unskilled workers who dug the tunnel through silica rock.

Working for extremely low pay, breathing carbon monoxide fumes as they rode into the tunnel every day, the workers also inhaled the heavy clouds of silica dust created by rock blasting in the tunnel. Engineers wore masks inside the tunnel, for the adverse effects of silica dust inhalation were even then known to health officials. But no masks were assigned to the workers. As increasing numbers of workers died from exposure to the dust, Rinehart Dennis, the subcontractor on the project, hired a local undertaker to bury the bodies at $55 per corpse.

When the U.S. Public Health Service probed the disaster in 1935, five years after its occurrence, it concluded that 476 men had died and 1,500 had been disabled. The case was eventually tried in the courts and congressional hearings were held, but the effective legal and legislative response was negligible. The settlements for survivors were extremely small; some defense lawyers were even caught accepting bribes from the company. The congressional hearings did not result in effective health regulations. And none of the companies involved—New Kanawha Power, Rinehart Dennis, and Union Carbide—ever faced official punitive action.

Despite recent legislation designed to protect the health and safety of workers, the classic cycle persists. Consider some of the facts about work and health in America today:

> The Public Health Service estimates that *each year* prolonged exposure to toxic chemicals, dust, noise, heat, cold, and radiation kills 100,000 workers and disables 390,000 more.
>
> A federally-sponsored, and more intensive, study of workers in a variety of factories and farms disclosed that 3 out of every 10 workers suffered occupationally related illnesses. Ninety percent of these illnesses were not reported through regular channels, suggesting that the Public Health estimates are seriously deflated.
>
> While Congress, the President, and the federal courts were all moving to reduce the ability of the Occupational Safety and Health Administration (OSHA) to protect workers from job hazards, another study showed that one out of every four workers in a sample of small businesses incurred an occupationally-related disease. Eighty-nine percent of these were not reported to the Labor Department. The diseases included chronic respiratory disorders, loss of hearing, eye cataracts, and increased lead absorption in the blood.[12]

Inside these global statistics are particular areas of extreme suffering and neglect:

> Three million workers in fabricated metals, stone, clay, and glass products suffer a very high incidence of irreversible respiratory diseases such as silicosis, bysinosis, and emphysema.
>
> The death rate among coal miners from respiratory diseases is five times higher than that of the general population.
>
> Asbestos workers are disproportionately afflicted with asbestiosis, which is in turn linked to cancer of the lung, stomach, colon, and rectum.
>
> Coke workers in steel factories assigned to the ovens for five years or more incur a risk of cancer 10 times greater than that of the general population.

[12] *New York Times*, March 4, 1974, May 12, 1975, April 28, 1975.

One out of every six uranium miners will die of cancer within ten years.

Employees in petroleum-based mineral oils suffer a very high incidence of cancer.[13]

Passage of the Occupational Safety and Health Act of 1970 seemed to promise rectification of this miserable record of worker illness and death, but the effectiveness of its administrative and research arm, OSHA, has been severely limited. Of the half-million synthetic substances introduced into the work environment, threshold limits had been established for only 250 by 1974. Though the agency proposed new standards for a variety of toxic substances in 1971, including inorganic lead, carbon monoxide, arsenic, and sulphuric dioxide, the standards had not been enacted by time of printing. Indeed, the Nader Health Research Group contended in 1974 that Nixon campaign strategists used the promise of relaxed OSHA controls to gain large contributions from business elites during the 1972 campaign. And, indeed, a memorandum published by the Senate Watergate Committee quotes a Nixon official promising that "no highly controversial standards (i.e., cotton, dust, etc.) will be proposed by OSHA" during the next four Nixon years.[14]

By 1974 OSHA was hamstrung in a variety of ways: with less than 800 inspectors in the field, the average employer will see an inspector once every 66 years; after three years of operation only two firms had been convicted of criminal violations; and the average fine for OSHA violations is twenty-five dollars.[15]

Clearly the workplace is a major locus of ecological assault, but just as clearly corporate and business elites use the impressive resources at their disposal to hide the facts about worker disease, to deflect pressures for reform of the work environment into other channels, and to malign those who would convert the oppressive conditions of work into a public issue. The U.S. Chamber of Commerce reflected this orientation nicely when it told health officials, "The health of American industry is eroded every time a new standard is issued."[16]

[13]These estimates, and others, are found in Frederick Wallick, *The American Worker: An Endangered Species* (New York: Ballantine, 1972); Jean Stellman and Susan Daum, *Work is Dangerous to Your Health* (New York: Vintage, 1973); Special Task Force Report to the Department of Health, Education and Welfare, *Work in America* (Cambridge: M.I.T. Press, 1973).

[14]David Burnham, "Nader Group Says Labor Department Lagged on Health Rules to Spur Gifts," *New York Times*, July 16, 1974. The same memo goes on to emphasize "the great potential of OSHA as a sales point for fund raising."

[15]*Wall Street Journal*, August 9, 1974.

[16]Ibid.

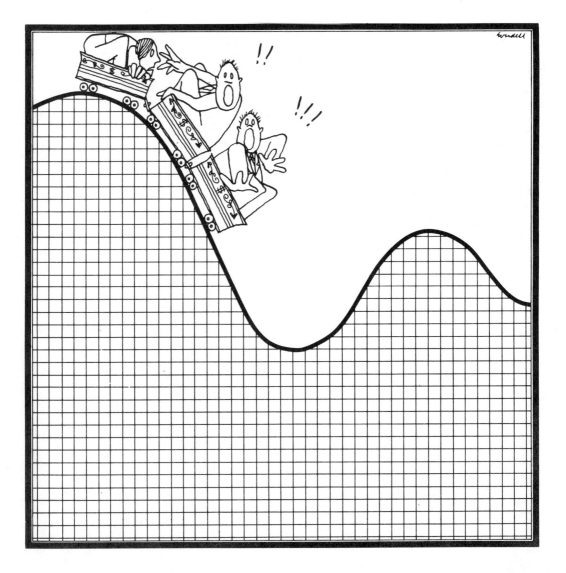

CHAPTER 12

Economic Crises

AFTER SEVERAL DECADES in which the term had rarely been mentioned in the United States, the reality of an "economic crisis" forced itself upon most Americans in the 1970s. Soaring rates of unemployment and inflation, declining levels of production and consumption, and widespread economic difficulties unmatched since the Great Depression of the 1930s shattered the prevailing myth that economic prosperity and stability could be taken for granted in a modern capitalist society. Uncomfortable as it may be for the many economists and politicians who had predicted a more or less continuously prosperous future for the American economy, we are now all obliged to come to grips with the persistence of capitalist economic crises.

What exactly do we mean by an economic crisis? In its broadest sense, an economic crisis refers to a period of serious economic difficulties during which the viability of a socioeconomic system comes into question. A capitalist economic crisis marks an historical turning point for the capitalist system: heightened economic problems generate rising social and political tensions, which can lead either to a revolutionary break with the past or to major changes within the system which provide at least temporary solutions to the problems raised.

During the history of capitalist development there have been a number of periods of economic crisis that have alternated with periods of general prosperity. In the first reading of this chapter, Eric Hobsbawm identifies three periods of generalized econo-

mic crisis for the world capitalist system during the past two centuries: from 1815 to 1848, from 1873 to 1896, and from 1917 to 1948. The economic difficulties of each of these periods led to a restructuring of the international capitalist economy that created the conditions for a subsequent period of economic expansion and prosperity. Although socialist revolutions have been successful in outlying parts of the world capitalist system, the industrialized center of the system—the capitalist metropolis—has thus far emerged from each crisis with renewed strength. Whether it can continue to do so after future crises remains an open question.

The period beginning in 1948 marked the most recent expansionary surge of the capitalist system. In a reformed world capitalist economy dominated by the economic and political power of the United States, the capitalist nations as a whole attained unprecedented rates of sustained economic growth.[1] U.S. hegemony guaranteed a stable international monetary system which encouraged the rapid growth of world trade, and it contributed to the availability of cheap supplies of energy and raw materials by enabling multinational corporations to obtain very favorable terms for the exploitation of natural resources in third-world countries and territories. At the same time capitalist govern-

[1]The (unweighted) average annual rate of growth of total output in eight of the biggest capitalist nations was roughly 3 percent from 1865 to 1950 and 5 percent from 1950 to 1967. See Table 9-A, p. 365, of the first edition of this book for documentation.

ments took on a greatly expanded role in managing the capitalist economies, and by applying Keynesian techniques of economic stabilization[2] they succeeded in staving off major economic downturns and assuring a more or less continuous upward trend in economic activity. Yet this latest period of relatively untroubled capitalist expansion lasted little more than two decades.

THE CRISIS OF THE 1970S

Since the late 1960s, it has become apparent that the capitalist nations are again in serious economic difficulty. The 1970s have marked another period of crisis for the capitalist system, and major changes will be necessary if the conditions for a renewed period of economic expansion and prosperity are to be restored within a capitalist framework.

The crisis of the 1970s has appeared as a cluster of several different economic problems. These problems have affected virtually all of the nations within the world capitalist system simultaneously, and they have had a strong impact on the U.S. economy. First of all, the long-term trend rate of growth of real economic output (correcting for changes in the level of prices, and abstracting from cyclical fluctuations in the level of output) has slowed down. The rapid rate of expansion of the world capitalist economy in the 1950s and 1960s will not be matched in the 1970s, nor is it likely to be matched well into the future. Even if estimates of gross national product do rise again as fast as they did in past decades, they will not reflect an equivalent rise in real material standards of living because of growing environmental costs of growth which escape the quantitative measures of total output.[3]

[2]The British economist John Maynard Keynes, in *The General Theory of Employment, Interest and Money* (New York: Harcourt Brace and Co., 1936), developed the now orthodox theory of national income and output determination which underlies the macroeconomic stabilization policies of capitalist governments.

[3]See Weisskopf, Section 11.1, p. 395, for a discussion of the limitations of gross national product as a measure of economic well-being.

Second, the crisis of the 1970s has been characterized by rapid price inflation throughout the capitalist world. Moreover, this inflation has proven unusually resistant to orthodox capitalist anti-inflationary policy. Until the late 1960s the rate of inflation became excessively high only at times when unemployment was very low. To reduce inflation to a tolerable level, it was sufficient to slow down economic activity and to cause a limited rise in the rate of unemployment. Such Keynesian techniques worked fairly well in maintaining overall price stability with moderate levels of unemployment. But since the late 1960s inflation has been more rapid than at any other time in the postwar period, and it has persisted even under conditions of relatively high unemployment.

The third and final major element of the crisis of the 1970s is a high rate of unemployment. The mid-1970s witnessed the most severe cyclical economic downturn in the capitalist system since the Great Depression, as levels of gross national product dropped sharply and rates of unemployment rose higher than at any other time since World War II. Even aside from its cyclical peak around 1975, unemployment (like inflation) appears to have become a more serious problem in most capitalist economies than it was in the earlier postwar period. Thus the crisis of the 1970s has produced a new phenomenon in capitalist history: "stagflation," which combines the economic stagnation and high unemployment characteristic of cyclical downturns with the inflation characteristic of booms.

SOURCES OF THE CRISIS

Like all capitalist economic crises, the manifold crisis of the 1970s grew out of certain contradictions that developed in the preceding period of expansion. The unprecedented postwar boom in the world capitalist economy had several significant consequences which ultimately put an end to the boom itself. In the following paragraphs, we discuss two of the most important contradictions that contributed to the crisis of the 1970s.

First of all, the postwar expansion of the world capitalist economy was dependent to a large extent on the hegemonic position of the United States. The U.S. government used its authority to establish and to maintain a system of international monetary arrangements conducive to the expansion of capitalist trade and foreign investment, and it used its power to guarantee favorable access to raw materials. While the United States gained special economic advantages by virtue of its dominant position in the world economy (for example, by having dollars join gold as the basic international currency), all of the advanced capitalist nations benefited from the general economic stability and cheap raw materials which U.S. hegemony provided. Yet the resulting economic expansion laid the basis for the ultimate erosion of the power relations upon which the expansion had been based.

On one side, the postwar boom enabled the advanced capitalist nations of Western Europe and Japan to build up their economic strength after the devastation of World War II; by the late 1960s they could successfully challenge the United States in markets that it had previously dominated. On the other side, the postwar expansion helped to strengthen the bargaining power of certain third-world nations possessing key natural resources—especially the oil-producing states—because it increased their ability to play off rival industrial powers and corporations. The hegemonic position of the United States was further eroded by third-world liberation movements, most notably in Indochina, which limited the American power to police the capitalist world. The growing economic strength of other advanced capitalist nations, the increased bargaining power of raw material exporters, and the rising military challenge from the third world combined to undermine the international monetary system that had prevailed for two decades. Stable international arrangements were needed for continued economic expansion, but by

the early 1970s the United States was no longer powerful enough to impose such stability on the international capitalist system.[4]

The decline in U.S. hegemony has contributed to a slowdown in economic growth and to inflation throughout most of the capitalist world by causing general international instability and by helping to bring to an end the era of cheap energy and raw materials. The impact of these developments on the U.S. economy has been especially serious, because the United States has suffered not only from the generalized difficulties of the world capitalist economy but also from the loss of many of the special economic advantages that accrued to it by virtue of its dominant position. The decline in the ability of the U.S. government and U.S. corporations to obtain especially favorable terms for trade and investment in the rest of the world has led to some redistribution of the benefits of capitalist economic activity to rival capitalist powers and to those third-world nations whose raw material export earnings have boomed—primarily the oil-producing states. But for most countries such redistributive gains have not made up for the losses attributable to the crisis as a whole.

The second important contradiction growing out of the postwar boom involved the ability of national capitalist governments to control their own domestic economies. The successful application of Keynesian stabilization policy to maintain relatively full employment with limited inflation in most of the advanced capitalist nations eventually created conditions that undermined the continued effectiveness of the policy. For the commitment of the capitalist state to maintain relatively high levels of employment has an increasingly inflationary impact on the econ-

[4]In principle several strong nations could join forces to ensure the stability of the world capitalist economy and to defend the interests of the advanced capitalist nations. Thus far, however, international rivalries have made it impossible to substitute for the dominant role of a single state that was played by Great Britain for a long period in the nineteenth century and by the United States in the period following World War II.

omy, if only because it limits the application of the most reliable anti-inflationary mechanism: a major downturn. With the prospect of a severe downturn ruled out, both capital and labor push harder for increases in prices and wages and resist more successfully any decreases. Along with other developments in the advanced capitalist economies—e.g., the growing concentration of capital—this has contributed to increasing inflationary pressures at any given level of unemployment.

At the same time, the growing internationalization of the capitalist system as a whole has reduced the degree of control any individual government can exercise over domestic economic activity. Foreign investment by multinational corporations, international flows of short-term capital, overseas money markets, etc. have increased by leaps and bounds and blurred the lines between national economies. As a result, both inflation and economic downturns tend to become generalized throughout the world capitalist system. Differing conditions in different countries no longer tend to offset one another; instead, the problems are amplified by their simultaneous occurrence in many countries. Moreover, the ease with which commodities and money move from one country to another tends to frustrate the macroeconomic policies applied by any single capitalist state. This conflict between nationally based economic policies and an increasingly international economy is made worse by the decline in U.S. hegemony: the U.S. is now less able to coerce other capitalist governments into pursuing mutually needed but individually costly policies.

The contradictory consequences of the Keynesian strategy of economic stabilization, and the growing weakness of the standard tools of capitalist macroeconomic management, have been major contributing factors to the unprecedented combination of inflation and unemployment—the stagflation—that has characterized the crisis of the 1970s. Inflation and unemployment can no longer be kept near tolerable limits simultaneously; to

reduce one, it is necessary to increase the other to an unprecedented degree. The severity of the economic downturn of the mid-1970s can be attributed in part to the extraordinary extent to which the economy must now be slowed down in order to curb inflation. And recent evidence suggests that the downturn was not even strong enough to put an end to the inflationary surge that has characterized this period of crisis.[5]

PROSPECTS FOR THE FUTURE

If the past history of capitalist crises can serve as a guide to the future, it is likely that the most recent crisis will last in one form or another for many years to come. Earlier crises of the capitalist system required several decades to be adequately resolved. It is hard to predict how long the crisis that began in the 1970s will last, but we can assert that major reforms in the capitalist system will be required if the world capitalist economy is to enter into a new period of prosperity and expansion.

The capitalist system clearly needs a new and effective international institutional framework to replace single-nation hegemony as a basis for managing the increasingly open and interdependent world economy. Such a framework might be built upon a supranational agency with broad powers to control the world economy, much as national governments have in the past controlled domestic economies. Alternatively, a new international framework might be based on some form of joint management by a closely cooperating group of major capitalist powers. But either of these solutions is fraught with difficulties and potential sources of tension, so that it remains highly uncertain whether the re-establishment of a strong international

[5]During and after the downturn in the U.S. economy in 1974–1975, prices have continued to rise at rates much higher than in similar phases of the business cycle in the past. See Figures 12-A and 12-B, pp. 444–445.

capitalist order can be accomplished very quickly.[6]

The capitalist system also clearly needs a new kind of domestic order to prevent the conflict between capital and labor from generating intolerable levels of unemployment and/or inflation. In effect, what is required is a "social contract" whereby labor would curtail its wage demands while capital would moderate its price increases and the age-old struggle over shares of the pie would be kept under close control. Such a contract could only be enforced by means of a greater degree of government intervention into the economy than in the past: Keynesian techniques of (indirect) control would have to be replaced by a much more direct form of planning. While some advanced capitalist nations(e.g., Sweden, the United Kingdom) have already begun to move in this direction, there remain very substantial political and economic obstacles to its successful implementation.[7]

If such reforms in the international capitalist economy and within the capitalist nations are not forthcoming, there is a possibility that more revolutionary changes will occur. For it is precisely during times of crisis that class struggles become most intense and revolutionary movements have their greatest opportunity for success.

The readings in this chapter pursue in much greater detail the issues raised in this introduction. The first reading defines the concept of a crisis and presents a broad historical account of past crises of the capitalist system as a whole. The remaining three readings focus on the United States economy and explore both the international and the domestic aspects of the crisis of the 1970s.

[6]See Fred Block, "Contradictions of Capitalism as a World System," *The Insurgent Sociologist*, 5, No. 2 (Winter 1975), for a thorough analysis of the difficulties faced by the advanced capitalist nations in restructuring the world capitalist economy after the decline of U.S. hegemony.

[7]The prospects and problems of capitalist planning in the United States are discussed by William Tabb, "We Are All Socialists Now: Corporate Planning for America," in the Union for Radical Political Economics, *Radical Perspectives on the Economic Crisis of Monopoly Capitalism* (New York: Union for Radical Political Economics, 1975).

12.1 *Capitalist Crises in Historical Perspective*

To understand the nature of the economic crisis that has afflicted the world capitalist system in the 1970s, it is important to place the crisis in an appropriate historical perspective. In this first reading of the chapter, Eric Hobsbawm reviews the alternate periods of prosperity and crisis that have characterized the history of capitalist development since the Industrial Revolution in England. Hobsbawm's analysis represents an excellent example of the Marxist method of historical materialism (introduced in Chapter 2); he shows how each stage in the process of capitalist development generates certain contradictions, whose ultimate resolution paves the way for a new and more advanced stage of development.

The following is excerpted from "The Crisis of Capitalism in Historical Perspective" by ERIC HOBSBAWM. From *Marxism Today*, 19, No. 10 (October 1975). Reprinted by permission of the author.

Everyone has known for a long time that the operations of the capitalist economy generate various types of periodic disturbances which give it a sort of jerky rhythm. The best-known of these rhythms is the so-called trade-cycle, namely the slump,[1] which was discovered by radical and socialist economists from the 1830s on, and analysed by the orthodox from 1860 on. Sometimes it has been more dramatic than at other times, sometimes—and notably in the years since the Second World War—it has been so mild that people have seriously doubted whether it was still in operation. Certainly it has been much less visible and important than ever before in capitalist history. However, though some of these slumps were catastrophic in their impact, both on business and on different classes of the people, with one exception none of them by themselves has looked like putting the capitalist system itself at risk on a world scale, nor possibly in any individual country. That exception is, of course, the slump of 1929 to 1933.

PERIODICAL FLUCTUATIONS

Once the rhythm of the trade-cycle was recognised, slumps were, for the best part of a century, regarded as inevitable but temporary interruptions, analogous to the less predictable, but certainly periodic cycle of harvests which dominated the lives of pre-industrial societies. Capitalism lived with them, capitalism lived through them, capitalism survived them. However, perhaps it is less well known that there also appears to be a rather longer kind of periodical fluctuation in the course of capitalism, which the Russian economist, Kondratiev, tried to analyse in the 1920s, and which is still called by his name. Periods of 20 to 30 years or so—the exact length doesn't really matter—appear to alternate, marked until the present by the different movements of prices. Deflations succeeded inflations for fairly long periods. Then we may also detect a longer trend of this kind,

[1]Editors' note: A "slump" is another word for a short-run cyclical economic downturn, which must be distinguished from the long-run crises discussed in this reading. The short-run cyclical behavior of a capitalist economy is examined in the next reading by Weisskopf, Section 12.2, p. 441.

a general tendency of prices to fall from the beginning of the 19th century, the end of the Napoleonic Wars, until almost the end, and a general trend of prices to rise, of which we are only too well aware—a long-term trend—since the beginning of the 20th century.

Periods of prosperity and capitalist expansion have thus alternated with periods of economic, and, as we shall see, with periods of political and social troubles. . . . From the beginning of the Industrial Revolution to the end of the Napoleonic Wars was one such period of long-term [upward] trend. It was followed, until the middle or late 1840s, by a period of difficulties, though of rapid economic growth, and this in turn by the golden years of the mid-nineteenth century, the high point of capitalist, liberal, economics. From 1873 until almost the end of the century there was a period of difficulties called by contemporary business observers and also by some economic historians the "Great Depression", although, of course, it had only very small similarities with the Great Depression of the 1930s, which is what we know by this name. It was followed by another period of lengthy boom which lasted, I suppose, until the end of the First World War; thereafter came the depressed inter-war years which did not really end until after the Second World War, and lastly the greatest of all global booms in the 1950s, 1960s and early 1970s, reaching its peak, as far as we can see, in 1973.

It looks as though we have now entered another period of general economic difficulties. . . . [E]ach of these periods of troubles in the past was in some sense the result of the successes of the previous period. Each boom created the conditions which, as we now see, led inevitably to the subsequent difficulties. But I am also bound to point out that, until the present, each of these periods of trouble led to changes within the capitalist system which in turn provided solutions for the problems previously raised, and created the conditions for the subsequent secular boom.

Now the point I wish to make is that the times when the viability of the entire capitalist system could be questioned have occurred during these rather lengthy periods of trouble, between 1815 and 1848, between 1873 and 1896, and between 1917 and 1948. It is during these periods that we can speak of a crisis of capitalism.

TYPES OF SOCIAL AND POLITICAL CONFLICTS

I have so far talked in what looks like entirely economic terms, but of course we are not talking about the economic mechanism in isolation, even on a world scale; we are talking about societies divided into classes and other social groups, organised in a system and a hierarchy of states with particular forms of political institutions. Moreover, we are not only concerned with the interaction within the international system, but with all these at a particular phase of history. For even if, from the Industrial Revolution on, we can speak of a world dominated by capitalism, we cannot yet speak of—in fact we can never speak of—a uniformly and homogeneously capitalist world. Capitalism, or bourgeois society, captured the world progressively, transformed its various parts which were in very different phases of their own development at various times, and what is more, progressed and still progresses at an uneven rate. This is true of the poor countries of the capitalist system, and of the so-called developed or industrialised countries of the West, and later Japan. All this is familiar. The Industrial Revolution before 1848 was virtually confined to Britain, Belgium and a few patches in Western Europe and the European seaboard. The Industrial Revolution in Germany and most of the US occurs after 1848, in Scandinavia even later, in Russia from the 1890s, and so on.

So what we are confronted with is a global, historical process, producing at least three types of social and political conflicts, in addition to, or rather in combination with, economic contradictions within capitalist development and complicated, moreover, by the unevenness of the transformation and timing in the various parts of the world. The first of these conflicts is the development, within the developed and developing countries, of a working class and its movements which are in conflict with the capitalists. The second is the resistance and developing rebellion of the dependent world, colonial and semi-colonial, against the domination of, or conquest by, the handful of developed countries. One might perhaps also add at this stage yet another contradiction—though it tends to be of a slightly different kind—the resistance of pre-capitalist strata such as the peasants and petit-bourgeoisie in the developed or semi-peripheral countries, to the process of capitalist development which destroyed their traditional economy and social order.

And finally there is the conflict between the [developed countries of the world, an international conflict involving the] various core states of capitalism themselves [and—since World War II—the USSR.]

THE AGE OF BRITISH POWER

I do not wish to suggest that these three conflicts exhaust the analysis, but for the sake of simplicity let us just concentrate on them. Now, until about the last quarter of the 19th century none of these three major conflicts could be expected to be acute on a global scale: industrialisation was only just beginning to produce massive proletariats, except in very few places such as Britain. Again, with certain exceptions, capitalism was only beginning to seize hold of the under-developed world from the middle of the 19th century on, and to engage in intensive capitalist investment there. Very little of the world was actually colonised, occupied and ruled from abroad, the major exceptions being India and what today is Indonesia. And since there was for more than half a century only one major industrial power, one workshop of the world and world trader, one power with a genuinely global policy and the means to exercise it—mainly through a global navy—the scope for major international conflict such as general, European or world war, was rather small. In world history this era, stretching from the defeat of Napoleon to the 1870s, perhaps to the end of the century if you like, may be described as the age of British power. It is this sort of world control of which the US has dreamed ever since 1941, and which it thought it had established in the 1950s and 1960s; but if the British era lasted little more than half a century, three-quarters perhaps, what the Americans call the American century turns out to have lasted little more than 25 years. But this is by the way. At all events, the moment when world capitalism was entirely successful, confident and secure, was comparatively brief, the mid-Victorian period, which may possibly be prolonged towards the end of the 19th century. In history this period is preceded by [an age] of revolution . . . from, say, 1776, the date of the American Revolt, to 1848, about 70 odd years. . . .

Why was it revolutionary? Because, as we see, looking back on it, it was a transition to the era of modern industrial capitalism, to bourgeois society; and what made it revolutionary was not only the attempt to break the fetters of earlier social and political orders which were believed to stand in its way, to construct an international system suited to the expansion of capitalism, but, I suggest, two further factors. First, the mobilisation of the common people which this revolutionary transition implied; that is why some phases of it have sometimes been called the age of democratic revolution; peasants, artisans, small shopkeepers, miscellaneous poor, were drawn into the drama of history as actors, rather than simply as crowd extras. Second, difficulties of developing industrial capitalism itself, which still found itself hampered by the very narrowness of the front on which it had broken through. It therefore . . . created . . . unusually acute social problems, unusual hardships for the emerging, exploited working class, a mass of people whom at this stage it was better at uprooting than at finding work, not even work at the modest wages then believed to be adequate. It also created difficulties for business. All this made the 1830s and the 1840s a period of unusually persistent and acute crisis; so much so that many—

not least among the capitalists themselves—feared that the first stage of successful industrial capitalism might also be its last. The spectre of Communism haunted Europe.

Looking back we can see that this was not the end of capitalism but what today would be called in the jargon "teething troubles." But we can properly consider this as the first era of general capitalist crisis. From this crisis capitalism emerged in the 1850s, the years of railways, iron and free trade, and above all the era when the world as a whole was opened to capitalist development (which did not necessarily mean industrialisation), or the exploitation by the developed and developing industrial powers.

MID-NINETEENTH CENTURY BOOM

The giant and prolonged boom of the mid-nineteenth century was not based on a new technological breakthrough; by and large it utilised and acknowledged and developed the first Industrial Revolution, coal as a source of energy, the steam-engine as motor-power, iron rather than steel as the basic raw material for capital goods such as machinery and so on. But this technology was now used on a far greater scale internationally both in the countries which were now entering industrialisation, and also to create what is nowadays called an infrastructure in colonial and semi-colonial under-developed areas, railways, port installations—all that sort of thing. These allowed them to be integrated, mainly as suppliers of primary products into the capitalist world economy.

Hence the three major consequences of this boom: first, it replaced industrial world monopoly by Britain, by what you might call world industrial oligarchy by a handful of competing industrial powers among whom the USA and Germany were rapidly overhauling Britain. We shall see that this situation has some parallels with the present. So long as the technology and methods of the first Industrial Revolution were very basic to industrialisation, this did not diminish the industrial role of Britain, but eventually it would do so. Second, in making possible through railways, steamships, etc., an economic trade in bulk goods from hitherto inaccessible areas, it created a number of potential mass exporters of primary products, generally specialising in one or two commodities—American and South Russian wheat, Argentinian and Australasian meat, South Asian tea, Latin American coffee, etc. —each dependent on the developed industrial world for their outlets. When these became actual rather than just potential mass exporters, the result would be a major disruption of agriculture, both in the exporting and importing countries, and also the development of dependent, mono-culture export economies like the banana and coffee republics of Latin America. . . .

Third, and in consequence of the first two developments, the boom enormously expanded imports and exports of both goods and capital. This world trading and payments system continued to hinge on Britain and in this respect the British economy continued to occupy a key position even after its industrial role began to diminish. However, the boom was particularly quick in getting under way because of two further factors: a rather large reserve of hitherto under-utilised resources, notably the labour which had been uprooted but was available for fairly short-term employment, and the discovery of vast supplies of precious metals, mostly gold, in California and Australia, but also silver in the USA.

The reserves of labour, although reinforced by a considerable degree of immigration from agriculture to industry and to the cities, were still only a small part of what was really available in the world. . . . The precious metals as well as the enormous expansion of the international market for goods, whose output may have somewhat lagged behind the demand, helped to create a moderate inflation of prices—it's the only period between 1850 and the end of the century when prices were not tending to drop—and, in short, there was no pressure on business profits. Quite the contrary. Except for greatly im-

proved employment, the workers got little enough out of this boom, but on the whole conditions in developed countries improved after 1860 at least, and the prospects of capitalism looked extremely rosy.

LAST QUARTER OF NINETEENTH CENTURY

As I have already implied, the great boom created its own troubles which became obvious in the last quarter of the 19th century. But, with some qualifications which I shall shortly be making, these troubles were, as we can see in retrospect, not fundamental. This is why most economic historians today take the phrase "The Great Depression," which was then widely used, with a very large pinch of salt, and many actually refuse to accept that it was a depression at all. What we find is not a general crisis of capitalism but a shift within it: from the technology of steam and iron and a limited knowledge of chemistry to electricity and oil, steel alloys and non-ferrous metals, turbines and internal-combustion engines; from competitive small firms to corporations, cartels and trusts; from free trade to protection and the partition of the world; from one industrial economy to several rival industrial economies; in short, from mid-19th century capitalism to imperialism or monopoly capitalism. Expansion in terms of output and trade continued faster than before, even during the period when businessmen complained of the squeeze on profits and the rate of interest. Probably agriculture rather than industry took the main brunt of the crisis, but incidentally the consequent rapid fall of the cost of living benefited a lot of workers, notably in Britain.

.   .   .

AFTER 1900

Now, even in a purely economic sense, capitalism seemed set for a long and untroubled future around 1900. Even British capitalism, which was by now lumbered with a lot of old-fashioned plant and methods, and both slow-ing down and falling behind the Germans and Americans, enjoyed the profits of being both the largest empire and increasingly the world's financier, shipper, insurance-broker, and in general the advantages of a world sys-tem which rested on the pound sterling. And, in fact, of the three major areas of conflict within the capitalist system, the one which had seemed most dangerous before 1848 now appeared to become quite manageable. Dur-ing the so-called "Great Depression" mass trade union and labour movements developed in all industrial countries, even to a sub-stantial extent in the USA, mostly socialist and indeed largely Marxist. But, in fact, though these Marxist mass movements con-tinued to salute the flag of revolution every time their leaders opened their mouths in public, we know that they rapidly turned into harmless, social-democratic movements, though not, of course, in the illegal and marginal movements in the peripheral and under-developed countries such as Russia.

On the other hand, the two other types of conflict now became increasingly dangerous. The pressures of imperialism on parts of the colonial and semi-colonial world, including countries on the margins of capitalist devel-opment, such as Tsarist Russia, became intolerable. Between 1905 and 1914 a break-ing-point was reached in three areas. One, the traditional structures of pre-capitalist empires in the Islamic world and Asia col-lapsed under the pressure of western penetra-tion and conquest: Tsarist Russia, in so far as it belonged to this group, Persia, Turkey and, most significant of all in 1911, China.

Second, social revolution of peasants and workers broke out in Tsarist Russia, the first major social revolution of the 20th century. And, third, in Mexico in 1910 there occurred the first anti-imperialist social revolution in which the workers played no significant part because they did not form a significant part of the population.

These developments constitute the begin-nings of the 20th century age of revolutions. At the same time the tensions of the state sys-tem led directly towards an era of interna-tional wars such as had not existed since the 18th and early 19th century. The first of these wars, expected, predicted, and in spite of great efforts not avoided, ended the era of triumphant confidence. After 1914 nothing would ever really be the same again. Then after 1917 one-sixth of the world's surface moved out of the capitalist economy and after the Second World War large regions of Europe and Asia joined this movement. Capitalism was not destroyed as a world sys-tem, but the First World War opened an era when all three of the main types of conflict became for a time apparently dominant and unmanageable.[2] The threat of social revolu-tion dominated the politics of most of the highly developed capitalist states, though the operative factor at times was not so much the reality of this threat of social revolution as the fear of revolution in the minds of an uncer-tain, frightened, demoralised ruling class. This was particularly so in the period fol-lowing the October Revolution and during the Great Depression. International conflict became endemic as a second and even greater world war followed the first after barely 20 year's interval of a very uncertain peace. And the great empires into which the world had been divided at the end of the 19th century now lived on borrowed time. Their end could be predicted.

But what made this entire period so dra-matic a crisis was the breakdown of the inter-national capitalist economy which had, by and large, had such an astonishing run for its money—the money being the pound sterling —until 1914. The attempt to reconstruct this international liberal economy after the First World War in the 1920s failed. For one thing

[2]Editors' note: The fact that the United States enjoyed a period of prosperity in the 1920s may appear incon-sistent with the view that the entire period from 1917 to 1948 was one of crisis. But the U.S. economic boom was exceptional and short-lived. For almost all the other capitalist nations and for the world capitalist economy as a whole, the 1920s represented a period of political and economic instability which ushered in the all-encompassing Great Depression of the 1930s.

the keystone of the whole structure, Britain, was no longer in a position to bear its weight: the great slump of 1929 to 1933 showed just how unsuccessful this attempt had been, and brought the system close to actual collapse for a brief moment. To give you a single illustration: in 1938 world trade was little more than two-thirds of what it had been in 1913, and in 1948 European trade was about 15 percent below this modest level. There had been no setback of this kind since the beginning of the Industrial Revolution.

The period of depression, flanked on either side by war and revolution, remains to this day the only time when the future of the world capitalist system really looked as though it was in imminent danger. It did not seem unrealistic to speak in the words of a contemporary book-title of *This Final Crisis*. But, as we can see now, the immediate and urgent danger to capitalism was not due to the fact that the system had come to the end of its possibilities either economically or politically; it had merely come to the end of the possibilities of its 19th-century international structure and the assumptions on which its policy had then been based. The slump forced one country after another to abandon these, and Keynes—who you may remember set out to save rather than to undermine bourgeois society—provided the most familiar, theoretical reasoning behind this change. Actually, in all countries, even including Scandinavia, this change took place through a combination of experiment, accident and the discovery that even the slump of 1929 to 1933 ended of its own accord, and of course subsequently by the necessity of an economy of total war.

.   .   .

THE NEW GREAT BOOM

The capitalist states of the new great boom moved back to some variant or other of an admittedly very much more bureaucratised and, so to speak, state-administered bourgeois parliamentarianism. We thought that declin-

ing capitalism would be unable to compete successfully with the rising rival socialist[3] economy, especially one so much larger than before. But the opposite happened. Capitalism outproduced socialism and even began to re-infiltrate and re-integrate socialist economy from outside by virtue of its technological superiority and greater wealth. And so on. So it is clear that the foundations of capitalism have not been fatally undermined by the era of crisis, profound though that crisis was. What happened is rather that capitalism abandoned the old assumption of a self-regulating, competitive market economy and changed its structure accordingly. In the first place the state expanded its economic function in all developed countries, including the USA, to the point where it deliberately planned and managed the economy to a large extent, including an enormous public sector, and in many countries, even a largely nationalised industry. In the second place, the developed economies abandoned the economies of cheap labour and market control of unemployment, thus incidentally making possible a vast extension of the market for consumer goods. In the third place, the concentration of capital created the phenomenon of the modern, super-giant, largely self-financing, independent-of-the-market, transnational corporation. The developed countries entered the era of state monopoly capitalism and welfare capitalism inasmuch as welfare is implicit in full employment as a major government policy which automatically maintains workers' incomes.

I do not want to describe or analyse these far-reaching changes further; but I want just to point out that phrases like "state capitalism" or "state monopoly capitalism" obscure one very important aspect of this new relation between the state and the large corporations which increasingly and in all developed countries constitute the "private sector." The corporations both need the state—I mean

[3]Editors' note: In this essay Hobsbawm uses the term "socialist" to describe what we prefer to call the "state socialist" nations of the modern world: the USSR, the Eastern European nations, China, etc.

the national state—and break its boundaries. They need it, and not only for various other purposes, but because it controls the conditions of political stability which makes the operation of the system possible in the post-1930 period, i.e., full employment and social security. These conditions depend on a constantly rising level of state expenditure. In the USA, for instance, it has risen from about 24 percent of GNP in 1948 to about 32 percent in 1969. And every time it drops, unemployment rises.

But at the same time the operations of the giant corporations become steadily more transnational, whatever their local base (which in most cases is American), and therefore to some extent they come into conflict with the interests of the economic policy of the national states; for instance, in the matter of the balance of payments. The fact that the United States has run an enormous deficit for many years—in the 1950s and 1960s—which in the end undermined the position of the dollar, was of considerable negative importance to the US Government, but it was an undoubted advantage to the American transnational corporations which used this fact to buy themselves into foreign economies. Hence, incidentally, the post-war international economy has not on the whole been one of mere mercantilism, as some Keynesians anticipated, but a sort of world restoration of free trade and free investment for the benefit of what is now, one might say, the major dynamic element in the capitalist economy, the large transnational corporations.

Given this restructuring of capitalism, its recovery was facilitated by the large reserve of unused resources, industrial capacity and labour available at the end of the war, and by the disproportion which had widened during the period of economic crisis, between the growing capacity to produce and the stagnation of world trade. It was also made possible by the systematic reconstruction, in which incidentally Keynes also took a leading part, of an international trade and payments system in the immediate post-war years. As I have already suggested, this system was in

some respects a reversion to the mid-19th century order, only it rested on a US world monopoly instead of a British, on the dollar instead of on the pound sterling. But the unparalleled expansion of capitalism could not have occurred but for important changes in the level of the means of production, just as the previous expansions also occurred not simply by a widening of the market and changes in the structure, but also by changes in the means of production; changes comparable to cotton in the first Industrial Revolution, to railways and iron in the mid-19th century, to the new technology that I have sketched above of the early 20th century.

THREE KEY FACTORS

I would like to suggest three changes of this kind, not necessarily in order of importance. First, in addition to the generalisation of the internal combustion engine, the spread of the car from being virtually an American phenomenon to being a world phenomenon, there were the consequences of the technological revolution—in the field of light consumer goods—of electronics and plastics. Most of these, incidentally, like most of the technological revolutions which paid off in the later periods of boom, were made during the inter-war period, or at least during the period of crisis.

The technological revolution in light consumer goods, electronics and plastics, created an enormous number of new consumer goods, and increasingly cheapening consumer goods —you may observe that among the very few goods which still continue, even in the period of inflation, to become cheaper, are things like colour television sets. If we look at a country like Japan, the consumer society there is based much less on the car than on the camera and the television set. That was a development in the fifties and sixties.

Second, there is something which perhaps made possible what I have just described, a really quite unprecedented development—at least unprecedented on this scale—an enormous, massive process of urbanisation or sub-urbanisation, the emptying of the country-side. In the 1950s and particularly in the 1960s, for the first time in Western and Cen-tral Europe, the old—not only Marxist—prediction of the disappearance of the peasant appeared to be coming true. . . . This phe-nomenon is not necessarily confined only to developed countries; urbanisation, sub-urbanisation, the consequent road-building and all the rest of it, also occurred in the peri-pheral and even in many of the under-developed countries, very notably in a region like Latin America.

Third, I think we have the systematic ex-ploitation, again on quite an unprecedented scale, of ultra-cheap energy. This was not energy that had previously been unknown, because oil, after all, had been significant in the past. However, there was now exploita-tion of oil on a scale, particularly after the late fifties, which simply had no precedent. Alternative sources of energy were run down —coal mines, for instance, shut down, right, left and centre—in order to use the benefits, the advantages of this bonanza of ultra-cheap oil. We may also, however, note that capi-talism began to do two things, one old and one new: first, unlike the inter-war periods, it once again relied very largely on immigrant labour, the abundant and cheap labour on its fringes. There were no longer such large reserves in central capitalist countries with full employment where the only unused labour capacity was that of married women—the percentage of employed married women shot up dramatically. Again there was no prece-dent for this post-war period rise in women's employment. We now find immigration, very notably controlled immigration in some in-stances, in Europe, from places as far away as Turkey, or Syria, in some instances, not to mention Asia and the West Indies. But we also find a new phenomenon: the export of the actual plant and industry to the areas where the reservoir of cheap labour was, to places like South Korea, Taiwan, Singapore. In the last ten years such transfers have taken place on a large scale, certainly in industries

like electronics and cameras. In short, the exploitation of the under-developed world, both in labour and raw materials, by the developed world contributed to an important extent—and some would argue fundamental-ly—to the great boom of the 1950s and 1960s.

Now during this golden age of capitalism we may note that two out of the three main conflicts I have talked about ceased to be acute, at least for this period. After a few years of sharp confrontation, the USA and the USSR developed a stable *modus vivendi*, and in spite of bloody local wars an immediate world conflict has for several years appeared to be unlikely. Similarly the working class movements in the developed countries, whether under social-democratic or Marxist leadership, also established—there was little else to do—a *modus vivendi* with the existing system, which they screwed for all they were worth for the higher wages and better condi-tions which at that period the system was per-fectly able to grant. . . .

Only the tension between the industrial and the under-developed countries remained alive, given the widening gap between the two and the role of exploitation in the world boom. But once again, with a few localised exceptions such as Cuba and Vietnam, we cannot really regard this conflict as unman-ageable in the period, let us say, between 1950 and 1973.

INTERNAL CONTRADICTIONS

It is not my business to analyse the internal contradictions which led to the end of this golden age, though I will in passing point out three: first, the United States was incapable of maintaining its overwhelming economic and political supremacy, and consequently of maintaining the dollar in its position as the basis of the international payment system. That system, visibly shaken since 1968, is at present on the point of breakdown. The revival or rise of other capitalist economies, notably those in the EEC and Japan, puts the US today in a similar relationship to them as Britain was from the end of the 19th century in relation to Germany and the USA. It is no longer true to think of the USA as the overwhelmingly dominant, or even the technologically dominant, country. . . .

International rivalry and tensions, therefore, revived as American hegemony declined. Second, it is now clear that capitalism can choose either unemployment or inflation. However, while a moderate degree of inflation is rather good for business, an excessive amount produces, as we know too well, considerable social and economic political troubles. Moreover, it is possible . . . that the structure of capitalism has changed in such a way as to make it increasingly difficult to control either inflation by means of unemployment, or the other way round. Or rather that one would need an unpredictably greater amount of unemployment than was previously believed necessary to control inflation and the other way round.

And third, the now politically independent countries which happen to be sitting on scarce raw materials discovered how to turn the tables on the industrial world by using monopoly themselves, as in the oil crisis. In short, the era when capitalist corporations could operate at their will in a Third World of cheap resources was bound to end. And it did.

THE PRESENT PERIOD

So we are once again at the end of another bout of capitalist expansion. I do not say of capitalism, since, again speaking in purely economic and technical terms, the system has not exhausted its possibilities. For instance, it could quite easily extend the method of exporting industrialisation to the underdeveloped world, which it has already started to do, and it would then acquire a very large, cheap labour force once again, for a while. It can, and it almost certainly will, invest heavily in the search for new sources of energy, nuclear and other, and such a massive investment programme might well open up

yet another phase of rapid development. Its immediate weaknesses are a combination of the economic and the political, and its vulnerability lies in this combination and not in the insolubility of any specific economic difficulties taken in isolation. Thus the reconstruction of the international monetary system has so far been prevented—and this is for at least four years—essentially by political frictions between the US and the European countries, with the socialist countries and the Third World countries intervening, since they also have their interests in this matter. The USA is no longer in the position it was at the end of the war to impose its own solution.

No one is able to impose a solution in a situation of tension between rival groups. We may take it that even if the control of inflation by unemployment were technically possible, which, as I have suggested, is not certain, a return to mass unemployment on the inter-war scale is simply politically *not* on, both because governments in industrial countries fear the political consequence, and because the strength of organised labour movements in several of these countries makes such a course extremely difficult, if not impossible. If mass unemployment occurs again, it will not be the result of policy but of the breakdown of policy. The decline of the USA which has led to more freedom of action in smaller countries combined with the general atmosphere of uneasiness and fear—not least in the USA—has once again led to a much more explosive or potentially explosive international situation, from which once again major international conflicts may spring. The Vietnam War was terrible, but nobody seriously expected that it would widen into a world conflagration for more than the occasional moment. On the other hand, the Middle Eastern situation, particularly today and particularly in the last two years, is one which might well become a world crisis, into which the powers might quite well be drawn and from which they might not be able to escape. In this sense, once again, a period of economic difficulties and a period of political and international tensions combine and coincide.

. . .

How shall I end this historic survey? Marx showed that the basic contradiction of the system was between the social nature of production and private appropriation. Capitalism got as far as it could by uncontrolled private enterprise until, say, the end of the 19th century. Thereafter it entered a severe crisis. It emerged from this only by turning itself into a managed, monopolist, state capitalism, i.e., by involving as much social organisation as was compatible with it in the system, and by eliminating a large amount of the element of competition and of the market economy. Yet the contradiction remained. It remains within countries and, above all, on a global scale. It is clearly not impossible for capitalism to go yet further along the road of social organisation and planning of production, but while it remains capitalism there must be limits for this process, though at present it would be unwise to make a firm statement about what these limits are. The main strength of the system has evidently lain in the impressive viability and stability and, above all, the powers of recovery of a hard core of the old industrialised economies, Western and Central Europe, the USA and Japan. Let us not under-rate the blows that some of them have suffered; wars, slumps and so on, and from which they have so far recovered with one or two exceptions. . . . Its main weakness . . . has lain both in the peripheral countries, such as Tsarist Russia once was, and in its relation with the underdeveloped world. However, such breakaways from world capitalism, as there have been, have not so far destroyed the general dominance on a world scale of the capitalist economy. Its main vulnerability has lain in the combination of economic difficulties with internal and international political conflicts. All of these have tended, and perhaps increasingly tended, to combine during the periodic down-swings of the alternating long waves, and at the turning points between these long-term periods, which I sketched at the beginning of this [essay].

12.2 *Sources of Cyclical Downturns and Inflation*

We turn now from the discussion of long-term periods of boom and crisis to an analysis of the short-run cyclical behavior of a capitalist economy. Cyclical fluctuations in economic activity characterize periods of boom as well as crisis in capitalist societies, but the most severe cyclical downturns tend to occur during periods of crisis. Thus the crisis of the 1970s has included the worst downturn since the Great Depression of the 1930s; it has also involved an unusually rapid and persistent inflation.

To contribute to an understanding of this latest crisis, Thomas E. Weisskopf provides in the following reading a general theoretical framework within which to analyze cyclical downturns and inflation. Weisskopf's essay also suggests explanations for the cyclical and inflationary behavior of the U.S. economy since the late nineteenth century. Some of the issues raised in this reading are treated in greater detail in the next two readings, which focus on developments in the U.S. economy since World War II.

I. INTRODUCTION

Wherever it has occurred, capitalist economic growth has been marked by short-run cyclical fluctuations in economic activity around a long-run upward trend line. Periods of rapid expansion are followed by periods of contraction, which in turn give way to new bursts of expansion that carry the economy beyond its previous peak.

The most useful single indicator of overall economic activity in a capitalist economy is the gross national product (GNP). GNP is a measure of the *actual* output of the economy; in analyzing economic downturns it is important to distinguish this from the *potential* output. The potential output is the level of GNP that could be reached with reasonably full utilization of the available productive resources. Potential output increases more or less continuously over time as the size of the labor force grows, as more and better equipment is used in production, as improved techniques of production are applied, etc. Actual output, on the other hand, is subject to cyclical upward and downward movements that bring it alternately closer to and farther from the rising level of potential output.

An economic downturn occurs, by definition, whenever the GNP of an economy declines after having risen for a period of time.[1] Since potential output is always rising, such a downturn necessarily involves a growing gap between actual and potential output. This implies that productive resources in the economy—labor, machinery, raw materials, etc.—are underutilized. Periodic downturns are thus a major source of waste in capitalist societies, distinct from and additional to the waste embodied in the production that does take place.[2]

But the most significant consequence of capitalist economic downturns, from a human point of view, is that many workers suffer all the hardships associated with unemployment. For in a capitalist society there is no arrangement for sharing the available job opportunities among those people who have been employed, nor is there any arrangement for providing additional job opportunities to all the people who want to work.[3] Thus, as the gap between actual and potential output gets larger, there will be more idle productive capacity and a higher rate of unemployment.[4]

Figure 12-A provides a visual impression of cyclical fluctuations in the U.S. economy from 1890 to 1975. The upper half of the figure charts the ratio of actual to potential output, and the lower half charts the rate of unemployment. Figure 12-A is based on U.S. government estimates of unemployment which seriously understate its true magnitude, because they ignore people who have given up looking for work and they count part-time workers as fully employed even if they want but cannot get full-time work.[5] However, the

---

[1]When discussing changes in output levels in this essay I will always refer to "real" values of output—i.e., values measured in constant prices so as to avoid including changes due to price changes rather than output changes.

[2]See Chapter 11 for an analysis of the waste involved in capitalist production.

[3]The idea that the government should directly guarantee everybody a job has been raised in some capitalist societies, usually in the form of a political demand by working people. But such proposals have invariably been rejected—or greatly watered down—because of their essential incompatibility with the operation of a capitalist economy.

[4]Just how great a gap between actual and potential output, or how high a rate of unemployment, is necessary to describe an economic downturn as a "depression" is somewhat arbitrary. Any shortfall of actual below potential output, or any level of unemployment above a minimum reflecting simply people's transition to new jobs, involves waste and hardship that a rational and humane society would avoid. But downturns that last for a relatively short time (one or two years) and that involve only moderate increases in the rate of unemployment (a few percentage points) are usually characterized by the milder term, "recession." The term "depression" is applied to downturns that last somewhat longer and that involve more sharply increasing rates of unemployment.

[5]Correcting for such factors ignored by the U.S. government estimates of unemployment, the true unemployment rate has been estimated at more than twice the official rate in recent years. For details, see "What's the Real Unemployment Rate?", *Dollars and Sense* (November 1974), pp. 12–13.

official figures do provide an adequate indication of changes in employment conditions over time. Both indicators in Figure 12-A display a continuous pattern of ups and downs; the negative correlation between the two is very strong, since the rate of unemployment measures the rate at which the major productive resource—labor—is not utilized.

The most severe economic downturn since 1890 was clearly the "Great Depression" of the 1930s, during which the official rate of unemployment reached roughly 25 percent. Other major downturns occurred in the 1890s and, briefly, in the early 1920s. Since World War II there have been a series of minor recessions, but not until the mid-1970s did another major downturn develop. This recent downturn led to unemployment rates unmatched since the recovery from the Great Depression.

In addition to cyclical fluctuations in the rate of overall economic activity, capitalist economic growth is marked by varying trends in the average level of prices. Figure 12-B shows how prices have changed in the United States from 1890 to 1975. The lower part of the figure traces an index of the general price level, and the upper part shows the corresponding annual rate of price inflation. Since the turn of the century the long-term trend of prices has been decidedly upward. But the rate of inflation has varied greatly from one period so another, producing a cyclical pattern somewhat akin to the pattern of overall economic activity.

A comparison of Figures 12-A and 12-B suggests a strong negative correlation between the annual rate of inflation and the corresponding rate of unemployment: this relationship is often termed the "Phillips Curve." But there are some exceptions to this rule, most noticeably within the last decade. Virtually every previous rise in the rate of unemployment had been associated with a fall in the rate of inflation. But between 1969 and 1975 the unemployment rate rose sharply while the rate of inflation accelerated to heights unmatched since the 1940s. This combination of unemployment and inflation constitutes the "stagflation" that has been unique to the economic crisis of the 1970s.

When an economic downturn occurs, it is obvious that there is a loss to the economy as a whole and a much more significant loss to certain groups of people. The economy as a whole loses to the extent that potentially producible output is not actually produced; many workers suffer because they are thrown out of work. When inflation occurs, it is somewhat harder to determine the consequences. Inflation need not cause any loss to the economy as a whole, for price rises help sellers at the same time they hurt buyers. But rapid inflation can hurt the performance of the economy by reducing exports to foreign countries with slower rates of inflation; and changing rates of inflation have adverse economic effects by creating new uncertainties for capitalists and by disrupting regular patterns of economic activity. It is difficult to determine which classes within a capitalist society have the most to lose by inflation, for much depends on the particular context in which the inflation occurs. But one can say that in any period of change and uncertainty it is likely to be the poorest and politically weakest groups that are least able to defend their economic position or to take advantage of the situation.

In the remainder of this essay I will seek to analyze the sources of cyclical downturns and inflation in the U.S. economy. Section II is devoted to downturns, and section III is devoted to inflation.

II. CYCLICAL DOWNTURNS

During the course of economic growth in the United States, periods of rapidly expanding output and high employment have always been followed by periods of declining output and growing unemployment. Why is it that a capitalist economy cannot sustain full use of its productive capacity and maintain full employment? Why must periods of economic prosperity inevitably be followed by periods of economic stagnation?

Figure 12-A Changes in output and employment in the U.S., 1890–1975

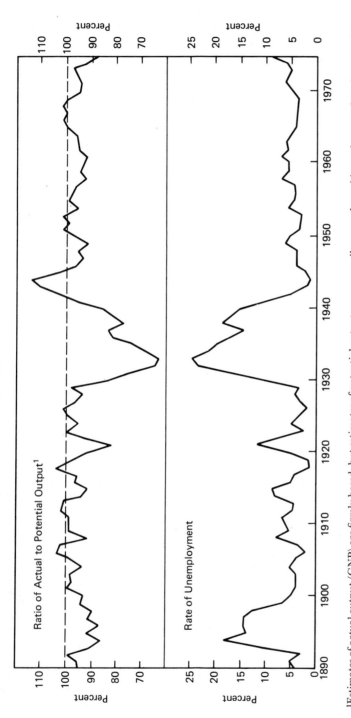

[1]Estimates of actual output (GNP) are firmly based, but estimates of potential output are necessarily somewhat arbitrary because there is no precise way to determine "the level of GNP that could be reached with reasonably full utilization of the available productive resources" (as potential output was defined on p. 442). Normally actual output must be less than or equal to potential output, but it may temporarily be greater if the labor force and the existing productive capacity are utilized more intensively than usual (e.g., during World War II).

SOURCES: The data on which Figure 12-A is based were drawn from the following three sources: U.S. Department of Commerce, *Long Term Economic Growth, 1860–1970* (Washington, D.C.: U.S. Government Printing Office, 1973), hereinafter referred to as *LTEG*; and the *Economic Report of the President*, 1975 and 1976, hereinafter referred to as *ERP-75* and *ERP-76*.

Annual data on actual output (GNP) in 1958 dollars were obtained for the years 1909–1968 from *LTEG*, Series A-2; figures for 1890–1909 from *LTEG*, Series A-1, were linked at 1909 to the series used for the subsequent years; figures for 1969–1972 were obtained directly from *ERP-75*, Table C-2; and figures for 1972–1975 (in 1972 dollars) from *ERP-76*, Table B-2, were linked at 1972 to the series used for the preceding years.

Annual estimates of potential output in 1958 dollars were obtained for the years 1952–1970 from *LTEG*, Series A-5; figures for 1909–1952 (in 1954 dollars) from *LTEG*, series A-4, were linked at 1952 to the series used for the subsequent years; and it was assumed (on the basis of comparative figures for GNP in years with similar rates of unemployment) that potential output increased at an annual rate of 3 percent from 1905 to 1909 and 4 percent from 1890 to 1905 and from 1970 to 1975.

Annual data on the rate of unemployment for the period 1890–1928 were obtained from *LTEG*, Series B-1; for the period 1929–1970 from *LTEG*, Series B-2; and for the period 1971–1975 from *ERP-76*, Table B-22.

Figure 12-B Changes in prices in the U.S., 1890–1975

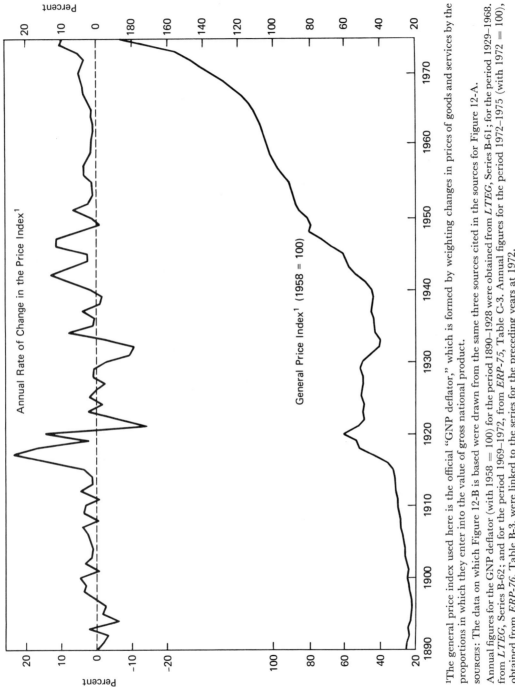

¹The general price index used here is the official "GNP deflator," which is formed by weighting changes in prices of goods and services by the proportions in which they enter into the value of gross national product.

SOURCES: The data on which Figure 12-B is based were drawn from the same three sources cited in the sources for Figure 12-A.

Annual figures for the GNP deflator (with 1958 = 100) for the period 1890–1928 were obtained from *LTEG*, Series B-61; for the period 1929–1968. from *LTEG*, Series B-62; and for the period 1969–1972, from *ERP-75*, Table C-3. Annual figures for the period 1972–1975 (with 1972 = 100), obtained from *ERP-76*, Table B-3, were linked to the series for the preceding years at 1972.

The annual rate of change in the GNP deflator was calculated directly from the series itself (with 1958 = 100), obtained as described above.

The answer has been succinctly summarized by Roger Alcaly:

> *In the most basic sense, crises can be said to dominate the dynamics of capitalist development because capitalism is a system of production for profit rather than production for use. This means, of course, that anything which endangers profits will eventually lead to cutbacks in production and rising unemployment—in short, to economic crises. Thus, the formal possibility of crises which exists in any economic system in which the acts of purchase and sale are not identical and hence are capable of rupture is vastly enhanced under capitalism where production will only take place if it expands the value of capital.[6]*

The crucial point is that in a capitalist economy most production is organized and most jobs are made available by private capitalists, who will choose to set the process in motion if and only if they expect it to be sufficiently profitable. When profits are expected to be high, capitalists will be encouraged to produce at full capacity and to invest in expanding their productive capacity, thereby creating more jobs. When the outlook for profits is gloomy, capitalists will cut back on their production and investment plans and thereby reduce the number of available jobs.

To say that the cyclical behavior of a capitalist economy is attributable to a cyclical pattern in the expectations of capitalists is not to advance a purely psychological theory of the process. Although there are no doubt some subjective psychological elements at work, the profit expectations of capitalists are grounded in what is objectively happening to the economy in general and to profit rates in particular. Capitalists put much effort into assessing the profitability of alternative activities (in the form of market research, cost

studies, etc.); when they nonetheless turn out to be wrong in their anticipations, they will soon find out and act accordingly. Thus to understand the reasons for the periodic contractions of a capitalist economy, we must investigate the forces that periodically cause a fall in the average rate of profit in the economy as a whole.

Broadly speaking, there are two potential sources of declining profitability for an individual capitalist: *inadequate demand* and *rising costs*. First, if the demand for the output of a given industry (at currently prevailing prices) fails to rise as rapidly as the supply, the firms in that industry will find it impossible to sell all their output without lowering prices; they will then suffer reductions in realized profits on account of unsold output and/or output sold at reduced prices. Second, even if the demand for the output of an industry is sufficient to permit individual firms to sell all of their output at the prevailing prices, the firms's profits may be squeezed if they face rising costs of production which cannot simply be passed on to consumers (in the form of higher prices) without undermining the demand for the output.

For either of these sources of declining profitability to affect the economy as a whole, they must be sufficiently widespread to affect simultaneously a large number of industries, and they must not be offset by sources of rising profitability elsewhere in the economy. Inadequate demand for the output of the economy as a whole arises, by definition, when aggregate demand falls short of potential output.[7] Rising costs of production occur simultaneously for large numbers of firms when the price of a commonly used input goes up (without any corresponding increase in the output obtained from it). The most significant input in this context is labor power itself —both because labor accounts for a substantial share of production costs in most

---

[6]Roger Alcaly, "Capitalism, Crises and the Current Economic Situation," in the Union for Radical Political Economics, *Radical Perspectives on the Economic Crisis of Monopoly Capitalism* (New York: Union for Radical Political Economics, 1975), p. 120. Alcaly uses the term "economic crisis" synonymously with "economic downturn."

[7]See Weisskopf, Section 11.1, Part III, p. 399, for a detailed discussion of the sources of aggregate demand and its relationship to potential output in a capitalist economy.

industries, and because an increase in labor cost per unit of output, unlike an increase in the cost of any other input, involves a net loss to the capitalist class as a whole.[8] In the case of nonlabor inputs, a rise in price means higher costs for the input-using industries, but this is generally offset by correspondingly higher profits for the input-supplying industries. Thus, in considering declining profitability due to rising costs, I will focus primarily on the "*wage* squeeze on profits."

A useful starting point for analyzing the periodic economic downturns that have characterized capitalist economies is the theory of "underconsumption."[9] This theory emphasizes inadequate aggregate demand as the main source of the declining profitability that precipitates downturns. The essential tenet of underconsumption theory is that there is a secular (i.e., long-run) tendency for aggregate demand to fall short of potential output in a capitalist economy. This tendency results from the inequality of income inherent in capitalism, which concentrates a large fraction of total purchasing power in the hands of people (e.g., capitalists) who use only a fraction of it for their own consumption purposes and who save the rest of it.

To maintain a level of aggregate demand equal to potential output, it is necessary to find nonconsumption sources of demand suf-

ficient to offset the level of saving that occurs when the potential output is actually produced. The prime source of nonconsumption demand is investment demand. But investment demand itself is ultimately dependent on the growth of consumption demand, since investment increases the capacity to produce commodities that must be sold on the market. Given the limits on consumption demand inherent in a capitalist economy, it is questionable whether the investment demand of private capitalists will be high enough to sustain a level of aggregate demand equal to potential output. The problem is particularly acute in the stage of monopoly capitalism, because the incentive of monopolistic firms to invest is likely to be diminished by fear of spoiling the market.

This analysis leads to the expectation that the normal state of a capitalist economy is one in which aggregate demand is below potential output, and that periods of prosperity must be explained by specific historical forces that serve to raise aggregate demand above its normal level. Such forces include far-reaching technological innovations (e.g., the railroad, or the automobile) that stimulate a new wave of investment activity, or wars that require a massive upsurge in military spending. These forces would periodically (although not regularly) raise the overall profitability of the economy and lead to booms in economic activity; downturns would result from the subsequent reversion to the normal condition of inadequate aggregate demand.

This underconsumption theory of the cyclical behavior of capitalist economies is reasonably consistent with the historical experience of the United States economy during the past century.[10] Periods of economic prosperity have generally coincided with surges of aggregate demand due to particular historical circumstances—e.g., the automobile boom in the 1920s, and the major wars in which the United States has been involved.

[8]The net loss to the capitalist class does not necessarily imply a corresponding gain for the working class, for the rise in labor cost per unit of output could result from a decline in worker productivity, or from an increase in employment taxes, as well as from an increase in wages actually taken home by workers.

[9]The theory of underconsumption represents one of three different approaches to the explanation of capitalist crises which have been developed by scholars working in the Marxist tradition. Roger Alcaly, in "Capitalism, Crises and the Current Economic Situation," provides a useful discussion of the three variants of Marxist crisis theory. For a more detailed exposition of underconsumption theory, see Paul Sweezy, *The Theory of Capitalist Development* (New York: Monthly Review Press, 1942), Chap. 10. The underconsumption approach is reflected also in Paul Baran and Paul Sweezy, *Monopoly Capital* (New York: Monthly Review Press, 1966).

[10]For a discussion of the empirical evidence on this point, see Baran and Sweezy, *Monopoly Capital*, Chap. 8.

Periods of stagnation have been marked by the absence of major innovations or wars.

World War II marks a significant turning point in the analysis of underconsumption tendencies in the United States, as in other advanced capitalist economies. For since then the working classes have become much stronger in their demands on the capitalist state to promote full employment, and the ruling authorities have learned how government policy can be used to generate some of the nonconsumption demand needed to balance private saving and avoid large shortfalls in aggregate demand. In all of the advanced capitalist nations government purchases of goods and services have become a major source of aggregate demand, and capitalist governments have used Keynesian fiscal and monetary policies to gain some control over the level of aggregate demand. The fact that the postwar period has not witnessed a downturn on the scale of the Great Depression may be attributed in considerable part to the conscious use of Keynesian policies by capitalist governments determined to avoid the seriously adverse political and economic consequences of mass unemployment while preserving the basic (unequal) framework of a capitalist society.

Yet cyclical economic downturns have persisted in the United States since World War II, albeit on a smaller scale than in the past. These downturns cannot be explained by means of an underconsumption theory alone, for the U.S. government has had the capacity to maintain aggregate demand at a level high enough to sustain reasonably full utilization of productive capacity and full employment. To explain postwar cycles it is therefore necessary (1) to identify sources of periodically declining profitability which are not attributable solely to inadequate demand, and/or (2) to explain why a capitalist state may be unable or unwilling to maintain a consistently high level of aggregate demand.

At this point it is helpful to consider an alternative perspective on capitalist downturns that focuses on the second source of declining profits mentioned earlier: the wage squeeze on profits.[11] This perspective places primary emphasis on changing conditions in the labor market during the process of economic growth. At the beginning of a period of expansion the "reserve army of the unemployed" is plentiful, labor's position is weak, and capitalists can make high profits. The favorable climate for profits encourages production and accumulation, and the economy grows rapidly. As capital accumulation takes place, more and more workers are drawn into active employment. Sooner or later the reserve army diminishes to the point at which it is difficult for capitalists to find additional workers to hire. This tightness in the labor market increases the bargaining power of labor vis-à-vis capital; it permits workers to bid up their money wages more successfully or to cut down on the intensity of their work effort with relatively little fear of being laid off. As long as labor productivity (output per worker) rises as fast as money wages, labor costs per unit of output will not rise and capitalists' profit margins will not be threatened. But an acceleration of wage increases and/or a slowdown in productivity increases will lead to higher unit labor costs and lower profit margins for capitalists.

To offset these higher costs, capitalists will want to raise their output prices. But unless there is a very buoyant demand for their products, capitalists will not be able to pass all of their rising costs on to consumers in the form of higher output prices without suffering a loss in sales. Firms involved in competition with foreign producers will clearly have to limit any increases in their output prices, for

[11]The theory of the periodic exhaustion of the reserve army of the unemployed, which leads to a wage squeeze on profits, represents another one of the three variants of Marxist crisis theory discussed by Roger Alcaly in "Capitalism, Crises and the Current Economic Situation." This general approach has been developed in great detail by Andrew Glyn and Bob Sutcliffe, *Capitalism in Crisis* (New York: Pantheon, 1972), in the context of the British economy, and by Raford Boddy and James Crotty, "Class Conflict and Macro-Policy: The Political Business Cycle," *Review of Radical Political Economics*, Vol. VII, No. 1 (Spring 1975), in the context of the U.S. economy.

their foreign competitors will not be under the same pressure to raise prices. The overall effect of the higher labor costs, then, is likely to be a combination of higher prices and lower profits. The fall in profitability results sooner or later in a contraction of business activity, which leads to a replenishment of the reserve army and a corresponding weakening of labor's position. This restores the basis for profitable activity by capitalists, and another expansion can begin.

The central point of this analysis is that in a normally functioning capitalist economy full employment is incompatible with private profit maximization. As full employment is approached it is a wage squeeze, not inadequate aggregate demand, that first begins to reduce profits and consequently causes a downturn in economic activity. Once the process begins, however, it is reflected in declining aggregate demand because businesses curtail their demand for investment goods (in the face of reduced profit expectations) and consumers may also curtail their demand for consumer goods (in the face of higher prices). In principle the government might be able to forestall the downturn by raising government demand sufficiently to offset the decline in private demand and to permit producers to pass on all of their rising labor costs in correspondingly higher output prices. Such a policy, however, would obviously have highly inflationary consequences and would soon lead to many related problems: business uncertainties, balance of payments deficits resulting from rising imports and falling exports, etc.

Thus, in a situation in which profits are squeezed on the cost side rather than the demand side, Keynesian techniques of aggregate demand management are inadequate to maintain prosperity. To reinvigorate the economy in the face of what amounts to a strike by capitalists, a government has few options. Unless it is willing and able to take over virtually the entire private sector and operate it on a less profitable basis, it must try to restore the basis for private profitability. The simplest way to do this is to acquiesce in

an economic downturn that performs the curative function of disciplining labor by throwing workers out of work.[12] Even though both workers (via unemployment) and capitalists (via reduced profits) suffer during the depth of the downturn itself, the downturn sets the stage for a highly profitable period of expansion in which workers' wages are lower than they would have been otherwise. Herein lies a critical reason why the capitalist state may not seek to avoid periodic downturns even if it has the capacity to do so.[13]

This analysis of the impact of a wage squeeze on profits is essential for understanding recent economic downturns in the United States. But capitalist business cycles are complex phenomena, and no single line of explanation is adequate to explain their persistence. The postwar cylical behavior of the U.S. economy can be better understood by integrating the wage squeeze on profits into

[12]This is not to argue that a capitalist state will always support a downturn after a period of expansion, for at some times there may be other overriding state priorities that dictate an expansionary government budget. This is what happened in the late 1960s when the U.S. government chose to undertake massive new military expenditures to defend the U.S. empire in Vietnam rather than to encourage a developing contraction in the economy (See Crotty and Rapping, Section 12.4, pp. 465–466, for details). At other times the state may prefer to adopt alternative means of disciplining labor—e.g., encouraging an inflow of immigrant workers, or establishing a system of direct wage controls—rather than accepting or promoting a cyclical downturn. The Nixon administration's "New Economic Policy" in 1971 involved an effort to use direct controls on wages, rather than an economic downturn, to discipline labor (See Crotty and Rapping, Section 12.4, p. 467.)

[13]The argument that profit maximization is incompatible with sustained full employment does not, by itself, imply that periodic downturns are profit-maximizing. Why should not the state, in the interest of the capitalist class, seek to maintain a more or less steady rate of unemployment that would keep the reserve army plentiful enough to discipline labor? The best answer to this question is provided by Raford Boddy and James Crotty, "Class Conflict, Keynesian Policy and the Business Cycle," *Monthly Review*, 26, No. 5 (October 1974), 10: because "the *rate of change* of unemployment, as well as the *level and duration* of unemployment, is a fundamental determinant of labor confidence and militancy."

an analysis that takes into account also what is happening to aggregate demand. Moreover, such an analysis must include consideration of the role of the banking system as well as international economic relations.

During the early phase of all expansions aggregate demand is generally buoyant; but after a period of time a situation of inadequate demand tends to develop. This inadequate demand serves to reinforce the adverse effect of a wage squeeze on profits in the latter phase of an expansion. The cyclical behavior of aggregate demand appears to be attributable in considerable part to the phenomenon of "overinvestment."

Overinvestment occurs when capitalists invest in the expansion of productive capacity to such an extent that total productive capacity exceeds the level of aggregate demand once the new capacity becomes operative. Rising rates of capacity utilization in the early phase of expansions followed by falling rates in the latter phase suggest that overinvestment (in the early phase) has been a typical feature of postwar booms in the United States.[14] There are several possible sources of overinvestment. On the one hand, it may be attributable to the favorable profit position of most businesses in the early phase of an expansion. On the other hand, it may be due to struggles among different firms in the same industry, each one seeking to expand its size and share of the market in order to improve its competitive position.[15]

In any event, investment has risen sharply in the early phase of postwar expansions with profits up, business confidence high, and banks quite willing to extend credit to allow firms to supplement their internal sources of finance with external borrowing. But once the new capacity becomes operative at a later stage in the upswing, many firms discover that they have overexpanded supply relative to the prevailing demand. Inventories begin to accumulate as sales are insufficient, and these firms have to lower their rate of capacity utilization in order not to produce too much. Thus a situation of excess supply/inadequate demand has developed in the latter phase of expansions, contributing to the erosion of profit margins. At the same time, the wage squeeze has operated on profits from the cost side. The fall in unemployment during the upswing eventually strengthens labor's bargaining position; increases in money wages lead to rising prices and to falling profits, and the distribution of income swings in favor of wages over profits in the latter part of the expansion.[16]

These imbalances on the demand and the cost side, which restrain profits after an initially buoyant upswing, have been exacerbated by concomitant developments in money markets and international trade. Excess capacity, higher prices, and declining profits lead to falling stock prices, greater need for external financing, and rising interest rates. Firms that borrowed heavily in the early phase of the expansion encounter increasingly onerous debt problems, and a general shortage of liquidity develops as the cost of loan repayment rises and internal sources of finance dry up. Furthermore, rapidly rising aggregate demand in the early phase of the expansion, and rising prices later on, lead to a much more rapid growth of imports than of exports. The resultant decline in net exports contributes to the weakening of demand for domestic output in the latter phase of the expansion, and the balance of payments comes under increasing pressure.

The natural effect of all these imbalances and strains that have developed during the

[14]See George L. Perry, "Capacity in Manufacturing," *Brookings Papers on Economic Activity*, 1973, No. 3, for evidence on cyclical fluctuations in the rate of capacity utilization in the U.S. economy.

[15]This theory of overinvestment, in which the competitive struggle forces a rate of capital accumulation so high as to cause a falling rate of profit, is related to the third variant of Marxist crisis theory discussed by Roger Alcaly in "Capitalism, Crises and the Current Economic Situation."

[16]See Raford Boddy and James Crotty, "Class Conflict and Macro-Policy: The Political Business Cycle," *Review of Radical Political Economics*, 7, No. 1 (Spring 1975) for data on the shift in the distribution of income between profits and wages over the course of postwar business cycles in the United States.

course of continuing expansions is to under-mine profits and turn the expansion into a downturn. The downturn serves an essential curative function for the economy by restor-ing the conditions necessary for a renewed expansion: lower labor costs, higher profits, price stability, improved liquidity, lower interest rates, an improved balance of trade, etc. Because the downturn plays such a func-tional role, there has been strong pressure not to try to oppose it with government fiscal and monetary policy. In fact, during the period since World War II the U.S. government has supported almost every naturally developing cyclical downturn with restrictive macro-policy after periods of expansion.[17] The restrictive macropolicy has generally been justified as an anti-inflationary measure, but its true purpose is to combat all of the imbal-ances discussed above (including inflation) which threaten the continued profitability of the accumulation process. Thus government policy-makers have sought not to eliminate the business cycle, but to guide it in the long-term interest of the capitalist class. In so do-ing, they have not allowed the downturns to assume anything like the scale of the Great Depression; for that would provoke so much social and economic turmoil as to threaten the foundations of the whole system.

In conclusion, it appears that in the con-temporary U.S. capitalist economy sustained full employment is incompatible with high rates of profit. It takes high profits to stimu-late the expansion of output and employment, but the expansion of output and employment sooner or later reduces profits. The result is a cyclical pattern of overall economic activity that favors long-run profits at the cost of periodic downturns and unemployment. Only a substantial change in the structure of the economy, involving an unprecedented degree of government control over employment, wages, and prices, could relieve the U.S. economy of its need for periodic downturns.

III. INFLATION

Inflationary pressures in a capitalist economy can be attributed to one of three general sources. "Demand-pull" inflation occurs when aggregate demand (at currently pre-vailing prices) exceeds the potential output of the economy. Under these circumstances, everyone's demand cannot be satisfied be-cause "too much money is chasing too few goods." Many producers will find more than enough demand for all they can produce; hence they will be able to raise their output prices and still sell all their output, and an inflationary surge will result. This source of inflation is simply the opposite of the situation of inadequate demand that leads to economic downturns. Just as conventional Keynesian wisdom calls for an expansionary macro-economic government policy to increase aggregate demand when an economic down-turn is imminent, so it calls for a deflationary policy to decrease aggregate demand when inflation begins to accelerate.

The second possible source of inflation is the pricing policy of powerful monopolistic corporations. Even in the absence of any excess aggregate demand, it is generally the case that there is excess demand for the output of certain industries and excess supply of the output of other industries. In a world of com-petitive capitalist producers, such imbalances would lead to price increases where there is excess demand and price decreases where there is excess supply. These differential price movements would offset one another and the overall price index would remain constant, as long as aggregate demand was not excessive. But in the contemporary monopoly stage of capitalism, in the United States and other advanced capitalist societies, most large cor-porations tend to resist market pressures to lower their prices.[18] As a consequence, prices are free to rise where demand is high but they generally do not fall where demand is low,

[17]See Boddy and Crotty, ibid., for more details; as noted above in footnote 12, the Vietnam War buildup in the late 1960s constitutes an exception to the general rule.

[18]See Chapter 4, and especially Baran and Sweezy, Section 4.3, p. 134, for an analysis of the pricing policy of large corporations that explains their resistance to price reductions.

and the end result is an upward trend in the overall price index. This type of inflation can be termed "profit-push" inflation, since it results from the tendency of powerful corporations to maintain their prices and profit margins even when market forces call for a reduction in prices.

The third source of inflation is rising costs, which may also occur whether or not there is any excess aggregate demand. "Cost-push" inflation can result either from a general rise in labor costs or from a rise in the cost of some significant material inputs. Labor costs (per unit of output) rise when money wage rates increase more rapidly than the corresponding increases in worker productivity. This kind of cost push is precisely the source of the wage squeeze on profits discussed earlier; it will tend to occur when labor's bargaining position is relatively strong. The other kind of cost push, attributable to rising material costs, may simply reflect profit-push or wage-cost-push inflation in the input-supplying industries. But there is also a potentially important independent source of rising material costs in the acquisition of primary raw materials. The real cost of certain raw materials may rise because of an increasing global scarcity of the relevant natural resources, or because of poor harvests due to temporary or permanent climatic deterioration. And the real cost of certain raw materials to a particular economy may rise because changing political and economic conditions result in less favorable access to foreign sources of the materials than in the past.

Whatever the source of the cost push, it gets translated into general inflation only to the extent that producers protect their profit margins and pass on the cost increases to consumers in the form of higher output prices. In other words, the cost push can result in either lower profits or higher prices; it is most likely to result in some of each. The lower the level of aggregate demand, the more difficult it will be for producers to raise prices and the more likely it will be that the cost push cuts into profits. Conversely, the higher the level of aggregate demand, the more likely it will

be that prices go up. Thus, various sources of inflation—like different sources of economic downturns—tend in practice to be intertwined and therefore difficult to distinguish clearly.

Irrespective of its origin, once an inflationary surge continues for a period of time it becomes increasingly difficult to arrest it. This is because an "inflationary psychology" emerges as everyone comes to expect continuously increasing prices. Labor unions negotiate contracts with "escalator clauses" tying future wage increases to rises in the cost of living; capitalists seek to protect their profit margins by raising prices more rapidly; and so on. The state comes under considerable pressure to accommodate the rise in prices by pursuing "easy money" policies that allow for an expansion of the money supply and a growth of the credit system sufficiently rapid to prevent interest rates from rising to prohibitive levels.

In principle, any capitalist government can prevent an inflationary surge—whatever its source—from getting out of hand by adopting a strongly deflationary macroeconomic policy. By cutting down its purchases and/or increasing taxes, and by slowing down the growth of the money supply and causing interest rates to rise, the government can eliminate any demand-pull pressures and make it difficult for businesses to sell all their output if they engage in profit-pushing or seek to pass on a cost push. But in practice there are several possible obstacles to the pursuit of such a deflationary policy for a sufficiently long time to harness an inflation. First of all, it is bound to cause an economic downturn and a rise in unemployment; this may not always be politically feasible for the ruling authorities. Second, if it comes after a period of growing indebtedness, a deflationary policy could bankrupt major corporations and banking institutions and cause severe economic dislocations. Finally, even when a government is trying to carry out a deflationary domestic macropolicy its efforts may be thwarted by international money movements; for example, rising interest rates accompanying a tight money policy may well attract short-term capital inflows from abroad which serve to expand credit and offset to a large extent the restraint on the domestic money supply.

Turning now to an examination of the sources of inflation in the United States since the turn of the century, we can see in Figure 12-B that there were five periods in which an inflationary surge reached an annual rate of 10 percent or more. The first four of these periods of rapid inflation (1915–18, 1919–20, 1940–43, and 1945–48) were periods in which the rate of unemployment was either sharply falling or relatively low. These inflationary periods can be explained primarily in terms of demand-pull forces: the first and third periods involved sudden step-ups of military spending associated with World Wars I and II, while the second and fourth periods involved surges of private consumer demand that had been pent-up during wartime. Up until the late 1960s even the milder surges of inflation were almost always coincident with falling or relatively low rates of unemployment, which lends further support to the relevance of the demand-pull explanation. And the only two periods in which the price level declined significantly (1920–22 and 1929–33) were periods of rapidly rising and/or unusually high rates of unemployment.

When-we approach the last of the periods of rapid inflation (1973–75), we encounter an entirely new situation. From 1969 to 1975 the overall trend of the unemployment rate was upward, especially after 1973. Yet throughout this period the price level continued to mount, at a rate of roughly 5 percent from 1969 to 1973 and 10 percent from 1973 to 1975. To explain this most recent inflationary surge a simple demand-pull analysis is clearly inappropriate. The inflation of the 1970s is no doubt largely attributable to some combination of cost-push and profit-push forces, sufficiently strong to produce rapidly rising prices in spite of sluggish aggregate demand and a rising rate of unemployment.

Popular explanations of the recent inflation have placed great emphasis on certain unusual and apparently random events in the early 1970s, all of which increased the cost of significant inputs into the U.S. economy. These events include the organization of the oil-exporting nations, which brought about a fourfold increase in the price of imported oil; poor harvests around the world, which helped to push up the prices of agricultural products; and the devaluation of the dollar, which increased the price of all imported commodities. Each of these events did contribute to the severity of the inflation in the 1970s, but it is a mistake to conclude that the whole thing was simply a matter of bad luck.

In the first place, these apparently unpredictable events had much to do with the decline of U.S. hegemony in the world capitalist system which manifested itself increasingly from the mid-1960s on.[19] Weakened in its relationship to the third world, the United States in the early 1970s was in no position to resist the exercise of joint monopoly power by the oil-exporting nations. And weakened in economic competition with other advanced capitalist nations, the U.S. government was obliged to devalue the dollar and to promote an agricultural export drive; this exacerbated the rise in domestic food prices by limiting the supply of agricultural commodities available to U.S. consumers.[20]

Secondly, the inflationary trend was already established by the late 1960s—well before the above events took place. In part the upward trend of prices that developed in the late 1960s may be attributed to the economic stimulus provided by the inflationary financing of Vietnam War expenditures from 1966 to 1968. (The magnitude of the war itself was another reflection of declining U.S. hegemony). But prices continued to rise fairly rapidly during the period of contraction that began in 1969. Rather than emphasizing only exogenous forces that have

[19]The decline in U.S. hegemony is discussed in detail in MacEwan, Section 12.3, p. 455.

[20]The sources and consequences of the U.S. agricultural export drive are analyzed in Raford Boddy and James Crotty, "Food Prices: Planned Crisis in Defense of Empire," *Socialist Revolution*, 5, No. 1 (March 1975).

impinged on the U.S. economy, it is important to recognize that the inflationary surge
of recent times has resulted to a significant
extent from endogenous forces generated by
the development of modern capitalism itself.

Since the turmoil of the Great Depression,
the ruling authorities in advanced capitalist
nations have been determined not to risk the
danger of mass unemployment again. But the
very success with which they have applied
Keynesian   macroeconomic   stabilization
policies in the postwar period has imparted a
significant new inflationary bias into virtually
all the capitalist economies. Precisely because
capitalist governments have become more
committed and able to prevent major economic downturns such as the Great Depression, they have inhibited the operation of
traditional   anti-inflationary   mechanisms.
Knowing that the government is committed
to sustaining high long-run levels of aggregate demand, businesses are under much less
pressure to reduce prices (or to hold back
price increases) when demand falls off in the
short run. Similarly, knowing that the government cannot afford to allow the unemployment rate to go too high, labor unions are
under less pressure to moderate their wage
demands. As a result, both profit-push and
wage-cost-push inflation have been growing
in intensity, and they manifested themselves
strongly in the United States by the late
1960s.

The political commitment of capitalist
governments to avoid high rates of unemployment may also contribute to the persistence
of inflation insofar as deficit spending is used
to mitigate the normal cyclical contractions
of the economy. For deficit spending requires
increased government borrowing; and if the
increased public spending is not to be offset
by reduced private spending, the government
will have to step up the rate of increase of the
money supply and to encourage a general
expansion of the whole system of credit and
debt. But the more such a process continues
to advance, the more vulnerable businesses,
banks, and consumers become to any contraction in the supply of credit and in the

economy as a whole. In order to avoid a
series of financial disasters, the government
comes under great pressure to inject more and
more credit into the system and thereby keep
the inflationary spiral going. Thus the growth
of total debt in the economy becomes itself
a major obstacle to the restraint of inflation.

Such a process was clearly at work in the
U.S. economy from the mid-1960s to the
mid-1970s.[21] Beginning with the financing of
the Vietnam War in the late 1960s, the U.S.
government resorted increasingly to deficit
spending and the U.S. credit structure became increasingly bloated as the government
refused to allow any downturn to take its full
and natural course. In doing so, however, it
was only postponing the day of reckoning:
sooner or later the inflation had to be brought
under control or the viability of the whole
economy would be threatened.

The Keynesian strategy of macroeconomic
stabilization is thus a contradictory one.[22] It
can work for a certain period of time, but
eventually it generates an accelerating rate of
inflation which increases the need for an
economic downturn to restore the basis for
profitable private capital accumulation. In
1971 the Nixon administration introduced a
"new economic policy" which sought to
avoid this contradiction by using wage and
price controls to hold down the rate of inflation while simultaneously encouraging the
economy to expand. By 1973, however, it
became clear that this approach could not
work without much greater government control over the private sector of economy than
the administration was willing to consider.
After more than a decade in which only a
minor contraction had been allowed to occur
(in 1969–71), the U.S. economy sorely needed
a major downturn to curb the rampant
inflation, to discipline labor, to restructure
the overextended credit system, and in

[21]For details, see the editorial, "Keynesian Chickens
Come Home to Roost," in the *Monthly Review*, 25, No.
11 (April 1974).

[22]The contradictory character of the Keynesian strategy
is forcefully elucidated in Jacob Morris, "The Crisis of
Inflation," *Monthly Review*, 25, No. 4 (September 1973).

general to correct all of the imbalances that inhibited the renewal of a profitable process of expansion.

The economic downturn did finally come about in 1974–75, with the support of the U.S. government. The severity of the downturn, in comparison with earlier postwar cycles, is attributable to the long period of government resistance to contraction that preceded it and the consequent accumulation of imbalances in the economy. Yet even though the rate of unemployment soared to heights unprecedented in the postwar period, the rate of inflation remained very high throughout the downturn. The continuation of inflation under these circumstances—the stagflation of the mid-1970s—is due to the enormous buildup of inflationary pressures during the previous decade.

Although the rate of inflation did eventually begin to slow down in the wake of the downturn, it remains very questionable whether the downturn was deep enough and long enough to perform fully its restorative function. Popular resistance to high unemployment forced the U.S. government to shift gears in 1975 from an anti-inflationary to an anti-recessionary policy. As the U.S. economy begins to regain its expansionary momentum in the late 1970s, there is every likelihood that strong inflationary pressures will again develop—long before anything close to full employment is reached. For the underlying source of inflation remains in effect: the contradictory Keynesian strategy of stabilization, which encourages both wages and profits to push up prices in a continuing inflationary spiral. Sooner or later the United States will again face a choice between accelerating inflation, another economic downturn, or a significant change in the structure of the economy.[23]

[23]See the concluding part of the essay by Crotty and Rapping, Section 12.4, pp. 467–469, for a more thorough discussion of future options for the U.S. economy.

12.3 *World Capitalism and the Crisis of the 1970s*

In this chapter we have mentioned three internal contradictions which helped to turn the postwar period of capitalist expansion into the crisis of the 1970s. These are: (1) the decline of U.S. hegemony and the rise of rivalries among the major capitalist powers; (2) the increasing difficulty of controlling simultaneously unemployment and inflation; and (3) the growing economic power of some of the resource-rich third-world nations.

We examined the second of these contradictions in the context of the U.S. economy in the previous reading. We consider the impact of the first and third of the contradictions on the U.S. economy in the following reading, as Arthur MacEwan reviews the international dimensions of the prosperity of the 1950s and 1960s and the crisis of the 1970s.

The following is excerpted from "Changes in World Capitalism and the Current Crisis of the U.S. Economy" by ARTHUR MACEWAN. From *Radical America*, Vol. 9, No. 1, Jan.–Feb. 1975 (P.O. Box B, N. Cambridge, MA 02140). Reprinted with minor revisions by permission of Arthur MacEwan and *Radical America*.

The period since World War II has been characterized by a continuous increase in the integration of the world capitalist system. However, throughout the period, forces have been building towards the destruction of the stability of that system. By the beginning of the 1970's, those forces had come into their own, and the basis for stability—U.S. hegemony—had been eliminated.

The simultaneous *integration* and *destabilization* of the world capitalist system constitutes an important contradiction that has far-reaching implications. In particular, the operation of this contradiction has put the U.S. economy of the 1970's in a precarious position.

In this essay, I intend to describe some central features of the operation of world capitalism during the post–World War II period and to explain how the very success of those years was creating the conditions for the disruption of the system. I will then be in a position to relate the current crisis of the U.S. economy to the important changes in world capitalism and show how international affairs have played a central role in the development, precipitation and continuation of the crisis.

CREATION OF U.S. HEGEMONY

At the end of World War II, the United States was in a particularly fortunate position. While the economies of the other advanced nations—victors and vanquished alike—had been devastated by the war, the U.S. economy had flourished. Consequently, in 1945, the U.S. held a position of unique and unchallenged political-military and economic power among capitalist nations.

An era of U.S. hegemony had begun. The U.S. government was able to dictate economic and political policies within the world capitalist system.[1] Accordingly, it was possible to reestablish an international order which had been lacking for over half a century—

since the time when other nations had begun to seriously challenge Britain's pre-eminence.

The new era of U.S. hegemony expressed itself in several new institutional arrangements. Most frequently noted are the set of monetary arrangements imposed on the other capitalist nations in 1944 at the Bretton Woods Conference. In the earlier periods of colonial expansion, each colonial power had imposed its currency—pound, franc, mark—within its empire. Now, after World War II, the U.S. established the dollar as the principal reserve currency throughout the capitalist world.

The role of the dollar was closely connected to the rapid international growth of U.S. business. The expansion of U.S. banking abroad highlights the general picture. In Europe, for example, U.S. banks had only 20 to 30 branches in the 1920's, and during the 1930's and the War most of these were closed down. The 1950's and the 1960's saw a steady advance to the point where by 1968 U.S. banks had 326 branches in Europe.[2]

The largest industrial corporations were central actors in the post-War overseas expansion. In 1950 General Motors was annually producing less than 200,000 vehicles abroad. By 1952 it had expanded production to approximately 600,000 units. In another year, with European production being supplemented by Australian and Brazilian expansion, GM was producing over one million vehicles in its foreign plants. And the boom continued on into the 1960's: between 1963 and 1964 GM's overseas production grew by a quarter of a million.[3]

Aggregate data show the same general picture of rapid growth of U.S. foreign investment in the 1950's and 1960's. The value of all U.S. direct investment abroad stood at roughly $11 billion in 1950; by 1960 the total

---

[1]The ability of the U.S. government to dictate was, of course, limited in the ways that the power of any dictator is limited. A dictator must compromise sometimes, must cajole reluctant followers, and must smash rebellions. But as long as he is successful in maintaining the foundation of his power, the dictator remains a dictator.

[2]See J. P. Koszul, "American Banks in Europe," in C. P. Kindleberger, ed., *The International Corporation* (Cambridge, Mass.: MIT Press, 1970), pp. 274–75.

[3]See J. W. Sundelson, "U.S. Automotive Investment Abroad," in C. P. Kindleberger, ed., *The International Corporation*, p. 256.

had risen to over $30 billion; and in 1970 the figure was over $70 billion.[4]

The absolute growth of U.S. business interests abroad is impressive, but it should be seen in the context of the establishment of overwhelming U.S. dominance in the international capitalist economy. In Latin America, for example, just prior to World War I, only 18% of foreign private investment and less than 5% of public debt was held by U.S. interests. British interests held 47% of private investment and 70% of public debt. In the early 1950's, direct investment in Latin America from sources other than the U.S. was negligible, and in the early 1960's the U.S. still accounted for roughly 70% of new foreign investment in Latin America. As to foreign public debt, the U.S. was supplying about 70% in the early 1950's and still more than 50% in the early 1960's.[5]

Not only has the U.S. replaced the European nations as the leading economic power operating in the Third World, but the post-War years saw a substantial penetration of the European economies by U.S. business. The value of direct U.S. investment in Europe tripled between 1950 and 1959 (from $1.7 billion to $5.3 billion), then quadrupled (to $21.6 billion) by 1969, and doubled again to $44.5 billion by the end of 1974.[6]

On the political and military level, U.S. expansion kept pace with economic interests. Economic aid, military aid, and the establishment of overseas military bases helped provide a political environment conducive to corporate penetration. Throughout the European colonial world, the U.S. ambassadors began to replace the European colonial administrators as the dominant political figures. And in line with the new world order European colonies were transformed to independent nations under the aegis of U.S.

neocolonialism. More and more, the British and French military networks were replaced by U.S. centered "alliances" such as SEATO and CENTO.

The U.S. took on the role of maintaining an international police force to maintain "law and order" throughout the capitalist world. Moreover, it became the organizer and chief participant in the general effort of capitalist nations to contain and harass the socialist bloc.

BENEFITS OF HEGEMONY

This hegemony had its distinct advantages for U.S. business. To begin with, foreign activity has been a significant and growing source of direct profits. As a proportion of after tax profits of U.S. corporations, profits from abroad rose steadily from less than 10% in 1950 to about 25% at the beginning of the 1970's.[7] Moreover, these profits accrue disproportionately to the very large firms in the U.S. economy.[8] . . .

In addition to these direct benefits of international activity, the maintenance of an open and stable international capitalist system under U.S. hegemony has provided important elements in the structural foundations of the post–World War II expansion of the U.S. economy.

It has been generally recognized that having the dollar as the central currency of world capitalism assured that U.S. businesses would always have ample funds to undertake foreign activity. With the dollar-based monetary system, businesses in other nations had an increasing need for dollars in order to carry out their own international transactions. In the 1960's for example, the growth of dollars held outside the U.S. averaged about $2 billion a year. As a result, U.S. business could make purchases abroad with dollars without having all of those dollars redeemed by

---

[4]See Table 13-A, p. 476.

[5]See United Nations Economic Commission for Latin America, *External Financing in Latin America*, 1965, pp. 16–17, 147–48.

[6]These figures can be derived from Table 13-C, p. 478.

[7]See Table 13-B, p. 477.

[8]For documentation, see MacEwan, Section 13.1, p. 488, and Table 13-E, p. 480.

equivalent purchases by foreigners in the U.S. The rest of the world was effectively extending credit, to the tune of $2 billion more each year of the 1960's, to U.S. business.[9]

Monetary matters are, however, only the beginning of the story. The story continues with the impact of international activity on domestic power relations and with the importance of access to and control over resources and markets.

Manufacturing has been the most rapidly growing sector of U.S. foreign investment.[10] Foreign expansion of manufacturing has been motivated by the dual goals of obtaining a foothold in foreign markets and exploiting cheaper labor. The process has a structural impact on power relations that goes far beyond its direct impact on corporate profits. The ability of capital to move abroad greatly strengthens its hand in disputes with labor. Labor, whether demanding higher wages or better working conditions, is threatened by the possibility that management will choose to close shop and relocate abroad (or simply cease domestic expansion). The effectiveness of the threat has been demonstrated by the extensive expansion of overseas operations by U.S. manufacturers. And that extensive expansion has been greatly facilitated by U.S. hegemony.

Consequently, we may say that one of the elements establishing labor discipline in the domestic economy is the international mobility of manufacturing capital. The labor discipline—or the power relations between capital and labor which it represents—has been a central element upon which the successful domestic expansion of the U.S. economy has been based.[11]

Another structural basis for economic growth has been provided by foreign investment based on natural resources. While not as rapidly growing as manufacturing investment, resource-based foreign investment has by no means been stagnant.[12] The central issue in assessing the importance of natural resource based investment is *control*. In the first place, as recent experience with oil makes clear, natural resource prices—of copper, bauxite, and so forth, as well as oil—are determined within a fairly wide range by power relationships. The low prices of certain resources which have been important to the post-War growth of the U.S. economy can now be seen to have rested on the combined economic and political power of U.S. corporations in the context of U.S. hegemony.

A second factor explaining the importance of natural resource control is that control provides a basis for security, for both the nations and companies involved. The U.S. military apparatus is dependent on several imported strategic raw materials, e.g., nickel and

[9]For more on this, see F. Ackerman and A. MacEwan, "Inflation, Recession and Crisis," *Review of Radical Political Economics*, 4, No. 4 (August 1972). By holding dollars as reserves, foreigners were allowing the dollar to be overvalued (i.e., the demand for dollars as reserves pushed the price of the dollar above what it would have been as a result simply of the demand for U.S. goods and services); foreign assets were accordingly cheaper to U.S. firms than they otherwise would have been.

[10]The value of manufacturing assets abroad rose from 33 percent of the total in 1950 to 43 percent of the total in 1974. See Table 13-C, p. 478.

[11]The argument here should be distinguished from another argument sometimes put forth by opponents of the runaway shop—to wit, that capital mobility means a slower overall growth of jobs in the U.S. economy. It is not at all clear that in the aggregate and over time capital mobility means fewer jobs. Of course, workers immediately affected by a runaway shop are thrown out of work. But the overall effect of foreign investment is to increase the surplus available for investment within the U.S. In any given year, profits returned from former foreign investment exceed the outflow of new foreign investment and, accordingly, contribute to the expansion of the U.S. economy including the aggregate expansion of jobs. However, regardless of the aggregate long-run impact of foreign investment, at any point in time the existence of options for capital weakens labor because the threat of joblessness for a particular group of workers at a particular time means it is less able to make effective demands on capital. Moreover, the sector of labor most immediately affected tends to be the most thoroughly organized, for it is in those cases relatively more advantageous for capital to move abroad.

[12]The value of foreign assets in petroleum and mining and smelting tripled between 1950 and 1959 (from $4.5 billion to $13.3 billion) and had almost tripled again by 1974 (to $36.3 billion). See Table 13-C, p. 478.

chromium.[13] Thus, the position of the military and all that it implies is tied to the control of certain natural resources. From the point of view of the corporations, control of resource supplies provides security for their monopoly positions, both domestically and internationally. In oil, in aluminum, in copper, the major companies have used "vertical integration"—i.e., involvement in all phases of the industry from crude material production to sales of final products—as a basis for their power.

In numerous other types of industries as well, international activity is bound up with monopoly power. Domestic monopoly power provides the basis for successful international expansion, and the international expansion further enhances size and power which secure the original monopoly position. A description of the drug industry's activities has been provided by no less a source than Senator Russell Long, speaking in 1966: "For more than a dozen years, American drug companies have been involved in a world wide cartel to fix the prices of 'wonder drugs' . . . the conspirators have embarked on an extensive campaign to destroy their competitors."[14]

All of these benefits that have been obtained by U.S. business during the era of U.S. hegemony in world capitalism have not, of course, been theirs alone. Other advanced capitalist nations have participated in and their businesses have gained from the international stability. The U.S. may have led, but the followers have done well for themselves. And therein lies one of the problems.

CONTRADICTIONS IN THE SYSTEM

The good times for U.S. business could not last because the successful operation of the system was, from the outset, leading towards

[13]See Harry Magdoff, *The Age of Imperialism* (New York: Monthly Review Press, 1969), pp. 45–54.

[14]Quoted by Richard Barnet and Ronald Müller, *Global Reach* (New York: Simon & Schuster, 1975), p. 187, from the *Congressional Record—Senate*, February 10, 1966, 2886–94.

its own destruction. Simply insofar as the U.S. used its power to maintain stability, it allowed the reconstruction of the other capitalist nations. Success for the U.S. meant stability, but stability would allow its competitors to reestablish themselves.

In fact, the U.S. did far more than simply maintain stability. For both economic and political reasons, the success of the U.S. required that it take an active role in rebuilding the war-torn areas of the capitalist system. Economically, U.S. business needed the strong trading partners and investment opportunities that only reconstruction could provide. Politically, the U.S. needed strong allies in its developing confrontations with the Soviet Union and China.

Consequently, throughout the post–World War II period, the other capitalist nations were able to move toward a position where they could challenge the U.S., both economically and politically. As early as the late 1950's and early 1960's, it was becoming clear that Japanese and European goods were beginning to compete effectively with U.S. products. And other nations began to grumble about the costs of supporting a world monetary system based on the dollar. It was only a matter of time before the economic challenge would become serious, and the other nations would no longer allow the U.S. to dictate the rules and policies for the operation of international capitalism.

Still, "a matter of time" can be a long time or a short time. If the only challenge had been that from the expansion of other advanced capitalist nations, the U.S. might have maintained its position of hegemony for many more years. That was not, however, the only challenge.

The successful extension of capitalism into new geographic areas is—especially in the era of the rise of socialism—a process involving considerable conflict. In providing the police force for world capitalism, the U.S. government has been obliged to engage in numerous direct and indirect military encounters. Greece, Iran, Guatemala, Lebanon, the Dominican Republic only begin the list of nations that have felt the effect of U.S. coercion. In many cases, the overwhelming military capacity of the U.S. was sufficient to prevent serious military conflict from developing.

Indochina, however, presented a different story. The liberation forces in Vietnam were not so easily contained, and the U.S. became more and more deeply involved. A particular dialectic was thus created which had far-reaching implications. On the one hand, unable to win in Vietnam, the U.S. was forced to act in a way that undermined its economic strength. On the other hand, as its economic position deteriorated, the U.S. government was less able to pursue a successful military policy in Vietnam.

This dialectical process combined the contradiction between the U.S. and other advanced capitalist nations and the contradiction between the U.S. (as the central power among the advanced nations) and the periphery of the system (i.e., the Third World). The combined operation of these contradictions has ended the era of U.S. hegemony in a manner that will be shortly described.

First, however, it should be pointed out that the operation of these two contradictions established the foundation for the operation of still another contradiction. Success in the era of U.S. hegemony meant the integration of world capitalism, the creation of a system in which business was less and less constrained by national boundaries, a system in which capital could move freely. Consequently, a general interdependence has developed within world capitalism. The continued operation of a system of interdependence requires stability and coordination. Without U.S. hegemony the basis for stability and coordination no longer exists. The resulting contradiction between an integrated capitalist system and a capitalist system that has destroyed its basis for stability plays a central role in the crisis of the 1970's.

· · ·

The new situation of the 1970's was marked by both political and economic disruption of U.S. world power. Politically, the experience in Vietnam has demonstrated the inability of the U.S. to effectively police the world. Economically, the shift in the balance of U.S. international trade brought the new reality into stark relief. In the period 1960 through 1965, U.S. power had been reflected in large trade surpluses, averaging $5.8 billion. The trade surplus began to decline in 1966, and for the 1966 to 1971 period averaged only $1.4 billion. In 1971, 1972 and 1973 the U.S. ran trade deficits of $2.7 billion, $6.9 billion, and $0.7 billion, respectively.[15]

The challenge from Europe and Japan, which had been on the horizon in the early 1960's, had now arrived. Its coming was greatly hastened by the economic problems which the U.S. economy suffered as a consequence of the Vietnam War. In this sense, the two contradictions of international capitalism had come together to effect an alteration of the system. The formal alteration of international capitalism came with Nixon's declaration in 1971 of the New Economic Policy,[16] the devaluation of the dollar, and the destruction of capitalism's international monetary system.

· · ·

In concluding this paper it is useful to take particular note of the complications that international instability combined with integration creates for the formulation of government monetary and fiscal policy. Quite simply, under the present circumstances the implications of any particular policy are at best unclear.

Most obvious are the difficulties in formulating monetary policy. When in 1971 the U.S. lowered its interest rates relative to those in Europe, a huge, unprecedented outflow of capital took place. That experience showed the degree to which capital markets have become integrated and the speed at which

[15]From the *Economic Report of the President, 1974* (Washington: U.S. Government Printing Office, 1974).

[16]Editors' note: The New Economic Policy involved a set of domestic wage and price controls accompanying the devaluation of the dollar. See Crotty and Rapping, Section 12.4, p. 467, for more details.

money managers respond to interest rate variations. The situation would seem at least as senstive today with the large amount of "oil money" moving around the system. Accordingly, it makes little sense for the U.S. or any other major nation to formulate monetary policy and adjust interest rates on its own. In 1974 all of the major nations did, in fact, act in the same manner, maintaining high interest rates and tight money policies. There is, however, no reason to believe that in the absence of coordination they will continue to choose the same policies; different governments will face different circumstances and will act differently. Yet it is not clear how any coordinated policy would be developed.

The problems for fiscal policy are only slightly less immediate. It is at least a possibility that in carrying out expansionary programs designed to encourage investment, the U.S. government will find itself competing with the other advanced nations to see which can provide the most favorable investment climate. The result could be a substantial expansion of overseas investment, lacking any substantial direct and immediate impact on the U.S. economy.

Moreover, under conditions of international integration and instability, the impact of any policy is difficult to predict. When the time comes again for counter-inflationary actions, a deceleration of the economy could lead to a much greater cutback of investment than the government would be aiming for. If other governments were not following similar deflationary policies, overseas options might attract an unexpectedly large amount of U.S. capital. The results of the U.S. action could then be inflation-exacerbating shortages and the development of another round of recession.

The list of uncertainties and possible problems could be continued. Different nations may attempt to solve their own problems by raising tariffs; other nations might follow suit and a serious disruption of trade patterns could occur. Alternatively, a series of competitive devaluations may take place, or some nations might impose more stringent foreign exchange controls. Each such action would present new problems for the U.S. economy.

The governments of the leading capitalist nations are not unaware of the dangers in the current situation, but awareness and ability to cope are not the same thing. In his much publicized *Business Week* interview, Kissinger put the problem simply: "One interesting feature of our recent discussions with both the Europeans and Japanese has been the emphasis on the need for economic coordination. . . . How you, in fact, coordinate policies is yet an unresolved problem."[17]

Thus, international instability of an integrated world capitalism will continue to plague the U.S. economy for some time to come. Policy problems, trade and monetary instability, price shocks, and other unforeseeables will all be part of the new agenda.

[17]*Business Week*, January 13, 1975, p. 76.

12.4 *Class Struggle, Macropolicy and the Business Cycle*

In this last reading of the chapter James Crotty and Leonard Rapping analyze the formulation of U.S. government macropolicy and the cyclical behavior of the U.S. economy since World War II. Their analysis is based upon the wage-squeeze-on-profits approach (introduced in Section 12.2), which stresses the fundamental incompatibility of continuous full employment with profit maximization in a capitalist economy.

Crotty and Rapping develop the argument that the major downturn of the mid-1970s was needed by the U.S. capitalist class in order to restore the basis for profitable capital accumulation which had been eroded by years of expansion and inflation. The unusual severity of this downturn, as compared with earlier postwar downturns, is attributable in part to the fact that it was delayed for a long time by other policy considerations—most importantly the U.S. effort to maintain its dominant position within the world capitalist system. As we have argued earlier in this chapter, the need for a major downturn was also due to the growth of inflationary pressures which have increased the amount of deflation in economic activity needed to bring down the rate of inflation.

In the last part of their essay Crotty and Rapping address themselves to future macropolicy options facing U.S. policy-makers in the context of the stagflation of the 1970s. Just as the capitalist system faced a crisis of stagnation in the 1930s which could ultimately be resolved only by restructuring capitalist economies so as to allow for a major new role for the state (in maintaining aggregate demand via Keynesian fiscal and monetary policies), so the capitalist system in the 1970s appears to require major changes if it is to cope with the new crisis of stagflation. Crotty and Rapping suggest that once again the resolution of the crisis is likely to involve a much larger role for the state, this time in undertaking new and much more comprehensive forms of economic planning. Whether such a resolution will prove to be purely reformist, by strengthening the underlying capitalist relations of production, or whether it can become revolutionary, by transforming those relations, depends on the course of the political struggle to come.

The following is excerpted from "The 1975 Report of the President's Council of Economic Advisers: A Radical Critique" by JAMES R. CROTTY and LEONARD A. RAPPING. From the *American Economic Review*, 65, No. 5 (December 1975). Reprinted by permission of the authors and the American Economic Association.

CLASS CONFLICT AND MACROPOLICY

While it is undoubtedly true that the working class has achieved important political victories in modern American history, the process of macropolicy formulation in the post–World War II era has been dominated by the interests of the capitalist class. Organized labor has represented a constraint limiting the policy choices available to capital, but by no means has it been an equal partner in the formation of macropolicy. The main objective of policy has been to protect and extend corporate profits.

. . .

Capital's control of macropolicy and its quest for maximum corporate profits would be a secondary issue were the impact of policy always class-neutral. [Bourgeois economists generally assume] that policy choices exist that are optimal for both capital and labor. In particular, this harmonious view assumes that labor's key objective, sustained full employment, and capital's objective, maximum profits, are compatible. According to this reasoning, reaching the twin objectives of full employment and maximum profits involves mainly technical problems, and it is assumed that the basic structure of the economy is consistent with the simultaneous achievement of both goals.

. . .

An alternative to [this] view of macropolicy, one based on capital-labor conflict, maintains that the basic structure of the economy precludes the simultaneous attainment of labor's and capital's objectives. The existence of a conflict between full employment and profit maximization is supported by empirical evidence from the past twenty-five years. The typical pattern of the post–World War II business cycle shows that the profit share of income and even the absolute level of real profits have fallen in the latter phase of the expansion. This full employment profit squeeze helps explain both the failure of capitalist-oriented macropolicy to sustain full employment prior to 1965 and the consequences of full employment during the Vietnam War period of the late 1960's.

The primary problems with sustained full employment from the perspective of the capitalist class are that it creates conditions which lead to the continuous decline of profits and profit margins, to an increase in labor's share of national product, to domestic financial instability, and to the erosion of the international financial institutions through which the American empire was developed and is maintained. Intermittent recessions are a necessary condition for the maintenance of satisfactory profits and the health of financial institutions. The tradeoff between profits and full employment enables the state to partially mediate this capital-labor conflict through macropolicy. Control of the policy-making apparatus therefore becomes central in determining the influence of macropolicy on the outcome of this conflict. The state cannot be expected to pursue full employment since those who formulate macropolicy are primarily concerned with the welfare of capital and the preservation of capitalist institutions.

PROFITS, WAGES, PRODUCTIVITY, AND THE CYCLE

In the absence of wage-price controls, full employment and high profits are incompatible. This contradiction is a cornerstone of Marxian business cycle theory. Consider the economy emerging from a recession and entering the early phase of an expansion. Wages are rising moderately, but productivity growth is very rapid, so that stable or moderately rising prices yield increasing profits and profit margins. Capacity utilization is rising but is not yet so high that shortages develop. Credit is cheap and readily available, but credit demand is moderate because cash flow is sufficient to accommodate most business needs. Investment is rising, business and consumer confidence is strong, and the stock market is buoyant. Trade and payments accounts are improving. Employment is growing and with a lag the rate of unemployment begins to decline from its recession highs.

When relatively full employment is approached, however, a series of distortions develop which, in Wesley Mitchell's words, "cause a slow accumulation of stresses within the balanced system of business . . . that ultimately undermine the conditions on which prosperity rests. . . ."

The reduction of the reserve army of the unemployed which accompanies the expansion, strengthens the bargaining position of the working class in its labor market confrontation with capital. Workers can then struggle successfully for higher wages. In the latter part of the expansion, moreover, the rate of increase in productivity decreases and consequently unit labor costs rise rapidly. While the growth in unit labor costs drives corporations toward labor saving capital equipment, the resulting productivity gains are only realized in the early phase of the next expansion when the new capital is actually installed. Although developing "technical" bottlenecks and inefficiencies partially explain the productivity slowdown, knowledgeable observers of the labor scene have pointed directly to an increasingly obstreperous labor force as an explanatory factor. Full employment affects not only wage rates, but also quit rates, strikes, and labor militancy in general. It has been a longstanding observation that such favorable conditions for labor evoke less effort on the shop floor. For example, a plant superintendent testifying before the Commission on Labor in 1904 had the following to say:

> *Five years ago men did not restrict their output,
> union or non-union men, because they wanted to hold
> their jobs and a man would do anything and all he
> was told to do. Now a man knows that all he has to
> do is to walk across the street and get another job at
> the same pay. During the hard times we took contracts
> at any price we could get, and in some places and cases
> men were driven at high speed to get this work out, so
> as to lose as little money on it as possible. Men will not
> keep up that speed rate in these days.*[1]

In this phase of the expansion, inflation accelerates, but not enough to prevent profit margins from deteriorating. Although there is no unique and universally accepted hypothesis that explains why prices do not keep up with costs, the fact that they do not is of extreme importance. For profits and profit margins end up being squeezed toward the top of the boom. The termination of the expansion and the rebuilding of the reserve army is required to relax this profit squeeze. . . .

Empirical evidence from the post–World War II era supports the hypothesis that there is indeed a full employment profit squeeze.[2] Profits tend to peak, both in relative and absolute terms, approximately halfway through the typical expansion. Profitability is eroded during the latter part of this phase as labor markets tighten and continues to decline during the contraction. This pattern is discernable in each of the post–World War II cycles. However, the expansion of the 1960's is the only one in which there was prolonged full employment. It therefore provides us with the best opportunity to test the full employment profit squeeze hypothesis. The evidence of this period dramatically supports the hypothesis, whether profitability is measured as a share, as a rate of return, or in dollars. Net profits before taxes as a percent of gross product originating in nonfinancial corporations rose steadily from 14.5 in 1961 to a peak of 17.0 in 1965, then fell steadily to a postwar low of 9.8 by 1970. Compensation of employees, on the other hand, declined from 65.1 percent in 1961 to 62.6 in 1965, rising thereafter to 65.1 in 1969 and 67.2 in 1970. As reported by Nordhaus,[3] the rate of return on nonfinancial corporate capital rose from 11.8 percent (before taxes) in 1961 to 16.3 percent in 1965; it then fell steadily to a post–World War II low of 9.1 percent in 1970. Before tax corporate profits for all industries in current dollars rose from $50.3 billion to $82.4 billion between 1961 and 1966. They were $79.8 billion and $69.2 billion in 1969 and 1970, respectively. In real terms, they declined steadily and strongly from 1966 through 1970.

The full employment squeeze on profits means that continuous expansion would undermine the accumulation of profits. It is the profit squeeze, not inflation per se, which motivates capitalists to eventually demand restrictive macropolicies during periods of full employment. The fact that profits are lowest in recession has often been used to argue the preposterousness of the charge that recessions are desired by capital. Indeed they would prefer to avoid them. But the recession is a necessary condition for establishing the basis of the highly profitable first phase of the expansion and for avoiding the highly unprofitable consequences of sustained full employment. Recessions also provide the political context within which the government grants fiscal incentives to capital. Under the impact of recession-induced corporate tax reductions, the post–World War II period has witnessed a secular decline in effective corporate tax rates.

Of course other problems also develop during the expansion. The deterioration of profitability in the latter phase of the expansion means that corporations turn increasingly to external sources to finance investment in plant, equipment, and inventories. Rising

---

[1] Quoted in W. Mitchell, *Business Cycles and Their Causes* (Berkeley: University of California Press, 1941), p. 113.

[2] Evidence in support of the full-employment profit squeeze may be found in R. Boddy and J. Crotty, "Class Conflict and Macro-Policy: The Political Business Cycle," *Review of Radical Political Economics*, 7, No. 1 (Spring 1975).

[3] W. Nordhaus, "The Falling Share of Profits," *Brookings Papers in Economic Activity*, 1974, No. 1.

prices and the fear of shortages accelerate inventory accumulation, while inventory profits and depreciation at historical costs increase the effective tax rate on corporate profits. Debt accumulates just when interest rates are highest. Moreover, serious balance of trade problems develop as the rising price of *U.S.* products retards exports and, aided by strong aggregate *U.S.* demand, stimulates imports.

Eventually of course lower profits and associated stresses restrain production and investment and thus, before long, the expansion tends to abort. Macropolicy can work by either acquiescing in this tendency toward contraction or can extend the expansion for months or even years beyond its "natural" life. In the 1945–65 period, the government reacted to the decline in profits, the rise in inflation, and the problems in the international sector as we would expect—by reinforcing the recessionary pressures developing in the private sector.

The economic function of recession in a capitalist economy is to create the preconditions for a new expansion of profits. By taking away the jobs of millions of people, and by threatening the jobs of millions of others, recessions reduce worker demands. Unit labor costs are brought under control, the decline in profit margins is eventually stopped, and inflationary pressure weakens. During recessions inventories are cut, loans are repaid, corporate liquidity positions are improved, and the deterioration in the balance of payments is reversed. All the statements of Keynesian economists to the contrary notwithstanding, recessions are inevitable in the unplanned economy of the United States because they perform an essential function for which no adequate substitute has thus far been available.

WORLD CAPITALISM, U.S. HEGEMONY, AND MACROPOLICY

The preceding analysis assumes that when capital controls the process of macropolicy making, the primary concern of policy is the profitability of major corporations. However, [U.S.] corporate profits—domestic as well as foreign—are fundamentally dependent upon the condition of the international economy and the relative position of the United States therein. The [U.S.] state, therefore, must formulate macropolicies which support and sustain world capitalism as a system, and, simultaneously, attempt to maximize the strength of the United States vis-à-vis its capitalist rivals.

. . .

Pressures on macropolicy emanating from the international sector can be placed in two general categories: (1) the "normal" month-to-month and year-to-year dynamics of trade, investment, and financial capital flows; and (2) the inevitable wars and lesser military skirmishes which arise as a natural result of the United States' role as capitalist policeman of the third world and defender of the international capitalist system against the encroachment of socialism. Between 1945 and 1965 there existed a rough correspondence between domestic macropolicy requirements and the requirements of the international system. The behavior of the economy over the cycle generated simultaneous pressures to relax the economy for both domestic and "normal" international objectives. The refusal of the macropolicy authorities to follow expansionary policies during the recession of 1957–59 is an important historical example of this coincidence of objectives. There is, of course, no systematic reason to expect the changes in military expenditures necessitated by *U.S.* international objectives to coincide with domestic economic needs. Yet, the military expenditures on World War II and on the Korean War did help to revive a sagging economy.

The first dramatic conflict among these policy objectives occurred in 1965. Late that year, as 4 percent unemployment was attained, profit margins peaked and the trade surplus began to deteriorate. Both domestic and normal international interests required a recession and the Council of Economic Advisers called for more restrictive policies. The Johnson Administration, however, with the approval and support of corporation owners and managers, had already made the fateful judgment that a military victory over the revolutionary forces in Vietnam was essential to the maintenance of the world capitalist system and the protection of the American place in it.

· · ·

The administration's decision to escalate the war was a momentous gamble. Unless the government compensated for the sharp rise in military expenditures with either increased taxes or greatly reduced domestic spending, the war-related expenditures would eventually generate domestic economic instability, would place a severe strain on international financial institutions, and would jeopardize the special status of the United States in the world capitalist system. But the administration was constrained. It was unable to reduce domestic spending because of explosive unrest in the black urban areas, and it was unwilling to raise taxes because of fear that this would fuel incipient political opposition to war policies. Except for the delayed and ineffective tax surcharge of 1968, the Johnson Administration chose to let inflationary war finance run its course. . . .

The gamble failed. Yet the fact that it was undertaken, given the enormous political-economic costs involved, indicates how important the defense of the empire was to the policy makers. No other single event speaks so eloquently and convincingly in support of the hypothesis that the international interests of *U.S.* corporations are of paramount importance in the objective function of macro-policy authorities.

By the end of 1968 the costs of the Vietnam War had become obvious. The domestic economy had been severely strained by long years of expansion and dangerous pressures were building on the world payments system. Profit margins were low, labor's share was growing, interest rates were high, inflation was accelerating, and the *U.S.* balance-of-payments position was deteriorating. Certainly it must have appeared that a recession lasting as long as three or four years would be

required to curb the pressures and end the dislocations generated by eight years of continuous expansion and five years of continuous tight labor markets. In 1969, the incoming administration began to deal with these problems by means of classic recessionary policy.

The actual recession of 1969–70 was rather short, lasting only five or six quarters. Restrictive macropolicy was eased in 1970 because profits, squeezed first by five years of tight labor markets and then by the initial impact of the recession, were in need of immediate relief; because its continuation would have led to a rate of unemployment so high that it could not possibly have been reduced to a politically acceptable level in time for the 1972 presidential election; and because the debt and liquidity structure of many corporations and banks raised questions as to whether they could survive the usual recessionary medicine.

· · ·

The policies of the Vietnam period hastened the decline of the American monopoly of international capitalist power, consequently destroying the basis on which international stability rested. The unprecedented length of the *U.S.* expansion created an environment in which the export-oriented economies of Europe and Japan could sustain their own derivative expansions and accelerate their assault on our balance-of-trade surplus and our share of world export markets. The decade-long expansion in the world capitalist system in turn laid the foundation for a worldwide raw material or commodity inflation. In concert with the declining ability of the United States to control world events, the world commodity boom created the necessary preconditions for the coming economic and political revolt of the third world producers of raw materials, most significantly that of the oil-exporting countries. The balance-of-payments deficits and inflation-exportation of this period clearly hastened the demise of the existing international economic and financial institutions leaving little hope, in the power vacuum that existed, for a set of substitute institutions and arrangements.

In short, the expansive macropolicies chosen in the late 1960's to accommodate the defense of *U.S.* hegemony in the end accelerated its demise, leaving by August 1971 a legacy of international instability and an unmet need for a prolonged recession in a domestic system that seemed incapable of easily surviving one. It is thus clear why the administration was forced to abandon exclusive reliance on orthodox macropolicy. On the one hand, the system needed expansionary macropolicy to stimulate short-run profits and investment and to keep unemployment from rising too high. On the other hand, it needed restrictive policy to curb inflation, kick interest rates back up, improve the trade balance, and get labor fully under control. By August 1971 there was simply no combination of standard macropolicy tools capable of achieving these contradictory objectives. . . . The emergency in the international monetary system—a cornerstone of *U.S.* international hegemony—would not permit a delay in action. The administration's response was the New Economic Policy (*NEP*).

· · ·

THE NEP AND THE
DOWNTURN OF 1974–75

The *NEP* was an innovative policy undertaken by a capitalist government to achieve the complementary objectives of regaining America's international hegemony and restoring "balance" to the domestic economy. The mechanism was to be an economic expansion immunized against inflation and a profit squeeze through wage and price controls. It basically failed on both fronts. The *NEP* carried over unresolved into 1974 many of the domestic and international problems facing the *U.S.* economy in August 1971, and it severely exacerbated or created several others: inflationary pressures in general, and food price inflation in particular; debt and liquidity problems; shortages, speculative inventory buildups, and commodity inflation; secular profit and cashflow problems,

temporarily alleviated by the controlled decline in real wages; the domestic inflationary impact of the declining value of the dollar; a fundamental, unresolved instability in the international sector. The basic problems of the economy in 1971 remained as 1974 began. The economy suffered from severe imbalances and disproportions requiring a massive recession it might not be able to withstand, and was situated in an international context of declining *U.S.* power amid system instability.

· · ·

Except for the introduction of extensive economic planning, the administration had no option other than to permit the economy to recess in late 1973. The stakes were high. The accumulated pressures described in the preceeding [paragraphs] were more severe in 1973 than in late 1969. The controls were under extreme market pressure; the financial structure of businesses was imbalanced because of extensive debt financing; the rate of inflation was accelerating; and the international economy was in disarray. Nothing short of a major recession-depression could eliminate these imbalances from the system. While the impact of recessionary policies was uncertain, these policies were viewed as less risky than any of the perceived alternatives. The economy had to be purged. First fiscal and then monetary policy accommodated to this need. Fiscal policy was restrictive beginning in the middle of 1973 and remained so throughout 1974. Monetary policy tightened in the second half of 1973 and became severely restrictive in the second half of 1974. The macropolicy authorities were attempting to generate a severe economic contraction. Skyrocketing unemployment rates in late 1974 left no doubt of their success. . . .

PROSPECTS FOR
THE FUTURE

The Office of Management and Budget has . . . provided the administration's projections for [the remainder of the 1970's] and they present a dismal picture for working people. Starting from the optimistic assumption that the economy will witness an uninterrupted growth in real *GNP* averaging about 6 percent a year from 1976 through 1980, they project an average reported unemployment rate for the period of almost 7 percent, making the 1970's a decade of joblessness. To perceive the human impact of these forecasts, consider that the fraction of the work force who experience unemployment at some time during the year may be three or more times the average unemployment rate.

These projections, however, are not accompanied by any serious political-economic analysis of the forces likely to be operating on the *U.S.* economy over the remainder of the decade. Yet powerful secular pressures will clearly influence policy and performance. There will be a drive to reassert American control over a restabilized international economy, to reverse the decade-long decline in *U.S.* productivity, to close the gap between the percent of output channelled into capital accumulation here relative to Europe and Japan, to obtain . . . "energy security," and to increase the rate of profit and decrease the growth of corporate debt. These objectives will not only influence policy but may lead to class struggle at home and rivalry and conflict abroad. They may also, in concert with the generally abysmal performance of the system over the past decade, induce major institutional change.

Given the conjunction of these pressures with . . . economic stagnation, every option confronting those who control economic policy involves economic contradictions and policy conflict. American capital must engineer a long, noninflationary, balanced economic expansion within which the rate of capital accumulation dominates consumption growth. There appears to exist no single policy, and certainly no monetary-fiscal mix, that can achieve these objectives.

One option would be to initiate a strongly expansionary macropolicy which would generate full employment rather quickly. But this would lead to rapidly accelerating inflation, something neither the domestic nor the international economy can tolerate. A rapid *U.S.* expansion would lead to an international economic revival retriggering commodity inflation and a large increase in the world demand for oil—an ominous prospect indeed. Too many structural imbalances remain in the domestic economy to make possible a repeat of 1961 to 1965.

Another option would be to generate a long, gradual expansion much like the one projected in the budget in the hope that the years of high unemployment would hold wages down while production slowly edged upward. Meanwhile, the drive for a discrete jump in the rate of capital accumulation would be aided by fundamental changes in the tax system. Capital's demand for corporate tax relief has been widely supported. Every week brings new proposals by economists, politicians, or influential individual or organizational business spokesmen to lower the effective rate of corporate taxation and/or the income tax rate of the wealthy. A further move in the direction of a higher investment-consumption ratio may also be discerned in the current fiscal crises of state and local governments. In the context of budget crises, state and local governments are in the process of purging their welfare and employment rolls. The federal government apparently does not desire to relieve these fiscal pressures. This process, should it continue, will transfer resources from the public to the private sector and, by adding to the reserve army of the unemployed, will increase the downward pressure on wage rates.

The gradual expansion option has contradictions. Not only would it fail to guarantee price stability, but its long years of intolerable unemployment rates raise the prospect of heightened class conflict in the United States. Although the leaders of organized labor have been incredibly docile up to this point, they may not be able to restrain rank and file anger for the duration of the decade. . . .

Alternatively, the government might initiate an incomes policy of wage-price and perhaps profit and interest rate controls administered in a manner similar to those of the *NEP*. These controls might be used to augment one of the monetary-fiscal strategies discussed above. . . . If we add an unusually high target rate of capital accumulation, a reduction of labor's share would be necessary.

Such an augmented incomes policy poses difficult questions. Can demand be sustained in the face of a declining share of income for labor? Will labor tolerate a lower share of output? An incomes policy, moreover, is essentially self-contradictory in the context of a capitalist economy. . . . Unless more extensive micro or sectoral planning is introduced, a permanent system of wage-price controls is untenable.

Economic planning may be the wave of the future, even under capitalism; it represents an option, perhaps *the* option in the long run. Several notable planning proposals have already been made but they do not envision a fully planned economy as we normally understand this concept. They deal more with gathering information, making forecasts, using some tax and subsidy incentives and marginally altering resource allocation. But it is clear to us that if planning is to help resolve major contradictions in the domestic economy, it must achieve a significant substitution of administrative for market processes. Genuine planning could involve not only the setting of wages and prices, but government-directed allocation of raw materials and credit, a detailed system of tax subsidies and penalties, antistrike or even anticollective bargaining legislation, and administratively coordinated investment strategies among firms and industries.

Although pressure toward planning is likely to continue, it will not be steady. While a brief period of relatively trouble-free expansion may temporarily silence supporters of planning, renewed outbreaks of inflation, rising unemployment, credit crises, and/or shortages will intensify this pressure. Planning may represent the only way to eliminate recurrent crises from the domestic economic system and to successfully pursue the goal of *U.S.* domination of the world capitalist system. Only within a planned economy is it potentially possible to achieve full employment and price stability and at the same time restrain wages and consumption in support of capital accumulation. But planning demystifies economic power relations and transfers the stresses and strife of the market system into the political arena. It therefore portends political conflict of the highest order—conflict within the capitalist class as well as between capital and labor.

Within the present array of political forces in the United States, the development of economic planning will undoubtedly mean corporate control of the planning process, just as the introduction of federal regulatory agencies has historically meant control by and for the regulated industries. It is, therefore, more important than ever before that the political balance of power be changed and the power of the corporate elite broken. Working people and their allies must defend the interests of the majority of the American people against the fundamentally antagonistic interests of the corporations and the super-rich who own and control them.

CHAPTER **13**

Imperialism

CAPITALISM, BY ITS VERY NATURE, cannot be contained within national boundaries. Since its origin, the rise of capitalism has been associated with the displacement of relatively self-contained local economies by an increasingly international network of social and economic relations. And the more that the capitalist system has developed over time, the greater the extent to which market relations and capital movements have eroded national boundaries and linked distant areas together within one and the same world capitalist economy.

Not only has the capitalist system always been essentially *international* in character, but also it has always been characterized by *unequal* international relations. Capitalism is a system built upon hierarchy and inequality, and this applies at the international level as well as at the level of the nation or the firm. It is for this reason that the term "imperialism" is used to characterize international relations within the world capitalist system. Imperialism connotes a relationship of dominance/subordination between a stronger and a weaker nation or people. In the context of the capitalist system, imperialism refers to the dominant relationship of the most powerful nations within the world capitalist economy to other nations and territories with which they enter into social, political, and economic relations.[1]

At any given time one can (at least roughly) divide the capitalist world into a "center" and a "periphery." The center includes those nations from which capital accumulation is propelled—i.e., the major sources of economic management, financial control, and technological progress. The periphery refers to those countries and territories that are linked to the center in an economically subordinate manner. Today, for example, the capitalist center includes the rich and industrialized nations of North America, Western Europe, and Japan, while the periphery includes much—but not all—of Asia, Africa, and Latin America.

With the passage of time and the evolution of the world capitalist system, both the nature of the basic imperialist relationship and the delineation of the center and the periphery have been changing. In the following paragraphs we review briefly the way in which imperialism has changed as the capitalist system has developed since its origin.

THREE STAGES OF IMPERIALISM

The capitalist world system has evolved through three broad stages of imperialism in

---

[1]The dominance of weaker nations by a stronger nation is of course not unique to the capitalist system. A reading of world history suggests that empire-building has been the rule rather than the exception for human

societies. The point of this chapter is not to argue that imperialist drives arise only out of a capitalist society, but to examine the particular form that imperialism takes under capitalism. This concern is warranted both by the dominant position of capitalism in the modern world and by the particularly tenacious character of imperialism within the world capitalist system.

which first plunder, then trade, and finally direct investment have been most representative of the economic relations between the center and the periphery. In each stage of imperialism the periphery has played an important role in contributing to the growth of the capitalist economies in the center. But the effect of the imperialist relationship on the periphery has varied from one stage to another.

The capitalist mode of production arose initially from the interstices of feudal society in Western Europe; it developed most rapidly in England, where it became the dominant form of socioeconomic organization by the eighteenth century.[2] To a significant extent the rise of capitalism in England and elsewhere in Western Europe was predicated upon the overseas exploits of explorers and traders. The European explorations of the fifteenth, sixteenth, and seventeenth centuries were motivated largely by a spirit of adventure, acquisition, and plunder rather than by any desire for capital accumulation. Nonetheless, they did serve as an important source of "primitive accumulation" (i.e., original capital accumulation) as the profits from foreign ventures returned home and ultimately helped to stimulate the rise of the new capitalist class.

Marx described this early phase of capitalist history as follows:

> The discovery of gold and silver in America, the extirpation, enslavement and entombment in mines of the aboriginal population, the beginning of the conquest and looting of the East Indies, the turning of Africa into a warren for the commercial hunting of blackskins, signalized the rosy dawn of the era of capitalist production. These idyllic proceedings are the chief momenta of primitive accumulation.
>   •   •   •
> The treasures captured outside Europe by undisguised looting, enslavement, and murder, floated back

to the mother-country and were there turned into capital.[3]

In this first stage of imperialism, the capitalist center (which then included England and a few coastal regions of Continental Europe) made use of the periphery (Asia, Africa, and the Americas) primarily as an object of plunder or a source of exotic products and slaves. This predatory relationship between the center and the periphery was dominant for several centuries following the initial overseas explorations of the late fifteenth century. By the beginning of the nineteenth century, changes in the character and the needs of capitalism in the center were leading to changes in the nature of imperialism in many parts of the world. There ensued a second broad stage of imperialism in which the increasingly capitalist nations of Western Europe began to industrialize on a significant scale and became interested in the periphery primarily as a partner in trade, supplying food and raw materials in exchange for industrial manufactures.

By this second stage many of the American territories previously colonized by the European powers had become politically independent nations. But in the Caribbean, in Asia, and (by the end of the nineteenth century) in Africa the Europeans strengthened their political control, establishing direct rule over their overseas territories and forming a worldwide system of rival colonial empires.

In spite of the differences in political status of different parts of the periphery, the economic relations between center and periphery were quite similar throughout the world. Each major European power sought to preserve for its own capitalists the economic gains accruing from trade with those parts of the periphery which it dominated, either as colonial ruler (e.g., England in India, France in Indochina) or as principal trader (e.g., England in South America). In the process of promoting a rapid growth of world trade, capitalists from the center exported increasing

---

[2]For an analysis of the transition from feudalism to capitalism, see Hunt, Section 2.3, p. 54. Near the end of Section 2.3 Hunt discusses the phenomenon of primitive accumulation to which the first stage of imperialism contributed.

[3]Karl Marx, *Capital*, Vol. I, Part VIII, Chapter 31.

amounts of capital to the periphery. With the aid and protection of their national governments they invested in mines, plantations, and related infrastructural facilities designed to improve access to needed raw materials and to create expanded markets for the export of manufactured goods from the center. In this way the peripheral economies were shaped to meet the needs of the center.

Marx expected that when the center began to take an active interest in promoting productive enterprise in the periphery (rather than simply plundering it or trading with it), the imperialist relationship would favor the extension of the capitalist mode of production and the promotion of economic growth in the periphery. Impressed with British plans for the development of Indian railways, he wrote that:

> *"England has to fulfill a double mission in India: one destructive, the other regenerating—the annihilation of old Asiatic society, and the laying of the material foundations of Western society in Asia.*
>
> . . .
>
> *I know that the English millocracy intend to endow India with railways with the exclusive view of extracting at diminished expenses, the cotton and other raw materials for their manufactures. . . . [But] you cannot maintain a net of railways over an immense country without introducing all those industrial processes necessary to meet the immediate and current wants of railway locomotion, and out of which there must grow the application of machinery to those branches of industry not immediately connected with railways. The railway system will therefore become, in India, truly the forerunner of modern industry.*
>
> . . .
>
> *All the English bourgeoisie may be forced to do will neither emancipate nor materially mend the social condition of the mass of the people, depending not only on the development of the productive powers, but of their appropriation by the people. But what they will not fail to do is lay down the material premises for both. Has the bourgeoisie ever done more? Has it ever effected a progress without dragging individuals and peoples through blood and dirt, through misery and degradation?*[4]

Thus Marx viewed capitalist penetration of the periphery as an unambiguously progressive force: at a high cost in human misery, to be sure, imperialism would lay the basis for the capitalist development of the periphery.

As it turned out, however, Marx's expectations were not realized in most of the periphery during the second stage of imperialism. Only in a few areas of European settlement— the United States, Canada, Australia, and New Zealand—and in Japan did the capitalist mode of production begin to flourish and promote a process of sustained capital accumulation and rapid economic growth. Moreover, these parts of the periphery were unusual in several respects. In the first place, they were among the countries that had become politically independent well before the twentieth century. In the four countries of European settlement the settlers virtually destroyed the pre-existing native peoples rather than ruling over them, as they did elsewhere in Asia, Africa, and Latin America. And Japan was unique in the third world in having resisted altogether any form of colonial domination by the Western powers. Thus it was only under exceptional circumstances that a few nations emerged from the periphery to form part of the capitalist center, which consisted by the early part of the twentieth century of Western Europe, North America, Australia, New Zealand, and Japan.

At the same time, the rest of Asia, Africa, Latin America,[5] and Southern and Eastern Europe remained in the periphery. Throughout these peripheral areas, imperialism in its second stage had the effect of inhibiting the development of the capitalist mode of production and blocking industrialization. As explained by Thomas Weisskopf in the third reading of this chapter, this regressive effect was due largely to the fact that capitalists and their governments in the center found it advantageous to maintain the local power

---

[4]Karl Marx, "The Future Results of British Rule in India," reprinted in Shlomo Avineri, ed., *Karl Marx on Colonialism and Modernization* (New York: Doubleday & Co., 1968), pp. 132–39.

[5]Throughout this chapter the term "Latin America" will be understood to include the Caribbean as well as Central and South America.

of traditional elites in the periphery and to promote production based on pre-capitalist social relations rather than wage-labor.

The second stage of imperialism was characterized by intense rivalries among the major capitalist powers. In seeking to facilitate their own economic and political expansion, they competed with one another to carve up the rest of the world into their respective colonial empires or spheres of influence. This competition contributed greatly to the tensions that led to World Wars I and II and ultimately resulted in a major transformation of the world capitalist system.

A third stage of imperialism has emerged in the second half of the twentieth century, following the disruptions of the two world wars and the rise of state socialist rule in most of Eastern Europe and mainland East Asia. The weakening of the European colonial powers led to the dissolution of their colonial empires; within a few decades of World War II almost all of the former colonial territories had gained their political independence. Imperialist relations between the center and the periphery are no longer mediated by colonial rule; instead, they operate in a "neo-colonial" manner between formally independent nation-states. Moreover, the emergence of the state socialist nations has removed a substantial part of the world from the capitalist orbit. Thus the periphery is now confined to Latin America, Southern Europe, Africa, and Asia, exclusive of Japan, China, and the adjacent smaller state socialist nations.[6]

The period since World War II has been characterized by a rapidly increasing integration of the world capitalist economy. With the erosion of colonial barriers and the establishment of a new international economic framework under the leadership of the United States,[7] economic relations among the nations of the capitalist center and between the center and the periphery have developed on an unprecedented scale. This increasing integration has involved a great expansion of foreign trade, but it is most dramatically manifested in the rapid growth of direct foreign private investment. Rather than simply exporting their products to foreign markets, capitalist firms have found it increasingly profitable to set up or buy out production facilities in foreign countries and territories. Thus the "multinational corporation" has become the hallmark of modern capitalism and the primary vehicle of imperialist relations between the metropolis and the periphery.

The dominance of the center over the periphery in the contemporary stage of imperialism has been maintained not by direct political control but by virtue of the economic power of the center nations and their multinational corporations. Virtually all of the foreign investment within the world capitalist economy has been undertaken by corporations based in the center nations; it has been directed both to other center nations and to the periphery. As the dominant capitalist power in the postwar period, the United States has accounted for the lion's share of the foreign investment since World War II. Of a total value of direct foreign private investment assets estimated (conservatively) at $165 billion in 1971, slightly over 50 percent was owned by U.S.–based multinational corporations.[8] British firms held roughly 15 percent of the total, and no other country accounted for more than 6 percent. In a statistical appendix following this introduction, we present a series of tables designed to document the growth and nature of U.S. private investment in foreign countries.

---

[6]It is difficult to draw a precise line between the center and the periphery, for there are always some nations that may be in transition from a subordinate to a more independent status within the world capitalist system. Countries such as Israel and South Africa share some of the attributes of both the center and the periphery and could be classified either way.

[7]See MacEwan, Section 12.3, p. 455, for a discussion of the international economic framework that emerged within the capitalist system following World War II.

[8]Estimates of the distribution of direct foreign private investment by source country in 1967 and 1971 are given in the United Nations, Department of Economic and Social Affairs, *Multinational Corporations in World Development* (New York: United Nations, 1973), Table 5.

The rapid growth of direct foreign private investment in the world capitalist economy since World War II was facilitated by the economic, political, and military hegemony of the United States.[9] Diplomatic pressures, economic sanctions, covert operations, and military interventions have all played a role in the process whereby the U.S. government has sought to maintain a favorable international climate for capitalist activity in the periphery without a system of formal colonies. Yet the economic recovery of the rival capitalist powers of Western Europe and Japan, and the growing success of anti-imperialist movements (most notably in Indochina), have weakened considerably the dominant position of the United States. Today the center continues to subordinate much of the periphery, but rivalries among center powers and challenges from some of the peripheral nations—e.g., the oil-exporting countries—are beginning to change some of the characteristics of this third stage of imperialism.

The three readings in this chapter are intended to illuminate several important dimensions of modern imperialism, focusing on the role of the United States as the major imperialist power within the world capitalist system. The first reading locates the roots of American imperialism in the expansionary needs of a capitalist economy. The following reading investigates the nature of the multinational corporate system that has emerged with the integration of the world capitalist economy in recent decades. The final reading examines the new relationship between the center and the periphery that has developed in the period since World War II, and considers to what extent Marx's view of the progressive impact of imperialism on peripheral economic development may now be valid. All three readings conclude with an examination of contradictions that seem to be arising in the current stage of imperialism in the capitalist system.

[9]See MacEwan, Section 12.3, p. 455, for an analysis of the rise and subsequent decline of U.S. hegemony in the postwar period.

Statistical Appendix

THE GROWTH OF U.S. PRIVATE INVESTMENT ABROAD

Table 13-A presents data on the growth of U.S. private investment assets in foreign countries from 1950 to 1974. The total value of foreign private investment includes not only direct investment assets (equity capital invested in enterprises located abroad) but also other long-term assets (loans for a year or more) and short-term assets (loans for less than a year). Long-term assets account for the bulk of the total value of U.S. private investment abroad, and direct investment represents over 60 percent of the total. Total assets, long-term assets, and direct investment abroad have all multiplied by roughly ten times in the twenty-four-year period, growing at average rates of more than 10 percent per year.[1]

Table 13-A also lists the annual value of capital outflow and the corresponding balance of payments inflow associated with U.S. direct private investment abroad. A major share of this investment is financed in foreign countries, both from local sources and from reinvested earnings of the foreign affiliates of American enterprises. Thus the annual outflow of direct investment capital from the United States is much less than the corresponding annual increase in the value of U.S. direct investment assets abroad. The return flow from abroad includes both investment income (that part of the income from existing foreign investment that is repatriated back to the United States) and royalties and fees (the various payments for licenses, technological know-how, managerial services, etc., made by

[1]All the data presented in this reading are based on dollar values at current prices. Thus real rates of growth are overstated by the amount of price inflation that took place in the period under consideration. From 1950 to 1974, the U.S. GNP price deflator rose by an annual average of roughly 3 percent per year (see *The Economic Report of the President*, 1976, Table B-3). Thus in real terms the growth of U.S. foreign investment has averaged roughly 7 percent per year.

TABLE 13-A THE GROWTH OF U.S. PRIVATE INVESTMENT ABROAD, 1950–1974

	Value of Assets (billions of dollars at end of year)			Direct Investment Flows (billions of dollars during year)		
Year	Total	Long-Term	Direct	Capital Outflow	Total Inflow[1]	Investment Income
1950	19.0	17.5	11.8	0.6	1.5	1.3
1955	29.1	26.8	19.4	0.8	2.1	1.9
1960	49.4	44.4	31.9	1.7	2.9	2.4
1965	81.5	71.4	49.5	3.5	5.2	4.0
1970	116.4	103.6	75.5	4.3	7.9	6.0
1974	196.6	160.0	118.6	7.5	20.7	17.7

[1]Includes investment income plus royalties and fees.
SOURCE: U.S. Department of Commerce, *Survey of Current Business* (monthly), annual articles on U.S. foreign investment.

foreign affiliates to their American parent companies). As shown in Table 13-A, both the outflow of new investment capital and the inflow of investment income plus royalties and fees have increased greatly from 1950 to 1974, but the latter has been consistently higher than the former. There has thus been a continuous (and indeed steadily increasing) net capital inflow associated with U.S. direct private investment abroad.[2]

With the recovery of the West European and Japanese economies from the devastation of World War II, the primacy of the United States in the world capitalist economy has come increasingly under challenge.[3] The decline in U.S. hegemony has become quite evident in the 1970s, and is reflected in, among other things, a growth of direct investment by foreign corporations in the United States. By 1974 the value of foreign direct investment assets in the United States had

reached a total of $21.7 billion,[4] almost 20 percent of the value of the corresponding U.S. assets abroad.

Table 13-B attempts to place the postwar growth of U.S. direct private investment abroad into an appropriate perspective by comparing it with the growth of total corporate business activity in the United States. The figures show that investment abroad not only has grown rapidly in absolute terms but also has grown substantially in relative terms. Between 1950 and 1972 the value of U.S. direct private investment assets abroad doubled from 5 percent to roughly 10 percent of total corporate investment assets (at home and abroad). The rise in the share of foreign profits[5] in total after-tax corporate profits was even more dramatic: from roughly 7 percent in 1950 to about 25 percent in 1972. The fact that the foreign share of profits was sub-

[2]This net capital inflow belies the notion that private capital from the United States adds directly to the capital resources available to the rest of the world. In fact the return flow of profits exceeds the outflow of new capital. But foreign private investment has indirect as well as direct effects on the availability of capital in foreign countries. An estimate of the overall impact of United States' private investment abroad would have to take account of its net contribution to domestic income, the extent to which it displaces or inhibits domestic capital formation, and other such variables that affect the availability of capital in foreign countries.

[3]See Chapter 12, and especially MacEwan, Section 12.3, p. 455, for a discussion of the decline in U.S. hegemony since the late 1960s.

[4]This estimate is drawn from the article on foreign investment in the United States published in the U.S. Department of Commerce, *Survey of Current Business* (October 1975).

[5]As Frank Ackerman has pointed out in his review of Harry Magdoff's *Age of Imperialism* (*Public Policy*, 19, No. 3, Summer 1971), it is necessary to make some adjustments on the reported data on foreign earnings in order to make them comparable with domestic after-tax profits. The data available from the Department of Commerce show foreign earnings after foreign taxes but before U.S. taxes. Because U.S. tax laws allow firms to deduct from their U.S. taxes an amount equal to foreign taxes paid on repatriated income (provided foreign tax rates do not exceed the U.S. tax rates), the effective U.S. tax rate on foreign earnings is much lower than the rate (about 50 percent) that applies to domestic profits.

TABLE 13-B THE RELATIVE SIZE AND PROFITABILITY OF U.S. DIRECT PRIVATE
INVESTMENT ABROAD: 1950–1972

Year	Total Investment			Investment Abroad			Foreign/Total Ratios	
	After-tax Profits (billions of dollars)	Invested Capital	Profit Rate (%)	After-tax Profits (billions of dollars)	Invested Capital	Profit Rate (%)	After-tax Profits (%)	Invested Capital (%)
1950	24.9	223.6	11.1	1.8	11.2	16.3	7.3	5.0
1957	26.0	344.4	7.5	3.7	23.9	15.4	14.2	6.9
1960	26.7	409.0	6.5	3.9	30.8	12.7	14.6	7.5
1965	46.5	536.0	8.7	6.3	47.0	13.4	13.5	8.8
1970	39.3	752.0	5.2	10.2	73.2	13.9	26.0	9.7
1972	57.7	887.0	6.5	14.1	86.7	16.2	24.4	9.8

SOURCES: Corporate after-tax profits: from U.S. Department of Commerce, *National Income and Product Accounts* (published annually in July issue of *Survey of Current Business*), Table 6.15.

Corporate invested capital: from U.S. Internal Revenue Service, *Statistics of Income: Corporate Income Tax Returns* (annually), data on net worth of corporations.

After-tax profits from foreign private investment: calculated by multiplying before-tax profits by 94% for reason explained in footnote 5. Before-tax profits obtained by adding together repatriated investment income, royalties and fees, and undistributed profits (reinvested earnings), as reported in U.S. Department of Commerce, *Survey of Current Business* (monthly), annual articles on U.S. foreign investment.

Foreign private invested capital: figures for each year represent the average of the year-end book value of direct investment assets for the preceding and given year, as reported in *ibid*.

Profit rates and foreign/total ratios: calculated directly from the corresponding values in the table.

stantially higher than the foreign share of invested capital throughout the period reflects the consistently higher average profitability of foreign as compared to total (and *a fortiori* domestic) business activity. The average foreign profit rate ranged between 12 and

According to Table 4 in "The Multinational Corporation and the World Economy," a staff report published in the *Hearings before the Subcommittee on International Trade of the Committee on Finance, U.S. Senate, 93rd Congress, 1st Session* (February/March 1973), the taxes paid to the U.S. government on income from foreign investment averaged approximately 6 percent of that income in 1968 and 1970. Using this figure, after-tax profits from U.S. foreign private investment have been calculated in Table 13-B by multiplying the available data on profits (before U.S. taxes) by 94 percent in all years.

It should be noted that even these adjusted figures tend to understate the profitability of foreign investment. On the one hand, profits made by overseas affiliates can be disguised by artificially high prices charged for the supply of inputs imported from the parent company. Such over-invoicing has the effect of transferring the profits from the accounts of the overseas affiliate to the accounts of the parent company in the United States. On the other hand, the reported value of foreign assets may well overstate the true value of the invested capital because of overpricing of the capital equipment and/or capitalization of costless assets such as brand names, etc.

17 percent from 1950 to 1972, while the corresponding average overall profit rate ranged between 5 and 11 percent. Indeed, the relative profitability differential in favor of foreign investment seems to have increased during the postwar years.

The geographical and sectoral distribution of U.S. direct private investment abroad is tabulated in Table 13-C for the years 1929, 1950, 1959, 1969, and 1974. The absolute figures in the table reflect the dramatic increase in the total value of direct investment both in the center and the periphery. But the percentage figures show significant shifts in the distribution of this investment among areas and sectors. The share of direct investment assets in the center has increased from roughly one-half in 1929 to roughly three-quarters in 1974, while the corresponding share in the periphery has dropped from about one-half in 1929 to about one-quarter in 1974. The major area for U.S. foreign investment has shifted from Latin America in 1929 and 1950 to Canada in 1959 and to Western Europe in 1969 and 1974. These geographical shifts have been accompanied by an increasing emphasis on invest-

TABLE 13-C THE DISTRIBUTION OF U.S. DIRECT PRIVATE INVESTMENT ASSETS ABROAD BY AREA AND SECTOR: 1929–1974

	1929	1950	1959	1969	1974
ALL AREAS	$7.5 b.	$11.8 b.	$29.7 b.	$70.8 b.	$118.6 b.
Center	49%	52%	61%	72%	76%
Canada	27	31	34	30	24
Western Europe	18	15	18	31	37
Japan	*	*	1	2	3
Others[1]	4	6	8	9	12
Periphery	51%	48%	39%	28%	24%
Latin America	47	39	30	19	16
Middle East	*	1	2	3	2
Africa[2]	*	2	3	3	2
Asia[3]	4	6	4	3	4
Mining & smelting	16%	9%	10%	8%	5%
Petroleum	15	29	35	28	26
Manufacturing	24	33	32	42	43
Other sectors	45	29	33	22	26
CENTER	$3.7 b.	$6.1 b.	$18.2 b.	$50.8 b.	$90.1 b.
Mining & smelting	12%	7%	7%	6%	4%
Petroleum	11	20	29	24	25
Manufacturing	41	49	44	48	47
Other sectors	36	24	20	22	24
PERIPHERY	$3.9 b.	$5.7 b.	$11.5 b.	$20.0 b.	$28.5 b.
Mining & smelting	19%	13%	14%	12%	7%
Petroleum	19	37	44	39	29
Manufacturing	8	15	14	26	32
Other sectors	54	35	28	23	32

*Denotes less than 0.5%.

[1]Includes South Africa, Australia, New Zealand and International.

[2]Excluding South Africa.

[3]Excluding Japan and the Middle East.

SOURCES: 1929 and 1950 data: S. Pizer and F. Cutler, *U.S. Business Investment in Foreign Countries* (Washington, D.C.: U.S. Government Printing Office, 1960).

1959, 1969, 1974 data: U.S. Department of Commerce, *Survey of Current Business*, articles on U.S. foreign investment in issues of September 1960, October 1970, and October 1975.

ment in the manufacturing sector in the postwar period. From 24 percent of total foreign investment assets in 1929, the share of the manufacturing sector rose to 43 percent by 1974. Within the center the share of manufacturing investment has remained close to 50 percent, while within the periphery it has risen from 8 to 32 percent. The extraction of raw materials (petroleum and mining and smelting) has long been more significant than manufacturing for foreign investors in the periphery. However, the steady growth in the importance of manufacturing investment, and a decline in the importance of raw mate-

rial investment in recent years,[6] will soon reverse their relative position.

The remaining two tables are intended to illustrate the extraordinary power of leading multinational corporations within the world economy. Table 13-D ranks the top ninety nations and corporations together according

[6]The decline in the importance of U.S. investment abroad in petroleum and mining and smelting is partly the result of increasing nationalization of such assets by third-world nations, which in turn is attributable to their enhanced bargaining power since the late 1960s. See Weisskopf, Section 13.3, p. 499, for further analysis of this phenomenon.

TABLE 13-D RANKING OF NATIONS AND CORPORATIONS BY SIZE OF ANNUAL PRODUCT: 1971

Rank	Economic Entity	Product[1] ($b.)	Rank	Economic Entity	Product[1] ($b.)
1	United States	1068.1	46	Pakistan	8.2
2	USSR	343.1	47	*Chrysler*	8.0
3	Japan	223.0	48	Nigeria	7.9
4	West Germany	196.8	49	Thailand	7.8
5	France	172.0	50	Chile	7.6
6	United Kingdom	135.8	51	*Texaco*	7.5
7	China	128.1	52	U.A.R.	7.5
8	Italy	100.6	53	*Unilever*[2,3]	7.5
9	Canada	89.4	54	*ITT*	7.4
10	India	60.6	55	Portugal	7.1
11	Poland	44.1	56	Bulgaria	7.0
12	Brazil	43.9	57	New Zealand	6.9
13	Spain	37.4	58	Peru	6.7
14	Mexico	36.7	59	Israel	6.6
15	Australia	36.4	60	Taiwan	6.4
16	Netherlands	34.6	61	*Western Electric*	6.1
17	East Germany	34.5	62	*Gulf Oil*	5.9
18	Sweden	34.3	63	Algeria	5.2
19	Czechoslovakia	30.7	64	*British Petroleum*[2]	5.2
20	Argentina	29.0	65	*Philips Gloeilampen*[3]	5.2
21	Belgium	28.7	66	*Standard Oil (Cal.)*	5.1
22	*General Motors*	28.3	67	Puerto Rico	5.1
23	Switzerland	22.9	68	*Volkswagen*[4]	5.0
24	*Standard Oil (N.J.)*	18.7	69	*U.S. Steel*	4.9
25	South Africa	18.4	70	Bangladesh	4.7
26	Denmark	17.2	71	*Westinghouse*	4.6
27	Austria	16.5	72	Malaysia	4.5
28	*Ford Motor*	16.4	73	Ireland	4.5
29	Rumania	15.2	74	North Korea	4.4
30	Yugoslavia	15.1	75	Cuba	4.4
31	Iran	13.4	76	South Vietnam	4.3
32	*Royal Dutch/Shell*[2,3]	12.7	77	*Nippon Steel*[5]	4.1
33	Hungary	12.4	78	*Standard Oil (Ind.)*	4.1
34	Turkey	12.3	79	Morocco	4.0
35	Norway	12.2	80	*Shell Oil*	3.9
36	Finland	12.0	81	*duPont*	3.9
37	Greece	11.3	82	*Siemens*[4]	3.8
38	Venezuela	11.2	83	Saudi Arabia	3.8
39	Indonesia	9.5	84	*Imperial Chem. Ind.*[2]	3.7
40	*General Electric*	9.4	85	*RCA*	3.7
41	Philippines	9.1	86	*Hitachi*[5]	3.6
42	South Korea	8.3	87	*Goodyear*	3.6
43	*IBM*	8.3	88	Hong Kong	3.6
44	Colombia	8.3	89	Iraq	3.6
45	*Mobil Oil*	8.2	90	*Nestle*[6]	3.6

[1]Gross national product for countries and gross sales for corporations.

[2-6]Corporations based outside the United States, in: (2) the United Kingdom; (3) the Netherlands; (4) West Germany; (5) Japan; or (6) Switzerland.

SOURCES: Gross national product figures from the *World Bank Atlas* (Washington: World Bank, 1973).

Corporate sales figures from United Nations, Department of Economic and Social Affairs, *Multinational Corporations in World Development* (New York: United Nations, 1973), Table 3.

to the size of their respective gross national product (GNP) or gross annual sales in 1971. Such figures do not measure precisely the relative economic strength of the different entities, for national governments control only a part of the income from their country's GNP and corporate directors control only a part of the revenues from their company's gross sales. Nonetheless, the table does convey a rough idea of the comparative power of nation-states and corporations.

Table 13-D indicates that in 1971 the top eight industrial corporations (seven of them based in the United States) ranked among the top thirty-nine nations whose GNP exceeded $8 billion. The majority of these thirty-nine are in the capitalist center; only fourteen are in the periphery. Among the top ninety economic entities in the rank-ordering by GNP or sales are twenty-nine corporations and sixty-one nations, of which only thirty-one are in the periphery. Thus a substantial majority of the hundred-odd peripheral nations and territories (those not listed in the table) ranked behind the largest twenty-nine corporations in economic power.

Table 13-E presents detailed information on the extent to which the twenty-five largest

TABLE 13-E FOREIGN OPERATIONS OF THE TOP 25 INDUSTRIAL CORPORATIONS: 1971[1]

Rank	Corporation	Sales ($b.)	Foreign Content as % of			
			Sales[2]	Assets	Earnings	Employment
1	General Motors	28.3	14[a]	15[a]	19	27
2	Standard Oil (N.J.)	18.7	68[a]	56[a]	52	
3	Ford Motors	16.4	36[a]	40[a]	24	48
4	Royal Dutch/Shell	12.7	79			70
5	General Electric	9.4	16	15	20	
6	IBM	8.3	30[a]	34[a]	54[b]	36
7	Mobil Oil	8.2	45	46[a]	51	51
8	Chrysler	8.0	21[a]	31[a]		24
9	Texaco	7.5	40		25	
10	Unilever	7.5	80	60		70
11	ITT	7.3	47[a]	47[a]	35	72
12	Western Electric	6.0				
13	Gulf Oil	5.9	45	38[a]	21	
14	British Petroleum	5.2	88			83
15	Philips Gloeilampen	5.2		53		73
16	Standard Oil (Cal.)	5.1	45	9	43	29
17	Volkswagen	5.0	69			18
18	U.S. Steel	4.9	54	48		
19	Westinghouse	4.6				
20	Nippon Steel	4.1	31			2
21	Standard Oil (Ind.)	4.1		16		
22	Shell	3.9				
23	duPont	3.9	18	12		
24	Siemens	3.8	39			23
25	Imperial Chem. Ind.	3.7	35	25		27

[1]Sales figures in $ billion are for 1971; foreign content figures in % are for various years, mostly in the early 1970s.

[2]Sales to nonaffiliate firms outside the home country.

SOURCES: Sales in $ billion from United Nations, Department of Economic and Social Affairs, *Multinational Corporations in World Development* (New York: United Nations, 1973), Table 3; and from *Fortune* (May 1972) Directory of the Top 500 Industrial Corporations.

Foreign content in % from United Nations, *ibid.*, except where superscript indicates (a) J. Fred Weston and Eugene Brigham, *Managerial Finance*, 4th ed. (New York: Holt, Rinehart and Winston, 1972), p. 627; (b) *Business Week*, January 12, 1974, p. 53.

industrial corporations in the world (ranked by gross sales in 1971) are involved in foreign operations. Eighteen of these twenty-five corporations are based in the United States. The available data on the foreign share of total sales, assets, earnings, and employment show varying degrees of foreign involvement for these corporations. It is clear, however, that the foreign share of total economic activity is higher for most of the U.S. corporations on the list than it is for the U.S. economy as a whole. It follows that foreign economic activity is highly concentrated among a relatively small number of major corporations in the United States.[7]

[7]It has been estimated that in 1970 the income derived from foreign operations by the top ten U.S. industrial corporations (ranked by foreign sales) represented 30 percent of the total foreign earnings of all U.S. industrial corporations, and the income derived by the top fifty accounted for roughly half of the total. For documentation, see Thomas E. Weisskopf, "American Economic Interests in Foreign Countries: An Empirical Survey," Discussion Paper #35, Center for Research on Economic Development, University of Michigan (April 1974), p. 16.

13.1 Capitalist Expansion and the Sources of Imperialism

Since the Vietnam War assumed major proportions in the 1960s, most Americans have become aware of the reality of U.S. imperialism. Yet the very magnitude and horror of the U.S. involvement in Vietnam has suggested to many observers that this is a unique phenomenon, an aberration rather than a natural consequence of American capitalism.

In the following essay Arthur MacEwan argues to the contrary that the Vietnam War is only the most obvious example of a consistently imperialist American foreign policy, and that imperialism necessarily arises in a capitalist system. MacEwan shows first that the logic of capitalist expansion leads inevitably to the flow of capital across national boundaries and that large monopolistic firms tend to dominate the expansionary process. He then goes on to discuss the role of the state in the expansion of capitalism, and he illustrates this role with a brief look at the history of United States foreign policy since the turn of the century. Finally, he examines modern imperialism, emphasizing the critical role of capitalist ideology in supporting an imperialist foreign policy.

In developing his argument, MacEwan identifies three stages of expansionary activity during the process of the internationalization of capital: the development of national economies, the formation of colonies and spheres of influence, and the integration of the world capitalist economy. These three stages correspond to the three stages of imperialist relations between the center and periphery discussed in the introduction to this chapter.

The Vietnam War, its profound impact on U.S. society, and the final defeat of the United States in Vietnam have led us all to ask many questions about the foreign policy of the United States. Such an inquiry reveals that the United States has a long history of intervening—militarily, politically, economi-cally—in the affairs of other nations. The intervention in Vietnam was unusual only in that it developed into a full-scale war which the United States lost.

In order to understand the origins of the Vietnam War, it would thus be an error to confine oneself to the history and immediate bases of that particular *military* intervention. The Vietnam War should be examined in the context of the entire history of U.S. foreign involvement. This history reveals the extent to which U.S. business and the U.S. govern-ment have extended control over other nations. It is this extension of control, in all its aspects, that I shall describe by the term "imperialism."

While U.S. imperialism operates in many spheres—political, economic, cultural—it is in its most fundamental sense an economic phenomenon. That is, this international extension of control has its basis in the eco-nomic organization of American society. Within a capitalist economic system—and the United States is the most advanced capi-talist system in history—there are basic forces that push that system toward expansion. This expansion carries with it an extension of con-trol; hence, a capitalist system necessarily develops into an imperialist system.

THE EXPANSION OF CAPITAL

The fundamental principle of operation for the capitalist firm is the search for profits.[1] This search takes on many forms. One form is the introduction of new techniques of pro-duction and organization which allow cost reductions. The introduction of new tech-niques is often associated with a dependence upon expansion in the size of the enterprise's operation. For example, an extension of the division of labor—that hallmark of capitalist efficiency—is almost always dependent upon an expansion of sales. In this manner, tech-nical change in the production process is often intricately bound up with another form of the search for profits—namely, the search for new markets. Whether or not cost-cutting innovations are introduced, the opening of new markets allows an expansion of sales without a corresponding decline in price. In the absence of increasing costs, new markets thus provide a basis for expanding profits.

Particularly important for the purposes of this essay is that the search for markets will often involve an expansion of the geographic sphere of operations. Geographic expansion has many advantages. For a firm operating in a competitive industry, geographic expansion allows the exploitation of markets where the downward pressure on prices is not so severe. For firms selling a relatively new product, the size of the local market may not be sufficient to take advantage of economies of scale, and international sales are necessary if produc-tion is to be profitable. In each case profitability is, of course, the criterion of geographic expansion, but profitability is often limited by uncertainty, lack of information, and political or economic instability. These factors can be significant barriers to the geo-graphic expansion of the small firm.

For the large monopolistic firm, such matters of information, uncertainty, and instability are of less importance. In con-fronting each of these problems, the large firm has a natural advantage. It has the facil-ities to gain knowledge and gauge the pos-sibility for profits, and it can help insure its investments against instability. There are additional reasons why the monopolistic firm is apt to place particular importance upon international expansion of its markets.[2] First, simply in order to maintain its monopolistic position, it must control markets outside its original sphere of operation. Otherwise new firms may develop in those areas and even-tually threaten the original base of operation.

[1]For an analysis of the profit-making drive of the capi-talist firm, see Edwards, Section 3.3, p. 99.

[2]The argument presented here and in the next para-graph is developed more fully, in the context of a "product-cycle" model by T. Moran, "Foreign Expan-sion as an 'Institutional Necessity' for U.S. Corporate Capitalism," *World Politics,* 25, No. 3 (April 1973).

The consequences of a failure to control new markets is clear from the development of the European and Japanese automobile industries and their subsequent inroads on U.S. markets. While U.S. firms did attempt to control through the purchase of some European firms (e.g., Opel) they were unable to halt the European competition.[3]

Second, in the same manner that it will search for new products rather than expand its own product line, the monopolistic firm will seek to expand in new markets rather than expand and cut profits (through a lowering of the price) in its basic market. This is exemplified by the pharmaceuticals industry, which is notorious for its monopolistic practices in the United States and which has become a leader in the development of international markets.[4]

In addition to the search for new markets, there are other forms of the international search for profits. The availability of raw materials has always drawn capitalist enterprises throughout the world. While a firm of any size may be attracted by the profitability of obtaining raw materials, it is the large monopolistic firm that is particularly active and successful. In the first place, the exploitation of raw materials often requires large capital resources. Second, the large firm that is vertically integrated (e.g., the bauxite-aluminum-aluminum products companies) and thus uses the raw materials and sells the final product often has a special advantage. Third, and perhaps most important, the monopolistic firm is concerned about control. Whatever the narrow profitability of obtaining particular raw materials, controlling their supply is often important to the large firm which must continue to insure that other firms do not make inroads on its realm. The petroleum industry is the most prominent example of an international exploiter of raw materials, and it exhibits each of these advantages of monopolistic operation. Aluminum, copper, and other mineral industries also provide good examples.[5]

Another form which the internationalization of business takes is the extension to new areas of the production process itself. On the one hand, the establishment of production operations in new areas is a means to exploit the markets of those areas. Sometimes the nature of the product is such that it is necessary or desirable to undertake production, or at least the final stages of production, close to the market in which it is sold. The refining of oil, the processing or packaging of food products (Coca-Cola!), the provision of a service, and construction projects all provide examples. Sometimes legal restrictions of the host country—tariffs, for example—require that a product be produced in the area where it is to be sold. This is true of the automobile industry in Mexico and in several other Latin American countries. Insofar as the establishment of production operations in a new area is based on such motives, it often involves not a complete operation but only the final assembly of a product.

On the other hand, production activities are frequently established in a new area in order to exploit the relatively low-cost labor in that area. The assembly of electronic components in Taiwan, punching IBM cards in Hong Kong, making shoes in Italy, and hand typesetting in several countries have all been developed by U.S. industries to avoid the relatively high labor costs at home. As with other types of international expansion, we can expect the monopolistic enterprise to take the lead in the international exploitation

[3]Ernest Mandel, in *Europe vs. America* (New York: Monthly Review Press, 1970), provides much information and an analysis of the competition for markets among enterprises from advanced capitalist nations.

[4]Michael Kidron, in *Foreign Investments in India* (New York: Oxford University Press, 1965), Chap. 4, Section 5, provides a particularly interesting description of the inroads of Western pharmaceutical firms into the Indian market.

[5]For accounts of the operations of the petroleum industry that develop these points see: M. Tanzer, *The Political Economy of International Oil and the Underdeveloped Countries* (Boston: Beacon Press, 1969); R. Engler, *The Politics of Oil* (New York: Macmillan & Co., Inc., 1961); H. O. Connor, *World Crisis in Oil* (New York: Monthly Review Press, 1962).

of labor. In terms of its ability to control and to transfer technology, its ability to secure sufficient demand for the new production enterprise, and its political ability to cope with the local population as a work force, the large firm has marked advantages.

In summary, the basic method of operation of the capitalist firm leads to international expansion in several ways. While the overall motivation is always profit, the particular medium through which the profits are gained can be the extension of markets, the obtaining of raw materials, or the exploitation of new sources of labor. In general, monopolistic enterprises can be expected to take the leading role in the internationalization of capital.

The internationalization of capital is a process that does not take place in a political vacuum. Capital requires direct protection and the institutions through which it operates must be protected. Thus the expansion of the area of operation of capital is always associated with an expansion of the political influence of the state with which that capital is associated. In the following section I shall examine the historical operation of state and capital in the expansionary process.

THE ROLE OF THE STATE

In the history of capitalist development, we may distinguish three broad stages of expansionary activity. These stages, while they do not conform in a precise way to historical eras, are useful analytical tools for examining the internationalization of capital. In each of the stages the state can be seen providing the essential framework for expansion.

First is the stage of creating *national economies* in which the locus of economic activity moves from cities or small regions toward a national framework. Second is the stage of *colonialism and spheres of influence* in which the business interests of advanced nations extend their control beyond their own boundaries but with each nation operating in separate geographic areas. Third is the stage of *inter-national capitalist integration*, in which barriers to economic activity among capitalist countries tend to be eliminated and firms from each nation have access to the economies of all of the geographic areas within the world capitalist orbit. In this third stage it is possible for a single dominant capitalist power to exercise economic hegemony over the entire capitalist world, as the United States did for the first few decades after World War II. But in more recent times several European nations as well as Japan have gained enough strength to challenge U.S. hegemony, so the third stage of international capitalist integration is now increasingly characterized by a new form of competition among rival capitalist powers.

The First Stage: The Development of National Economies

The early development of capitalism required the expansion of the size of the capitalist economic unit. In this expansion the state played a crucial role.

The key aspect of capitalist production is that the worker must be separated from the control of any productive factors other than his or her own labor and that the production process must be controlled by the owner of capital.[6] The process of separating workers from their means of production, and thus forcing them into the labor market and into capitalist production relationships, was facilitated by the power of the state. The state was instrumental in the development of capitalism in England, for example, through promotion of the enclosure movement in the eighteenth century and through legislation forcing the poor to enter the work force in the nineteenth century. It played a similar role in other parts of Western Europe and in Japan (after the Meiji Restoration in 1868), where the persistence of feudal institutions threatened to impede the growth of capitalism.

[6]See Chapter 3, and especially the introduction, p. 75, for a more detailed description of the capitalist mode of production.

The profitable use of a developing labor force by the capitalist firm depends upon an expansion in the size of the unit of production. The division of labor that provides the basis for capitalist efficiency could not take place in a small craft shop of the pre-capitalist era. However, an enterprise could be profitably expanded only to the extent that there was a market for increased output. (This was true, for example, of the development of textile mills in England: a national market was necessary to support these harbingers of the factory system.) Thus it was necessary for capitalist development that local restrictions on trade be broken down, that means of transportation and communication be developed, that a uniform system of law and order be established over a wide area—in short, it was necessary that national economic units be developed and strengthened.

The Second Stage: Colonies and Spheres

The stage in capitalist development that followed the political and economic development of the nation was characterized by colonial expansion and the creation of spheres of influence. As in the preceding stage, the economic integration of a larger geographic area was the key to the expansion process. However, while the need for markets and labor played some role, the effort to develop sources of supply for important foodstuffs and raw materials became particularly important in the second stage. The role of the state remained as before: to break down local restrictions on economic activity; to create a labor force; to create means of transportation and communication; to insure stability through the imposition of law and order.

Britain, for example, united the regional economies of India and opened the whole subcontinent to penetration by British capital. Each colonial power established its own currency as the medium of exchange throughout its realm. The European colonial powers in Africa imposed monetary taxes on the indigenous people, forcing them to leave the traditional economy and enter the capitalist labor force to earn cash incomes to pay the taxes. Throughout the colonial world, railways directed toward import-export activity were given priority. Britain, France, Germany, and all of the colonial powers backed up their economic decisions in the most direct manner—with armed force.

In organizing trade within its particular sphere, each nation reserved for its own capitalist class special economic privileges—with respect to both the subordinate areas in its control and other leading capitalist powers. Thus, for example, Portugal prohibited the development of manufacturing in Brazil, reserving the market for goods produced in the parent country, and England restricted the trade of its North American colonies with other European powers.

The Third Stage: International Capitalist Integration and the Role of the United States

It is not surprising that the United States was a latecomer in building spheres of influence and establishing colonies. First, the United States itself had been under the control of Britain and became a nation only when many European nations were well-established as international powers. Second, as long as the United States was able to expand westward within the North American continent, there was little pressure for the more typical overseas expansion.

As continental boundaries were reached, the United States began to enter seriously the competition among the big powers for new areas of exploitation. Around the turn of the last century, the United States and Britain were instrumental in ushering in a new era of capitalist international relations. The policies of the new era were typified by the U.S. demand for an "open door" in the Far East. With several European powers scrambling to establish control in China, the United States in 1899 demanded that all countries be allowed commercial access to this area—that the door be left open to all. This policy signified a movement away from national spheres of influence toward a single integrated international capitalist economy. Two world wars were to be fought, however, before this final stage would be firmly established.

Part of the reason that the U.S. government took a diplomatic lead in altering the relations of international capitalism was that U.S. business interests were latecomers to international activity. Thus, short of all-out war with other imperialist powers, the government had no way other than diplomatic initiative to gain access to many areas for U.S. business. More important, the government's demand for open access and equal terms was natural since the nation was rapidly becoming the world's greatest economic power. Under conditions of open access, the emerging political and economic strength of the United States would insure that its interests would prevail more often than not.

Coincidentally with the rising international power of U.S. business, the U.S. government engaged in numerous military interventions around the beginning of the century. The Spanish-American War led to the establishment of formal U.S. colonies in Puerto Rico and in the Philippines (an important stepping stone for establishing influence in China) and virtual colonial control over Cuba (only nominally independent). In each of these areas, the extension of U.S. political control was followed by a rapid increase of U.S. economic interests.[7]

In 1912 the United States intervened militarily in Nicaragua in order to assure that the interests of U.S. banks financing a railway were not interfered with. In 1915 the United States occupied Haiti in order to insure that the Haitian government "honor" its obligations to U.S. bankers. In 1916, the U.S.

Marines were sent to Santo Domingo and seized control of the customs and treasury of that nation in order to insure that obligations to American companies would be fulfilled. And again in 1916, when U.S. oil interests were threatened in Mexico, the Marines were sent to the scene. While the majority of U.S. military interventions in this period were in the Caribbean, they were by no means limited exclusively to that area. In 1911 and 1912, and later in 1924 and 1926, U.S. armed forces made their presence felt in China in order to protect U.S. private property during civil disturbances there; these military actions provided the backdrop for the growth of U.S. trade and financial interests in China.[8]

Military interventions, however, should not necessarily be taken as typical of the operation of U.S. imperialism. More often than not, control has been exercised through economic power or through nonmilitary political pressure.

[7]See S. Nearing and J. Freeman, *Dollar Diplomacy* (New York: Monthly Review Press, 1966), for the details of the early period of U.S. military interventions. An exhaustive list of U.S. military interventions abroad from 1900 to 1975 is given in the Appendix to Section 1.7, p. 33.

[8]This era is summed up in the following statement by a retired Marine commander:

I spent thirty-three years and four months in active service as a member of our country's most agile military force—the Marine Corps. I served in all commissioned ranks from a second lieutenant to major-general. And during that period I spent most of my time being a high-class muscle man for Big Business, for Wall Street, and for the bankers. In short, I was a racketeer for capitalism. . . .

Thus I helped make Mexico and especially Tampico safe for American oil interests in 1914. I helped make Haiti and Cuba a decent place for the National City Bank boys to collect revenues in. . . . I helped purify Nicaragua for the international banking house of Brown Brothers in 1909–1912. I brought light to the Dominican Republic for American sugar interests in 1916. I helped make Honduras "right" for American fruit companies in 1903. In China in 1927 I helped see to it that Standard Oil went its way unmolested.

During those years I had, as the boys in the back room would say, a swell racket. I was rewarded with honors, medals, promotion. Looking back on it, I feel I might have given Al Capone a few hints. The best he could do was operate his racket in three city districts. We Marines operated on three continents.

Major-General Smedley D. Butler, *Common Sense* (November 1935), as quoted by L. Huberman and P. Sweezy in *Cuba: Anatomy of a Revolution* (New York: Monthly Review Press, 1960).

MODERN IMPERIALISM

Economic power provides the basis for control in a modern imperialist system. Imperialism results from the internationalization of capitalist economic relations, and it involves the internationalization of capitalist power relations. In the first place, the rationale of commodity markets is that those who can sell products the cheapest will hold the dominant position. Thus, important sectors of the economies of secondary capitalist countries are dominated by the more advanced enterprises of the primary imperialist nations. While such domination has an impact at all levels of the international system, it takes on its most overt form in the poor countries.[9]

Second, international capitalism tends to develop or reinforce a class structure in poor countries that serves its interests. Classes in subservience to and alliance with international capital tend to control the political apparatus; their power derives directly from their association with international capital. Both directly through the market and indirectly through the class structure, the economic power of the capitalist elite in the advanced capitalist nations enables them to dominate the economies of the poor countries.

The rapid growth in recent years of multinational corporations has greatly enhanced this economic power. The multinational corporations have a great deal of bargaining power in setting the terms on which their capital will be deployed in host countries simply because they have numerous options. They control technology and can regulate its dissemination according to their own priorities. They have the power, through internal pricing and bookkeeping adjustments, to artificially adjust the international location of their revenues and outlays and thereby affect the finances and balance of payments of host countries. The international capitalist market is like any national capitalist market: those who dominate the control of the means of production dominate the economy.

Imperialist control operates through political as well as economic channels. First, day-to-day control operates through normal diplomatic channels. The role of U.S. diplomatic missions throughout the world is defined as looking after the interests of its nationals, and this means in practice looking after the interests of U.S. business. Second, long-run control operates through the determination of the institutions of the international capitalist economy. Good examples are the negotiation of trade agreements favorable to U.S. capital and the establishment of an international monetary system in which the dollar is key. Such operations serve to maintain the long-run international hegemony of U.S. capital.[10]

Finally, the dominance of the world capitalist economy by the United States is backed up by tremendous military strength. Modern imperialist operations depend on the actual deployment of the military only when problems arise which economic power and quiet political dealings cannot handle. But today imperialism is being presented with serious challenges, and as these challenges become a threat to the entire system, military responses become increasingly necessary.

The Socialist Challenge

With the Russian Revolution in 1917—but more clearly following World War II when the Soviet Union emerged as a major world power, socialism "spread" to Eastern Europe, and successful socialist revolutions occurred in China, Korea, Vietnam—the political position of international capitalism has been severely altered. The system has been forced to move from a purely offensive political strategy toward a defensive posture.

[9]For an analysis of the impact of imperialism on the poor countries of the capitalist periphery, see Weisskopf, Section 13.3, p. 499.

[10]For elaboration and substantiation of the assertions of this paragraph see Harry Magdoff, *The Age of Imperialism* (New York: Monthly Review Press, 1969), Chap. 3 and 4.

In the early part of this century the state functioned to establish and to assure the operation of capitalist relationships in areas where those relationships had not been fully established or were unstable. This was true of the numerous Caribbean military interventions cited above. Failures by foreign governments to honor contractual commitments with U.S. business, an elementary condition of capitalism, brought on the U.S. military. In the post–World War II era, however, the dominant concern of U.S. foreign policy has been the prevention of moves toward socialism by countries within the capitalist system. Thus, the interventions in Iran in 1953, in Guatemala in 1954, in Cuba in 1961, and in the Dominican Republic in 1965 should be seen primarily as defensive efforts against the threat—real or perceived—that the nations in question would opt out of the international capitalist system. The same is true of the long and ultimately unsuccessful U.S. military involvement in Indochina, and the intervention of the C.I.A. in Chile which helped to overthrow the leftist government of Salvador Allende in 1973.

As the major capitalist power emerging from the debacle of World War II, the United States assumed most of the burden of protecting the world capitalist empire. But the preservation of international capitalism is a goal in which not every American citizen has an equal interest. On a direct and material level, the income returned to the United States from direct foreign investment amounts to roughly one percent of national income.[11] In terms of its direct contribution to overall employment or its contribution to individual income, this figure would indicate that the international involvement of U.S. business is not very important. However, this income

from international activity goes predominantly to those who obtain their income from profits. As a share of after-tax corporate profits, income from direct foreign investment has been growing rapidly and exceeded 25 percent by the early 1970s.[12] If one examines the very large corporations, the importance of the international economy becomes even more apparent. Standard Oil (N.J.), IBM, Mobil Oil, Singer, Sperry Rand, Coca-Cola, and many other major corporations derive more than 50 percent of their earnings from overseas.[13] In 1972, the First National City Bank, the world's first bank to earn over $200 million in a single year, earned $109 million abroad.[14]

These data support two points. First, U.S. business in general, and large firms in particular, have a very real interest in international operations taken as a whole. They clearly benefit from the foreign policy described above. Second, people who earn their income from sources other than capital, and even a good deal of the business community, do not significantly depend directly on the preservation of international capitalism. This mass of the population should not find such great appeal in a foreign policy explicitly based on the concept that the government must protect and facilitate the search for profits overseas. Where economic interest is lacking, however, a popular form of the ideology of capitalist expansion provides the domestic support for the U.S. government's foreign policy.

The Role of Ideology

The ideology of capitalist expansion—the set of ideas that justify and support the system—has developed out of the needs of the expansionary process. In providing support for the system, one of its most important functions is to establish criteria for judging

---

[11]Table 13-A, p. 476, presents figures on the inflow of income from abroad associated with direct private foreign investment. Comparing these figures with the corresponding levels of GNP in current dollars published in Table B-1 of the *Economic Report of the President*, 1976, one can see that 1974 was the first year that the ratio of foreign investment income to GNP exceeded 1 percent.

[12]See Table 13-B, p. 477.

[13]See Table 13-E, p. 480, and the sources cited therein.

[14]See R. J. Barnet and R. E. Müller, *Global Reach* (New York: Simon & Schuster, 1975), p. 28.

political activities. Thus, growing out of an economic process, the capitalist ideology provides a basis for unifying the economic and political realms of the system and for facilitating their joint operation.

The expansionist ideology is based on the functioning of the capitalist enterprise, and its primary element is simply the belief that the function of economic enterprise is the pursuit of profit. As was argued in the first part of this article, acceptance of the pursuit of profit as a guiding principle means that the behavior of capitalist firms will be expansionary. In order for capitalist expansion to be successful, it is necessary that basic capitalist institutions be created and maintained: the labor market and other basic factor and commodity markets; private property; legal sanction for economic contracts; control of the work process by the owners of capital. According to the ideology of capitalism, these institutions promote "economic freedom." Actions taken by the state that preserve this "freedom" or that facilitate its operation become synonymous with actions that preserve a decent society.

Translated into the realm of foreign policy, the task of the capitalist state then becomes that of facilitating and protecting the international business activities of its nationals. On the level of particular interests, for example: the U.S. diplomatic mission in India sees to it that U.S. pharmaceutical companies are allowed to produce and sell under "reasonable" conditions; in Bolivia and Peru, when U.S.-owned oil companies are nationalized, it is the business of the U.S. government; when Brazilian coffee producers begin to sell instant coffee below the price at which U.S. companies can produce, the U.S. government "encourages" the Brazilian government to impose an export duty.[15] On a broader level, the government provides

mechanisms for the general expansion of U.S. interests abroad: the U.S. government encourages foreign governments to lower tariffs for U.S. goods and to enter reciprocity arrangements with the United States; the U.S. government provides insurance against nationalization or other political "disasters" in unstable areas; the international sections of various government departments—e.g., commerce, labor—devote themselves to providing U.S. business with investment and trade information on countries throughout the world. Finally, on the broadest level, the the role of the U.S. government in protecting the international business interests of its citizens is the protection of the system that allows those interests to operate—i.e., the protection of international capitalism.

The keystone of the ideology of capitalist expansion during the post–World War II period has been anti-communism. Communism has been presented to the American people as an international conspiracy which has as its design the enslavement of all the peoples of the world and the consequent destruction of everything that they are taught to hold dear, from the private family and religion to freedom of speech and the two-party system. Such a threat must be fought at every step of the way, partly to protect those immediately in danger, but ultimately to protect the American people themselves. The fact that communism presents a systematic threat to the uninhibited operation of international capital is not emphasized in the popular form of the ideology.

Anti-communism is not the only form in which the ideology of expansionist policy has been popularized. At an earlier time, Christianity, Manifest Destiny, and the White Man's Burden have all done service to imperialist strategy. Indeed, today, as the force of anti-communism has begun to wane, a new set of popular justifications for U.S. interventions is taking form under the heading of "modern liberalism." At its base lies the sentiment that it is the task of the rich, powerful United States to help the poor, backward countries of the world in their quest for

[15]The Indian example is discussed by Kidron in the book cited above in footnote 4. The Brazilian example is from *The Economist*, February 24, 1968, and is cited by Harry Magdoff in *The Age of Imperialism* (New York: Monthly Review Press, 1969), p. 163. The Bolivian and Peruvian cases are well-known.

development. Economic advisory missions, foreign investment, the Peace Corps, and ultimately military involvement can all be justified on this basis.

In any society, over time the dominant class molds ideology in terms of its own interests. We need only mention various ways in which the U.S. business community shapes ideas about foreign affairs to indicate how all-pervasive is its influence. First, the individuals who hold foreign policy positions in the U.S. government are drawn heavily from the business community. The point here is not the importance of these individuals in making particular decisions but rather their role over a long period in shaping the institutions and developing the criteria by which decisions are made.[16] Second, by its control over resources, directly or through foundations, the business community sponsors in conjunction with the government virtually all of the writing, research, and teaching that is done in the area of foreign affairs. Here, the concept of "a marketplace of ideas" is truly apt. As in any commodity market, the goods demanded by those who control resources and who have purchasing power are the ones that continue to be produced. By this process, not only are the dominant ideas reinforced and strategy and apologia developed for actions, but the growth of any ideological counterforce is severely limited. Other means by which the business community can shape concepts of foreign policy include its control over the media, its sponsorship of the Council on Foreign Relations and lesser organizations of policy consideration, and its extensive lobbying practices. In each case, power rests not on any formal arrangements but on the control over resources and on a common objective interest in the general design of policy.

Having established the conceptual framework for U.S. foreign policy, the U.S. busi-

[16]See Domhoff, Section 6.4, p. 242; or, for a more detailed study, G. William Domhoff, "Who Made American Foreign Policy, 1945–1963?", in David Horowitz, ed., *Corporations and the Cold War* (New York: Monthly Review Press, 1969).

ness community can expect relatively little difficulty in having its way in most cases. Thus, to explain the U.S. government's actions, from aid-giving to military intervention, we need not argue that any particular interests are being served, nor even that business interests have been directly involved in the development of policy. A powerful ideology provides a guide to action, the link between economic interests and political policy. When the integrity of the world capitalist system is threatened and the rules of international capitalist operation are in jeopardy, the ideology of capitalist expansion propels the U.S. government into action to preserve international capitalism.

The Case of Vietnam

So it was with Vietnam. Prior to the late 1960s, U.S. business had relatively few direct economic interests in Vietnam, or even in the rest of Indochina. While one could point to its economic potential or argue that Vietnam was the key to a much larger economic realm, an argument that explains U.S. intervention in Vietnam in terms of particular economic interests is clearly inadequate. There was simply not very much at stake for U.S. business in Vietnam. However, in terms of the general interest of maintaining the integrity of the international capitalist system, of which South Vietnam was a small but recognized part, there was very much at stake. The United States, as the dominant capitalist power, had to make every possible effort to prevent the rise in South Vietnam of a government and social system that would break all the rules of international capitalism.

The fact that the United States was ultimately unsuccessful in defending the capitalist empire in Vietnam does not detract from the cogency of the above argument. The loss of South Vietnam to capitalist enterprise has not caused any fatal damage to those firms whose assets were lost; much less has the loss of these assets had a serious direct impact on the U.S. economy as a whole. However, the impact of the loss of South Vietnam on the integrity of the international capitalist system has in fact been quite profound. For one thing, the neighboring countries of Laos and Cambodia quickly followed South Vietnam out of the capitalist orbit. And throughout Asia and the rest of the third world, anti-imperialist forces gained in strength.

The point is that what was at stake in Vietnam was *not just some business assets or a piece of capitalist territory, but a set of rules and the integrity of an international system.* A violation of the system is a serious threat in and of itself. In order to function effectively, a social system must be supported by a set of beliefs regarding its legitimacy and its durability. These beliefs constitute the ideological support for the system. If violation or destruction of any part of the system occurs, then those beliefs are called into question and the whole system is in danger.[17]

CONCLUSION

The explanation of imperialist state activity that has been offered in this essay is, of course, an economic explanation. It is not economic in the simple sense that immediate economic interests directly determine state policy. The argument has been the somewhat more complex one that the economic organization of a capitalist society generates an ideology which, in turn, provides the framework for state action. The state thus responds indirectly to the needs—both immediate and general—of the capitalist class.

[17]An analogy may be useful. Suppose that the Cincinnati Reds are playing the San Diego Padres in the last game of the regular season. Cincinnati has already secured the pennant by twenty-five games and the Padres are in last place by an equal margin. Cincinnati is ahead by a score of 31 to 2; there are two outs and no men on in the last of the ninth. The Padre at bat, who is batting .208 for the season, has two strikes. He swings and misses a third pitch. But instead of walking off, the batter turns to the umpire and says, "How about a fourth strike?" He alludes to the above-mentioned facts, and he points out that no one's interests can possibly be seriously jeopardized by giving him a fourth strike. No immediate interests are at stake, but is it conceivable that such a violation of the rules of the game, a violation of the system, would be allowed?

The whole process of international capitalist expansion and its associated state intervention reveals some fundamental contradictions of capitalism. A successful capitalism is a geographically expanding capitalism. But the process of geographic expansion generates resistance in the form of conflicts among advanced powers and, as in Vietnam, conflicts with indigenous liberation movements. While these conflicts can often be contained, they will at times develop into major military engagements. In those cases, they can threaten the basic stability of the system.

The dependence of the expansionary process on an ideological link between economic interests and state action can exacerbate the contradictions of expansion. Were interventions to be carried out on a hard-nosed, carefully calculated basis, and related directly to economic interests, it would then be conceivable for a government to disengage when a venture became too costly. For example, when in Vietnam the United States found itself unable to win and the domestic costs of the war—both social and economic—became extremely burdensome, we might have expected a "rational" disengagement. Because the policy was based on an ideological link, however, "rational" disengagement proved difficult. The *immediate* basis of action was ideological, not economic, and military setbacks and domestic difficulties could not easily or quickly alter that ideological basis.

In the wake of the U.S. defeat in Vietnam, we may now begin to appraise the implications of the whole experience. At first, it might appear that in spite of military defeat, the contradictions contained in the conflict were overcome; the world capitalist system still stands. However, U.S. capitalism and the international empire which it dominated have been profoundly altered. Partly as a result of events set in motion by the Vietnam War, the U.S. government no longer has a free hand to suppress rebellions abroad (as recent events in Angola have illustrated); the oil-producing nations wield a new power in world affairs and have imposed severe constraints on the economies of the metropolitan capitalist powers; the international monetary system was disrupted and weakened; and world capitalism entered into its most serious economic crisis since the 1930s.[18] In short,

[18]See Chapter 12 for an analysis of the economic crisis of the 1970s; MacEwan, Section 12.3, p. 455, focuses on the international aspects of the crisis.

the era of international capitalist integration under U.S. hegemony has come to an end. World capitalism has entered a new period of instability, in which rival capitalist powers are competing with one another for economic influence and the future of the international capitalist system is clouded with uncertainties.

13.2   *The Multinational Corporate Capitalist Economy*

In an earlier reading[1] Stephen Hymer analyzed the evolution of the representative capitalist firm from its origin as a small workshop to its present status as a multinational corporation. In the next reading Hymer goes on to describe the nature of the modern capitalist world economy, increasingly dominated by multinational corporations based in the capitalist metropolis. It is these multinational corporations which have served as the primary vehicles for integrating the world capitalist system and establishing the international structure of hierarchy that now characterizes it.

[1]Hymer, Section 4.1, p. 120.

The following is excerpted from "The Internationalization of Capital" by STEPHEN HYMER. From the *Journal of Economic Issues*, 6, No. 1 (March 1972). Reprinted by permission of the *Journal of Economic Issues*.

The multinational corporation, or the multinational corporate system, has three related sides: international capital movements; international capitalist production; and international government.

By international capital movements I refer first to the direct investment of corporations in their overseas branches and subsidiaries, which [amounted in 1971] to about [$85] billion for American multinationals and about [$80] billion for non-American multinationals.[1] Second, I refer to the associated flows of short-term, long-term, and equity capital stimulated by the multinational corporation, which in turn stimulate the growth

[1]Editors' note: New estimates of the value of foreign investment have been supplied here, drawn from the source cited in footnote 8 of the introduction to this chapter, p. 474.

of international finance, that is, deposits in foreign banks, investments in the Eurocurrency and Eurobond market, investments in corporate stock of multinational firms by nonnationals, and so forth. The direct foreign investment by corporations has served as a base for a vast superstructure of credit drawing capital from all over the world; the associated noncorporate private capital flows from one country to another are at least as large as direct investments by corporations, and probably are growing faster.

International capitalist production refers to the incorporation of labor from many countries into an integrated worldwide corporate productive structure. American firms, for example, directly employ from 5 to 7 million people in foreign countries, and a growing but unknown number indirectly through subcontracting, licensing, and so forth. By comparison, the total employment of the 500 largest American firms is 13 or 14 million (this figure includes some, but not all, foreign employees), which means that many large corporations have 30, 40, or 50 percent and more of their labor force outside the United States.[2]

International government refers to the erosion of the traditional powers of nation-states and the emergence of international economic policy instruments in line with the tendency of the multinational corporation to internationalize capital and labor. When a corporation invests abroad, it not only sends capital and management out, but also establishes a system for drawing foreign capital and labor into an integrated world network. When many firms from many countries do this together on an expanded scale, as has been true over the last decade and will be increasingly true in the next, they are forming a new world system. They are unifying world capital and world labor into an interlocking system of cross-penetration that completely changes the system of national economies that has characterized world capitalism for the past three hundred years. This process reduces the independence of nation-states and requires the formation of supranational institutions to handle the increased interdependence. To create a world market where state frontiers disappear, a world system is needed in which the separate interests, laws, governments, and systems of taxation and regulation are lumped together into a unified code of laws on the rights and limits of international private property.

This three-pronged process is far from complete and is anything but smooth, but it has moved further and faster than is commonly realized. The outlines of a new international system already can be discerned, and, it must be quickly added, so can its cracks. American firms have been in the vanguard, but Euro-pean corporations are close on their heels; Japanese corporations, who have just started, are moving very quickly. International capital markets and international banking also are growing by leaps and bounds, and the combined movement of these forces is rapidly reducing the autonomy of governments. The pressure for international governmental agencies is very great and a start has been made on many fronts, but the process has been zigzagging and is far from off the ground.

In this essay I wish to concentrate on the political economy of the process, that is, the political consolidations accompanying the multinationalization of business. In the last analysis, markets come out of the barrel of a gun, and to establish an integrated world economy on capitalist lines requires the international mobilization of political power.

The central image of my analysis is the pyramid of power, and the focus of study is the merging of the separate pyramids of nation-states into an international pyramid. "When two primitive feudal states amalgamate," wrote Franz Oppenheimer in his classic treatise on the state, "their social layers stratify in a variety of ways, which to a certain extent are comparable to the combinations that result from mixing together two packs of cards." The process of integration now going on in the international economy may be thought of in a similar way—as the interpenetration of national corporation and capital into a new multinational system of ownership and control. The shuffle is neither random nor even, nor are the decks of the same size. Aces, kings, and queens are trying to remain on top, but instead of lording over their separate piles, they are cross-penetrating into a more complex structure.

I have chosen the image of cross-penetration instead of American imperialism pure and simple because I believe that the American hegemony which characterized the past twenty-five years has ended with the recovery of Europe, Japan, and Russia. American capital may well be able to retain a position of dominance, but it is under severe challenge

[2]Editors' note: These figures are for the early 1970s. See Table 13-E, p. 480, for estimates of the foreign share of employment for selected major corporations.

and will have to share power with other capitalists far more than it has done in the past.

I wish in my analysis to stress how competition in the product and capital market helps forge a unified interest among capitalists, while the corporate hierarchy and competition in the labor market divide and weaken popular power. The dynamic of the multinational corporation is thus a contradictory one. True, it expands the social nature of production to a world level; but only on the basis of minority power, and a conflict emerges between the general social power into which capital develops, and the private power of individual capitalists over these social conditions. As capital unites many workers in production and collectivizes many capitals in ownership, it becomes an alienated independent power which stands opposed to society and checks the full development of human productivity and its universal application.

. . .

INTERNATIONALIZATION OF CORPORATIONS

. . .

The two powerful levers for concentrating capital into larger and larger aggregates and then integrating these aggregates into a unified whole are *competition* and *credit*. Competition drives firms to continuously reinvest their profits and extend their markets as a means of self-preservation. The credit system unites individual capitals and stimulates further increases in their size. It acts as an immense social mechanism above that of the individual firm for the centralization of capital and the preservation of its collective interest. The market forces are now operating on a world scale and leading to the internationalization of corporations and capital.

. . .

[The threat of competition] played an important role in the postwar expansion of American firms in foreign countries. The American giants who were or became multinational possessed numerous advantages in organization, technology, access to capital, and product differentiation. They could supply some of the foreign market through exports, gaining a certain protection for their secrets from the long distance between production and consumption. The recovery of Europe and Japan soon challenged them, and they began to see many foreign firms using their technology and methods, or improving upon them. They could see their own expansion being thwarted by the formation of new capitals in other countries, and they discovered their advantages would be short-lived if they did not undertake foreign investment to preserve them.

These firms had three motives for expansion: (1) they saw a rapid growth in the *markets* for goods in which they specialized; (2) they saw *cheaper labor* (productivity divided by wage) which made it profitable to produce abroad; and (3) they saw *foreign competitors* growing faster than themselves and gaining an increased share of the world market.

To the individual firm these might appear as separate phenomena, but they are closely connected to each other through the labor market. Europe and Japan emerged from the devastation of the war with consumption patterns and expectations well below the American standard. However, their potential productivity was not nearly as far below that of America's, given the work habits and levels of skills of the labor force. A large surplus was available if the labor force could be organized and consumption kept from rising too fast.

. . .

American firms were thus presented with an opportunity and a challenge. Growth of foreign markets and labor supply made it attractive to invest abroad; growth of European and Japanese firms made it necessary. American firms did not invest substantially in continental Europe and Japan in the late forties and early fifties when they had the most political influence. Only after the development of the Common Market did they make their greatest effort, just as it was serious competition from Japanese firms that spurred the great drive to get into Japan. . . .

The world economy now presents new opportunities and challenges. The unlimited supply of labor in Europe is drying up as they exhaust their own populations and the possibilities for importing cheap labor. Twenty years of prosperity have changed labor's expectations about consumption standards and work intensity. . . . A similar tendency toward labor shortage, that is, a decline in the margin between labor's production and consumption, is emerging in Japan. In the United States resistance to work seems about to reach acute proportions from capital's point of view. Firms from all these countries are looking more and more toward labor in outlying fields.

In Eastern Europe, low consumption standards and a great expansion of infrastructure, health services, and education have resulted in a potentially very high rate of surplus value now bogged down in undemocratic socialism. The managers of these economies are trying, through economic reforms, to channel this surplus into the accumulation of capital and wealth. They could provide a great challenge to Free World capitals. (The threat would be greater, but different, if these countries chose socialist development.) The scramble for East–West trade and technical agreements is an attempt to change this challenge into an opportunity. China, less advanced and less amenable, also presents an important commercial and industrial challenge. (This article was written with a perfect replica of a Parker pen—as far as I could tell —manufactured in China; it sells in Iran for 50 cents, and in Singapore for 40 cents.) The scramble for China's surplus labor is just beginning.

The Third World also will be an important battleground in the coming years. . . . Large absolute numbers of people . . . [are] concentrated in the cities, ready, able, and willing to sell their labor power. Standards of consumption have remained low due to the large supply of this free labor, while potential productivity has increased substantially due to the . . . expansion of education, urban and industrial infrastructure, and other services.

Potential surplus labor is large, while the local capitalist class is weak, due to the restraints placed on it during the colonial period. Many multinationals have begun to tap this cheap labor supply, originally to displace imports, but now to expand exports to other underdeveloped countries and to the developed world. This phase of international investment is just beginning, but is likely to grow rapidly when one considers the plentiful supply of labor. The big danger to the multinationals is the possibility of socialism or state capitalism which will prevent the transformation of commodity production into capitalist commodity production. . . .

The large firms of the world are all competing for these various sources of future growth, but in an oligopolistic rather than in a cutthroat way. They recognize their mutual interdependence and strive to share in the pie without destroying it. As they do so, they come to be less and less dependent on their home country's economy for their profits, and more and more dependent on the world economy. Conflicts between firms on the basis of nationality are thereby transformed into international oligopolistic market sharing and collusion.

INTERNATIONALIZATION OF CAPITAL MARKETS

The second great lever of capital concentration and centralization is the credit system. The formation of a world capital market has only begun, but if its development continues at the present rate, it soon will be a factor of great significance in the world economy.

The multinational corporation and the international capital market should be seen as parallel, symbiotic developments. The multinational corporation's need for short-term loans and investment arising from the continuous inflow and outflow of money from all nations, never quite in balance, has encouraged international banking and has helped integrate short-term money markets; its long-term financial requirements and excellent credit rating have broadened the demand for international bond and equity capital. This provides an impetus for free international capital mobility.

The Eurobond market, for example, attracts capital from all over the surface of the globe (a significant portion comes from underdeveloped countries, particularly the oil wealth of the Middle East and the war wealth of Southeast Asia), concentrates it in an organized mass, and redirects it via multinational corporations and other intermediaries back to the country from which it came. It then bears the stamp of international capital and its privileges.

The development of the international capital market, in turn, gives multinational corporations increased access to the savings of many nations, enables larger undertakings to be formed, and fosters mergers and consolidations. Most important, it helps forge an identity of interests between competing national capitals, a vital ingredient for the survival of the multinational corporate system.

The overseas expansion of American firms, for example, has substantially diversified the investment portfolio of American shareholders internationally. In addition, Americans have purchased stock in non-American corporations, or invested in land or other assets abroad, and thus further transferred their interests from the United States to the world as a whole. Given the prospects for industrial growth outside the United States and the social and political problems within the United States, this diversification is likely to continue as a sort of capital flight. At the same time, capitalists from other countries have been buying corporate stock in the United States, lending money to multinationals in regional or local capital markets, and in this way shedding their national character and becoming part of international capital.

An analogy might be made here to the development of the national corporation and national capitalism in the United States at the turn of the century. Prior to that time, the typical industrial enterprise was the closed family firm with only a few outside shareholders. With the merger movement and the development of a national capital market for industrial equity stock, the modern corporation began to emerge with many shareholders, none of whom owned a majority of stock.

Much has been written about how the dispersion of ownership and the lessening of direct control over management by owners has created an autonomous technostructure which operates independently of the specifically capitalist character of the production process. However, it seems to me to be more appropriate to look upon this process in exactly the opposite way. From the point of view of the large capitalists, that is, the 1 percent of the population that owns the vast majority of corporate stock, the modern corporation was an institutional device for maintaining their control and ensuring the continued accumulation of their wealth.

What happened, in effect, was that the wealthy exchanged shares among themselves, thus forging a common front. Far from relinquishing their interests, they generalized them. Instead of each family capital being locked into a specific firm, it became diversified over many firms and over other assets, such as government bonds and land. In this system, competition more or less assures the equalization of the rate of return; and each capital, if it is sufficiently diversified and prudently managed, will share in the general social surplus, according to its size. Rivalry remains as each capitalist strives to obtain an above-average rate of return, but a dominant general interest in the aggregate rate of profit emerges.

·   ·   ·

Without the multinational corporate system, the growth of American capital, and European and Japanese capital, would be thwarted by the growth of new capitals or new socialisms based on the increasing productivity of world labor. With the multinational corporate system, the interests of the

1 percent can be better preserved as they absorb and co-opt some of their potential creditors while crowding out others.

. . .

In sum, the wealthy of the world have a strong interest in internationalism in order to preserve their position. Freedom to intermingle and compete in the world capital market allows them to diversify their holdings and escape supervision of national governments, that is, control by the majority. It thus protects them from the vagaries of specific markets and specific governments and gives them diversified, general interests in the maintenance of the capitalist system as a whole. This continued flow of aggregate profit is then divided among them more or less in proportion to their wealth, as equalization of world rates of profit is brought about by competition.

INTERNATIONAL DIVISION OF LABOR

As we have just seen, market forces lead corporations and capitalists toward internationalization and a greater recognition of their mutual harmony of interests. At the same time, they divide labor, to whom increased cooperation appears as increased competition. The expansion of the market does not, for the most part, help labor diversify and expand, as it does capital; rather, in many cases it takes away their security and stability.

In order for the multinational corporate system to survive and expand, it must maintain the rate of profit. At its most fundamental level this depends on the state of the labor market and the gap between the productivity of labor and the share labor is allowed to control. Capital can be threatened within the system by labor's unwillingness to work efficiently at a "reasonable wage," and ultimately it is threatened by political revolution which would destroy private property as the basis of income and investment.

To maintain the separation between work and control, capital has erected elaborate corporate superstructures to unite labor in production, but divide it in power. . . . Upon its various bases of national labor, the multinational corporation constructs local hierarchies to supervise and manage day-to-day operations, regional administrations to coordinate national branches, and, at the top, strategy apexes to give overall guidance and direction through the use of budgetary controls. At the bottom of this vertical hierarchy, labor is divided into many nationalities. As one proceeds up the pyramid, nationality becomes more homogeneous and increasingly north European.

The work of this hierarchy has a twofold character. In part, it fulfills functions of coordination and unification which are necessary wherever larger numbers cooperate; in part it fulfills functions that arise from the alienated nature of work in capitalist production. Under capitalism, the laborer does not think socially about his work, his machines, or his product. He regards his work as something he would rather not do, except that he needs the money. Because he does not participate voluntarily, each day is a constant struggle over labor time. The capitalist, or his representative, tries to get the laborer to do something he does not want to do. The laborer tries not to do it.

. . .

The vertical stratification of the corporation rests on a division of mental and manual labor. The higher-level intellectual functions concentrate at the top and vanish on the bottom. In the natural body, head and hand wait upon each other. In the corporation, they part company and become deadly foes. Although the multinational corporation spreads production over the world, it concentrates coordination and planning in key cities, and preserves power and income for the privileged.

The power of the bottom is thus weakened by the spatial division of labor. Each national or regional labor force performs a specialized function which is only meaningful to the integrated whole, yet it has no understanding of the whole. Its integration with other groups is not of its own doing, but is the act of capital (the head) that brings them together; it remains an isolated group whose connections to other groups are matters foreign and external to it. Even its national leaders—its government officials and local corporate executives—are only middlemen in a world system, and are themselves blocked from the information needed to obtain an overall picture. The national technostructures occupy an ambivalent position. On the one hand, they are in conflict with the top of the pyramid over their desire for better jobs or their nationalist identification with their country; on the other hand, they are subordinate and dependent because they lack the key ingredients of capitalist power—information and money.

The government may have apparent political sovereignty, but it too has limited real power and is forever looking to international corporations for technology and capital. It remains a weak state, subordinated to the dictates of the budget, the sternest taskmaster of all in a capitalist society. In this way, the corporate economy attempts to solve its dilemma: it requires an expanding state to solve its problems, but must prevent the state from coming under the actual control of the majority, who have formal control in a democratic state. . . .

The weakening of the state is a two-edged sword; it incapacitates the government from fulfilling social needs which require active participation, support, and understanding from the population as a whole. The demonstrative effect of capitalist growth creates rising expectations which it is unable to fulfill. In older established areas, resistance and unity grow, forcing capital to tap new untainted sources as a spatial industrial reserve army. Hence the contradictory nature of industrialization of the Third World.

The spread of technology potentially should make everyone better off, but it appears to labor in advanced countries as a conflict for jobs. This is because their jobs and income are in fact threatened by international competition since under capitalism the burden of adjustment is placed on them. The cycle of depressed areas and depopulation which happened when textiles left the northern United States, for example, now might well be occurring on a world scale. As capital leaves one group of workers for another, in a process resembling slash and burn agriculture, the advanced group is forced to lie fallow in unemployment for use later when their resistance has been weakened.

· · ·

CURRENT POLITICAL PROBLEMS

The current needs of capitalism are, first, a reduction of the conflicts between national capitalists, which initially helped but later plagued capitalist development. Second, and at the same time, the labor market must be maintained by pacifying the advanced workers in the developed countries and by tapping the latent reserve army in the underdeveloped countries. The three major sources of difficulty for international capitalism are contradictions between the centers, competition between the centers and the hinterland, and contradictions within the centers.

Contradictions between the Centers. Although the bitter memories of the Great Depression and war remain, national rivalry—the use by national capital of the protective state to foster its growth—is far from gone. There remains not only the problem of settling differences between the Free World powers of the United States, Europe, and Japan, but also the challenge of Russia and China. In addition, the capitalists of the underdeveloped countries, although weak in general, are strong in particular places (for example, the overseas Chinese, the Philippines, the large Indian capitalists), and somehow must be integrated into a supranational system.

It is not merely a question of avoiding war between the rivals, but also the much more intractable problem of creating an international government apparatus to prevent depression and inflation, to work out a balance between big and small, and to prevent, when the going gets rough, the tendency of capitalists to rely on their individual strength and cunning in place of collusion and cooperation.

Competition between the Centers and the Hinterland. Despite capitalism's advances, poverty remains a significant problem in the advanced world and an overwhelming problem in the underdeveloped nations. Even the most optimistic forecasters do not see great progress in this area over the next thirty or forty years, which, for political prognostication, is a rather long time. The excluded masses, united before in the national independence movements, are now united in much stronger forms of resistance. The United States [became] bogged down in one such struggle, and several more are on the horizon. . . .

Contradictions within the Centers. In order for an integrated worldwide system based on the relations of private property to exist, a vast imperial apparatus is necessary to administer the empire and to fight when necessary. During the [1950s and 1960s] the United States provided this apparatus. It now seems less able to carry on this function due to many internal struggles. Among these are: the revolt of the Blacks; the failure of some of the most promising youth to take up the call for which they were trained; a host of movements, such as the cultural revolution and women's liberation, which reject the whole social fabric of the society and the power system on which it is based; the low morale in the army; and other problems now manifested in drugs and an unwillingness to work hard, but soon perhaps to take political form.

Our present fiscal crisis at the municipal, state, and international level, . . . the switch in the allegiance of intellectuals, and a loss of self-confidence in the ruling class were the three major signs of a disintegrating *ancien regime* identified by Crane Brinton in his study of the anatomy of revolution.[3] No wonder a sense of foreboding is dawning that capitalism is no solid crystal, but an organism capable of changing. Some are hopeful, most are frightened, a few have everything to lose.

In sum, it is my view that although the first round (the fifties and sixties) went to the multinational corporation, the coming rounds (the seventies and eighties) will take a quite different course, as the arena shifts from economic integration to political battle. With the fall of the United States from its position of predominance, Europe and Japan may try to substitute some system for American hegemony, but their record of foreign rule is a bad one. Furthermore, their faith in growth as a solution to all problems has been challenged, and they all face many of the same internal problems as the United States. These, at bottom, seem to stem from the fact that twenty-five years of prosperity erode the compliance to capitalism built up by wars and depression, and that economic growth under capitalism is not satisfying and does not fulfill human needs.

[3]Editors' note: See Crane Brinton, *The Anatomy of Revolution* (New York: Random House, 1957).

13.3 *Imperialism and the Economic Development of the Third World*

We turn now from consideration of the sources of imperialism and the nature of the modern imperialist system to an examination of the consequences of imperialism for the capitalist periphery.

In this chapter we have distinguished between three broad stages of imperialist relations between the center and the periphery: an initial stage in which the center essentially plundered the periphery; a second stage in which the center promoted trade with the periphery as a means to further its own industrialization; and the present stage in which multinational corporations from the center have been rapidly expanding their direct investment abroad and bringing about a new form of international capitalist integration. The first stage clearly inhibited any form of economic development in the periphery. The second stage permitted only a few favored countries in the periphery to set in motion a dynamic process of capitalist development, while most of the periphery was locked into underdevelopment. With the transition to a new stage of imperialism since World War II, in which the periphery has been drawn ever more closely into the world capitalist system, the impact of imperialism on the periphery is likely to be qualitatively different than in the past.

In this third reading Thomas E. Weisskopf attempts to analyze the differences between the second and third stages of imperialism insofar as they affect the prospects for economic development in the periphery. He concludes that the present stage is likely to be somewhat more progressive than the previous one, in the sense that it is more conducive to the spread of growth-oriented capitalist relations of production. Yet he shows that the growth process that has begun to occur in some parts of the present-day periphery is very uneven, dependent, and authoritarian; it seems to be potentially unstable and, ultimately, vulnerable to socialist revolution.

I. INTRODUCTION

Since the early days of capitalism, the imperialist relationship between the center and the periphery has had an inherently dual, and consequently ambivalent, character. On the one hand, the center is in a position to dominate the periphery by virtue of its superior power. The result can be that the center exploits the resources of the periphery to the advantage of the former and to the disadvantage of the latter. On the other hand, the center, in the process of penetrating the periphery, can break down its traditional modes of production and promote the growth of a modern capitalist social and economic order. This result may be progressive in the sense that pre-capitalist barriers to development are destroyed and the basis for participation in world capitalist development is established. Which of these dual aspects of imperialism is predominant depends on the particular historical context and the geographical area under analysis.

In most parts of the third world,[1] at least until the middle of the twentieth century, the regressive aspect of the imperialist relationship dominated the progressive aspect. Economic relations with the major capitalist powers, and the gradual extension of the capitalist mode of production, did little to stimulate sustained economic growth in the countries and territories of Asia, Africa, and Latin America. The huge differences in current levels of per capita product shown in Table 13-F attest to the highly unequal participation of the center and the periphery in capitalist economic growth over the past few centuries.

[1] I will use the term "third world" synonymously with the "periphery"—i.e., all those nations and territories which do not belong to the capitalist center (the advanced capitalist nations) and which have not become state socialist nations.

TABLE 13-F PER CAPITA OUTPUT BY COUNTRY GROUPS: 1971

Area	Per Capita Output[1] (U.S. $)	Population (millions)	Total Output[1] (billion U.S. $)
North America	5,064	228	1,155
Australia, New Zealand	2,797	16	45
Western Europe	2,296	375	861
Japan, Israel, South Africa	1,890	132	249
U.S.S.R., Eastern Europe	1,358	371	504
Latin America	591	288	170
Middle East[2]	376	69	26
Africa[3]	170	343	58
Asia[4]	144	1,853	267
WORLD	907	3,675	3,335

[1]Output measured by gross national product at market prices, converted to U.S. $ at official exchange rates.
[2]Excluding Israel.
[3]Excluding South Africa.
[4]Excluding Japan and the Middle East.
SOURCE: *World Bank Atlas* (Washington, D.C.: World Bank, 1973).

In the last few decades, however, there is evidence that a significant number of third-world countries have begun to experience more rapid rates of growth than in the past.[2] Moreover, they have done so without breaking out of the world capitalist economic system. Indeed, many of them have intensified their economic relations with the major capitalist powers. This suggests that we may now be entering a new stage of imperialism in which the economically progressive aspect of the relationship may be dominating the regressive aspect in at least some parts of the third world.

In this essay I will examine recent trends in the relationship between the capitalist center and periphery in order to determine the extent to which the character of imperialism has changed. I will begin in section II by reviewing the nature of imperialism before World War II, and the reasons why it generally retarded the economic development of the periphery. In section III I will discuss certain changes in the world capitalist system which have significantly affected economic relations between the metropolis and the periphery in the postwar period. In section

IV I will describe the character of the economic development which has been taking place in the third world since 1950. Finally, in section V I will examine certain contradictions which seem likely to arise from contemporary imperialism.

II. SOURCES OF UNDERDEVELOPMENT IN THE PERIPHERY

The capitalist mode of production unquestionably generated a momentous long-run expansion of productivity and economic output in the nations of the present-day center. Why did capitalism not bring to the periphery the same growth stimulus that it brought to the center? The primary reason is that the shaping of the periphery to the requirements of the center resulted in a very different development of *class relations* in the two areas.[3]

In the center countries, capitalism was introduced and spearheaded by a dynamic

[2]See Tables 13-G and 13-H, p. 506 and p. 507.

[3]The analysis of underdevelopment outlined here is based on the work of neo-Marxist authors such as Paul Baran and Andre Gunder Frank.

indigenous bourgeois class that had to struggle persistently against the old feudal order in order to gain control of the state apparatus and win a dominant position within the society. It was very much in the class interest of the bourgeoisie to destroy the social and economic institutions of the feudal era and thereby to eradicate pre-capitalist fetters on the expansion of capitalist production. Bourgeois revolutions in England (the Civil War of the seventeenth century), France (the Revolution of 1789), and Japan (the Meiji Restoration of 1868) were part of this process; in North America, Australia, and New Zealand, no such revolutions were needed because white settlers from already bourgeois-dominated countries destroyed most of the precapitalist inhabitants and their institutions.[4] Either way, the stage was set for rapid and unrestrained capitalist growth.

In the periphery, however, nothing equivalent to a bourgeois revolution occurred because of the impact of Western colonization and economic domination by the capitalist center. Western colonialists and capitalists introduced certain features of capitalism—growing commercialization of the economy, increased domestic and foreign trade, new investments in raw material extraction and transportation—but they did not stimulate the development of an indigenous bourgeoisie or a free wage-labor force. On the contrary, colonial administrators reinforced the power of certain traditionally powerful classes—e.g., the landed aristocracy—in order to facilitate their rule. And foreign capitalists, benefiting from friendly governments and/or their greater wealth and experience, inhibited the emergence of local competitors. Consequently, to the extent that an indigenous bourgeoisie did arise in the peripheral areas, it was small, weak, highly dependent on foreign capital and/or the local

state, and quite unable to provide the dynamic leadership necessary for a thoroughgoing transformation of traditional society into an expanding capitalist economy.

As Paul Baran described it:

> *While in advanced countries, such as France or Great Britain, the economically ascending middle-classes developed at an early stage a new rational world outlook, which they proudly opposed to the medieval obscurantism of the feudal age, the poor, fledgling bourgeoisie of the underdeveloped countries sought nothing but accommodation to the prevailing order. Living in societies based on privilege, they strove for a share of the existing sinecures. They made political and economic deals with their domestic feudal overlords or with powerful foreign investors, and what industry and commerce developed in backward areas in the course of the last hundred years was rapidly moulded in the straitjacket of monopoly—the plutocratic partner of the aristocratic rulers. What resulted was an economic and political amalgam combining the worst features of both worlds—feudalism and capitalism—and blocking effectively all possibilities of economic growth.*[5]

Granted that there was no indigenous bourgeoisie capable of promoting economic growth in the periphery, why could not foreign capitalists play a progressive role in the development of the peripheral economy? In general, foreign capital could not promote long-run growth in the periphery because it was concentrated primarily in export-oriented extractive activities (e.g., mines, and plantations), with little positive impact on most of the peripheral economy. In effect, foreign investment typically created small enclaves geographically located in the periphery but economically representing simply extensions of the domestic economies of the center. Capital and technology were brought from the center to extract food products and raw materials from the periphery and ship them back home; very few of the material

---

[4]The "American Revolution" involved much less an anti-feudal than an anti-colonial struggle, in which the nascent national bourgeoisie and its allies threw off the fetters of British Imperial rule. For more details, see the introduction to Chapter 6, p. 217.

[5]Paul Baran, "On the Political Economy of Backwardness," in Charles K. Wilber, ed., *The Political Economy of Development and Underdevelopment* (New York: Random House, 1973), p. 84.

inputs were purchased from the domestic economy; very little of the output was sold there; virtually none of the profits remained there. Thus, the domestic society received little or nothing in exchange for the depletion of its natural resources.

Whether or not a colonial administration was formally in power, foreign investors sought to ally themselves with and strengthen reactionary domestic elites in order to preserve political stability and their own freedom to continue their extractive activities. Thus, parasitic landed and trading classes would be favored over potentially dynamic and productive entrepreneurs. Foreign capitalists and their indigenous allies did not promote the development of capitalist social relations of production in the periphery. Instead, they generally preferred to incorporate precapitalist relations into a system of international exchange dominated by foreign capital. Thus capitalism made use of—and in many cases helped to establish—pre-capitalist labor systems based on slavery, debt-serfdom, contract labor, and various other forms of unfree labor. These practices served to keep down labor costs in the production of agricultural and mineral commodities for export to the center, while they inhibited capitalist development in the periphery.

Thus the periphery remained primarily a supplier of cheap primary products to the center and a purchaser of manufactured products therefrom. Instead of fostering capitalist development, imperialism led to a form of underdevelopment in the periphery in which economic growth was limited and industrialization was blocked. In those few regions of the third world where rapid economic growth did occur, the growth was almost always linked to a boom in the export of primary products. Often the boom would eventually peter out, leaving the exporting region little better off than before. Even where the market for the exported products remained strong (e.g., in the case of oil), the economic growth was rarely accompanied by any significant degree of structural change that could lay the

basis for a sustained and diversified pattern of economic growth long into the future.[6]

This overall analysis of imperialism and underdevelopment is applicable to most of the periphery up to the time when the Great Depression and World War II disrupted the world capitalist economy and brought the second stage of imperialism to an end.

III. RECENT CHANGES IN RELATIONS BETWEEN THE CENTER AND THE PERIPHERY

The period following World War II ushered in several changes in the world capitalist system with potentially great significance for the periphery.[7] The most obvious change was the dissolution of the bulk of the European colonial empires in Asia, Africa, and the Caribbean. As a result, formally independent national governments assumed power throughout most of the third world. This development also had the effect of changing the character of rivalries among the major capitalist powers. Where in the nineteenth century each power maintained a degree of

[6]Andre Gunder Frank, in his essay "The Development of Underdevelopment," in Wilber, *The Political Economy of Development and Underdevelopment*, points out that the limited amount of industrialization that did occur in the third world before the second half of the twentieth century almost always happened when and where there were relatively *weak* links between the metropolis and the periphery. For example, spurts of industrial growth took place in Argentina, Brazil, and Mexico precisely when trade and investment relations with the metropolis were sharply reduced by the Great Depression and World War II. This negative correlation between the strength of imperialism and industrialization supports the argument that the economically regressive aspect of imperialism was dominant up to the postwar period.

[7]These changes, and their implications for the neo-Marxist analysis of imperialism and underdevelopment, have been forcefully spelled out by Bill Warren in his essay, "Imperialism and Capitalist Industrialization," *New Left Review*, No. 81 (September 10, 1973). Unfortunately, Warren's analysis tends to overstate the case; for a useful antidote, see Philip McMichael, James Petras, and Robert Rhodes, "Imperialism and the Contradictions of Development," *New Left Review*, No. 85 (May/June 1974).

economic monopoly over its own colonies and/or spheres of influence, in the modern postwar period there is much greater scope for economic competition in the periphery among the capitalist powers. This reality was only latent in the early postwar period when the United States dominated the international capitalist order, but it has become increasingly evident with the revival of the European and Japanese economies and the consequent intensification of "inter-imperialist" rivalries. Finally, a third important difference between the postwar period and earlier historical eras is that there now exists a substantial group of state socialist nations competing with the capitalist powers for influence in the third world. The international capitalist system no longer dominates the entire world but faces significant economic, military, and ideological rivalry from these socialist nations.

Such changes in the international setting have had several consequences for relations between the capitalist center and periphery. Governments of third-world countries have found themselves under mounting popular pressure to promote economic growth and industrialization as well as to reduce their dependence on the major capitalist powers. Political independence has meant that these governments have somewhat greater control over their domestic economies, and rivalries between capitalist powers and between capitalist and socialist states have improved their bargaining position vis-à-vis foreign states and corporations. Moreover, farsighted capitalists in the center now tend to see economic growth in the periphery as a possible antidote to socialist revolution. The significance of such changes has, of course, varied greatly from one country to another. For example, governments in small countries like Honduras or Malawi will necessarily remain in a much weaker position than in large countries like India or Brazil. But the direction of change is applicable to most of the third world.

These changing circumstances are reflected in corresponding changes in economic relations between the capitalist center and periphery. In the first place, the increased bargaining power of third-world governments has helped to bring about a substantial flow of financial aid from the rich to the poor countries.[8] To be sure, the aid is given not for altruistic reasons but to serve the foreign policy interests of the donors; much of the aid has been directed to support friendly governments and allied military establishments in the third world; and the real economic value of aid to the recipient countries is generally overstated by its nominal value. Nonetheless, the flow of aid from rich to poor capitalist countries does make available resources to third-world governments on an unprecedented scale; during the colonial era the flow of official capital was generally in the other direction, as colonial territories paid heavily to be administered by their rulers in the center.

A second significant development in the postwar period has been a change in the character of private foreign investment in the periphery (see Table 13-C, p. 478). The traditional type of investment in primary product extraction—especially petroleum—has continued to grow. However, its developmental impact is no longer so limited as it used to be because host governments have been able to capture, in the form of taxes, an increasing share of the huge monopoly profits generated by the petroleum and mineral companies.[9] The most dramatic change

[8]Since the early 1960s the annual flow of official development assistance funds from the capitalist metropolis to the periphery has ranged from roughly $5 billion to $10 billion; see Everett Hagen, *The Economics of Development* (Homewood, Ill.: Irwin, 1975), Table 17.4, for data from 1962 to 1972. For reasons discussed in detail by Gunnar Myrdal, *Challenge of World Poverty* (New York: Pantheon, 1970), Chap. 11, such figures overstate the actual value of the aid to the recipient countries.

[9]For example, Raymond Vernon, *Sovereignty at Bay* (New York: Basic Books, 1971), p. 54, reports that the host country share of pretax profits of foreign investors in oil and copper rose from roughly 10–15 percent in the 1920s to 65–70 percent in the 1960s; the percentage has no doubt increased further in the 1970s with the increasing power and collaboration of governments from the oil- and mineral-exporting nations.

in the character of investment in the periphery has resulted from a rapid growth of foreign investment in the manufacturing sector. Policies adopted by host country governments to promote industrialization—e.g., tariff protection for local industries—have induced multinational corporations to set up local subsidiaries to produce commodities within the countries whose markets are to be served. This has been especially true of those third-world countries with large internal markets—e.g., Brazil, Mexico, India—but it has occurred on a smaller scale in other countries as well. More recently there has been significant growth in a different kind of foreign investment in the manufacturing sector, known as "offshore sourcing." This involves the establishment by multinational corporations of enterprises in the periphery designed to produce certain intermediate products for re-export back to the center either for further processing or for sale on the domestic market. The point is to take advantage of cheap and disciplined labor in certain third-world countries to perform relatively labor-intensive activities, such as electronic component assembly, at a much lower cost than would be possible in the center. Countries such as Taiwan, South Korea, Singapore, and Mexico (especially near the U.S. border) have been among the major recipients of this kind of investment.

All of the above developments have greatly increased the extent of economic linkage between foreign capital and the domestic economies of the periphery. No longer does foreign investment simply create an export enclave that is but an extension of the home economy. Rather, foreign capital is now penetrating into the peripheral economies and inducing changes on a much greater scale. By the same token, the governments and capitalists of the center nations no longer necessarily support the traditional pre-capitalist elites of the periphery, nor the pre-capitalist relations of production with which they are associated. They now have more of an interest in collaborating with those classes in the periphery who will promote the growth of capitalism—its markets, its infrastructure, its labor force—so long as foreign capital retains access to the local economy.[10]

IV. CONTEMPORARY CAPITALIST DEVELOPMENT IN THE PERIPHERY

As a consequence of the changes described above, one would expect the impact of imperialism on the periphery to have become somewhat more favorable to economic growth and industrialization than in the past. In fact, the available data do tend to confirm the view that conditions within the world capitalist system are developing in such a way as to favor growth in the periphery.

Table 13-G presents some statistical evidence on rates of growth of aggregate output and manufacturing output in the capitalist center and periphery from 1950 to 1973.[11] According to the data in the table, aggregate output in the periphery as a whole grew at an annual rate of roughly 5 percent from 1950 to 1973; per capita aggregate output increased by roughly 2-1/2 percent per year, and manufacturing output by more than 7 percent per year. Although comparable figures are not available for earlier periods, there can be no doubt that these growth rates are much higher than ever before. Moreover,

[10]This is not to suggest that foreign capital always supports pro-capitalist forces in the periphery. Under certain circumstances pre-capitalist institutions can enhance the profitability of foreign investment—for example, by maintaining a semi-proletarianized labor force whose cost of reproduction is lower than that of a fully developed proletariat.

[11]The United Nations data from which these growth rates have been calculated are not perfectly reliable; for reasons suggested by Simon Kuznets, "Problems in Comparing Recent Growth Rates for Developed and Less Developed Countries," *Economic Development and Cultural Change*, 20, No. 2 (January 1972), the rates of growth in the periphery are probably overstated. Nonetheless, the broad conclusions that I draw from the data are adequately supported.

TABLE 13-G ECONOMIC GROWTH IN THE CENTER
AND THE PERIPHERY: 1950–1973

Area	Total Output[1]	Per Capita Output[1]	Manufacturing Output
	(Average annual % rate of growth, 1950–1973)		
Capitalist world[2]	4.7	2.6	5.5
Center	4.5	3.4	5.4
Periphery	5.1	2.6	7.2
Latin America	5.4	2.6	7.0
Middle East[3]	7.8*	4.8*	10.5*
Africa[4]	4.9*	2.3*	7.0*
Asia[5]	4.4	2.0	7.1

*Figures apply to the period 1960–1973 only.

[1]Output measured by gross domestic product.

[2]Defined here to exclude the U.S.S.R., Eastern Europe, China, Mongolia, North Korea, and North Vietnam.

[3]Excluding Israel.

[4]Excluding South Africa.

[5]Excluding Japan and the Middle East.

SOURCE: Growth rates calculated from index numbers published in the United Nations, *Statistical Yearbook, 1968* and *1974* (New York: United Nations, 1969 and 1975), Table 4.

they compare very favorably with the performance of the center in the postwar period. Aggregate output and manufacturing output actually grew more rapidly in the periphery than in the center.

Rapid as the growth of output has been in the periphery as a whole, it has not been rapid enough to prevent a widening of the gap between average levels of living in the center and the periphery. The best single quantitative measure of the average level of living in a country is its per capita income, equivalent to its per capita output.[12] To reduce the enormous differentials shown in Table 13-F, it would be necessary for per

[12]Many elements of economic welfare are not captured by per capita income figures—e.g., the distribution of income, nonmonetized sources of welfare, etc. Moreover, international comparisons of income levels are fraught with both theoretical and empirical problems. Still, the comparative figures in Table 13-F do provide a rough indication of the vast differences in average standards of living prevailing in different parts of the world.

capita output to grow more rapidly in the periphery than in the center. But as Table 13-G shows, the growth of *per capita* output in the periphery has been somewhat lower than in the center, even though the growth of *total* output has been higher. And, it is in the poorest areas of the periphery (Africa, and South and East Asia) that per capita output is growing the most slowly.

The above figures on aggregate economic growth suggest that imperialism has begun to have a more progressive impact on the periphery than in the past. It does appear that capitalism is now generating forces that are conducive to some degree of economic growth and industrialization in the third world. Any effort to analyze this phenomenon, however, must go beyond aggregate growth rates to study in more detail the *nature* of capitalist growth in the periphery. As we will see below, this growth—like all capitalist development—has been highly uneven and exploitative in character.

Before examining evidence on the character of capitalist development in the periphery, it will be useful to review the context of class relations in which this development is occurring. Although nationalist movements have taken over power from earlier colonial rulers in almost every part of the periphery, there has been in most cases no revolutionary redistribution of power among the indigenous classes. Workers and peasants, and the lower- and middle-income classes in general, have very little political influence. Power tends to be concentrated among various elite classes—landlords, indigenous businesspeople, highly placed bureaucrats, and foreign capitalists—in combinations that vary from one country to another. But, as writers like Baran have stressed, the indigenous bourgeoisie tends to be weak or virtually nonexistent, and it therefore cannot play the role of a dominant elite as it did in the capitalist center.

Yet since World War II, unlike in earlier times, economic growth and industrialization have not been stunted by the absence of a strong and independent indigenous bourgeoisie. It appears now that capitalist growth can be promoted in the periphery if foreign capitalists can be induced by the peripheral state to play the economically progressive role classically performed by an indigenous bourgeoisie. In fact, capitalist growth in the periphery has been largely dependent on foreign initiative, foreign technology, and—often—foreign capital. While some of the countries of the present-day capitalist center drew on foreign resources at various stages of their economic development, the growth process as a whole was led by an indigenous bourgeoisie with varying degrees of support from the state. In the present-day periphery the indigenous bourgeoisie has always been and remains relatively weak and ineffectual vis-à-vis the bourgeoisie from the capitalist center. The stimulus for growth and industrialization in the periphery has typically come from the state, which has had to turn to foreign enterprise for many of the key resources required for economic advancement. The multiplying rates of foreign investment shown in Table 13-C, p. 478, attest to the prominent role played by foreign *capital* in the growth of the periphery. These figures do not account for the ever-increasing dependence of peripheral economies on foreign *technology*, which can remain in effect even where local firms or the local state have financial control over productive enterprises.

It is precisely the need for an alliance between the peripheral state and capitalists from the center (with the peripheral bourgeoisie as a junior partner at best) that imparts to capitalist growth in the periphery a particularly uneven and repressive character. The class relations characteristic of the periphery no longer necessarily inhibit economic growth *per se*, but they serve to aggravate some of the negative qualities that have always characterized the capitalist growth process.

In the first place, economic growth in the periphery has been very unevenly distributed among the peripheral nations. Table 13-H

TABLE 13-H ECONOMIC GROWTH IN SELECTED PERIPHERAL COUNTRIES: 1950–1973

Rank	Country	Total Output	Per Capita Output
		(Average annual % rate of growth, 1950–1973)	
1	Libya	12.7	8.7
2	Israel	9.9	5.5
3	Saudi Arabia	9.8	7.8
4	Taiwan	9.3	6.0
5	Hong Kong	9.1	5.4
6	Iran	8.1	4.9
7	Singapore	8.0	4.6
8	Iraq	7.8	4.5
9	South Korea	7.6	5.0
10	Greece	7.0	6.3
11	Puerto Rico	6.9	5.7
12	Spain	6.7	5.7
13	Brazil	6.7	3.7
14	Thailand	6.7	3.5
15	Jamaica	6.6	5.1
16	Dominican Republic	6.5	3.2
17	Panama	6.4	3.4
18	Venezuela	6.4	2.7
19	Jordan	6.4	3.3
20	Mexico	6.3	2.9

SOURCE: Growth rates for the full period 1950–1973 calculated from growth rates for various subperiods presented in the World Bank *World Tables* (Washington, D.C.: World Bank, 1971 and 1976).

lists the twenty third-world nations (among those with populations exceeding one million) whose output has grown most rapidly since 1950. These are the "success stories" of the capitalist periphery, where the average rate of economic growth has exceeded 6 percent per year and per capita output has risen by roughly 3 percent or more per year. The remaining sixty-five peripheral nations and territories (with populations exceeding one million) have had at best very mixed success, with per capita output rising slowly or—in some cases—not at all. It is worth noting that among the twenty "success stories" are five major oil-producing nations (Libya, Saudi Arabia, Iran, Iraq, and Venezuela), two commercial city-states (Hong Kong and Singapore), five of the major per capita beneficiaries of U.S. foreign aid (Israel, Taiwan, Greece, Jordan, South Korea) and a U.S. territory (Puerto Rico). Needless to say, conditions for economic growth in these countries have been unusually favorable and atypical of the third world as a whole.

The uneven incidence of economic growth in different parts of the periphery can be explained largely in terms of the degree of interest shown by foreign capital in different third-world countries. For the investor from the center the most attractive countries are those with one or more of the following attributes: (1) large deposits of key industrial raw materials; (2) large internal markets for manufactured goods; and (3) a disciplined low-wage labor force.[13] Thus, major oil producers (e.g., Iran, Saudi Arabia, Venezuela) and aluminum producers (e.g., Jamaica), countries with relatively high levels of per capita income and population (e.g., Brazil, Mexico, Spain) and countries with reliable cheap labor (e.g., Taiwan, South Korea, Hong Kong) can expect to attract foreign capital on a considerable scale. Such countries then have at least the *potential* for generating economic growth and industrialization with the help of foreign capital, provided their respective governments can form a workable alliance—neither scaring away foreign capital nor becoming totally subservient to it. Countries that for political/strategic reasons received substantial amounts of foreign aid from the center (e.g., Israel, Jordan, Greece) clearly also have their growth potential raised. In countries with little appeal to foreign investors or governments, the prospects for economic growth would depend on the ability of the state itself to play the role of a dynamic bourgeoisie. This is a remote possibility as long as the dominant elites are still very much identified with past privilege and the old order.

[13]Note that these attributes correspond to the three types of foreign investment discussed earlier: investment in primary product extraction, investment in manufacturing for the local market, and investment in offshore sourcing.

Just as economic growth has been very unevenly distributed *among* peripheral nations, economic gains have been very unevenly distributed *within* these nations. In most areas of the third world both inequality and unemployment appear to be worsening. The available data show that income distribution is even more unequal in the capitalist periphery than in the center.[14] Data on the time trend of income distribution within countries is as yet rather unreliable, but what evidence there is suggests to most observers that there has been an increase in inequality in the great majority of the countries of the third world. Moreover, urban/rural disparities seem to be widening, as much of the economic expansion is concentrated in industries located in or near large cities. As a high official of the World Bank wrote, in introducing a volume on economic growth and income distribution:

> It is now clear that more than a decade of rapid growth in underdeveloped countries has been of little or no benefit to perhaps a third of their population. Although the average per capita income of the Third World has increased by 50 percent since 1960, this growth has been very unequally distributed among countries, regions within countries, and socio-economic groups.[15]

Evidence on trends in unemployment is similarly hard to come by, but again there seems to be little doubt among observers that the problem is becoming increasingly acute.[16] One fact is quite clear: the rate of growth of industrial employment in the periphery has been much slower than the rate of growth of industrial output, so that the ability of even a

[14]See Felix Paukert, "Income Distribution at Different Levels of Development: A Survey of the Evidence," *International Labor Review*, 108 (July–December 1973).

[15]Hollis Chenery, introduction to Chenery et al., *Redistribution with Growth* (London: Oxford University Press, 1974), p. xiii.

[16]For a detailed review of the evidence, see David Turnham and Ingeles Jaeger, *The Employment Problem in Less Developed Countries: A Review of the Evidence* (Paris: Organization for Economic Cooperation and Development, 1971).

rapidly growing industrial sector to provide employment opportunities has been rather limited. Moreover, the population in urban areas has been increasing much more rapidly than the availability of jobs in the modern sector of the economy, with the result that increasing numbers of urban dwellers have joined the ranks of the marginalized "lumpenproletariat." In general, the beneficiaries of capitalist economic growth in the third world appear to have been confined largely to the well-to-do classes, and particularly those living in major urban centers with close links to the capitalist center.

The persistence and exacerbation of inequalities among regions and socioeconomic classes withing third-world countries is a natural consequence of the nature of capitalist growth and the class relations that underlie it. The very logic of capitalist expansion is "to build on the best"—i.e., to invest in those areas and favor those people that are already the most economically advanced, because it is more profitable to do this than to try to develop backward areas or provide opportunities for the poorer classes. Inequality is inherent in the operation of capitalist institutions,[17] and it is often indispensable for capitalist accumulation because it concentrates income in the hands of those with the highest propensity to save and invest—the capitalist class. Similarly, unemployment plays a functional role in any capitalist society by holding down wages and maintaining labor discipline,[18] thereby stimulating capitalist profits and accumulation.

There are several aspects of the situation in contemporary third-world countries which tend to aggravate the forces that generate inequality and unemployment in any capitalist economy. The fact that economic growth and industrialization is propelled

largely by foreign rather than indigenous capital and technology means that types of products and techniques of production based on conditions in the center are likely to play an undue role in the periphery. In particular, relatively capital-intensive products and technology tend to be transferred to the periphery, where they generate large economic gains for a small and privileged group of people while displacing many local small businesspeople and workers and failing to provide alternative employment opportunities for them. At the same time, the domination of power by privileged classes limits the political effectiveness of demands for redistributive measures, employment-creating projects, and more equitable growth in general.

Finally, successful capitalist growth in the periphery has generally been associated with highly authoritarian political rule.[19] Many of the more rapidly growing nations in the capitalist periphery (listed in Table 13-H) are characterized by unusually repressive regimes —most notable are the examples of Taiwan, South Korea, Spain, and Brazil. Most of the remaining countries in the table have been subject to authoritarian and/or colonial rule for much of the postwar period. Only Israel stands out as a nation in which a wide range of bourgeois democratic rights have been maintained continuously since 1950 (and only for the majority Jewish population). Greece, Mexico, Jamaica, and Venezuela have at times had democratic institutions functioning with a moderate degree of effectiveness. But

[17]See the introduction to Chapter 8, p. 293, for an analysis of the relationship between capitalism and inequality.

[18]See Weisskopf, Section 12.2, p. 441, and Crotty and Rapping, Section 12.4, p. 461, on the role of the "reserve army of the unemployed" in maintaining profitability in advanced capitalist economies.

[19]Every capitalist society is authoritarian in the sense that the most important decisions reflect disproportionately the interests of the dominant capitalist class. But there are nonetheless real and significant differences in the degree of responsiveness of different kinds of political institutions to the will of the people. For all its shortcomings, a bourgeois democracy often permits sections of the working class to obtain certain concessions that could not be wrung from a fascist police state. For a detailed discussion and documentation of the degree of democracy and authoritarianism in different countries throughout the world, see the annual *Comparative Survey of Freedom* published by Freedom House (New York).

—with the exception of the special case of Israel—the most democratic political systems in the third world over the past twenty-five years are to be found in countries that are *not* among the capitalist success stories—e.g., in Ceylon, Chile (until recently), Costa Rica, India, Lebanon (until recently), and Uruguay (until recently).

The particularly authoritarian political context of capitalist growth in most third-world countries may be attributed in part to the absence of a revolutionary bourgeois triumph over the old order in those countries. Instead of being led by an indigenous bourgeoisie rebelling under a democratic banner against pre-capitalist bastions of privilege, capitalist growth in the periphery has been fostered by an alliance of elites—both traditional and modern—operating through a relatively powerful state. Even in some of the "late developers" among the nations of the center—notably Germany and Japan—the relative weakness of the indigenous bourgeoisie, its inclination to ally with rather than struggle against feudal elites, and the emergence of the state as a major force promoting capitalist growth had markedly authoritarian implications.[20]

In the third-world countries that are presently experiencing some economic growth, these same sociopolitical circumstances are modified primarily by the addition of foreign capitalists to the alliance of dominant classes. This modification serves only to reinforce authoritarian tendencies, for foreign capitalists and foreign governments have much to fear from the nationalist and populist forces that are likely to gain strength with the inclusion of middle and lower classes into the political process. It is no accident that so many of the authoritarian regimes of the contemporary third world—in Brazil, Chile, Indonesia, etc.—have come to power with the active assistance of the United States

government and its Central Intelligence Agency.[21]

Both foreign and domestic capitalists tend to see in strong, authoritarian regimes the best hope for political and economic stability in the periphery today. In a context of growing worker militance, increasing public demands for a wider distribution of economic benefits, and nascent as well as active revolutionary movements in many parts of the third world, political repression often seems to be the surest way to insure a docile labor force willing to work at wage levels that ensure a high rate of profit on invested capital. In the capitalist center, bourgeois democracy serves an important legitimizing function without seriously threatening capitalist economic interests.[22] In the capitalist periphery, however, democracy usually serves to inhibit the process of capital accumulation.

It is important to recognize that the inequality, the unemployment, the dependence, and the authoritarianism that have characterized capitalist development in the periphery are not inevitable requisites of economic growth. One need only study the example of the People's Republic of China to learn that it is possible for a poor third-world country to achieve rapid economic growth and industrialization while promoting a high degree of equity and self-reliance as well as full employment.[23] While China's political

[20]See Barrington Moore, Jr., *Social Origins of Dictatorship and Democracy* (Boston: Beacon Press, 1967), for a comparative historical analysis illustrating—among many other things—the importance of a bourgeois revolution for nonauthoritarian capitalist development.

[21]The experience of Chile provides a perfect illustration of this point. Chile's unusually democratic political framework resulted in a trend toward increasing nationalism and populism in public officials, culminating in the electoral victory of socialist Salvador Allende in 1970. Allende proved to be more than ITT or Henry Kissinger could stand, so three years later the U.S. government (via the CIA) helped to overthrow Allende and install one of the most brutal and repressive military governments in the third world.

[22]See Edwards and Reich, Section 6.5, p. 252, on the role of democracy in the United States.

[23]There is a rapidly growing literature on the development achievements of the People's Republic of China. For a brief survey of the Chinese experience, see John W. Gurley, "Maoist Economic Development: The New Man in the New China," in Wilber, *The Political Economy of Development and Underdevelopment.*

system remains authoritarian in important respects, there is also evidence of a substantial degree of popular participation in decision-making at the "micro" level of the neighborhood and the enterprise (farm, factory, or office). There is therefore good reason to believe that there are viable alternatives to the pattern of development that has occurred in the capitalist periphery; and the existence and awareness of such alternatives heightens the contradictions that are developing there.

In conclusion, it appears that the contemporary stage of imperialism has proven somewhat more progressive in its overall impact on the third world than earlier stages. To a greater extent than in the past, capitalism has begun to play in the periphery as well as in the center the historical role Marx foresaw for it in advancing the forces of production. Yet this does not imply that the unequal international relations of the world capitalist system will come to an end, nor that the periphery will come to resemble the center.

In the first place, capitalist growth is taking place only in certain favored regions of the periphery; the prospects for capitalist growth in many other regions remain highly uncertain. Secondly, even where it is taking place, capitalist growth in the periphery remains in many important ways dependent on the center and its capitalists. Thus the underlying hierarchy that characterizes imperialism remains a reality, although it is taking a new form. Especially because of continuing technological dependence, the capitalist success stories of the periphery will find it very difficult to join the center. Most of them can expect to become, at best, junior partners intermediate between the center and the periphery.

V. CONTRADICTIONS OF IMPERIALISM IN THE PERIPHERY

Even where imperialism is successful in advancing the forces of production in the periphery, it generates certain contradictions which threaten the stability of the process and offer opportunities for revolutionary change. These contradictions are more intense than those that arose out of early capitalist growth in the center because of the different setting in which growth now takes place in the periphery.

First, the unequal character of capitalist growth in the periphery is likely to give rise to serious tensions. When some classes in a society are quite obviously benefiting from economic growth while the masses of people see little improvement in their standard of living, discontent is bound to grow. The perception of inequality is heightened by continual improvements in transportation and communications media. The poor in the periphery are becoming more and more aware of the affluent standards of living enjoyed by some of their compatriots and by most foreigners resident in the periphery or at home in the center; as a consequence, their economic aspirations are raised. This so-called "demonstration effect" operates much more powerfully in the modern era than it did in the early stages of growth in the capitalist center.

Rising aspirations conflict with a largely unchanging reality for the masses of people who benefit little from economic growth. Thus demands for more widespread participation in economic progress begin to mount. In response, the dominant classes can either turn toward tighter repression or begin to share the benefits of growth. The first course will sooner or later lead to intensified conflict and possibly a revolutionary movement; the second course may threaten the foundations of capitalist growth by reducing the surplus available for accumulation and lowering the private profitability of investment. Only in countries where unusually favorable circumstances create the potential for very rapid economic growth can capitalist accumulation proceed while at the same time the standard of living of the masses rises appreciably. For most of the third world, the contradiction of unequal capitalist growth cannot long be circumvented.

A second contradictory aspect of capitalist growth in the periphery arises from its effect on the traditional socioeconomic structure. The increasing penetration of capitalist social relations serves to undermine the paternalistic and/or communal sources of security in traditional pre-capitalist societies. Peasants, serfs, and artisans are separated from their means of production and their niche in rural society and thrown into the impersonal free market for labor, seeking employment on large capitalist farms or in industrializing urban areas. The brutal proletarianization of the labor force is part of the history of capitalist development in every part of the world. But again it is particularly acute in the contemporary periphery because employment opportunities are now much scarcer than before. As I have argued earlier, new products and improved techniques of production, developed primarily in the rich countries, usually involve a capital-intensive bias appropriate to conditions in the center. Whether introduced by foreign capitalists or by local capitalists borrowing from abroad, these new products and techniques tend to have a limited potential for absorbing labor. Thus, capitalism in the periphery erodes traditional bases of stability without providing an adequate substitute in the form of wage employment. The ranks of the "reserve army" of unemployed or marginalized workers are growing, and they are exacerbating the conflict between capital and all but the (usually small) minority of workers who manage to get the limited number of secure jobs available.

A third contradiction arising out of capitalist growth in the periphery results from its politically authoritarian character. Repression can promote stability—but not forever. In the long run the most stable kind of capitalist society is one in which bourgeois democratic freedoms can thrive sufficiently so as to legitimize the *status quo* by obscuring the fundamentally authoritarian nature of the economic order. With few exceptions, the governments in third-world countries experiencing capitalist growth derive no legitimacy from popular involvement in the political process. What legitimacy they can claim is based upon their ability to deliver economic improvement, and even this source of legitimacy is compromised by the uneven distribution of the gains. Continued authoritarian rule with limited popular legitimacy is at best an uncertain and unstable proposition. It is likely to breed either popular revolt on the part of the repressed masses or military coups carried out in the name of the people or with the intent of "restoring stability." The recent history of third-world countries is replete with popular uprisings and sudden changes of government. While they do not always necessarily inhibit the process of capitalist economic growth, they can lead to serious economic reverses and the possibility of revolutionary upheavals.

To be sure, some of the negative aspects of capitalist economic growth that I have described as potentially contradictory in the periphery have also characterized capitalist growth in the center. Capitalism has always generated resistance from the many people who suffer from its expansion: those whose traditional kinship systems, communities, and occupations are destroyed; those who are excluded from the growing wealth of the economy; those who are thrown into the reserve army of the unemployed; those who experience directly the repressive arm of the state; and so on. Yet so far, at least, capitalism has proven durable in the center. For all of its potential contradictions, it has rarely been seriously vulnerable to a revolutionary challenge. Why should we expect capitalism to be any less viable in the contemporary periphery, as long as it does succeed in generating economic growth?

Part of the answer is that the potentially contradictory aspects of capitalist growth are stronger in the periphery today than they were in the center in the past. For reasons discussed earlier, inequality, unemployment, and authoritarianism are likely to be particularly acute in the circumstances under which capitalist growth can take place in the contemporary third world. Even more important, however, is the fact that there now exist concrete examples of an alternative to capitalism in the form of the state socialist nations of the world. These nations have not avoided all the shortcomings of capitalist economic growth. But their experience serves to heighten the contradictory elements of capitalist growth in the periphery and strengthen revolutionary anticapitalist movements in several ways.

First, the very existence of the state socialist nations is important in exploding the conservative myth that there simply is no alternative route to economic improvement than a capitalist one. Second, the model projected (if not always realized) by the state socialist nations provides a forward-looking inspiration for anti-capitalist movements. In the past history of the capitalist nations of the center, opposition to the growth of capitalist hegemony was usually doomed from the beginning because it was predominately backward-looking. It encouraged the smashing of machines and extolled the virtues of traditional ways of life; but it offered no vision of the future and could develop no positive program capable of resisting the increasing power that capitalism derived from its harnessing of technological progress. The socialist model, however, provides a socially, economically, and technologically progressive focus for anti-capitalist resistance in contemporary third-world countries. At the same time, some of the state socialist nations are in a positon to provide direct material assistance—as well as political and ideological support—to revolutionary movements struggling against capitalist domination in the periphery.

One final important new element in the contemporary situation is the *dependent* character of capitalist growth in the periphery. Because the indigenous elites and their state become dependent on foreign capital for much of the impetus to economic growth, they find it difficult to harness the forces of nationalism to their own advantage. The very presence of foreign capitalists and their growing role in the economy serve to inflame nationalist feelings on the part of the indigenous population. The elites must respond to growing nationalist pressures by at least an escalation of nationalistic rhetoric and a show of tougher bargaining with foreign capitalists and governments. Up to a point they may be able to improve the terms of their alliance with foreign capital, but they cannot afford to push too far. In the last analysis they are inextricably tied to an internationalist outlook and cannot maintain ideological hegemony over popular nationalist forces. Thus, their participation in the capitalist economic growth process makes them increasingly vulnerable to oppositional movements which can raise more effectively the banner of nationalism.

It is precisely the opportunity of anti-capitalist opposition movements to link their struggles with nationalism that gives them a potentially powerful basis for carrying out a successful revolution. Within the center—both in the past and at present—socialist movements have had to struggle primarily against an indigenous capitalist class, and nationalism could not play much of a role. But in the periphery anti-capitalist movements can be simultaneously anti-imperialist, and thereby draw upon a broader base of opposition to the *status quo*. It remains quite possible that indigenous national capitalists will attempt to use anti-imperialist struggles to serve their own ends and to co-opt potentially revolutionary socialist movements. But the logic of capitalist development in the periphery ultimately leads in an internationalist direction. In the long run, it is socialist movements that are likely to reflect most effectively the nationalist aspirations of third-world peoples.

In the foregoing discussion I have stressed the contradictions that arise even when imperialism is successful in stimulating capitalist economic growth in the periphery. In those parts of the third world where imperialism has yet to show much of its progressive side, significant contradictions are also likely to develop. In the first place, a lack of economic growth is likely to be a source of instability in itself, given increasingly widespread demands for economic improvement. Moreover, the slower the rate of economic growth, the less tolerance there will be for existing inequalities, the less successful will the economy be in providing employment opportunities, and the weaker will be the classes supportive of foreign capital. Where imperialism fails to build a local base of support by promoting some degree of capitalist economic growth in alliance with indigenous elites, it renders itself all the more vulnerable to nationalist opposition. Whether under these circumstances the anti-imperialist forces become anti-capitalist as well depends largely on the effectiveness of revolutionary socialist organization. And the success of any revolutionary socialist movement in the third world ultimately depends both on its own strength and on the ability and desire of the imperialist powers to defend their empire with military might.

PART VI

TOWARD AN ALTERNATIVE TO THE CAPITALIST SYSTEM

CHAPTER 14

From
Capitalism
to Socialism

THUS FAR IN THIS BOOK we have developed a critical analysis of the capitalist system, focusing especially on its operation in the United States. Our analysis is bound to raise some basic questions about alternatives to capitalism. What would a truly desirable society look like? How would it work? And how is it possible for us to get from here to there?

In this final chapter of the book, we will attempt to provide an initial basis for developing answers to these crucial questions. We will not try to provide definitive and comprehensive answers, for they do not yet exist. Instead, we urge you—our readers—to pursue these questions yourselves with the help of the readings in this chapter,[1] your own experience and imagination, and an open mind.

A VISION OF A SOCIALIST ALTERNATIVE

What kind of society might replace capitalism? What is our vision of a more decent and humane society?

We cannot present a blueprint or an exact specification of such a future society; nor

[1]For additional literature on the subject of alternatives to the capitalist mode of production, we recommend very strongly that you consult *Socialist Alternatives for America: A Bibliography*, selected, structured, and annotated, with an introductory essay, by Jim Campen (New York: The Union for Radical Political Economics, 1974).

should we attempt to do so, since constructing imaginary utopias bears little relation to the actual task of building a decent society. Any real alternatives to capitalism will be historically linked to the forces and movements that are successful in overcoming capitalist society itself. New institutions that liberate rather than oppress can only be created by real people confronting concrete problems in their lives and developing new means to overcome oppression. The political movements arising in opposition to capitalism therefore constitute the only means for society to move from its present condition to a new and more decent form, and only out of these movements will humane as well as practical new institutions be generated.

We can, however, explain what values would characterize a truly decent society and what goals should motivate the political movement for it. In a sense, the values underlying a decent society have been implicit throughout our analysis of capitalism. Our alternative society would be characterized by equality: equality rather than hierarchy in making social decisions; equality in sharing the material benefits of the society; and equality in society's encouragement to develop one's full potential. Work must cease to be a means of "making one's living" and become nonalienated, a part of one's living. Arbitrary distinctions by sex and race (or language or eye color) would cease to be criteria for particular forms of oppression or for tracking people into limited opportunities. The irrationality of production for profits would be transformed into the rationality of production to satisfy people's needs, and the unequal relations of imperialism would be replaced by a cooperative ethic recognizing people's responsibility to each other.

We call our vision of an alternative society *socialism*, because we identify with the humane values that have inspired generations of men and women to struggle for a socialist alternative to capitalism. But we wish to stress that our conception of a relevant and desirable socialist alternative to capitalism differs in certain important ways from most of the contemporary societies that are commonly referred to as socialist.[2]

For us, socialism is more than a set of humane values, and it is more than the substitution of public for private ownership of the means of production. We have in mind a socialism which means democratic, decentralized and *participatory* control for the individual: it means having a say in the decisions that affect one's life. Such a participatory form of socialism certainly requires equal access for all to material and cultural resources, which in turn requires the abolition of private ownership of capital and the redistribution of wealth. But it also calls for socialist men and women to eliminate alienating, destructive forms of production, consumption, education, and community and family life. Participatory socialism requires the elimination of corporate bureaucracies and all such hierarchical forms and their replacement, not by new state or party bureaucracies, but by a self-governing and self-managing people with directly chosen representatives subject to recall and replacement. Participatory socialism entails a sense of egalitarian cooperation, of solidarity of people with one another; but at the same time it respects individual and group differences and guarantees individual rights. It affords to all individuals the freedom to exercise human rights and civil liberties that

[2]In the introduction to this book, p. xi, we described briefly the relationship between our vision of socialism and various kinds of socialism currently in existence. See also the first part of Lerner, Section 12.3, p. 532.

are not mere abstractions but have concrete day-to-day meaning.

Our vision of a participatory socialist society is not one in which all problems miraculously disappear. Anti-social behavior, natural disasters, and necessary tradeoffs (e.g., between production and the environment) will undoubtedly continue. But participatory socialism should provide a way of life and a set of social institutions that *encourage* cooperative, egalitarian, and decent relations among people—quite a contrast to capitalist organization, which fosters their opposites. And over time, as people live and experience the new society, they themselves will likely be changed. Greed, alienation, racism, and other forms of anti-social behavior, which grow so naturally in capitalist society, will become like exotic hothouse flowers transplanted outdoors; no longer matched to their environment, they will wither and die.

To achieve this kind of participatory socialism clearly requires a radical transformation of the existing capitalist mode of production, for it calls for the elimination of each of the forms of oppression that gave us titles to Chapters 7 to 13. As we have seen, these forms of oppression are both integral and functional to capitalism, and they will persist as long as the capitalist mode of production prevails.

GETTING FROM HERE TO THERE

How is it possible to bring about the kind of fundamental social change that alone can lead to participatory socialism? In the first place, this requires a growing revolutionary movement that can become strong enough to resist and overcome the power of the capitalist class to maintain the capitalist system from which it benefits. As the class that comprises the great majority of the people in any capitalist society, and which stands to benefit most clearly from the transformation of capitalism, the working class must necessarily be in the forefront of a successful movement for participatory socialism. Only the working class, in its broadest sense, has the potential to become more powerful than the capitalist class in an advanced capitalist society such as the United States.

But unless the working class is fully conscious of the source of its oppression, and aware of both the necessity and the realistic possibility of transforming the capitalist mode of production, the movement for participatory socialism cannot be expected to grow in strength. In this matter there has been much pessimism among socialists in the United States. Yet one can point to many signs of popular opposition developing in response to the various forms of social oppression that capitalism generates and perpetuates. Victims of alienation, inequality, sexism, racism, irrationality, economic crises,, and imperialism are engaging in struggles to overcome their oppression. They are finding that capitalism is one of their principal enemies, and that their special problems are but manifestations of the *class* oppression suffered by the working class as a whole.

Outside the United States, socialist movements have already won important victories. In some parts of the underdeveloped world, capitalist domination has been successfully overthrown; in other parts, capitalism has been put in a defensive position. And in many advanced capitalist nations socialist movements have been growing in strength. The very existence of such challenges suggest that capitalism is neither a smoothly operating system in which little protest is heard nor a system unsusceptible to any change. On the contrary, the entire history of the capitalist era has been marked by resistance from those whom capitalism has sought to subordinate. Often this resistance has been overcome only through the use of violent force or coercion by the state.

Still, social systems do not fall simply because they are oppressive or considered by many to be unjust; the capitalist system has survived for a long time like this. There are countless examples of protests and rebellions

that have not succeeded in transforming capitalism because they were self-destructive, they struck at the wrong targets, or they became co-opted and commercialized as part of the capitalist system itself. Fundamental social change will occur only if a self-conscious revolutionary movement engages in organized political struggle in such a way as to challenge the basic capitalist relations of production. Moreover, the struggle must be carried out with an understanding of when, where, and why the capitalist system is relatively weak and vulnerable.

Dynamic forces within capitalist society insure that some social change will always be occurring; yet this social change will not necessarily or inevitably take the form of a fundamental transformation of the capitalist mode of production. Capitalism can be radically transformed only if and when it produces dysfunctional social forces that destabilize the system, weaken the power of the capitalist class, and thus encourage the growth of revolutionary opposition and contribute to its power. In short, a strategy for radical social change must begin with an understanding of the *contradictions* at work in a capitalist society.[3]

A contradiction of capitalism results when the very process of capitalist development produces simultaneously the conditions needed to transform it fundamentally; that is, when the successes of capitalist development create situations that are fundamentally antagonistic to capitalism itself. In Parts IV and V of this book we have discussed various kinds of contradictions which appear to be arising from the development of advanced capitalism.[4] Such contradictions tend to intensify with time, and they cannot be resolved

[3]The concept of a contradiction is a fundamental element of the Marxist method of historical materialism; see the introduction to Chapter 2, p. 39.

[4]The readings which deal most directly with the contradictory aspects of modern capitalism are Wachtel, Section 7.3, p. 283; Rowbotham, Section 9.4, p. 353; Baron, Section 10.2, p. 368; Weisskopf, Section 11.1, p. 395; Hobsbawm, Section 12.1, p. 431; and Weisskopf, Section 13.3, p. 499.

within the existing socioeconomic framework. Each contradiction creates dissatisfaction and tension among those people who are most directly and adversely affected by it, and it may become the locus around which opposition to capitalism can develop.

Thus, a radical transformation of capitalism into a better society can occur only if men and women understand the historical and social forces at work in a capitalist society and intervene actively and collectively in a conscious attempt to direct and control those forces and turn them to desired human ends.

The capitalist class is a privileged and exploiting class, and it is not about to give up its special place without resistance. When faced with a growing movement for participatory socialism, the capitalist class will try to obfuscate and mystify discontent, offer sham concessions, co-opt leaders and causes, divide the movement, and suppress movement organizations. What it cannot do, however, is resolve the contradictions of advanced capitalism; only a change in the mode of production can do that. This is the basis for our optimism that the movement for participatory socialism will ultimately succeed.

The readings in this chapter are intended to develop further our conception of a participatory socialist society, and to discuss some of the issues involved in trying to bring it about. The basic goals of participatory socialism are restated at the beginning of the first reading, and an effort to describe its operation in much greater detail is undertaken in the third reading. The first reading also reviews some of the principal contradictions arising in advanced capitalist societies. Both the first and second readings suggest certain strategic principles that should guide the political movement for a revolutionary transformation of the capitalist mode of production.

14.1 *Socialist Revolution in the United States: Goals and Means*

A revolution must have goals; it must have reason to believe that it can succeed; and it must have a strategy to achieve success. In this first reading, Samuel Bowles and Herbert Gintis address themselves to these preconditions for revolution in the United States by discussing the goals of socialism, the contradictions of capitalism, and strategies for social change.

THE GOALS OF SOCIALISM

The goals of . . . revolutionary socialism go beyond the achievement of the Soviet Union and countries of Eastern Europe. These countries have abolished private ownership of the means of production, while replicating the relationships of economic control, domin- ance, and subordination characteristic of capitalism. While the abolition of private property in the means of production has been associated with a significant reduction in economic inequality, it has failed to address [many] other problems. . . . The socialism to which we aspire goes beyond the legal question of property to the concrete social question of economic democracy as a set of egalitarian and participatory power relationships. While we may learn much about the process of building a socialist society from the experiences of the Soviet, Cuban, Chinese, and other socialist peoples—and indeed, may find some aspects of their work downright inspiring—there is no foreign model for the economic transformation we seek. Socialism in the United States will be a distinctly American product growing out of our history, culture, and struggle for a better life.

What would socialism in the United States look like? Socialism is not an event; it is a process. Socialism is a system of economic and political democracy in which individuals have the right and obligation to structure their work lives through direct participatory control. Our vision of socialism does not require as a precondition that we all be altruistic, selfless people. Rather, the social and economic conditions of socialism will facilitate the full development of human capacities. These capacities are for cooperative, democratic, equal, and participatory human relationships; for cultural, emotional, and sensual fulfillment. We can ascribe to a prospective U.S. socialism no fixed form, nor is socialism a solution to all the problems we have discussed here. Socialism directly solves many social problems, but, in many respects, it is merely a more auspicious arena in which to carry on the struggle for personal and social growth. Its form will be determined by practical activity more than abstract theorizing. Nevertheless, some reasonable aspects of socialism in the United States of direct relevance to the transformation of our society can be suggested.

The core of a socialist society is the development of an alternative to the wage-labor system. This involves the progressive democratization of the workplace, thus freeing the educational system to foster a more felicitous pattern of human development and social interaction. The ironclad relationship between the division of labor and the division of social product must also be broken: Individuals must possess, as a basic social right,

an adequate income and equal access to food, shelter, medical care, and social services independent of their economic position. Conversely, with the whip of material necessity no longer forcing participation in economic life, a more balanced pattern of material, symbolic, and collective incentives can, indeed must be developed. Essential in this respect is the legal obligation of all to share equitably in performing those socially necessary jobs which are, on balance, personally unrewarding and would not be voluntarily filled. An educational system thus freed from the legitimation of privilege could turn its energies toward rendering the development of work skills a pleasant and desirable complement to an individual's life plans.

The object of these changes in the social division of labor is not abstract equality, but the elimination of relationships of dominance and subordinacy in the economic sphere. There will certainly always be individual differences in ability, talent, creativity, and initiative, and all should be encouraged to develop these capacities to their fullest. But in a socialist system, they need not translate into power and subordinacy in control of economic resources. For similar reasons, historical patterns of racial, sexual, and ethnic discriminations must be actively redressed as socially divisive and unjust. What is now called household work will also be deemed, at least in part, socially necessary labor. This work, whether done in collective units or individual homes, must be equitably shared by all individuals.

Another central goal of socialism in the United States must be the progressive democratization of political life. From production planning, the organization of social services, and the determination of consumption needs at the local level right up to national economic planning and other aspects of national policy, decisions will be made in bodies consisting of or delegated by those affected by the result. We envisage a significant role for the national government: assuring regional economic equality; integrating and rationalizing local production, service and consumption plans; and, directly implementing other social and economic policies which are infeasible at the local level. The egalitarian and democratic nature of economic life should vastly increase the responsiveness and flexibility of governmental institutions. While mediating disputes between groups and regions will remain a central political function, economic equality will eliminate the need of the state to pander to interests and powers of a small minority who control production. Though political activity will not be a major preoccupation of most, the process of participation in work and community should dramatically increase the political sophistication, participation, and knowledgeability of citizens. Indeed, we venture to suggest that all of the glaring inadequacies of political democracy in the United States are attributable to the private ownership of the means of production and the lack of a real economic democracy.

It is a tenet of liberal thought that social equality can be purchased only at the expense of economic efficiency. Yet the evidence is less than persuasive. Democratic social relationships in production lead to highly motivated and productive workers, who will turn their creative powers toward the improvement of work and the satisfaction of consumer needs rather than profit. Moreover, democratic control of work can reorient technology toward the elimination of brutalizing jobs, toward a progressive expansion of the opportunity of attaining skills through on-the-job and recurrent education, and toward a breakdown of the division between mental and physical labor. The elimination of racial and sexual discriminations would liberate a vast pool of relatively untapped talents, abilities, and human resources for productive purposes. Comprehensive and rational economic planning leads to heightened efficiency through elimination of wasteful competition and redundancy in ·the provision of services (e.g., insurance, banking, and finance), the elimination of unemployment, rational programs of research and development, and a balanced policy of resource development with environmental stability.

The increased efficiency of socialist economic life should quickly reduce the workweek devoted to the production of social necessities, thus freeing individuals for creative leisure and more informal production. Indeed, this aspect of individual development in U.S. socialism will represent one of its most central successes—a veritable new stage in the history of humankind. Under capitalism, a true dedication to the fostering of individual capacities for creative leisure and craft production is incompatible with generating a properly subservient labor force. We expect the creative production and consumption of social amenities to form an ever-increasing portion of economic activity in socialist society. Thus, there must be a stress on the development of a vital craft and artistic sector in production as a voluntary supplement to socially necessary work. It can be organized on a master-apprentice or group-control line and open to all individuals. Far from being a neglected afterthought in socialist society, this sector will be a major instrument in channeling the creative energies unleashed by liberated education and unalienated work toward socially beneficial ends.

To those of us who envision economic equality and a social system dedicated to fostering personal growth, democratic and participatory socialism is clearly desirable. But is such a system of economic democracy feasible? The conventional wisdom in academic social science supports a negative reply. Yet . . . the cynicism bred by modern mainstream economics, sociology, and political science is based on a series of myths: that inequality is due to unequal abilities; that hierarchical authority is necessitated by modern technology; that capitalism is already meritocratic; and that the existing situation corresponds to people's needs and is the product of their wills.

Just as the philosophers of ancient Greece could not conceive of society without master and slave and the Scholastics of medieval times without lord and serf, so, today, many cannot conceive of society without a controlling managerial hierarchy and a subservient working class. Yet neither technology nor human nature bar the way to democratic socialism as the next stage in the process of civilization. Unalienated work and an equal distribution of its products is neither romantic nostalgia nor postindustrial Luddism. The means of achieving social justice and of rendering work personally meaningful and compatible with healthy personal development are as American as apple pie: democracy and equality.

· · ·

THE CONTRADICTIONS OF CAPITALISM

We have argued both the desirability and the feasibility of a socialist society. But is it possible to get from here to there? And if so, what form might a democratic socialist revolution take?

· · ·

A revolutionary transformation of . . . economic life in the United States is possible because the advanced capitalist society cannot solve the problems it creates. A social system which generates or awakens needs in people which it cannot fulfill is surely vulnerable to social upheaval. This is all the more true when the means to the satisfaction of people's felt needs are clearly available. Capitalism in the U.S. is indeed such a system. It both awakens and thwarts people's needs—needs for economic security, for mutual respect, and for control over one's life. Capitalism has, at the same time, developed a technological and material base which could successfully address these needs, though under a radically different social order. . . . [Yet] while capitalism vigorously promotes the development of production, its basic social institutions are not geared to translating this development into balanced social development for fostering general human fulfillment and growth.

· · ·

The uneven development of social progress results from the inability of the social relationships of economic life in U.S. capitalism to harness for social ends the productive forces to which it gives rise. This contradiction between the forces and social relations of production under advanced capitalism not only renders democratic socialism a progressive transformation of social life, but gives rise to some of the basic preconditions of such a transformation. We believe that the political and social upheavals of the 1960s— including the black and women's movements, radical student revolts, rank-and-file unrest in the labor movement, the rise of the counterculture, and a new mood of equality among youth—have ushered in a growing consciousness directed against the power relationships of the U.S. society. These are but manifestations of the contradictions that inevitably arise out of the system's own successes—contradictions that lead to social dislocation and require structural change in the social relations of production for the further development of the social system.

· · ·

First, the legitimacy of the capitalist system has been historically based, in no small part, on its proven ability to satisfy people's consumption needs. The ever-increasing mass of consumer goods and services seemed to promise constant improvement in levels of well-being for all. Yet the very success of the process has undermined the urgency of consumer wants. Other needs—for community, for security, for a more integral and self-initiated work and social life—are coming to the fore and indeed are the product of U.S. society's very failures. These needs are unified by a common characteristic: They cannot be met simply by producing more consumer goods and services. On the contrary, the economic foundations of capital accumulation are set firmly in the destruction of the social basis for the satisfaction of these needs. Thus through economic development itself, needs are generated that the advanced capitalist system is not geared to satisfy. The legitimacy of the capitalist order must increasingly be handled by other social mechanisms, of which the educational system is a major element. It is not clear that the latter can bear this strain.

Second, the concentration of capital and the continuing separation of workers—white-collar and professional as well as manual—from control over the production process have reduced the natural defenders of the capitalist order to a small minority. Two hundred years ago, over three-fourths of white families owned land, tools, or other productive property; this figure has fallen to about a third and, even among this group, a tiny minority owns the lion's share of all productive property. Similarly, two hundred years ago, most white male workers were their own bosses. The demise of the family farm, the artisan shop, and the small store plus the rise of the modern corporation has reduced the figure to less than 10 percent. Even for the relatively well-off, white, male American worker, the capitalist system has come to mean what it has meant all along for most women, blacks, and other oppressed peoples: someone else's right to profits, someone else's right to work unbossed and in pursuit of one's own objectives. The decline of groups outside the wage-labor system—farmer, artisan, entrepreneur, and independent professional—has eliminated a ballast of capitalist support, leaving the legitimation system alone to divide workers against one another.

Third, developments in technology and work organization have begun to undermine a main line of defense of the capitalist system; namely, the idea that the capitalist relations of production—private property and the hierarchical organization of work—are the most conducive to the rapid expansion of productivity. We have suggested[1] that in those complex work tasks that increasingly dominate modern production, participatory control by workers is a more productive form of work organization. The boredom and stultification of the production line and the

steno pool, the shackled creativity of technical workers and teachers, the personal frustration of the bureaucratic office routine increasingly lose their claim as the price of material comfort. The ensuing attacks on bureaucratic oppression go hand in hand with dymystification of the system as a whole. Support for capitalist institutions—once firmly rooted in their superiority in meeting urgent consumption needs and squarely based on a broad mass of property-owning independent workers—is thus weakened by the process of capitalist development itself. At the same time, powerful anticapitalist forces are brought into being. The accumulation of capital—the engine of growth under capitalism—has as its necessary companion the proletarianization of labor, and the constant increase in the size of the working class.

Fourth, the international expansion of capital has fueled nationalist and anticapitalist movements in many of the poor countries. The strains associated with the worldwide integration of the capitalist system are manifested in heightened divisions and competition among the capitalist powers, in the resistance of the people of Vietnam, in the socialist revolutions in China and Cuba, and in the political instability and guerrilla movements in Asia, Africa, and Latin America. The U.S. role in opposition to wars of national liberation—particularly in Vietnam—has brought part of the struggle back home and exacerbated many of the domestic contradictions of advanced capitalism.

Fifth, and cutting across all of the above, with the return of comparatively smooth capitalist development in the United States in the mid-1950s after the tumultuous decades of the 1930s and 1940s, the impact of far-reaching cumulative changes in the class structure is increasingly reflected in crises of public consciousness. The corporatization of agriculture and reduction of the farm population has particularly affected blacks; they are subjugated to the painful process of forceful integration into the urban wage-labor system. The resulting political instabilities are not unlike those following the vast

[1]Editors' note: See Bowles and Gintis, Section 7.2, p. 274.

wave of immigrants in the early decades of the century. Changes in the technology of household production and the increase in female labor in the service industries also portend a radically altered economic position for women. Finally, the large corporation and the state bureaucracies have replaced entrepreneurial, elite, white-collar, and independent professional jobs as the locus of middle-class economic activity. This effective proletarianization of white-collar labor marks the already advanced integration of these groups into the wage-labor system. In each case, the contradictions have arisen between the traditional consciousness of these groups and their new objective economic situations. This has provided much of the impetus for radical movements among blacks, women, students, and counterculture youth.

Sixth, even the vaunted material productivity of capitalism—its ability to deliver the goods—seems increasingly open to question. Inflation, commodity shortages, unemployed workers, and unmet social needs all attest to the growing inability of capitalism to meet people's needs for material comfort, economic security, and social amenity.

Lastly, in response to the unsolved—and we believe unsolvable—problems of capitalism, modern liberals have advocated, and won, significant extensions of the role of government in our society. . . . [T]he expansion of education is a prime example of this process. Increasingly, the government has taken responsibility for the attainment of social objectives unattainable within the capitalist economic framework: full employment, clean air, equality of opportunity, stable prices, and the elimination of poverty, to name only a few. The result: Social problems are increasingly politicized. People are increasingly coming both to understand the political origins of social and economic distress and to sense the possibility of political solution to these problems.

The assault on economic inequality and hierarchical control of work appears likely to intensify. Along with other social strains endemic to advanced capitalism, the growing tension between people's needs for self-realization and material welfare through work and the drive of capitalists and managers for profits opens up the possibility of powerful social movements dedicated to the construction of economic democracy.

STRATEGIES FOR SOCIAL CHANGE

. . .

Revolutionary social change is a serious affair. Responsible individuals and social groups with a sober respect for the inertial pace of historical progress do well to consider the tumultuous dislocation and uncertainties of revolutionary change only as a last resort. Gradualism and piecemeal reform represent normal and healthy responses to social problems, to be rejected only in the face of compelling evidence of their failure or unfeasibility.

Nonetheless, we support the development of a revolutionary socialist movement in the United States. However arduous the path to success, a socialist alternative can provide the sole access to a future of real progress in terms of justice, personal liberation, and social welfare. Revolutionary—even violent —changes have unleashed massive progressive forces in the past. Witness the French, Russian, Chinese, Cuban Revolutions and the American War of Independence. They will continue to do so in the future. . . . We need, in short, a second American revolution —and a more democratic, egalitarian, and participatory one at that.

How do we get there? This is the central question of political strategy. . . . We consider this a major task of socialists in the coming years—one to be dealt with in terms of both social theory and concrete political practice. In this section, we will restrict our remarks to [certain] aspects of socialist strategy [which we believe to be important].

Our analysis is inspired by three basic principles. First, socialism is the progressive strengthening and extending of the process of economic democracy, with its attendant continual transformation of the process of interpersonal relationships in work, community, education, and cultural life. Economic democracy includes such "events" as a change in the patterns of ownership of the means of production, or the adoption of particular institutional forms in work or education, but merely as aspects in the development process. Second, the nature of socialism will depend on the content of revolutionary struggle in this society. A socialist movement cannot subordinate means to ends and cannot manipulate and deceive to achieve success precisely because socialism is not an event. The consciousness developed in struggle is the very same consciousness which, for better or worse, will guide the process of socialist development itself. Thus a socialist movement while striving to obtain power, must do so through means which inexorably promote democracy, participation, and a sense of solidarity and equality. Third, a socialist movement must be based on the recognition of class struggle as its organizing principle. A revolution is a fundamental shift in the structure of power in the social system and, with it, a shift in those aspects of social life on which power is based and by means of which it is reproduced. A socialist revolution is the shift of control over the process of production from the minority of capitalists, managers, and bureaucrats to the producers themselves. The move toward democratic and participatory economic relationships makes possible the breakdown of the hierarchical division of labor and the antagonistic relationships among groups of workers vying for positions in the stratification system (e.g., between blacks and whites, men and women, white- and blue-collar workers). It unleashes the possibility of turning technology and organization toward unalienated social relationships. By undermining the social subordination of working people, it allows the emergence of a truly democratic consciousness—both political and economic—of the citizenry. By removing the economic base of class oppression, it permits the construction

of social institutions—such as schools—which foster rather than repress the individual's struggle for autonomy and personal development while providing the social framework for making this a truly cooperative struggle.

A revolutionary shift in power renders all this possible but not inevitable. A change which formally transfers power to workers but is not based on a spirit of socialist consciousness around the goals of economic democracy will merely reproduce the old power relationships in new forms. This is true also for the elimination of racism, sexism, and the fetishism of hierarchical authority.

A revolution may be violent or peaceful; it may succeed with the aid of existing political channels or in spite of them. Which characteristics predominate is of central strategic importance, but cannot be prejudged in one way or another as intrinsic to a revolutionary movement. Nevertheless, we must forcefully reject the notion that a revolution is a bloody putsch by a minority of political zealots. A socialist revolution in the United States cannot be a coup in which one small ruling minority replaces another. Nor can it be a result of the insurgency of a Messianic "vanguard." We have argued that those who will benefit from socialism are workers in all walks of life. We have also argued that, at the present time, the overwhelming majority of individuals are workers, and increasingly proletarianized workers at that. Hence, the new American revolution cannot succeed without being a truly democratic movement which ultimately captures the hearts of the majority of the people.

The question of violence, while clearly a weighty tactical consideration, must also be assigned to a position of secondary importance. A majoritarian revolution has no use for terrorism. The socialist alternative involves a struggle for power and the struggle will be bitter and hard-fought. It is almost inconceivable that a socialist revolution in the United States would not involve violence at some stage. But there is little reason to depend on violence as a basic strategic weapon. Rather, socialists must be prepared to counter violent measures taken against them; they must deploy all their resources to deflect and expose any such violent measures. Strong local and national victories, electoral or otherwise, by the socialist movement raise a strong probability that dominant elites will subvert the democratic process and attempt to draw on the might of the armed forces and the National Guard to restore order. This tactic can be countered only if military rank and file are on the side of the socialists and refuse to exercise a repressive role. The question of violence recedes into the background, for the only viable socialist strategy is to disable the military capacity of the capitalist class, rather than to develop the force to combat it on its own terms.

As we have suggested, the socialist movement is a social, not merely a political, movement as it deals with the transformation of daily life rather than the mere reorientation of political power. As such, the diversity of the U.S. working class lends a socialist movement immense potential for vitality and creativity. We expect socialist manual workers to use their extensive knowledge in reorganizing production and training others to do their share of manual work. We expect socialist women to be in the forefront of eliminating oppression in the home and demanding vital alternatives to traditional domestic patterns. We expect socialist artisans, architects, and planners to heighten the artistic and aesthetic powers of the rest of us in the process of pursuing their own struggles. We expect revolutionary health workers to open new horizons in health-care delivery, and revolutionary teachers to forge the liberating schools of tomorrow as major tactics in their struggles for power. Revolutionary athletes must teach us all to respect our bodies, and teachers our minds—all this and more the creative potential of the revolutionary movement derives from the diversity and resourcefulness of American workers.

The other side of the diversity of the U.S. working class is its lack of a unified consciousness. We [believe] that major aspects of U.S. society can best be understood in terms of the need of the dominant classes to fragment the work force and, by dividing, conquer [it]. The strategy is as old as civilization itself. In the United States today, the fragmention of consciousness is facilitated by racial, sexual, and socioeconomic antagonisms.

The overriding strategic goal of a socialist movement is the creation of working-class consciousness. Too frequently, this task is seen as simply making people aware of their oppression. Far from it! Most people are all too well aware of the fact of their oppression; what is lacking is a strategy to overcome it. The conviction that a change for the better is possible will arise only where the divisive and fragmented consciousness of U.S. working people is progressively replaced by an understanding that, beneath the all too real differences in needs, desires, and social prerogatives, all suffer oppression from the same source and stand to gain similarly from the socialist alternative. Toward the end, each group struggling for control over its conditions of production must deploy its forces to overcome immediate conflicts among the people. In part this can be done by each group extending its demands to embrace other potential allies and to protect their interests. Workers seeking higher pay and control of the enterprise must fight also to promote consumers' rights, to reduce pay differentials on the job, to eliminate the demeaning secondary-status jobs and discriminatory hiring, and to create free day-care centers for the children of employees. Pursuit of an integrated set of objectives broad enough to encompass most elements in the working class will of course require some form of coordination among popular groups. In the absence of a unified theoretical and programmatic framework, radical spontaneity may result in less rather than more unity among oppressed peoples.

.   .   .

A major strategic element of a socialist movement is the continual interjection of a broader vision of a socialist alternative into concrete struggles of all types. All too often, those with utopian visions of the Good Society have neither the capacity nor the inclination to engage in real social struggle. Conversely, those with an earthy sense of the arduous task of day-to-day struggle have either cynically or opportunistically buried their vision of the larger goals. Yet the propagation of a socialist vision in the context of down-to-earth politics is essential. Few in the United States will opt for a revolutionary change as a nothing-to-lose desperation assault on a literally unbearable status quo; life for most people is simply not that bad. People must choose, and choose to fight for, socialism as a positive alternative based on a serious, desirable, and feasible vision. This vision must develop in the course of struggle, but the struggle will not develop without it. Moreover, vague notions of socialism and economic democracy, however effective in producing change, will by no means insure that change will take desirable and ultimately progressive forms. As we are often reminded by our more conservative friends, revolutionary change can be a disaster, too—a disaster which buries the fondest hopes of the strongest supporters. Only a vigorous and creative effort at defining the course of socialist development before its ultimate victory, however extensively this course must be altered through the practical experience of people involved in the struggle, can minimize this possibility. Finally, the fragmentation of con-

sciousness of working people can be overcome only by offering an alternative in which the disparate objectives of different groups are simultaneously met.

The final strategic consideration we have in mind is the sober recognition that the preparatory phase of a revolutionary movement involves working in, and through, existing capitalist institutions. We cannot sit around and wait for a political cataclysm. We cannot rely solely on creating alternative institutions as ". . . little islands of socialism in a sea of capitalism." Rather, we must think in terms of building up working-class and popular power; creating arenas of social management and direct democracy in the major branches of production; conquering positions of strength in bodies such as unions, schools, the media, and government. In short, proper strategy requires what Rudi Dutschke called the ". . . long march through the institutions." This crucial aspect of movement strategy is necessary to prepare people for taking power in every area of their lives. It has two aims: (1) to weaken progressively the power of those who control economic life and undermine the functioning of oppressive capitalist institutions, and (2) to develop in people the facility for making cooperative decisions and for exercising power, an experience normally denied us in a capitalist society.

14.2   *Reforms and the Struggle for Socialism*

A perennial question facing revolutionary movements is whether or not to fight for reforms in the existing system which fall short of revolutionary change. It can be argued that such reforms merely serve to strengthen the existing system and make revolution more difficult to achieve. On the other hand, it is possible that the struggle for reforms can help to build a stronger popular base for future revolutionary change.

In the following reading Andre Gorz helps to resolve the dilemma of "reform or revolution" by drawing a critical distinction between *reformist* and *revolutionary* reforms. Gorz suggests that an important element of revolutionary socialist strategy must be to identify and fight for revolutionary reforms that can be imposed on a capitalist society yet at the same time contribute ultimately to its radical transformation.

The following is excerpted from the Introduction to *Strategy For Labor* by ANDRE GORZ. Copyright © 1964 by Editions de Seuil; English translation copyright © 1967 by Beacon Press. Reprinted by permission of Beacon Press.

The weakness of the working class and socialist movement in all capitalist countries . . . has up to the present been its more or less pronounced inability to link the struggle for socialism to the everyday demands of the workers. This inability is rooted in historical circumstances. For at least the past thirty years, the Communist movement has propagated the prophecy that capitalism would inevitably, catastrophically collapse. In the capitalist countries, its policy has been to "wait for the revolution." The internal contradictions of capitalism were supposed to sharpen, the condition of the toiling masses to worsen. Inevitably the working class would rise up.

This period has left deep marks. Working class leaders continue to fear that too great a victory in their everyday struggles will remove—or blunt for a long time—the workers' discontent and their revolutionary spirit. These leaders fear that a tangible amelioration in the workers' condition, or a partial victory within the capitalist framework, will reinforce the system and render it more bearable.

These fears, nevertheless, only reflect fossilized thinking, a lack of strategy and theoretical reflection. On the assumption that partial victories within the system would inevitably be absorbed by it, an impenetrable barrier has been erected between present struggles and the future socialist solution. The road from one to the other has been cut. These leaders act as if the solution to all problems could wait until the working class had seized power, and as if in the meantime there were nothing to do but to stoke the flames of revolutionary discontent.

However, this kind of attitude leads to an impasse. Lacking perspectives and positive accomplishments, the revolutionary flame begins to dim. Certainly, capitalism is incapable of fundamentally resolving the essential problems which its development has brought about. But capitalism can resolve these in its own way, by means of concessions and superficial repairs aimed at making the system socially tolerable. At present the working class and socialist movement finds itself cornered and on the defensive: having failed to impose its own solutions, it has lost the initiative. Having failed to anticipate the foreseeable problems and to define the solutions beforehand, the working class ceases to assert itself as the potential ruling class. Quite the contrary, it is capitalism itself which then grants the workers half-solutions. And with each of these concessions, capitalism—left at liberty to define for itself the nature and scope of its measures—strengthens its lead and consolidates its power.

. . .

Is it possible *from within*—that is to say, without having previously destroyed capitalism—to impose anti-capitalist solutions which will not immediately be incorporated into and subordinated to the system? This is the old question of "reform or revolution." This was (or is) a paramount question when the movement had (or has) the choice between a struggle for reforms and armed insurrection. Such is no longer the case in [the advanced capitalist countries, where] there is no longer an alternative. The question here revolves around the possibility of "revolutionary reforms," that is to say, of reforms which advance toward a radical transformation of society. Is this possible?

Straight off we must rule out the . . . objection [that, by definition, reforms cannot be revolutionary]. All struggle for reform is not necessarily reformist. The not always very clear dividing line between reformist reforms and non-reformist reforms can be defined as follows:

A reformist reform is one which subordinates its objectives to the criteria of rationality

and practicability of a given system and policy. Reformism rejects those objectives and
demands—however deep the need for them—
which are incompatible with the preservation
of the system.

On the other hand, a not necessarily reformist reform is one which is conceived not in
terms of what is possible within the framework
of a given system and administration, but in
view of what should be made possible in terms
of human needs and demands.

In other words, a struggle for non-reformist
reforms—for anti-capitalist reforms—is one
which does not base its validity and its right
to exist on capitalist needs, criteria, and rationales. A non-reformist reform is determined
not in terms of what can be, but what should
be. And finally, it bases the possibility of
attaining its objective on the implementation
of fundamental political and economic
changes. These changes can be sudden, just
as they can be gradual. But in any case they
assume a modification of the relations of
power; they assume that the workers will
take over powers or assert a force (that is to
say, a non-institutionalized force) strong
enough to establish, maintain, and expand
those tendencies within the system which
serve to weaken capitalism and to shake its
joints. They assume structural reforms.[1]

Nevertheless, is it not inevitable that
powers gained by the workers within the capitalist framework be reabsorbed by the system

---

[1]Each time I use the term structural reform, it should be
understood that this does not mean a reform which
rationalizes the existing system while leaving intact the
existing distribution of powers; this does not mean to
delegate to the (capitalist) State the task of improving
the system.

Structural reform is by definition a reform imple-
mented or controlled by those who demand it. Be it in
agriculture, the university, property relations, the
region, the administration, the economy, etc., a structural reform *always* requires the creation of new centers
of democratic power.

Whether it be at the level of companies, schools,
municipalities, regions, or of the national Plan, etc.,
structural reform always requires a *decentralization* of the
decision making power, a *restriction on the powers of State
or Capital*, an *extension of popular power*, that is to say, a
victory of democracy over the dictatorship of profit. No
nationalization is *in itself* a structural reform.

and subordinated to its functioning? This
question is essential for the Marxist movement, and the only possible answer . . . is the
following: the risk of subordination exists,
but subordination *is not inevitable*. The risk
must be run, for there is no other way. Seizure
of power by insurrection is out of the question,
and the waiting game leads the workers'
movement to disintegration. The only possible
line for the movement is to seize, from the
present on, those powers which will prepare
it to assume the leadership of society and
which will permit it in the meantime to control and to plan the development of the
society, and to establish certain limiting
mechanisms which will restrict or dislocate
the power of capital.

It is not, therefore, the opportuneness of
"counter-powers" which is in question, but
their nature and their relationship to the
power of the capitalist State. The alternative
is not between the conquest, exercise, and
constant enlargement of powers by the workers, on the one hand, and the necessarily
abstract will to seize power, on the other.
The choice is between subordinate powers
and autonomous powers.

By subordinate powers must be understood
the association or participation of workers in
an economic policy which urges them to
share the responsibility on the level of results
and execution, while at the same time it
forbids them to become involved in the decisions and the criteria according to which this
policy has been decreed. For example, the
union is invited to "participate" in a policy
predetermined by others on the company
level and to "share" in carrying out this policy. The union is permitted to "challenge"
the implementation, or even the effects of
capitalist administration. But it is hoped at
the same time that it will in fact not be able
to challenge the *effects*, since it has been made
an accomplice to the premises from which
they follow. And as an additional precaution,
management provides for an "arbitrator" to
make sure that the challenge to the effects
does not place these premises in question.

By *autonomous* power, on the other hand,
must be understood the power of the workers

to challenge, in opposing the effects and the methods of implementation, the very premises of the management's policy; to challenge them even in anticipation, because they control all the particulars on the basis of which the management's policy is elaborated. . . . Such autonomous power is a first step toward the subordination of the exigencies of production to human exigencies, with the conquest of the power of autonomous control as an ultimate goal.

The exercise of this kind of autonomous power cannot be restricted to purely negative opposition. But it is also clear that this power will never be granted, nor even conceded, by the employers without a struggle. This power must be won by force. And even when it is won . . . this power can be exercised only at the price of constant mobilization. Moreover, it will inevitably tend to extend beyond the framework of the large enterprise, because the policy of a monopoly or of an oligopoly is in such close reciprocal relation with the economic policies of the State, the life of the city, the community, and the region.

Far, then, from leading toward the integration and subordination of the labor movement to the State, the autonomous power of the workers—in the large enterprises, but also in the cities, the towns, public services, regional bodies, cooperatives, etc.—prepares the way for a dialectical progression of the struggle to a higher and higher level. Autonomous power is at once the generator and the indispensable relay station for the elaboration and pursuit of the integral objectives of a policy aimed at replacing capitalism.

Moreover, this autonomous power is an indispensable element in the training and education of the masses, making it possible for them to see socialism not as something in the transcendental beyond, in an indefinite future, but as the visible goal of a praxis already at work; not a goal which the masses are supposed to wish for abstractly, but one to aim for by means of partial objectives in which it is foreshadowed.

What is involved here is indeed a strategy of *progressive* conquest of power by the workers, a strategy which does not, however, exclude the possibility of or even the necessity for a revolutionary seizure of power at a later stage.

Is such a strategy a step backward, because it abandons the idea of seizing power right away, of installing socialism with one blow? That would be the case if a revolutionary seizure of power were possible, or if the preparation for this seizure maintained the masses in a state of mobilization. But such is not the case. It is impossible—above all for Marxists—to pretend to explain the masses' present state of demobilization by the absence of revolutionary fervor on the part of their leaders. In truth, the state of demobilization today is due to the fact that neither the possibility nor the form nor the content of the workers' potential political power has been defined.

As long as the condition of the workers was immediately and absolutely unbearable, the conquest of power was an immediate end in itself. At present, however, the conquest of power is not a goal which will gain support unless it is made clear toward what ends—unrealizable under capitalism—the workers' power will be *the means*. Why socialism? How will it be achieved?

The answer to these questions is today a necessary first step. Mobilization for the conquest of power and of socialism—abstract terms which no longer in themselves serve to mobilize the masses—must pass through the "mediation" of intermediate, mobilizing objectives. The struggle for partial objectives which arise from deep needs and bring into question the capitalist structure, the struggle for partial autonomous powers and their exercise should present socialism to the masses as a living reality alteady at work, a reality which attacks capitalism from within and which struggles for its own free development. Instead of dichotomizing the future and the present—future power and present impotence, like Good and Evil—what must be done is to bring the future into the present, to make power tangible *now* by means of actions which demonstrate to the workers their positive strength, their ability to measure themselves against the power of capital and to impose their will on it.

Certainly, socialism can be no less than the hegemony of the working class, the public ownership of the means of production. But in order to reach this goal, it is necessary first to aim at intermediate objectives by means of which socialism can be seen as possible, as having a concrete significance, as being within reach. If socialism is to result from the prolongation of the present day struggles and demands, it cannot be presented straight off as a whole system, as a solution which precedes all problems. It should be presented instead as the general direction in which concrete solutions to specific problems move.

14.3   *After the Revolution*

Because a participatory socialist society can only be built by *all* of its participants, people who are struggling to make it possible are reluctant to go beyond the formulation of goals and principles and to spell out in detail what the system would look like. Yet, if only to motivate others to join the struggle, there is clearly a need to talk about participatory socialism in terms more specific than goals and principles. Therefore we will conclude this final chapter of our book with a more detailed account, by Michael Lerner, of how participatory socialism might actually operate in the United States.

Excerpted from *The New Socialist Revolution: An Introduction to its Theory and Strategy*, by MICHAEL LERNER. Copyright © 1973 by Michael Lerner. Reprinted by permission of Delacorte Press.

What do we want? In a word, "socialism." Unfortunately, that word has been so misunderstood that it is often more confusing than illuminating to use it. We retain it because it is associated with a long history of human aspirations with which we essentially identify. But let us make clear what we mean by "socialism." Socialism is the ownership and control of the means of production, and, through that, the control of all areas of life, by the majority of people who work. So socialism is another way of saying "power to the people": power to control all the basic institutions that affect our lives. Socialism is radical democracy, democracy extended to every area of our collective lives.

· · ·

DOES THE SOVIET UNION HAVE SOCIALISM?

We do not believe that socialism now exists in any country in the world. Socialism means ownership and *control* of the means of produc-

tion, democratically by the people, rather than by a governmental bureaucracy. The critical element in our understanding of socialism is the democratization of the economy and of all areas of political and social life. In the Soviet Union, this does not exist. The Communist party runs everything, and the Party is not a democratic institution, but is dominated by a group of bureaucrats who in most respects fit the notion of a "new ruling class." The people are unable to organize any effective opposition elements, either inside or outside the Party, and hence have no effective way of making their will known, short of armed rebellion. Powerless to affect the decisions that affect their lives, the people in the Soviet Union are far from having socialism.

The Soviet Union does, however, have a high degree of welfare statism. And in this respect it is similar, though somewhat in advance of, Sweden and other countries that supply the minimum social welfare benefits all humans deserve. This feature should not be minimized. People in these countries are not deprived of medical attention because of the expense, people can get work to support themselves, their minds and bodies do not decay because they have too little money to buy food. These basic needs matter very much to those who cannot satisfy them, and in these respects the people in the Soviet Union are far better off than many people in America. But while it is a contingent fact that when socialism is established, all these basic human needs will be met, meeting these needs is not the defining essence of socialism. It is a necessary condition for people to be free and self-determining, but it is not a sufficient one. Slaves may be materially satisfied, but they are slaves nevertheless. Socialism is about power over one's life and circumstances; it is about freedom and self-determination, and these do not obtain in the Soviet Union. Nor is there any indication that the USSR is moving in that direction; the ruling class seems to have strengthened itself in the past decades sufficiently and to have retreated far enough from the ideals of socialism that it would be hard to envision anything short of a revolution establishing socialism in the Soviet Union. And, to the extent that other "socialist" countries are under the military or economic control of the Soviet Union, the same is true for them.

"But doesn't this show that revolution is no alternative, because a ruling class will always reemerge no matter what the original ideals of those who make the revolution?" No. This argument misses the historical context in which the revolutions in Russia, China, North Vietnam, Cuba, etc., developed. Marx predicted, accurately, that socialism would only be possible in an industrial society whose material base—the technology and factories and skilled workforce—was sufficiently advanced to make possible the elimination of scarcity. As Marx correctly saw, the advanced industrial societies had all the prerequisites necessary for abolishing forever the domination of man by irrational forces. But the countries that are now called socialist were all backward peasant countries, often prevented from developing by the capitalist countries that influenced their economic life.

The main task of their "socialist" revolutions was to build up the industrial bases to the point where it was possible to talk about the elimination of scarcity. But in trying to industrialize, these countries faced a hostile capitalist world which would attempt to isolate and destroy them. In 1919, for example, the last remnants of the economic infrastructure of Russia were destroyed by the crippling civil war that was spurred by the United States, Britain, and France.

.   .   .

The great disservice done by the Communist parties around the world was to describe the Soviet Union, developing under extremely difficult circumstances that put industrialization, not socialism, on the agenda, as "socialist." This discredited socialism with people everywhere, especially in the Soviet Union and Eastern Europe. In taking the real for the ideal, in making a virtue out of necessity, the Communist parties helped undermine people's confidence in the ideal. Add to that the continued apologies for a regime whose paranoid excesses were inexcusable and you have all the ingredients for the widespread disillusionment experienced by so many good idealistic people of the 1930s. The same thing will happen again if the American Left tries to identify its aspirations with any existing state, whether China, North Vietnam, or Cuba. These states have much to recommend them: They have begun to deal with many of people's basic material needs, and unlike the Western nations during their period of capitalist industrialization, they have a real concern for the welfare of working people and a real interest in promoting liberation for women within the limits imposed by continued material scarcity. The rulers of these countries, unlike the ruling class of the Soviet Union, are not interested simply in self-aggrandizement and stabilization but are committed to building a socialist world eventually. Nevertheless, these countries do have "rulers," and these rulers are not elected representatives of the people. The people do not control the economy and are rarely directly consulted on crucial issues. These countries may be moving toward socialism, but it would be a critical mistake to say that they have achieved it. There is no socialism until there are substantial procedures through which the workers decide the basic questions facing them.

· · ·

WHAT WILL THE TRANSITION TO SOCIALISM BE LIKE IN THE UNITED STATES?

The situation in which socialism will come to the United States is totally different from that in which it emerged in Eastern Europe and in Asia. The United States is an advanced industrial society whose material base is adequate to meet all the material needs of its citizens and those of people around the world. Furthermore, the agent of revolutionary change in this country will be a highly diversified working class, literate and intelligent, that is capable of running things for itself and deciding on seemingly complex issues.

Immediately the socialists take control of the U.S. economy a high level of material prosperity will be possible in the United States and much of the rest of the world. Because we are so highly industrialized, it will be possible to decrease dramatically the amount of time the worker spends in work, at the same time producing adequate material goods for ourselves and helping to advance the underdeveloped parts of the world. The revolution will be experienced not as a new but goodhearted taskmaster, but as a liberation and freeing from much that is unpleasant in life. In this situation, it will be impossible for a new ruling class to emerge that encourages people to delay gratification, while itself benefiting from the labor of the majority. Since the United States is the strongest military power in the world, with atomic weapons sufficient to destroy everyone else and hence sufficient to defend itself, no group will be able to argue that people must surrender their liberties or make other sacrifices in order to defend socialism from any "external threat."

The working class that will be part of the American revolution will have a high degree of intelligence and competence in running things. American workers have been heavily indoctrinated in anticommunism and hence are particularly sensitive to the mistakes created by a Stalinist direction. Moreover, one of their main motivating forces for making the revolution will be the desire to reclaim power over their lives; for many American workers, simple material scarcity is not a problem. Having fought for power in a real sense, having seen through strategies for "participation" and other cooptive schemes, such a working class will have developed the acuity not to be duped by a group of persuasive charlatans. To think otherwise is to believe that Americans are specially unintelligent—and I see no evidence of that. We must have enough faith in each other and our collective intelligence to believe that we can learn from the mistakes of the past and can transcend them.

· · ·

AFTER THE REVOLUTION

Those who are committed to the revolution have written almost nothing about what things will look like thereafter. And for a good reason. Socialism is the beginning of the epoch of human freedom and the end of the time when some men control all others. But once human beings are genuinely free, how can we know what they will choose to do? We can have some idea based on past behavior, but we cannot have a fixed blueprint. To the challenge, "What is your new society going to look like?" the first answer must be, "This is not *my* new society, but *our* new society, so what it will look like will in part depend on what you want it to look like." A liberal running for office may give a more satisfying answer; he will be able to make authoritative statements, since he is trying to put himself in a position where he will have power that others will not. But for the socialist revolutionary, the task is to build a society in which everyone together decides what it will be like.

Still, people have a good reason for asking the question. After all, if you are going to make sacrifices to build a new social order, you want to have some idea of what the order will be like. To say "We will all be free" is poetic, but contentless; people want to know *why* this freedom will produce desirable results for humanity. I cannot answer this question for everyone, but I can answer for myself, and I can tell you what I as one individual with one vote will argue for, and what kind of society I believe will be possible. I shall try to outline what will be possible after a fairly substantial period of control by the people, not what it will be like one or two years after the people have taken power, when the transition is still going on. So let me put forward one vision, among many, of what socialism could be like and would be like if others agree with me when we all get together to construct our new society.

POLITICAL AND ECONOMIC ORGANIZATION

Every important political question would be put directly to the people for their consideration and decision. We already have the technology to do this easily. Every home would have a very simple voting device, possibly attached to the phone or television receiver, which would send a message to a central computer in the city or area recording the vote. Prior to the vote, issues would be debated in newspapers and on television and in mass meetings in the community, with every major side given equal opportunity to present its position. At the local, regional, and national level there would be an elected body of delegates (each recallable to his district any time 10 percent of the voters signed a petition for a new election) whose responsibility would be to decide which issues would be put to the people and how to formulate them in the clearest possible way in order to maximize understanding and to bring out

the potentially controversial aspects of the proposal under consideration. Any group that felt some key question was not being put to the electorate or that some key viewpoint was not being represented publicly on television, at mass meetings, or in newspapers, would circulate a petition stating its viewpoint. Signatures of 1 percent of the voting population in the relevant area would give the group the right to (1) write its own proposal to be put directly to the people, and (2) air its views on the media (it would be given more time than any single position normally is, on the grounds that its view had not previously been given exposure in the usual debates on relevant issues). The government would have an executive branch, most of the key positions of which would be filled by elections. But the executive would have little originating power, since the key decisions on policy would always be put to the people. Because of human fallibilities and weaknesses, important decisions, which should have been presented to the people, might occasionally be made under the guise of simple bureaucratic or administrative decisions. But rarely would such decisions have severe consequences, because they could always be challenged by those who were affected by them and brought directly to the people, and the official could simultaneously (if his fault was judged malicious) be recalled.

· · ·

For the first hundred years, at least, the key decisions would probably remain in the area of production. Many economists argue that it would be possible to decentralize the economy without in the slightest decreasing its efficiency. But we would be in favor of decentralization even if it meant an additional cost. A decentralized economy would be easier to control and ecologically more sound. Regions of between 15 to 20 million people would be established to replace the present states, and those regions would themselves be composed of a variety of autonomous municipalities. In order to maximize the fulfillment of human needs and eliminate needless production, the economic area would be governed by a rational long-term plan developed every few years and approved by vote of the electorate. The plan would be developed from the bottom: each work unit and each consumer entity would submit its ideas and desires to a community board which would try to adjust them into a coherent whole, then resubmit the adjustments back to the populace for approval. Thereafter, they would be submitted to a regional board that took all the ideas and tried to develop a regional plan, which itself would be sent to a national board, which would try to adjust the regional plans. The last step would be to send that plan back to everyone for approval. Equally complex planning now takes place in the Department of Defense and other areas of the government, with one crucial difference: the people consulted are members of the boards of directors of large corporations instead of the people as a whole. Because the process would be complex, we would want two key qualifications on the procedure:

1. The plan would be voted on not only as a whole, but also with separable components (much as is the present budget before Congress) so that people who liked most of it could vote "yes" on the question of making the plan as a whole the basis of discussion, and could also vote against any section of which they disapproved.

2. Any plan would have to allocate a great deal of the social surplus to each locality, so that a significant part of the wealth created by each community was in its hands to use, hence avoiding a situation in which people from far away tell people who have worked to create wealth that they cannot use even part of it in ways in which they desire.

Every community must have enough resources to experiment with education, housing, creativity, etc. The regional and national plans should deal with the minimum necessary number of issues: e.g., where to build new cities, how to solve general ecological problems, how to arrange transportation between localities, foreign trade, taxation, and long-term financing. The regional and national plans would have as one key task the allocation and redistribution of resources in such a way as to guarantee that no one area suffers because it does not have adequate natural resources or because a main source of its economic strength (e.g., car manufacturing or mining) is shut down for reasons of preserving the ecology. But since the idea of giving each community a large sum initially for discretionary planning is key to this conception, the national plan is likely to be less complicated than the present federal budget in an unplanned economy, because so much that is now decided nationally will be decided at the local level.

The key unit in the plan is the local community, whose power and resources would be greatly expanded. The emphasis for each community will be on experimentation, and funds will be made available so that minorities and individuals within each community who do not like the drift of the majority can experiment on their own. Within each community, the key centers of power will be the workplaces. Each factory or office will be democratically controlled by those who work there. All decisions that primarily affect the workers (e.g., work conditions) will be totally under their control. On the other hand, we do not envision a society such as that developed in Yugoslavia, where workers' control of each factory was not balanced by community, regional, or national control of the economy. There, without central community planning, the workers in each factory and each area began to develop specialized interests and began to relate to other groups of workers as competitors. If an economy composed of factories, each run by the workers, is governed only by the free marketplace, it becomes nothing but a rerun of capitalism on a higher level. It would be unlikely, for example, that one group of workers would agree to shut down its factory because it was producing an unnecessary commodity; instead, the workers would try to convince people the commodity was necessary and even, perhaps, to conceal its harmful effects, if it had any. Only a larger regional and national framework can assure people that their talents will be used creatively and that they will never have to suffer want and hence will enable them to accept the closing of their workplace for the common good. So it is crucial that the productive life of a community be decided by a balance between the claims of the worker in the workplace, which are to be given much weight, and the interests of the community as a whole.

. . .

The conditions of work will be decided collectively, and workplaces will be governed by those who work in them. Given the present level of technology, much less the probable advances of the period ahead, it will be possible immediately after the people take control of the economy to reduce substantially the number of work hours for the individual without in any way reducing real wages. One way in which this will be done is to employ the unemployed in the production of necessary goods. But the most important way will be to eliminate all wasteful production. Production will be geared to goods that last instead of goods that fall apart to satisfy the need for new markets. When the economy is no longer geared to the trash can, the same amount of labor will produce more lasting social goods, so the total amount of work hours required to fill social needs will be less. Advertising will be seriously curtailed, duplication of production reduced, and consequently needs for new kinds of goods will be seriously reduced. Once production is geared to human needs, and needs are not artificially created, there will be much less production time necessary. For instance, vast rapid transit systems, built on ecologically sound models, can replace the production of automobiles. Sales jobs, insurance jobs, promotion and advertising jobs, and many governmental jobs will be seen as socially useless labor, and billions of hours of office work and secretarial work will be eliminated. The elimination of this kind of work in a capitalist framework would be frightening—because the people involved would simply be put on the job market to compete with everyone else. But the elimination of all this useless work in a socialist society would be coordinated as part of a plan for reemploying everyone, and reduc-

ing the total number of hours that all people had to work. Add to this the increase in automated work, which at this point would be welcomed rather than opposed by the workers (since automation would mean less work but not unemployment and economic insecurity), and it can be safely predicted that within a very short period of time, probably not more than twenty to thirty years, the average workday would be five hours and the workweek four days. And both would decrease progressively in the next period.

. . . In a socialist society, while the total amount of work will be greatly reduced, the work that remains will have to be shared by all. To a large extent work will seem much more meaningful because the work conditions are under the worker's control and he is working to serve his fellow human beings' needs, but some work will still be drudgery and some will be unpleasant. A just distribution of work will permit inequalities if, and only if, they improve the position of those who are worst off, and the offices and positions to which the inequalities attach are open to all. In general, this will mean that unpleasant labor and drudgery will be done by everyone in the community on a rotating basis. We do not, of course, want to call a doctor away from the operating table to collect garbage, but we do want to create enough medical schools and training programs so that, were a particular doctor unavailable, someone else would be able to take his place.

Not only the worst work, but also work in general, will be rotated to the greatest degree possible consistent with the wishes of the people doing it. This will involve two key societal changes:

1. Job categories will have to be much changed from the present, and many tasks that are now combined in the hands of a "professional" will be distributed to a number of trained personnel. For example, paramedical training could be given to a very large percentage of the population so that most of the work of the average medical doctor could be competently handled by people with a more limited but still proficient training. Or, to put it another way, people whose present jobs require only menial

work and limited use of their intelligence would be given broader training and jobs would be more broadly defined to give them opportunity to use their intelligence. So, for example, we might find that the design of a building was discussed and decided not merely by a group of architects, but also by the people who were involved in constructing it and the people who were going to use it. In some limited areas, special expertise and long training would still be called for. But every attempt would be made to share expertise, develop it widely, and to have the expert in a given area use at least part of his time to teach his talents to as many people as wanted to learn.

2. Job assignments would be rotated at given intervals, separated by vacation periods and periods to learn new skills and techniques. Rotation would allow people to experience several kinds of work in their lifetime, and the training periods would guarantee that they learned how to do different jobs well. Rotation would also ensure that new perspectives were brought to most assignments, to provide additional creativity in the work situation. Rotation would not operate merely in relation to similar kinds of jobs, but also to different ones: people would shift among managerial, labor, clerical, skilled, farm, and other work so that each person had a full variety of experiences.

To the greatest extent possible, consistent with getting all the necessary jobs filled, job allocation would be voluntary. People would choose the job they wanted to be rotated to, with the proviso that jobs with power over others (managerial, for instance) and jobs that were unpleasant could be held only for a limited number of years. In the case of the least pleasant jobs, there would have to be accompanying compensation so that people who did them even for a limited time had additional benefits, such as significantly short workweeks or longer vacation periods.

·   ·   ·

THE SOCIALIST COMMUNITY

·   ·   ·

Probably one of the first actions of a socialist government would be to make free such essential services as health care, transportation, utilities, and housing. All forms of cultural activity would be free, and one of the main tasks of local government or administration would be to provide plans for making cultural experimentation possible for everyone. As a beginning, of course, we want every neighborhood to be equipped with adequate musical supplies, sports supplies, painting supplies, sculpture supplies, knitting, embroidery, macrame, etc. Each neighborhood should have facilities for the development of film, and facilities for the presentation of concerts and plays, as well as printing presses for leaflets, poetry, books and community newspapers. One of the highest ideals of the socialist revolution is to liberate and actualize human creativity. That is why we can adopt the slogan that workers and students used in the 1968 French rebellions: All Power to the Imagination.

Education will be radically transformed in our socialist community. For one thing, schools for youngsters will no longer be prisons. While basic skills will be taught, the greatest energies will be placed on allowing students to develop their talents by exposing them to the greatest possible range of creative activities. There will be no grading, but comprehensive reports on each youngster's development. A key element will be helping young people learn how to work and act together, at the same time respecting each person's individuality and uniqueness. Particularly in the elementary school, there will be no pressure on people to learn isolated facts about the world: the main emphasis will be on learning how to play, how to create, how to be an individual, and how to live and work collectively. The course content in high school is likely to resemble that of today's best liberal arts colleges: an introduction to the full variety of human thought, science, art, music, literature, and history of the past, taught not as isolated subjects but from a point of view that integrates all these fields. It is only when this kind of basic appreciation of the achievements and disabilities of the past are fully assimilated that the student can begin to specialize. There is no reason that most of what is today taught in college cannot be learned as thoroughly and perceptively at an earlier age, providing the student has not gone through the systematically moronizing experience that now goes under the name of elementary and high school education. The next level is learning some series of skills, for one's first set of jobs, and this learning will be repeated periodically as jobs are rotated. Every time one learns a new skill, however, time will be allowed to pursue in-depth education in some other area of intellectual and artistic interest, so that one can use one's leisure more intelligently.

So far we have been talking about the structured periods in which education is the primary activity. But, after the socialist revolution, education will have a much broader role. Every community will begin to develop facilities for extensive educational opportunities in all areas of human intellectual life. Given that at least half of our day will be free, many of us will avail ourselves of this kind of opportunity, and education will become a permanent feature of life, not limited to the youthful period, or rotation intervals.

. . .

It should be clear that in our socialist community we place as one of our highest goals the full development of each person. And we understand that this is achieved only through the full development and liberation of all. Indeed, the one is inconceivable without the other, for one of the chief needs of each person will be that every other person be fulfilled and their potentialities developed to the greatest extent possible. People will be spurred to creativity and to invention, to the development of beauty and love, both because it is self-fulfilling and because it is a positive contribution to society. . . . We do not believe that collectivity should ever mean the sacrifice of one's talents or skills or the abandonment of one's individuality and uniqueness. It is precisely these things that make each human being precious and which a socialist society seeks to maximize. Collective sharing, collec-

tive living, collective activity, and collective loving must develop out of an appreciation and love for each individual member of the collective, and not out of the sense that the collective itself has a transcendent worth unrelated and far superior to the sum of the worth of individuals that compose it. . . .

But while today we can take only very limited steps in the direction of creating a collective life that respects the individual's uniqueness and creativity, once society is in the hands of the people, much will become possible. It is quite likely that a variety of new forms of living and working together will emerge that are unthinkable or unworkable today. For one thing, it is highly unlikely that the monogamous family will attract many people. Even today monogamy has so completely broken down that divorce rates in many states have reached 50 percent or higher. But divorce only accentuates the problem rather than solving it: the problem is built into the very idea that one other person can forever fulfill all the individual's needs for love and intimacy. The monogamous family today is kept together primarily by the fact that husbands and wives see each other as private property. But when property relations break down generally, and when people begin to treat one another as ends and not just as means to their own purposes, the whole syndrome of possessiveness that today appears to be part of "human nature" will largely disappear. As a result, most people are likely to have a variety of relationships of varying intensity, and to live in extended family units in which many people together share a living facility and some aspects of child rearing. There is likely to be some variety in the kinds of arrangements to which this will lead. Some will be large houses in which individuals each have their own room; there are no permanent couples and everyone shares the housework and the child rearing. Another possibility is the same arrangement composed of nonmonogamous couples who have a primary commitment to each other but also relate to others in the house. A third arrangement is monogamous couples who share the housework and child rearing with other couples or individuals in the house. A fourth arrangement, similar to many kibbutzim, is for couples to have small cottages with their own living and bedrooms and a small kitchen facility, and then to share with a larger community a common dining room, assembly hall, and library. This form might be the prototype of the urban commune. All these possible living arrangements would require serious changes in the architecture of homes and communities. As they are built today, most living units assume the monogamous couple as the basic unit. We need houses and neighborhoods where this assumption is not built into the structure of houses. It will be crucial to have facilities where common life can develop, and at the same time have private homes for the individuals or couples whose privacy is sacrosanct.

The complete and permanent liberation of women will be a first priority of the transition period, and is likely to be accomplished within two to three generations of the revolution. In the transition every effort will be devoted to eliminating sex roles that have been developed for both men and women, in every area from jobs and education to personal relations. In that period it is not unlikely that a strong independent women's movement will still function at every level of society to check on the progress in the battle to eliminate sexism and chauvinism. But after a few generations, this will be unnecessary. At that point, women will not be thought of as having any "group" characteristics that distinguish them from men, and much of what goes under the name of "masculinity" will also be transcended by men. Housework and child rearing will be completely shared, not because men think they "ought to help out" but because no one will see the slightest reason for women to have any greater role in these areas than men. There will be no economic dependence on men, and no assumption that a woman must find a man or else be thought of as strange or as a failure. In the transition period, many collective living arrangements will be composed only of women or only of men,

although this is likely to seem less important once sex roles have largely disappeared. Women's passivity will be completely dethroned, and women will as likely be initiators of sexual contact as men, or as likely to shape the lives of their men as vice versa. Since decent human relations will become one of the main foci of life, there will be a marked reduction in competition for the affection and love of other people. Once love becomes superabundant, competition for it makes much less sense.

                    .   .   .

One of the greatest beneficiaries of these possibilities will be children. No longer raised by parents who think of them as their own private property, children will have the opportunity to grow up in a more extended family where they come into contact with a variety of significant others, both adult and peer. Parents no longer will have the same need to make their children what they never could be, or to make their children feel and think like them. No longer will we be victimized by the desperate need of unhappy people to pretend that childhood is a utopian period full of innocence and free of frustration. It will thus be possible to see children for what they are. The mutual concern with and love for children expressed by the whole collective at once will give the child much more support and much more room for uniqueness and self-development, since there will be less consensus on "the right" path for him. Once the notion that children are not possessions is taken seriously, a variety of ways for them to become self-governing will develop, allowing them to maximize their own autonomy and to develop at their own pace, without in any way sacrificing the context of love and support. On the contrary, if children's ability to be independent and to define their lives for themselves is not considered a threatening sign of disrespect or lack of love for parents, the parent can begin to take pleasure in the child's development without feeling anxiety or rejection.

In talking about human relations I have suggested one style of relating which is likely to become common. But it will not be the only one. It is perfectly conceivable and even likely that there will still be many couples who like the monogamous family situation, and who want to live by themselves. This preference will also be respected. But its content and meaning for the individuals involved will inevitably be different from what it is today. In a context where other forms of living and relating obtain, no one will be forced to remain in the monogamous family for lack of an alternative. Hence monogamy is likely to be a free choice that can always be reversed without the tremendous pain and complications that attend divorce in modern America. Just as in questions of dress, appearance, art forms, work forms, etc., there will be plurality of life styles, each of which will be acceptable as long as it does not depend on some structural position which allows one person to exploit another. . . .

The same kind of principle will govern the existence of minority communities. Ethnic, religious, cultural, aesthetic, national, and historical differences embedded in common customs and traditions will be respected and there will be no attempt to uproot or displace them from the outside. Internationalism and human solidarity do not imply homogeneity. This point must be stressed again and again, not only because the reactionaries try to portray socialism as an extension of the trend, so marked in capitalist society, toward the suppression of individual and group differences, but also because some people in the New Left have given the most vulgar interpretation to what it means to fight "individualism." In the transition period especially, it is quite likely that minorities oppressed under capitalism will cling strongly to their culture as they join the general societal battle to smash the remnants of racism and other forms of prejudice. But even after racism and other prejudices no longer play any role in the consciousness or institutions of the new society, it is both probable and desirable that people take what is best in their cultural inheritance and build on it, rather than try to assimilate into one large homogeneous culture.

At several points in this account I have suggested forms of living, working, and community building that may not totally appeal to each reader of this [essay]. Hence, it is important to stress that what I have tried to do is to outline a vision of what could be and what *I* would probably vote for and try to influence others to want. But I will have one vote, just like everyone else, and I will not have any more access to instruments of influence and power than anyone else, so the view that will win out will be the one that succeeds in convincing the largest number of people. There is no guarantee that every decision made will be the best one, but there is a guarantee that the mistakes will be *our* mistakes, made in good faith, and rectifiable by *all of us* when we decide to do so. That kind of guarantee is a world of difference from a society in which decisions about what to do, insofar as they are not simply given by the structure, are made on the basis of the need of a small group to maximize their own wealth and power. In capitalist society, rationality and truth have no efficacy unless they happen to coincide with the needs of vested interests. In a socialist society, free conscious activity is finally possible for all of us: we become the masters of our own fate.

Bibliography

The following selective bibliography is designed to refer both teachers and students to books and major articles that we recommend for further study. We have divided the bibliography into sections corresponding to each chapter of the book. In order to save space, we have not included here all the sources from which we excerpted readings for our book, but we do recommend that interested readers follow up those sources as well as the additional materials listed below.

For more detailed bibliographies on a wide variety of topics in radical political economy, we suggest that readers consult the *Reading Lists in Radical Political Economics* published periodically by the Union for Radical Political Economics, 41 Union Square West, Room 901, New York, N.Y. 10003. In addition, we recommend the following journals (listed alphabetically) as particularly good sources of current work by radical political economists:

Insurgent Sociologist, published quarterly at the Department of Sociology, University of Oregon, Eugene, Oregon 97403.

Monthly Review, published monthly by Monthly Review, Inc., 62 West 14th Street, New York, N.Y. 10011.

New Left Review, published bimonthly by New Left Review Ltd., 7 Carlisle Street, London W1V 6NL, England.

Radical America, published bimonthly at 60 Union Square, Somerville, Mass. 02143 (mailing address: P.O. Box B, North Cambridge, Mass. 02140).

Review of Radical Political Economics, published quarterly by the Union for Radical Political Economics, 41 Union Square West, Room 901, New York, N.Y. 10003.

Socialist Review (formerly *Socialist Revolution*), published bimonthly by Agenda Publishing Co., 396 Sanchez Street, San Francisco, California 94114.

And, for a continuing topical review of current economic events from a socialist perspective, see *Dollars and Sense*, published monthly by the Economic Affairs Bureau, Inc., 324 Somerville Avenue, Somerville, Mass. 02143.

CHAPTER 1

Tepperman, Jean, *Not Servants, Not Machines: Office Workers Speak Out* (Boston: Beacon, 1976).

Harrington, Michael, *The Other America* (Baltimore: Penguin, 1963).

Lessing, Doris, *The Golden Notebook* (New York: Bantam, 1967).

Brown, Claude, *Manchild in the Promised Land* (New York: Knopf, 1965).

Commoner, Barry, *The Closing Circle* (New York: Knopf, 1971).

Terkel, Studs, *Hard Times* (New York: Pantheon, 1970).

Petras, James and Morris Morley, *The United States and Chile: Imperialism and the Overthrow of the Allende Government* (New York: Monthly Review, 1975).

CHAPTER 2

Amin, Samir, *Unequal Development* (New York: Monthly Review, 1977), Ch. 1–2.

Avineri, Shlomo, *The Social and Political Thought of Karl Marx* (New York: Cambridge University, 1968), Ch. 2–6.

Dowd, Douglas, *The Twisted Dream: Capitalist Development in the United States since 1776* (Cambridge, Mass.: Winthrop, 2nd ed. 1977).

Fleischer, Helmut, *Marxism and History* (New York: Harper Torchbooks, 1973).

Hobsbawm, Eric, *Industry and Empire* (Baltimore: Penguin, 1968).

Moore, Barrington, Jr., *The Social Origins of Dictatorship and Democracy* (Boston: Beacon 1966).

CHAPTER 3

Dobb, Maurice, *Capitalism, Yesterday and Today* (London: Lawrence Wishart, 1958).

Horowitz, David, *The Fate of Midas* (New York: Monthly Review, 1972).

Lichtman, Richard, "Marx's Theory of Ideology," *Socialist Revolution*, No. 23 (April 1975).

Marx, Karl, *Capital*, 3 volumes (New York: International Publishers, 1967).

O'Connor, James, *The Corporations and the State* (New York: Harper & Row, 1974).

Sweezy, Paul, *The Theory of Capitalist Development* (New York: Monthly Review, 1968).

CHAPTER 4

Adams, Walter, *The Structure of American Industry* (New York: MacMillan, 4th ed. 1971).

Averitt, Robert, *The Dual Economy* (New York: W. W. Norton, 1968).

Chandler, Alfred D., *Strategy and Structure* (New York: Doubleday, 1961).

DeVroey, Michel, "The Separation of Ownership and Control in Large Corporations," *Review of Radical Political Economics*, Vol. 7, No. 2, (Summer 1975).

Goulden, Joseph, *Monopoly: The Story of AT&T* (New York: Putnam, 1968).

Shepherd, William G., *Market Power and Economic Welfare* (New York: Random House, 1970).

CHAPTER 5

Brooks, Thomas R., *Toil and Trouble: A History of American Labor* (New York: Dell, 1971).

Edwards, Richard C., *The Great Transformation Inside the Firm* (forthcoming).

Edwards, Richard C., Michael Reich and David M. Gordon (eds.), *Labor Market Segmentation* (Lexington, Mass.: Heath, 1975).

Gutman, Herbert, *Work, Culture and Society in Industrializing America* (New York: Knopf, 1976).

Smuts, Robert W., *Women and Work in America* (New York: Schocken Books, 1971).

Wright, Erik O., "Class Boundaries in Advanced Capitalist Societies," *New Left Review*, No. 98, (July/August 1976).

CHAPTER 6

Best, Michael and William Connolly, *The Politicized Economy* (Lexington, Mass.: Heath, 1977).

Brecher, Jeremy, *Strike!* (San Francisco: Straight Arrow Books, 1972).

Domhoff, G. William, *The Higher Circles: The Governing Class in America* (New York: Vintage, 1970).

Miliband, Ralph, *The State in Capitalist Society* (New York: Basic Books, 1969).

O'Connor, James, *The Fiscal Crisis of the State* (New York: St. Martin's Press, 1973).

Wolfe, Alan, *The Seamy Side of Democracy* (New York: D. McKay Co., 1973).

CHAPTER 7

Blauner, Robert, *Alienation and Freedom* (Chicago: U. of Chicago, 1964).

Blumberg, Paul, *Industrial Democracy* (New York: Schocken Books, 1969).

Gorz, Andre (ed.), *The Division of Labor* (New York: Humanities, 1976).

Jenkins, David, *Job Power* (Garden City, N.Y.: Doubleday, 1973).

Marx, Karl, *Early Writings*, trans. and ed. by T. B. Bottomore (New York: McGraw-Hill, 1963).

Sheppard, Harold L. and Neal Q. Herrick, *Where Have All the Robots Gone?* (New York: Free Press, 1972).

CHAPTER 8

Bowles, Samuel and Herbert Gintis, *Schooling in Capitalist America* (New York: Harper & Row, 1976).

Kolko, Gabriel, *Wealth and Power in America* (New York: Praeger, 1962).

Lundberg, Ferdinand, *The Rich and the Super-Rich* (New York: Bantam, 1968).

Miller, Herman P., *Rich Man, Poor Man* (New York: Crowell, 1971).

Miller, S. M. and Pamela Roby, *The Future of Inequality* (New York: Basic Books, 1970).

Tuckman, Howard P., *The Economics of the Rich* (New York: Random House, 1973).

CHAPTER 9

Eisenstein, Zillah (ed.), *Capitalist Patriarchy and the Case for Socialist-Feminism* (New York: Monthly Review, 1978).

Engels, Friedrich, *Origins of the Family, Private Property and the State* (New York: International Publishers, 1962).

Mitchell, Juliet, *Women's Estate* (New York: Vintage, 1973).

Rowbotham, Sheila, *Women, Resistance and Revolution* (New York: Pantheon, 1972).

Ryan, Mary, *Womanhood in America from Colonial Times to the Present* (New York: Franklin Watts, 1975).

Socialist Revolution pamphlet, *Capitalism and the Family* (available from Agenda Publishing Co., 396 Sanchez Street, San Francisco, CA 94114.)

CHAPTER 10

Allen, Robert, *Black Awakening in Capitalist America* (New York: Doubleday, 1970).

Almaguer, Tomas, "Class, Race and Chicano Oppression," *Socialist Revolution*, No. 25, (July–Sept. 1975).

Boggs, James and Grace Boggs, *Racism and the Class Struggle* (New York: Monthly Review, 1970).

Genovese, Eugene, *Roll, Jordan, Roll* (New York: Random House, 1976).

Jacobson, Julius (ed.), *The Negro and the American Labor Movement* (New York: Doubleday, 1968).

Schwartz, Barry and Robert Disch (eds.), *White Racism: Its History, Pattern and Practice* (New York: Dell, 1970).

CHAPTER 11

Baran, Paul and Paul Sweezy, *Monopoly Capital* (New York: Monthly Review, 1966).

Commoner, Barry, *The Poverty of Power* (New York: Knopf, 1976).

Gordon, David (ed.), *Problems in Political Economy: An Urban Perspective* (Lexington, Mass.: Heath, 2nd ed. 1977).

Kapp, K. William, *Social Costs of Business Enterprise* (New York: Asia Publishing House, 2nd ed. 1963).

Lens, Sidney, *The Military-Industrial Complex* (Philadelphia: Pilgrim, 1970).

Weisskopf, Walter, *Alienation and Economics* (New York: Dutton, 1971).

CHAPTER 12

Block, Fred, *The Origins of International Economic Disorder: A Study of U.S. International Monetary Policy from World War II to the Present* (Berkeley and Los Angeles: U. of California Press, 1977).

Glyn, Andrew and Bob Sutcliffe, *Capitalism in Crisis* (New York: Pantheon, 1972).

Gordon, Robert A., *Business Fluctuations* (New York: Harper & Row, 2nd ed. 1961).

Magdoff, Harry and Paul Sweezy (eds.), *The End of Prosperity* (New York: Monthly Review, 1977).

Sherman, Howard, *Stagflation: A Radical Theory of Unemployment and Inflation* (New York: Harper & Row, 1976).

Union for Radical Political Economics (URPE), *Radical Perspectives on the Economic Crisis of Monopoly Capitalism* (New York: Union for Radical Political Economics, 1st ed. 1975, 2nd ed. forthcoming).

CHAPTER 13

Barnet, Richard and Ronald Muller, *Global Reach: The Power of Multinational Corporations* (New York: Simon & Schuster, 1974).

Barratt-Brown, Michael, *The Economics of Imperialism* (London: Penguin, 1973).

Magdoff, Harry, *The Age of Imperialism* (New York: Monthly Review, 1969).

Owen, Robert and Bob Sutcliffe, *Studies in the Theory of Imperialism* (London: Longman, 1972).

Rhodes, Robert (ed.), *Imperialism and Underdevelopment* (New York: Monthly Review, 1970).

Wilber, Charles (ed.), *The Political Economy of Development and Underdevelopment* (New York: Random House, 1973).

CHAPTER 14

Alperovitz, Gar and Staughton Lynd, *Strategy and Program: Two Essays Toward a New American Socialism* (Boston: Beacon, 1973).

Buber, Martin, *Paths in Utopia* (Boston: Beacon, 1958).

Campen, Jim (ed.), *Socialist Alternatives for America: A Bibliography* (New York: Union for Radical Political Economics, 1974).

Hunnius, Gerry, G. David Garson and John Case (eds.), *Workers' Control: A Reader on Labor and Social Change* (New York: Vintage, 1973).

Sweezy, Paul and Charles Bettelheim, *On the Transition to Socialism* (New York: Monthly Review, 1971).

Weinstein, James, *Ambiguous Legacy: The Left in American Politics* (New York: Franklin Watts, 1975).